Fr. Steph[...]

D0070025

W. C. Brann

BRANN
THE ICONOCLAST

A COLLECTION

OF THE

WRITINGS OF W. C. BRANN

IN TWO VOLUMES

WITH BIOGRAPHY BY J. D. SHAW

VOLUME ONE

Published by

HERZ BROTHERS

Waco, Texas, U. S. A.

1911

CONTENTS

CONTENTS

WILLIAM COWPER BRANN

William Cowper Brann was born in Humboldt Township, Coles County, Illinois, January 4, 1855. He was not raised in the home of his parents, though his father, Rev. Noble Brann, survived him, and is still living. His mother having died when he was two and a half years old, he was within the next six months placed in the care of Mr. William Hawkins, a Coles County farmer, with whom he lived about ten years. As to his childhood experiences on the Hawkins' farm nothing is now known. They were probably such as are common to children raised in the country. Of Mr. Hawkins he always spoke kindly, referring to him as "Pa Hawkins." His nature was not suited to farm life, however, and he finally made up his mind to see more of the world, hence without ever having disclosed his resolution to any one, he quietly walked away one dark and cheerless night, carrying in a small box under his arm all that he then possessed, and leaving behind him the friends of his childhood in the only place he had ever known as his home, thus entering upon the active struggle of life at thirteen years of age, without friends, destitute of means, and almost entirely uneducated.

The first position he obtained was that of bell boy in a hotel. Later on he learned to be a painter and grainer, then a printer, a reporter, and finally an editorial writer. He was energetic, industrious and painstaking in whatever he undertook to do, therefore always employed. Early in his struggle he realized the need of an education, in the acquirement of which he applied himself with eager diligence. Nature had endowed him with keen perceptive powers, a retentive memory and great mental vigor, by means of which he soon accumulated considerable knowledge. Every moment that could be spared from his daily toil was spent in reading books of science, philosophy, history, biography and general literature. In this way he became thoroughly informed on almost every important subject, as will be seen by the contents of this volume.

On March 3, 1877, at Rochelle, Illinois, he was married to Miss Carrie Martin, who, with their two children, Grace Gertrude and William Carlyle, is now living in the beautiful home, here at Waco, from which he was buried April 3, 1898.

During all the years, from the time he left the hospitable home of Mr. Hawkins, in 1868, until after he had successfully launched "Brann's Iconoclast," he suffered the harassing annoyances of extreme poverty, in the endurance of which he was cheerful, hopeful and diligent in the equipment of his mind preparatory to the work he always believed he would some day be able to accomplish.

Beginning his literary career as a reporter, he was soon made an editorial writer, in which capacity he became well-known throughout Illinois, Missouri and Texas. As such he was versatile, forceful and direct. There was no needless repetition or tiresome circumlocution in his composition. He possessed an inexhaustible vocabulary, from which he could always find the words best fitted to convey his meaning at the moment they were most needed, and every sentence was resplendent with an order of wit, humor and satire peculiar to a style original with himself.

In July, 1891, he issued at Austin, Texas, the first number of "Brann's Iconoclast." Only a few numbers appeared, when it was suspended and he resumed his editorial work, then on the "Globe-Democrat," of St. Louis, Missouri, and later on the "Express" of San Antonio, Texas. It was in connection with his first attempt to establish the "Iconoclast" that he delivered a few lectures that were well received. In later years he went upon the platform again with every prospect of a successful career in the lecture field.

In the summer of 1894 he settled here in Waco, and, in February of the following year, revived the "Iconoclast," which was successful from the first issue, having reached, at the time of his death, a circulation of ninety thousand copies. It was through the "Iconoclast" that his genius found full scope for development, and that he became best known to the public. In its columns he dared to be himself. There was now no restraint imposed upon him by timorous publishers. It belonged to him, and in it he gave full wing to his own thought. It was this intellectual freedom, sustained by the magic power and personality of a real genius, that gave to it such widespread popularity.

Mr. Brann has been classed as a humorist. This he was, and of a type peculiar to himself, but he was not content with merely having amused or entertained the people, he aspired to arouse public sentiment in the interest of certain reforms. He was a hater of shams and defied every form of fraud, hypocrisy and deceit. He made of his humor a whip with which to scourge from the temple of social purity every intruder there. He joined in no partisan schemes for place or power, but, confident of his own ground, he would stand alone in the defiance of popular humbugs and frauds. This heroic independence, while admired by many, made him a mark for the envy and hatred of such as feared him, and in the end proved to be the cause of his death.

But with all his uncompromising hatred of shams, there beat in the bosom of W. C. Brann a warm and generous heart for the world at large, and no man was ever a more devoted friend to the poor and needy. No beggar was ever turned away from his door empty handed, and no worthy cause ever asked his help in vain. His religion was to do whatever he believed to be right, and to defy the wrong even though it should be found parading in the garb and livery of righteousness.

Mr. Brann was fond of nature. He loved the mountains, the lakes, the rivers and the billowy sea. He loved to walk amid forest trees and watch the birds fly from bough to bough and warble their songs of love, but in all the wide, wide world, his home life was the most sacred object of his devotion, and when prosperity gave him the means to do so he found great delight in making it beautiful and pleasant. He was fond of his friends, but the love he bore his wife and children was sublimely beautiful, tender and affectionate.

His sudden death was a shock not only to his immediate friends, but to the hundreds of thousands who knew him through the "Iconoclast." Walking quietly along the street, talking with a friend, the bullet of an assassin pierced his body, entering through the back, and, although he had the courage, with strength enough, to turn and fatally wound his antagonist, he lived but a few hours, when all that remained of one of the most brilliant journalists on the American continent was followed to Oakwood Cemetery by probably the largest funeral procession ever witnessed in this city. There he was tenderly laid to rest in the embrace of our common mother earth, and under a mound of floral offerings, which though profuse and costly were but a feeble expression of the sincere grief that struck dumb with awe the thousands upon thousands who had learned to love him with an affection accorded to few men.

J. W. SHAW.

Waco, Texas, Sept. 10th, 1898.

WOMAN'S WICKEDNESS.

By the "social evil" is commonly understood illicit intercourse of the sexes, a violation of law or custom intended
to regulate the procreative passion.

The "evil" is probably as old as society, coeval with mankind. History—tradition itself—goes not back to a time
when statutes, confessedly human, or professedly divine,
were capable of controlling the fierce fires that blaze within
the blood—when all-consuming Love was cold Reason's
humble slave and Passion yielded blind obedience unto Precept. Although the heavens have been ever peopled with
threatening gods and the great inane filled with gaping
hells; although kings and courts have thundered their inhi-
bitions forth, and society turned upon illicit love Medusa's
awful frown, the Paphian Venus has flourished in every
age and clime, and still flaunts her scarlet flag in the face
of heaven.

The history of humanity—its poetry, its romance, its
very religion—is little more than a Joseph's coat, woven of
Love's celestial warp and Passion's infernal woof in the
loom of Time. For sensuous Cleopatra's smiles Mark
Antony thought the world well lost; for false Helen's favors
proud Ilion's temples blazed, and the world is strewn with
broken altars and ruined fanes, with empty crowns and
crumbling thrones blasted by the selfsame curse.

In many cities of every land abandoned women are so
numerous, despite all these centuries of law-making and
moralizing, that they find it impossible to earn a livelihood
by their nefarious trade—are driven by sheer necessity to
seek more respectable employment. The supply of public
prostitutes is apparently limited only by the demand, while
the number of "kept women" is constantly increasing, and
society becoming day by day more lenient to those favorites of fortune who have indulged in little escapades not in
strict accord with the Seventh Commandment. It is now
a common occurrence for a female member of the "Four
Hundred" who has confessedly gone astray, to be received
back on an equality with her most virtuous sisters. In
ancient Sparta theft was considered proper, but getting

caught a crime. Modern society has improved upon that peculiar moral code. Adultery—if the debauchee have wealth—is but a venial fault, and to be found out a trifling misfortune, calling for condolence rather than condemnation. It is not so much the number of professed prostitutes that alarms the student of sociology, as the brutal indifference to even the semblance of sexual purity which is taking possession of our social aristocracy, and which poison, percolating through the underlying strata, threatens to eliminate womanly continence from the world.

If, despite all our safeguards of law and the restraining force of religion, society becomes more hopelessly corrupt; if, with our advancing civilization, courtesans increase in number; if, with our boasted progress in education and the arts, women of alleged respectability grow less chary of their charms—if the necessities of poverty and the luxury of wealth alike breed brazen bawds and multiply cuckolds —it is a fair inference that there is something radically wrong with our social system.

It might be well, perhaps, for priests and publicists to cease launching foolish anathemas and useless statutes at prostitution long enough to inquire what is driving so many bright young women into dens of infamy,—for those good souls who are laboriously striving to drag their fallen sisters out of the depths, to study the causes of the disease before attempting a cure. I say disease, for I cannot agree with those utilitarians who profess to regard prostitution as a "necessary evil;" who protest that the brute passions of man must be sated,—that but for the Scarlet Woman he would debauch the Vestal Virgin. I do not believe that Almighty God decreed that one-half the women of this world should be sacrificed upon the unclean altar of Lust that the others might be saved. It is an infamous, a revolting doctrine, a damning libel of the Diety. All the courtesans beneath heaven's blue concave never caused a single son of Adam's misery to refrain from tempting, so far as he possessed the power, one virtuous woman. Never.

Governor Fishback, of Arkansas, recently declared that "houses of ill-fame are necessary to city life," and added: "If you close these sewers of men's animal passions you overflow the home and spread disaster."

This theory has been adopted by many municipalities, courtesans duly licensed, their business legitimatized and accorded the protection of the law. If houses of ill-fame be "necessary to city life;" if they prevent the overflow of the home of bestial lust and the spread of disaster, it follows as a natural sequence that the prostitute is a public benefactor, to be encouraged rather than condemned, deserving of civic honor rather than social infamy. Will Governor Fishback and his fellow utilitarians be kind enough to make a careful examination of the quasi-respectable element of society and inform us how large an army of courtesans will be necessary to enable it to pass a baking powder purity test?

Governor Fishback does not appear to have profited by Pope's suggestion that "The proper study of mankind is man," or he would know full well that the presence in a city of prostitutes but serves to accentuate the dangers that environ pure womanhood. He would know that they add fuel to Lust's unholy fires, that thousands of them are procuresses as well as prostitutes, and that one bad woman can do more to corrupt her sex than can any libertine since the days of Sir Launcelot. He would likewise know that so perverse is the nature of man that he would leave a harem filled with desirous houris more beautiful than ever danced through Mohammedan dream of Paradise, to dig pitfalls for the unwary feet of some misshapen country wench who was striving to lead an honest life. As a muley cow will turn from a manger filled with new-mown hay, and wear out her thievish tongue trying to coax a wisp of rotten straw through a crack in a neighbor's barn, so will man turn from consenting Venus' matchless charms to solicit scornful Dian.

What is it that is railroading so large a portion of the young women to hell? What causes so many to forsake the "straight and narrow path" that is supposed to lead to everlasting life, and seek the irremediable way of eternal death? What mad phantasy is it that leads so many wives to sacrifice the honor of their husbands and shame their children? Is it evil inherent in the daughters of Eve themselves? Is it lawless lust or force of circumstances that adds legion after legion to the cohorts of shame? Or has our boasted progress brought with it a suspicion that female chastity is, after all, an overprized bauble—that what is no crime against nature should be tolerated by this eminently practical age? We have cast behind us the myths and miracles, proven the absurdity of our ancestors' most cherished traditions and brought their idols beneath the iconoclastic hammer. In this general social and intellectual house-cleaning have we consigned virtue to the rubbish heap—or at best relegated it to the garret with the spinning-wheel, hand-loom and other out of date trumpery? Time was when a woman branded as a bawd hid her face for shame, or consorted only with her kind; now, if she can but become sufficiently notorious she goes upon the stage, and men take their wives and daughters to see her play "Camille" and kindred characters. This may signify much; among other things that the courtesan is creeping into social favor—even that a new code of morals is now abuilding, in which she will be the grand exemplar. As change is the order of the day, and what one age damns its successor ofttimes deifies, who knows but an up-to-date religion may yet be evolved with Bacchic revels for sacred rites and a favorite prostitute for high priestess?

Were I called upon to diagnose the social disease; did any duly ordained committee—from the numerous "Reform" societies, Ministerial Associations, secular legislatures or other bodies that are taking unto themselves great credit for assiduously making a bad matter worse—call upon me for advice anent the proper method of restoring to healthy life the world's moribund morality, I would probably shock the souls out of them by stating a few plain facts without troubling myself to provide polite trimmings.

You cannot reform society from the bottom; you must begin at the top.

Man, physically considered, is merely an animal, and the law of his life is identical with that of the brute creation. Continence in man or woman is a violation of nature's edicts, a sacrifice made by the individual to the necessities of civilization.

Like the beast of the field, man formerly took unto himself a mate, and with his rude strength defended her from the advances of other males. Such, reduced to the last analysis, is the basis of marriage, of female chastity and family honor. Rape and adultery were prohibited under pains and penalties, and behind the sword of the criminal law grew up the moral code. As wealth increased man multiplied his wives and added concubines; but woman was taught that while polygamy was pleasing to the gods polyandry was the reverse—that while the husband was privileged to seek sexual pleasure in a foreign bed, the wife who looked with desiring eyes upon other than her rightful lord merited the scorn of earth and provoked the wrath of heaven.

For long ages woman was but the creature of man's caprice, the drudge or ornament of his home, mistress of neither her body nor her mind. But as the world advanced and matter was made more subject unto mind—as divine Reason wrested the sceptre from brute Force—woman began to assume her proper place in the world's economy. She is stepping forth into the garish light of freedom, is realizing for the first time in the history of the human race that she is a moral entity—that even she, and not another, is the arbiter of her fate. And, as ever before, new-found freedom is manifesting itself in criminal folly—liberty has become a synonym for license.

The "progressive" woman—the woman who is not only well "up-to-date," but skirmishing with the future—is asking her brother: "If thou, why not I? If man is forgiven a score of mistresses must woman, blessed with like reason and cursed with kindred passions, be damned for one lover?" And while the question grates upon her ear, the answer comes not trippingly to the tongue. I do not mean that all women who imagine themselves progressive are eager to assume the same easy morals that from time immemorial have characterized the sterner sex; but this line of argument, peculiar to their class, while not likely to make men better, is well calculated to make foolish women worse. The sooner they realize that he-Dians are scarce in the country as brains in the head of a chrysanthemum dude; that such sexual purity as the world is to be blessed withal must be furnished by the softer sex, the better for all concerned. That they will eventually cease their altogether useless clamor that bearded men become as modest as blushing maids, and agree with the poet that "Whatever is, is right," the lessons of history bid us hope. When the French people threw off the yoke of the royalist and aristocrat they likewise loudly clamored for equality, fraternity and other apparently reasonable but utterly impossible things, until the bitter school of experience taught them better. The progressive women have not yet set up la Belle Guillotine—in Washington or elsewhere—for the decapitation of male incorrigibles; which significant fact confirms our old faith that the ladies rather like a man who would not deliberately overdo the part of Joseph.

But the female "reformer," with her social board of equalization theories, is but a small factor in that mighty force which is filling the land with unfaithful wives and the potter's field with degraded prostitutes.

When the people of a nation are almost universally poor, sexual purity is the general rule. Simple living and severe toil keep in check the passions and make it possible to mould the mind with moral precepts. But when a nation becomes divided into the very rich and the extremely poor; when wilful Waste and woful Want go hand in hand; when luxury renders abnormal the passions of the one; and cupidity, born of envy, blunts the moral perceptions of the other, then indeed is that nation delivered over to the world, the flesh and the devil. When all alike are poor, contentment reigns. The son grows up a useful, self-reliant man, the daughter an industrious virtuous woman. From this class comes nearly every benefactor of mankind. It has ever been the great repository of morality, the balance-wheel of society, the brain and brawn of the majestic world. Divided into millionaires and mendicants, the poor man's son becomes feverish to make a showy fortune by fair means or by foul, while his daughter looks with envious eye upon m'lady, follows her fashions and too often apes her morals. The real life is supplanted by the artificial, and people are judged, not by what they are, but by what they have. The "true-love match" becomes but a reminiscence—the blind god's bow is manipulated by brutish Mammon. Men and women make "marriages of convenience," consult their fortunes rather than their affections—seek first a lawful companion with a well-filled purse, and then a congenial paramour.

The working girl soon learns that beyond a few stale platitudes—fired off much as a hungry man says grace —she gets no more credit for wearing honest rags than flaunting dishonest silks; that good name, however precious it may be to her, is really going out of fashion—that when the world pretends to prize it above rubies it is lying —is indulging in the luxury of hypocrisy. She likewise learns that the young men really worth marrying, knowing that a family means a continual striving to be fully as fashionable and artificial as those better able to play the fool, seek mistresses rather than wives. She becomes discouraged, desperate, and drifts into the vortex.

Much is said by self-constituted reformers of the lachrymose school anent trusting maids "betrayed" by basehearted scoundrels, and loving wives led astray by designing villains; but I could never work my sympathies up to the slopping over stage for these pathetic victims of man's perfidy. It may be that my tear-glands lack a hairtrigger attachment, and my sob-machine is not of the most approved pattern. Perchance woman is fully as big a fool as these reformers paint her—that she has no better sense than a blind horse that has been taught to yield a ready obedience to any master—to submit itself without question to the guidance of any hand. Will the "progressive" woman—who is just now busy boycotting Col. Breckinridge and spilling her salt tears over his discarded drab—kindly take a day off and tell us what is to become of this glorious country when such incorrigible she-idiots get control of it? It is well enough to protect the honor of children with severe laws and a double-shotted gun; but the average young woman is amply able to guard her virtue if she really values it, while the married woman who becomes so intimate with a male friend that he dares assail her continence, deserves no sympathy. She is the tempter, not the victim. True it is that maids, and matrons too, as pure as the white rose that blooms above the green glacier, have been swept too far by the fierce whirlwind of love and passion; but of these the world doth seldom hear. The woman whose sin is sanctified by love—who staked her name and fame upon a cowardly lie masquerading in the garb of eternal truth—never yet rushed into court with her tale of woe or aired her grievance in the public prints. The world thenceforth can give but one thing she wants, and that's an unmarked grave. May God in his mercy shield all such from the parrot criticisms and brutal insults of the fish-blooded, pharisaical female, whose heart never thrilled to love's wild melody, yet who marries for money—puts her frozen charms up at auction for the highest bidder, and having obtained a fair price by false pretenses, imagines herself pre-eminently respectable! In the name of all the gods at once, which is the fouler crime, the greater "social evil:" For a woman to deliberately barter her person for gold and lands, for gew-gaws, social position and a preferred pew in a fashionable church—even though the sale be in accordance with law, have the benediction of a stupid priest and the sanction of a corrupt and canting world—or, in defiance of custom and forgetful of cold precept, to cast the priceless jewel of a woman's honor upon the altar of illicit love?

Give the latter woman a chance, forget her fault, and she will become a blessing to society, an ornament to heaven; the former is fit inhabitant only for a hell of ice. She has deliberately dishonored herself, her sex and the man whose name she bears, and Custom can no more absolve her than the pope can pardon sin. She is the most dreadful product of the "Social Evil," of unhallowed sexual commerce—is the child of Mammon and Medusa, the blue-ribbon abortion of this monster-bearing age.

A FINANIAL FETICH.

The gold reserve is at present making life a burden to
the powers that be. No African tribe deprived of its
stuffed snake, or maid forlorn despoiled of her virginity,
ever filled the circumambient ether with clamor more dol-
orous than that with which the Cleveland administration is
rending heaven's imperial concave because its blessed financial fetich is endangered. Its doleful jeremiads mount
heavenward night and day, while its piteous appeals to
Congress to come to the rescue of its god of gold and thereby
save the country from its impending doom, are sufficient to
melt a heart of adamant. The round earth reels beneath its
burden of agony and the tom-tom wildly beats to frighten
from its sacrilegious feast the omnivorous demon that is
devouring the great monetary moon which regulates the
commercial tides—and sometimes afflicts with lunar madness those politicians who repose beneath its horizontal
rays. Perhaps ere these mournful lines are committed to
cold type by the deft fingers of a fair compositor the dreadful danger will have passed, and Cleveland's wild alarums
and Carlisle's sad lament disturb our dreams no more.
Perhaps even a Democratic Congress can be prevailed upon
to come to the rescue of its imperilled country, and thereby
relieve the agonized President of the awful alternative of
letting it go to Hades, or appealing to his political foes for
saving grace—throwing the Goddess of Liberty into the
arms of Reed, who is supposed to have played Sextus Tar-
quinus to the old dame's Lucrece.

The Cleveland administration has already increased the
nation's interest-bearing debt $100,000,000 to galvanize
the moribund Gold Reserve, and now admits that it might
as well have poured a Houston *Post* editorial into a sieve,
or stored its watermelon crop in the vicinity of a nigger
camp-meeting. Perhaps in the fullness of time the idea
will worm itself even into the President's nice fat head that
when a brick block can be built on the point of a ten-penny
nail, $100,000,000 of gold will form a sufficient "basis" for
a two-billion dollar currency—that the Gold Reserve "pro-
tects the credit of our circulating media" much as a rabbit's
foot wards off headless hobgoblins, or compels the reluct-
ant smiles of Fortune.

Think of $100,000,000 of gold going "security" for more

Does not every man with sufficient intelligence to avoid standing under a waterspout like an inept gosling till he drowns, know that if the Gold Reserve were really necessary to the credit of our currency, capitalists would no more make war upon it than they would scratch a match in a powder house or gaily bestride a buzz-saw making a million revolutions a minute? Cannot even the most irremediable monetary mutton-head understand that if the integrity of our circulating media depended on the preservation of the Gold Reserve, Carlisle could gather into the treasury half the yellow coin of the country in a single week without issuing a single interest-bearing bond—that it would be forced upon him whenever there was the slightest suspicion that "the basis of our currency" was in danger? Cannot Secretary Carlisle himself understand that if his theory be correct Wall Street would even now be eager to exchange gold for paper instead of vice versa—would lend to the government without interest all the gold it could scrape together?

The very fact that it is possible for a few men to exhaust the Gold Reserve in a single day proves conclusively that it is not and cannot possibly be the "basis" of our currency's credit—that it is a ridiculous as well as an expensive nuisance. A security that may be destroyed any day, and which is at all times notoriously insufficient, is utterly useless so far as establishing confidence is concerned. If the government had possession of every gold coin in the country it could redeem but little more than one-half the outstanding paper currency. The people know full well that should they become fearful of their paper money and demand gold for it they could not get it, to-day, to-morrow or next year—that to redeem it dollar for dollar is a physical impossibility. Isn't that a fine "basis of credit?" And yet nobody appears to be seriously alarmed except the Cleveland administration, a few "cuckoo" newspapers—and those capitalists who bought the $100,000,000 worth of bonds!

The bulk of our currency consists of irredeemable paper —irredeemable because it exceeds all the gold and silver coin in the country! And yet it is accepted even more readily than gold itself—is "money current with the merchant" in every State of the American Union.

If all the gold and silver mined and minted since the days of King Solomon were sunk beneath the waters of the sea, our paper currency would continue to circulate and enjoy the same respect that it does to-day. Why? Because

than $1,600,000,000 of paper and silver; that were a "16 t[
1" ratio worth considering! There is not $600,000,000 ol
gold coin in the entire country; yet we are expected to
believe a paper dollar isn't worth a whoop in Hades unless
"backed by the yellow metal,"—that but for the "guarantee" of gold, silver would be discredited and lie down in
the middle of the road. Think of a bank with but $1,000
in ready cash, and whose entire assets amount to less than
$6,000 enjoying the entire confidence of an intelligent com-
munity that has more than $16,600 on deposit! Yet that
is the position of Uncle Sam to-day if gold be. in very
truth, "the basis of our currency." Turn Cheops upside
down and you get a fair idea of the present monetary situation as seen by those financiers whom God in his inscrutable wisdom has suffered to take charge of our affairs.

Suppose the theory of Cleveland and Carlisle be correct
—that the Gold Reserve is really the bulwark of our currency, and that should it be exhausted we would plunge to
the dreaded "silver basis" like Lucifer hurled headlong out
of heaven, and all our cartwheel and paper currency lose
half its purchasing power: Who, then, is most interested in
maintaining it unimpaired? Is it not the capitalistic, the
creditor class—the very men who are assiduously assaulting it and who have twice "forced" the administration to
issue bonds to replenish it? If the purchasing power of
the dollar be reduced one-half, the debtor is not damaged,
but the creditor is despoiled. The price of the farmer's
products and the wage of labor quickly adjust themselves
to the new conditions; but the man who has money loaned,
or corded up awaiting investment, finds half of it turned to
ashes and has absolutely no recourse. If the Reserve be of
so much importance to the capitalist why is he constantly
encroaching upon it—even locking up gold lest the government get hold of it, and with it ward off his impending
ruin? If the financial Samsons insist on pulling the monetary temple down about their ears why should Messrs.
Cleveland and Carlisle tearfully appeal to Congress to head
'em off? Why should we poor but honest Democrats who
are struggling—and not always successfully—to discharge
our debts, be expected to sit up o'nights and lament because
our creditors insist on forgiving half our obligations? Why
bribe the capitalist with interest-bearing bonds to refrain
from hoisting himself with his own petard. Let the
damphool but kerosene his coat-tails and apply a match before ascending, and he will make a very respectable sky-
rocket.

it serves the purpose for which it was created; because
commerce does not care whether it will exchange for any
other kind of money or not so long as it will expeditiously
effect the exchange of pork and potatoes, soap and sad-
irons; because it constitutes a claim on the entire wealth
of this mighty Yankee nation—a lien upon every bale of
cotton and bushel of corn, a claim upon every waving
wheat-field and ounce of ore—a mortgage on every acre of
sunny soil upon which falls the shadow of our flag.

What a man wants to know is that he can purchase with
the dollar as much of the world's wealth as he gives therefor. Assured of that, he slips it into his jeans and goes on
his way rejoicing. But, it will be asked what imparts this
virtue to a piece of paper? We have already shown that
it is not the Gold Reserve that does it—that a bank whose
liabilities are known to be double its total assets cannot
possibly command public confidence. If the creditors of a
concern should demand their money it would be compelled
to close its doors—and the very day that our paper currency is discredited by commerce that day redemption will
cease.

Upon what is confidence in our currency grounded if not
on gold? Upon confidence in the stability of the American
Government, upon experience, credit, necessity! Upon ocular demonstration that it is an efficient exchange medium,
an effective tool of trade.

The fear that our paper currency will depreciate in purchasing power if not redeemed in gold on demand can exist
only in the minds of those who are ignorant both of the lessons of history and the maxims of the foremost financiers
of the last two centuries. The currency of a country, no
matter of what it be made, only depreciates in purchasing
power when there is more money than business, more
trade-tools than trade—when the supply of the exchange
media exceeds the demand. Expansion of the currency reduces, contraction increases the purchasing power of the
dollar, whether it be made of paper or metal—just as the
scarcity of labor raises the wage-rate and a surplus reduces
it. Eliminate all our gold and silver coin, leaving to do the
money-work of the country only the paper currency now
extant, and instead of destroying its credit you enhance its
value. The money-work must be done; if not by one
agent, then by another.

But this line of reasoning—or rather these statements of
fact—do not necessarily lead into the "Greenback" camp.
It is one thing to point out that the credit of our paper

trade-tool is not dependent upon the precious metals, and quite another to conclude from this premise that it were advisable to entrust the currency of the country to a paper-mill, a job-press and an omnium gatherum of political odds and ends who draw their financial inspiration from the Forks-of-the-creek. The man who imagines that adding to our exchange media necessarily increases our wealth would double the grocer's stock by multiplying his gallon measures.

As the volume of currency dominates the standard of value, the most important of all our multifarious tools of trade, it should be controlled by commerce instead of by a partisan Congress. And such is, to a great extent, the case to-day. Not to exceed 6 per cent. of the exchange media employed by the commerce of this country bears the government stamp, and the amount is steadily decreasing. Commerce has practically taken the "Money Question" out of the hands of the politicians. While partisan polemics have perorated, and political conventions resoluted; while able editors have poured forth columns of foolish advice and obfuscated Presidents looked into leather spectacles and sagely shook their heads; while the gold age and the silver age have struggled for their innings and the "wild-cat" and "red dog" have plaintively meowed or assiduously bayed the moon, commerce has quietly cut the Gordian knot —has provided itself, without the adventitious aid of the pol-itico-economic "reformer," with that great desideratum of industry, a flexible exchange medium which automatically adjusts itself to the requirements of trade. The development of our banking business, of our system of credits—of what has been not inaptly termed a "deposit currency"— renders it possible to transact nearly the entire business of the country without the use of actual money. Nearly 95 per cent. of all exchanges of goods are effected to-day without the shifting of a single dollar. Except in trifling trans-actions money is now used, not as a medium of exchange, but only as a measure of value. And it is worthy of remark that all our monetary troubles are caused by the 5 or 6 per cent. of political money we still employ.

Mr. Cleveland imagines that he is confronted with a frightful condition, when he is only harassed by a foolish theory. He has not kept pace with the progress of mone-tary science—is pounding along in the dust far in the rear and imploring the procession to chase itself and catch up. We transformed the metal dollar into paper, and supposed it to represent so much coin—that did not exist. We just imagined it a dollar, and that, by some thaumaturgic feat or alchemistic process, the government might give us for it the gold it did not have and which we did not want, and found it served as well as tho' it weighed a pound—as tho' redemption were easy at any time instead of impossible at all times. Then we went further, and instead of a dollar "based on (non-extant) coin," we imagined a dollar without even a green-coated paper ghost, and "based," not upon supposititious gold, but on commercial credit. And it, too, worked well—is, in fact, doing nearly all our monetary work to-day, and doing it better and cheaper than metal ever did.

And yet President Cleveland professes to believe that if he once permits that Gold Reserve to get away, a people possessing such a monetary imagination would be unable to exchange a keg of sauer-kraut for a calico shirt, a mugwump vote for a mixed-drink jag. He doesn't understand the capabilities of this country. Why, if worst came to worst, we could imagine that on Mars or the Moon there was located so much gold, and with that as "basis" for a paper currency, continue in business at the old stand—continue to exchange commodities. And we would have the sweet satisfaction of knowing that our Gold Reserve was safe—that we wouldn't have to bribe Wall Street with all the 5 per cent. bonds it could carry to let our sacred hoodoo alone.

We sincerely trust that Mr. Cleveland will cease to worry about "the credit of our currency"—will not wear himself to a skeleton trying to protect the Gold Reserve. The currency will take care of itself if the politicians will but restrain themselves until a plan can be devised for placing it altogether under the control of commerce; and as for the Gold Reserve, he might as well let it go to join Symme's Hole, or the long exploded fallacy that the government can make a currency of any kind that is "good the world over." The commerce of this country gives coin the cold-shoulder, as being both costly and clumsy; and we have never yet been able to build a gold eagle that didn't lose its tail-feathers and become simply a commodity like pork and potatoes the moment it crossed our frontiers—worth so much a pound in the country to which it was carried. There is no more reason why the government should provide commerce with minted gold for export than that it should put hot-house bouquets on the beeves we send abroad.

The Iconoclast would suggest that instead of increasing the excise taxes to enhance the public revenues during the present business depression, the Gold Reserve be applied to defraying the legitimate expenses of the government. If there is anything calculated to discredit our paper and silver dollars it is the action of the government itself in discriminating against them in the sale of its bonds—in persistently advertising that unless it can do what now appears doubtful, they must infallibly depreciate 50 per cent. Confidence is the basis of all currency; hence persistent calamity-clacking —predictions by those high in authority that it would depreciate in purchasing power—were sufficient to make the people distrustful even of gold itself.

THE BEAUTEOUS REBECCA.

A BILLET D'AMOUR.

Miss Rebecca Merlindy Johnson, Care Post, Houston, Tex.

My Erstwhile Own:—Pardon me, Merlindy, dear, for addressing you thro' the columns of a great religious journal, instead of slipping my tender billy-doo under your back gate by the melancholy light of the gibbous moon. Conditions have arisen in this unkind and captious age which make it necessary that I should hang my torn heart upon my sleeve for daws to peck at, instead of following the lead of my soulful longings and enclosing my viscera in an antique envelope, perfumed with frangipanna, and firing it at my Merlindy thro' the mails. You know—or I will grant you do—the poet says, "What great ones do the less will prattle of." They are prattling of you and I Merlindy. In the first flush of our fond affections we did forget that fixed upon us was the curious gaze of the *hoi polloi,* and ere we were aware Dame Rumor had donned her Sunday gown and sailed abroad to pour into the prurient public ear another tale of a trusting maid undone by selfish man—had even hinted that you were playing Madeline to my Willie. 'Twas all my fault. You were so pure and unsuspecting, so little versed in the ways of this wicked world, and I should have guarded you with the thoughtful solicitude of a careful shepherd shielding from a sneaping frost the fresh-dropped female lamb. I should not have permitted you to patter about the public streets in male attire and call yourself Rienzi Miltiades—I should have bade you beware those cute little breeches and that bob-tail coat.

Heaven forfend that I should be the unhappy cause of your spotless character being called in question. God wotteth well that your fair name and fame are dearer to me

than the ruddy drops that visit my sad heart. (See Don-
nelly's Cryptogram.) But you are not bearing yourself
toward me in a manner to allay suspicion. The public is
quick to see the similitude of your treatment of the Apostle
and Miss Pollard's haughty scorn of her former paramour,
and is hinting that like causes produce like effects—is even
putting its tongue in its larboard cheek and suggesting that
"Hell hath no fury like a woman scorned." But don't you
believe, Merlindy, that the Apostle scorns you. He knows
your worth, and will stick to you, thro' good and evil report,
like a dead game sport to loaded dice.

> "My pen is pore, my ink is pail,
> But love for you shall never fale."

Tho' you have ceased to love me, and decline to be even
a sister to me, I cannot forget those dear old days that are
dead, before "Pinkie" of the Hill tribes crept into our ambrosial Eden like the odor of Buffalo Bayou into the boudoir
of a Houston belle. You should be more cautious, Merlindy. You should remember that the public is watching
you as intently as a nigger preacher eyes the plug hat circulated for the capture of small coin. Tho' your heart may
break to-morrow you must be all smiles to-night. If you
desire to spill your fond affections on a blond vacuum
chained to an Aurora Borealis you should do it unostentatiously, and thereby dodge the damning suspicion that your
life is wrecked and that you are throwing away the fragments in a fit of hilarious desperation. You should not advertise the fact that you turn the hose on me when I seek
to warble some pathetic roundelay or work off an Ella
Wheeler yearn under your dormer window. You should
not bruit it abroad that you whistle on your lily-white fingers for the police when I attempt to unbosom my pent-up
agony to the sympathetic moon in your back yard.

Rebecca Merlindy, my soulful bird of Paradise, if you
have really soured on me—if our ecstatic yum-yum was too
intoxicatingly sweet for a steady diet—I shall not upbraid
you; but you should not with your dainty tootsie-wootsies,
trample on a true heart, nor play fast and loose with a pure
affection that has unwittingly warped itself about your lovely
diaphragm like a boa-constrictor encircling a yearling calf.
You have a right to discard me, Rebecca; but no right to
drive me to drink by turning up your patrician gold-cure
nose as I pass humbly by, then filling the white horse moustache of Epictetus Paregoric Hill with hyblaean honey.

But I will not complain. 'Twere better to have loved and

lost than ne'er to have loved at all. Instead of hanging my
harp on the willows I will attune it to the soul-sob key and
pour forth my sad lament like the bulbul warbling to the
red, red rose, while she presses the cruel thorn ever deeper
into her wounded heart. I will return good for evil, because
I am built that way. Instead of answering scorn with scorn,
as little souls would do, I will bend all my poor talents and
wobbly energies to the holy task of making you immortal.
And I will succeed, or burst a suspender in the sacred enterprise. I will dramatize our tale of true love turned awry,
and "Pinkie" shall play the heavy villain—shall hypnotize
you with the splendor of his sunset hair and make you err
against your better judgment. I will weave you into song
and story like a thread of burnished gold in a somber carpet
of rags, or a clean cuspidore in a Populist sanctum. The
ages yet to be shall remember you as the Apostle's sweetheart, even as the present recalls the Laura of Petrarch, the
Heloise of Abelard and the Dulcinea of Don Quixote. Tho'
parted in life we will be united in death. Posterity will attend to that—will scoop together our pathetic dust and plant
it in some romantic spot, where the shadow of the quivering aspen falls and the bull-frog's melancholy croak makes
life not worth the living. And every lover throughout the
wide, wide world whose affection has slipped its trolley-pole,
will come apilgriming as to some sacred shrine, pull off an
unpainted picket and drop upon our lowly mound the sympathetic sob and scalding tear.

Ah, Merlindy, you may not be so beautiful as Ida Wells,
nor so intellectual as Mrs. Lease; but my soulful song shall
so gloss your imperfections o'er that in the unborn ages yet
to be you'll loom up on the sensuous cigarette or soothing
"hardware" sign a very Hebe, and no living picture exhibit
will be complete without some counterfeit presentment of
your personal pulchritude, attired in hand-me-down pants.
Adios, but not farewell.

"THE APOSTLE."

THE BUCK NEGRO.

I once severly shocked the pseudo-philanthropists by suggesting that if the South is ever to rid herself of the negro
rape-fiend she must take a day off and kill every member
of the accursed race that declines to leave the country. I
am not wedded to my plan; but, like the Populists, I do in-

sist that those who object to it are in duty bound to offer
something better.

We have tried the restraining influence of religion and the
elevating forces of education upon the negro without avail.
We have employed moral suasion and legal penalties; have
incarcerated the offenders for life at hard labor, and hanged
them by the neck in accordance with statutory law. We
have hunted the black rape-fiend to death with hounds, bored
him with buckshot; fricasseed him over slow fires and flayed
him alive; but the despoilment of white women by these
brutal imps of darkness and the devil is still of daily occur-
ence. The baleful shadow of the black man hangs over
every Southern home like the sword of Damocles, like the
blight of death—an avatar of infamy, a decree of damnation.

There is not to-day in all this land of Christ an aged
mother who is safe one single hour unless guarded by watchful sons, a wife who may rest secure beyond the reach of her
husband's rifle, a female infant but may be sacrificed to feed
some black monster's lust the moment it leaves its father's
breast.

In the name of Israel's God, what shall we do?

This condition of affairs is becoming intolerable. A
man's first duty is not to an alien and inferior race, but to
his family. It is much better to shoot a negro before he
commits an irreparable crime against the honor of a family
than to hang him afterwards.

Drive out the "nigger"—young and old, male and female
—or drive him into the earth! It may be urged that the
"good negro" would suffer with the bad. It is impossible to
distinguish the one from the other until it is too late. It
were better that a thousand "good negroes"—if so many
there be—should suffer death or banishment than that one
good white woman should be debauched. We must consider ourselves first, others afterwards. The rights of the
white man are paramount, and if we do not maintain them
at any cost we deserve only dishonor.

During the slavery regime the negro kept his place like
any other beast of the field. He no more dreamed of co-
habitation with white women than does the monkey of mating with the swan; but when his shackles were stricken off
and he was accorded political equality with his old-time master he became presumptuous, insolent—actually imagined
that the foolish attempt of fanatics to humanize him had
been successful—that a law of nature had been repealed by
act of Congress! If we could but restore the negro to his

old ante-bellum condition of involuntary servitude and give him time to forget the social fallacies with which he has been inoculated by misguided theorists, all might be well with Sambo; but that is out of the question. We do not want to re-enslave him—he is not worth it. And if we desired to do so, the world, which is crazed with its own foolish cackle of "equality and fraternity," would not permit it.

No, we could not revive old customs if we would. There are too many long-haired men and short-haired women picking up a more or less honest livelihood by experimenting with Sambo at our expense, his wonderful "progress," his divine "rights" and his devilish "wrongs," to permit serious consideration of what is really best for him.

The negro is to the American social organism what a pound of putty would be in the stomach of a dypseptic. The sooner we realize this fact and spew him out, the better. It were as wise to make the eagle and the crow tenants of the same eyre as the white and black man of the same territory; as sensible to yoke Pegasus and a plow-horse as to make the Caucasian and the African co-rulers of the same country. The attempts of sociologists to "harmonize the races" are as absurd as trying to bring into the same diapason the twanging of a jewsharp and the music of the spheres—the effort to make the negro an element of strength to the nation's energy as misdirected as the labors of Gulliver's scientists at the academy of Lagado. The American nation would be billions of dollars better off to-day had Ham failed to get into the ark. The negro has been the immediate cause of more bitterness and bloodshed than his entire race, from its genesis to the present, is worth, and he will continue the fruitful cause of trouble so long as he is permitted to remain.

The XIVth amendment to the Constitution is a flagrant violation of natural law—of the law that the greater and less cannot be equal, that matter must be subject unto mind, that wisdom was born to rule and ignorance to obey. To deny that the greater shall govern the lesser intellect is to abrogate man's right to rule the beast and God's authority over Adam's sons.

The greatest injury ever done the people of the South was self-inflicted—the introduction of negro slavery. The next greatest was the act of the Federal Government in making the black man co-ordinate sovereign of the State. It would have been a thousand times better for the Southern people had they adopted paganism or polygamy instead of negro slavery—a thousand times better for them and the nation at large had the Federal Government confiscated every foot of soil in the insurgent States, put the torch to every dwelling, destroyed every factory and filled every harbor with the wreck of railroads and the debris of business blocks instead of putting the ballot in the hands of the black. The ruin wrought by torch and torpedo could have been quickly repaired; the damage done by the XIVth amendment is well-nigh irreparable. Burning with the accursed lust for political power, the Republican party, like another shameless Tarquin, held the knife at the throat of the Southern Lucrece while it robbed her of her honor, made her an object of contempt, her name a byword and a reproach. Pitifullest blunder of all the ages! Most damning infamy ever perpetrated since the dawn of Time! Fearfullest penalty brave men ever paid for daring death for conscience's sake!

This is a republic. The supreme power is, ostensibly at least, vested in the people. The voter is the sovereign. Suppose that it were an absolute monarchy: Would it not be a mistake unparalleled, a crime unspeakable to take from an ignorant, brutal slave his shackles and place upon his stupid head a crown? The Republican party did even worse. A sovereign cannot long oppress a brave and spirited people. Let him issue an edict that meets with general disapproval and it is laughed to scorn. Should he attempt to enforce it he is dragged from the throne. But the Republican party corrupted a sovereign from whose edict there is no appeal. It has debased the great army of voters, poisoned the political organism by injecting into it a vast mass of ignorance destitute of even the saving grace of virtue.

Had the negro been naturally the intellectual peer of the white man, it would have been a grievous blunder to give him the ballot, to force political responsibility upon him until at least a generation after his emancipation. He was an untutored savage in his native land, making no appreciable progress. He was captured, like any other wild beast, brought to America and sold into slavery. Here he was taught, not how to wisely rule, but to servilely obey. It required a thousand years of education to fit the thoughtful Saxon and the quick-witted Celt for the duties and responsibilities of American sovereignty; the stupid Ethiopian was fitted for them by the scratch of a pen and a partisan vote! Transformed from semi-savagery to super-civilization by the power of a political fiat! From slave to sovereign by the magic wand of genie! Fitted for American sovereignty! He was not fitted for it. Ten thousand years of civilization and education could no more qualify the negro for self-government than it could raise to the intellectual level of a lousy ape the piebald jackass who presides over the destinies of the Houston Post. True, it is that there are some negroes with a suggestion of intellect; but they are usually negroes only in name—mongrels in whose veins flows the blood of some depraved Caucasian bum. The pure blood blacks who have exhibited intellectual and moral qualities superior to those of the monkey, are few and far between. And yet the pure-blood Ethiop is generally a much better and safer member of society than the "yaller nigger," who appears to inherit the vices of both races and the virtues of neither.

The negro vote is dangerous because of its ignorance, doubly so because of its venality. It is utterly irresponsible, altogether reckless, knows little of principle, cares less, and will follow wherever the most blatant demagogue or the most liberal purse will lead. Is it any wonder that there is occasional "bulldozing" at the polls in the Black Belt—that men whose ancestors wrung Magna Charta from King John and recognition of American independence from King George, should decline to be dominated by the bastard spawn of white bummers and black bawds?

The presence of the negro in the South has kept this section a century in arrears of what it would otherwise be. It has prevented white immigration; it has kept out capital; it has bred a contempt among the Southern whites for labor; it has fomented strife between sections and is still fostering provincial prejudice, fanning the fires of sectional hate. The South could afford to give the negro, black and "yaller," a hundred millions of money to leave the country and never return. The negro is, for a verity, the bete-noire of the South, a millstone about her neck, tending ever to drag her down into the depths of social and political degradation. Every Southern man, every man of whatever clime, long resident here, and not sans eyes, ears and understanding, knows this to be true.

Does the Southern press proclaim it? Not at all. The Southern press, believing the black man a fixture—that the disease is incurable—with a burst of optimism that discounts that of the man who thanked God for the itch because of the luxury of scratching, proclaims his presence an inestimable boon, a transcendent blessing. Every day we are told that the negro is "the natural laborer of the cotton, cane and rice field"—whatever that novel economic theorem may mean. If it meant thereby that white labor is not adapted to those industries, it needs no further refutation than a glance at existing conditions. In every Southern State and county white men are performing identically the same kind of labor as the black, and performing it better. There is not a spot within the broad confines of the United States where the African can live and labor that the Caucasian cannot live as well and labor with more effect.

Remove the negro from the South and this section will quickly become the most populous, prosperous and progressive portion of the American Union. But will the negro be removed? Not at all. The two great political parties need him in their manufacturing industry—the making of political "issues."

The negro will remain right where he is, wear the cast-off clothes of the white man, steal his fowls, black his boots and rape his daughters, while the syphilitic "yaller gal" corrupts his sons. Yes, the negro will stay, stay until he is faded out by fornication—until he is absorbed by the stronger race, as it has absorbed many a foul thing heretofore.

A VISION OF HEAVEN.

It was in the year of our Lord 1893, the seventh day of the ninth month, hour midnight. The editor had toiled all day trying to harmonize the two wings of the Texas Democracy—had held out the olive branch of peace until his arm ached. He was now reclining on a pile of exchanges in the sanctum, listening to the dreamy rhythm of the music that floated in from an adjacent beer garden, the monotonous clickety-click of the Mergenthalers and the impromptu observations of the office cat to a visiting Thomas feline on the back gallery. The music of the beer garden orchestra gradually swelled into a mighty anthem, and the office cat's sad complaint became a paean of praise, the rat-tat-tat of the Mergenthalers, the click of golden slippers, keeping time to celestial music on the ballroom floor of a house not built with hands, and the fitful gleam of an arc light, filtering through the dust and grime of an uncurtained window a Jacob's ladder, on the top rung of which a seraph poised with outstretched wings, like a blue jay on the top twig of a Washingtonian cherry tree.

"Ascend," he commanded, and the editor complied.

"What's the matter now?" he asked the seraph, as the latter gave him a lift and pulled in the ladder like a country belle taking the cube-root of a yard of gum. "Has another rebellion broken out in Heaven?"

"Naw," said the seraph with a shrug of his wings; "I thought perhaps you'd like to write up our town. Of course, if you do so it must be for its news features. We are not placing any advertising at present. Times are too hard, and corner lots in the New Jerusalem are not what they were in the city's boom days. Immigration has fallen off to such an extent that St. Peter says the entrance fees don't pay for greasing the hinges of the gate, and he's thinking of padlocking it and applying for a new job. The committee on ways and means say we'll have to pave the streets with silver and set the throne with stage jewels if business doesn't improve pretty soon."

"What's the matter?"

"Too much hide-bound orthodoxy and too little Christianity. Now, were you to suggest that St. John had a bad case of the jimjams when he saw all those funny things, the people down below would probably mob you. The preachers would thunder against you from the pulpit, and Deacon Twogood pronounce you a blasphemous atheist. Of course, every man's an atheist who doesn't see God through Deacon Twogood's telescope, and every man a blasphemer who applies historical criticism to the Bible—who attempts to separate the word of God from the folly of the redacteurs. Still, these good people continue to build palatial churches in which to practice hypocrisy, while men with families to support are glad of a chance to toil from sun to sun three times a week for a dollar a day! A man in that condition naturally becomes an anarchist, if not a criminal, and if his children do not turn out thieves and his wife a prostitute it is no fault of either society or the Church. I think the Almighty is getting tired of lending His name to such religious layouts, and I don't blame Him. If He ever asks my advice I'll tell Him to smash with His thunderbolts every church on earth that costs more than $5,000 and start the fool-killer on the trail of every preacher who prattles about blasphemy while children are begging bread and women are dying of want. What the old world needs is a religion of humanity —one broad enough and liberal enough to take up into its bosom every creature created in the image of God."

By this time the editor and the other seraph had reached a narrow gate, over which was inscribed in golden capitals: "Orthodox Heaven." The seraph pulled the bell and St. Peter peeped out through the wicket. Seeing that it was a newspaper man he threw wide the gate and removed his crown as a mark of respect.

"I'd best give you a return check," he said. "You're from Texas, and you'll want to go back in an hour or two."

"Where's Judas Iscariot?" asked the traveler.

"Oh," said the man on the door, "Judas has been in hell nearly 2,000 years. You see, he sold his Saviour for thirty pieces of——."

"Yes, yes; but he had the decency to go hang himself. Now there was another disciple who went back on his Master because he feared the rabble would ride him on a rail, then sat down and bawled like a spanked baby because he was a born coward and——"

But St. Peter was pointing out to a Populist the shortest road to Perdition and evidently did not hear. A man of majestic mien and carrying a golden harp came forward and grasped the wanderer's hand.

"Do they still read my poetry down below?" he asked eagerly. "What do the modern critics say of it?"

"Permit me to introduce King David," said the seraph. "Davy, this is the editor of the Great Religious." The psalmist was delighted and wanted to present the pilgrim to Mrs. David, No. 923, but the editor checked him. He didn't care to make female acquaintances in a strange city.

"Let's see; aren't you the party who despoiled Uriah's wife, then had that gentleman murdered to conceal your crime?"

"Oh, please don't put that in the papers," pleaded Saul's successor. "Of course, on earth little things like that are charged up to a fellow, but they make no difference in the orthodox heaven. If a man is only pious and strictly orthodox, all things are forgiven him. Ah, here is my distinguished ancestor, Father Abraham. Allow me to present you."

"Come nestle in this bosom with Lazarus," said the patriarch; but the pilgrim, being somewhat choice of his bedfellows, dodged the embrace.

"Are you the party who gave up his wife to the lustful Orientals, saying, 'She is my sister?' Are you the party who preferred the life of a cuckold to the death of a gentleman?" But he had already seized a harp and joined in the serpentine dance about the throne, crying with his cracked voice, "Holy, holy, holy."

Lot and his two daughters came tripping by to the sound of timbrel. The seraph beckoned the husband of the pillar of salt and he came to a standstill.

"You are the party whose righteousness saved him when Sodom and Gomorrah did the Herculaneum act?" He nodded. "Well, I'd just like to ask you, for the information of a medical fraternity, how a man who is dead drunk can accomplish what you did in the cave at——"

"Don't mention it," pleaded the beloved of the Lord, and he blew a blast on a golden trumpet, pulled his crown about his ears and joined in the sacred dance with his youngest daughter for partner.

"Who are those people bearing down upon us with crashing cymbals and loud hosannahs?" asked the scribe.

"That," replied the seraph, "is Murderers' Band. Those people were all hanged for infamous crimes; but when they found they were in for it—that they could not get a commutation of sentence to life imprisonment—repented and were jerked to Jesus. That fellow who leads the procession and whose hallelujah is particularly unctuous, murdered his mistress, a sweet little girl whom he had debauched, and whom he compelled to enter a house of infamy to supply him with whisky money. The papers printed an account of the crime and his execution some time ago."

"Catch the celestial bird and give him to me," pleaded the scribe. "I long to hear him warble." He came with his ambrosial locks streaming wide on the celestial air, a song in his mouth, an instrument of melody in his hand.

"Hello, Jim! How did you break in here? Where's Julia?"

"Oh, Julia's in hell," said Jim gaily, as he swept the strings of his instrument and cried, "Glory, glory, glory!"

"You see, she didn't have time to repent. She tried to shake me and I brained her with a hatchet. I got religion, and here I am, with two pair of reversible wings—came direct from the scaffold. But Julia's frizzling in everlasting fire. Strike the timbrel, blow the trumpet and let there be a joyful noise unto the——"

"Whoa! Shut off that sanctified Ta-ra-ra Boom-de-aye and tell me about Julia. She was a child pure as a lily, sweet as the incense that rises from Buddha's altar. You led her astray. You dragged her down to the lowest depths ever touched by womankind. You beat her. You brought Chinamen to visit her, took the price of her shame, bought whisky, and murdered her because she dared plead with you not to further humiliate her. You say that she is in hell. Do you ever go to see her? Do you ever carry a cup of cold water to cool her parched lips? Does her agony haunt you? Does it cause the anthem to die on your lips and the hot tears to scald your cheeks? Do you pray God to allow you to change places with her?"

"What are you giving me? T'ink I'm a chump? We 'uns up here don't worry about der lost. That's their biz; see?" And he was gone—chanting Solomon's assignation song.

Just then John Calvin came along. "Where's Servetus?" asked the scribe. "Where should he be but in hell?" retorted John. "He was a heretic and I burned him. Of course, he was an honest, truthful, kindly-hearted man, with more brains in his little finger than I had in my head; but he got wrong in his scriptural views, and, as in duty bound, I made a bonfire of him. Praise the Lord God Almighty, who is a merciful God!" And he drifted on to meet Henry VIII, who was gaily whistling, "Catharine, my Catharine."

"Have you any respectable people up here?" asked the scribe pulling the seraph aside by one of his pin-feathers.

"Well," said he, glancing about apprehensively, "to give you a straight deal, I think the respectable people are all in hell. And to tell you truly, I believe they are far happier down there than this job-lot of pious murderers and sanctified hypocrites up here. Of course, the climatic conditions are not conducive of ecstasy, but the society is infinitely more select, and there's such a thing as human sympathy and love among the lost. Of course, I don't want you to give me away, but——"

"Nine columns short—wires all flat—two machines kerflummixed—news editor tearing his hair—foreman cussin' a blue streak—what'n Helen Blazes we goin' o' do? Say?"

It was the "devil." The "Vision of Heaven" vanished, and the weary editor cried out in agony, "This is hell!"

APOSTLE VS. PAGAN.

Col. R. G. Ingersoll:

My Dear Colonel:—I have not picked up my pen for the express purpose of annihilating you at one fell swoop. Even were such the case, I do not flatter myself that your impending doom would cause you to miss meals or lose sleep, for you have become somewhat used to being knocked off the Christmas tree by theological disputants from the back districts. At least once each lunar month for long years past your quivering diaphragm has been slammed up against the shrinking face of nature by mental microbes, or walked on by ambitious doodle-bugs, who wondered next day to learn that you were absorbing your rations with clock-work regularity and doing business at the same old stand. I once saw

an egotistical brindle-pup joyfully bestride the collar of an
adult wild-cat, and the woeful result convinced me that Ambition and Judgment should blithely foot it hand in hand.
That is why, my dear Colonel, I approach you by siege and
parallel, instead of capering gaily down your right-o'-way
like a youthful William goat seeking a head-end collision
with a runaway freight train.

Without any view of paving the way for a future loan, I
tell you frankly that I admire you very much. Your public
record and private life prove you to be one of God's noblest
—and rarest—works, an honest man. That you are the
equal morally and the superior mentally of any man who
has presumed to criticise you must be conceded. The prejudices of honesty are entitled to consideration and the judgment of genius to respect bordering on reverence; but in
this age of almost universal inquiry we cannot accept any
man, however wise, as infallible pope in the realm of intell-
lect and declare that from his *ipse dixit* there shall be no
appeal. That were intellectual slavery, the most degrading
species of bondage, and it is your greatest glory that you
have ever been the apostle of liberty—liberty of the hand
and liberty of the brain. More than all other men of your
generation you have fostered independence of thought and
the search for new truth; hence you cannot complain if the
fierce light which you have taught the world to turn full and
fair upon cults and creeds, should be employed to discern
the false logic of the great critic himself.

In your warfare upon hypocrisy and humbuggery I am
with you heart and soul. I will set my foot as far as who
goes farthest in the exposure of frauds and fakes of every
class and kind, tho' hedged about with the superstitions of
a thousand centuries and licensed by prescriptive right to
perpetrate a brutal wrong; but it does not follow because
some church communicants are hypocrites that all religion
is a humbug; that because the Bible winks at incest and robbery, murder and slavery, the book is but a tissue of foolish
falsehoods; that because Almighty God has not seen proper
to reveal himself in all his supernal splendor to Messrs.
Hume and Voltaire, Pan and Ingersoll the world has no good
reason for belief in his existence—that because the dead do
not come back to us with a diagram of the New Jerusalem it
were folly to believe the soul of man immortal.

My dear Colonel, your mighty intellect has not yet com-
prehended the philosophy of religion. Oratorically you soar
like the condor when its shadow falls upon the highest peaks
of the Andes, but logically you grope among the pestilential

shadows of an intellectual Dismal Swamp, ever mistaking shadow for substance. You are frittering away your mighty intellectual strength with the idiosyncrasies of creeds and the clumsy detail of cults, instead of considering the psychological phenomena of religion in its entirety. You descend from the realm of philosophy to assume the role of scholastic—to dispute with little men anent points of doctrine, to wrangle with dogmatists regarding their conception to the Deity.

An ignoramus believes the Bible because of the miracles, and because of the miracles an Ingersoll disbelieves it—and both are equally blind. A cult is simply an expression, more or less crude, of the religious sentiment of a people, the poor garment with which finite man clothes Infinity. Would you quarrel with Science because it is not yet made perfect? Would you condemn music because of an occasional discord? Would you reject history altogether because amid a world of truth there are preserved some fables such as tempted the satire of Cervantes? Would you banish the sun from heaven because of its spots or declare Love a monster because born of Passion?

The real question at issue is not whether the miracles be fact or fable; Mahomet, the duly ordained prophet of Allah, or an ignorant adventurer; Jonah a delegate of the Deity or the father of Populism—whether Christ was born of an earthly father or drew his vigor direct from the loins of omnipotent God. Let us leave these details to the dogmatists, these non-essentials to the sectarians. Let us consider the religion of the world in its entirety, with the full understanding that all sects are essentially the same.

The core of all religion is the worship of a Supreme Power, and the belief in man's immortality. That is the central idea, around which the imagination of man has woven many a complicated web, some beautiful as Arachne's robe, some barbaric and repulsive, but all of little worth. The wise man, the true philosopher, will not mistake the machinery of a religion for the religious idea, the garment which ignorance weaves for Omniscience, for God himself.

Even if we grant that the Creator never yet communicated directly with the creature; that man has not seen with mortal eyes beyond the veil that shrouds the two eternities, it does not follow that religious faith is but arrant folly, that God is non-extant and man but the pitiful creature of blind force. The dumb brute knows many things it was never taught, and might not man, the greatest of the animal creation, be gifted with a knowledge not based upon experience? So far as observation goes, there is provision for the satisfaction of every passion, and the most powerful of all passions is the dread of annihilation—the longing for continual life. If death ends all then here is a violation of "natural law"—a miracle! And you, my dear Colonel, do not believe in miracles. If we discard Revelation and take Reason for our supreme guide, we must infallibly conclude that the devotional instinct implanted in the heart of the entire human race has its correlative—that the longing for immortal life which burns in the breast of man was not a brutal mistake, else concede Nature a poor blunderer and all this prattle anent her "immutable laws" mere nonsense.

Before ridiculing Revelation and mocking at Inspiration were it not well to determine their true definition? What is genius but inspiration? and a new truth bodied forth to the world but a revelation? Were it not possible for a genius—an inspired man—to trace the finger of God in the sunset's splendor as easily as upon tables of stone? to hear the voice of Omnipotence in the murmur of the majestic sea as well as in the thunders of Sinai? to read a divine message of undying love in a mother's lullaby as readily as in the death and resurrection of a Deity? If God can teach the very insects wisdom and gift even the oyster with instinct, can He communicate with man only by word of mouth or the engraver's burin? Examine the most beautiful woman imaginable with a powerful microscope and you will turn from her with a disgust similar to that of Gulliver when the Brobdingnagian maid placed him astride the nipple of her bosom. Her skin, so fair to the natural eye and velvety to the touch, becomes beneath the microscope suggestive of the hide of a hairless Mexican dog. Religion is a beautiful, an enchanting thing if you do but look at it with the natural eye; but when you employ the adventitious aid of the skeptic's microscope you find flaws enough. It were doubtful if even our boasted American Government, of which you are so proud, could stand such an examination and retain your confidence.

No, my dear Colonel; you will never banish worship from the world by warring upon non-essentials. You may demonstrate that every recorded miracle is a myth—that the founders of the various cults were but mortal men and the writers of every sacred book but scheming priests. You may make it gross to sense that the Creator has never held direct communication with the creature, and you have but stripped religion of its tattered vestments—have not laid the weight of your hand upon the impregnable citadel, the universal Fatherhood of God and Brotherhood of Man. You have never yet talked to the real question. You reject religion because

Moses and Mahomet, Luther and Calvin entertained crude ideas of the plans and attributes of the Creator. You pose as an agnostic—a religious Knownothing—because the Almighty has not taken you completely into his confidence. Because the blind have sometimes led the blind and both have fallen into the foul ditch of fanaticism and cruelty, you infer that not one gleam of supernal glory has pierced the dark vale of human life. While posing as the apostle of light, you will obscure the scintillations of the stars because the sun is hid; while apotheosizing Happiness you would banish Hope, that mother of which it is born.

But your labors have borne good as well as evil fruit. While your siren eloquence has led some doubting Thomases into the barren desert of Atheism, you have driven others to seek a better reason for their religious faith than barbarous tradition and the vote of ecumenical councils. Bigotry has quailed beneath the ringing blows of your iconoclastic hammer, dogmatism become more humble and the priesthood well-nigh forgotten to prate of a hell of fire in which the souls of unbaptized babes forever burn. Without intending it, perhaps, you have done more to promote the cause of true religion, more to intellectualize and humanize man's conception of Almighty God, than any other reformer since the days of Christ.

FAITH AND FOLLY.

"LET US HAVE PEACE."

In sixty centuries of earnest toil, with infinite pain and tearful prayer, what knowledge have we gained of God, oh brother mine, that we should quarrel about his plans or attributes? As yet we can but touch the hem of Divinity's robe; we can but hear His voice in dreams or catch in fleeting visions glimpses of His glory.

Why quarrel about our faiths, and declare that this is right or that is wrong, when all religions are, and must of necessity ever be, fundamentally one and the same—the worship of a Superior Power, the great

"Father of all, in every age, in ev'ry clime adored,
By saint, by savage and by sage, Jehovah, Jove, or Lord!"

Cult wars with cult, and sect with sect, while all unite to damn the independent worshipper; yet every man who bows the knee or breathes a prayer to any God of whatsoever name; every Egyptian bending at Isis' fanes and every Phenician sacrificing unto Baal; every Gueber worshipping his god of fire, and every Catholic following the sacred cross; every Peruvian adoring the rising sun and every Methodist agonizing at the mourner's bench, is a member of the same great church. They may accredit their God with different attributes and worship him in diverse ways; but their faiths, when stripped of non-essentials, are one and the same—their Deities are identical.

Men of our day, who from the dizzy heights of modern learning, hurl their logical thunderbolts at Mahomet's incoherent mouthings and Moses' solemn confabs with the Almighty anent matters of no possible moment; who sneer at Guatama's four-fold path to a Celestial Nowhere and denounce the worship of an illiterate carpenter as foolish blasphemy, forget that all things must have a beginning—that e'en proud Science sprang from the womb of stupid Ignorance, and stumbled, awkwardly enough, through long ages of Folly before she could firmly plant her feet upon the eternal rock of Fact.

I have no word of condemnation for any religious faith, however fatuous it may appear to me, that has cast one gleam of supernal glory into the dark vale of human life; but I regard with unspeakable contempt the man of these modern days who decries all religious progress and brands as blasphemers those who would take one step beyond the crude faiths of former days—insists that religion is too sacred to be handled by human reason, that mother of which it was born! It were folly to expect a people whose wisest men believed this world the centre of the universe and the stars mere ornaments of the night, to evolve a perfect religion, or form an intelligent conception of the great First Cause.

The Sacred Books of all the centuries are essentially the same—the half articulate voice of the world crying for light, the frantic efforts of man to learn whence he came and whither he goes, to lift the veil that shrouds the two eternities—to see and know! I gather them together—the Old Testament and the New, the Koran and the sacred Vedas, the northern Sagas and the southern Mythologies; I search them through, not to scoff, but to gather, with reverent soul, every gleam of light that since the birth of Time has been vouchsafed to man. I read the Revelations and ponder the Prophecies; I listen once again to the voice in the burning bush and the mystic whisperings of the Dodona Oak; I descend into the Delphic cave, or stand with uncovered head to hear the voice of Memnon answer to the rosy fingers of the morn. I sit with Siddartha beneath the Bodhi tree and follow the prophet of Islam in all his pilgrimings; I stand with Moses on Sinai's flaming crest and listen to the prayer of Christ in the Garden of Gethsemane, then I go forth beneath the eternal stars—each silently pouring its stream of sidereal fire into the great realm of Darkness—and they seem like the eyes of pitying angels, watching man work out, little by little, thro' the long ages, the mystery of his life.

THE AGE OF CONSENT.

Are the various legislatures of this alleged land of Christ composed chiefly of "chippy chasers," of lecherous libertines eager to despoil little school-girls—of unclean creatures who would violate the very cradle to feed lust's unholy fires?

No? Then why is it they persistently decline to give the little girls legal protection from moral destruction? Why is it that they deliberately disregard public opinion and turn a deaf ear to the pleading of ten thousand mothers, if they have not formed "a league with death and a covenant with hell?"

I will be told that our law-builders, like Brutus and his brother conspirators, are "honorable men." Did an honorable man ever yet decline to protect youth and innocence to the utmost of his power?

What is the record of the American legislatures anent this important matter? Most of them fixed the age of consent at ten years. Think of it, ye men with daughters completing their first decade! The men chosen by popular vote to make laws for a people boasting of their enlightenment, declared that a girl scarce old enough to prepare her trundle-bed or dress her dolls, was amply qualified to pass upon the most momentous question that can confront her between the cradle and the grave! One state actually fixed seven years as the age at which a girl may legally "consent" to carnal intercourse, her ravisher, tho' a full-grown man, not being liable to punishment for rape. And this is the country that is building laws to shield from desecration the "Christian Sabbath," sending missionaries to the antipodes to carry prayer-books and Bibles to barbarians—tithing itself to build palatial churches and provide legislative bodies with perfunctory prayer!

God of Israel, what a gall!

I lay it down as an impregnable proposition that the men who enacted these laws were knaves or they were fools. They were either corrupt to the heart's core, or it were fulsome flattery to brand them as burros. If fools they should have been caged, if knaves they should have been hanged. Their infamous legislation has left a foul blot on American civilization which centuries cannot erase. When the antiquarian of the future finds those revolting statutes in the ruins of our marble capitols he will decline to dignify us by calling us barbarians—he will brand us brutes!

A decade ago the age of consent in England was thirteen years. A careful investigation resulted in the disclosure of crimes against children that appalled the civilized world. Parliament promptly raised to sixteen the age at which a female may legally part with that priceless jewel of her soul, her chastity. Gladstone insisted on eighteen years, but was overruled by the younger members, many of whom had mistresses under that age. The agitation spread to America, where for ten years the ladies, supported by public opinion, the pulpit and the press, have attempted to secure legal protection for their little daughters.

In twenty-nine States and Territories the age of consent still ranges from ten to fourteen years. A few States have been induced, after an heroic struggle, to raise it to sixteen, even eighteen, years, and, now, as if ashamed of this concession to common decency, are trying to reduce it again. The Texas legislature did finally consent a few years ago to increase from ten to twelve the age at which a babe is privileged to become a bawd; but the victory cost the ladies a severe struggle. The matter has been brought forcibly to the attention of the present Legislature, and the Senate has actually succeeded—after much industrious lobbying by the ladies—in passing, over powerful opposition, a bill raising the age of consent to fifteen years; also one prohibiting the sale of cigarettes to "children under sixteen!" What the fate of this bill in the House will be I do not at this writing (February 12) know; but it is safe to say the most potent, grave and reverend jackasses—who consider cigarette smoking a crime and fornication but a venial fault—will consent to no improvement.

As matters now stand in Texas an unmarried woman of twenty cannot legally purchase a bottle of beer or sell a foot of land. At seventeen she cannot legally contract an honorable marriage without the consent of parents or guardian; she is an infant in the purview of the law—for every purpose but prostitution! She is not mistress of her property until twenty-one, but mistress of her person at twelve!

I lay down the proposition that when a girl is old enough to be entrusted with the guardianship of her virtue she is old enough to contract a marriage without asking permission of any one; that when she is old enough to become an unclean prostitute she is old enough to become an honorable wife—that when she is old enough to dispose of her person she's old enough to dispose of her property.

The man who will have carnal intercourse with a child under fourteen years of age, with or without her consent, should be burned alive. The man who will be criminally intimate with a girl under seventeen years of age should be castrated—then shot. Yet all the American States but three decline to consider him guilty of rape.

In Texas the child of twelve is placed on a parity with the woman of forty, so far as sexual intercourse is concerned. When Congressman Breckinridge seduced a grown woman, well versed in the ways of the world, millions of people cried "Shame!" Yet his offense was no greater in the eye of the law than tho' he had coaxed some twelve-year-old Texas child with a box of bon-bons to submit to his brutish desires. When a middle-aged married woman is "led astray" we denounce her "destroyer" as worthy of death; yet we take precious good care to protect with the law the life of the lecherous brute who despoils her young daughter.

I do not know of a single reason why the age of consent should not be at least seventeen years in every State of the Union; nor can I understand why any law-maker, laying the slightest claim to respectability, should object to raising it to that figure. I believe that if the question were submitted to a vote of the very bagnio keepers and blacklegs it would carry by a big majority, for they still retain some respect for pure womanhood, and are not sunk so low in the scale of human degradation as to deny legal protection to children. I can understand the man who considers that when a girl has reached maturity she is lawful prey for whosoever can despoil her; I cannot understand why the Legislature of any State should decline to protect little school-girls in every possible manner, unless it be dominated by lecherous demons more utterly depraved than those that inhabit the amen-corner of hell.

JONAH'S GOURD.

Circumstances over which he seems to have had no control made Jonah the prototype of the modern panic-builder; *facile princeps* of chronic kickers, the high priest of professional calamity howlers. He received a call to cry against Nineveh because of its cussedness, but seems to have had a presentment that the job wouldn't pay, and made a desperate attempt to jump it. We are not advised what awful wickedness the city planted by Ninus and watered by Sennacherib had been guilty of. Perhaps a Democratic Congress had declined to add $500,000,000 to the interest-bearing burden of the people for the special behoof of the plutocracy. The people may have blasphemed the Golden Calf, declared for the money of the constitution, or hinted that they were better off when wrestling with the flesh-pots of Republicanism than trailing a mugwump king across barren deserts to a Babylonian captivity. Or they may have neglected to give the first fruits and fat of the land to the Lord—via the larders of the Levites. Certain it is that Nineveh had gotten off on the wrong foot, and Jonah was sent to "cry against it" and enable it to strike the proper gait. Like all the Jews of his generation, Jonah supposed that Jehovah ruled over but a small territory—that by crossing a State line he could get beyond his jurisdiction and into the bailiwick of other gods; so he boarded a packet plying between Joppa and Tarshish and "fled from the face of the Lord." It did not occur to the good man that Jehovah might have an extradition treaty with the Tarshish deity, or that he might make an excursion into foreign territory and recapture the runaway at the imminent risk of precipitating a celestico-international complication. Jonah probably did not suppose that Jehovah was cooped up in the Ark of the Covenant like the fisherman's genie in the vessel of copper, and uncorked only when the enemies of Israel became troublesome or some new people were to be despoiled of their corn and cattle, their vines and virgins; still, he imagined, like many people of the present day, that the Almighty clung pretty close to the amen-corner. But before the patron saint of amateur fishermen and professional falsifiers could get clear of the legal three-mile coast limit of Israel's God, that potentate pulled down on him with a double-barreled hurricane and a muzzle-loading leviathan. The aim was true, and Jonah tumbled. When he found himself in the belly of the big fish our peripatetic prophet from Galilee—which appears to have been the

ancient Georgia—repented of his sins. We all do when they
fail to pay the expected dividends. Jonah decided that he
would rather go to Nineveh and found a Cleveland calamity
club than travel, a perpetual passenger, in the prototype of
Jules Verne's Nautilus; so he offered up penitential prayers,
made fair promises and was permitted to go ashore.

"The Lord spake to the fish and it vomited Jonah upon
dry land."

Pictures of the prophet walking ashore, with the lower
jaw of the whale for gang-plank, are quite plentiful; but his
remarks on that occasion have not been preserved.   The
kodak fiend seems to have been waiting for him, but the
ubiquitous interviewer failed to get in his graft. Perhaps it
is just as well; but it gives us a poor opinion of ancient journalism. During the three days and nights the prophet was a
cabin passenger his whaleship must have swallowed a vast
variety of the denizens of the deep, and it were interesting
to know if Jonah lived happily with them, and if they came
ashore when he did, or continued their voyage.   Perhaps
some devout defender of the inerrancy of the Bible will yet
consent to be swallowed by a whale for a few days in order
to give the world a realistic account of Jonah's remarkable
journey.

But although our hero vigorously objected to becoming
a calamity howler he took a wonderful interest in his work
when he once got into harness. He was only commissioned
to conduct a camp-meeting revival in Nineveh and rail
against its moral rottenness; but he determined to "bring a
corollary rather than want a spirit," so he began to bawl in
the streets.

"Yet forty days and Nineveh shall be overthrown."

Such a calamity cry as that, coming from a man whom we
have no evidence had taken a bath or changed his shirt since
associating with the whale, was enough to frighten a marble caryatid into convulsions. The entire population, from
the King on his throne to the wingless buzzard who wrote
anonymous communications to the editor of the Nineveh
Morning Bazoo, informing him that he was an iridescent ass,
donned their sackcloth suits, sat in the ashes and failed to
come up to their feed. In those old days a man who filled
his hair with hickory ashes and boycotted his barber and his
belly, was supposed to be an especially agreeable sight to the
good God; hence we can hardly wonder that he promptly repealed the act authorizing the free coinage of calamities.
Just what awful punishment would have been inflicted upon
the fair city had the people refused to rend their garments

and run their noses in the sand, we are left to conjecture. The Lord might have sunk it beneath a sea of bitter waters as he did Sodom, sent the seventeen-year locusts, or saddled it with a mugwump administration. But the God of the Jews seems to have ever been open to conviction. That's where he differed from Grover Cleveland. The Lord eventually pulled his prophet of evil off the perch; but Cleveland strives manfully to fulfill every panic-breeding prediction of his faithful cuckoos.

After the hot wave prognosticator had put out his bulletins he got him out of the city, so as not to slip on his own banana peel, built a jackal a considerable distance from the spot where his curse was to get action, and deliberately sat him down to see the show. He expected nothing less than the utter destruction by a gracious God of the city in which were 60,000 infants—"also much cattle."

The summer climate of Nineveh was almost as sultry as that of St. Louis; and as Jonah lay in his hut with his tongue hanging out the Lord took pity on him and caused a gourd to spring up to comfort him with its shade. There Jonah lay, day after day, we are led to suppose, looking off toward Nineveh, eager to see fire and brimstone descend from heaven on a million happy homes—to inhale the sweet incense of three score thousand helpless babes burned alive! On the morning of the fortieth day we may well suppose that he arose bright and early. This is the day that is to prove him a true prophet and assure him the patronage of princes and potentates, or proclaim him a garrulous old guy with a disordered liver and an ill-balanced head. Either Nineveh or the prophet must be overthrown.

Beyond the Tigris the heralds of the sun are flaming in the sky. Now the great day-god shows his shining disc, lingers a moment as tho' loth to leave Aurora's loving arms, then wheels upward in stately majesty and pours his golden splendors full upon Assyria's mighty capital. The people awake from refreshing slumber, and the streets resound with the same drowsy hum that for a thousand years has been heard in that ancient centre of civilization. The merchant goes about his business, the gude house-wife borrows soap and sad irons of her neighbor and gossips with her over the back fence about the new priest of Baal; the King and his courtiers go forth to hunt the wild boar and the bride bedecks herself for the nuptial rites. Jonah begins to fidget beneath his gourd and glances often upward, wondering if the consignment of blazing brimstone has been side-tracked by another celestial revolution, such as that of which Milton

sings. The sun sinks like a globe of gold into the plain far
beyond the Zab, and the crescent moon is trying to clasp
Love's brilliant star to her concave breast. The ring of the
hammer and the shrill cry of the herdsmen are hushed, and
from park and garden come peals of mirth and music, the
dreamy cadence of dancing feet on polished cedar floors, and
the sensuous perfume of dew-bespangled flowers. Pyramus
is bending his steps to old Ninus' lonely tomb to meet his
lovely Thisbe; in the banquet hall the golden goblet brims
with nectarous wine such as Samos never knew, and perfumed lamps cast a ruddy glow on giant warriors and women
fair as ever cast in mortal mold. The hour grows late, the
music ceases; the hum dies slowly out, and the midnight
quiet is broken only by the prayer of an ascetic worshipping
the host of heaven, and the yoop of an unhappy married man
going home from the primaries in charge of a pair of policemen. Nineveh is going to bed just as tho' no whale had
swallowed Jonah—then puked him up when it discovered
that he had "a call to preach."

When Jonah learned that the show for which he was acting as press agent had collapsed, he proceeded to file a vigorous kick. That was perfectly natural. No matter how
terrible a prophet's predictions may be, he earnestly desires
that they come to pass. Jonah had shrieked calamity until
his tongue was parched, yet nothing serious had happened.
No wonder that he felt that his star was evil—that through
no fault of his own a great three-cornered hiatus had been
kicked in his political fences. So he went to the Lord, we
may fairly infer from the trend of the narrative, and said:

"Look here, you've busted me up in business. I'd a been
a hanged sight better off had I taken my stand squarely on
the Chicago platform and defended the money of the constitution instead of joining the mugwumps and clamoring
for currency contraction."

The Lord said unto Jonah, in substance, tho' probably not
in these exact words:

"The calamity clacker, like the cut-worm and the cholera
microbe, hath its uses. Here was Nineveh growing careless.
It had been prosperous so long under Republican paganism
that it was losing sight of the eternal principles of Jeffersonian Democracy. The old town had become deaf to argument
and indifferent to political duty; so I stirred up you to grow
a crop of anarchical whiskers, an abnormal gall, and spout
calamity from the beer-kegs at the corners. You have
served my purpose. I will now cut down your gourd, and
you must sing small or the sun will shine into and sour you."

A CARNIVAL OF CRIME.

During the year 1894 there were about 9,800 homicides and but 132 legal executions reported in the United States. I have no later statistics at hand; but it is conceded, I believe, that crimes of this kind are steadily on the increase, while the disproportion between the number of homicides and hangings continues to grow greater. As matters now stand, one might slay a fellow mortal every year and stand an excellent chance of dying of old age, so far as the courts are concerned. You may go upon the streets, insult a man, provoke him to offer you violence, shoot him down like a dog, and, if able to employ eminent counsel to behedge you with legal technicalities and befuddle the jury, go scot free; or failing in that, put the public to an expense of several thousand dollars in excess of what your cowardly carcass is worth, and escape with a short term in some comfortable penitentiary, where you will be well cared for, taught a good trade and regularly prayed for at the expense of law-abiding people. What is the result? The people, despairing of legal protection from the armed thug, take the law into their own hands—invoke the power of Judge Lynch to defend their right to life, liberty and the pursuit of happiness. There are more lynchings than legal executions. In 1894 the first reached the appalling number of 190. That is indeed a terrible record of lawless violence, but it were idle to declaim against the effect without removing the cause. The American people are naturally law-abiding; but above and beyond their respect for courts is their inherent sense of justice— paramount even to the law of the land is the law of self-preservation. Theorists may protest and sentimentalists rend their nether garments and spill their ready tears; but so long as the assassin is white-washed by the courts and the rape-fiend turned loose to prey upon pure homes, Judge Lynch will continue to hold his midnight sessions—the shotgun will continue to roar in the hands of maddened mobs and the lonely tree groan beneath its grewsome burden. Is it any wonder that the people lose patience? In Judge Lynch's court there is no eminent counsel skilled in the esoteric art of protecting crime; no change of venue; no mistrials; no appeals; no postponements to give important witnesses time to die or get away; no one-year terms in the penitentiary for the brutal assassin or infamous rape-fiend. We have "reformed" our jurisprudence until the contention of the courts with the great tide of crime suggests Dame Partington's unequal combat with the sea. By assiduously trundling her mop she was able to fill her bucket with brine; and by laboriously grinding, the courts succeed in cramming the penitentiaries—with small-fry thieves and people too poor to employ skilled counsel. Our courts have become mere circumlocution offices, winding and unwinding red tape, instead of the sinewy arm of justice wielding the unerring sword. Our judges are usually learned and upright, our juries eager to administer justice, our officers active and the public heart in the right place; but it avails not—our system is all wrong. We make too many laws, then involve them in a mass of legal verbiage which permits a skilled sophist to demonstrate to the untrained mind that they mean what best serves the interest of his client. It is common cant that "the people make the laws." They do not. The lawyers make them, and that with the full understanding that the more intricate the legal machinery may be, the more need of experts, the fatter the harvest of fees. All the criminal laws this country needs could be printed in a pamphlet no larger than the Iconoclast, together with full instructions for their enforcement; made so plain that the most stupid juror could understand them— and in simplicity there is strength. "Thou shalt not kill," says the Bible; and the sentence stands out like a star. The penalty for violation of this law was death, unless it plainly appeared that the killing was accidental or done in self-defense. The trial was immediate, and, if conviction followed, the culprit turned over to the "avenger of blood." No provision for experts to pass upon the sanity of the prisoner, no prattle of hypnotism, no searching of the community for the greatest numbskulls to determine the case, no reversals on legal technicalities, no penitentiary and convict labor prob· lem—no lawyers! A careful, common sense inquiry, honorable acquittal or conviction and immediate execution. The jury constitutes the chief feature of our legal machinery, a feature in full accord with our theory of popular sovereignty; but we have so hedged it about with foolish restrictions that, instead of being the ancillary of Justice, it has become a veritable bulwark of Crime. We select as jurors, not those who know most about the case, but those who know least. When an atrocious crime is committed we set aside as unavailable those who have kept in touch with current events, and select a jury from the residue. In these days of rapid transit and daily papers all men of average intelligence are soon informed of every crime of consequence committed in their county, even in their State; and no one gifted with a thinking apparatus can avoid arriving at some conclusion regarding all he sees and hears. As a rule, we get together twelve of the most consummate blockheads in the county—a dime museum of mental freaks—permit them to be further obfuscated by artful counsel, whose business it is to "make out a case" for or against, as goes the fee, then lock them up until the most obstinate jackass in the corral dominates the herd or compels a compromise. Sometimes there are two or more burros of equal obstinacy; a mistrial results, and the case goes over to the next term of court. The public loses interest in it—is absorbed in the contemplation of new crimes —and if the culprit is eventually convicted and properly punished the people regard it as a special dispensation of Providence. Punishment, to have a repressive effect, must be not only sure but swift. The law's delay—coupled with its uncertainty—encourages crime. More than five years ago, and on several occasions since then, the Iconoclast suggested that jurors be elected by the people like other county officers— that every county select nine men of approved worth to try criminal cases, and establish the majority rule. This would relieve the citizen of a disagreeable duty for which he is often in nowise qualified, and insure for jury service men capable of analyzing evidence and arriving at just conclusions. Let the vote of the jury in criminal cases be made a matter of public record, and thereby fix the responsibility for every miscarriage of justice. Only attorneys employed by the State should be permitted to appear in criminal cases. These should be skilled lawyers, but in no sense prosecuting attorneys, intent only upon securing conviction and pocketing a comfortable fee. Their business should be to elicit facts for the jury to pass upon, and act as counsellors to the court in questions of law. The attorney who will, with equal readiness, employ his skill to acquit a felon or hang an innocent man, should speedily become a forgotten factor in our criminal jurisprudence. In March, 1895, I called attention to these needed reforms, and well-nigh in the same words; but a question involving the lives of 10,000 Americans annually cannot be too frequently called to the attention of our publicists and the people.

THE APOSTLE'S BIOGRAPHY.

I am pleased to learn from some of my contemporaries that I am an ex-convict, who tramped into Texas carrying a false trade-mark; that I have been driven out of several cities, and fired by various managers of morning newspapers; that I have been thrashed by aged cripples, and compelled to make retractions in the public prints. That is by no means the entire catalogue of my high crimes and misdemeanors, as set forth by my industrious biographers; but is sufficient to show that as an original sinner neither St. Paul nor Sam Jones was a circumstance to myself. To become chief of the rogues in this era of rampant rascality were indeed a distinction; but being a modest man, I shall refrain from assuming the post of honor in the nether pantheon until my right thereto is fully established.

My biographers are sadly derelict in their duty, or they would have discovered my pre-Texas cognomen and the location of the prison in which I clanked my chain. The cities from which I was expelled should be marked on the map, and sworn statements by reputable citizens anent these interesting episodes made matters of record. The affidavits of publishers who have willingly dispensed with my services, would give to the work an historical accuracy calculated to impress the public. Photographs of all the aged cripples who have walked my log should illume the book, while a facsimile of some retraction I have printed would make an appropriate frontispiece.

From the foundation of the world the falsehood has been the defensive weapon of the fool. Assail him with logic and he answers with lies; lash him with sarcasm and he retorts with calumny; impale him on the rapier of ridicule and he deluges you with brutal defamation.

While it is true that no creature rising to the moral level of the mangy coyote, the intellectual altitude of an acephalous louse, will utter a malicious lie, it is likewise true that no one within whose heart there pulses one drop of gentle blood; within whose brain there was ever born a noble thought; within whose soul there is enshrined the instincts of a manly man, will retail a story calculated to injure a fellow craftsman—even if he knows it to be true. The respectable journalist, the well-bred gentleman, is ever ready to break a lance in intellectual tourney—to prove his powers on the Field of the Cloth of Gold—but he leaves the throwing of stink-pots to Chinamen, the exploitation of night-soil to scavengers, the peddling of stale falsehoods to fools, the concocting of unclean calumnies to cowards.

BLUE AND GRAY.

AN ADDRESS TO THE OLD VETERANS.

[The following summary of Mr. Brann's address to the United American Veterans, San Antonio, Feb. 22, 1894, is published by request.]

It occurs to me that the time is not an appropriate one for lengthy speeches. This is a love-feast, and I have noticed that when people are much in love they are little inclined to talk. Perhaps I have been called upon because I'm a professional peacemaker, an expert harmony promoter. Were I not as meek as Moses and patient as Job I certainly would weary in well-doing—become discouraged and give o'er the attempt to inaugurate an era of universal peace and general good will; for when I go North I am denounced by the partisan press as an unreconstructed rebel seeking to rip the federal government up by the roots, and when I come South I'm pointed out as a dangerous Yankee importation with the bluest of equators. The Democrats insist that I'm a Republican, but that party declines the responsibility; the infidels call me a religious crank, the clergy an Atheist, and even the Mugwumps regard me with suspicion. But let me tell you right here that whatever I may or may not be, I am an American from the ground up—from Alpha to Omega, world-without-end. I may be a man without a party and without a creed; but so long as Old Glory blazes in God's blue firmament I will never be a man without a country.

I can no more imagine a man loving only the north or south half of his country than I can imagine him loving only the right or left side of his wife. If I had to love my country on the instalment plan I'd move out of it. The man who is really a patriot loves his country in a lump. There's room in his heart for every acre of its sunny soil, its every hill upon which the morning breaks, its every vale that cradles the evening shadows, its every stream that laughs back the image of the sun.

When a man feels that way you can safely trust him with an office—and most of us are perfectly willing to be trusted.

As an American citizen I am proud of every man, of whatever section, who, by the nobility of his nature or the majesty of his intellect, has added one jot or tittle to the fame of his fair land, has increased the credit of our common country, has contributed new power to the car of human progress. They are my countrymen, friends and brethren.

Are you of the North? Then I claim with you a joint interest in your entire galaxy of intellectual gods. At the shrine of Lincoln's broad humanity, of Webster's matchless power, of the cunning genius of your Menlo wizard I humbly bow. Are you of the South? Your Jefferson, Jackson and Lee are mine as well as thine, for they too were Americans —lords in that mighty aristocracy of intellect that has, in four generations, made the New World the wonder of the Old with its cumulative greatness of forty centuries.

I have watched the progress of the United American Veterans' Association with uncommon interest, because it is distinctively a national organization, in which shriveled sectionalism and party prejudice find no place. Its cornerstone is American manhood, its object fraternity, its principles broad as the continent upon which falls the shadow of our flag. Do you know what that association means?—had you thought of its significance? It means that when brave men sheathe the sword the quarrel's done. It means that peace hath its triumphs no less than war. The world's annals furnish forth no parallel to that association whose guests we are to-night. Men have fought ere this and patched up a peace; but where, in all the cycles of human history, have they waged war more relentless than did Rome and Carthage, then, without a murmur, accepted the arbitrament of the sword and swung into line, shoulder to shoulder, a band of brothers, one flag, one country, one destiny and that the highest goal of human endeavor?

My attention has been especially attracted to this association because it is a practical illustration of what I have so often urged in print: That the pitiful sectional prejudices which we see here and there coming to the surface both north and south; that the petty hatreds, which appear to transform some hearts into bitter little pools in which Justice perishes and divine Reason is quite overthrown, have no lot or part among the soldiers who made the civil war the grandest event in modern history—one from which the world will mark time for centuries yet to be. I have yet to hear an ex-federal who met Lee's veterans at the Wilderness or Gettysburg, speak disrespectfully of the man who wore the gray. I have yet to hear an ex-confederate who mixed it with "Old Pap" Thomas at Chickamauga, or Joe Hooker above the clouds, speak disparagingly of those who wore the blue. It is those who stayed at home to sing, "We'll hang Jeff Davis on a sour apple tree," and those who damned "Old Abe" Lincoln at long range who are doing all the tremendous fighting now. They didn't get started for the front until after Appomattox; but having once sailed in for slaughter all Hades can't head 'em off! If a merciful Providence doesn't soon interpose, these mighty post-bellum warriors will either break a lung or wreck the majestic world. They are more dreadful in their destructive awfulness than the farmer's two he-goats, that "fit an' fit" until there was nothing left of 'em but a splotch o' blood and two belligerent tails. Those who exchanged compliments at Corinth and Cold Harbor; those who received informal calls from Kilpatrick's cavalry, who we are told "rode like centaurs and fought like devils"; those who saw Grant's intrepid Westerners hurl themselves against Vicksburg's impregnable heights; those who were slammed up against Jackson's "Stone wall" or picnicked with Johnston's cartridge-biters on grapeshot pie and deviled minnie balls, now treat each other with the studied respect which the Kansas farmer paid the cyclone. He felt sure that the Lord was on his side and that with such help he could more than hold his own; still he was in no wise anxious to steer his theory against a condition that was making a million revolutions a minute and hadn't yet brought up its reserves.

In commingling thus in a common brotherhood, those who followed the fortunes of the confederacy until human fortitude could no further go, and those who, with the sword's keen point, held every gleaming star in Old Glory's field of blue, are furnishing a commendable example to all our countrymen, to all humanity. It is an echo, nay, an incarnation of those words of Grant, the grandest that ever fell from victorious warrior's lips: "Let us have peace." The battlefield was sown long since with kindlier seed than dragon's teeth, has blossomed and borne the fruits of Life where Death reigned paramount. The flowers of our Southern fields are no longer dyed with the blood of the contending brave, but drip with heaven's own dews; the sullen battery has gone silent on our purple hills and the crash of steel resounds no more amid our pleasant valleys. No longer the Northern child waits and watches for the soldier sire whose lips have felt the touch of God's own hand; no longer the Southern woman wanders with bursting heart amid the wreck and wraith of the fierce simoon, brushing the battle grime from cold brows, seeking among the mangled dead for all that life held dear. The curse has passed: "Let us have peace."

The civil war was a national necessity. It was the fiery furnace in which Almighty God welded the discordant elements of the New World into one homogeneous people.

For generations the Puritan hated the Cavalier, and the latter gave back scorn for scorn and added compound interest. This mutual dislike was a rank, infectious weed that first took root across the sea and ripened into that revolution which sent Charles the First to the block and invested Cromwell with more than regal power. Some of this virus, distilled in stubborn hearts by religious and political intolerance, was carried by the Puritan to Plymouth and by the Cavalier to the banks of the James, and it survived even the fires of patriotism and the frosts of Valley Forge. Bone of the same bone and flesh of the same flesh, the religio-political doctrinaires had succeeded in casting our forefathers in different molds—each colossal, masculine, heroic, but radically antagonistic. Together they followed Washington through those eight long years of blood and tears of which human liberty was born. Together they laid broad and deep the foundation of the Republic and reared thereon that wondrous superstructure which—please God—shall endure forever, and together they poured their blood in one unstinted tide upon its sacred shrine. But the Puritan was still a Cromwell and the Cavalier a lord. That people so widely divergent in customs and character could long dwell at peace as one political household were preposterous. The one had his "convictions," the other his "institutions," and neither would yield the right-o'-way. When such opposing trains of thought try to pass on a single track there's going to be trouble sure. The friction, evident even in the early days of the Republic, grew and gathered fire until the nation burst forth in that mighty conflagration whose pathetic ashes repose in a million sepulchers. It had to come. Let us thank God that the fierce baptism of fire is in the past and not yet to be; that the bitter cup can never be pressed to our children's lips; that never again while the world stands and the heavens endure will Americans meet in battle-shock; that never again will our rivers run red with the blood of Columbia's brave, poured forth by her own keen blade—that the last stumbling-block hath been removed from our path of progress; that we can now move forward with a giant's stride to that high destiny for which the chastening hand of God hath fitted us, the greatest nation and the grandest people in all the mighty tide of Time!

I rejoice to see the veterans setting the example of reconciliation, for they, more than all others, have most to forgive and forget. I am doubly gratified that the good work should have begun in Texas, which has such cause to entertain the kindliest feelings toward every section of our common country, for each and all contributed to her past glory and present greatness. Among those who cast their lot in Texas when every step was a challenge to destiny and every hour was darkened by a danger; who faced unflinchingly the trials of frontier life and carved out an independent republic with the sword, were men from every State of the American union. One instance will suffice (though scores might be cited) to illustrate the cosmopolitan character of that band of heroes who made the early history of Texas one of the noblest cantos in the mighty Anglo-Saxon epic. The New Orleans Grays was the first military company to come from the States to the aid of the struggling Texans. It got its first baptism of fire in this city, being a part of that band of 300 Spartans who followed Old Ben Milam to attack General Cos and his 1,500 veterans. From the roster of the Grays I learn that the company numbered but sixty-four men, yet represented sixteen sovereign States and six foreign countries! Think of it! Twenty-five came from north of the Ohio, twenty-four from the Southern States, fourteen across far seas to fight for Texas liberty, while one brave lad came from God knows where, but he got there just the same! General Cos never inquired where Milam's men were born. He knew where his own were dying, decided that San Antonio had been overrated as a health resort and took to the chaparral.

As most of those daring spirits who flocked hither to fight for Texas remained, and ever since a steady human tide has poured in from all parts of the Union, and every country of Western Europe, we have become a mixed people, scarce daring to throw a rock in any direction lest we hit our relatives. And the cosmopolitan character of our people—the fact that the Puritan and the Cavalier have blended here as nowhere else—will be found a powerful factor in the attainment of a glorious future.

It is particularly appropriate that the Blue and the Gray should unite in observing the day that marks the birth of Washington, that soldier-statesman who marshaled our fathers under one flag and led them forth to the defense of human liberty. Whatever may have since mischanced, the trials and the triumphs of the Revolution are our common heritage. As the Greeks of old, divided among themselves, united to face a foreign foe, so did the Americans, North and South, unite beneath the banner of Washington and hurl down the gage of battle to Britain's mighty power, and no historian has yet presumed to say which was the better soldier. Washington belongs to no section. He was truly an

American, pre-eminently a patriot. The nobility of his character was his very own; the dazzling splendor of his undying fame is the brightest jewel in Columbia's crown of glory, for it was born of the dauntless valor and nurtured with the priceless blood of a people whom kings could not conquer nor sophists deceive.

A husband and wife, long estranged, met at the grave of their firstborn, the child of their youthful strength. Their strife had been bitter, their love had turned to hate, and they elected to tread life's path apart. They stood, one on either side, and looked coldly upon each other. Then they looked down upon the little mound that held the broken link with which God had bound their hearts. They knelt and bowed their faces upon the cold sod that covered the sacred dust of their dead. They stretched forth their hands across the little grave, each to the other, and the Angel of God washed all the bitterness of the years from their hearts with a rain of penitential tears, and sent them down life's pathway hand-in-hand, as in the old days when Love was lord of their two lives and the lost babe was cradled upon its mother's breast.

This day the North and the South kneel at the grave of Washington, their best beloved. The estrangement is forgotten, the bitterness of the years passes like an uneasy dream, they reach their hands each to the other across the tomb, and the benediction of God falls upon a reunited people.

A MAID'S MISTAKE.

A Defense of the Beauteous Rebecca.

The King of Corea is anxious to found a harem, and it is hinted that he has dispatched agents to Houston to see if Miss Rebecca Merlindy Johnson, of the Post, is really so pretty as report hath painted her.—*Waco News.*

Ye gods! has American journalism come to this? O tempora! O mores! Oh, mamma! How can our representative dailies deliberately mock the misfortunes of a fair young maid, simply to make a hoodlum holiday? Rebecca may have erred; but can she be reformed by drawing a rat-tail file across her milk-white teeth and coupling her name in brutal jest with that of a barbaric Mongol, who wears his eyes cut bias and the narrative of his nether garments floating wide upon the wandering air? True it is that Re-

becca's unhappy custom of donning male attire and posing
as a man, at press conventions and on the public streets, is
a great temptation to the sacrilegious paragraphers to let
slip the biting epigram and ribald jest; but they should remember that while Rebecca is beautiful as a spotted pup
she was never bright, and pass her little idiosyncrasies over
in silence.

Although Rebecca has gone astray the Iconoclast feels
for her only the profoundest pity, and it will permit no one
to make her a target for the chilly sneer or heap upon her
humbled head great wads of withering scorn. Dear! dear!
how sad it seems that one so young should feel the heavy
hand of unkind fate—Hope's fair morning overcast with the
dun clouds of grim despair! How pitiful that the bright
dream of a young life should be dispelled, the cloud-capped
temple of Love, in which she expected to wander ever, but
a frightful Fata Morgana—the golden Apples of Hesperides for which in holy faith and trust she held out her blue-
veined hand, turned to bitter Dead Sea fruit! Alas! The
great heart of the Iconoclast bleeds for Houston's unfortunate belle, once so imperial in her pride, now brought so
low that the very dogs will no longer pause in front of her
office, despite the seductive sign, "Houston Post." How
often, oh how often, as her sad romance came rushing thro'
our mind like an unhappy ghost shrieking and sobbing
thro' Fancy's incorporeal halls, have we put aside our goose-
quill pen and corncob pipe and retired to the dim seclusion
of the woodshed to uncork by stealth the briny tear and tie
loose the melancholy moan. It may be unmanly, but we
always feel better, nobler, purer afterwards—better qualified
to instruct the legislature and lead the State out of its financial follies.

Born beneath the sometimes sunny skies of the great
Goober State, of poor but honest parents, Rebecca grew up,
neglected but beautiful, soulful, an impulsive child of nature. A liberal diet of 'possum, peanuts and corn pone, encouraged in its onward course by gourds of buttermilk and
an occasional nip from a moonlight still, rapidly rounded
out the lissom form, and running barefoot over the red hills
in joyous sport with the young coons, gave to her a majestic
carriage which Juno might have envied. Thus the happy
years sped on, as years are wont to do, until the heroine of
this thrilling novelette had reached the age of consent, when
many a young gallant awooing came and sought to toll the
matchless beauty forth to candy pullings, singin' skules, log
rollings and other hilarious gatherings where the youth

and beauty of back districts meet, to slobber over each other, or chase the glowing hours with flying feet.

But Rebecca was ambitious and scorned the clumsy advances of the wool-hat boys. She yearned for the glory of fame and the glamour of wealth. Her soul mounted above such plebeian occupations as boiling soft-soap, deodorizing diapers and building crackling bread. Poor child! She could not understand as yet that the hand that wields the slipper is the hand that rocks the world; hence she turned her back upon domestic joys and sought fame and fortune on the mimic stage—played Pauline in Claude Melnotte with such effect that soon she wore as cestus a string of bleeding hearts. Pity that she failed to heed the solemn warning so often given.

"Pauline, thro' pride angels have fallen ere thy time."

Rebecca's triumph on the stage but fired her fond ambition for loftier flights. She was no longer content to parrot the words of others, but would write—would dally with the delusive pen, weapon more powerful than the sword. The sock and buskin were exchanged for the gilded sanctum, and here the proud beauty and the "Apostle" met. The queen of the stage, who had resisted the temptations of the green-room and the seductive rhythm of Cracker poetry, surrendered at discretion, and entered, with all the ardor of a woman whose charms are waning, upon that intoxicating yet dangerous dream of bliss that—oh lackaday!—was too sweet to last.

While Menelaus was far from home, assiduously hustling the wherewithal to discharge the family butcher bills, old Priam's roving son did steal away the matchless Helen— and history repeats itself. While the "Apostle" was absent —trying to enforce the Sunday law in San Antonio and cording up shekels wherewith to purchase a gilded cage for his bright Bird o' Paradise—Epictetus Paregoric Hill did abstract from him the fond affections of the fair Rebecca. Nor was this all. Paregoric proceeded to uncork himself in the columns of the Houston Post and add insult to injury. He cried aloud unto the powers that be to tie the saintly "Apostle" up and spread upon his shrinking diaphragm nine-and-thirty cruel lashes, for no other crime than that he had loved, not wisely but too well. As Paregoric's fierce appeal was pigeon-holed, perhaps he'll yet conclude to tackle the job himself—will lift the "Apostle's" cuticule and make thereof a silken purse for his old sweetheart.

But we bear Epictetus Paregoric no shade of malice. He could not help loving Rebecca. If he will but deal honestly by her all will be forgiven. Whether he has done so thus far we do not know; but the poor girl's sad demeanor and the fact that she has been an inmate of an asylum for the erring, leads us to fear the worst. Her conscience is evidently hurting her, and day by day that exuberant gladness, that was once her glory, is departing, leaving her moody and abstracted as the man who fails to keno. It is possible that she regrets the days that are no more? That in the stilly night she dreams of the "Apostle" and smiles again—thinks him still at the old desk, grinding out editorial copy, for which she cheerfully takes the credit? When she wakes and finds it all a dream, does she wish that she had awaited his return, even as Penelope waited for Ulysses, instead of playing Annie to his Enoch Arden and tying fast to a pink-haired plug whom God in his inscrutable wisdom has permitted to accumulate a little wealth, while brainier men are trailing the meek-eyed mule in the lowly cotton-path?

Poor Rebecca! Did mischievous Puck pour into the soulful eyes of the "Apostle's" fair Titania some curst decoction that caused her to dote on a pie-bald ass and mistake his ears for angel's wings, his fiery muzzle for a seraph's radiant nimbus? Or do you possess beneath that fair exterior all the frailties of Hamlet's desiring dam, who is supposed to have left a celestial bed to prey on garbage? We do not know; but be it as it may, the "Apostle" will remain forever your guardian angel—will gather you beneath his wing even as the careful hen gathereth some other bench-legged gosling, and protect you from the wintry scorn of those cruel papers, that cannot understand that tho' you have sinned you have also suffered. Be virtuous, Rebecca, and you may be happy yet.

OPTIMISM VS. PESSIMISM.

The Preacher and the "Apostle."

I am in receipt of a long letter from a Missouri minister, in which, to my surprise, he says: "I regret to note that you are a Pessimist. Permit me to express the hope that so powerful a journal as the Iconoclast will yet espouse the sunny philosophy of Optimism, which teaches that all that is accords with the Plan of the Creator, and works together for the ultimate good."

"God moves in a mysterious way his wonders to perform."

I had not hitherto suspected that I was inoculated with the awful microbes of Pessimism, but if my reverend friend is a professor in the sunny school of Optimism, I certainly do not belong to that sect. If "all that is accords with the Plan of the Creator," did not Christ deserve to be crucified for bringing about new conditions, and Gallileo to go to jail for interfering with the stupid ignorance of certain Catholic cardinals? Can even the Missouri minister be held guiltless when he attempts to turn my thinking apparatus around and make it operate from the other end? Surely he should not interfere in even so slight a particular with the "Plan of the Creator," who may have been moving "in a mysterious way his wonders to perform" when he gave the supposedly pessimistic bent to my mind. Nay, if my Christian friend do but have the rheumatism, should he not refrain from poulticing himself, lest he throw the celestial machinery out of gear? If changes wrought in religion, science, government, etc., constitute a portion of the "Plan," we must concede it to have originally been a very faulty affair—quite upsetting the optimistic theory that "Whatever is is right."

The terms Pessimism and Optimism are handled very loosely in these latter days. In the modern acceptance of the terms, the first may be defined as a chronic intellectual bellyache, the latter as an incurable case of mossbackism. The thorough Pessimist believes the world is going in hot haste to the demnition bowwows, and that nothing short of a miracle can head it off; the full-fledged Optimist carries concealed about his person an abiding faith that "God ordereth all things well"—that he not only designed the mighty universe, but is giving his personal attention to the details of its management. Really, I do not believe I am Pessimist to hurt, or that my reverend critic is so dangerously ill of the Optimistic disease as he imagines. Perhaps he has been living too high for great intellectual effort. Were he in the condition of some millions of his fellow creatures, the cuticle of whose abdomens is flapping against their vertebrae like a wet dish-rag warping itself around a wire clothes-line, perhaps there would not be quite so much sunshine in his philosophy. The man with whom the world goes well is apt to prattle of the "ultimate good" when considering the woes of other people.

The basis of Optimism is foreordination, the foolish faith

that before God created the majestic universe and sent the
planets whirling about the blazing sun; that before the first
star gleamed in the black, over-hanging firmament or a
single mountain peak rose from the watery waste, he calmly
sat him down and mapped out every act of moral man—
decreed every war and pestilence, the rise and fall of every
nation, and fixed the date of every birth and death. That
may be excellent "orthodoxy," but it is not good sense. I
reject the theory that all the happenings here below "accord
with the Plan of the Creator—work together for the ultimate good." Hence, I am not an Optimist. I dare not
accuse my Creator of being responsible for all the sin and
sorrow, suffering and shame that since the dawn of history
has bedewed the world with blood and tears.

I do not believe the "Plan of the Creator" contemplated
that millions of people should perish miserably by war, and
famine and pestilence. I do not believe the black buck who
ravishes and murders a white babe is one of the great moral
agents of the Almighty, nor that the infamous act has any
possible tendency to promote "the ultimate good." And
did I so believe, I would keep my shotgun loaded just the
same. I do not believe that the blessed God intended there
should ever be a liar or a thief, a prostitute or a murderer
in this beautiful world. I do not believe that the Creator
entered into a compact with the devil or a covenant with
the cholera. And if not, then all that is does not "accord
with the Plan of the Creator." If that be Pessimism, make
the most of it.

That there is a Divine Plan I do not doubt; but I believe
it to be broader, deeper, more worthy of the great Demiur-
gus than that which pictures him telling a priest how to carve
his pantaloons or sacrifice a pair of pigeons, than standing
idly by with his hands under his coat-tails, while some
drunken duffer beats the head off his better half with a boot-
jack, or a bronze brute rips the scalp from a smiling babe.
If that's the kind of a hair-pin who occupies the throne of
heaven, I don't blame Lucifer for raising a revolution. I
would have taken a fall out of him myself, even had I known
that my viscera would be strewn across the face of the
shrinking universe.

God gave us life, and this grand old globe for habitat.
He stored it with everything necessary to the health and happiness of the human race—poured his treasures forth with
a hand so bounteous that tho' its population were doubled,
trebled, it might go on forever and no mortal son of Adam
need suffer for life's necessaries. The gaunt spectres of

Want and Pestilence are not of his creation; they were born of Greed and Ignorance. God sent no devil with hoofs and horns to torment or tempt us; he gave to us passions necessary to the perpetuation and progress of the race and divine Reason wherewith to rule them—then left us to work out our own salvation, aided by those silent forces that are pressing all animate and inanimate life onward to perfection. Reason needs no celestial guide, no heavenly monitor, for it is the grandest attribute of God himself. Where Reason sits enthroned God reigns!

For more than half a million years man has been toiling upwards, impelled by that mysterious law that causes the pine to spring towards the sun. Sometimes the advance is by leaps and bounds, as when some giant intellect—some Son of God, especially gifted with the attributes of his Sire—brushes aside the obstructions at which lesser men toil in vain; sometimes the Car of Progress stands still for a thousand years, else rolls slowly back toward brutishness, there being none of sufficient strength to advance the standards further up the rugged mountain-side—nearer the Celestial City. Thus, ever in ebb and flow, gaining and losing, only to regain; nations rising and falling but to serve as stepping-stones whereon mount a nobler race, a grander people, the irrepressible conflict of the God-like with the Beast-like in man goes bravely on.

In half a million years we have come far—won many a fair field from the dominion of Darkness. We no longer dwell in caves and hollow trees, fighting naked with the wild beasts of the forest for our prey. We have erected temples to that God who dwells, not only in the heavens, but here on earth—in the brain and heart of the human race. We have made matter so far subject unto mind that Nature's mighty forces have become our obedient bond-slaves. We have built societies, nations, weighed the world and measured the stars. We have acquired not only knowledge and power, but love and modesty. The procreative passion no longer crawls, a hideous thing, but soars aloft, a winged Psyche. Thus, one by one, through the long ages, have we built up within ourselves the attributes of the Most High, toward whom our feet are tending. Life is no longer mere animalism, content to gorge itself with roots and raw meat and sit in the sun. The ear craves melody, the eye beauty, the brain dominion, while the soul mounts to the very stars!

Thus far have we come out of the Valley of Darkness, led on, not by those who believe that "all that is accords with the Plan of the Creator," but by those whose battle-cry has ever been,

> "Forward, forward let us range,
> Let the great world spin forever
> Down the ringing grooves of change."

Every reformation yet wrought in religion, science or politics, was the work of men who declined to accept the doctrines, enunciated by the Missouri divine. If I am a Pessimist I am in such excellent company as Confucius and Christ, General Washington and Mr. Gladstone, Prof. Morse and Dr. Pasteur, while my critic is training with the gang that poisoned Socrates, bribed Iscariot and crucified the Savior. And the world persists in judging a man by the company he keeps!

BALAAM'S ASS.

And Other Burros.

> "Force first made conquest, and that conquest, law;
> Till Superstition taught the tyrant awe,
> Then shared the tyranny, then lent it aid,
> And gods of conquerors, slaves of subjects made.
> She, from the rending earth and bursting skies,
> Saw gods descend and fiends infernal rise;
> Here fixed the dreadful, there the blest abodes;
> Fear made her devils and weak hope her gods;
> Gods partial, changeful, passionate, unjust,
> Whose attributes were rage, revenge and lust;
> Such as the souls of cowards might conceive,
> And, formed like tyrants, tyrants would believe.
> Zeal then, not charity, became the guide;
> And hell was built on spite, and heaven on pride."
> —Pope.

Kind reader, have a care! For aught I know this article may be the rankest blasphemy, and reading it may wreck your immortal soul—granting of course, that you are in possession of such perishable property. I submitted it to several of my brother ministers and sought their opinion as to the propriety of publishing it; but while some assured me that it was calculated to purify the moral atmosphere somewhat and foster respect for true religion, others were equally certain that Satan had inspired it—that it was, in fact, a choice bit of immigration literature for the lower regions. Finding even the elders unable to decide what should be done with Balaam's Ass—whether it should be turned loose upon the land like another evangelist, or consigned to the flames as a hopeless heretic—I determined to give it the benefit of the doubt. The animal may break into the preserves of some unctuous hypocrites and trample a few choice flowers of sacerdotal folly; but I opine that no honest man of average intellect will find herein occasion for complaint. I would not wantonly wound the sensibilities of those earnest but ignorant souls who believe the very chapter headings of the Bible to have been inspired; who interpret literally every foolish fable preserved therein—"like flies in amber"; but the Car of Progress cannot roll forward without crushing an occasional pismire. We cannot bid it stand forever in the same old rut, like an abandoned road-cart or "Jeffersonian Democrat," because across its shining pathway lie the honest prejudices of zealous stupidity.

The Bible is a great gold-mine, in which inexhaustible store of yellow metal is mixed with much worthless rubbish that must be purged away by honest criticism before the book becomes really profitable—even fit for general circulation. I would rather place in the hands of an innocent girl a copy of the *Police Gazette* or *Sunday Sun* than an unexpurgated Bible. It is a book I value much, yet keep under lock and key with Don Juan and the Decameron. It contains both the grandest morality and most degrading obscenity ever conceived in the brain of mortal man. There are passages whose beauty and power might cause the heart of an angel to leap in ecstacy, others that would call a blush of shame to the brassy front of the foulest fiend that ever howled and shrieked thro' the sulphurous valleys of hell.

The man who rejects the Bible altogether because it is honey-combed with barbarous traditions, rank with revolting stories and darkened by the shadow of a savage superstition, is cousin-german to him that casts aside a priceless pearl because it is coated with ocean slime. He that accepts it in its entirety—gulps it down like an anaconda absorbing an unwashed goat; who makes no attempt to separate the essential from the accidental—the utterance of inspiration from the garrulity of hopeless nescience; who forgets that it is half an epic poem filled with the gorgeous imagery of the Orient, may, like the ass which Balaam rode, open its mouth and speak; but he never saw the Angel of the Lord; he utters the words of emptiness and ignorance.

Had the Bible been taught intelligently and truthfully the entire world would have accepted it centuries ago. Its very worst enemies are those who insist upon its inerrancy —who strive by some esoteric alchemy of logic to transmute its every fragment of base metal into bars of yellow gold, the folly of the creature into the wisdom of the Creator. During the Dark Ages hide-bound orthodoxy prevailed and practically every man was a church communicant; it is paramount to-day only in those countries that have failed to keep pace with the Car of Progress. It is a sad commentary upon all religious faiths that they flourish best where ignorance prevails—that Atheism is rapidly becoming the recognized correlative of education. By presuming to know too much of God's great plan; by decrying intelligent criticism and attempting to seal the lips of living students with the dicta of dead scholastics; by standing ever ready to brand as blasphemers those who presume to question or dare to differ, the dogmatists are driving millions of God-fearing men into passive indifference or overt opposition.

Ignorance is not a crime *per se;* but it is the mother of Superstition and Intolerance, those twin demons that have time and again deluged the world with blood and tears; that for forty centuries have stood like ravenous wolves in the path of human progress; that with their empoisoned fangs have torn a thousand times the snowy breast of Liberty—that have done more to inspire Doubt and foster Infidelity than all the French *philosophes* that ever wielded pen. The logical, well-informed man who to-day becomes a church communicant does not so because of the doctrine promulgated by the average pulpiteer, but despite of it.

The long night of intellectual slavery has not altogether passed, but on the higher hills already flame the harbingers of Reason's glorious morn. Gone is the Inquisition with its sacred infamies—the Christian rack is broken and the thumb-screw rusted in twain. The persuasive wheel no longer whisks the non-conformist into full communion, the Iron Virgin has ceased to press the writhing heretic to her orthodox heart. The faggot has fallen from the hand of the saintly fanatic and the branding iron from the loving grasp of the benevolent bigot, while Superstition, that once did rule the world with autocratic sway, can only shriek her impotent curses forth and flourish her foolish boycott at Reason's growing flame.

If I can but enable sectarians to understand that all so-called sacred books are essentially the same—that Brahma

and Baal, Jupiter and Jehovah are really identical; if I can
but make them cognizant of the crime they commit in decrying honest criticism; if I can but convince them that the
man who is

> "Slave to no sect, who takes no private road,
> But looks thro' nature up to nature's God,"

is not necessarily an active emissary of evil whom it is their
duty to denounce; if I can but create a suspicion in the
minds of the clergy that perhaps they know no more of the
Omnipotent than do other men—are possibly mistaking bile
for benevolence, gall for godliness and chronic laziness for
"a call to preach"—I will feel that these few hours expended grooming Balaam's burro have not been cast away.

*   *   *

Our information concerning the Rev. Mr. Balaam and
his burro is very limited. Although the latter was endowed
with the gift of gab it appears to have spoken but once and
then at the especial bidding of an angel, which fact leads us
to suspect that the voluble jackasses now extant have de-
teriorated at both ends since the days of their distinguished
ancestor—have parted with all their brain as well as with
half their legs. Bro. Balaam does not appear to have
"syndicated" his sermons or made any special bid for notoriety. If he ever hired half-starved courtesans *a la* Park
hurst—to dance the can-can, then hastened into court to file
complaint against the very bawds he had filled with booze
and dandled naked on his knee; if he called the ladies of
his congregation "old sows" after the manner of Sam Jones;
if he got himself tried on a charge of heresy or became en-
tangled with some half-wit sister whose religious fervor
led her to mistake Levite for the Lord, no record of the
shameful circumstance has been preserved. He appears
to have attended pretty strictly to the prophet business, and
we may presume, from such stray bits of his biography as
have come down to us, that he prospered.

The Israelites, who had gotten out of Egypt between two
days with considerable of the portable property of other
people concealed about their persons, had gone into the
Bill Dalton business under the direct guidance—as they
claimed—of their Deity, and were for some time eminently
successful. Wholesale murder and robbery became their
only industry, arson and oppression their recognized amusement. They had swiped up several cities—"leaving not
a soul alive"—and were now grinding the snickersnee for

Moab and Midian. The people of the petty nations of Palestine—whom God's anointed received an imperative command to "utterly destroy"—had builded them happy homes and accumulated considerable property by patient industry. They appear to have been peaceably disposed and devout worshippers of those deities from whom the better attributes of Jehovah were subsequently borrowed. The Israelites had not struck a lick of honest labor for forty years. They had drifted about like Coxey's "Commonwealers" and developed into the most fiendish mob of God-fearing guerrillas and marauding cut-throats of which history makes mention. Compared with Joshua's murderous Jews, the Huns who followed Atilla were avatars of mercy and the Sioux of Sitting Bull were Good Samaritans. A careful comparison of the crimes committed by the Kurds in Armenia with those perpetrated by "God's chosen people" in Palestine will prove that the followers of Allah are but amateurs in the art of courage. Doubtless any other people, brutalized by centuries of bondage, then turned loose without king or country, with only ignorant prophets for guides and avaricious priests for law-givers, would have become equally cruel—would have adopted a divinity devoid of mercy and a stranger to justice. The god of a people is, and must of necessity ever be a reflection of themselves, an idealization of their own virtues and vices—a magic mirror in which, Narcissus-like, man worships his own image.

The Jews are one of the grandest people that ever dwelt upon the earth. A more intellectual and progressive race is unknown to human history; but, like all others, it had its age of savagery and its epoch of barbarism before it reached the golden era of civilization. I am not criticising the Jews for their treatment of the Canaanites during that century when crass ignorance made them credulous and bondage rendered them brutal; but to assume that the excesses of semi-savages were heaven-inspired were a damning libel of the Deity. I rather enjoy being lied about by malicious lollipops; but did I sit secure in some celestial citadel, holding the thunderbolts of heaven within my hand, it were hardly safe to assert that I instigated such unparalleled atrocities as were perpetrated by the emancipated Israelites in Palestine. I would certainly be tempted to take a pot-shot at an occasional preacher who persisted in defaming me with his foolish dogmatism.

Balak, the king of Moab and Midian, saw that he was not strong enough to withstand the sacred marauders, and

well knew that surrender meant a wholesale massacre—
that those who had dared to defend their homes would be
placed under harrows of iron—that the silvery head of the
aged grandsire would sink beneath a sword wielded in the
name of God; that unborn babes would be ripped from the
wombs of Moabite women and the maidens of Midian
coerced into concubinage by their heaven-led captors. In
this dire extremity Balak bethought him of Bro. Balaam,
who was not "a prophet of God," as popularly supposed,
but a priest of Baal, the deity devoutly worshipped in Moab
and Midian. It were ridiculous to suppose that the king,
princes and elders of Moab and Midian would appeal for
aid to the God of their enemies instead of to their own
divinity, for in those days the principal business of a deity
was to wage war in behalf of his worshippers. Balaam
was a Midianite, and Balak sent messengers to him "with
the reward of divination in their hand," and begged that
he would kindly come over and knock the Israelites off the
Christmas tree with one of his smooth-bore, muzzle-loading
maledictions; "for, said he, with a pious fervor that proves
he was addressing a priest of his own faith, "I wot that he
whom thou blesseth is blessed, and whom thou curseth is
cursed." He evidently believed that Balaam carried the
celestial thunderbolts concealed about his person—that when
he turned them loose those on whom they alighted frizzled
up like a fat angle-worm on a sea-coal fire. The good man
said he would see what could be done to help Balak out of
the hole.

And God came unto Balaam and said, What men are these with
thee?"

As Balaam was evidently expecting the visit we may conclude that the caller was Baal, as Jehovah was not at that
time on visiting terms with the Gentile priests—was busily
engaged pulling down their altars and putting them to the
sword. Balaam gratified the very natural curiosity of his
celestial visitor, and the latter, after learning all the particulars, cautioned his diviner or priest not to make any bad
breaks. Balaam sent the ambassadors back with word that
Baal was a trifle shy of curses at that particular time.
Balak evidently understood the situation, for he sent other
agents with larger offerings. Balaam still insisted that he
had received no permission to wipe up the Plain of Moab
with the ex-brick builders, but saddled his ass and went
along, promising to do the best he could for his bleeding
country. He evidently desired to size up the situation and

be quite sure that none of his curses would come home to roost. Doubtless he also desired to see if Balak was bidding all he could afford for celestial aid, for we have no reason to believe that Bro. Balaam was in the prophet business for his health or peddling curses for recreation. While en route his companions probably informed him that the Jews were as frequent as jugs in a Prohibition precinct—that they had slaughtered the people of Ai, driven Og into the earth, overcome Ammon and were making the rest of the Canaanitish nations hard to catch, for the good man was seized with a sudden desire to take the back track. His burro balked and Balaam told his fellow travelers that an angel was interfering with his transportation facilities. Perhaps the princes of Moab made ribald remarks anent the celestial obstruction—even hinted that Balaam had best get a Maud S. move on him or he might contract a vigorous case of unavailing regret. Then the burro began to blab. Like many of the old pagan priests, Balaam was doubtless an adept in the art of ventriloquism. That may have convinced the ambassadors and bulled the price of curses; for then, as now, it was no uncommon thing for the utterance of an ass to be mistaken for that of an oracle. Or some Doubting Thomas may have twisted the burro's tail. For some reason not set forth by the sacred chronicler, the angel withdrew his objections and the prophet proceeded on his way, but still protesting that no permit had been accorded him to put a kibosh on Joshua's free-booters.

Balaam was entirely too smart to pray for rain when the wind was in the wrong quarter—altogether too smooth to launch his anathemas at an army he knew could take Moab by the back-hair and rub her nose in the sawdust. He counted the campfires of Israel and concluded that Balak's promises of high honors were worth no more than a camp-meeting certificates of conversion—that he would soon be hoofing it over the hills with his coat-tails full of arrows; so, after working his patrons for all the spare cash in sight, he made a sneak, leaving his sovereign to wage war without the aid of supernatural weapons. Like many of his sacerdotal successors, Balaam took precious good care to get on the winning side.

*   *   *

Ever since the days of Bro. Balaam there has been considerable trading of curses for cold cash. The industry has been patiently built up from humble beginnings to a magnificent business. From an itinerant curse peddler, trotting about on a spavined burro and resorting to the methods of the mountebank to create a market for his merchandise, it has become a vast commercial concern with costly establishments in every country. The first curses, as might have been expected, were very crude affairs—little more than hoodoos, intended to promote the material welfare of the purchaser at the expense of other people. A king of ye olden times bought a curse and turned it loose upon his enemies—"played the god an engine on his foe"—much as a modern prince might a gatling-gun; but it seems to have slowly dawned upon the royal ignorami that the Lord is usually on the side of the heaviest battalions—a fact which Napoleon emphasized. The practice of fencing in a nation with a few wild-eyed prophets, or sending a single soldier forth with a hair-trigger hoodoo and the jawbone of a defunct jackass to drive great armies into the earth, gradually fell into disuse—curses and blessings became a drug in the market.

About this time the Jewish priesthood began to take kindly to the doctrine of future rewards and punishments. This theological thesis—promulgated before the age of Abraham—had influenced to some extent the religious thought of the entire eastern hemisphere. That the Jews were among the last to admit the immortality of the soul was doubtless due to the fact that, because of their long enslavement, they did not emerge from semi-savagery so soon as did the other divisions of the great semitic family. Furthermore, for a long period after their emancipation the Jews seem to have received the rewards of their peculiar virtues here on earth and were little inclined to defer their happiness to the hereafter—were amply able to punish their enemies and had no occasion to delegate that pleasant duty to a Superior Power. Finally, however, the fortunes of war began to go against them. They were no longer able to make on earth a heaven for themselves and a hell for other people. Instead of despoiling others they discovered an occasional hiatus in their own smoke-house. Instead of burning the cities of their inoffensive neighbors their own began to blaze. The priests and prophets insisted that these evils befell them because they had neglected their Deity; but the more devout they became— the more fat kids, fine meal and first fruits they referred to the Levite larder as "offerings to the Lord"—the more deplorable became their condition. The people began to drift to the more reasonable religion of their neighbors and even the wisest of their kings could not be held to the faith of their fathers. The Jewish priesthood gradually adopted the old Parsi doctrine of heaven and hell—a doctrine unrecognized by Abraham, Isaac and Jacob and having no place in the theology of Moses.

The Jews eventually discovered that robbery was wrong and assassination a crime—that the practice of ripping open pregnant women and putting prisoners of war under harrows of iron was displeasing to the Lord. It was a forcible illustration of the ancient axiom that it makes a great difference whose ox is gored. Instead of founding a mighty nation as predicted by their prophets, the Jews were conquered, scattered, enslaved.

Palestine was filled with foreigners; had become a religious Babel, a theological chaos. The time was ripe for a religious revolution such as had been inaugurated in India six centuries before. It was accomplished and, as might have been expected, the result was a curious composition; a religious olla-podrida in which the profound wisdom of Zoroaster and the childish superstition of western barbarians, grand morality and monumental absurdity elbow each other like spectres in a delirium—in which is heard both "the still small voice" of Omnipotent God and the megalophanous bray of Balaam's Ass.

Jehovah, the national God of the Jews, supplanted Jove and Baal, Ashtaroth and Oromasdes, and with their thrones took many of their attributes. The doctrine of future rewards and punishments became the corner-stone of the new theology, while further concessions were made to ethnic creeds in various stages of decay by the adoption of the Trinity, Incarnation and Resurrection. The Jewish prophets were accepted by the composite cult—which Christ may have originated, but certainly did not develop—but their every utterance was given a new interpretation of which the Hebrew hierarchy had never dreamed. The great kingdom which they had predicted was to be spiritual instead of temporal; the Jerusalem predestined to become the capitol of a powerful prince, to whom all nations should acknowledge allegiance—and pay tribute—was not the leprosy-eaten old town among the Judean hills, but a city not made with hands, existing eternal in the heavens. Christianity does not contain a single original idea. It borrowed liberally on every hand, but chiefly of Parseeism in which faith, as taught by Zoroaster—Aristotle says 6000 years before Plato—may be found its most important features. It owes absolutely nothing to Judaism but the name of its God and an idle string of misinterpreted prophecies

—is, from first to last, essentially a "Gentile" faith. There never was a religion instituted upon the earth that the priesthood failed to transform into arrant folly, to debase until it finally fell into disrepute. Such was the fate of that established by Zoroaster, and upon the ruins of the grandest theology this world has known, Siddartha Guatama erected the Buddhist credo, which is really a revolt to first principles—a search for happiness here on earth, the attainment of Nirvana. So, too, the priesthood has corrupted the teachings of Christ until the logical mind revolts from the jumble of self-evident absurdities, rejects Revelations as a nursery tale and seeks by the dim light of science to find the cause of all Existence.

The new cult was not regarded kindly by the old priest-hoods, and the methods adopted for its suppression were almost as rigorous as those it in turn employed some centuries later for the discouragement of other "blasphemers" and "heretics"; hence it is not surprising that the old Hebrew doctrine that whom the Lord loves he makes mighty, gives wealth in plenty and concubines galore, power over his enemies and privilege to despoil his neighbors, should have been early transformed into "Whom the Lord loveth he chasteneth." The doctrine of temporal rewards and punishments revived somewhat as Christianity became powerful, but has remained a subordinate feature. As not a sparrow falls to the earth without a special permit from the Almighty, it follows, as a natural sequence, that every brutal crime is gracefully permitted—if not ordained—by that dear Lord whose protection we daily pray, and whose apostles we support. If we inquire why this is so we are cautioned not to commit blasphemy—some worthy brother of Balaam's Ass bids us beware the Angel of the Lord.

* * *

The claim of the ancient priesthoods to support was based on the presumption that they promoted the national welfare of the people by keeping the national deity in good humor. Whenever he contracted a case of the sulks the smell of fresh blood would usually bring him around all right. Sometimes the butchery of a few innocent birds and beasts would do the business; but it not infrequently became necessary to commit a number of homicides to get him actually gay. When even the sweet incense of blazing cities and roasting babes failed to restore his hilarity the prophets sounded the alarm much as the weather bureau gives warning of approaching cyclones and other atmospheric

disturbances. In case the dire predictions failed to mater-
ialize the Lord had listened to their protestations that he
was not doing the proper thing and "repented him"—the
Immutable had changed his mind! The prophets were supposed to make a man prosperous as a Tammany politician
by blessing, or poor as a *Houston Post* editorial by laying
a curse upon him. As civilization advanced the people
able to pay "the rewards of divination" became too intelligent to be taken in by the transparent tricks of Bro. Balaam,
hence the new priesthood devoted itself chiefly to the spiritual welfare of the people—made a specialty of the hereafter business. For obvious reasons, it is the safer enterprise.

Man was now told to believe thus-and-so and he would
be blessed eternally, but if he believed not he would be
cursed everlastingly. The rewards promised by the early
priesthoods had, by centuries of evolution, developed from
good crops and fat cattle, fruitful vines and successful villainy, into mansions in heaven; the punishments from a
protracted drought or descent of the Assyrians, a bad case
of buck ague or boils into a hell of fire where the souls of
aged unbelievers and unbaptized babes forever burn. This
was the old *argumentum ad hominem* in a new Mother
Hubbard; but the masses were still ignorant, and those who
could not be bribed with the fruits of heaven were bluffed
with the fires of hell. The old priesthoods were crushed
and kings became the sworn defenders of the new faith,
even propagated it with the sword—dispensed saving grace
with gallows' ropes and with the bludgeon drove heaven
inspired precepts into the heads of unbelievers. Wisdom
could not withstand such logic—the philosopher yielded to
the unanswerable argument of the Inquisition. As no one
could disprove the comforting doctrine of eternal damnation, and there is a strong vein of superstition in even the
best of men, the ignorant populace cowered in terror most
pitiful at the feet of a presumptuous priesthood. And to
this good day men who have managed in some mysterious
manner to dodge the mad-house, believe that priests or
preachers are the special deputies of the Deity, that a criticism of the clergy is an insult to the Almighty—that if you
dare dissent from the foolish opinions of some wooden-
headed dominus anent the Divine Plan you might as well
"curse God and die."

Once this old ethnic cult in a new dress became well established—and the source of considerable revenue to the
latter day Levites—its most glaring absurdities were able to

withstand for a time even the invention of the printing press and the general dissemination of knowledge; for "that monster custom, of habits devil," is very potent in shaping the minds of men and retarding human progress. Thus we find, in this so-called enlightened age, millions of men defending the rights of certain scorbutic families of indifferent minds and muddy morals, to sway the sovereign's sceptre. Mental collosi—men who tower up like Titians in the world of intellect—are proud to acknowledge themselves the "dutiful subjects" of some brainless fop or beery old female who chanced to be born in a royal bed while their betters were ushered in as the brats of beggars. So, too, we find men possessing clear judicial minds defending with all the fervor of Fifteenth century fanatics, not the Christian faith *per se,* but some special interpretation thereof; not the philosophy of religion, but the inconsequential theorems of some sacerdotal "reformer" who has added to the world's discord by founding a new "faith." These various religious divisions have become little more than rival commercial establishments, each peddling its own peculiar brand of saving grace—warranted the only genuine—and dealing damnation round on all dissenters.

Dogmatism begat Doubt, and men began to study the Bible, not to search out its wisdom and its truth, but its folly and its falsehood. They represent the recoil from one extreme to the other—from blind belief to unreasoning skepticism, from intellectual slavery to liberty degenerated into license. Instead of judging the Bible by God they judge God by the Bible, and finding by this ridiculous formula that he is little better than a brutal maniac, they reject him altogether and try to account for the creature without the Creator, to explain an effect without an efficient cause. If we could but muzzle the dogmatists Infidelity would quickly die. .

* * *

The essentials of the Christian religion do not depend upon the inerrancy of the Scriptures. They do not depend upon direct Revelation or the Miracle, the Incarnation or the Resurrection of Jesus from the tomb of Joseph of Arimathea. In fact, these very "Evidences" adduced in behalf of the "True Faith," produce all the Doubt with which it is called to contend. Let us grant that Moses was not called to Sinai's flaming crest to receive laws promulgated centuries before Joseph was carried a captive into Egypt; that the Bible is but the history of a barbarous people—a compendium of their poetry, religion and philosophy; that

the Incarnation and Resurrection are but myths borrowed
from decaying ethnic cults, and what have we lost? Simply
indefensible non-essentials—the tawdry garment with which
Ignorance has bedecked her poor idea of the Infinite. What
matters it whether we call our Creator Jehovah or Jupiter,
Brahma of Buddha? Who knoweth the name by which
the Seraphim address him? Why should we care whether
Christ came into the world with or without the intervention
of an earthly father? Are we not all sons of the Most High
God—"bright sparkles of the Infinite?" Suppose that the
story of the Incarnation (older than Jerusalem itself) be
literally true—that the Almighty was the immediate father
of Mary's child: Is not the birth of each and all of us as
much a mystery, as great a "miracle," as tho' we sprang
full-grown from the brow of Olympian love? Is it necessary that the Creator should violate his own laws to convince
us that he does exist? Is it more wonderful that the sun
should stand still upon Gibeon and the moon in the Valley of
Ajalon than that the great world should spin forever, bringing the night and the morning, the seed-time and the harvest? Is not a "miracle"—an interruption of nature's harmony—rather calculated to make a man of logical mind suspect that he is the sport of chance than believe himself the
especial care of an Omniscient Power that "Ordereth all
things well?" When this great globe hangs motionless in
space and the rotting dead arise in their cerements; when
great multitudes are fed with a few small fishes and virgins
are found with child, then, and not till then, will I relinquish
faith in an intelligent Architect and acknowledge lawless
Force the only Deity.

Man is but a microbe lost in immensity. He peers about
him and, by the uncertain light of his small intelligence,
reads here a word, there a line in the great Book of
Nature, and, putting together these scattered fragments,
makes a "Faith" which he defends with fanatical fervor.
Dare to call in question its most inconsequential thesis
and you are branded as an heretic; deny it *in toto* and you
are denounced as an enemy of the Almighty! The curses
of Brother Balaam no longer kill the body, but they are
expected to play sad havoc with the soul! When the
priest of Baal was *en route* to Moab's capitol for cursing
purposes an angel tried to withhold him, and even his
burro rebuked him; but neither angels nor asses are exempt
from the law of evolution. Now when a priest or preacher
lets slip a curse at those who presume to question the supernal wisdom of his creed, the angels are supposed to flap their

wings until heaven is filled with flying feathers, while
every blatant jackass who takes his spiritual fodder at
that particular rick unbraids his ears and brays approvingly.

A TOUCH OF HIGH LIFE.

THE PRESS AND THE PARVENUES.

There was a time when the principal business of the
American press was the publication of important news
and the expression of opinion anent matters of moment.
In those days it posed as a "public educator," and the
self-bestowed title was not altogether inappropriate; but
it has, for the most part, dropped its high pretensions and
is now notoriously "out for the stuff." The "great dailies"
that once went in for glory and aspired to decency, that
"molded public opinion" and "saved the country" semi-
occasionally, are not averse to accepting a fat fee for
championing some particular interest, regardless of the
general welfare. When it was proven that the *Galveston-
Dallas News* had sold its alleged editorial influence, it
had the audacity to defend the practice as legitimate journalism! A majority of the other morning papers of Texas
are not of sufficient importance to justify the public in
keeping tab on them. If they should succeed in selling
their souls for a copper cent the public would only pity
the purchaser. When the great dailies are not "pulling
the leg" of some corporation with a legislative axe to
grind, or inflating with a pneumogastric bellows some
political boomlet born of a bank account, they are courting the parvenues—who are ever ready to pay for publicity—puffing society belles for a consideration, obse-
quiously bowing to cymling-headed dudes with more dollars than sense and gathering in the golden shekels from
every available source.

The marriage of Miss Anna Gould—a very commonplace young person—to a French butterfly whom we have
no evidence ever did aught to entitle him to existence
upon the earth, afforded the "independent" American
press an opportunity to slop over in great shape, and it
slopped. Tons of toads were eaten with evident relish,
fulsome flattery fairly overran the column rules, and the
disgusting tide of eulogistic dish water is now but slowly
ebbing.

Some of the bridegroom's ancestors had once borne petty titles—out of which the *tiers etat* unceremoniously kicked the sawdust; but the nice little thing, who is of less importance to the world at large than a blind wiggle-tail, still clings to his title like a spendthrift to a canceled pawn ticket—calls himself the "Count de Castellane"—and spends his time painting, primping and puttering about like a girl inoculated with the matrimonial itch. And the great American dailies, which are supposed to be the very avatars of rugged republicanism, "dearly love a lord" even tho' his title be worth no more than a draft on a broken bank or a cook book to a starving hobo. Miss Gould was the rather stupid daughter of an American sovereign who began life as a map-maker and mouse-trap architect, and who succeeded, by very questionable methods, in amassing an enormous fortune. "Nobility and wealth!" That were indeed a combination sufficient to cause the average American editor to bow his face to the earth and lick boots until he resembled a tame duck with its mouth full of dried mud! The great dailies informed us when the little "Count" went to bed and when he got up. They told us what he ate for breakfast and how he spent each day, but even "journalistic enterprise" could not catch him in the water closet. The press watched the little parvenue who had purchased him as narrowly as a hungry buzzard could a spoiled beefsteak. "It was a love match, pure and simple," they informed the world—then wondered in the next paragraph if she would utilize the trousseau purchased less than a year ago, when she was engaged to wed some other gilly. But she didn't. She could afford a new one—the mouse-trap of her sire had been set for suckers as well as for ravenous rodentia. The trousseau purchased when she made that other "love match, pure and simple," was not nearly good enough in which to be tied fast to a titled dude—like a living man to a dead mule. The cable was kept hot ordering new "dreams of loveliness" from the he-milliners and mustachioed mantua-makers of "Paree," and the great dailies had to tell us all about it—just how each gown was cut and what it cost, how many suits of silk lingerie the bride-elect had ordered and their colors. Whether the "Count" ordered any extra underwear for the occasion the newspapers neglected to state, which omission leads us to suspect that he was not addicted to the luxury of lingerie and the expense of pajamas before he succeeded in trading his Confederate bond title and mortgaged chateau for fifteen millions of Jay Gould's ill-got gold. The Associated Press —the champion toad-eater of the universe—informed us, however, that before ze "Count" could obtain a special dispensation from his theological boss to bag the eager heiress she had to sign an agreement not to interfere with the religious faith of Frenchy and consent that their kids be brought up Roman Catholics. If His Holiness had but seen his niblets he would probably have considered the latter stipulation entirely unnecessary—a work of supererogation, so to speak. In about two years we may expect to see the "Countess" come sneaking back to her own countree in company with a divorce case and a tale o' woe that would wring the briny from a bust of Sitting Bull. It is the usual way. She will have the experience, the "Count" will have the cash and the newspapers will have another scandal with whiskers on it that trail the shrinking earth.

*　　*　　*

In the hurly-burly of getting Miss Gould married, the newspapers rather neglected the divorce case of Mr. and Mrs. Willie K. Vanderbilt—only giving us a column or so each day as condiment. But they had been hammering at it for lo! these many moons—had already told us, several times, all they knew about it and pretty much everything that a morbid imagination could guess at. Willie and his wife separated some time ago for reasons which they succeeded in keeping within the sacred Vanderbiltian circle. It was known that Willie resembled Solomon in that he "loved many strange women," and that was usually supposed to constitute the *casus belli;* but Mrs. Willie did not trot to any alarming extent in the same class with Cæsar's wife. That they quarreled and fought like some drunken "canary," and his drab was understood; but, by a liberal use of money they kept the divorce proceedings out of the papers, so it is not generally known whether the separation was caused by "incompatibility of temper" or mutual fornication. The pot probably grew aweary of calling the kettle black, and the latter of animadverting on the complexion of its companion, so a legal separation was secured and each can now indulge in those propensities peculiar to social swelldom untrammeled by marital ties. Mrs. Vanderbilt is one of three sisters, each of whom found a husband an inconvenient handicap. Willie and his ex-wife, buoyed up by boodle, will continue to float in the *creme de la creme*—where adultery seems to be the rule and decency the exception—and the great dailies to

deluge a defenseless public with highfalutin hogwash
anent their most inconsequential doings, just as tho' the
common people cared a tinker's dam whether Mrs. Vanderbilt was yum-yumming with Alphabet Belmont in
London while Willie was dallying with the Neustetter
nymph du pave in Paris. Cornelius Vanderbilt, a cross-
grained old curmudgeon with his bump of acquisitiveness
abnormally developed, went into business and prospered.
Had he failed the great dailies would trouble themselves
but little about his descendants. Those who got hanged
or divorced might get a few lines gratis, the marriage and
death notices would cost the usual dollar per line—set in
solid nonpareil and sandwiched between market reports
and pure patent medicine advertisements.

*   *   *

Jno. W. Mackay is said to have begun life by peddling
bock beer over a pine bar. This occupation probably required intellectual effort to which he found himself unequal, for he exchanged the barkeeper's apron for the
miner's overalls; the bung-starter for the quartz breaker.
He was a good fellow and the Goddess of Fortune favored
him. When he "struck it rich" his wife, who appears to
have been general manager of a miners' hash-factory,
forthwith blossomed out as a "sawsiety" butterfly. A
dinner of "biled" turnips and bull beef, a calico Mother
Hubbard and a red bandana had formerly been the *ultima
thule* of her ambition; but with millions at her command,
nothing America could produce satisfied her sybaritic
tastes. She obtained an establishment in "Paree," and
there she is in the habit of dispensing Lucullean luxuries
to the hungry horde of high-toned hoodlums who regard
a fresh-picked American parvenue as an oasis in the
Sahara of semi-starvation. And the daily press, which
would not have given her a two-line personal when she
was slinging hash and building slumgullion, began to
gush like a cask of fermenting molasses, to crawl on its
belly before the Mackay millions. Mrs. Mackay could not
purchase a poodle or old John cut his corns without the
fact being cabled across the ocean and peddled to eager
papers by the Associated Press—accompanied by the
usual cackle about its own remarkable "enterprise."
Finally Miss Mackay persuaded papa to purchase a little
macaroni prince for her to play with, and the press proceeded to have ecstatic spasms. The "Prince and Princess
Colonna" loomed up by the page in all important news-

papers, accompanied by double-column before-and-after-taking portraits. More space was devoted to this foolish young female and her titled lazzarone than to all the authors and artists, inventors and educators upon the earth. One would have supposed that when, in consideration of some millions of money, the Prince Colonna consented to occupy the same bedroom with the American heiress, a new and happier era had dawned upon the human race—that the millennium was at hand. But when the Prince had wrapped his scorbutic diaphragm around a few square feeds—at his wife's expense—he became so vicious that a self-respecting dog could not have endured him, and his purchaser was compelled to turn him loose. A few months of poverty usually brings him around all right, however, and a "happy reunion" results. Colonna would rather live with his plebeian wife occasionally than clean cuspidores or manipulate a hurdy-gurdy for a living. Every time the Prince patches up a truce—for the purpose of acquiring more boodle to blow in on the gamblers and courtesans of European capitals—the American people are compelled to learn all about it, else boycott the daily papers. Just how much the Dago dudelet has cost old honest John will probably never be known; but the latter has doubtless regretted a dozen times that the law does not allow him to take the scurvy scion of a titled but ignoble family out behind the wood shed and knock out his seldom brains by slugging him beneath the coat tails with a brogan built for that especial business.

* * *

As these lines are penned the readers of the daily press are getting another dose of the disreputable Mrs. J. Coleman Drayton, *nee* Astor. Old John Jacob Astor embarked in the skin business and, being an artist in that particular line, soon accumulated enough money to purchase property in Manhattan Island when it was worth about as much as a West-Texas goat walk. New York grew into a great city and the "unearned increment" made the family he had incidentally founded—while trading tin tomahawks and firewater for the Aborigines' furs—as rich as a fat pork pie. Three generations have sufficed to rub the grease off his gold and transform the aggressive effluvia of his hide house into odors of Araby the Blest. J. Coleman Drayton distinguished himself by capturing one of the Astor heiresses, then started in to enjoy life regardless of expense, while the great dailies gushed and slopped,

toadied and taffied. The girl was no great shakes, but her
bank account was a bute. J. Coleman was nothing to
speak of, but with an Astorian fortune at his fingers' ends
he quickly became an object of absorbing interest to our
"public educators." But, like Othello, the gentleman who
parts his name on the side and his hair in the middle became suspicious. The green-eyed monster straddled his
neck, rode him around the donjon keep of the Astorian
castle and permitted the portcullis to fall upon him with a
dull, sodden plunk. Not caring to "keep a cistern for foul
toads to knot and gender in," he gave his alleged better
half the bounce. It was expected that he'd borrow an
axe and carve a great three-cornered orifice in the anatomy of her paramour; but he concluded to tell his troubles
to the court. An opera-bouffe duel grew out of the affair;
but the cuckold was nursing his mental anguish and kept
well out of the way while a brace of society swells wounded the atmosphere and attracted the world's attention to
the frailties of his wife. Meanwhile the press fairly stag-
gered beneath the burden of the sensation—a crisis
seemed to have suddenly arisen in the history of the
human race! We were almost led to expect that the
world would cease revolving and the entire solar system
slip an eccentric because a female descendant of an ignorant old fur trader had been dallying with the dudes—
had strayed from home in her reckless pursuit of happiness.

And so it goes. The daily press is ever at the feet of
the parvenues, always cringing before the Golden Calf.
Its boasted "backbone" is made of gutta-percha, it is as
deficient in moral force as a mangy yellow fice. It has
degenerated from a public educator into a professional
scandal-monger, from an inculcator of independent American manhood to a pitiful flunkey that serves for hire,
panders to a vitiated public taste for stray pennies, flatters
Mammon for its fodder and slobbers over everything with
a title simply because it has no better sense. That is
strong language; but it will find an echo in the heart of
this mighty Yankee nation—composed, not of princes and
pimps, lords and lackeys, counts and cuckolds, but of
American sovereigns who do not depend upon boodle to
make them respectable; who are superior, morally, mentally and physically, to the very kings of foreign countries. The proudest European nobleman is a Subject; the
humblest American citizen is a Sovereign! The American
who cannot understand that fact—whether "able editor"

of a great daily or heiress seeking social distinction—
should be castrated or killed. We are breeding entirely
too many title-worshippers, toadies and intellectual tomtits—too few self-reliant, manly men, who realize that
below them are all things, animate and inanimate, above
them only the eternal King of kings.

EVOLUTION OR REVOLUTION.

The Plutocrat and the Pauper.

"For Christ's sake, Cap, give me the price of a sandwich!"

I stopped and surveyed the speaker, not because the
request was unusual, but because the applicant for aid had
not acquired the beggar's whine. He was a large, powerful man, evidently a mechanic, for every trade leaves its
peculiar stamp upon its followers.

"Why should I give you a dime? You are far more
able to work than I. A man with half your strength
should be ashamed to beg."

"Work?" he retorted, bitterly. "Give me a job—at anything—and see if I do not prove myself a man."

"But I have nothing for you to do."

"A dozen men have told me that to-day. You sneer at
me because I do not earn the bread I eat, yet decline to
give me an opportunity to do so."

I steered him against a lunch counter and watched him
chisel desolation into a silver dollar, then listened to his
story—one that I had heard a hundred times within the
year. Thrown out of employment by the business depression, he had tramped in search of work until he found
himself penniless, starving in the streets of a strange city.
He handed me a letter, dated St. Louis, written by his
wife. Some of the words were misspelled and the bad
chirography was blotted as if by falling tears, but it
breathed the spirit of a Roman matron, of a Spartan
mother. Both the children were ill. She had obtained a
little sewing and provided food and some medicine, but
two months' rent were due and the landlord would turn
them out unless it was promptly paid. She would do the
best she could, and knew that her husband would do the
same. Then thro' the blinding tears came a flash of nether
fire. Transformed into respectable English it read:

"Were I a man I would not tramp from city to city begging employment only to be refused. Were I a man I would not see my babies starve while people are piling up millions of money which they can never need. In this country there should be an opportunity for every man to make a living. Were I a man I would make an effort to release myself and my unhappy fellows from this brutal industrial bondage, this chronic pauperism— if it cost my life. I have two sons, whom God knows I do dearly love; but I would consecrate them to the holy cause of human liberty if I knew they would perish on the scaffold. I would rather see them die like dogs than live like slaves."

He sat a long time silent after returning the letter to his pocket, then said as tho' speaking to himself:

"I wonder if the rich people ever pause to reflect that there's a million brawny men in my condition to-night— a million men who only lack a leader? I wonder if they think we'll stand this kind o' thing forever? Don't talk to me about patriotism," he interrupted, fiercely. "No man can be a patriot on an empty stomach! Why should I care for the preservation of a government of, for and by the plutocrat? Let it go to the devil across lots! D—n a flag beneath which a competent and industrious mechanic cannot make a living. Anarchy? Is anarchy worse than starvation? When conditions become such that a workingman is half the time an ill-fed serf, and the other half a wretched vagabond, he's ready for a change of any kind—by any means. I am supposed to be entitled to 'Life, Liberty and the Pursuit of Happiness.' I have Liberty—to starve—and I can pursue Happiness—or rainbows—to my heart's content. There's absolutely no law prohibiting my using the horns of the moon for a hatrack if I feel so disposed!"

*   *   *

The optimists who are depending upon the "conservatism" of the American people to maintain intact our political and industrial systems; who proclaim that the present too apparent spirit of unrest is but the ephemeral effect of a few professional agitators, are of the same myopic brood as those French aristocrats who declared that all was well until the crust over the tartarean fires— steadily eaten away from beneath, steadily hammered upon from above—gave way with a crash like the crack of doom and that fair land was transformed as if by infernal magic into a high-flaming vortex of chaos, engulfing all forms and formulas, threatening the civilization of a world.

"After us the deluge!" cried those court parasites, who, with more understanding than their fellows, read aright the *mene, mene, tekel upharsin* traced upon the walls of royalty. But the deluge waited not upon their convenience. Like another prodigy of Death gendered by Pride in the womb of Sin, it burst forth to appall the world. But the American multi-millionaires mock at the "deluge"—can in nowise understand how it were possible for the thin crust that holds in thrall the fierce Gehenna fires to give 'way beneath *their* feet, dance they upon it never so hard.

The American nation is trembling on the verge of an industrial revolution—a revolution that is inevitable; that will come peaceably if it can, forcibly if it must. So ripe are the American workingmen for revolt against the existing order of things; so galled are they by the heavy yoke laid upon them; so desperate have they become that it but needs a strong man to organize and lead them, and our present industrial system—perhaps our political, also—would crumble like an eggshell in the grip of an angry Titan.

Nor is the dissatisfaction confined to the industrial class, the farmer, that Atlas upon whose broad shoulders the great world rests, is in full sympathy with every attack made upon the Cormorant by the Commune. While not ready for a revolution by force, he would not take up arms in defense of the prescriptive rights of the plutocrat from the assaults of the proletariat. Yet the American press proclaims that all is well! The "able editor" looks into his leather spectacles —free trade or high tariff brand—and with owl-like gravity announces that if the import tax on putty be increased somewhat, or fiddle-strings be placed on the free list, the American mechanic will have money to throw at the birds—that mortgages and mendicancy will pass like a hideous nightmare, and the farmer gaily bestride his sulky plow attired like unto Solomon in all his glory.

*   *   *

What is wrong? In God's name, what is right? Here we have the most fertile land upon the globe, the best supplied with all things necessary to a prosperous people. Our resources are not half developed; there is no dearth of capital; our working people are the most intelligent, energetic and capable upon which the sun ever shone. Man for man the world never contained their equal. Their productive capability is the marvel even of this age of industrial miracles. And yet, with every nerve strained to its utmost tension; toiling, saving—at very death-grips with destiny—they are sinking year by year deeper into the Slough of Despond—into that most frightful of all Gehennas, the hell of want!

Nor is this all. While those who toil are but fighting a losing battle—wearing out hand and heart and brain for a crust that becomes ever scantier, ever more bitter—there are thousands and tens of thousands who cannot even obtain the poor privilege of tramping in this brutal tread-mill, but must stand with folded arms and starve, else beg or steal. All this might be borne—would be endured with heroic fortitude—if such were the lot of all; but while the opportunity to wear out one's strength for a bare existence is becoming ever more a privilege to be grateful for, we are making millionaires by the hundreds. While the many battle desperately for life, the few are piling up fortunes beside which the famed wealth of ancient Lydia's kings were but a beggar's patrimony. The employer is becoming ever more an autocrat, the employee ever more dependent upon his good pleasure for the poor privilege of existing upon the earth.

*   *   *

To say that the "conservatism" of the American workingman will cause him to patiently endure all this is to brand him a spiritless slave, deserving not only slavery, but the shackles and the knout. He will not endure it much longer, and when his patience reaches its utmost limit—when he tires of filling his belly with the East wind supplied him in such plentitude by aspiring politicians and "able editors," look ye to see something break.

*   *   *

The problems for our statesmen to solve are, First, how to insure to every person able and willing to work an opportunity to earn an honest livelihood; Second, to effect a more equitable distribution of the wealth created among the factors engaged in its production. All other problems now engaging the attention of publicists sink into insignificance beside these. They are to practical statecraft what the immortality of the soul is to theology. They must be solved; at least, some progress must be made in that direction or force will ere long attempt it. The trouble with such convulsions is that they invariably produce temporary evil, but do not always compensate it with permanent good. They are a kind of social *mania a polu,* racking the whole organ-

ism, debilitating it—good chiefly as frightful examples of
what evil customs lead to.

To diagnose the disease and prescribe a remedy were no
easy task. There is infinitely more the matter than a mal-
adjustment of the tariff, inflated railway stocks or a dearth
of white dollars. It is a most difficult, a wonderfully intricate problem—one entirely without precedent. The rapid
development of America; the still more remarkable advancement in the science of mechanics, conjoined to a political organism not yet fully developed, but half understood, yet marking an epoch in man's social progress; commercial customs of by-gone days surviving in the midst of
much that is new—really when you come to think of it you
may well wonder that we have got thus far without more
than one great convulsion! Clearly it is no place for cathol-
icons.

That a comparatively small class of men are absorbing
the wealth of the country as fast as it is produced, leaving
to those who create it scarce a bare subsistence, is patent
to all; that the vast body of the people, clothed with political
power and imbued with the spirit of "equality," will not
permit such conditions to long continue, any thoughtful
man will concede. Even in European countries, where the
working people have come to regard privileged classes as a
matter of course, there are mutterings of a coming storm
that will only gather fresh terrors by delay. In Europe the
change will probably be wrought by revolution; in America
it may be achieved by peaceful evolution if the monied aristocracy does not, with its checks and repressions—with its
corrupted judiciary, purchased legislators and obsequious
press—drive a people, already sorely vexed, to unreasoning
madness.

*   *   *

What shall we do? We must avoid the two extremes—
that of the radical reformer and the apostle of *laissez faire*.
We will find a middle course safest and best—will need to
proceed with caution, but by no means with cowardice. The
politico-economic school that would at once change the existing order of things with as much sang-froid as a miller
substitutes steam for water-power forgets that society is not
a machine; that it was not made to order like a newspaper
editorial, and that to attempt by a radical process to make
it other than what it is—to change its genius arbitrarily—
were as fatuous as trying to transform a wolf into a watch-
dog by a chemical process or surgical operation. But while

the radical "reformer"—the man who would ignore the lessons of history and launch boldly out upon the tempestuous sea of experimentalism—is one dangerous extreme, we must remember that it is not the only one. In avoiding Scylla we must not forget Charybdis. If we are to look ever to the past, to make no experiments, to become the bondslaves of precedent, then progress is at an end and society must petrify, retrograde or consume itself in fierce fire whirlwinds.

When the American people emancipate themselves from party-slavery—than which there is none more debasing; when they cease to fight the battles of ambitious place-hunters and begin in true earnest to fight their own, then, and not till then, will the faults of our social organism be rapidly reduced to the minimum. When the common people of this country decline to be divided into two or more hostile camps by "issues" carefully concocted by political harlequins, then will the combined wisdom, purified of partisan prejudice, evolve the best possible national policy.

How many of the hard-working people of this nation who are now assiduously assailing or defending the dogma of protection or free trade—or any other of the many "issues" evolved from time to time by professional politicians as a kind of Pegasus upon which they fondly hope to ride into power—ever carefully considered the question in all its bearings; studied it from a national, sectional or even individual standpoint. Questions upon which Adam Smith and Auguste Compte, Jefferson and Hamilton disagreed, are settled by the dicta of a partisan convention—composed chiefly of political hacks and irresponsible hoodlums—with less trouble than a colored wench selects a calico gown.

The American people, as P. T. Barnum long ago pointed out, have a weakness for humbugs. They are the natural prey of the charlatan, and in nothing more so than in matters political. Despite their boasted intelligence, they will follow with a trust that partakes of the pathetic the mountebank who can perform the most sleight-of-hand tricks, the demagogue who can make the most noise. They think, but are too busy or indifferent to think deeply, to reason closely. They "jump at conclusions," assert their correctness stubbornly and prove the courage of their convictions by their ballots. They demonstrate their "independence" by choosing their political fetich, their confidence in the infallibility of their judgment by worshiping it blindly. Herein lies the chief danger—danger that the American workingman will follow this or

that *ignis-fatuus,* hoping thereby to find a shorter north-
west passage to impossible spice islands, until poverty
has degraded him from a self-respecting sovereign into a
volcanic *sans culotte;* until he loses hope of bettering his
condition by whereases, resolutions, trades-unions, acts of
Congress, etc., and, like another blind and desperate Samson, lays his brawny hands upon the pillars of the temple
and pulls it down about his ears.

SPEAKING OF GALL.

Gall is a bitter subject, and I shall waste no time selecting sweet words in which to handle it. There's no surplus of sweet words in my vocabulary anyhow. I have
never yet been able to rent my mouth for a taffy mill.
Webster gives several definitions of Gall; but the good
old etymologist was gathered to his fathers long before
the word attained its full development and assumed an
honored place in the slang vernacular of the day. It was
needed. It fills what editors sometimes call "a long-felt
want." Gall is sublimated audacity, transcendent impudence, immaculate nerve, triple-plated cheek, brass in
solid slugs. It is what enables a man to borrow five dollars of you, forget to repay it, then touch you for twenty
more. It is what makes it possible for a woman to borrow her neighbor's best bonnet, then complain because
it isn't the latest style or doesn't suit her particular type
of beauty. It is what causes people to pour their troubles
into the ears of passing acquaintances instead of reserving
them for home consumption. It is what makes a man
aspire to the governorship, or to air his asininity in the
Congress of the United States when he should be fiddling
on a stick of cordwood with an able-bodied buck-saw. It
is what leads a feather-headed fop, with no fortune but
his folly, no prospects but poverty—who lacks business
ability to find bread for himself—to mention marriage to
a young lady reared in luxury, to ask her to leave the
house of her father and help him fill the land with fools.
Gall is what spoils so many good ditchers and delvers to
make peanut politicians and putty-headed professional
men. It is what puts so many men in the pulpit who
could serve their Saviour much better planting the mild-
eyed potato or harvesting the useful hoop-pole. It is what
causes so many young ladies to rush into literature in-

stead of the laundry—to become poets of passion instead
of authors of pie.

Gall is a very common ailment. In fact, a man without a liberal supply of it is likely to be as lonesome in this
land as a consistent Christian at a modern camp-meeting,
or a gold-bug Democrat in Texas. Nearly everybody has
it and is actually proud of it. When a young man is first
afflicted with the tender passion; when he is in the throes
of the mysterious mental aberration that would cause him
to climb a mesquite bush and lasso the moon for his
inamorata if she chanced to admire it, he is apt to think
it love that makes the world go round. Later he learns
that Gall is the social dynamics—the force that causes
humanity to arise and hump itself.

Gall has got the world grabbed. Politics is now a high-
class play, whose pawns are power and plunder; business
is becoming but a gouge-game wherein success hallows
any means. Our mighty men are our most successful
marauders; our social favorites minister in the temple of
Mammon, our pillar of cloud by day and of fire by night
the follics and foibles of the "Four Hundred," our God the
Golden Calf. The standard by which society now measures men is the purse; that by which it gauges greatness
the volume of foolish sound which the aspirant for immortal honors succeeds in setting afloat, little caring
whether it be such celestial harp music as caused Thebe's
walls to rise, or the discordant bray of the ram's horn
which made Jericho's to fall. This century, which proudly
boasts itself "heir to all the ages and foremost in the files
of time," doffs its beaver to brazen effrontery, burns its
sweetest incense on the unhallowed shrine of pompous
humbuggery, while modest merit is in a more pitiable
predicament than the traditional tomcat in Tartarus without teeth or toenails.

We make manifest our immeasureable Gall by proclaiming from the housetops that, of all the ages which
have passed o'er the hoary head of Mother Earth, the
present stands pre-eminent; that of all the numberless
cycles of Time's mighty pageant there was none like unto
it—no, not one. And I sincerely hope there wasn't. Perhaps that which induced the Deity to repent him that he
had made man and send a deluge to soak some of the
devilment out of him, was the nearest approach to it. We
imagine that because we have the electric telegraph and
the nickel-plated dude, the printing press and the campaign lie, the locomotive and the scandal in high life; that

because we now roast our political opponent instead of the guileless young missionary, and rob our friends by secret fraud instead of despoiling our foes by open force, that we are the people *par-excellence* and the Lord must be proud of us.

Progress and improvement are not always synonyms. A people may grow in Gall instead of grace. I measure a century by its men rather than by its machines, and we have not, since civilization took its boasted leap forward, produced a Socrates or a Shakespeare, a Phidias or an Angelo, a Confucius or a Christ.   This century runs chiefly to Talmages and Deacon Twogoods, pauper dukes and divorce courts—intellectual soup and silk lingerie.

* * *

The poets no longer sing of the immortal gods, of war and sacrifice, while the flame mounts to manhood's check, red as the fires of Troy: They twitter of lovies and dovies, of posies and goose-liver pie, while pretty men applaud and sentimental maids get moonsick. Cincinnatus no longer waits for the office to seek the man: He sells his brace of bullocks and buys a political boom. No more the Spartan mother gives her long black hair for bowstrings: She blondines it, paints, powders and tries to pass as the younger sister of her eldest daughter.   The Norse viking no longer plows the unknown wave, his heart wilder than the wat'ry waste, his arm stronger than tempered steel: He comes to America and starts a saloon. No more the untamed Irish king caroms on the Saxon invader with a seasoned shillalah: He gets on the police force and helps "run the machine," or clubs the head off the harmless married man who won't go home till morning.   In these degenerate days the philosopher retires not to the desert, and there, by meditation most profound, wrings from the secret treasure-house of his own superior soul, jewels to adorn his age and enrich the world: He mixes an impossible plot with a little pessimism, adds a dude and a woman whose moral character has seen better days, spills the nauseous compound on the public as a "philosophical novel" and works the press for puffs. Indeed we're progressing; going onward and upward— like the belled buzzard dodging a divorce scandal. Greece had her Pericles, but it was left for us to produce a Parkhurst. Rome had her Cicero and her Caesar, but was never equal to a Culberson or a Corbett. The princes of old conquered the earth, but the modern plutocrats put a mortgage on it. Cleopatra drank pearls dissolved in wine, but whisky straight is said to be good enough for some of her successors. Samson slew the Philistines with a jawbone of an ass; but a modern politician, employing the self-same weapon, would have got 'em to elect him governor. We've got no Helen of Troy; but our "Hell'n Blazes" is a bird o' the same feather. We've got to yield the palm in poetry and philosophy, art and architecture; but when it comes to building political platforms that straddle every important issue and slinging princely style on a pauper income we're out of sight.

How can the acorn become a mighty forest monarch if planted in a pint pot and crossed with a fuzzy-wuzzy chrysanthemum? How can the Numidian lion's whelp become a king of beasts if reared in a cage and fed on cold potatoes, muzzled and made to dance to popular music? How can the superior soul expand until it becomes all-embracing, god-like, a universe in itself, in which rings sweet sphere-music and rolls Jovinian thunder—in which blazes true Promethean fire instead of smoulders the sulphurous caloric of the nether world—when its metes and bounds are irrevocably fixed for it—when it can only grow in certain prescribed directions, painfully mapped out for it by bumptious pismires who imagine that their little heads constitute the intellectual Cosmos?

*　　*　　*

Hamlet, Prince of Denmark, lamented that he lacked Gall; but the melancholy Dane was dead years before the present generation of titled snobs appeared upon the scene. None of the princes or dukes of the present day appear to be short on Gall; none of the nobility seem to be suffering for lack of it. Not long ago a little Duke who owes his title to the fact that his great-grand-aunt was the paramour of a half-wit prince, kindly condescended to marry an American girl to recoup his failing fortunes. A little French guy whose brains are worth about two cents a pound—for soap-grease—put up a Confederate-bond title for the highest bidder and was bought in like a hairless Mexican pup by an American plutocrat. Now half-a-dozen more little pauper princelings and decadent dukelings are trying to trade their worthless coronets for American cash. But the fact that many a man boasting of his American sovereignty will dicker with a titled young duke, instead of using the forecastle of a No. 9 foot to drive his spinal column up thro' his plug-hat like a presidential lightning-rod; will actually purchase for his daughter some disgusting little title upon which rests the fateful bar-sinister of a woman's shame, and is encumbered by a dizzy young dude, too lazy to work and too cowardly to steal—too everlastingly "ornery" to raise a respectable crop of wild oats—proves that the young lollipop lordlings haven't a monopoly of the Gall of the Globe.

*   *   *

A most shameful exhibition of Gall is the practice now coming into vogue with certain society ladies of encouraging newspapers to puff their charms—even paying them so much a line for fulsome praise. Not a few metropolitan papers reap a handsome profit by puffing society buds whom their fond parents are eager to place on the matrimonial market, hoping that they will "make good matches;" in other words, that they will marry money—its possessors being thrown in as *pelon.* Even married women, who are long on shekels but short on sense, sometimes pay big prices to get their portraits in the public prints—accompanied by puffs that would give a buzzard a bilious attack.

But the Gall of the girl who puts her picture in the papers, accompanied by a paid puff of her "purty," scarce equals that of the conceited maid who imagines she has only to look at a man and giggle a few times to "mash him cold"—to get his palpitating heart on a buckskin string and swing it hither-and-yon at pleasure. How the great he-world does suffer at the hands of those heartless young coquettes—if half it tells 'em be true! David said in his haste that all men are liars. And had he carefully considered the matter he would have come to the same conclusion. Washington may have told his father the truth about that cherry-tree; but later in life he became entirely too popular with the ladies for a man unable to lie.

It is natural for men to pay court to a pretty woman as for flies to buzz about a molasses barrel; but not every fly that buzzes expects to get stuck, I beg to state. The man who doesn't tell every woman who will listen to him —excepting, perhaps, his wife—that she's pretty as a peri, even tho' she be homely enough to frighten a mugwump out of a fat federal office; that she's got his heart grabbed; that he lives only in the studied sunshine of her store-teeth smile and is hungering for an opportunity to die for her dear sake—well, he's an angel, and he-seraphs are almighty scarce I beg of you to believe. Since Adonis died and Joseph was gathered to his fathers none have appeared that I am aware of. These young gentlemen were all right, I suppose; but I'd like to see either of them get elected now-a-days on the Democratic ticket in Texas.

But feminine conceit, fed on flattery, were as milk-shake unto mescal, as a kiss by mail to one by moonlight compared with the insufferable egotism of the "pretty man" who puts his moustache up in curl-papers and perfumes his pompadour; who primps and postures before an amorous looking-glass and imagines that all Eve's daughters are trying to abduct him. Whenever I meet one of these male irresistibles I'm forcibly reminded that the Almighty made man out of mud—and not very good mud at that. The two-legged he-thing who makes a clothes-horse of himself and poses on the street-corner perfumed like an emancipation day picnic; who ogles a pretty woman until the crimson creeps into her cheek, then prides himself on having captured her heart like the boy caught the itch,— because he couldn't help it—when she's only blushing for the mother who bore the pitiful parody on manhood; who imagines that every maid who deigns to waste a smile on him is sighing her soul out for his sweet sake, has allowed his Gall to go to his head and curdle his brains.

*   *   *

More than a moiety of our so-called great men are but featherless geese, possessing a superabundance of Gall— creatures of chance who ride like driftwood on the crest of a wave raised by forces they cannot comprehend; but they ride, and the world applauds them while it tramples better men beneath its brutal feet. Greatness and Gall, genius and goose-speech, sound and sense have become synonyms. If you fall on the wrong side of the market men will quote the proverb about a fool and his money; if on the right side you're a Napoleon of finance. Lead a successful revolt and you are a pure patriot whose memory should be preserved to latest posterity; head an unsuccessful uprising and you are a miserable rebel who should have been hanged. "Nothing succeeds like success." Had the Christian religion failed to take root, Judas Iscariot would have been commemorated in the archives of Rome as one who helped stamp out the hateful heresy, and had Washington got the worst of it in his go with Cornwallis he would have passed into history as a second Jack Cade.

Alexander of Macedon was great, as measured by the world's standard of eminence. After two-and-twenty centuries our very babes prattle of this bloody butcher, and

even his horse has been enshrined in history. In our own
day Father Damien left kindred and country and went
forth to die for the miserable lepers in the mid-Pacific,
but he is already forgotten—his name and fame have
faded from the minds of men. Yet greater and grander
than all the blood-stained princes and potentates of earth;
nobler, more god-like than all the proud prelates that ever
aired their turgid eloquence at Christian conference or
ecumenical council was that young priest; but no cenotaph rises to commemorate his sacrifice—silent as his own
sealed lips is the trumpet of fame.

But for Gall of the A1, triple X brand, commend me to
the little pot-house politician who poses as a political
prophet and points out to wiser men their public duties.
We have to-day in this land of the free and home of the
crank, thousands of self-important little personages who
know as little of political economy as a parrot of the
power of prayer, prating learnedly of free-trade or protection, greenbackism or metallic money. Men who
couldn't tell a fundamental principle from their funny-
bone, an economic thesis from a hot tamale—who don't
know whether Ricardo was an economist or a corn-doc-
tor—evolve from their empty ignorance new systems of
"saving the country," and defend them with the dogmatic
assurance of a nigger preacher describing the devil—make
gorgeous displays of their Gall. I have noticed that, as a
rule, the less a man knows of the science of government the
crazier he is to go to congress. About half the young statesmen who break into the legislature imagine that Roger Q.
Mills wrote the Science of Economics, and that Jefferson
Davis was the father of Democracy.

But the Gall is not confined to the little fellows—the big
political M D's have their due proportion. The remedies
they prescribe for Uncle Sam's ailments remind me of the
panaceas put on the market by the patent-medicine men—
warranted to cure everything, from a case of cholera-morbus to an epidemic of poor relations. We have one school of
practitioners prescribing free-trade as a sure-cure for every
industrial ill, another a more drastic system of protection.
One assures us that the silver-habit is dragging us down to
the demnition bow-wows, another that only an heroic dose
of white dollars will save us from industrial death. Political claptrap to corral the succulent pie—"issues" to get office. We have had high and low tariff, the gold and silver
standard, greenbackism and "wild-cat" currency; we have
had presidents of all shades of political faith and congresses

of every kind of economic folly; yet in a single century America has risen from the poorest of nations to the wealthiest in all the world. True it is that wealth is congested—that willful Waste and woeful Want go hand in hand—that the land is filled with plutocrats and paupers; but this distressing fact is due to the faults of our industrial system itself, and can never be reformed by placing fiddle-strings on the free list or increasing the tariff on toothpicks.

Gall? Ye gods! Look at the platform promises of the blessed Democratic party—then at its performances! Look at the party itself—a veritable omnium-gatherum of political odds and ends, huddled together under the party blanket like household gods and barn-yard refuse after a hurricane. High and low tariffs and free-traders; gold-bugs, greenbackers and bi-metallists; Cleveland and Croker, Altgeld and Olney, Hill and Hogg, Waco's Warwick and Colonel Culberson's kid, all clamoring to be dyed-in-the-wool Democrats! When I get a new main-spring put in my vocabulary I'm going to tackle the Gall of the Populists and Republicans.

* * *

Some specimens of Gall amaze me by their greatness, some amuse me, while others only spoil my appetite. Of the latter class is the chronic kicker who is forever fuming about feminine fashions. If the hoop-skirt comes in this critic is in agony; if the "pull-back" makes its appearance he has a fit and falls in it. Ever since Eve attired herself in a few freckles and fig-leaves he's been reforming the fashions. Don't mind him, ladies. Like a peacock crying in the night, he's disagreeable, but not dangerous. Adorn yourselves as you see fit; follow such fashions as seem good in your sight, and have no fear that the sons of men will ever forsake you because of your clothes. When you find a man dictating to the ladies what they shall wear you're pretty apt to see his head housed in a stove-pipe hat—the most inartistic and awkward monstrosity ever designed by the devil to make the Almighty ashamed of his masterpiece. In all history there's no record of a great idea being born in a beegum. I never saw a statue of a hero or picture of a martyr with a plug hat on. Imagine the Lord laying aside a silk cady preparatory to preaching that Sermon on the Mount—or Napoleon apostrophizing the pyramids in a plug! Before finding fault with the fashions of the ladies just imagine Apollo in the make-up of a modern society swell, loafing into court on High Olympus! Why Jove would hit him with a thunderbolt so hard there'd be nothing left of him but a wilted chrysanthemum and a pair o' yaller shoes!

* * *

For a specimen of Gall that must amaze the very gods commend me to a crowd of pharisaical plutocrats, piously offering, in a hundred thousand dollar church, prayers to him who had nowhere to lay his head; who pay a preacher $15,000 per annum to point the way to Paradise, while in the great cities of every Christian country children must steal or starve and women choose between death and dishonor. New York is crowded with costly churches that lift their proud spires into the empyrean, that part the clouds with golden fingers—monuments which Mammon rears as if to mock the lowly Son of God. Their value mounts up into the millions; yet I learn—from a religious paper, mark you—that 100,000 men, women and children were evicted in New York alone last year for the non-payment of rent; turned into the streets to suffer summer's heat or winter's cold—to beg, or starve, or steal, as they saw fit. I find these startling statistics in the same column with a tearful appeal for more money to send missionaries to black barbarians—on the same page with a description of a new church that must have cost a cold half-million of cash. That's what I call sanctified assurance—gall masquerading as grace. And what is true of New York is true, in greater or less degree, of every town from Plymouth Rock to Poker Flats, from Tadmor-in-the-Wilderness to Yuba Dam. Everywhere the widow is battling with want, while we send Bibles and blankets, prayer-books and pie, salvation and missionary soup to a job-lot of lazy niggers whose souls aren't worth a soumarkee in blocks-of-five—who wouldn't walk into heaven if the gates were wide open, but once inside would steel the eternal throne if it wasn't spiked down. Let the heathen rage; we've got our hands full at home. I'd rather see the whole black-and-tan aggregation short on Bibles than one white child crying for bread.

While Europe and America are peddling saving grace in pagan lands—and incidentally extending the market for their cheap tobacco, snide jewelry and forty-rod bug-juice— they are also building warships and casting cannon—preparing to cut each other's throats while prating of the prince of peace! The idea of countries that have to build forts on their frontiers and keep colossal standing armies to avoid being butchered by their own Christian brethren; that are full of divorce courts and demagogues, penitentiaries and poorhouses, sending young theological goslings, who be-

lieve that all of divine revelation can be found in one book,
to teach the philosophic Hindu the road to heaven! Gall!
Why the men we are trying to convert were preaching the
immortality of the soul when the Hebrew prophets were
putting people to the sword for accepting it; they were
familiar with all the essential features of the Christian faith
a thousand years before the crucifixion of Christ. Charity
begins at home. In our own country children are coming
up in ignorance and crime, while sect vies with sect in the
erection of proud temples in which polite society may display its Parisian finery while pretending to worship One
who broke bread with beggars and slept in the brush.

I haven't much use for gold-plated godliness. Christ
never built a church, or asked for a vacation on full pay,—
never. He indulged in no political harangues—never told
his parishioners how to vote—never posed as a professional
Prohibitionist. He didn't try to reform the fallen women
of Jerusalem by turning them over to the police, a la Parkhurst. Although gladitorial shows were common in his
country—and that without gloves—he didn't go raging up
and down the earth like some of our Texas dominies, demanding that these awful crimes against civilization should
cease. There is no record of his engineering a boycott
against business men who dissented from his doctrine. I
think he could have read a copy of the Iconoclast with far
more patience than some of his successors. Human or
divine, he was the grandest man that ever graced the mighty
tide of time. His was a labor of love, instead of for lucre.
The groves were his temples, the mountain-side his pulpit,
the desert his sacristy and Jordan his baptismal font.

* * *

Then there's the unconscious Gall of the pious parrot
who is quite sure that the only highway to the heavenly
hereafter is outlined by his little sect, macadamized by his
creed; that you've got to travel that or get into trouble,
perhaps fall into the fire.

Just imagine that dear Lord, who so loved sinners that
he died to save them from death eternal, looking over
heaven's holy battlements and observing a miserable mortal
plunging downward to his doom, leaving behind him a
streak of fire like a falling star, his face distorted with fear,
his every hair erect and singing like a jewsharp. He asks
St. Peter:

"Who's that?"

"Oh," says the man on the door, "that's old John Smith."

The Lord goes over to the office of the Recording Angel

and turns the leaves of the great ledger. He finds the
name, "John Smith, No. 11027," and on the credit page
these entries: "He was fearless as Caesar, generous as
Macaenas, tender as Guatama and true to his friends as the
stars to their appointed courses. He was a knight of
nature's nobility, a lord in the aristocracy of intellect, cour-
tier at home and a king abroad. On the debit page he
reads: "Went fishing on Sunday. There was a miscue on
his baptism. He knew a pretty woman from an ancient
painting, a jack-pot from a prayer-book, and when smitten
on one cheek he made the smacker think he'd been smuck
by a cyclone." Good-bye, John!

It may be that the monarch of the majestic universe
marches around after every inconsequential little mortal,
note-book in hand, giving him a white mark when he prays
for the neighbor who poisons his dog, or tells his wife the
truth regardless of consequences; a black one when he bets
his money on the wrong horse or sits down on the sidewalk
and tries to swipe the front gate as it goes sailing by; but
I doubt it. If I could make the sun, moon and stars in one
day and build a beautiful woman of an old bone, I'd just
like to see the color of that man's hair I'd waste much time
and attention on.

* * *

Why should we quarrel about our faiths and declare that
this is right and that is wrong, when all religions are, and
must of necessity ever be, fundamentally one and the same—
the worship of a superior power, the great

"Father of all, in every age, in ev'ry clime adored,
By saint, by savage and by sage, Jehovah, Jove, or Lord."

* * *

Man's cool assumption that the Almighty made him as
his "master-piece" should be marked Exhibit A in the
mighty aggregation of Gall. That after millions of years
experience in the creation business—after building the arch-
angels and the devil; after making the man in the moon and
performing other wondrous miracles, the straddling six-foot
biped who wears a spike-tail coat and plug hat, a silk surcingle and sooner tie; who parts his name on the side and
his hair in the middle; who sucks a cane and simpers like a
school-girl struggling with her first compliment; who takes
it for granted that he knows it all, when his whole life—
including his birth, marriage and death—is a piece of ridiculous guess-work; who insists that he has a soul to save, yet
labors with might and main to lose it; protests that there's

a better land beyond the grave, yet moves heaven and earth to keep from going to it so long as he can help it— the assumption, I say, that this was the best the Creator could do, is *prima facie* evidence of a plentitude of Gall of the purest ray serene.

The calm assurance of man that the earth and all it contains were made for his especial benefit; that woman was created solely for his comfort; that the sun was made to give him light by day and the moon to enable him to find his way home from the lodge at night without the aid of a policeman; that the heavens were hung with a resplendent curtain of stars and the planets sent whirling thro' space in a majestic dance about the God of Day, simply to afford him matter for wonder or for amusement when too tired to talk politics or too bilious to drink beer, evinces an egotism that must amuse the Almighty.

Master-piece indeed! Why, God made man, and, finding that he couldn't take care of himself, made woman to take care of him—and she proposes to discharge her heaven-ordained duty or know the reason why. Tennyson says that, "as the husband is the wife is;" but even Tennyson didn't know it quite all. When wives take their hubbies for measures of morality, marriage will become an enthusiastic failure and Satan be loosed for a little season. We acknowledge woman's superiority by demanding that she be better than we could if we would, or would be if we could.

We are fond of alluding to woman as "the weaker vessel;" but she can *break* the best of us if given an opportunity. Pope calls man the "great lord of all things"—but Pope never got married. We rule with a rod of iron the creatures of the earth and air and sea; we hurl our withering defi in the face of Kings and brave presidential lightning; we found empires and straddle the perilous political issue, then surrender unconditionally to a little bundle of dimples and deviltry, sunshine and extravagance. No man ever followed freedom's flag for patriotism (and a pension) with half the enthusiasm that he will trail the red, white and blue that constitute the banner of female beauty. The monarch's fetters cannot curtail our haughty freedom, nor nature's majestic forces confine us to this little lump of clay; we tread the ocean's foam beneath our feet, harness the thunderbolts of imperial Jove to the jaunting car, and even aspire to mount the storm and walk upon the wind; yet the bravest of us tremble like cowards and lie like Cretans when called to account by our wives for some of our cussedness.

But you will say that I have wandered from my text—have followed the ladies off and got lost. Well, it's not the first time it's happened. But really, I'm not so inconsistent as I may seem; for if the gentler sex exceeds us in goodness it likewise surpasses us in Gall. Perhaps the most colossal exhibit of polite and elegant audacity this world can boast is furnished by that female who has made a *marriage of convenience;* has wedded money instead of a man,—practically put her charms up at auction for the highest bidder —yet who poses as a paragon of purity; gathers up her silken skirts—the price of her legalized shame—lest they come in contact with the calico gown of some poor girl who has loved, not wisely, but too well.

Marriage is the most sacred institution ever established on earth, making the father, mother and child a veritable Holy Trinity; but it is rapidly degenerating into an unclean Humbug, in which Greed is God and Gall is recognized high-priest. We now consider our fortunes rather than our affections, acquire a husband or wife much as we would a parrot or a poodle, and get rid of them with about as little compunction. Cupid now feathers his arrows from the wings of the gold eagle and shoots at the stomach instead of the heart. Love without law makes angels blush; but law without love crimsons even the brazon brow of infamy.

* * *

But the fact that so many selfish, soulless marriages are made is not altogether woman's fault. Our ridiculous social code is calculated to crush all sentiment and sweetness out of the gentler sex—to make woman regard herself as merchandise rather than as a moral entity, entitled to life, liberty and the pursuit of happiness. The average woman must select a husband from a narrow circle; must make choice among two or three admirers or elect to live a loveless old maid—to forego the joys of motherhood, the happiness of a home. Man is privileged to go forth and seek a mate. The world is before him, a veritable "Dream of Fair Women." He wanders at will, as amid a mighty parterre of flowers, sweet as the breath of morn, and finally, before some fair blossom he bows the knee—pours forth the incense of his soul to the one woman in all the world he would make his wife. True, she may refuse him and marry some other fellow; but he is at least privileged to approach her, to plead his cause, to employ all the art and eloquence of love to bring her into his life. Woman enjoys no such privilege. She must wait to be wooed, and if her king comes not she must take the best that offers and try to be content.

Every daughter of Eve dreams of an ideal,—of a man tender and true, who will fill her life with love's own melody; his word her law, his home her heaven, his honor her glory and his tomb her grave. And some day, from these castles in the clouds he comes—these day-dreams, golden as the dawn, become the halo of a mortal man, to whom her heart turns as the helianthus to the sun. At last the god of her idolatry doth walk the earth; but she must stand afar,—must not, by word or act, betray the holy passion that's consuming her, lest "that monster custom, of habits devil," doth brand her bold and bad. Love ofttimes begets love, as the steel strikes fire from the cold flint, and a word from her might bring him to her feet; but she must stand with dumb lips and assumed indifference and see him drift out of her life, leaving it desolate as the Scythian desert, when it should have budded and blossomed like the great blush rose. So she drifts desolate into old maidenhood and the company of Maltese cats; else, when hope is dead in her heart—when the dream of her youth has become dust and ashes—she marries for money and tries to feed her famished heart with Parisian finery, to satisfy her soul with the Dead Sea fruit of fashion.

No; I wouldn't give woman the ballot—not in a thousand years. I want no petticoats in politics—no she-senators or female presidents; but I'd do better by woman; I'd repeal that ridiculous social law—survival of female slavery— which compels her to wait to be wooed. I'd put a hundred leap-years in every century, give woman the right to do half the courting—to find a man to her liking and capture him if she could. Talk about reforms! Why, the bachelors would simply have to become Benedicts or take to the brush, and there'd be no old maids outside the dime museums. But I was speaking of Gall.

* * *

Gall is usually unadulterated impudence; but sometimes it is irremediably idiocy. When you find a man pluming himself on his ancestors you can safely set it down that he's got the disease in its latter form, and got it bad. I always feel sorry for a man who's got nothing to be proud of but a dead gran'daddy, for it appears to be a law of nature that there shall be but one great man to a tribe—that the lightning of genius shall not twice strike the same family tree. I suppose that Cleveland and Jim Corbett, Luther

and Mrs. Lease, Homer and J. S. Hogg had parents and
gran'parents; but we don't hear much about 'em. And
while the ancestors of the truly great are usually lost in the
obscurity of the cornfield or cotton-patch, their children
seldom succeed in setting the world on fire. Talent may
be transmitted from father to son; but you can no more inherit genius than you can inherit a fall out of a balloon.
It is the direct gift of that God who is no respecter of persons, and who sheds his glory on the cotter's child as freely
as on those of monarchs and of millionaires.

We have in this country three aristocracies: The aristocracy of intellect, founded by the Almighty; the aristocracy of money, founded by Mammon, and the aristocracy
of family, founded by fools. The aristocracy of brains
differs from those of birth and boodle as a star differs from
a jack-o'-lantern, as the music of the spheres from the bray
of a burro, as a woman's first love from the stale affection
hashed up for a fourth husband.

To the aristocracy of money belong many worthy men;
but why should the spirit of mortal be proud? The founder
of one of the wealthiest and most exclusive of American
families skinned beeves and made weinerwurst. The calling
was an honest and useful one. His sausages were said to
be excellent, and at a *skin* game he was exceptionally hard
to beat; but his descendants positively decline to put a calf's
head regardant and a cleaver rampant on their coat-of-arms.
A relative much addicted to the genealogical habit once
assured me that he could trace our family back 600 years
just as easy as following the path to the drugstore in a
Prohibition town. I was delighted to hear it, to learn that
I too had ancestors—that some of them were actually on the
earth before I was born. While he was tracing I was
figuring. I found that in 600 years there should be 20 generations—if everybody did his duty—and that in 20 generations a man has 2,093,056 ancestors! Just think of it!
Why, if he had gone back 600 years further he might have
discovered that I was a lineal descendant of Adam, perhaps
distantly related to crowned monarchs—if not to the Duke
of Marlborough. As my cousin couldn't account for this
job-lot of kinsmen—had no idea how many had been hanged,
gone into politics or written poetry, I rang him off. Those
people who delight to trace their lineage through several
generations to some distinguished man should be tapped for
the simples. When John Smith starts out to found a family
and marries Miss Jones, their son is half Smith and half
Jones. The next crop is nearly one-fourth Smith and at the

end of a dozen generations the young Smiths bear about as much relation to the original as they do to a rabbit.

* * *

There are various grades of Gall; but perhaps the superlative brand is that which leads a man to look down with lofty scorn upon those of his fellow mortals who have tripped on Life's rugged pathway and plunged into a shoreless sea of shame. I am no apologist for crime—I would not cover its naked hideousness with the Arachne-robe of sentiment; but I do believe that many a social out-cast, many a branded criminal, will get as sweet a harp in the great hereafter as those who have kept themselves unspotted from the world. It is easy enough to say grace over a good square meal, to be honest on a fat income, to praise God when full of pie; but just wait till you get the same razzle-dazzle the devil dished up for Job and see how your halle-hallelujahs hold out before exalting your horn. Victory does not always proclaim the hero nor virtue the saint. It were easy enough to sail with wind and tide—to float over fair seas, mid purple isles of spice; but the captain who loses his ship mid tempests dire, mid wreck and wrath, may be a better sailor and a braver than the master who rides safe to port with rigging all intact and every ensign flying. With

> "The boast of heraldry, the pomp of power,
> And all that beauty, all that wealth e'er gave,"

it were easy enough to be a good citizen and a consistent Christian. It is poverty and contempt, suffering and disappointment that try men's souls—that proclaim of what metal they are made. Faith, Hope and Charity are man's triune transcendent—"and the greatest of these is Charity." A pharisee is either a pious fraud or a hopeless fool—he's either short on "gumption" or long on Gall.

* * *

Half the alleged honesty of this world is but Gall, and must be particularly offensive to the Almighty. We have oodles of men in every community who are legally honest, but morally rotten. Legal honesty is the brand usually proclaimed as "the best policy." Only fools risk the penitentiary to fill their purse. The smart rogue is ever "honest within the law"—infamous in strict accord with the criminal code.

Dives may attire himself in purple and fine linen and

fare sumptuously every day, while Lazarus lies at his door for the dogs to lick, vainly craving the crumbs that fall from the millionaire's table, and still be legally honest, even a church member in good standing; but his loyalty to legal forms will avail him but little when he finds his coat-tails afire and no water within forty miles.

The girl who flirts with a featherless young gosling till he doesn't know whether he's floating in a sea of champagne to the sound of celestial music, sliding down a greased rainbow or riding on the ridge-pole of the aurora borealis, then tells him that she can only be a kind of Christmas-present, opera-ticket sister to him; who steals his unripe affections and allows 'em to get frost-bitten—carries him into the empyrean of puppy-love, only to drop him with a dull plunk that fills his callow heart with compound fractures—well, she cannot be prosecuted for petit larceny nor indicted for malicious mischief; but the unfortunate fellow who finally gets her will be glad to go to heaven, where there's neither marrying nor giving in marriage.

The man who preaches Prohibition in public and pays court to a gallon jug of corn-juice in private; who damns the saloon at home and sits up with it all night abroad, may not transcend the law of the land, but if his Gall should burst the very buzzards would break their necks trying to get out of the country.

The druggist who charges a poor dunderhead a dollar for filling a prescription that calls in Latin for a spoonful of salt and an ounce of water, may do no violence to the criminal code, but he plays ducks and drakes with the moral law.

The little tin-horn attorney, whose specialties are divorce cases and libel suits; who stirs up good-for-naughts to sue publishers for $10,000 damages to 10-cent reputations; who's as ready to shield Vice from the sword of Justice as to defend Virtue from stupid violence; who's ever for sale to the highest bidder and keeps eloquence on tap for whosoever cares to buy; who would rob the orphan of his patrimony on a technicality or brand the Virgin Mary as a bawd to shield a black-mailer—well, he cannot be put into the penitentiary, more's the pity! but it's some satisfaction to believe that, if in all the great universe of God there is a hell where fiends lie howling, the most sulphurous section is reserved for the infamous shyster—that if he cannot be debarred from the courts of earth he'll get the bounce from those of heaven.

The woman who inveigles some poor fool—perhaps old enough to be her father—into calling her his tootsie-wootsie

over his own signature, then brings suit for breach of promise—or the Seventh Commandment; who exhibits her
broken heart to the judge and jury and demands that it be
patched up with Uncle Sam's illuminated anguish plasters;
who plays the adventuress, then poses in the public prints as
an injured innocent—sends a good reputation to join a bad
character in hope of monetary reward—well, she too may
be legally honest; but it's just as well to watch her, for no
woman worth powder to blow her to perdition ever did or
ever will carry such a case into court.   When a woman's
heart is really hurting her money is not going to help it;
when she's truly sorry for her sin she tells her troubles to
the Lord instead of to policemen and reporters.

The man who sues a fellow-citizen for alienating his
wife's affections, instead of striking his trail with a bell-
mouthed blunderbuss and a muzzle-loading bulldog; who
asks the court to put a silver lining in the cloud of infamy
that hangs over his home; who tries to make capital of his
shame and heal with golden guineas the hurt that honor
feels—well, he too may be a law-abiding citizen; but ten
thousand such souls, if separated from their Gall, might
play hide-and-seek on the surface of a copper cent for a
hundred years and never find each other.

* * *

Dignity is but a peculiar manifestation of Gall.   It is the
stock in trade of fools.   If Almighty God ever put up great
dignity and superior intellect in the same package it must
have got misplaced.   They are opposing elements, as antagonistic as the doctrines of infinite love and infant damnation.   Knowledge makes men humble; true genius is ever
modest.   The donkey is popularly supposed to be the most
stupid animal extant—excepting the dude.   He's also the
most dignified—since the extinction of the dodo.   No pope
or president, rich in the world's respect; no prince or po-
tentate reveling in the pride of sovereign power; no poet or
philosopher bearing his blushing honors thick upon him ever
equaled a blind donkey in impressive dignity.   As a man's
vision broadens; as he begins to realize what a miserable
little microbe he is in that mighty immensity, studded with
the stupendous handiwork of a power that transcends his
comprehension, his dignity drains off and he feels like asking to be recognized just long enough to apologize for his
existence.

When I see a little man strut forth in the face of heaven
like a turkey-cock on dress parade; forgotten aeons behind

him, blank time before him, his birth a mystery, his death
a leap in the dark; when I see him pose on the grave of
forgotten races and puff himself up with pomposity like the
frog in the fable; when I see him sprinkled with the dust
of fallen dynasties and erecting new altars upon the site of
forgotten fanes, yet staggering about under a load of dignity
that would spring the knee-joints of an arch-angel, I don't
wonder that the Lord once decided to drown the whole lay-
out like a litter of blind puppies.

*   *   *

A lecture on Gall were woefully incomplete without some
reference to the press, that "archimedean lever" and "moulder of public opinion." The average newspaper posing as a
"public educator" is a specimen of Gall that cannot be properly analyzed in one evening. Men do not establish newspapers for the express purpose of reforming the world, but
rather to print what a large number of people in a particular
community want to read and are willing to pay for. A
newspaper is simply a mirror in which the community sees
itself, not as it should be, but as it actually is. It is not the
mother, but the daughter of public opinion. The printing
press is a mighty phonograph that echoes back the joy and
the sorrow, the glory and the shame of the generation it
serves. I have no more quarrel with editors for filling their
columns with inanities than casting shadows when they
stand in the sun. They know what kind of mental pabulum
their people crave, and they are no more in business for their
health than is the merchant. They know that should they
print the grandest sermon that ever fell from Massillon's
lips of gold not 20 per cent., even of the professedly pious,
would read it; but that a detailed account of a fragrant divorce case or international prize-fight will cause 99 per cent.
of the very elect of the Lord to swoop down upon it like
a hungry hen-hawk on an unripe gosling and fairly devour
it, then roll their eyes to heaven like a calf with the colic
and wonder what this wicked old world is coming to. The
editor knows that half the people who pretend to be filled
to overflowing with the grace of God are only perambulating
pillars of pure Gall. He knows that the very people who
criticise him for printing accounts of crimes and making
spreads on sporting events, would transfer their patronage
to other papers if he heeded their howling—that they are
talking for effect thro' the crown of their felts.

Speaking of prize-fights reminds me that a governor who,
after winking at a hundred brutal slugging matches, puts his

state to the expense of a legislative session to prevent a pair
of gladiators pounding each other with soft gloves, is not
suffering for lack of Gall; that those pious souls who never
suspected that pugilism was an insult to our civilization until they got a good opportunity to make a grand-stand play,
then whereased and resoluted themselves black in the face
anent its brutality, should be presented with a medal of pure
brass. Politics is said to make strange bed-fellows, but I
scarce expected to see a shoe-string gambler and would-be
Don Juan lauded by ministerial associations as "our heroic
young Christian governor."

Gall? Why, Geo. Clark presumes to give Bismarck
pointers and congress advice. Nobody knows so well how
to manage a husband as an old maid. A bachelor can give
the father of a village pointers on the training of boys. Our
Northern neighbors know exactly how to deal with the
nigger. The man who would starve but for the industry of
his wife feels competent to manage the finances of the country. People who couldn't be trusted to wean a calf, tell
us all about the Creator of the Cosmos. Sam Jones wants
to debate with Bob Ingersoll, and every forks-of-the-creek
economist takes a hard fall out of Henry George. The
A. P. A. agitators prate loudly of freedom of conscience and
insist on disfranchising the Catholics. We boast of religious liberty, then enact iron-clad Sunday laws that compel
Jew and pagan to conform to our creed or go to prison.
The prohibs want to confine the whole world to cold water
because their leaders haven't sufficient stamina to stay sober.
Men who fail to make a living at honest labor insist on
entering the public service. Political parties charge up to
each other the adverse decrees of Providence. Atheists
deny the existence of God because he doesn't move in their
set, while ministers assume that a criticism of themselves is
an insult to the Creator.

* * *

But to detain you longer were to give a practical illustration of my text. I will be told that Gall is a necessary evil;
that a certain amount of audacity, of native impudence, is
necessary to success. I deny it. Fame and wealth and
power constitute our ideal of success—folly born of falsehood. Only the useful are successful. Father Damien was
the grandest success of the century; Alexander of Macedon
the most miserable failure known to human history—with
the possible exception of Grover Cleveland. Alexander
employed his genius to conquer the Orient and Cleveland

his stupidity to ruin the Occident. The kingdom of the one went to pieces, and the party of the other is now posing as the lost tribe of the political Israel!

Success? A Gould must give up his gold at the grave, the sovereign surrender his sceptre, the very gods are in time forgotten—are swallowed up in the voiceless, viewless past, hidden by the shadows of the centuries. Why should men strive for fame, that feather in the cap of fools, when nations and peoples perish like the flowers and are forgotten —when even continents fade from the great world's face and the ocean's bed becomes the mountain's brow. Why strive for power, that passes like the perfume of the dawn, and leaves prince and pauper peers in death? Why should man, made in the mortal image of immortal God, become the subservient slave of Greed and barter all of time for a handful of yellow dross to cast upon the threshold of eternity? "Poor and content is rich," and rich enough. With a roof to shelter those his heart holds dear, and table furnished forth with frugal fare; with manhood's dauntless courage and woman's deathless love, the peasant in his lowly cot may be richer far than the prince in his imperial hall.

Success? I would rather be a fox and steal fat geese than a miserly millionaire and prey upon the misfortunes of my fellows. I would rather be a doodle-bug burrowing in the dust than a plotting politician, trying to inflate a second-term gubernatorial boom with the fetid breath of a foul hypocrisy. I would rather be a peddler of hot peanuts than a President who gives to bond-grabbers and boodlers privilege to despoil the pantries of the poor. I would rather be a louse on the head of a lazar than lord high executioner of a theological college that, to preserve its reputation and fill its coffers with filthy lucre, brands an orphan babe as a bawd. I would rather watch the stars shining down thro' blue immensity, and the cool mists creeping round the purple hills, than feast my eyes on all the tawdry treasures of Ophir and of Ind. I would rather play a corn-stalk fiddle while pickaninnies dance, than build, of widows' sighs and orphans' tears, a flimsy bubble of fame to be blown adown the narrow beach of Time into Eternity's shoreless sea. I would rather be the beggar lord of a lodge in the wilderness, dress in a suit of sunburn and live on hominy and hope, yet see the love-light blaze unbought in truthful eyes, than to be the marauding emperor of the mighty world, and know not who fawned upon the master and who esteemed the man.

INCOME TAX DECISION.

The Supreme Court of the United States has taken a whirl at the income tax law and left it looking like a picnic suit after a shower. The bigwigs agreed to disagree on pretty nearly every point in controversy, deciding only two, and these in utter disregard of the laws of logic and the dictates of common sense. Chief Justice Fuller gravely declares that incomes derived from state, county and municipal bonds, (amounting to $65,000,000 per annum) "are not proper subjects for the taxing powers of Congress." If not, why not? The federal government is supported by revenues drawn from the people who constitute the various local governments, and upon whom congress is empowered by the constitution to levy a direct tax. Any property is depreciated in value by the amount of the tax laid upon it. Then wherein is it more objectionable for Congress to depreciate the value of Texas bonds than the value of the property pledged for their redemption? The difference would seem to consist in the fact that state, county and municipal securities yielding a revenue of $65,000,000 per annum have passed into the hands of the monied aristocracy who must be protected, while the property from which so much interest is yearly wrung is largely in the possession of the masses— who are "proper subjects for the taxing power of Congress." If I own a little home in Waco I am taxed to pay interest on bonds issued by state, county and municipality, and may be mulcted for the support of the federal government; but the millionaire into whose plethoric purse the interest goes must not be troubled by Uncle Sam's tax collectors. So says the court. The income of A, derived from cultivating cotton or planting hogs, is a "proper subject for the taxing power of Congress," while the income of B, derived from state, county or municipal six per-cents, is not! Had the law been upheld, buyers of future bond issues would unquestionably shift the tax upon the people emitting them; but to urge their exemption on that account were a plea for the exemption of merchants and manufacturers, telegraph companies and common carriers. Had the law been upheld the tax upon that $65,000,000 per annum now derived from state, county and municipal bonds, and amounting to more than $1,300,000, would have been borne exclusively by the holders—would have constituted a true income tax as intended by Congress, because it could not have been shifted to other shoulders. The best clause in the entire law—

granting the wisdom of an income tax—has been knocked out, not because it was unconstitutional, (for the Chief Justice did not so declare it), but because it displeased the court, which appears to have made the plutocrat its especial protege. The second point decided by the court was that a tax on incomes derived from land were equivalent to a direct tax upon the land itself, therefore, inadmissible unless apportioned as provided by the Constitution. If this be sound logic, then the Supreme Court has stricken out the enacting clause of the law in question; it is dead from nozzle to narrative, and we might just as well call off the collectors. With this utterance of Chief Justice Fuller for premise, the conclusion must inevitably follow that a tax on income derived from any class of property whatsoever is equivalent to a direct tax, therefore, unless apportioned, unconstitutional and void. It were clearly absurd to say that a tax on income derived from land is "direct," while that on incomes derived from buildings, mines, cattle, newspapers, professions, etc., is "indirect." That kind of hair-splitting would disgrace a forks-of-the-creek economist or professional shyster. If a tax on rent is a direct tax, what the devil is a tax on salary—the reward of individual effort? "What," asks Chief Justice Fuller, "is the land but the profit on it?" And what, we ask, is any class of property, profession or occupation but "the profit on it?" The idea of the framers of the income tax law was to compel every man to contribute to the support of government according to his abilities rather than his necessities; but the Supreme Court has practically declared that "Unto every one that hath shall be given, and he shall have abundance; but from him that hath not shall be taken away even that which he hath."

SANCTIFICATION AND THE SWORD.

ANOTHER "TEA PARTY" PENDING.

One of the leaders of the crusade for disestablishment in Wales writes the Iconoclast from Manchester, England, as follows:

"I hope to live to see the complete separation of church and state throughout the civilized world. I am a churchman, but the church and state should be kept as far apart as possible. America is my ideal. There the government of man and the government of God are separate and distinct, the one compulsory, the other entirely a matter of conscience."

I much fear that my English friend is not a close student of American institutions or he would look elsewhere for his "ideal." He has yet to learn that even here—in this boasted land of liberty—"the government of man and the government of God" are still starring as Siamese twins and that the latter is no less compulsory than its companion. He has evidently not heard that the American citizen, whether he be Jew or Gentile, Christian or Atheist, is compelled to cough up an extra sum to the tax collector in order that hundreds of millions of dollars worth of church property may escape the government mulct and legislative bodies be provided with matin prayers—paid for at the rate of $5 a minute from the public purse. He has probably never seen a great American state selling a widow's home or auctioning off her cow to satisfy a tax assessment, while the bells of a costly church in the same block pealed merrily, as tho' praising God that it had a "pull" on the government. Nor has he carefully examined the Sunday laws here in force or he would not assert that with us "the government of God is entirely a matter of conscience." Uncle Sam has evidently deceived our correspondent—and has well nigh humbugged himself—with his foolish boasts of "religious liberty," "freedom of conscience," etc. Our states are practically theocracies, our legislatures ecumenical councils by which those religious dogmas entertained by the majority are declared the law of the land and enforced by judicial process, the *posse comitatus* and the entire military force at the command of the government. We might at least expect that beneath the Lone Star, that especial child of liberty, the state would eschew the sacerdotal character and confine itself strictly to secular matters; yet our legislatures are fully persuaded that they are in duty bound to guard both the spiritual and temporal welfare of the citizen—that they have been duly ordained to administer the government of both man and God. Texas plumes herself on being "the banner democratic state," has much to say anent personal liberty and local self-government and never tires of pointing the finger of scorn at sumptuary laws; yet her statutes make it a misdemeanor punishable by fine—which the offender must lay out in prison if he cannot pay—to labor, sell goods, or open a place of amusement in any section of the state, regardless of the religious predilections of the people. Here we have a conservation of the spirit of the Spanish Inquisition showing itself as boldly as it dares, the fag-end of that early New England fanaticism and tongue-boring cropping out where a big democratic majority is swinging

its sombrero and cracking its lungs howling for personal
liberty!

Think of throwing an American citizen into jail in this,
the last decade of the Nineteenth century, for shaving a
"sovereign" or selling a cigar on Sunday; for an offense,
not against his fellow man but against that great God who
created the heavens and the earth and incidentally "made
the stars also"—threw them in as lagniappe! Yes, think of
it; then contemplate a people boasting their independence
and posing as the very apotheosis of progress, tamely sub-
mitting to such a flagrant infringement of their divine rights
and constitutional prerogatives!

But "the old order changeth, yielding place to new." Our
English correspondent has probably heard that it changed in
1776. At this time there was in Great Britain a fat-headed
fellow who played the divine racket on the American people much as the priests and preachers are doing to-day.
He assumed that he had been divinely ordained to decide
what was best for them—that they were in duty bound to
obey, pay taxes and look pleasant. They took his presumption in good part for a great many years, but when he got
to rubbing it in they grew restless and began to file protests—much as they are doing now, and with the same unsatisfactory results. At that time to question the prerogative of princes to do as they pleased with the common people
was regarded as almost as great a sin as "Sabbath desecration" is to-day, and as King George was in the majority he
simply sneered at the recalcitrants, rubbed a little more holy
oil on his divine right and went ahead with his hog-killing.
Finally the famous tea party, which had been so long brewing, was held in Boston harbor and for eight long years
there was h—l to pay and a distressing stringency in the
money market. Another tea party is rapidly getting ripe,
and when it is over and the cups and saucers returned to the
cupboard there'll be no "blue laws" in Uncle Sam's baili-
wick, costly churches will be taxed just the same as the poor
man's cottage, and legislators who desire to indulge in the
luxury of $5-a-minute Protestant prayers will not rob Cath-
olic, infidel and Jewish pantries to pay the sacred wind-
jammer, but go down into their own jeans for the price of
saving Grace.

We could stand taxation for church purposes without
representation in the amen corner if our sanctified brethren
would refrain from adding injuries that benefit nobody, then
presenting us with choice specimens of unprovoked insolence simply to reduce their superabundant stock; but when

a man cheerfully puts up his pro-rata for perfunctory prayers and the exemption of church property from all taxation,
then finds himself persistently boycotted both in politics and
business by the people he has befriended, denounced from
the pulpit as an emissary of the devil by flannelmouthed
preachers who are indirectly fattening upon his substance,
and rendered an abject slave one-seventh of his life by the
laws of his native land simply because an emperor who died
1,500 years ago was an unmitigated ass, he feels like exchanging his stock of Christian charity for a stuffed club
and asserting his rights as a free-born American citizen.

Nearly nineteen centuries ago Christ informed the Pharisees that "the Sabbath was made for man, and not man for
the Sabbath," but that extensive sect of sacred mummers
still cling tenaciously to the interdicted dogma. They de-
.clare it criminal to do on Sunday what is eminently proper
on other days, and, being in a majority, they enact an iron-
clad law compelling Jew and Gentile to conform to their
theological faith. And what excuse have they to offer for
this insolent interference with individual liberty, the abrogation of that "freedom of conscience" guaranteed us by
the Conscript Fathers? Sam Jones sums it up when he
says: "The citizen has no right to do wrong." True, oh
reverend blather-skite; but who authorized you to decide for
the American citizen what is right and wrong, theologically
considered? Produce your credentials, Sir Garrulity, or
come off the grass. Another lippy member of the black
army—Talmage, I believe—has told us that "the majority
has a right to say how the Sabbath shall be observed." Indeed? Then it also has a right to say what day shall be
accepted as the Sabbath by the entire people; hence it follows that if the Jews and Seventh Day Adventists should
eventually find themselves in the majority they would be
privileged to make Saturday the legal Sabbath and compel
its rigid observance as such by all other sects. The consistent Christian could then harvest his hooppoles or dig
fishbait on the first day of the week "in the fear of the
Lord." Having issued his *ipse dixit,* we invite Brother
Talmage to loaf around it and see how he likes it. This
being the country of majority rule in religion as well as in
matters mundane, it follows that what is sauce for the Christian goose is sauce for the Hebrew gander.

Good soul, who made thee thy brother's keeper? Where
in the constitution of your country or the teachings of your
Saviour do you learn it to be your duty to lay violent hands
upon a worldling and drag him, squirming and kicking—

perhaps cursing—to the Throne of God? Produce your authority for employing the jails of this country to propagate the Christian religion—for cramming its forms and symbols down the throat of thy fellow man with a policeman's bludgeon. What is it to thee if I till my field, sell my goods or list to some aspiring Roscious spout Euripides on Sunday? Does it compel thee to do likewise? Does it interfere with your freedom or abridge your prerogatives, endanger your health or cost you a copper? Will the blessed Saviour compel you to answer for my sins and send you to hades as a "vicarous atonement" while I roost on some roseate cloud in company with a halo and a harp and attended by a choice assortment of she-angels! No? Then please to forbear further interference in my affairs. If I feel the need of your assistance to reach the Throne of Grace I'll so inform you. I may prefer to deal with the Almighty direct and without the officious intervention of a middle-man—to map out my own path to the heavenly hereafter without the assistance of a theological surveyor. Your religion is really bile instead of benevolence. Instead of a crown you need a cathartic. You have mistaken an abnormal itch for meddling for the promptings of the Holy Spirit. You prattle about the "desecration of the Sabbath" when the very niggers know that Christ had no more to do with its establishment than Moses with making the Fourth of July an American holiday—that it was not sanctioned by the Father, the Son or any of the original Saints. You would, if clothed with plenary power, compel every son of Adam to accept your narrow-gauge creed and worship God according to the dictates of your so-called conscience instead of his own. You have altogether mistaken the spirit and ignored the letter of that message which Christ brought to mankind. It was a message of Love and Liberty, while you are the apostle of Slavery, the apotheosis of Persecution.

"Come unto me, all ye that labor, and are heavy laden, and I will give you rest," saith the Lord. "Jog along to your Jesus or go to jail," says the state. When encompassed by his enemies in the Garden of Gethsemane Christ rebuked that follower who employed force in his defense.

"Put up again thy sword into his place; for all they that take the sword shall perish by the sword."

Yet his so-called followers here in Texas rely upon the sword, not to protect their dear Lord from ignominious death, but to prevent some impecunious publican wrecking the New Jerusalem and throwing Omnipotent God into a fit of the sulks by selling a popcorn ball on Sunday. They

assume that every utterance of the Saviour was a divine
truth which must, perforce, be fulfilled to the very letter,
yet persist in playing with edge-tools.

That religion which must rely upon secular law is inher-
ently rotten. That religion which appeals to brute force to
secure respect is not of God but the devil, therefore, not
worthy of the devotion of a yaller dog.

"But Sunday laws are necessary as a police regulation,"
I am told. Indeed? Is there aught in the Lord's day calculated to multiply criminal deeds? Is it possible that extra
precautions must be taken on Emperor Constantine's "Holy
Sabbath" to stay the hand of the homicide? Can it be that
when a million Christian prayers are ascending like incense
to the Throne of God—and ten thousand preachers turning
an honest penny—that people are seized with an unnatural
impulse to despoil their neighbors? This being the conceded
effect of the Christian Sabbath it would appear desirable to
abolish it altogether "as a police regulation," and the quicker
the better.

NO CROSS-EYED CLERGYMEN.

The Methodist Episcopal Conference, recently assembled
in New York, created something of a sensation by rejecting
a candidate for clerical honors because he was cross-eyed.
He had studied three years for the ministry and outstripped
all his classmates, was admittedly intelligent and of unex-
ceptionable morals; but strabismus was regarded by the theological solons as an insuperable objection, and he was rejected. Many worthy brethren have sharply criticised the
action of the conference, but The Iconoclast is inclined to
commend it. No man who can look two ways at once has
any business in the Methodist ministry; he might see too
much for a successful exponent of sectarianism. Furthermore, those sanctified gentlemen who assembled in the metropolis of the most enlightened nation the world ever knew,
were obeying the imperative command of the Creator as
expressed in the Bible, hence a criticism of their action were
akin to blasphemy. In the Twenty-first chapter of Leviticus
we learn that

"The Lord spake unto Moses, saying, Speak unto Aaron saying,
Whosoever he be of thy seed in their generations that hath any
blemish, let him not approach to offer the bread of his God; for
whatsoever man he be that hath a blemish, he shall not approach:

A blind man, or a lame, or he that hath a flat nose, or anything superfluous; or a man that is broken-footed, or broken-handed, or crook-backed, or a dwarf, or that hath a blemish in his eye, or be scurvy, or scabbed, or hath his stones broken . . . he shall not go into the vail nor come nigh unto the altar, because he hath a blemish; that he profane not my sanctuaries."

No intellectual qualifications whatever were suggested, they evidently being considered as superfluous—it was simply stipulated that the priest, like the sacrificial bull, should be a perfect animal, and that he attire himself in "garments for glory and beauty." To the credit of the various religious denominations be it said that in selecting their priests and preachers they have adhered pretty closely to the original plans and specifications. Whenever they have departed therefrom in any marked degree a heresy trial has been sent to trouble them—a swift and awful "judgment" for their sin.

Whether the Lord really gave such a command to Moses, or the latter dreamed it while lying in the dusky arms of his Ethiopian wife, it is not my province to determine; but as a general law, intended to cull out the slick stock for the clergy, it has much to commend it. It were clearly absurd to select the finest specimens of physical manhood to defend the country from fellow mortals, leaving the "scurvy" and the "scabbed" to lead the scattering army of the Lord against the legions of the devil. Whether flat heads be preferable to flat noses, crooked morals to curved backs and spavined intellect to procreative impotence, can not be considered by the truly orthodox as a debatable question.

Now that the Methodist church has undertaken to make its ministry conform to the Mosaic standard we trust that it will not weary in well-doing, but make thorough work of it. The Iconoclast, as the unswerving friend of religious reform, suggests that each candidate be subjected to a rigid medical examination and a system of physical tests in order that the ministerial stud may consist exclusively of thoroughbreds. It would first be necessary to take the aspirant's altitude, as "Little Giants" were not considered eligible by the God of the Jews. Having found that his coat-tails hung sufficiently far from the earth, the next step will be to bring him *in puris naturalibus* before the board of examiners, who will determine whether he has "anything superfluous," then either fire him out or forward him on to the officiating Muldoon to be tested in wind and limb. Having passed this ordeal successfully, his eyes will be examined by an expert oculist, and if it be found that he can look through a keyhole with both at once, this fact will be duly certified and a civil engineer appointed to survey his proboscis and make report.   If he finds that it is an incipient mountain peak instead of a lowly campagna the candidate will be duly licensed to preach—to carry saving grace to godless sinners.

It is imperative that we have in our fashionable pulpits preachers who will harmonize with their recherche surroundings.   Placing a hunchback, a cross-eyed man or one with an amorphous snout like that of old Socrates amid the gorgeous trappings of a hundred thousand dollar temple were an insufferable sin against the estheticism of the age.   True, Christ was no brute, if we may believe Isaiah, who we are assured was referring to the Saviour when he said: "His visage was more marred than any man, and his form than the sons of men."   The Jews "saw no beauty in him," and the Rev. George C. Needham, in his appendix to the Bible, intimates that physically he was a fright. St. Paul was so horribly homely that the ladies avoided him, and he played for even by putting a time-lock on their mouths and discountenancing marriage.   None of the Apostles, so far as we can gather, were calculated to adorn a fashionable pulpit or cause the hearts of the sisters to palpitate with suspicious piety.   They traveled extensively, but not on their shape.   But we are building neither churches nor ministers on the model supplied us by the Son of Mary.   This is "a progressive age"—and the Methodist church has at last caught up with Moses.

THE MONROE DOCTRINE.

The so-called Monroe Doctrine has kept Uncle Sam in hot water for three-quarters of a century and bids fair to embroil him in one of the bloodiest wars known to the world's history if he persists in exploiting it.   In 1823, when it was suspected that the Holy Alliance would attempt to re-establish Spain's dominion over her revolted colonies, President Monroe, in a message to Congress, enunciated the "doctrine" that bears his name, but which doubtless emanated from that eminent jingoist, John Quincy Adams, then Secretary of State.   Monroe declared that the American continents "are henceforth not to be considered as subjects for future colonization by any European Power," and particularly warned the respective members of the Holy Alliance that "we should consider any attempt on their part to extend their system to any portion of the western hemisphere as dangerous to our peace and safety." Then, to make his meaning so plain that none might mistake it, he added, referring to the cisatlantic governments then struggling for life, that "we could not view any interposition for the purpose of oppressing them or controlling in any other manner their destiny, by any European Power, in any other light than as the manifestation of an unfriendly disposition toward the United States."

If that means anything whatsoever it means that the United States has established a quasi-protectorate over the smaller American governments, so far as Europe is concerned—that Uncle Sam is the self-constituted bouncer of the western hemisphere and proposes to serve without salary. Several Texas dailies have consumed considerable editorial space trying to give it a different construction; but unless we agree with Talleyrand that "language was made to conceal thought," we must concede that the Monroe pronunciamento means exactly what it says. Jefferson was consulted on the subject by the Monroe administration before the delivery of the message and he declared, after referring to the importance of the question, that "we should never suffer Europe to intermeddle with cisatlantic affairs." Webster, who certainly understood the English tongue, gave it this interpretation and his hearty endorsement so far as those countries bordering on the Mexican gulf are concerned. It is urged by certain political sophists that, even conceding the message to have meant all it said, and to constitute our policy to-day, it does not follow that we would take up arms to enforce it. To assume that Uncle Sam would solemnly warn European governments to keep off the cisatlantic grass, then fail to back his bluff with powder and ball; that he would suffer his "peace and safety" to be endangered without writing his protest in blood if need be, were to brand him a cowardly bully.

The Monroe Doctrine declares in diplomatic but unequivocal language that if Europe monkeys with any portion of the western hemisphere which has set up political housekeeping for itself, she will run afoul of the American eagle, and there'll be, as Sam Jones would say in his aesthetic pulpit vernacular, "blood and hair and the ground tore up." It assumes our right to inquire into such controversies as that of England vs. Venezuela, and to interfere, if need be, to prevent "oppression" by the transatlantic Power, or any tampering with the "destiny" of the little Republic. Such is the common-sense construction of the Monroe Doctrine by the world's diplomats; so it has been understood for two-and-seventy years by the people of every American government.

The Monroe Doctrine, like a defunct feline in the family cistern, can not be explained away; it must be removed. It is illogical, useless, productive of nothing but international ill-will. A protectorate implies responsibilities. If we will not permit European Powers to forcibly collect their dues of our neighbors or chastise their insolence, we become morally bound for their debts and responsible for their behavior. The Monroe Doctrine not only denies to Spain the right to reconquer Mexico, but would prevent the latter again becoming a Spanish province by the expressed will of her people, hence it is the tool of tyranny as well as the aegis of Liberty.

What can this country hope to gain by playing continental policeman at its own expense? Monroe declares that we must consider the extension of European authority "to any portion of this hemisphere as dangerous to our peace and safety." But that was seventy-two years ago, when Uncle Sam was in his swaddling clothes and, quite naturally, much concerned about the character of his neighbors. But time has amply demonstrated the uselessness of Monroe's anxiety. England owns everything to the north and other European Powers once controlled everything to the south and west of us, including a large tract of our present territory, yet the bird o' freedom never moulted a feather. If John Bull should put all South America into his capacious political pocket it would in nowise endanger the "peace and safety" of Uncle Sam. The Briton could not turn the wild beasts and reptiles of that practically unpopulated region loose upon us as he did the redskins during the Revolution. In case of war such possession would weaken him, and he would be unable to hold it after it became worth the having. As soon as the American colonies quit calling on him for troops to defend their frontier they arose and smote him in the umbilicus, and we have to close the door to keep Canada from coming into the Union—and bringing her sky-scraping Dominion debt with her. Spain lost Mexico and her South American possessions and is having a hades of a time holding Cuba. Brazil slipped through the fingers of Portugal like a greased pig, France has practically faded from the map of the New World, and even the kindly offices of Grover Cleveland could not keep monarchy alive in the mid-Pacific.

Really we need not worry about any seed the European monarchies may sow in American soil. The climate is not adapted to that kind of a political crop. About the time it gets a good start and promises to make a bale to the acre a revolutionary cyclone rips it up by the roots. It is not necessary that this government—the most powerful on the g obe—should "view with alarm" every European footprint in the western world, nor is it under any obligation to afford protection at its own expense to opera bouffe Republics. About the first thing a Spanish American government does after donning its initial diaper, is to flagrantly insult the American flag. Uncle Sam had serious trouble with Mexico, and the heteroscian pismires are continually crawling up the old man's pants. There is not a country between our southern boundary and the Antartic circle in which an American citizen is safe from official insult; yet whenever a European Power proposes to hold one of these single-shovel "Republics" up by the ear and pound the impudence out of it, it turns to us for protection. They are Republics *de jure* but despotisms *de facto,* and the cause of Liberty would suffer no loss if they were all made subject to the Russian czar. Madame Roland truly said that many crimes are committed in the name of Liberty, but even she never dreamed of aught so damnable as the wholesale sacrifice of Anglo-Saxons at the foolish shrine of a mongrel despotism masquerading in the robe of Freedom. Uncle Sam has been starring in the ridiculous role of Don Quixote quite long enough, and should now give the Spanish cavaleros and half-civilized Aborigines to the south of us to distinctly understand that they must work out their own salvation; that he desires "Peace, commerce and honest friendship with all nations—entangling alliances with none."

THE LOCOMOTIVE ENGINEER.

The locomotive engineer is to the village-bred boy of to-day what the stage-driver was to the youth of his grandsire. The brakeman who can ride all day on top of a box car, and the passenger-train conductor, with his gaudy cap and Mardi Gras lantern, pale into insignificance beside the man who manages the iron horse. Machinery possesses a weird fascination for the American youth, and the locomotive is to all other mechanism what a shotgun is to a "nigger-shooter." It adds to its attractions the romance of travel—is to the boys of the interior what a ship is to those reared within the sound of the sea.

At the age of ten I was so infatuated with locomotives that to get possession of one I stole an entire freight train. It was standing on the main track in my native village, the crew had abandoned it to investigate a big watermelon which the station agent had opened, and I improved the opportunity to penetrate the mysteries of the engineer's cab. I had no intention of meddling with the iron monster, but when I got my hand on the lever the temptation to set the big drivers in motion was too strong to be resisted. The train started so easily that it did not attract the attention of the hilarious crew in the freight-house until it went roaring across Flat Branch bridge and on towards Mattoon at a good round gait. I decided that I might as well be hanged for an old sheep as a lamb, and pulled the throttle open a little wider, whistling and ringing the bell for all the crossings and pretty much everything else in sight. A mule got on the track in front of me, and I was so fearful he would escape that I gave the lever another lusty pull. The train fairly bounded forward and the telegraph poles seemed thick as fence posts. I got the mule—spread him all over the smoke-stack. By this time I had the lever down among the tallow pots—was making the highest speed the machine was capable of. The great iron monster swayed and groaned, the cars seemed bowing to both sides of the right-o'-way, and I was delirious with joy. Mattoon was in sight, and I determined to go through the town like a whirlwind, on to Cairo and take a look at the two big rivers. I was leaning out of the cab window trying to make out the figures on the mile-posts when I was suddenly pulled by the ear. Instead of joining the watermelon debauch the conductor had lain down in the caboose and gone to sleep. When the "dog house" began to dance on one wheel he awoke and realized that there was something wrong. He crawled over the boxes at the imminent risk of his life to expostulate with the engineer. While he was bringing the train to a standstill I debated whether I should run away or go back home and take the worst licking of my life. The conductor solved the problem for me; I went back. I have a very vivid recollection of the events immediately subsequent thereto, but as they could not possibly possess that absorbing interest for the general public that they did for me I will let them pass.

The locomotive engineers constitute a peculiar class that is neither understood nor appreciated by the general public. Sober, silent, alert, with the time-table for their Bible and the train dispatcher's written orders for their creed, they discharge their dangerous duty. If a soldier loses his little finger in the service of his country he is voted a hero and given a pension. When a locomotive engineer deliberately goes to his death to protect the lives of others and the property committed to his care, his reward is a few lines in the daily press. Such occurrences are too common to excite comment.

If all the dangers of the rail were as patent to the public as to the man at the throttle there would be precious little traveling for "pleasure." The public hears only of the accidents that occur, not of the thousands averted by the cool judgment and leonine courage of the man in the cab. Mounted upon his iron steed, with its heart of fire and breath of flame, he goes rushing through the midnight storm at the rate of 50 miles an hour, dragging in his wake a heavy train filled with precious human freight. He may know that the speed is too rapid for either the track or rolling stock, but the time-table calls for it and it must come. Perhaps around the next curve he will find a culvert washed out or the track obstructed by a "cave-in." The rails may spread out at any moment, or the next switch be misplaced. Sleepy dispatchers sometimes blunder and a collision may occur; but he can only keep his eye on the slippery track, his hand on the lever, and go plunging on. If an accident occurs those in the coaches must escape with only a shaking up, regardless of what happens to him. He must stand at his post like a Roman sentinel tho' the heavens rain fire.

To the man at the throttle his engine is no dull, dead piece of mechanism, but a living, sentient creature, to be praised when it does well and rebuked when it does ill. It responds to his touch like a well trained steed and he becomes devotedly attached to it—talks to it as a good jockey does to his horse.

It is the end of a long night run with a heavy train, on a sinuous, ill-constructed track—a veritable serpent of rust resting upon rotten ties. The engineer has scarce spoken a word except to quote a little sacred blank verse when the new brakeman, who had turned a switch to let him in on a siding, turned it back to let him out. Even his orders to the fireman are given by a motion of the hand. But as we strike the stiff home grade his demeanor changes. He

uncurls from his bench and looks back at the train, then
surveys his engine as though measuring its strength.

"Now, old girl, you've got to hustle for it. Pull yourself
together and sand your feet. Here, here! no skirt-dancing,
madam! This is no John Bell joint. Steady, old girl—
steady."

The great machine plunges at the grade and struggles
like a living creature, the sharp puffs waking the echoes
far and wide amid the sombre pines, upon whose tall tops
rests the morning mist, reddened by the rising sun. The
engineer coaxes, as a driver might a willing horse, and the
machine, which seems to understand him, responds with
greater exertions, but the heavy loads roll slower and slower, the drivers slip despite the sand, emitting a million metallic sparks—the "old girl" is stalled. A short, sharp
whistle, that sounds like the shriek of some sentient animal
for aid, the three rear brakes are hard set, and up on this
buttress the train rolls slowly back. The engineer is preparing to "take the slack." His engine is no longer "old
girl" and "sweetheart," but the most disreputable drab that
ever inhabited Happy Hollow—or got listed in the blue
book of New York's Four Hundred. Locomotive engineers are not much addicted to gab—they are nothing if
not epigrammatic—and when they speak are liable to say
something. The engine stands for a minute as tho' heartily
ashamed of itself, panting like a brown roadster, then
springs forward with a bound. The cars follow, each in its
turn, with a rattling jerk that tests the drawheads, until
the last are reached, when the brakes are quickly released,
and "madam," having retrieved her moral character, goes
puffing proudly into port.

A year later I sat by the bedside of the same engineer
while he breathed his life away—crushed and scalded at the
post of duty. Again he was out on his "run," striving
desperately to make time with a heavy train.

"The last grade, my girl; climb that and we're home.
Molly's waiting, and so are the kids, to see you come round
the curve. What! Can't keep your feet? You must do
better than that or we'll never get in. How dark it is!
Tom, did you douse that glim? I can't see the rails! There's
the station light—now we roll—now—we—" and he had
climbed the "last grade."

No one troubled with what is sometimes called "nerves"
has the least business with a locomotive. To manage one
and at the same time enjoy good health requires not only
superior courage, but a stoicism worthy of a Sioux warrior.

The locomotive engineers shoulder graver responsibilities and face more dangers than almost any other class of men that could be mentioned. And this for a salary that would not satisfy a competent book-keeper.

One night, while northbound with the Fast Mail, we received orders to look out for a brakeman who was supposed to have fallen from a southbound freight.

"Who is it?" asked the engineer.

"Damfino," replied the pert young operator. "Think it's the Scotchman they call Sandy. What's the matter, old man? Seen a ghost?" But the engineer climbed into the cab without a word. There was something in his throat that would not permit of words.

"You d—d fool, Sandy's his son," said the conductor as he gave the signal to go ahead. I offered to handle the engine, but he only shook his head.

We are an hour late and are expected to move as fast as "66" can turn a wheel. A heavy fog is hugging the earth and at a hundred yards the headlight resembles a splotch of luminous vapor—a tallow dip whose flame had liquified. We tear through the fog like a thunderbolt rending the clouds, the buildings gliding by like ghosts, the engineer's eyes fixed steadily upon the dripping rails that come rushing out of the gloom. He knows to an inch what space he can stop, to a foot how far he can see into the fog. Sandy is safe so far as "66" is concerned. Ten miles, twenty, thirty, and still no sign of the missing man, and I can see the father is beginning to hope that it is a false alarm; but suddenly a prostrate figure, lying right across the rails, comes rushing into view, so near that an involuntary cry bursts from the lips of the fireman and he averts his face. Quick as the lightning's flash the engine is reversed and the air applied—but the latter will not work! The engineer shrieks for the hand brakes, but it is too late. The reversed drivers churn the rails to a red heat, but the terrible momentum of the heavy train cannot be overcome. Sandy waves his hand to us, he half rises, his white face showing ghastly beneath the headlight's glare. The sire dashes thro' the cab window as tho' to snatch the son from the very jaws of death, but ere he can reach the pilot it strikes the upturned face, and we feel the jar of the engine and hear the hiss of blood on the fire-box as he is ground beneath the wheels.

BRANN VS. SLATTERY.

[Ex-Priest Joseph Slattery, in his lectures at Waco, Texas, in the interests of the A. P. A., having bitterly denounced the Iconoclast, Mr. Brann replied to him as follows:]

Fellow Americans: The Iconoclast does not please ex- Priest Slattery, "Baptist minister in good standing," and I am not surprised. Its mission, as its name implies, is to expose Frauds and abolish Fakes, to make unrelenting war upon Humbugs and Hypocrites; hence it is not remarkable that Slattery should regard its existence as a personal affront. It is ever the galled jade that winces; or, to borrow from the elegant pulpit vernacular of the Rev. Sam Jones, "it's the hit dog that yelps."

Slattery would have you believe that I'm a rank atheist who's trying to rip religion up by the roots and bang it across a barbed wire fence in close companionship with the hides of Protestant preachers This charge has been hurled at me by various sectarian papers and malicious ministers; but not one iota of evidence has ever been submitted. It is simply a bald assertion born of sanctified malice, a brazen libel, similar to that which charges the Pope with trying to subvert the American government. I defy Slattery and all that unclean brood of moral vultures, assassins of character and thieves of reputation which trail in his wake and applaud his infamies, to produce one line I ever wrote, or quote one sentence I ever uttered disrespectful of *any* religion, Pagan, Protestant or Catholic. If in the wilds of Central Africa I should find a man bowing down to a dried toad, a stuffed snake or a Slattery, I'd remove my hat as a tribute of respect, not to his judgment, but to his honesty. I have no word of condemnation for any religious faith, however fatuous it may appear to me, that has comforted the dying or consoled the living—that has cast one gleam of supernal sunshine into the dark vale where grope, each beneath his burthen of sorrow, the sons of men. I am not warring upon religious faith, but on falsehood; not upon Christ, but on those who disgrace his cause—who mistake bile for benevolence, gall for godliness and chronic laziness for "a call to preach."

Nor have I taken the Pope of Rome under my apostolic protection. The Popes managed to exist for a great many years before I was born, and, despite the assaults of Slattery, will doubtless continue in business at the old stand for several years to come. I was raised a Protestant, and—thank

God!—I'm no apostate. I learned Protestantism at my
mother's knee, and from my father's pulpit; but I did not
learn there that the Church of Rome is the "Scarlet
Woman," nuns unclean creatures and priests the sworn
enemies of my country. I learned that but for the Church
of Rome the "glad tidings of great joy," which Christ
brought to a dying world, would have been irredeemably
lost in that dismal intellectual night known as the Dark
Ages. I was taught that for centuries the Church of Rome
was the repository, not only of the Christian faith, but of
civilization itself. I was taught that the Catholic is the
mother of the Protestant church, and that no matter how unworthy a parent may be, a child should not become the herald of its mother's shame.

And while being taught my duty as a Protestant, my education as an American citizen was not neglected. I was
taught that this was a land of religious liberty, where every
man is privileged to worship God in his own way, or ignore
him altogether; that it was my duty to insist upon this right,
both for myself and for my fellows.

That is why I am the uncompromising enemy of the A.
P. A.

Any attempt to debar an American citizen from the honors and emoluments of a public office because of his religious faith, or non-faith, is a flagrant violation of a fundamental principle of this Republic. And no patriot; no
man in whose veins there pulses one drop of the blood of the
Conscript Fathers, or who would recognize the Goddess of
Liberty if he met her in the road; no man imbued with the
tolerant spirit of the Lord Jesus Christ will aid or abet such
an un-Christian and un-American movement. The A. P.
A. is the bastard spawn of Ignorance and Intolerance, was
conceived in sin and brought forth in iniquity.

There may be some honest men connected with the movement; but if honest they should get their heads trepanned
to give their brains room to grow. They are as unable as
a mule-eared rabbit to comprehend either the broad principles upon which this government is grounded, or its political and religious history. No man—not even Judas
Iscariot Slattery—is to blame for his ignorance; so we
should humbly pray, Father forgive them, they know not
what they do. Nor is the Church of Rome responsible
for the shameless apostate's lack of information. It did all
that it could to transform him from an ignorant little beggar
into an educated gentleman—but even the Pope cannot
make a silk purse of a sow's ear. It is no fault of the

Church of Rome that he's densely ignorant of the very text-
book truths of history; that he knows less than nothing of
that Reformation of which he talks so glibly; that he is unable to comprehend the genius of the government upon
which he has conferred his more or less valuable citizenship.
The fault, if fault it be, lies with the Almighty, who gave
him a bad heart and a worse head.

*   *   *

American Protective Association, eh? That signifies
that Uncle Sam is in need of protection. I had hitherto
supposed that the gentleman in the highwater pants and
star-bespangled cutaway was able to protect himself; but it
now appears that unless he crawls under the aegis of the re-
doubtable Slattery he is—to again borrow from the most
popular of all Protestant divines—"a gone sucker." Think
of placing Uncle Sam under the protection of a man who is
an apostate in religion and a renegade in politics—of an
Irishman who apostrophizes the British flag! Think of that
kind of a bird presuming to tell the grand-sons of Revolutionary soldiers their duties as American citizens.

Slattery assures us that we need protection from the
Pope. There was a time when the proudest monarchs of
Europe trembled at the Papal nod; but gradually the Pope
has been shorn of temporal power, confined ever more to
the realm of spiritual, until to-day he exerts about as little
influence on the political destiny of this world as does Dr.
Cranfill with his little Prohibition craze. But Slattery will
have it that the Pope is gradually undermining American
institutions—leads us to infer that, sooner or later, he'll blow
our blessed constitution at the moon and scatter fragments
of the Goddess of Liberty from Dan to Beersheba, from
Cape Cod to Kalamazoo. The Pope, it appears, is a veritable Guy Faux, who is tunnelling beneath our national
capitol with a keg of giant powder in one hand and a box
of lucifer matches in the other. What's the evidence? Why,
out in San Francisco, so Slattery says—but as Slattery's
been convicted of lying it were well to call for papers—a
Catholic school-board was elected and employed only Catholic teachers. The same awful thing happened in Detroit—if
Slattery's telling the truth, which is doubtful in the extreme.
Then what? With a pride worthy a more American act,
this illogical idiot informs us that "when the Protestants captured the school-boards of those cities they discharged every
one of the Catholic teachers and put only good Protestants
on guard." And at that Baptist brethren—with water on

the brain—who boast of Roger Williams, cheered so loudly as to be in danger of lockjaw. In the exuberant imagination of Slattery and his dupes there appears to be a wonderful difference between tweedledum and tweedledee. It doesn't seem to have occurred to them that what is sauce for the Protestant goose should be sauce for the Catholic gander. They damn the Catholics for doing the very thing for which they commend the Protestant. That's the logic of the A. P. A.—the Aggregation of Pusillanimous Asses. In my humble opinion both were engaged in very small business. The only difference in the offenders that I can see is that while the Catholics are saying nothing, the Protestants are loudly boasting of their vicious subversion of the American principle of religious liberty. The circumstance is a sharp reminder that if we are to preserve a government of the people, for the people and by the people, we've got to keep religion of *all* kinds out of our politics, just as the framers of the federal constitution intended that we should do. Mixing religion and politics is like mixing whisky and water—it spoils both.

Slattery would have you believe that our Catholic citizens are simply emissaries of the Pope, to whom they owe allegiance both spiritual and temporal, and that they will, at the first opportunity, subvert American institutions and make this Nation simply a satrapy of the Vatican.

The American Catholic takes his theology from Rome; he takes his politics from the ecumenical council of his party—from the national convention of that partisan organization to which he may chance to belong.

That there can be no "Catholic conspiracy" against the free institutions of this country must be evident to every man of common sense from the simple fact that Catholics are divided among all the political parties—are continually voting against each other. Now I appeal to your judgment—lay aside your religious prejudices for the moment and look at the matter from a non-partisan, non-sectarian standpoint: If our Catholic fellow citizens be under the thumb of the Pope politically, as the apostate now evangelizing for the A. P. A. would have us believe; and if the Pope desires to make himself temporal ruler of this land, or in any manner direct its affairs, would they not be found voting as a unit—a mighty political machine—instead of being as badly divided on secular questions as the Baptists themselves? San Antonio is a Catholic stronghold, yet a prominent Roman Catholic was overwhelmingly defeated in the last mayoralty election. And I could cite you hundreds of instances where Catholics have voted against men of their own religious faith and elected Protestants or infidels.

Again: If the Pope is plotting against America; and if all manner of crime be considered a virtue when committed by Catholics in furtherance of his ends, as Slattery would have you believe, then it were well to keep a sharp eye on apostate priests. How are we to know that they are not emissaries of the Vatican, commissioned to stir the Protestants up to persecute their brethren in Christ and thereby solidify the Catholic vote? No one, not even Slattery, has accused the Pope of being a fool; and certain it is that the A. P. A. movement, if persisted in, will have the effect of driving the Catholics of this country to political unity in self-defense. Persecution, political ostracism for religious opinion's sake, will infallibly bring about those very conditions which Slattery, Hicks, et al. declare that the Pope desires. The communicants of the Church of Rome will no longer vote as Democrats or Republicans, but as Catholics —and then? With unlimited wealth, and such a political machine at the command of a man so ambitious and unscrupulous as we are asked to believe the Pope to be, the capture of the federal government and the political domination of this country were as easy as lying! The Protestants, divided into a hundred warring factions, many of them farther apart theologically than Episcopalianism and Catholicism, could offer no resistance to such a political machine, and they would receive but cold comfort from the liberal element, which has suffered so long from their petty persecutions.

And I tell you Protestants right here, that if it be the intention of the Church of Rome to transform this government into a theocracy by fair means or by foul, then the Pope is the real founder of the A. P. A. and Slattery's a Papal spy.

*   *   *

According to the story of this self-constituted protector of the American government, he studied Roman Catholic theology for years, then officiated as a priest for eight more before discovering anything immoral in the teachings of the Mother Church, when it suddenly occurred to him that it was but a tissue of falsehoods, a veritable cesspool of rottenness. His transformation appears to have been almost as sudden as that of Saul of Tarsus—or that of Judas Iscariot. I have no objection to his leaving the Catholic priesthood—his bishop stopped his pay. Like the servant maid caught pilfering, he "gave notice, with the missus a pintin' at the door." If Slattery believes that the Protestant Through Line runs more comfortable cars to the great hereafter, he's welcome to take his ticket over that route; but I would have thought better of him had he made the change quietly and refrained from assaulting with the vindictiveness of a renegade that church to which he owes his education, such as it is; had he treated the religion of his mother with decency if not with respect.

I thought I had met all manner of men; men hardened in crime—men destitute of even a semblance of shame; but never before did I behold one with the hardihood to stand up before American women and boast that he had incurred a mother's curse. When a man falls so low in the scale of human degradation that his own mother disowns him it were well to watch him. When a creature asks strangers to accept him because his relatives have rejected him; when, for the sake of gain, he snaps like a mangy fice at the hand that once fed him, and stings like a poisonous adder the bosom that once nurtured him; when, to promote his personal ends, he will use his best endeavors to exterminate religious liberty and precipitate a bloody sectarian war, I tell you he was not born a man but begotten a beast.

From the very foundation of this government the Catholics have been its firm defenders. Their wisdom and eloquence have adorned its councils from the signing of the Declaration of American Independence to this good day, and its every battlefield, from Lexington to the Custer massacre, has been wet with Catholic blood. Nine Roman Catholics signed the Declaration of Independence, and the Roman Catholics of New York contributed so liberally of their blood and treasure to the cause of the new-born Nation that Washington wrote them a letter praising their patriotism. Several Roman Catholics helped frame the Federal Constitution, and the interpretation of that wonderful instrument by a Roman Catholic chief-justice to-day constitutes the fundamental law of the land. Yet Slattery and that ridiculous organization of which he boasts himself a member, would have you believe that the American Catholics would, at a nod from the Pope, ruthlessly trample under foot that flag in whose defense they pledged their lives, their fortunes and their sacred honor—that they would wreck without remorse and ruin without regret that Nation they helped place on the map of the world. How do you old Confederates, who followed Pat Cleburne, relish having this

blatant tramp defame your dead commander? Can you
believe, on the unsupported testimony of this mendacious
mountebank, that Father Ryan's tribute to the Stars-and-
Bars was rank hypocrisy—that the poet-priest was the political tool of a foreign power?   Sherman died a Catholic.
Fighting Phil Sheridan was a Catholic. Old Pap Thomas,
"the Rock of Chickamauga," was a Catholic. The "Bloody
Sixty-ninth" New York was a Catholic regiment, and its
heroism at the Battle of Bull Run forms one of the brightest
pages in the military history of this nation.   Strange it
never occurred to those demoralized Protestant regiments
which took refuge behind the bayonets of the Sixty-ninth
that they were throwing the Vatican between themselves
and the Confederate forces!

Slattery assures us that the number of Irish Catholics on
the police force of our great cities is evidence that the
Church of Rome is on mischief bent. I am not surprised
that an Irish Catholic with a club in his hand should prove
rather alarming to Bro. Slattery. But, although he says,
"meet a policeman and you'll see the map of Ireland in his
face," those same policemen have several times saved his
worthless bacon. When he was mobbed in St. Louis for
defaming Catholic nuns, the police formed a cordon around
his infamous carcass and saved him from a well-merited
trouncing at the hands of the slandered women's relatives.
Probably the police did not relish the job overmuch, but
they had sworn to uphold the laws, and although Slattery
insists that a Catholic oath amounts to nothing, they risked
their lives in his defense.

We have many nationalities in this country, and each of
them, as every observant man well knows, manifests a pre-
dilection for some special occupation. Thus the Jews take
to trade, the Germans to agriculture, the Norwegians to
lumbering, the French to catering and the Irish to politics.
Make a Freewill Baptist or a Buddhist of an Irishman and
you do not change his nature—he'll turn up at the next political convention just the same. And the man who's too
good to take a hand in practical politics; who's too nice to
mingle with the horny-handed at the ward primaries; who's
too busy to act as delegate to the convention—who deliberately neglects his duty as an American citizen—finds that
Pat's activity has been rewarded with a place on the police
force, and blames it all on the Pope.

* * *

It is not my province to defend Roman Catholic theology

—I suppose that Slattery said all that could be urged in its behalf before the apostatized. Perhaps the Catholics really believe the Pope infallible; and if they do, it is certainly no worse than for certain Waco Protestants to believe that Slattery's infallible. I noticed that at his lecture last week they cheered every charge he preferred against either the Pope or the "Apostle," and that without asking for an iota of evidence. When I arose at the stag party with which he wound up the intellectual debauch, and questioned his infallibility, the good brethren cried, "Throw him out!" Why did they so unless they believed that to question the supernal wisdom and immaculate truth of aught a Baptist minister might say, were sacrilege—a sin against the Holy Ghost?

Here was I, their fellow citizen of Waco. I had done them no harm; yet when a strolling vagabond, wearing God's livery, and whose forte is the defamation of women, made a statement, which if true, would forever disgrace me in the eyes of the world; when he preferred this charge against me within two blocks of where my babies lay sleeping, they wanted to mob me for branding him then and there as an infamous liar and a cowardly blackguard.

Mark you, I'm no tramp in America. This is the house of my fathers. They helped hew it out of the Virginia wilderness. They helped put Old Glory in the heavens, and to keep it there for more than a hundred years; still it appears that I have no rights in this country which a foreigner with the smell of the steerage still upon him is bound to respect, if he chances to be a Baptist preacher.

Talk to me about the Church of Rome muzzling free speech when the A. P. A. would mob an American citizen for defending his character from the infamous falsehoods of a foreign tramp! "Throw him out!" Why throw him out? I'll tell you: The sanctified buzzards had gone there with appetites sharpened for a mess of carrion, and they were afraid I'd kill their cook. "Throw him out!" But I noticed that those who were splitting their faces as wide as Billy Kersands' were glued to their seats. They wanted somebody else to throw him out. They were anxious to see a gang of three or four hundred sanctified hoodlums trample upon me, but there was not one among the self-constituted protectors of this mighty American Nation with sufficient "sand" to lead the mob. If there were no better Americans than those trailing in the wake of the Rev. Joseph Slattery, like buzzards following a bad smell, I'd take a cornstalk, clean out the whole shooting-match and stock the country with niggers and yaller dogs. If such cattle were sired by

Satan, dammed by Sycorax and born in hell they would dishonor their parents and disgrace their country.

Slattery insists that Catholics believe thus-and-so, and
that no man with such a faith concealed about his person
can be a good American citizen.   I don't know about that;
but I do know that if the Catholic act in strict accordance
with their religious creed they are the only people in this
country that do so.   I've learned that you can't judge a
man by his catechism.   Slattery assures us that he has discarded the Pope and taken Christ for his immediate guide.
The latter commands his followers to pray for those who
despitefully use them; but if Slattery did any praying for the
"Apostle" during his sojourn in this city he managed to
keep that fact a profound secret.   Christ enjoins patience
and humility.   He tells his followers to turn the other cheek
to the smiter; yet Slattery assured the ladies Wednesday
night that he was "a great believer in muscular Christianity."   Then he placed his 250 pounds of stall-fed beef in
fighting attitude and declared he'd "like to have his enemies
come at him one at a time"—to be prayed for, I presume.
If Christ taught "muscular Christianity" I have inadvertently overlooked a bet.   Christ commands us to love our enemies, but doesn't suggest that we should manifest our affection by lying about 'em.   He rebuked those who tattled
about a common courtesan, yet Slattery defamed decent
women.   No, you can't judge a man by his creed.   If the
allegiance of the Catholics to the Pope is of the same character as that of Slattery to the Lord Jesus Christ, Uncle Sam
need not lie awake o' nights to worry about "Papal plots."

Had Slattery been truly a Christian, instead of black-
guarding me when protected by the presence of ladies, he
would have put up a fervent prayer for my immediate conversion to the Baptist faith.   But his milk of human kindness had soured—he was short on Christian charity and long
on gall.

"Faith, hope and charity," says St. Paul; "and the greatest of these is charity."   And he might have added that it's
also the scarcest.   Perhaps that's what makes it so valuable
—the supply is never equal to the demand.

Speaking of charity reminds me of my experience with
the Protestant preachers of San Antonio, some of whom, I
understand, are aiding and abetting this A. P. A. movement,
"designed to preserve the priceless liberty of free speech."
While editor of the morning paper of that city I was in the
habit of writing a short sermon for the Sunday edition, for
the benefit of those who could not go to church, I supposed

that the ministers would sanction my clerical efforts, but
they didn't. They wanted no assistance in saving souls,
considered that they should be accorded a monopoly in that
line and were entitled to all the emoluments. They proceeded to thunder at me from the pulpit, and sometimes
three or four perspiring pulpiteers were pounding away at
me at the same time—and incidentally making me very popular. I dropped into a swell church one Sunday morning
to get a little grace—a building that cost up in the six figures
while people were living in $4 jackals and subsisting on 50
cents a week within sound of its bells—and the minister was
holding a copy of the *Express* aloft in one hand and a Bible
in the other and demanding of his congregation: "Which
will you take—Brann or God?" Well, they seemed to think
that if they couldn't have both they'd best take God, tho'
some of the sinners on the back seats were a trifle subsequent
in making up their minds.

I kept hammering away—preaching to my little congregation of fifteen or twenty thousand readers every Sunday,
as I now do to ten times that many a month—until finally the
Ministerial Association met, perorated, whereased, resoluted
and wound up by practically demanding of the proprietor of
the *Express* that I be either muzzled or fired. And all this
time the Catholic priests said never a word—and San Antonio is a Catholic city. But the Baptist ministers were
running a sneaking boycott! Yet the Church of Rome is
the boa-constrictor that's trying to throttle the American
right of free speech!

The Y. M. C. A. invited me to lecture on Humbugs, and
that scared the Ministerial Association nearly to death.
They thought I was after 'em now sure, so they went to
the officials of the Y. M. C. A. and made them cancel the
date. And the only Protestant minister in the entire city
who did not join in this attempt to throttle free speech
was an Episcopalian—and the Episcopalians are not
Protestants to hurt. Yet when these ministers, who are
now so fearful that the Church of Rome will muzzle
somebody, found that they couldn't drive me out of town;
that they couldn't take the bread from the mouths of my
babes because I had dared utter my honest thoughts like
a freeman; that I was to continue to edit the *Express* so
long as I liked, they came fawning about me like a lot of
spaniels afraid of the lash! But not one of them ever tried
to convert me. Not one of them ever tried, by kindly argument, to convince me that I was wrong. Not one of
them ever invited me to church—or prayed for me, so far

as I could learn. Perhaps they, thought I was past redemption.

*   *   *

Slattery cautions you not to send your children to convent schools, declaring that he "never yet saw a nun who
was an educational woman." That statement, standing alone,
ought to convince every one blessed with a thinking apparatus that Slattery's a fraud. Some of the best educated women in this world have entered convents. Women upon whose tuition fortunes have been expended are
now making convent schools deservedly popular with the
intelligent people.

He says ignorance is the correlative of Catholicism, and
points to Spain as proof of this startling assertion. There
was a time when Spain stood in the very forefront of civilization, in the van of human progress, the arbiter of the
world's political destiny,—and Spain was even more
Catholic then than it is to-day. Nations and civilizations
have their youth, their lusty manhood and their decay,
and it were idle to attribute the decline of Spain to Catholicism as the decadence of Greece to Paganism. The Catholic church found Spain a nation of barbarians and brought
it up to that standard of civilization where a Spanish monarch could understand the mighty plans of Columbus. It
was her Catholic Majesty, Queen Isabella, who took from
her imperial bosom the jewels with which to buy a world
—who exchanged the pearls of the Orient for the star of
Empire. The Catholic church found England a nation of
barbarians and brought it up, step by step, until Catholic
barons wrung from King John at Runnymede the Great
Charter—the mother of the American Constitution. It
found Ireland a nation of savages and did for it what the
mighty power of the Caesars could not—brought it within
the pale of civilization. But for the Roman Catholic
Church Slattery might be wearing a breech clout, digging
roots with his finger nails and gorging himself with raw
meat in Ireland to-day instead of insulting the intelligence of American audiences and wringing money from
fanatics and fools by warring upon the political institutions of their fathers.

*   *   *

Slattery was horrified to learn that some of the nuns
were inclined to talk about each other. I sincerely trust

that he will find none of the Baptist sisters addicted to the same bad habit.

From what I could gather of his discourse,—before I was "put out"—and from the report of his alleged wife's lectures, I infer that this delectable twain impeach the virtue of the Roman Catholic sisterhoods. Malice, like death, loves a shining mark, and there is no hate so venomous as that of the apostate. But before giving credence to such tales, let me ask you: Why should a woman exchange the brilliant parlor for a gloomy cell in which to play the hypocrite? Why should a cultured woman of gentle birth deliberately forego the joys of wife and motherhood, the social triumph and the freedom of the world and condemn herself to a life of labor, a dreary round of drudgery, if her heart's impure? For shame!

Who is it that visits the slums of our great cities ministering to the afflicted, comforting the dying, reclaiming the fallen? When pestilence sweeps over the land and mothers desert their babes and husbands their wives, who is it that presses the cup of cold water to the feverish lip and closes the staring eyes of the deserted dead? Who was it that went upon the Southern battle-fields to minister to the wounded soldiers, followed them to the hospitals and tenderly nursed them back to life? The Roman Catholic sisterhoods, God bless them!

One of those angels of mercy can walk unattended and unharmed thro' our "Reservation" at midnight. She can visit with impunity the most degraded dive in the Whitechapel district. At her coming the ribald song is stilled and the oath dies on the lips of the loafer. Fallen creatures reverently touch the hem of her garments, and men steeped in crime to the very lips involuntarily remove their hats as a tribute to noble womanhood. The very atmosphere seems to grow sweet with her coming and the howl of hell's demons to grow silent. None so low in the barrel-house, the gambling hell or the brothel as to breathe a word against her good name; but when we turn to the Baptist pulpit there we find an inhuman monster clad in God's livery, saying, "Unclean, unclean!" God help a religious denomination that will countenance such an infamous cur!

As a working journalist I have visited all manner of places. I have written up the foulest dives that exist on this continent, and have seen Sisters of Charity enter them unattended. Had one of the inmates dared insult them he would have been torn in pieces. And I have sat in the opera house of this city—boasting itself a center of culture—and heard a so-called man of God speak flippantly of the Catholic sisterhoods, and professing Christians applaud him to the echo.

Merciful God! if heaven is filled with such Christians, send me to hell, with those whose sins are inhuman! Better everlasting life in a lake of fire than enforced companionship in Paradise for one hour with the foul harpies that groaned "awmen" to Slattery's infamous utterances. God of Israel! to think that those unmanly scabs, those psalm-singing vultures are Americans and our political brethren!

*   *   *

I know little about the private lives of the Catholic priesthood; but this I do know: They were the first to plant the standard of Christian faith in the New World. They were the first to teach the savages something of the blessings of civilization. I do know that those of them who were once Protestants are not making a specialty of defaming the faith of their fathers. I do know that neither hardship nor danger can abate their holy zeal and that hundreds of them have freely given their lives in the service of the Lord. And why should a man devote his body to God and his soul to the devil? I do know that one of them has given us the grandest example of human sacrifice for others' sake that this great world affords. Even Christ prayed in the Garden of Gethsemane, "If it be possible, let this cup pass from me;" but Father Damien pressed a cup even more bitter to his own lips and drained it to the dregs—died for the sake of suffering mortals a death to which the cross were mercy.

The Protestants admit that they are responsible for the inoculation of the simple Sandwich Islanders with the leprosy; yet when those who fell victims to the foul disease were segregated, made prisoners upon a small island in the mid-Pacific, not a Protestant preacher in all the earth could be found to minister to them. The Lord had "called" 'em all into his vineyard, but it appears that he didn't call a blessed one of them to that leper colony where people were rotting alive, with none to point them to that life beyond the grave where all the sins and corruptions of the flesh are purged away and the redeemed stand in robes of radiant white at the right hand of God. I blame no man for declining the sacrifice. To set foot upon that accursed spot was to be declared unclean and there confined until death released you—death by leprosy,

the most appalling disease in all the dreadful catalogue
of human ills, the most dreaded arrow in the quiver of the
grim Destroyer. Yet Father Damien, a young Roman
Catholic priest, left home and country and all that life
holds dear, and went deliberately forth to die for afflicted
barbarians. There he reared an humble temple with his
own hands to the God of his fathers, there, thro' long
years of confinement, he ministered to the temporal and
spiritual wants of the afflicted; there he died, as he knew
he must die, with his fingers falling from his hands, his
flesh from his bones, a sight to appall the very imps of
hell. No wonder the Protestant ministers held aloof.
Merciful God. I'd rather be crucified!

We are all brave men when the war-drum throbs and
the trumpet calls us to do battle beneath the eyes of the
world,—when, touching elbows with our fellows and clad
in all the glorious pomp and circumstance of war we seek
the bubble of fame e'en at the cannon's mouth. When the
music of the battery breeds murder in the blood, the electric order goes ringing down the line, is answered by the
thrilling cheer, the veriest coward drives the spur deep
into the foaming flank and plunges, like a thunderbolt,
into the gaping jaws of death, into the mouth of hell; but
when a man was wanted to go forth alone, without blare
of trumpet or drum, and become a life-prisoner in a leper
colony, but one in all the world could be found equal to
that supreme test of personal heroism, and that man was
a Roman Catholic priest. And what was his reward?
Hear what Thos. G. Sherman, a good Protestant, says in
the New York *Post:*

"Before the missionaries gained control of the islands
leprosy was unknown. But with the introduction of
strange races, leprosy established itself and rapidly increased. An entire island was properly devoted to the
lepers. No Protestant missionary would venture among
them. For this I do not blame them, as, no doubt, I
should not have had the courage to go myself. But a
noble Catholic priest consecrated his life to the service of
the lepers, lived among them, baptized them, educated
them, and brought some light and happiness into their
wretched lives. Stung by the contrast of his example, the
one remaining missionary, a recognized and paid agent of
the American Board, spread broadcast the vilest slanders
against Father Damien."

So it appears that the world is blessed with two Slat-
terys.

There are three kinds of liars at large in the land: The harmless Munchhausen who romances for amusement, and whose falsehoods do no harm; the Machiavellian liar, whose mendacity bears the stamp of original genius, and the stupid prevaricator, who rechews the fetid vomit of other villains simply because he lacks a fecund brain to breed falsehoods to which he may play the father. And Slattery's a rank specimen of the latter class. When he attempts to branch out for himself he invariably comes to grief. After giving a dreadful account of how Catholics persecute those who renounce the faith, declaring that they were a disgrace to the church while within its pale, he produced a certificate from a Philadelphia minister to the effect that he—the Philadelphian—had visited Slattery's old parish in Ireland and the Catholics there declared that he was a good and faithful priest! What Slattery seems to lack to become a first-class fraud is continuity of thought. He lies fluently, even entertainingly, but not consistently.

The apostate priest would have the various Protestant denominations throw down the bars that separate them and mark off their theological bailiwicks "with little beds of flowers." The idea is a good one—and I can but wonder where Slattery stole it. Still I can see no cogent reason for getting all the children together in happy union and leaving their good old mother out in the cold.

Throw down all the bars, and let every division of the Great Army of God, whether wearing the uniform of Buddhist or Baptist, Catholic or Campbellite, Methodist or Mohammedan, move forward, with Faith its sword, Hope its ensign and Charity its shield. Cease this foolish internecine strife, at which angels weep, swing into line as sworn allies and, at the command of the Great Captain, advance your standards on the camp of the common foe. Wage war, not upon each other, but on Poverty, Ignorance and Crime, hell's great triumvirate, until this beautiful world's redeemed and bound in very truth,

"With gold chains about the feet of God."

TRILBY AND THE TRILBYITES.

The Trilby craze has overrun the land like the "grip" bacillus or the seven-year locust. Here in America it has become almost as disgusting as the plague of lice sent upon Egypt to eat the chilled steel veneering off the heart of

Pharaoh the fickle. Everything is Trilby. We have Trilby bonnets and bonbons, poses and plays, dresses and drinks. Trilby sermons have been preached from prominent pulpits, and the periodicals, from penny-post to pretentious magazine, have Trilbyismus and have it bad. One would think that the world had just found Salvation, so loud and unctious is its hosannah—that Trilby was some new Caaba-stone or greater Palladium floated down from heaven on the wings of Du Maurier's transcendant genius; that after waiting and watching for six thousand—or million—years, a perfect exemplar had been bequeathed to the world.

I have read Du Maurier's foolish little book—as a disagreeable duty. The lot of the critic is an unenviable one. He must read everything, even such insufferable rot as "Coin's Financial School," and those literary nightmares turned loose in rejoinder—veritable Rozinantes, each bearing a chop-logic Don Quixote with pasteboard helmet and windmill spear. I knew by the press comments—I had already surmised from its popularity with upper-tendom—that "Trilby" was simply a highly spiced story of female frailty; hence I approached it with "long teeth"—like a politician eating crow, or a country boy absorbing his first glass of lager beer. I had received a surfeit of the Camillean style of literature in my youth, before I learned with Ecclesiastes the Preacher—or even with Parkhurst—that "all is vanity."

So far as my experience goes the only story of a fallen woman that was worth the writing—and the reading—is that of Mary Magdalen; and it is not French. Her *affaires d' amour* appear to have ended with her repentance. She did not try to marry a duke, elevate the stage or break into swell society. After closing her *maison de joie* she ceased to be *"bonne camarade et bonne fille"* in the tough de tough quarter of the Judean metropolis. There were no more strolls on the Battery by moonlight alone love after exchanging her silken *robe de chambre* for an old-fashioned nightgown with never a ruffle. When she applied the soft pedal the Bacchic revel became a silent prayer. So far as we can gather, the cultured gentlemen of Judea did not fall over each other in a frantic effort to ensnare her with Hymen's noose. If the Apostles recommended her life to the ladies of their congregations as worthy emulation the stenographers must have been nodding worse than Homer. If the elite of Jerusalem named their daughters for her and made her the subject of public discussion, that fact has been forgotten. And yet it is reasonably certain that she was beautiful—even more beautiful than Trilby, the bones of whose face were so attractive, the pink of whose tootsie-wootsies so irresistible. The Magdalen of St. Luke appears to have been in many respects the superior of the Magdalen of Du Maurier. She does not appear to have been an ignorant and coarse-grained she-gamin who frequented the students' quarter of the sacred city, posing to strolling artists for "the altogether," being, in the crowded atelier like Mother Eve in Eden, "naked and not ashamed." We may suppose that the sensuous blood of the Orient ran riot in her veins—that she was swept into the fierce maelstrom by love and passion and would have perished there but for the infinite pity of our Lord, who cast out the seven devils that lurked within her heart like harpies in a Grecian temple, and stilled the storm that beat like sulphurous waves of fire within her snowy breast.

"And behold, a woman in the city, which was a sinner, when she knew that Jesus sat at meat in the Pharisee's house, brought an alabaster box of ointment, and stood at his feet behind him weeping, and began to wash his feet with tears, and did wipe them with the hairs of her head, and kissed his feet and anointed them with ointment."

How stale, flat and unprofitable the modern stories of semi-repentant prostitutes beside that pathetic passage, which shears down into the very soul—penetrates to the profoundest depths of the sacred Lake of Tears! And yet this ultra orthodox age—which would suppress the Iconoclast if it could for poking fun at Poll Parrot preachers—has not become crazed over Mary Magdalen—has not so much as named canal-boat or a cocktail for her.

Du Maurier says of his heroine: "With her it was lightly come and lightly go and never come back again. * * * * Sheer gaiety of heart and genial good fellowship, the difficulty of saying nay to earnest pleading * * * so little did she know of love's heartaches and raptures and torments and clingings and jealousies," etc. A woman who had never been in love, yet confessed to criminal intimacy with three men—and was not yet at the end of her string! Not even the pride of dress, the scourge of need, the fire-whips of passion to urge her on, she sinned, as the Yankees would say, simply "to be a-doin' "—broke the Seventh Commandment "more in a frolicksome spirit of camaraderie than anything else." That's the way we used to kill people in Texas. Still I opine that when a young woman gets so awfully jolly that she distributes her favors around promiscuously just to put people in a good humor, she's a shaky piece of furniture to make a fad of—a doubtful example to be commended from the pulpit to America's young daughters. The French enthusiasts once crowned a courtesan in Notre Dame as Goddess of Reason and worshipped her; but I was hardly prepared to see the American people enthrone another as Goddess of Respectability and become hysterical in their devotion. I am no he-prude. I have probably said as many kindly things of fallen humanity as Du Maurier himself, but I dislike to see a rotten drab deified. I dislike to see a great publishing house like that of Harper & Bros. so indifferent to decency, so careless of moral consequences, that, for the sake of gain, it will turn loose upon this land the foul liaisons of the French capital. I dislike to see the mothers of the next generation of Americans trying to "make up" to resemble the counterfeit presentment of a brazen bawd. It indicates that our entire social system is sadly in need of fumigation—such as Sodom and Gomorrah received.

Trilby, the child of a bummy preacher and a bastard bar-maid, was born and bred in the slum of the wickedest city in the world. Little was to be expected of such birth and breeding. We are not surprised that she regards fornication as but a venial fault—like cigarette smoking—and sins "capriciously, desultorily, more in a frolicsome spirit of camaraderie than anything else." Girls so reared are apt to be a trifle frolicsome. We are not shocked to see her stripped stark naked in Carrel's atelier in the presence of half a hundred hoodlums of the Latin quarter—seeming as unconcerned as a society belle at opera or ball with half her back exposed, her bust ready to spill itself out of her corsage if she chance to stoop. We even feel that it is in perfect accord with the eternal fitness of things when these wild sprouts of Bohemia, "with kindly solicitude, help her on with her clothes." We can even pause to admire the experienced skill with which they put each garment in its proper place—and deftly button it. That she should have the ribald slang of the free-and-easy neighborhood at her tongue's end and be destitute of delicacy as a young cow might be expected; but we are hardly prepared to see one grown up among such surroundings so unutterably stupid as not to know when her companions are "guying" her. Trilby croaking "Ben Bolt" for the edification of *les trois Angliches* were a sight worthy of a lunatic asylum. It was even more ridiculous than the social performance of that other half-wit, Little Billee, in Carrel's atelier. Stupidity covers even more sins than charity, hence we should not judge Du Maurier's heroine too harshly. As weak intellects yield readily to hypnotic power, Svengali had an easy victim. I have no word of criticism for the poor creature. I do not blame Du Maurier for drawing her as he found—or imagined—her, nor can I blame popular preachers, "able editors" and half-wit women for worshiping the freckled and faulty grisette as a goddess; for does not Carlyle truly tell us that "what we see, and cannot see over, is good as Infinity?" Still I cannot entertain an exalted opinion of either the intelligence or morals of a people who will place such a character on a pedestal and prostrate themselves before it.

I confess my surprise at the phenomenal popularity of the book among people familiar with Dickens, Scott and Thackerary, triune transcendent of fiction. I had hoped when "Ben Hur" made its great hit that the golden age of flash fiction was past—that it could henceforth count among its patrons only stable boys and scullions; but the same nation that received "Ben Hur" with tears of thankfulness—thankfulness of a priceless jewel of spotless purity ablaze with the immortal fire of genius—has gone mad with joy over a dirty tale of bawdry that might have been better told by a cheap reporter bordering on the jimjams. Has the American nation suddenly declined into intellectual dotage—reached the bald-head and dizzy soubrette finale in the mighty drama of life?

I can account for the success of Du Maurier's book only on the hypothesis that "like takes to like"—that the world is full of frail Trilbys and half-baked duffers like Little Billee, who, Narcissus-like, worship their own image. They don't mind the contradictions and absurdities with which the book abounds; in fact, those who read up-to-date French novels are seldom gifted with sufficient continuity of thought to detect contradictions if they appear two pages apart. The book is ultra-bizarre, a thin intellectual soup served in grotesque, even impossible dishes and highly flavored with vulgar animalism—just the mental pabulum craved by those whose culture is artificial, mentality weak, and morals mere matter of form. The plot was evidently loaded to scatter. It is about as probable as Jack and the Beanstalk, and is worked out with the skill of a country editor trying to "cover" a national convention. The story affords about as much food for thought as one of Talmage's plate-matter sermons —is fully as "fillin' " as drinking the froth out of a pop-bottle, and equally as exhilarating. Like other sots, the more the literary bacchanal drinks the more he thirsts—appetite increased by what it feeds upon. We can forgive Byron and Boccaccio the lax morals of their productions because of their literary excellence, just as we wink at the little social lapses of Sarah Bernhardt because of her unapproachable genius; but Du Maurier's book is wholly bad. It could only have been made worse by being made bigger. It is a moral crime, a literary abortion. The style is faulty and the narrative marred—if a bad egg can be spoiled—by slang lugged in from the slums of two continents with evident labor. Employed naturally, slang may serve—in a pinch— for Attic salt; but slang for its own sake is smut on the nose instead of a "beauty-spot" on the cheek of Venus—sure evidence of a paucity of ideas. A trite proverb, a non-translatable phrase from a foreign tongue may be permissible; but the writer who jumbles two languages together indiscriminately is but a pedantic prig. It were bad enough if Du Maurier mixed good English with better French; but he employs in his bilingual book the very worst of both—obsolete American provincialisms and the *patois* of the quartier latin side by side. To the cultured American who knows only the English of Lindley Murray and scholastic French, the book is about as intelligible as Greek to Casca or the "doglatin" of the American school-boy to Julius Caesar.

His characters resemble the distorted freaks of nature in a dime museum. They may all be possible, but not one of them probable. Taffy and Gecko are the best of the lot. The first is a big, good-natured Englishman who wants to see his sweetheart married to his friend, weds another and supports her quite handsomely by painting pictures he cannot sell; the latter a Pole with an Italian's temperament, yet who sees the woman he loves in the power of a demon—by whom she is presumably debauched—and makes no effort to rescue her, is not even jealous. Svengali is the greatest musician in the world, yet cannot make a living in Paris, the modern home of art. He is altogether and irretrievably bad—despite the harmony in which his soul is steeped! Think of a hawk outwarbling a nightingale—of a demon flooding the world with melody most divine! We may now expect Mephistopheles to warble "Nearer My God to Thee" between the acts! Trilby can sing no more than a burro. Like the useful animal, she has plenty of voice, and, like him, she can knock the horns off the moon with it or send it on a hot chase after the receding ghost of Hamlet's sire; but she is "tone-deaf"—can't tell Ophelia's plaint from the performance of Thomas' orchestra. Svengali hypnotizes her, and, beneath his magic spell she becomes the greatest cantatrice in Europe. Hypnotism is a power but little understood; so we must permit Du Maurier to make such Jules Verne's

excursions into that unknown realm as may please him.
Had Svengali made a contortionist of the stiff old Devon-
shire vicar we could not cry "impossible." The Laird of
Cockpen is a good-natured fellow to whom Trilby tells her
troubles instead of pouring them into the capacious ear of a
policeman. He is a kind of bewhiskered Sir Galahad who
goes in quest of Trilby instead of the Holy Grail, and having found her, sits down on her bed and cheers her up while
she kisses and caresses him. As she is in love with his
friend, the performance is eminently proper, quite platonic.
The Laird advises Trilby to give up sitting for "the altogether;" yet Du Maurier assures us that "nothing is so chaste
as nudity"—that "Venus herself, as she drops her garments
and steps on to the model-throne, leaves behind her on the
floor every weapon by which she can pierce to the grosser
passions of men."

Then he informs us that a naked woman is such a fright
"that Don Juan himself were fain to hide his eyes in sorrow
and disenchantment and fly to other climes." How thankful Cupid must be that he was born blind! Still the most of
us are willing to risk one eye on the average "altogether"
model. Du Maurier—who is a somewhat better artist than
author—illustrates his own book. He gives us several portraits of Trilby, all open-mouthed, with a vacant stare.
Strange that he did not draw his heroine nude as she sat on
the bed hugging and kissing the Laird—that he did not
hang up "on the floor every weapon" by which even Venus
herself "can pierce to the grosser passions of men." But
perchance he was afraid the Laird would "hide his eyes in
sorrow and disenchantment and fly to other climes." He
could not be spared just yet. Despite his plea for the nude,
I think he exercised excellent judgment in leaving Trilby
"clothed and in her right mind"—such as it was—while the
Laird roosted on her couch in that attic bed-room and was
—to use a Tennysonianism—mouthed and mumbled. Even
New York's "400" might have felt a little squeamish at seeing this pair of platonic turtle doves hid away in an obscure
corner of naughty Paris *in puris naturalibus*—even if "there
is nothing so chaste as nudity."

Du Maurier says that Trilby never sat to him for "the altogether," and adds: "I would as soon have asked the
Queen of Spain to let me paint her legs." If nudity be so
chaste, and Trilby didn't mind the exposure even a little bit,
why should he hesitate? And why should he not paint the
legs of the Queen of Spain—or even the underpinning of the
Queen of Hawaii—as well as her arms? But if we pause to

point out all the absurd contradictions in this flake of ultra-French froth we shall wear out more than one pencil.

Little Billee is a very nice young man who has been kept too close to his mother's apron-strings for his own good—a girlish, hysterical kind of boy, who should be given spoon-victuals and put to bed early. Of course he wants to marry Trilby, for he is of that age when the swish of a petticoat makes us sea-sick. She is perfectly willing to become his mistress—although she had "repented" of her sins and been "forgiven" but a few days before. She has sense enough—despite Du Maurier's portraits of her—to know that she is unworthy to become a gentleman's wife, to be mated with a he-virgin like Little Billee. But she is over-persuaded—as usual—and consents. Then the young calf's mother comes on the scene and asks her to spare her little pansy blossom—not to blight his life with the frost of her follies. And of course she consents again. She's the great con-senter—always in the hands of friends, like an American pol-itician. "The difficulty of saying nay to earnest pleading" prevents a mesalliance. Trilby skips the trala and Little Billee—who has no chance to secure a reconsideration cries himself sick, but recovers,—comes up smiling like a cotton-patch after a spring shower. He is taken to England, but fails to find that "absence makes the heart grow fonder." He gets wedded to his art quite prettily, and even thinks of turning Mormon and taking the vicar's daughter for a second bride, but slips up on an atheistical orange peel, something has gone wrong with his head. Where his bump of amativeness should stick out like a walnut there is a dis-couraging depression which alarms him greatly, and worries the reader not a little. But finally he sees Trilby again, and, the wheel in his head, which has stuck fast for five years, begins to whizz around like the internal economy of an alarm clock—or a sky terrier with a clothes-pin on his tail.

Of course there is now nothing for Trilby to do but to die. They could be paired off in a kind of morganatic mar-riage; but it is customary in novels where the heroine has been too frolicsome, for her to get comfortably buried instead of happily married,—and perhaps it is just as well. Even a French novelist must make some little mock con-cession to the orthodox belief that the wage of sin is death. So Trilby sinks into the grave with a song like the dying swan, and Little Billee follows suit—upsets the entire Christian religion by dying very peaceably as an atheist, without so much as a shudder on the brink of that outer darkness where there's supposed to be weeping and wailing and gnashing of teeth. Svengali has also fallen by the wayside, a number of characters have been very happily forgotten, so the story drags along to the close on three not very attractive legs, Taffy, the Laird and Gecko. It is a bad drama worse staged, with an ignorant bawd for heroine, a weak little thing for leading man, an impossible Caliban for heavy villain and atheism for moral. Such is the wonderful work that has given this alleged land of intelligence a case of literary *mania a potu,* set it to singing the praises of a grimy grisette more melodiously than she warbled, "mironton, mirontaine" at the bidding of the villainous Svengali. Such is this new lion of literature who has set American maids and matrons to paddling about home barefoot and posing in public with open mouths—flattering themselves that they resemble a female whom they would scald if she ventured into their back yard.

THE AMERICAN DRUMMER.

THE APOSTLE OF CIVILIZATION.

The "Drummer" is distinctively an American institution. If we did not invent we developed him. He is not unknown to other lands, but the practice of "drumming trade" has been brought to the highest perfection in this hustling, pushing Republic of the West. The American merchant, like Mahomet, will go to the mountain if the altitudinous realty declines to skate over to him. Instead of bestriding a gum stump, like Patience on a monument, and waiting for some accommodating cow to back up to the milk-pail, he sends his agents out to round up the procrastinating bovine. He agrees with the poet that "all things come to him who waits"—including unpaid bills and bankruptcy. The day has gone by when it were possible to build up a profitable business without hard and persistent hustling—and that's what the Drummer is here for.

But he is more than an important trade factor; he is an apostle of civilization, nay, of religion itself— the religion of humanity. He penetrates every city, town and hamlet, bringing the people of the various sections of our common country into closer fellowship, making stupid provincialism impossible. He has wiped out Mason and Dixon's line, and had he been so progressive and powerful a century ago, would have prevented the growth of that sectional bitterness which culminated in blood. He is a public educator, a disseminator of new ideas, an inculcator of tolerance for the opinion of others, which, with the fear of God, is "the beginning of wisdom." He binds the people of the North and the South, the East and the West, together with the golden chains of commerce, of mutual interest, which are stronger than sentiment, paramount even to patriotism. He carries into the country the polish of the city, into the city the vigor of the country. With all due respect to the "cloth," I believe that we could better spare the D. D's for a thousand years than the Drummers for one day. The labor of the first has a tendency to produce faction, that of the latter to bring the entire people into a common brotherhood. If the books were balanced it would perhaps be found that every copper cent contributed by the ministers of America to feed the orphan and shelter the widow has been covered by the Drummers with a silver dollar. While the preacher has prayed the commercial pilgrim has worked—and "faith without works is dead."

To catalogue the noble deeds of the American Drummers would require a volume larger than Webster's Unabridged or the Bible. Their purses have ever been open to the needy,—they are the knights-errant of the new civilization, ever ready to succor the distressed, to shelter the weak and uplift the fallen. Nearly a score of them have laid down their lives for others,—not for relatives or friends, but for men whose hands they had never pressed, for children whose lips they had never touched, for women whose names they did not know. No cenotaph rises to commemorate their sacrifice, no flowers are strewn by a grateful nation upon their graves. No orator with lips of gold commends their heroism, no poet with heart of fire trills forth their praise—the muse of history passes in silence the lowly mounds where reposes the dust of men whose names should be immortal.

It is a popular superstition that the life of the Drummer is one dizzy round of pleasure—that his time is about equaly divided between paying attention to charming young ladies met on the train and picking his teeth in front of swell hotels, drawing on his house and being entertained by progressive merchants who are delighted to see him, and who give him carte blanche to stock 'em up. I dislike to bring the Drummer down from that ecstatic empyrean where public opinion has placed him; but really, the road angel's wings were not intended for Icarian flights. Should he go sailing "up among the little stars, all around the moon," he'd soon get a note from the head of his house intimating that he might as well fly across the ocean, birdie. He is expected to keep very close to the grass, but to avoid its growing under his feet.. Will Carleton's catalogue of the qualities necessary to make a competent editor aptly summarizes those of a successful Drummer.

"Is your son an unbound edition of Moses and Solomon both?
Can he compass his spirit with meekness and strangle a natural oath?
Can he courteously talk to an equal and browbeat an impudent
    dunce?
Can he keep things in apple-pie order and do half a dozen at once?
Does he know how to spur up his virtue and put a check-rein on
    his pride?
Can he carry a gentleman's manners within a rhinoceros' hide?"

The prospective purchaser who's the pink of politeness cannot pay his bills, while the cash customer's a veritable porcupine who must be approached by siege and parallel. The railway sandwich and gutta-percha pie smite him by day, while the pestilence that walketh in darkness crawls out of its lair and besieges him by night. One day he fares as sumptuously as Dives ever did, and he next dines on bull beef, stale bread and Pefferian butter, then bivouacs in a stuffy room, furnished with a three-legged chair and mouldy bed that smells like a second-hand coffin from a nigger cemetery. One day he is cared for like a king and charged two dollars, the next he is required to cough up three-cart wheels for being treated as an intruder and fed like a tramp. The servants in one hotel are paid by the proprietor, required to show guests every possible attention and told to use their Trilbys if caught angling for a tip; in the next they are mere slot-machines into which the Drummer is expected to drop four-bits to get a second-class dinner for which he's afterwards required to pay a dollar. Just about the time he gets his stomach educated to accept anything without a protest, and has become able to sleep on a corn-cob mattress without getting kicked out of his pajamas by a prowling nightmare, he falls in love with some sweet-faced girl, and the thought that he can visit her but once in 90 days, while his rival's fluttering about her four times a week, makes his heart as heavy as his sample-case at the subsequent end of a summer's day. Finally he is wedded and at once begins to look forward to the time when he can leave the road and enjoy the shade of his own vine and fig tree— where he can hear the whistle of a train at 2 o'clock in the morning without instinctively reaching for his clothes; but he now has a valuable trade established, which as a man of family he cannot afford to sacrifice. So he kisses the semi-widowed wife and the babes who regard him almost as an alien, and goes plodding over the old route, ever longing for the day of his emancipation, which too often comes only with a summons to exhibit his samples to St. Peter.

* * *

Comparatively few Drummers are to be found in American prisons, which proves that even the semi-homeless life they lead has not demoralized them, as it would the majority of men. In fact, were they not men of sterling honesty, brains and culture they could not retain their present responsible positions. I think it will be conceded by all careful students of sociology that the intelligence of the commercial travelers, as a class, is higher than the average in any other occupation. This is not the result of accident; it is the natural effect of a well-defined cause. There was a time—and especially here in the South— when the tendency of the best intelligence was to the professions and politics. The class spirit inherited from European ancestors was still strong within us, and the "tradesman," no matter how cultured or prosperous, was assigned to a lower position than the veriest mutton-head among professional men. The learned professions constituted the nobility of the New World, and, as Pride is ususally the handmaid of Intellect, drew to them the best minds of the Nation. Socially the merchant ranked with the mechanic, the mechanic the laborer, and all the journalist, who was regarded as a ne'er-do-weel—a mere literary scullion. But class distinction, grounded on vocation, was a European cult, in nowise adapted to the American atmosphere, which vibrated to the cry of "liberty, equality and fraternity." It perished, and for a nobility founded on occupation was substituted one of brains, and now men are expected to adorn their vocation instead of vice versa. Not only has the "tradesman" been placed on a social equality with his professional brother, but the mechanic has also taken his place in the "American house of lords," the once despised journalist become a multi-millionaire and, in his own opinion at least, arbiter of the destiny of the Nation. Our successful merchants and miners, inventors and journalists are even crowding the D. D's, M. D's and LL. D's for social pre-eminence. The rewards of commerce are greater than those of the professions, and the better intelligence of the country, being in nowise indifferent to the almighty dollar nor restrained by social scruples, "goes into trade" and prospers, instead of hanging its shingle on the outer wall and sitting down to semi-starvation. And the very best and brightest minds that commerce can command are put "on the road." There's where they are needed. The most stupid blockhead may learn routine duty in a great mercantile establishment; but the man sent out in these days of sharp competition and close margins to extend trade, must not only know a hawk from a handsaw and the cost of each, but have an accurate knowledge of human nature. He must be a strategist—be able to win the confidence, even friendship of men of antithetical dispositions, tastes and habits, for the proverb that "there's no sentiment in trade" is far from true. Other things being equal, our custom and our affections keep close company. Pope was probably viewing the Drummer with prophetic eye when he declared that, "The proper study of mankind is man."

We have carried the division of labor too far for the perfect intellectual development of the race. If it once took nine tailors to make a man, it now requires even more "specialists." Each devotes himself to some particular line, whether it be the curing of corns or the expounding of constitutional law, and follows it so assiduously that he usually knows little of anything else. It now requires about a dozen different kinds of doctors to keep the human mechanism in perfect running order—each of the important organs must have its specialist—and the same rule of subdivision obtains in every trade and profession. The specialist usually becomes a one-faculty man instead of a fully developed intellectual athlete. One may know comparatively nothing beyond theology, or some single division of law or medicine, and become wealthy and distinguished if he but know that one thing well; but the drummer who attempts to do business without a good supply of general information is going to get strung at the quarter-pole. It is an important part of his stock-in-trade—he must be able to interest the prospective purchaser, no matter what his hobby. Shakespeare assures us that "home-keeping youths have ever homely wits." However that may be, certain it is that the intellect of man is sharpened by frequent contact with his fellows, is strengthened by that stubborn "battle of life" in which the weakest go to the wall.

* * *

The Travelers' Protective Association of America was organized in 1882, "For the purpose of furthering the interest of commercial travelers, by giving them better hotel accommodations, cheaper rates of travel and greater allowance of baggage." It got considerably in debt after eight years' existence, and at the convention in Denver in 1890, St. Louis merchants offered to pay the indebtedness, amounting to $2200, if the headquarters were located in that city, and this offer was accepted. That year the annual membership fee was raised from $2 to $10 and an insurance feature added, allowing $3000 in case of death by accident and $15 a week in case of partial disability. At the reorganization Texas had about four times the membership of any other state. It was, in fact, greater than all the rest combined. Texas was "the banner state" at the close of the first year after reorganization, when the total membership of the National Association amounted to some 1800. Next year the convention met at Little Rock, and the membership approximated 2500. The following year it was held at Old Point Comfort, Va., and the membership was about 3000. In 1893 it was held at Peoria, Ill., and the membership had increased to nearly 4000. The death indemnity was raised to $4000 and the weekly indemnity, in case of disability resulting from accident, made $25. In 1894 the National convention was held at Milwaukee, Wis., and the membership had increased to over 7000. The death benefit was raised to $5000, the weekly indemnity remaining as before, $25. It is believed that the membership now exceeds 11,000—a mighty army of "hustlers" marshalled beneath the banner of Commerce, keeping step to the music of Progress.

The National Convention of the T. P. A. will be held this month in San Antonio, the metropolis of Texas, the most interesting city on the American continent. The "boys" will fall in love with San Antonio, because, like themselves, it is broad-gauged, hospitable, little addicted to the vice of hypocrisy. Many of them who come from the older states will probably expect to find a wild and woolly frontier town, where bad whisky's four-bits a drink and the festive cowboy chases the elusive longhorn through the principal streets, shoots out the kerosene street-lamps, and rides his broncho up to the bar when yearning for a compound of tarantula-juice and creosote; to be met at the train by a deputation of

leading citizens who wear their pants in their boots and boycott their barbers, and welcomed by Mayor Elmendorf from
the hurricane deck of a cayuse with an oration somewhat as
follows:

"Well, fellers, y're at the end o' the trail. We've got y'
corraled an' we're agoin to treat y' white. That's what.
We've laid in two dozen skins o' mescal fur the occasion,
histed the American flag an' fixed to hang a horsethief fer
your amusement. After he's swung off and has quit kicking we'll rope a steer jist to show you how it's done, have a
bull-fight in Main Plaza an' then adjourn t' the saloon of
Alkali Ike an' enjoy a fandango. If any o' youens feel like
chancin' yer pile y'll find the squarest poker game at Ike's
you ever sot into. Play 'er stiff as y' like. Make yourselves t' home. If Broncho Pete or Grizzly Bill goes to
shootin' holes in yer plug hats without an invite jist report
t' me, alcalde of the burg, an' me'n Bryan Callaghan 'll
straighten the cusses out in two shakes of a maverick's tail.
We'll now have some music by the Jewsharp quartette, with
Mesquite Charlie workin' in the lead. You'll then take a
drink with his-zonner, which is me, after which we'll adjourn to my hacienda over on the Nueces and hist in a few
slugs o' Kansas bacon and biled yerbs."

But those who come expecting to "rough it" will be happily disappointed. They will find a cultured city possessing all the modern improvements, including a municipal
debt—a grand old commonwealth gleaming in the glorious
sunlight of West Texas, a jewel pendant from the fringe of
Civilization's robe. They will find there, as nowhere else
in the New World, a romantic blending of the past and
present—the Sixteenth and Nineteenth centuries existing
side by side "in harmonious discord." They will find that
San Antonio is not so ultra-progressive as some of her sister
cities—that her people have not yet cast aside humanity and
anointed themselves with hypocrisy, like ancient runners
with oil, for that race whose guerdon is gold. San Antonio
puts on few frills. Her hospitality is of the old-fashioned
sort that may be felt as well as seen. She does not give the
stranger a stereotyped two-for-a-quarter smile, an ice-cream
handshake and expect to be repaid with a paean of praise
that will send the price of real estate up ten per cent. If
he is worthy she takes him to her great warm heart and
treats him so well—and so often—that, like the worn voy-
ageurs in the lotos-eaters' land, he's loth to longer roam.
Of course there are whining Uriah Heeps with itching fingers, and hypocrites with frappe hearts in the Alamo City,

as elsewhere; but she has put them on a "Reservation,"
figuratively speaking, with other disreputable characters—
banished them to a social trans-San Pedro, so to speak, and
framed her rule of conduct without their assistance.

San Antonio possesses for the poet, the philosopher and
the student an inexpressible charm. Its skies are brighter
than those of France, its airs softer than those of Italy.
There Anglo-Saxon chivalry rose to its glorious zenith.
There was fought America's Thermopylae, there Ben Milam
led his Spartan band against the fortifications and five-fold
force of General Cos, and fell, crowned with the victor's
wreath. There was planted the standard of Christian faith
when Texas was peopled by wild beasts and still more savage men. On the ancient battlements of San Antonio have
floated the banners of six nations, and through her streets
for an hundred and fifty years has ebbed and flowed the
crimson tide of war.

We must have several days—and nights—for sight-seeing
in San Antonio. We must dream about the ruined missions where, before our grand-sires' day, the savage was
taught to humble himself before the sacred cross; about the
Alamo, that charnel house of chivalry. We will be shown
a dozen different places where Bowie bled and Crockett
died; but no matter—it's all holy ground. We must have
a Mexican supper in the open air and a talk with the chile
queens. We must have hot tamales, with ice cold beer on
the side to temper the internal fires, listen to the music in
Alamo Plaza and witness the Battle of Flowers. And above
all, we must see San Antonio by moonlight—see it from the
roof of some tall building when, bathed in the silver flood
it becomes a veritable vision of beauty, the apotheosis of
romance, a fairy city which, like the baseless fabric of a
dream, we expect to fade from sight with the coming of the
sun. Beneath the magic rays of the southern moon the
grimiest adobe is transformed into Parian marble, the meanest jacal becomes an Edenic bower. The turreted postoffice
looms up a mighty mediaeval castle, the placid river a
tangled ribbon of burnished silver, a magic mirror, reflect-
ing the unreal. A brace of mocking-birds call to each other
from the depths of umbrageous foliage, then pour forth
a flood of melody such as Orpheus never equaled; the fire-
flies gleam in the cool gardens; there comes the rhythmic
pulse of dancing feet on oaken floors; the sensuous perfume
of dew-bespangled flowers hangs heavy in the air and sinks
into the blood like voluptuous music, while overhead rides
serene the silver Queen of Night, midway between the

sleeping earth and "the star-domed City of God." But, as
the governor of North Carolina remarked to the chief exe-
cutive of—Here's hopin'.

* * *

I once attempted to become a road angel, but found the
flying a trifle too laborious for my feeble wings. I had
attained to the mature age of seventeen years when I determined to become a knight of the grip and go forth conquering and to conquer. I noticed that they usually wore good
clothes and rode in the ladies' coach; so, with a sigh, I
surrendered my cherished ambition to become President of
this great Republic and pass my name down to posterity as
one of the numerous stepfathers of my country, and devoted
all my energies to the accomplishment of my new destiny.
I secured a position with an Indianapolis printing house—
on commission—and sallied forth into the small towns. I
was a Drummer at last and felt, with Monte Cristo, that
the world was mine. But it wasn't—at least not just yet.
The first merchant I tackled seemed delighted to see me.
His "What can I do for you to-day," was unctious as the
Song of Solomon, as oily as a keg of cotton seed butter;
but my reply seemed to freeze the genial current of his soul.
His encouraging smile faded like artificial beauty in a picnic shower, his suavity slipped its trolley-pole, his milk of
human kindness shrunk from a gallon an hour to half a pint
a day. I talked to him and he listened with the ennuied air
of a man to whom life is a burden and heaven not his hope.
I learned that he was a Presbyterian, and rung in a few
impromptu remarks on original sin without seeming to
interest him. Even a short disquisition on foreordination
failed to fetch him. I persuaded him to examine my samples
and he finally gave some faint signs of life, gradually grew
interested and asked for prices. After an hour's seance I
was sure of a big C. O. D. order, but he was called to serve
a customer, and I waited—trembling on the verge of my
first triumph. I was glad that I hadn't killed him during
the first ten minutes. I said to myself that with patience for
a lever and good-nature for a fulcrum I could move the
world. While I was congratulating myself my prospective
patron slipped out the back door and went to dinner,
leaving a stuttering clerk in charge, who tried to tell me
what had become of the boss, but sprung his pneumatic-tire
at the half-way house and had to withdraw. When the
merchant returned with his surcingle extended a notch or
two he told me that he had more stationery than he knew

what to do with—had no intention of placing an order.
Then I was sorry that I hadn't killed him when I could have
proved justifiable homicide. As I slowly packed my samples I resolved never to be polite and patient again—and
I haven't. I began to inspect the clothing with which his
tables were piled. He at once became interested. Did I
want to buy a suit? I hardly knew. I became distant, reserved, and he set to work to thaw me out. I asked for
prices and his politeness fairly oozed out at the pores—his
milk of human kindness increased momentarily in geometrical ratio. I was persuaded to try on various suits—became
well nigh enthusiastic in the matter of dress. For two
hours he perspired and tumbled his stock, trying to find
something that would satisfy my McAllisterian taste, then
I told him I was overstocked with clothes—had no intention
of ordering more, and departed, feeling that I had tied in
the ears of an unconscionable ass a double bow-knot that
wouldn't come out in a hurry. By working hard the rest
of the day I managed to take one order—for a pack of
visiting cards. I told the merchant that I would ship them
f. o. b. and draw on him in 30 days. Then I threw my
sample-case in the river and hoofed it home. If I ever
become a successful Drummer it will be as a member of
the Salvation Army.

CASH VS. COIN.

Coin, a free silver advocate, and Cash, a hardshell gold-
bug, have been conducting suppositious schools for the instruction of the common people in the so-called "science
of money." When first informed that their foolish little
books were having an extensive sale, I supposed that the
people regarded them simply as satires and read them to be
amused; for not even a controversy between Mesdames
Partington and Malaprop across the back-yard fence anent
the proper method of making soft-soap or skinning eels
could be more excruciatingly funny. But I learned somewhat to my surprise, that many people take them seriously
—even study them with attention, hoping to gain valuable
information therefrom. I would not now be surprised to
hear that Munchausen and Mother Goose had been adopted
as text-books by our universities. Coin should be soundly
spanked for his presumption and placed in the A B C class
of economics, and Cash sentenced to the dunce-block for

at least a dozen years. There is some hope for the first—
he may outgrow his vagaries; but the latter signs a dozen
certificates to his own irremediable idiocy. He begins with
a false premise and closes with a stolen currency plan. He
brazenly makes misleading statements, then appears to take
a fiendish delight in exposing his own falsehoods. Not
being a metallist, I might be expected to regard the merry
war now raging between the gold and silverites much as the
old woman did the controversy between her husband and
the bear; but of two evils there is always a least. If we
must have a money that will either scale the mighty fortunes
of the millionaires or ruthlessly despoil the pantries of the
poor, in God's name give us the first. A depreciating currency is always an evil. It has ever been the *bete-noire* of
the ultra conservative economists; but I defy them to point
to one nation it has irremediably ruined, to one people it
has hopelessly impoverished. Yet the strand of Time is
thick-strewn with wreck and ruin wrought by an appreci-
ating currency,—a currency that concentrated the wealth
of mighty nations in the hands of a favored few and made
of the masses miserable bondmen—compelled them to
choose between the bread of charity and the blood of revolution.

The free and unlimited coinage of silver would be a mistake *per se*, but wisdom personified compared with gold
monometallism. It would not induct the toiling millions
into an economic millenium; but it would constitute a step
in the emancipation of the industrial Israel. It were better
to wander forty years in the monetary wilderness, and at
last reach a fair Canaan, than to content ourselves with
Egyptian bondage and the making of bricks without straw.
Such being the case, it were well to look with a tolerant eye
on the "mistakes of Moses"—who means well—and align
our batteries full upon old Pharaoh. I have no doubt that
selfish monarch and his obsequious ministers talked to the
groaning Israelites much as the money kings of to-day talk
to the slaves of our industrial system. I can easily imagine
them saying:

"What would ye; leave the flesh-pots of Egypt—whose
savor ye are permitted to smell—and take to the desert?
Would ye follow to your certain destruction this bewhiskered fanatic, this foolish Midianite whose calamity clacking
hath made ye discontent? Behold the plagues already
brought upon the land by him! See how much better off ye
are than was labor four centuries ago. Why, we can prove
it by the government statistics! Jacob and his sons lived in

tents and came near starving to death, while ye inherit houses which ye have builded for yourselves, and for which ye pay rent—and there's a free soup joint in every city. Talk about being oppressed! Why, the value of farm property has doubled, and there was never a time when ye could purchase so much with a talent of gold—if ye have the talent."

The continual cry of the plutocrats through their newspapers and bipedal phonographs that the condition of labor is better to-day than in times past, is calculated to give sensible people a chronic case of ennui. It should be better —much better. The workman of today can create more wealth in a week than could his grandsire in a month, and the more he creates the more he should enjoy. The condition of the laborer, the farmer and the mechanic should have improved more than 300 per cent during the past century. But has it? A century ago there was work for all and labor was sure of its reward. There was no such thing as able-bodied pauperism. How is it to-day? The Chicago *Tribune,* an ultra-conservative paper of the gold-bug school, estimated not long ago that a million American workmen were out of employment—subsisting on the crumbs that fall from Dives' banquet-board and accepting his cast-off clothing with obsequious thankfulness.

Cash opens his school with an object lesson intended to be very impressive. He informs us by means of diagrams that the wage of labor well-nigh doubled and its purchasing power almost trebled from 1860 to 1892. I had no idea the workman was getting along so well! If he keeps up that lick for a few years he will be living in brown stone fronts and clipping bond coupons—instead of going hungry to bed and wondering where in the Devil's name he is to get the money to meet the interest on his mortgage or make the monthly payment on the little jag of cheap furniture he purchased on the installment plan. With Cash's diagrams before us it is difficult to understand how it chanced that a million men were taking up their belly-bands a notch for breakfast, dining on free soup and sucking their breath for supper. The average of wages is higher to-day than in 1890, but lower than in 1870. From 1875 to 1892 the average advanced one-half of one per cent—then dropped fully 15 per cent? You can hire labor cheaper to-day than a quarter of a century ago, and there are more men waiting for jobs. Yet in a quarter of a century the wealth-creating power—the value—of labor has almost doubled. Does not that clearly demonstrate that there's something radically wrong? Despite the fact that the wealth-creating power of labor has more than trebled during the century, the fact remains—a fact as gross to sense as the sun at noon to-day—that never before in the history of this nation, barring the acute stages of two or three panics, was it so difficult for the laborer, the mechanic and the farmer to make an honest living, or for the debtor to discharge his obligations. The gulf that separates Dives and Lazarus is wider than ever before—and this despite the fact that the average of wages is higher and their purchasing power greater than forty years ago. As civilization advances the standard of living rises. Our ancestors lived on roots and raw meat, inhabited caves and hollow trees and attired themselves in a streak of red paint for winter overcoat and a few freckles for summer ulster; but as the world made progress from pure animalism the luxuries of one generation became the necessities of the next—a fact which Cash has not dreamed of in his philosophy. He assures us that the principal cause of the panic of 1893 was "the decreased cost of production." In other words, when the people discovered that they could produce two bushels of wheat and two bolts of cloth with the expenditure of the same energy that was required in former times to produce one bushel of wheat and one bolt of cloth, they became panic-stricken—were so badly scared that they proceeded to go naked and hungry! He first points to the increased purchasing power of wages as a boon enjoyed by the workingman, then assures him that the decrease in the cost of commodities was what turned him into a tramp! It seems almost like cruelty to animals to criticise such a consummate idiot. It is only a lurking suspicion that Cash is more knave than fool—that he has been duly employed to pull wool over the eyes of the ignorant—that leads the Iconoclast to dignify his ridiculous book with this review. I have some respect for an honest ignoramus, but when a man possessing the faintest adumbration of intellect employs it in assisting Greed to despoil Need, he deserves to have his shirt-tail set on fire.

Cash "admits that we are in the midst of a great financial and industrial depression"—precipitated by an increased ability to create wealth—but would not have us become discouraged. He assures us that "this panic will not always last." Let us hope not; but if we may judge the future by the past—and cuckoo economics still prevail—it will scarce have blown itself out before another is ripe. In twenty years we have had three panics, and the depression which follows these crashes usually lasts from three to seven years. In other words, the workman can depend upon being employed at fair wages and the planter confidently expect to purchase with his cotton enough Paris green to poison the worms, about one year in four. And it is the occasional oasis in the industrial desert which Cash employs to prove that labor is fairly reveling in Lucullean luxury—that those who are striving to emancipate it from poverty are a pack of pestiferous demagogues. To illustrate how rapidly the man with the hoe is becoming a gold-plated plutocrat, he points out that the increase of the value of farm property in Minnesota during the past ten years amounts to more than $176,000,000, while the mortgage debt increased but $4,000,000 during the same time. He neglects, however, to mention that Minnesota is a new state, that the immigration has been very large and the increase in farm values chiefly due to augmented population. According to his figures the increase in land values represents about five-sixth of the total, but as he fails to state how much of this represents improvements and how much "unearned increment" his statistics are utterly worthless. The increase in land values may be entirely due to increase in population for aught he shows to the contrary, which would leave about $30,000,000 to represent the reward of labor in one of the greatest agricultural states for a period of ten years. Had Cash been seeking the truth instead of something to bolster up a preconceived theory, he would have taken for illustration one of the older agricultural States. He might as well have selected Oklahoma and argued from the rapid increase of farm values that the American agriculturalists are becoming veritable Astors! Having given the increase in farm debt, he should have given the amount of mortgage foreclosure. There is nothing in his statistics to show that half the arable area of Minnesota has not passed into the ownership of Eastern capitalists during the decade. Figures do not lie, to be sure, but—to quote from Cash—"they are the best friends a financial liar ever had."

He tells us, and quite truly, that "the credits of the country are based on the property of the country"—that the debts of the country are paid with the products of the soil and the handicrafts of the people." To the query, How can we repay the wealth we have borrowed from John Bull, he replies: "We will send the Englishman something to eat and to wear." That being the case, what has our currency to do with our foreign trade? Yet he tells us to reject currency plans "when they propose a money good enough to use at home, but which the foreigner will not take." Did

we ever make a money that the foreigner would "take?"
Has the foreigner made money since the establishment of a
purely American currency system that we would "take?"
If Cash had a hatful of British guineas he couldn't buy a
beer with them in the entire city of Chicago. He could
doubtless find some one to purchase them by weight, just as
he could go on the market and dispose of a carload of pork
or pig-iron.

Cash undertakes to demonstrate to a doubting world
that gold, instead of increasing, is actually decreasing in
value. He assures us that a day's labor is the measure of
value,—in fact the only one—declares that "it will buy
more than one and a half times as much gold as it would
forty years ago, and closes with the triumphant cackle of
an old hen that, by laborious effort, has succeeded in laying a new egg. Accepting a day's labor as the best possible measure of value, what does Cash prove by it?
Simply that gold, instead of having diminished in value,
has greatly increased. His assumption that a day's labor
will buy a third more gold than it would forty years ago
might be easily disproved; but granting that his premise
is correct, his conclusion is wrong. Labor is valuable only
as it is productive, and Cash assures us that a given
amount of human effort will produce three times as much
wheat and more than three times as much cotton cloth as
it would forty years ago. We know that the same rule applies to almost every line of human endeavor—because
Cash has told us so. What does this signify? Simply that
in forty years labor has about trebled in value; yet a
given amount, instead of buying three times as much
gold, will purchase but a trifle more than one and-half
times as much. Does Cash catch the idea? If his conclusion that gold has decreased in value more than 50 per
cent in forty years be correct, I submit that as a measure
of value it is a miserable failure and we had best find a
better one.

A suspicion that gold and paper currency bottomed
thereon do not constitute the best possible exchange medium seems to have occurred to Cash, for he suggests one
composed of greenbacks "convertible into a 2 per cent
government bond—an intercontrovertible bond which
may be exchanged for the greenbacks again upon the demand of the holder," then adds: "The proposed credit
money would constitute a flexible currency which would
always answer the demands of business. It would increase and decrease according to demand, and no cur-

rency famine could occur so long as there were outstanding bonds."

Cash has appropriated, without so much as by-your-leave, the currency plan which I proposed in the Iconoclast for December, 1891, and elaborated in a widely circulated pamphlet entitled "Dives and Lazarus," published June 1, 1894. It was this plan which the financiers of Germany discussed and approved at Berlin in 1893. I would feel highly gratified by an endorsement of my interconvertible bond-currency plan by the spokesman put forward by the American gold monometalists had he not taken the precaution to spoil it by stipulating that we "keep as the standard of value the gold dollar of present weight and fineness"—which he assures us has fluctuated more than 50 per cent in forty years! Still I am grateful for the direct admission by the gold-bugs that it is not necessary to bottom our paper money on metal, and for the tacit admission that a currency so constituted cannot possibly be a flexible currency, answering to the demands of business and preventing money famines. But just how we are to retain the fluctuating gold dollar as the standard of value when we have a currency in nowise dependent upon the yellow metal is beyond my philosophy. I fear that Cash has brooded over the money problem until his little think-tank has got full of logical wiggletails. If the bond-currency plan works it will soon be adopted by all enlightened nations and the monetary occupation of gold will be gone. The decreased demand will cause a slump in price greater than Cash figures out has occurred in the last forty years.

To emancipate our measures of value from the laws which govern commodities and make it as immutable as the multiplication table, I suggested the plan which Cash seems unable to comprehend. For his benefit I will restate it as briefly as possible:

Let the government sell just as many one per cent interconvertible bonds as the people desire, the proceeds constituting a redemption fund. Any one having United States currency of any kind could exchange it for these bonds redeemable on demand. Add full legal tender treasury notes to the volume of currency just so long as the increase will remain in the channels of trade. When people are buying bonds the currency is redundant; when they are selling bonds the volume of currency is too small to properly serve the ends of commerce. In the bond redemption fund we have an infallible indicator of the currency requirements of the country. When the volume of currency is too small its purchasing power increases until equal to the work required of it; when redundant its purchasing power decreases until all is employed. By this system the volume of currency would adapt itself automatically and infallibly to the requirements of commerce and our measure of value remain immutable."

Cash lays it down as a fundamental principle that "intrinsically valuable money only is a measure of value," yet commends a currency plan that would either prove a flat failure or drive all intrinsically valuable money out of existence. He prides himself on "disagreeing with all the great economists of the world" regarding the quantitive theory of money, yet approves a currency plan based exclusively upon that theory. The bond-currency plan would make our measure of value a theoretical dollar—purely a trade tool. Its value would not depend upon cost of production but on utility—on supply relative to demand.

Cash has something to say about "the science of money." They all do. It is supposed to be something very esoteric, quite beyond the comprehension of the *hoi polloi*. The metalists prattle of "redemption money," and "money of final payment," and "gold as a standard of value," until, like a half-baked sophist, they become completely lost in a fog of their own making and proceed to inflict a suffering public with books filled from *imprimus* to *finis* with foolish contradictions and self-evident absurdities. I have neither space nor inclination for a dissertation on money, but will drop the befuddled Cash a line to enable him to find his way out of the labyrinth in which he is lost. Should he inadvertently hang himself with it afterward "the science of money" will not have lost much. A dollar, whether it be of gold, silver or paper, is simply a check which the people in their official capacity gave against the entire wealth and credit of the nation. Unless it be redeemed on demand in the necessaries or luxuries of life it is absolutely worthless. There can be no "money of final payment." When you exchange a paper dollar for a gold dollar you have simply traded one government check for another—the gold dollar awaits redemption in commodities. One dollar is simply a figure of speech by which we express the commercial relation which one commodity bears to others. Every exchange made is upon this basis, but by using metal as an exchange medium all deferred payments become speculations—deals in futures. One great fault of Cash is jumping at conclusions, spraining his logical sequence in mid-air and landing on both sides of the goal. He has heard that the "per capita circulation of money is approximately two and one-half times as much in France as it is in England, while the prices of the great staples do not vary very much in the two countries." That is what causes him to joyfully bestride the celluloid collars of "all the great economists of the world" on the quantitive theory of money. It is another sad illustration of the axiom that "a little learning is a dangerous thing." Cash has heard of improved machinery in agriculture and the industrial arts, but is evidently not aware that in some portions of the world it is applied to exchange. A given quantity of currency will do double the money work in England that it will in France, perhaps ten times what it will in China. Exchanges to the amount of hundreds of millions sterling are effected without the handling of a single coin or the passing of a pound note. If we would abolish our banks and clearing houses here in the United States we would require a currency of at least $250 per capita to expeditiously transact our present volume of business. In every civilized country money is becoming ever less an exchange medium, while retaining its attribute as a measure of value. If we could so perfect our exchange system as to transact all our business without the use of money there would be no need of the interconvertible bond-currency plan, for the very thing at which it aims—to take currency altogether out of the control of politicians and place it in the hands of commerce—would be accomplished.

But this is probably as large a lesson as Cash can digest in a single year. When he has thoroughly mastered it I will explain to him, in words adapted to his understanding, that while the free and unlimited coinage of silver is an awkward and uncertain step, it is still a step forward; but that gold monometalism is an unequivocal step backward. The first is a misdirected blow for liberty; the last a strengthening of the chains that bind America's industrial slaves.

TEXAS AND INTOLERANCE.

CRANFILL SUPERSEDES CHRIST.

A subscriber at Savannah, Ga., sends me a newspaper containing an account of the attempt made by the ministers of Hoboken, N. J., to prevent Col. Robt. G. Ingersoll delivering a lecture in that city, and asks, "Can't you touch up those intolerant Jerseyites?" I could, and it would afford me some satisfaction to do so; but it would be firing away ammunition without effect. Professing Christians who believe that God Almighty needs their guardianship—that he can be injured by the ablest agnostic on the earth—are not amenable to reason, and the Iconoclast is not so well provided with pearls that it can afford to cast them before swine. When ministers imagine that the religion planted by the toil and watered by the tears of the Immaculate Son of God can be uprooted by a single scoffer; that it cannot stand the fierce light which beats upon Reason's forum and defy all the ballistae and battering-rams of human logic; that it must be sheltered from the puny attacks of mortal men lest they prove it a fraud and make it a by-word and a shaking of the head to the nations, their faith must be wofully weak or their lives a brazen fraud. Truth does not hide away in dark corners, but seeks the garish light of the noonday sun. It does not fear the attacks of Falsehood, but stands ever in the world's arena, courting the conflict. The Christian religion is true or it is false. It is of God or it is of the devil. If true it will stand the severest test. If of God it is indestructible as the law of gravitation. Then why do its ordained defenders take refuge behind long forgotten laws born of brutish ignorance, and with the policeman's bludgeon strive to close the mouth of honest criticism? The poet assures us that "Thrice armed is he who hath his quarrel just"; yet the leaders of the armies of the Lord will not fight, even on compulsion. Instead of meeting logic with logic and the fallible reason of man with the authoritative decrees of God, they answer every attack of infidelity with a tirade of foul calumny, then appeal to the laws of the land to protect them in their pitiful weakness. They shriek "infidel" when it was infidels whom Christ toiled and suffered to save. They howl "blasphemer," when their great Master forgave even those who nailed him to the cross and mocked his agonies. The tactics adopted by the church to crush those who presume to question or dare to differ is making infidels by the million. The day has gone by when men of intelligence were content to close their eyes, open their mouths and swallow without question every foolish assertion of clerical fatheads. Formerly they builded their Reason on their Faith; now they are grounding their Faith upon their Reason—that infinitesimal fragment of Godhood which burns, more or less brightly, in every human brain. They are demanding that the Christian religion be cast into the crucible where every assumption of science is tried by fire, and either comes forth in deathless splendor or is relegated to the rubbish heap.

Yes, it were a real comfort to "touch up those intolerant Jerseyites"; but my correspondent must excuse me. There's an old adage to the effect that those who live in glass houses should not throw stones—and Texas can furnish forth more hidebound dogmatists, narrow-brained bigots and intolerant fanatics in proportion to population than can any other section of these United States. That is why the Iconoclast located in Texas. It came, not to call the righteous, but sinners to repentance. When it has thoroughly reformed the Texas ministry it will be time enough for it to tackle that of other States. We are somewhat inclined to sneer at the old-time Puritans of New England and the exuberant cranks of Kansas. Ever and anon some able editor mounts to the roof garden of his donjon keep and thanks God that we are not as other people; but the cold hard fact remains that Massachusetts and Kansas combined cannot furnish so large a contingent whom it were unsafe to trust with power to persecute for religious opinion's sake. Of course Texas has many as broad-gauged and progressive people as any land or clime can boast; but she is cursed with a grand army of Me-and-god creatures of the Cranfillian type, who would, if invested with plenary power, establish a strict censorship of the press and permit nothing to be published that was not considered ultra-orthodox—that did not begin with hypocritical groans and end with blasphemous "amens"; who would require Jews and Catholics to recant on pain of death and place heretics under harrows of iron. In most States the church has made grand progress, broadened, become more tolerant, more Christ-like —calling science, art and education to its aid while casting non-essentials aside; has realized that

"New occasions teach new duties,
    Time makes ancient good uncouth;
They must upward still and onward
    Who would keep abreast of truth."

But the Texas division seems to have become hopelessly stuck in the Serbonian bogs of a brainless bigotry. It is not content to care for the spiritual welfare of man, but insists upon usurping the functions of the State and providing for his temporal well-being also. It would make him devout, not by God's love, but by due process of law. Having made it a criminal offense for him to pursue his usual vocation on Emperor Constantine's "holy Sabbath," it now aspires to close all fairs and other places of instruction on that day, and we may soon expect it to send a constable after those who fail to attend divine service and cannot furnish a doctor's certificate of inability so to do. It has banded itself together in a political party with the avowed purpose of dictating what man shall drink, and will doubtless next prescribe the cut of his clothing and limits his library to Slattery's and Sam Jones' sermons, a Protestant Bible and the "Baptist Standard." And the most remarkable phase of it all is that Cranfill has become infinitely more sacred than Christ, the political tenets of the church militant holier than the Ten Commandments. You may declare the Garden of Eden episode a myth, and even hint that the Immaculate Conception is but an old pagan legend in a new dress, and be allowed to live; but one doubt regarding the efficiency of Prohibition were sufficient to damn you, while to suggest that either Cranfill, Jones or Slattery are out for the long green and have as little religion as a rabbit, were rankest blasphemy—a sin against the Holy Ghost.

Fortunately the liberal element dominates in Texas, as it does in every civilized country, and the fiendish wolf of fanaticism can only tug at its chain and show its venomous teeth. Not being permitted to put men and women to the torture for uttering their honest convictions in a land of so-called religious liberty; to flay them alive for daring to dissent from some ridiculous dogma cooked up by half-crazed dunderheads during the Dark Ages; to drag them at the cart's tail and bore their tongues with hot irons in the name of a beneficent Deity, these professed followers of the Man of Galilee resort to sneaking boycotts, petty annoyances and cowardly calumnies. They prove in every way possible that their hearts, instead of being full to overflowing with the grace

of God and the catholic charity of Christ, are bitter little
pools in whose poisonous waters and fetid scum writhe
and wriggle unclean reptiles such as Dante saw in, the
desolate regions of the damned. That the picture is not
overdrawn every one who has chanced to provoke the
ire of the ultra-religious element of Texas knows too
well. It were equivalent to invading a den of rattlesnakes
or stirring up a rabid skunk. Tom Paine was a devout
Deist. At the shrine of the Most High God he humbly
bowed the knee. He never penned an irreligious line nor
uttered an immoral sentiment. He was an intellectual
Colossus, towering head and shoulders above even the
Titans of his time. He was the unfaltering champion of
freedom, the guide, philosopheɋ and friend of the new-
born nation. But for his fearless pen, whose path of fire
led on to liberty, the sword of Washington might have
slumbered in its sheath. Paine did more than all the
preachers of his day to nerve the eagle's wing for its
imperial flight—to fling Freedom's banner, like a burst of
glory, into the leaden sky. But he chanced to disagree
with the orthodoxy of his day, and for a hundred years
he has been denounced and damned as an enemy of God
and a curse to mankind. Even his dying bed has been
heaped with brutal lies, and across his grave still beat and
break the accursed waves of "Christian" calumny. In
many portions of the country the church has ceased to
belittle and belie Tom Paine; but the ultra-orthodox of
Texas still insist that he was an atheist and an outlaw
who repented of his foul crimes too late to escape the
horrors of hell.

The New England Puritans who hanged witches and
persecuted Quakers felt that they were discharging a disagreeable duty. They were the creatures of an ignorant and
superstitious but God-fearing age, and their cruelties, which
have left so dark a stain upon the annals of the Christian
church, were performed more in sorrow than in anger. If
they inflicted tortures in the name of religion they were willing to suffer death in its most terrible form in defence of
their faith. With them religion was a serious thing and
morality its synonym. If ignorant they were honest, and
if brutal they were brave. They despised the rewards of
this world, trampled its frivolities beneath their iron-shod
feet, loved God with their whole hearts and hated a liar and
a hypocrite as they did the imps of hell. How is it with
the Texas intolerants? Instead of fixing their eyes stead-
fastly upon the Kingdom of God, they are the most per-

sistent seekers after the almighty dollar, the most eager for
social preferment and political advancement of any class in
the commonwealth. They will give blows, but will not
stand to receive them, and instead of regarding with kingly
contempt that man who would swerve one iota from the
truth to preserve his life, they have made of lying a powerful lever with which they hope to overthrow religious liberty, transform the state into a theocracy and force free-born
American citizens to submit to the petty slavery of sumptuary laws. Their preachers, instead of serving without
salary and looking forward to a heavenly reward as did the
Apostles, are ever seeking "calls" to fatter financial pas-
tures. When the legislature is to select a brace of chaplains
to insult Almighty God with perfunctory prayers—paid for
at the rate of $5 a minute by men glad of an opportunity to
earn a dollar a day—there's a wild rush of the sanctified
time-servers to the capital city, and the methods they adopt
to corral the succulent sinecure would disgrace a railroad
lobby or cause a bunco-steerer to blush. They have di--
vorced morality from religion and substituted unadulterated
gall for the fear of God. Had the religious fervor of the
Puritans dominated the world we would have had men of
mistaken methods but of iron mould; should the fashionable
politico-religiosity of Texas prevail we would have, to borrow from Macaulay, "the days of dwarfish talents and
gigantic vices, the paradise of cold hearts and narrow minds,
the golden age of the coward, the bigot and the slave."

Unquestionably there are many worthy church communicants in Texas, as elsewhere; but they appear to be in a
hopeless minority—a few grains of sound corn in a pile of
compost. There are broad-gauged men in the Protestant
ministry here—men who serve the Lord in spirit and in
truth, and by their kindly acts, progressive ideas and noble
tolerance dignify his cause; but they are the exception instead of the rule and are almost invariably unpopular with
the great body of church communicants, whose ideal appears to be a preacher "with just ability enough to deceive
and just religion enough to persecute." During the recent
Prohibition campaign in McLennan county a minister of the
gospel, believing sumptuary laws violative both of the spirit
of the Christian Bible and the American constitution, spoke
and worked against it. What happened? Did a committee of his brethren in Christ wait upon him and strive by
kindly argument to convince him that he was wrong? Did
the other preachers offer up public prayers that he be
brought within the pale of their political party? Not a bit

of it. They poured out upon him the seven vials of their
wrath—attacked him with the vindictive hatred of a pack of
demons torturing a lost soul, or a drove of mangy jackasses
kicking a dead lion. They belabored him from the pulpit
and the rostrum, and turned the sectarian press into a reeking sewer that emptied upon him the foulest filth. These
"Christians," these professed followers of the meek and
lowly Nazarene, who was all love and charity and gentleness, reached for his vitals with beaks and claws like famished vultures, then served him as the unclean Yahoos did
the hapless Gulliver when they found him beneath their
roost in Houyhnhnm land. And so they serve every man
who declines to permit them to do both his religious and
political thinking for him; who refuses to take his place
among the intellectual goslings and trail blindly in the wake
of some flat-headed old ministerial gander, squawking when
he squawks and fluttering when he flies. There are ministers occupying prominent Texas pulpits who haven't originated an idea in forty years, and who would not recognize
the Incarnate Son of God if they met him in the road. It is
not necessary that a man should possess an iota of intellect
to become a popular preacher. In fact, brains are but in
his way, for in orthodoxy there is absolutely no room for
reason. He needs only to become a prohibitionist—not necessarily a teetotaler—cultivate a sanctified whine calculated
to curdle milk, grab the crank of some pitiful little gospel
mill and begin to grind. Let him but select the heavenly
turnpike on which he suspects there will be the most travel,
set up his little toll-gate, do the Jeremiah act and he'll soon
have a mob of sanctified nonentities about him who shame
the devil at his own game on week-days and try to bunco
the blessed Saviour on Sunday. I have noticed that those
who were most fearful that I would commit the awful sin
of blasphemy, or "desecrate the Christian Sabbath" by playing ball with the boys or dancing with the girls were the
people I had to watch closest in a trade; but those who sat
up nights to agonize lest the young be led astray by some
awful atheist, could tell the smoothest falsehood with the
straightest face; that those who wept the most copiously because the heathen of foreign lands had no Bible, were a
trifle backward in supplying the heathen right here at home
with bread; that those who cried "awmen" the loudest at
camp-meetings were usually expert circulators of calumnies.
If we could trade our ham-fat preachers for Good Samaritans at a ratio of 16 to 1, our brass-collar orthodoxy for
pure morality, and about three hundred thousand brainless

bigots and canting hypocrites for a yaller dog and lose him, Texas would be infinitely better off.

A DAMNABLE DECISION.

The decision of the Supreme Court in the income-tax case has placed this nation twenty years nearer a revolution that may terminate in a Reign of Terror. It has issued to the plutocrat a patent of nobility—declared that he belongs to a privileged class in nowise amenable to the laws that govern the proletarian. It has erected a barrier between Dives and Lazarus, drawn the line of battle between the Cormorant and the Commune. It has transformed the Federal Constitution from a palladium of liberty into an instrument of oppression, the tool of tyranny. That decision is a challenge to destiny, a red blanket in the face of an infuriated bull, a mockery of Samson by foolish Philistines as he stands, blind and desperate, his brawny arms encircling the pillars of our political temple. It is a crime against the common people, a poisoned dirk driven into the very vitals of the American Republic, a foul blasphemy of Liberty, Equality and Fraternity, the terrestrial Trinity of our fathers.

Doubtless the occupants of the Supreme Bench resemble Brutus in that they are "all honorable men;" but if such a halting, illogical and every way infamous verdict had been brought in by a petit jury there would have been more than a suspicion of bribery. The decision as handed down by Chief Justice Fuller reads like the special pleading of a jackleg lawyer, employed to defend a rich but notorious robber caught despoiling the pantries of the poor. Talleyrand declares that language was made to conceal thought; but even the opaque verbal flood in which the decision floats like a grisly skeleton in a sea of slime, cannot conceal the fact that Fuller knew the ruling was both dangerous and damnable. Like the lady in the play, he doth protest too much—consumes an hour in a dismal failure to establish a radical difference between tweedledum and tweedledee. It reminds one of the plea of Queen Elizabeth that she possessed a cavalry regiment of which neither horse nor man could be hurt, viz., a regiment of tailors on mares. He is too evidently arguing to his own conscience, which, like the dead Banquo, will not down.

The four dissenting justices did not accuse their associates of corruption; but they did charge them with having committed a crime—with having instituted a despotism of wealth, with having deliberately endangered the existence of the American government by an abortive science of definition. Never before in the history of the Supreme Court did the dissenting justices express such indignation over a decision or intimate so plainly that their associates were either fools or knaves. The vigorous, almost insulting protests of the dissenting justices; the tremendous monetary interests at stake, together with the scholastic hairsplittings, argumentative writhing and illogical twistings and turnings that distinguish the decision, may mean much or little according to the strength of the critic's confidence in the incorruptibility of the court. For my own part, I do not believe that the betrayal of the people was the result of direct bribery, as in the case of Benedict Arnold; but I do believe that such pressure was brought to bear by the plutocracy upon our court of last resort as to shamefully defeat the ends of justice. All men are more or less malleable, and several members of our Supreme Court exceptionably so—veritable Trilbys in pants, who find it "difficult to say nay to earnest pleadings."

The decision is simply an official notification that upon the shoulders of the poor must continue to rest the burthen of taxation. The court decided, by a vote of 5 to 4, that a tax on income arising from interest or rent is "direct," therefore unconstitutional unless apportioned among the several states on a basis of population; while a tax on income derived from labor, professional service or merchandizing is "indirect" and may be imposed at the pleasure of Congress and without apportionment. The gross injustice of such a ruling is too palpable to require comment, while its utter absurdity must be evident to every man capable of reasoning from a premise to the simplest conclusion. A has an annual income of $1,000,000, derived from the rental of real estate or interest on capital invested in securities; B has an income of $1000, derived from the occupation of merchant or machinist, butcher or baker. Congress, according to the Supreme Court, may, by a simple "Be it enacted," tax the petty income of B, but is forbidden to touch the colossal income of A, except by apportionment, when it becomes the province of each State to say how its pro rata shall be provided. A tax on the individual earnings of B is "indirect," while a tax on the revenues of A, drawn second-hand from the efforts of others, is "direct"—perhaps on the theory that "two negatives make a positive." The Federal gov·

ernment can shove its hand as deeply as it likes into the
pocket of labor, but cannot touch one penny in the thousand
pounds in the overflowing coffers of the capitalist.   So
says the court.   How is that for the fundamental law of
a land that poses in the face of heaven as "the refuge of
the world's oppressed?"

And what is the reply to this complaint?   "Apportionment."   Apportion hell—between the West and South!
Justice Harlan truly says that "No such apportionment can
possibly be made without doing monstrous, wicked injustice
to the many for the benefit of the favored few in particular
States."   Do those "able editors," short-horse politicians
and other intellectual animaculae now echoing the word
like lost burros braying for company, know what constitutional apportionment of the public burden means?   It
means that when the Federal government desires to raise a
sum of money by such method each State must contribute
thereto, not in proportion to its taxable wealth, but according to its population, no matter how poverty-stricken its
people.   It means that one state must put up as much for
a mechanic out of employment, or a farmer with a mortgaged crop, as another for a Rockefeller or a Gould.   The
privilege of taxing the great incomes by the method of apportionment simply means that labor is at perfect liberty to
bite off its nose to spite its face, then leap from the frying
pan into the fire.   No political party will ever dare perpetrate such an infamy as the apportionment of the income
tax.   Not even the Supreme Court—that pitiful cat's-paw
of the plutocracy—had the audacity to indorse it.

While a portion of the law was declared constitutional, it
was all killed—the tail was permitted to go with the hide.
The law was aimed at large incomes, many of which are
drawn neither from rent nor interest; but the court denied
the axiom that "half a loaf is better than no bread."   It
practically decided that should the government draft two
men for war, and one escape, it would hasten to discharge
the other, instead of mustering him in and sending a sergeant after the runaway.   The decision means that we cannot compel men to contribute to the support of government
according to their means until we have a constitution which
the plutocrat, with friends at court, cannot possibly pervert
—or the people decide that patience has ceased to be a
virtue.   It means that Wealth has decreed that Consumption shall bear the burden—that tariff reform and reduced
excises are, for the present at least, "an irridescent dream."
It means that no matter how imminent the peril of the gov-

ernment, or pressing its need, it is powerless to compel the plutocrat to contribute of his means to the defense of our flag. It means, as Justice Brown expressed it, "The submergence of the liberties of the people in a sordid despotism of wealth." It means that the people who have ever looked to the Supreme Court for protection from outrage and oppression, will henceforth regard it as the slave of their enemies. It means general dissatisfaction and growing unrest, until, despairing of righting his wrongs in the name of reason, the Titan will put forth his terrible strength, and the government of the United States of America will thenceforth live "only in the tomb of the world's history."

A BIBLICAL BEAR STORY.

The Bible is fruitful of snake and fish stories, replete with dreadful tales of ghosts and goblins, giants and chimerae dire; but no biblical narrative possessed for my childhood such absorbing interest as that of Elisha and his brace of anthropophagous bears. In early youth, as in later years, I resembled the Lord in that I was no respector of persons. There may have been other points of resemblance, but they were not sufficiently pronounced to excite remark. I had a bad habit of giving "back talk" to my elders, believing that youth has some rights which even age is bound to respect; hence I was frequently warned to beware the sad fate of those bad little boys who made ribald remarks anent Elisha's seldom hair.

This interesting animal appears to have long been Elijah's under-study, his man Friday, so to speak. Like Mary and her little lamb, everywhere that Elijah went Elisha was sure to go. He stuck to him like a cockle-burr to a merino buck, or an importunate creditor to a bankrupt. I rather suspect that Elijah went on that celestial excursion to get rid of him. I think that I would have ridden in a chariot of fire, or even straddled a streak of lightning to cut such bad company. Elijah tried to side-track his prophetic shadow at Gilgal, but it was no go. Elisha trotted along to Beth-el—wherever that may be—to Jericho and beyond the Jordan, despite the express orders of his master, much as a persistent pup trails its expostulating human property, but whether for genuine love of Elijah, or to appropriate his garments when the latter put on celestial raiment, deponent saith not. He got his master's mantle when the latter was swiped by a marauding whirlwind, and seems to have been well content,—to have shed no tears over the enforced absence of its former occupant. Several other people who witnessed the ascension were quite sure that Elijah was the victim of an infant cyclone and insisted on searching for the body, but to this Elisha strenuously objected. He may have considered it wasted effort; and, again, he may have feared that it would endanger his story anent that chariot of fire—which had inadvertently escaped the notice of the other eye-witnesses.

Having parted the river Jordan with his second-hand mantle—the waters fleeing affrighted from the unusual visitor—he was accepted by the simple people of Jericho as Elijah's legitimate successor and honored accordingly. He had tramped so long, however, that the spirit of the professional hobo as well as the spirit of prophesy was upon him, and he longed to be jogging along the dusty lanes and foraging his fodder, so he set out for Beth-el afoot. He does not appear to have had any business in Beth-el, but that was all the more reason why the old vagabond should go there. The prophets of his time were not in the habit of tarrying very long in one place, but kept swinging round the circle and living on the country, much like the modern evangelists.

The children of Jericho appear to have resembled the Nineteenth century youngsters in their unappeasable appetite for fireworks. They had heard about Elijah going up like a Fourth of July rocket, but had not been permitted to witness the pyrotechnic display. They knew that Elisha had fallen heir to the business and raiment of the original aeronaut, and naturally watched him with considerable interest, fully expecting that he would eventually take a header into the blue empyrean with a pair of flaming horses, scattering a stream of sparks behind them. But Elisha has packed his red bandana and is leaving the city—they are about to be disappointed. They cannot surrender the long anticipated circus without a protest, at least an appeal, so they follow him beyond the gates of the city, crying in their shrill treble.

"Go up, thou old baldhead! Go up, thou old baldhead!" They doubtless do not mean to be disrespectful, but are dreadfully eager to see the show. They have discussed it and dreamed of it for many days,—have trailed every little whirlwind to see if it was hunting for Elisha and scrutinized each horse headed in his direction, to see if it was on fire. They have heard that Elijah went out into the wilderness beyond Jordan to make his ascent instead of doing the aeronautic act from the market-place and getting all the caravans to give excursion rates, and they suspect that Elisha is sneaking out to board a whirlwind at some obscure way-station. What wonder that they grow clamorous and cry:

"Go up, thou old baldhead!"

But the duly ordained prophet of God does not take the curtain calls of the gallery in a kindly spirit. He is evidently sensitive about his scarcity of hair and considers their remarks not only an affront to his dignity but an insult to the Deity. Perhaps while dozing at the town pump the godless gamins had painted a face on the rear elevation of his cranium, so that it was difficult for people to determine in what direction the prophet was steering. Or the peddlers of hair rejuvenators may have persecuted him until his naturally sunny disposition had soured. Anyway, the allusion to his opera bouffe certificate was too much for his Christian charity. Instead of gathering the little gamins about him and explaining the significance of Elijah's translation, instructing them to lead worthy lives and thereby become an honor to their parents and a blessing to the world; instead of carrying with him to Beth-el the love and best wishes of the little ones and praying God to protect them from evil;—

"He turned back and looked on them, and cursed them in the name of the Lord. And there came forth two she-bears out of the wood and tare forty and two children of them."

Then Elisha continued on his mission of love, recking not the blood of the butchered babes—left the poor little bodies for the bears and buzzards. Forty and two little children lie torn and mangled in the wild-wood, their white faces upturned to an angry God. There is woe and wail in Jericho as the sun goes down that day, mothers weeping for their children and refusing to be comforted because they are not; men who have led the forlorn hope and looked unawed into the lion's angry eyes, are prostrate in the dust, bewailing their first born; the Lord of the universe is branded as a bloodthirsty beast, whose company a self-respecting devil would decline to keep, but the bald head of Israel's peripatetic prophet is avenged!

I sincerely trust that I will not be burned as a heretic, or even expelled from the church if I declare my doubts anent the Rev. Mr. Elisha's bear story. It is just possible that such a personage existed; tho' there does not appear to have been any necessity for his creation. It is conceivable that the gamins of Jericho regarded him as a harmless half-wit hobo, used him for their support until they got him "raw." It may be that while they were plaguing him a brace of ravenous bears set upon them. I can scarce blame the prowlers for preferring the tender children to the tough old prophet; still I regret that they didn't dally with him long enough to abate the insufferable nuisance. Elisha's bear story is one of those barbarisms which I shall cut out of the Bible when I re-write it, as I intend one of these days to do. It is not only a criminal libel of the Creator, but an insult to common sense.

BEAUTY AND THE BEAST.

Or the Ladies and the Apostle.

[A synopsis of Mr. Brann's address to the Ladies' Reading Club, San Antonio, Texas.]

I have been asked to lecture to the ladies of the Reading Club, but shall do nothing of the kind. That were to admit that you require improvement, and I would not have you better than you are. We would have to clip your wings or keep you in a cage. Besides, I never saw a woman whom I could teach anything—she already knew it. I have been going to school to the ladies all my life. My mother carried me through the kindergarten, lady preceptors through the intermediate grade, and my wife is patiently rounding off my education. When I graduate I expect to go direct to heaven. As near as I can figure it out, the inhabitants of the New Jerusalem will consist of several million women—and just men enough to fill the municipal offices.

"I would not live always, I ask not to stay."

No lecture then, but an informal talk, without text or subject—a vagrant ramble thro' such fields as tempt us. If we should find fruit, or even flowers, let us be thankful. If we encounter only briars, it will not be the first half hour we have wasted.

The fact that you are members of the Reading Club indicates that you are seeking knowledge. I trust that you are finding it,—that every stroke of the intellectual pick turns up a golden nugget; but do not make the mistake of supposing that all the wisdom of the world is bound in calf.

You may know all that was ever penned in papyrus or graved on stone, written on tablets of clay or preserved in print and still be ignorant—not even know how to manage a husband. As a rule people read without proper discrimination, and those who are most careful often go furthest astray. I once knew a woman with no more music in her soul than a rat-tail file, who spent three laborious years learning to play the piano, then closed the instrument and never touched it again. One day I said to her:

"Mary, what good did all the patient practice do you?"

"Lot's o' good," she replied; "I used to be dreadfully ashamed to have people know that I *couldn't* play." And a great deal of laborious reading is undertaken on the same principle that Mary learned to play the piano—and is of just as little benefit. Many people are with books as with medicine—imagine that whatever is hardest to get down will do them the most good. No mortal man—and, as the preacher correctly stated, the men embrace the women—ever yet got any permanent good out of a book unless he enjoyed its perusal. Jno. J. Ingalls says that everybody praises Milton's Paradise Lost, but nobody reads it. Ingalls is mistaken. Everybody making any pretension to culture has read the book—as a disagreeable duty; but that man don't live—at least outside of the lunatic asylum—who can quote a dozen lines of it. Same with Dante's Divine Comedia and a host of other books with which people are expected to inflict their brains. Read few books and those of the very best,—books that you enjoy. Read them thoroughly; make them your very own—then forget them as soon as possible. Having submitted to the mental or moral discipline of another, decline to lean on him, but stand up in your own independent individuality. Don't be a copy. There is on earth no more pitiable person than

"The bookful blockhead, ignorantly read,
With loads of learned lumber in his head."

Do not interpret too literally. What I warn you against is the habit, all too common, of imagining ourselves rich because we have counted the golden hoard of others. One may admire the Medicean Venus without becoming a sculptor, or have Plato at his fingers' ends and ever remain a fool. Were I an artist I would study with attention the works of all the great masters; but when I put my hand to my own task I would turn my back upon them all and my face to nature. My work would then be a "creation," not a copy. Did I aspire to be truly learned I would study the words of the world's wisest—then dig for wisdom on my own behoof, I would thus become a philosopher instead of a parrot.

* * *

I have been frequently called an iconoclast, and bad as the title is popularly supposed to be, I trust it is not altogether undeserved. I have striven to break foolish idols and shatter false ideals, to hurl unclean gods from their pedestals in the public pantheon. A work of destruction is not, I admit, of a high order. Anybody may destroy; it requires genius to build up. The wonder of the ancient world sank to ruin irremediable beneath the torch of a morbid dude who had rather be "damned to everlasting fame" than altogether forgotten. A hungry wolf may destroy a human life which Almighty God has brought to perfection thro' long years of labor. But destruction is sometimes necessary. The seas must be cleared of pirates before commerce can flourish; the antiquated and useless building must come down before the schoolhouse or business block can occupy the site. In the great cities are men who do nothing but destroy old buildings—professional wreckers of those works of man that have outlived their usefulness. They build nothing; but are they, therefore, to be condemned? So in the social world, a man may be a professional wrecker, without the constructive ability to build a political platform on a piecrate, and still be useful, indispensable. The wrecker of bad buildings does not contract to put good ones in their places; nor is the iconoclast under any obligation to find a heavenly grace for every false god that falls beneath his hammer, a saint for every sinner he holds up to scorn, a new truth for every old falsehood he fells to earth. He may, if he thinks proper, leave that labor to others and go on, with brand and bomb, bludgeon and bill-hook, wrecking, destroying—playing John the Baptist to a greater to come after.

A great many good people have taken the trouble to inform me that I am a pessimist. Perhaps so; but I am not worrying much about it. A pessimist is a person somewhat difficult to define. The fool who smokes in powder-house, or believes that his neighbors always speak well of him behind his back; the wife who encourages her husband to pay court to other women on the supposition that no harm can ensue; the banker who accepts a man's unsecured note because he is a church member and powerful in prayer, and the servant girl who lights the fire with kerosene—then goes to join the angels taking your household goods and gods with her—are certainly not pessimists; they are only idiots.

It is easy enough to say that a pessimist is a person afflicted with an incurable case of mulligrubs—one whom nothing in all earth or heaven or hades pleases; one who usually deserves nothing, yet grumbles if he gets it. But we should not forget that every reform this world has known; every effort that has lifted man another notch above the brute level; every star in our flag of freedom; every line and letter in our constitution of human liberty; every gem of knowledge that gleams in the great world's intellectual crown of glory; every triumph of science and religion, philosophy and mechanics was the work of pessimists, so-called —of men who were not satisfied with the world's condition and set determinedly to work to better it. They strove with their full strength against those conditions panegyrized and poetized by the smirking optimists of their time, and thereby incurred the enmity of pedants and self-sufficient purists,—were denounced and denied, belittled and belied.

But, says the enthusiastic optimist, things are not what they used to be. When a college of cardinals gave Galileo to the gaoler for maintaining that "the world do move;" when Christ cast forth the money manipulators and purged the porches of the temple of the disreputable dove dealers; when Luther raised the standard of revolt and the Puritan packed his grip there were cruel wrongs to right. But look at us now! We've got a constitution and a Confession of Faith, prize rings and Parisian gowns, sent missionaries to Madagascar and measured Mars' two moons. Of course we've made some mendicants, but please admire the multifarious beauty of our millionaires! Who can doubt that we've triumphed over the world, the flesh and the devil? Have not the Spanish inquisition and the English Court of High Commission gone glimmering? Do we bore the tongues of Quakers or amputate the ears of non-conformists as in Auld Lang Syne? Do we not run troublesome wives into the divorce court instead of into the river, as was once our wont,—scientifically roast our criminals with electricity instead of pulling their heads off with a hair halter? Do we not fight our political battles with wind instead of war clubs? Have not our great partisan paladins substituted gall for Greek fire?

Progressing we certainly are, but the devil has adapted the Fabian tactics and is leading us a wild dance thro' unprofitable deserts. While we have been shattering ethnic images he has been building new idols. While we have been dragging the Phalaris Bull from its pedestal the Golden Calf of ancient Israel has reached maturity and maternity and its progeny is now worshipped in a thousand pantheons.

Everywhere the false and the true, the good and the evil, the lambent light of heaven and the sulphurous shadows of hell meet and blend. Nowhere, yet everywhere, floats the white veil and flaming ensign of the modern Mokanna— and we stand wrangling about the proper cut of a collar; debating whether the Gadarenes, whose swine the outcast devils drowned, were Jews or Gentiles; dogmatizing anent the proper form of baptism; doubting with which hand we should tip the hat; wondering if Joseph's coat were a sack or a swallow-tail—ninety-and-nine out of every hundred wasting upon childish trifles the strength given us to do the work of demi-gods—and every foolish breath, every heartbeat bearing us across Time's narrow sands into the broad bosom of that sea which hath no shore!

What does the all-seeing sun that has for so many centuries glared down upon this wretched farce-tragedy, think of it all? And yet man boasts that he is the mortal image of immortal God! It was for this trifling, straddling biped, intent only upon getting his goose-head above other foolish geese, that the Regent of the universe suffered ignominy and death! I sometimes think that had the Almighty cast the human horoscope he would never have given Noah a hint to go in out of the wet.

*   *   *

I am no perfectionist. I do not build the spasmodic sob nor spill the scalding tear because all men are not Sir Galahads in quest of the Holy Grail, and all women angels with two pair o' reversible wings and the aurora borealis for a hat-band. I might get lonesome in a world like that. I do not expect to see religion without cant, wealth without want, and virtue without vice; but I do hope to see the human race devote itself to grander aims than following the fashions and camping on the trail of the cart-wheel dollar. I want to see more homes and fewer hovels, more men and fewer dudes. I want to see more women with the moral courage to brave the odium of being old maids rather than the pitiful weakness to become loveless wives. I want to see more mothers who would rather be queens of their homes than the favorites of fashionable circles; women who would rather have the love of their husbands than the insolent admiration of the whole he-world—women who do not know too much at 15 and too little at 50.

I want to see more men who are not a constant reminder

of a monkey ancestry. Some philosopher once remarked: "As between men and dogs, give me dogs." I have been often tempted to indorse the sentiment—and I am not much of a lover of dogs either. I want to see men who are not fops in their youth, fools in their prime and egotists in their old age—a race of manly men to whom life is not a lascivious farce; whose god is not gold; who do not worship at the shrine of the Pandemian Venus nor devote their lives to the service of Mammon, "the least erect of all the angelic host that fell from heaven." I want to see men who scorn the pusillanimity of the policy-prayer, who,—like Caesar, dare tell greybeards the truth e'en tho' it cost a crown; men of leonine courage, men of iron mould, men strong of hand and heart, who defiantly throw down the gage to destiny—who can trample hell itself beneath their proud feet, even while it consumes them.

* * *

The dream may be Utopian. I much fear it will never be made a blessed reality by either philosophy or religion. We have had both for forty centuries, yet the fool has become ever more offensive and the liar has overrun the land. Yet we imagine that because we no longer live in caves and fight naked with the wild beasts of the forest for our food we are away up at the head of the procession, with Greek civilization distanced and all the other times and half times nowhere.

Human development, like the earth, the sun, the stars—like all things brought into being by the breath of Omnipotent God—travels ever in a circle. Savagery and ignorance, barbarism and ambition, civilization and sybaritism, dudeism and intellectual decay; then once more savagery and ignorance proclaim the complete circle,—that we have traveled from nadir to zenith and from zenith to nadir—when once again we begin with painful steps and slow to repace the path which carries us to the very verge of godhood and wreathes our brows with immortal bays, then brings us down—even while we think we mount—until we touch a level beneath the very brute. Such has ever been the world's history, and such it will ever be until a force is found that can transform this circle into a straight line—that can blend the rugged manhood of the barbarian with the graces of our higher civilization and give us wisdom without weakness and culture without cowardice; that can incorporate us as corpuscles in the social organism without eliminating every spark of God-like individuality, making us helpless dependents upon social, political and religious precedent.

If the Car of Progress travels in a circle—and history says it does; if neither science, philosophy nor religion can deflect it from its seemingly predestined path—and the condition of their birth-place proclaims their failure so to do— where is hope? Must the human race forever go the weary round of birth and death, like Buddhist souls wandering thro' all that's fair and foul, until it finds Nirvana in the destruction of the world? Not so, for there is a hope—a blessed hope—that like

"A poising eagle burns above the unrisen morrow."

That hope is in the union of all the mighty forces that make for the emancipation of mankind,—a union of religion and philosophy, science and woman. And of these the first is the last and the last is the first in point of power and importance.

* * *

When I reflect that until within comparatively recent times women were slaves, I don't much wonder that the old civilizations went to the dogs—that the millennium is not yet due. Trying to make a civilization that would stick without the help of woman were like building a cock-tail with a basis of buttermilk. God gave her to man to be an helpmeet, not a plaything. I don't think that she can help him much by going into politics, or becoming a crusading she-Peter-the-Hermit while her own children need her care; but I do believe that the wife and mother—that erstwhile ignorant drudge, raised by God's great mercy to royalty— made Queen of the home, and thereby absolute Empress of the great round earth—is to be the dynamics of a new and grander civilization that can never recede; that the womanly woman, self-poised as a star, pure as the polar snows, fit companion for the true nobleman of nature, is to be the Providence that will lead humanity, step by step, ever onward and upward, until our cruel age of iron is transformed into an age of gold in which there'll be neither millionaire nor mendicant, master nor slave—in which Selfishness will be considered the worst of crimes and Love the all-powerful law.

Such, ladies, is my dream of the future. You see, with true mannish instinct, I throw the work of the world's salvation upon the women. I don't know, however, but it's retributive justice. If you got us fired out of the first Paradise it is your duty to find another and put us in possession. But really with all due respect to Sacred Writ, I could never accept that serpent story without considerable salt. My observation—and experience—has been that men are much more addicted to the snake habit than are women. I gather from Genesis that after the Edenic reptile had done the damage it was condemned to go upon its belly all the days of its life. That indicates that it was not only a good conversationalist, but had legs. Now I submit it to you in all seriousness: which member of the original family was most likely to see such a serpent as that? I think I should have given Adam the Keeley cure, then crossexamined him a little before laying the burden of the blame on Eve. If the latter was really the tempter she was probably trying to reach the heart of her hubby by that direct route, the stomach—lost heaven for love, as too many of her daughters have since done. The fact that Adam was not willing to father her fault proved him unworthy his wife, and the bad example he set is too often followed by many of his sons— who attribute all their trials and tribulations to the patient wives whose watchful care keeps them out of the penitentiary. Whatever may have been Eve's fortune, Adam was no great loser by being ejected from Eden, for the man who possesses the love of a good woman carries Paradise with him wherever he goes. A woman's love can transform a hovel into a heaven and fill it with supernal sunshine—and her scorn can make perdition of a palace and put in all the fancy touches.

Woman is the only thing extant, if Genesis be believed, that was not evolved from a solid slug of nothing. That I presume, is why she amounts to something. Nothing was good enough raw material of which to make the father of mankind; but when the Almighty came to create our common mother he required something more substantial than a hole in the atmosphere.

I always bank on a boy who has a good mother, regardless of what the old man may be. The fathers of philosophers have sometimes been fools, but their mothers never. A wise man may beget dudes or a good man practical politicians; but it's his misfortune, not his fault. The good Lord expects no man to gather grapes of thorns or figs of thistles. I have yet to hear of a single man who became distinguished in any line of human endeavor according to his father the credit for his greatness. Character is moulded at the mother's knee, and in the light of her loving eyes is born that ambition which buoys man up in a sea of troubles

—that drives him on thro' dangers and difficulties, straight to the shining goal.

The Nineteenth century marks the culmination of an era of human triumphs, a brilliant coruscation of victories over the cohorts of Ignorance and Prejudice; but its crown of imperishable glory is the recognition that woman was created to be man's companion and co-laborer instead of his chattel, his joint sovereign of the earth instead of his slave. Fronting the dawn of a grander day, her hand ungyved and her brain unfettered; with broader opportunities for usefulness and boasting a nobler beauty than during the dark and dreary centuries that lie behind her like a hideous dream—such is the woman of the Nineteenth century, and upon the shapely shoulders of this new Pallas I hang my second Providence, to her loving hands I commit the destiny of the race, to her true heart the salvation of the world.

PUGILISM VS. HYPOCRISY.

The announcement that Corbett and Fitzsimmons will meet in the fistic arena at Dallas to determine which is the better man, has, as might have been expected, provoked a veritable deluge of sanctified "gush" and sentimental "rot." The press and pulpit of Texas were immediately seized with moral jimjams and began to cut fantastic capers before high heaven. One would suppose from their doleful jeremiads and frantic protests that the bottom was about to be knocked out of the Christian cosmos, mortality sent careening over the ropes, civilization swiped from the face of the shrinking earth and chaos come again. Consistency is a jewel not found in the casket of the latter-day Jonahs. For years past slugging-matches have been of frequent occurrence in Texas, and have provoked scarce a protest from those goody-goodies who are now having a conniption fit every fifteen minutes over the Corbett-Fitzsimmons affair. It is a well-known fact that the less science fistic combatants possess the more liable they are to do each other serious bodily harm. A "mill" between unskilled sluggers resembles nothing so much as a kicking match between a brace of vicious mules, in which the beast that can stand the most punishment wins the battle, while a contest by well-trained athletes were like the fine sword-play of expert fencers. The pending bout is not likely to be nearly so "brutal" as many "mills" fought in Texas during the past half-dozen years, and duly reported by the very papers that want the visiting champions put in the penitentiary. The professional "moral element" is entirely too subsequent in getting its Ebenezer up, and I suggest that it be pulled down before a disgusted world expectorates upon it. Having swallowed a whole herd of mangy camels, the self-styled "moral element" should not employ a brass band to call attention to the fact that it is now straining so hard at a gnat that its umbilical cord is in danger of collapse. The abuse heaped upon the progressive city of Dallas because it made a bid for the great contest, is but the dishonest vaporings of a canting hypocrisy, accentuated by morbid minds and bilious livers. If Dallas were making deliberate preparation to violate a well-established law of the land it were well enough to criticise her; but the statute anent prize-fighting, like many other enactments by Texas legislatures, is not considered by competent lawyers as one whit more reliable than a camp-meeting certificate of conversion. And it is reasonable to suppose that if the law in question would stand the crucible of the courts, those busy little souls who consider themselves pious because they dislike to see other people enjoy themselves, would have clamored for its enforcement long ere this.

The Iconoclast is not the apologist of pugilism. Its voice is ever for peace—peace in its most virulent form. I have had a sneaking respect for Grover Cleveland ever since he sent a substitute to fight the Southern Confederacy while he remained at home to play pinocle with the pretty girls. It proved that while he may not be much of a statesman in time of peace, there's no picnic ants on his judgment in time of war. But I do insist that if we are to have prize fights here in Texas they should be contests between expert boxers instead of awkward clowns who pound each other to a pulp to make a hoodlum holiday. Nor is a fistic encounter between first-class athletes altogether an unmixed evil. It inoculates our young men with a desire for physical development, and is a splendid object lesson in the very necessary art of self-defence. Every boy should learn to box; it is a manly accomplishment, necessary to the perfect physical development of the race. It is infinitely better that a boy should get a black eye or a bloody nose occasionally, and grow up masculine and self-reliant, than run to chrysanthemums and creased twousahs, flash dickeys and effeminate dudeism. Those who make super-goodness a paying profession sneer at the claim that pugilism is a "manly sport." However that may be it is certainly preferable to employing brazen apostates to defame Catholic nuns—or raping infants in Baptist universities. Nothing is more conducive to continence than severe athletic training: hence it might not be a bad plan to make a hot whirl with the gloves a part of the daily devotional exercise of all professing he-Christians. While boxing does not insure morality, it is infinitely more profitable than empty dogmatizing. While the world may not fully approve of Corbett and Fitzsimmons facing each other in the "squared circle" like contending Titans, it will certainly esteem them above the cymling-headed lollipops whose highest accomplishment is the nursing of canes. The proposed "'mill," while not so elevating, perhaps, as a slumgullion editorial in the *Houston Post,* or an official $5-a-minute prayer, is calculated to inspire respect for nature's weapons and thereby assist in relegating the six-shooter to the rear. Personal encounters will be of occasional occurrence so long as man inhabits the earth; hence it might not be amiss for even "Christian Texas" to take an occasional lesson in the art of self-defense from men who do not gouge out eyes, chew off ears or bestride the brisket of a fallen foe and pound his face to a pumice. Whatever may be said against the "ring," it is one place where a man gets absolutely fair play, and that is more than can be said of the journalistic arena—or a mob of Baptist brethren assembled to hear one of their number back-cap his betters and descant upon the awful iniquity of the Church of Rome.

Striving to eliminate these contests of strength and skill were much like trying to tie up John Barleycorn with a Prohibition string. Man is naturally combative. As far back as we can trace his history he has rejoiced in trials of physical force. The Greeks of Homer's day fought with the terrible cestus; when Rome ruled the world every citizen was expected to be a soldier; the English could not get fighting enough in the tented field and resorted to tilt and tourney. Despite our so-called civilization man is very much a savage. "The glory of the young man is his strength," just as it was when Solomon sat upon the throne of ancient Israel, and it is well. There is hope for a warlike and aggressive people. Such are the characteristics of an advancing civilization, while dudeism is certain evidence of decay. That man who doesn't relish a rattling fight— e'en tho' it be only a dog fight—should be put in petticoats and his place in the world's economy supplied by the "coming woman." He is better qualified to lead a pug around with a pink ribbon and deodorize diapers than to sway the

sceptre of American sovereignty. Half those who damn
prize-fighting in public would swim a river to obtain a newspaper containing a write-up of an important "mill" by
rounds. When Sullivan bested Kilrain I chanced to be
stopping with a devout deacon who was particularly severe
on pugilism. He said an editor who would print an account of a prize fight ought to be put in the penitentiary—
meaning me; yet on the morning after the mill I found
that good old man with his nose buried in a newspaper, and
he wasn't reading the religious column, either. He was
fairly wallowing in counters and uppercuts, stingers and
stand-offs. He swooped down upon it like a hungry hen-
hawk on an unripe gosling, read it through to the last line,
then rolled his eyes to heaven like a calf with the colic and
wondered what this wicked old world was coming to. Had
I declined to print it he would have written me a compli-
mentary letter—and transferred his patronage to some other
paper.

There must be some vent for the combative spirit which
permeates the American people, and the glove contest is the
most satisfactory and the least dangerous yet discovered.
Statistics prove that a dozen men are killed and as many
crippled at football where one is seriously injured in the
fistic arena. At inter-collegiate football games it is customary to have a surgeon present to care for the wounded;
but I have yet to see one in attendance in his official capacity at a prize fight. In view of these facts the sanctified
hullabaloo now heard because of the pending event in the
world of pugilism is calculated to make sensible people long
for the coming of the fool-killer.

ANTONIA TEIXEIRA.

The Iconoclast is not in the habit of commenting on particular social ulcers and special sectarian scandals. It prefers to deal with broad principle rather than individual offenders. To even catalogue the sexual crimes of professing
Christians and people of social pre-eminence—to turn the
calcium for even a moment into all the gruesome closets of
"respectability" and upon every sectarian cesspool redolent
with "the odor of sanctity"—would consume the space of
such a periodical, while proving about as profitable as pointing out each festering pustule on the person of a Hot
Springs habitue trailing blindly in the wake of the Pande-

mian Venus; but once or twice in a decade a case arises so
horrible in conception, so iniquitous in outline, so damnable
in detail that it were impossible to altogether ignore it.   Such
a case has just come to light, involving Baylor University,
that Bulwark of the Baptist Church.   I fain would pass it
by, knowing as I do that a criticism, however dispassionate
and just, will be misconstrued by those good Baptist brethren who tried to muzzle me while ex-Priest Slattery foully
defamed me, and whose religion teaches them that "with
what judgment ye judge ye shall be judged; and with what
measure ye mete it shall be measured to you again."   But
on this point they have naught to fear.   Had they, for every
sneaking lie they have told about me, spawned a thousand;
and had "Brother" Slattery, in the fullness of his Baptist
Charity, branded me as a horse-thief and proved it, I could
not, tho' vindictive as Thersites and gifted with the vocabulary of a Carlyle, do even and exact justice to the case of
Antonia Teixeira.   Crimes similar in some respects have
been committed in White Chapel and on Boiler avenue;
but, to borrow from Macaulay, "When we put everything
together—sensuality, poltroonery, baseness, effrontery, mendacity, barbarity—the result is something which in a novel
we should condemn as caricature, and to which, we venture
to say, no parallel can be found in history.   It is a case
wherein "the qualities which are the proper objects of hatred, and the qualities which are the proper objects of contempt," preserve an exquisite and absolute harmony.   Three
times I have essayed to write of this enormous iniquity, this
subter-brutish crime against the chastity of childhood, and
thrice I have laid down my pencil in despair.   As there is
a depth of the sea to which the plummet will not descend, so
are there depths of human depravity which mind cannot
measure.   Language hath its limits, and even a Dante could
only liken the horrors of hell to earthly symbols.   It were
as impossible to describe in print the case of Antonia Teixeira as to etch a discord or paint a stench.   Before justice
can be done to such a subject a new language must be invented—a language whose words are coals of juniper-wood,
whose sentences are woven with a warp of aspics' fangs and
a woof of fire.

We all remember the coming to Texas of Antonia Teixeira, the dove-eyed heteroscian, and the brass-band display
made of the modest little thing by the Baptist brethren,
whose long years of missionary labor in Brazil had snatched
her from the Papal power—a veritable brand from the burning.   A tardy consent had been wrung from her widowed

mother that Antonia should be brought to Texas. The child was to be given five years' schooling, then returned to her native land to point out to her benighted Catholic countrymen the water route to the Celestial City. Relying upon this promise, the simple Brazilian woman consigned her little wild-flower to the bosom of the Baptist church. Five years! What an eternity! How they would miss her at home—how they would count the days until she returned to them, a cultured lady, as wise even as the strange priests who spoke the English tongue! It must be for the best, she thought; so the poor woman crushed her heart in the name of Christ and took up her cross. And Antonia? How bright the world before her! To be educated, and useful and honored both in this world and the world to come, instead of an ignorant little beggar about the streets of Bahia. Bearded men prayed over her and sentimental women wept to know that she was saved—saved from the purgatorium of Popery! And then she was "consecrated" and began her studies at Baylor, the duly ordained "ward of the Baptist church." Not yet 13 years old, and such honors paid her —what might she not expect in the years to be? How the poor little heart must have swelled with gratitude to the good Baptist brethren, and how she must have loved everything, animate and inanimate, that the good God had made. But ere long she found herself in Dr. Burleson's kitchen instead of the class-room. Instead of digging Greek roots she was studying the esculent tuber. Instead of being prepared for missionary work, this "ward of the Baptist church" was learning the duties of the scullion—and Dr. Burleson has informed the world through the public prints that as a servant she was not worth her board and clothes. But then she was not brought hither to sling pots, but to prepare for the saving of souls. Surely the blessed Baptist church will provide its little "ward" with board and clothes. Perhaps the poor child thought that scrubbing floors and playing under-servant was part of a liberal education, for she made no complaint to her self-constituted guardians. After some three years of the kitchen curriculum she was examined in the office of a secular official and it was there found that she had not made much progress toward effective missionary work. She had heard something of the Protestant faith and salvation by water, but did not understand it. And in two years more her "education" would be complete—the promise made to her mother redeemed! But suddenly it was discovered that the "ward of the Baptist church" was about to give birth to a babe. Day by day this mournful fact became more in evidence, and finally her dish-rag and scrub-broom studies were suspended because of a press of more important business. She was sneaked off to a private house and nothing said about her condition to the secular authorities—no steps taken to bring the destroyer of this child in short dresses to justice. But the meddlesome officials concluded to look after the "ward of the Baptist church" a little, and the poor child told them, reluctantly enough, how she had been dragged from her culinary class-room, drugged and three times criminally assaulted— how she complained, "but nothing was done about it." A medical examination demonstrated conclusively that she had been the victim of foul play. What did the aged president of Baylor, that sanctum sanctorum of the Baptist church, do about it? Did he assist in bringing to justice the man who had dared invade the sanctity of his household and despoil the duly ordained "ward of the Baptist church?" Not exactly. He rushed into print with a statement to the effect that the child was a thief and "crazy after the boys"— that he had "prayed and wept over her" without avail. Are prayers and tears the only safeguards thrown around fourteen-year-old girls at Baylor? They do those things differently in Convent schools—supplement prayers and tears with a watchful care that makes illicit intercourse practically impossible. No matter how "crazy after the boys" a girl in short dresses may be, she is not permitted to go headlong to the devil—to be torn to pieces and impregnated by some lousy and lecherous male mastodon. Dr. Burleson considered the idea that Antonia had been ravished as ridiculous, yet the doctors declare it one of the most damnable cases of outrage and laceration within their knowledge— and in matters of this kind a wicked and perverse generation is more likely to believe doctors of medicine than doctors of divinity. The students at Baylor declare that instead of being "crazy after the boys" Antonia was particularly modest and 'womanly. But had she been the brazen little thing which Dr. Burleson hastened to brand her, what were his duties in the premises: to guard her with especial care, or give the "boys" an opportunity to work their will, then turn her out with a Baptist bastard at the half-developed breast? Enciente at 14, among strangers who had promised her mother that no harm should befall her. A mother while still in short dresses, and branded in the public prints as a bawd by people who worship One who forgave Mary Magdalen! We might have expected the very devils in hell to weep for the pity of it, but "Christian charity" had

not yet reached its *ultima thule*. Another Baptist reverend
had to have his say. He was somewhat interested in the
matter, his brother having been named by Antonia as her
ravisher. This reverend gentleman tried to make it appear
that the father of her unborn child was a negro servant and
her accepted paramour. Had this been true, what an "ad."
for Baylor University—that fourteen-year-old girls committed to its care conceived children by coons! But even
Baylor did not deserve the terrible censure of Dr. Burleson's pious son-in-law, and Antonia replied to this insult
added to injury by putting a white child in evidence—a child
with the pale blue eye and wooden face characteristic of
those who thus defamed her. When the girl's condition
became known the men about town—"publicans and sinners" such as Christ sat with, preferring their society to that
of the pharisees—raised a handsome purse to provide for
her and the young Baptist she was about to bring into the
world, while those who should have guarded and protected
her were resorting to every artifice human ingenuity could
devise to blacken her name, to forestall pity, prevent charity and make an impartial trial of the case impossible.
While men who never professed religion, who never expect
to wear feathers and fly thro' Elysian fields, could not talk
to each other about the case without crying, those wearing
God's livery were eager to trample her down to the deepest
hell to preserve the credit of their denomination. If there
is anything on earth calculated to make a public prostitute
of an unfortunate girl it is the treatment the Baptist brethren
have accorded Antonia Teixeira.

At this writing (June 27) the preliminary trial awaits the
convalescence of the child mother. I would not pre-judge
the case. I know not who is the guilty man; but I do know
that this child was brought from her faraway home by men
who promised to protect her and transform her into a cultured and useful woman, and who so far neglected their duty
that she was debauched at Baylor University and her young
life forever blighted. Better a thousand times that she
should have remained in Brazil to say her pater nosters in
the Portugese tongue; better that she should have wedded
a water-carrier in her native land and reared up sturdy sons
and daughters to the Church of Rome, than to have been
transported to Texas to breed illegitimate Baptists. I do
know that at the very time "Brother" Slattery was writing
us against the awful dangers of convent schools—and im-
peaching the chastity of the Catholic sisterhoods—and the
Waco Baptists were crying "awmen"—this 14-year-old girl

was growing great with child at Baylor University! I do know that while we were being assured that among all the nuns there was not one educated woman—not one competent to superintend the education of a child—a girl was completing her third year in the greatest educational institute the Baptists of Texas can boast, and in all that time she had learned but little, and that little she could have acquired almost as well in "Hell's Half-Acre." I do know that Antonia is not the first young girl to be sent from Baylor in disgrace—that she is not the first to complain of criminal assault within its sanctified walls. I do know that should a girl meet with a mishap at a convent school the Catholic priests would not turn against her and insult her family and her race by trying to fasten the fatherhood of her unborn babe upon a negro servant. I do know that instead of trying to drive the unfortunate girl to the "Reservation" with cowardly calumnies, they would draw around her the sacred circle of the Church of Rome, and if there remained within her heart one spark of noble womanhood it would be fanned by the white wings of love and charity into ethereal flame. I do know that if Antonia Teixeira was a Catholic instead of a half-baked Baptist, every man within that church would be her brother, every woman her sister,—that every church bearing the cross would be her house of refuge. I do know that so far as Baylor University is concerned the day of its destiny is over and the star of its fate hath declined; that the brutal treatment the Brazilian child received at its hands will pass into history as the colossal crime of the age, and that generations yet to be will couple its name with curses deep as those which Roman matrons heaped on the head of Sextus Tarquinius—"he that wrought the deed of shame."

DANCING TO THE DEVIL.

THE GREAT SALTATORIAL SIN.

Just at present many "progressive" preachers are bringing all their powers to bear upon what they denominate the dance evil. Even before Sam Jones began to blackguard the ball-room in his so-called sermons, various Protestant divines were vociferously denouncing this species of divertisement as a worship of that trinity of wickedness—the World, the Flesh and the Devil; but the Cracker peddler of pseudopiety is the recognized Peter-the-Hermit of the anti-saltatorian crusade.

There was a time when it was considered a mortal sin to be merry—when professing Christians refrained from harmless jest and healthful laughter lest they displease the Deity. Some ultrapietistic people eschewed ornament, wore unbecoming clothes and cultivated an expression such as pertains to those afflicted with cramp colic or torpid livers. The idea appears to have been that by making themselves and everybody else unnecessarily miserable in this world their ecstacy would be enhanced in the great hereafter. The theater was tabooed, the ball-room placed under the ban, the euchre-deck banished and young people expected to do their courting with a solemnity befitting the making of contracts in a coffin-factory. All the joy and sweetness was crushed out of life by the iron hand of a pessimistic orthodoxy; the sunshine of the heart turned into clammy London fog by spectres born in the chaotic brain of pious fools; the pleasant valleys and purple hills transformed into monster-bearing deserts, the refreshing springs into bitter pools, the fragrant flowers into cruel throngs by those too blind to see that the cult of Christ is the law of love, the unfailing fount of joy, the bloom of eternal spring, the song of birds and the merry laughter of men and maids.

But eventually the world rebelled against the pessimistic brand of piety—concessions were made, perforce, to the renaissance of reason. Gradually the dark clouds fled from the hills and the dismal mists from the valleys; the crash of cymbals and the rythmic pulse of dancing feet supplanted groans and moans—again birds sang, flowers bloomed and perfumed fountains cast their grateful spray in the terrestrial vineyard of our God. It was no longer a crime to be happy, laughter ceased to be a sin—a sunny face came to be regarded as an outward evidence of an inward grace. Toleration born of intelligence budded and burgeoned like the proverbial green bay tree, and men whose fathers thought a fiddle but another Red Piper to lure souls to hell, felt their hearts swell with paternal pride as they looked on happy sons and graceful daughters marking time with nimble feet to music that swept with Orpheus-figures every chord of the human heart.

But as there still be men who believe the world is flat, so are there others, even in this enlightened age, who take it for granted that a loving God revels in the sweet incense of sighs, is pleased with a paean of groans—that a beneficent Deity looks with dire displeasure on every bright oasis

Life's worn voyageur finds between the cradle and the grave. They are preachers and teachers who have failed to keep pace with the procession—who can not realize that religion, like all else called into being by the Creator, must be progressive. Poor preterists, with their faces to the past, they would repace every step in the path of human progress, and across the sunlight of the noon cast the shadows of the night.

Most of these anti-dancing dominies make uncompromising war upon the so-called evil in all its forms, from the stately minuet to the Irish jig, from the stomach contortions of the Midway Plaisance to the nervous "jerks" of the Methodist camp-meeting; but the latest preacher to declaim against the ballroom is not quite so bigoted as his crusading brethren. We gather from the Galveston *News* that Rev. J. W. Lowber has been holding forth on the subject in the Central Christian Church of that city, and some of his pious observations may be worth attention by this, the ministerial organ of Texas. We approach him with considerable caution, however, for, by whatever name they are known—whether as Christians, Disciples or Campbellites—the members of that disorganized organization are great " 'sputers," and relish nothing so much as an interminable debate, whether anent forms of baptism or the shortcomings of other sects. Parson Lowber is evidently harboring the hallucination that when he has eliminated dancing, as now indulged in by the sons and daughters of men, the world will be redeemed and the millennium due. Like the Prohibitionist who approved of punch if the spirits were left out, he can tolerate dancing if each sex will but indulge in terpsichorean exercise by itself. He has ascertained, in some mysterious manner which he does not divulge, that when Miriam, the sister of Moses, tripped the light fantastic she had no partner to caress her patent health corset, and that David, the son of Jesse, indulged in the stag-dance. That would appear to most people about as unsatisfactory as a single-handed game of baseball or a boxing bout with one's own shadow—pre-eminently stale, flat and unprofitable. Parson Lowber has decided, in the goodness of his heart, to permit that kind of gayety, but when

> "youth and beauty meet
> To chase the glowing hours with flying feet,"

he becomes alarmed for the morals of the community and relieves Jeremiah of his job. He assures us that "if men and women will dance apart no harm can ensue." We fear

the worthy parson is theorizing in utter ignorance of conditions—that he has never accompanied Dr. Parkhurst in
his nocturnal visits to the Tenderloin district, and witnessed
the can-can as danced for the special delectation of doctors
of divinity. Evidently he has never participated in the hilarious "stag-party," observed the

> "Midnight shout and revelry,
> Tipsy dance and jollity,"

that characterize these gatherings, and compared the wild
orgies with the Chesterfieldian courtesy and princely bearing of the same men when subjected to the mild censorship
of woman's eyes. Each sex values the good opinion of
the other, and right acting begets right thinking. The correctness of this premise conceded, the conclusion is plain
that the good of the race demands that the sexes be brought
together as much as possible, whether at work or play—that
it were unwise if not unsafe to leave either to its own resources.

Parson Lowber assures us that "the modern dance is a
great waste of time and money." Perchance he has never
heard that "all work and no play makes Jack a dull boy"—
has not suspected that some preachers toil so hard to attain
a little cheap notoriety that they can not comprehend the
plain teachings of Christ. Is time expended in social pleas-
ures really wasted? Is it not rather true that time is wasted
when devoted to the attainment of wealth in excess of our
needs, to foolish dogmatizing, to denouncing a harmless
custom as old as the human race—while children are suf-
focating in the slums of our great cities, men are hesitating
between beggary and crime, and the face of the world is
wet with tears? Oh ye pitiful triflers who would be teachers
—heaven-ordained doctors who give a moribund world
bread pills to ward off the Black Death! Ye Davids of the
new Israel, are there no Goliaths of Gath, that ye must
stone sheep?

These soldiers of the Lord who are valiantly charging
down upon the dance and euchre-deck remind me of a
hound with which I once hunted wolves. His lust for blood
before we flushed our quarry was terrible to contemplate,
and every cow and calf along his route was made to feel his
fangs; but when the great black beast turned savagely at
bay the hound would neither bark nor bite. So some
preachers assail society's venial faults with fury, but when
the host of hell stands forth beneath the blood-red banner

of Greed, these lions of the Lord "roar as softly as suck-ing doves."

Is money wasted when employed to bring elasticity to the limb, brightness to the eye and happiness to the heart? A greater than Parson Lowber has assured us that "the spend-thrift saves, the miser is prodigal." The man who devotes every shining hour to the service of Mammon, "the least erect of all the angelic host that fell from heaven," begrudg-ing every moment claimed by the goddess of Joy, is the real spendthrift. He squanders, not his substance, but his life—turns his back upon the fond delights of the Vale of Tempe and wanders to the end of his days in the burning desert. I fear that Parson Lowber is more pedant than philosopher—that he has overlooked the true significance of life. While doctors of medicine are beseeching us to abate that unre-mitting toil which wears out hand and heart and brain before their time, here is a doctor of divinity reproving us for every breathing spell in the "demnition grind." While philosophers insist that a life ungemmed with social pleas-ures is not worth the living, here is a preacher pleading that every hour is "wasted" if not burthened with a care.

Parson Lowber objects to the sexes dancing together be-cause it has, he thinks, a tendency to sensuality and is a severe strain on the Seventh Commandment. That a man should take hold of a young lady's hand, touch her waist with his finger tips and guide her thro' the mazes of the dreamy waltz, fills the good doctor's head with foolish dreams of a world forever lost in the wild chaos of lust. He has somewhere heard of mesmerism, and fears the dancer will exercise that strange power on his fair compan-ion to her hurt. If he will but reflect a little he may con-clude that there's infinitely more danger in the "sitting-down waltz" in a darkened parlor than in the salutations of the brilliantly lighted ball-room. Dancing may be of the devil, but there is no intimation in Holy Writ that the Prince of Darkness ever danced. He did not cause the downfall of Mother Eve by the "arm-clutch" or the poetry of motion. According to Milton, Ithuriel found him "squat like a toad," distilling poison in the ear of Adam's credulous mate,—and we may safely assume that most of the wreck and ruin since wrought among the gentler sex has been by the quiet distillment of poison by human toads in the ears of confid-ing maids.

The truth is there is a tendency to sensuality in most things which minister either to the physical or spiritual life of men. Even that good living—of which the average preacher is so fond—inflames the passions, and the sacred music which throbs thro' our great churches makes voluptuaries as well as votaries. While it is true, as Parson Lowber points out, that some girls trace their downfall to dancing, others attribute it to singing in fashionable choirs and the hypnotic influence of popular preachers. The ancient Greeks recognized two kinds of music—that which makes soldiers and that which makes sybarites. The savagery in man may be refined away by education and religion; but sensuality grows with civilization's growth and strengthens with its strength. Generally speaking, that which tends to make man less a servant of Mars tends to make him more a slave of Venus. No savage nation was ever noted for licentiousness—that is the curse of civilization.

The bewildering beauty of a summer night's high noon; the melody of a half-awakened mocking-bird calling to its mate; the sensuous perfume of dew-bespangled flowers, were lost upon the savage, solely animal; but they sink into the supersensitive soul like Cleopatra's mad'ning kiss and burn within the blood with celestico-infernal fire. In such moods—when the whole being is ablaze with passion, half demoniac, half divine—man climbs Parnassus' rugged steeps and stands, poised in mid-heaven, like a star. In such moods the orator is gifted with lips of gold and in the poet's heart there rings the melody of the spheres. In such moods man hears the still small voice of Omnipotent God giving a new message to mankind, and lo! another sacred book is born—another Mecca established as fingerpost for toiling millions treading, with bleeding feet, the path of Life! But not every man may drive Apollo's steeds and safely guide the chariot of the sun. The same strange power that lifts man to the highest heaven may dash him to the deepest hell. Love that should illume the world may become lawless as that of a Grecian god, and Promethean fire perverted is a destructive brand—the Star of Bethlehem becomes a blighting thunderbolt and man a demon instead of a demi-god.

Clearly we cannot exterminate everything which causes the sexes to gravitate to each other, else were the Song of Solomon hushed, beauty banished, poetry forbidden and the grander rhythm of the great prose masters—that sensuous tide which bears us away on its bosom

"O'er the ocean wild and wide—"

placed under the ban. The great sun itself—that parent and perennial store-house of passion—were blotted from the heavens, and a lawless universe reduced to cosmic dust—go floating once more thro' space in snow-cold purity!

Marriage is a good or it is an ill. If good, those things which lead man to choose a mate and rear up sons to perpetuate his name, should be encouraged rather than repressed. If the dance drives some to lawless love, it must, in the very nature of things, impel more to matrimony. If contact of the sexes in the waltz, the music, the mesmeric touch of hands and wild thrill of heart pulsing against heart arouse those longings common to all animate nature, then indeed is the ball-room the enemy of celibacy and the builder of homes; for we must concede that in a country professedly Christian—and which sends missionaries to the heathen—the procreative passion will go right as the rule and wrong as the exception. I know that it will be urged by some pseudo-psychologists—who have but a vague suspicion of what really ails them—that love and passion are as distinct as the daylight and the dark; that, to borrow from Plato, there is a Uranian as well as a Pandemian Venus. Love purified of all earthly dross is a pretty conception, but it's a barren ideality. "Love is love forevermore," and, refine it as we may, disguise it as we will, the basic principle of that force which draws the sexes together is the procreative passion. When drunk with the perfume and beauty of the blush-rose we think not of the compost in which its roots lie buried. When the wine of Samos sparkles in the crystal cup, or the must foams

"'Round the white feet of laughing girls"

we forget the mouldering bones that nurtured the purple clusters. But compost and bones are there, and right well the gardener knows that but for them the great white light of the moon and the red glory of the sun would beat and break in vain—that the rose would not enrich the vagrant air, nor the vine pour its empurpled tide into the veins of kings. We think not of the Creator's divine command to be fruitful and multiply—nor of the method he employs to compel obedience—when, amid a wilderness of flowers, the fair bride and gallant groom accept the sacred vows; but the command is there, and the wedding-bells send answer back—"God's will be done." The sexes must be brought together under circumstances mutually agreeable ere Hymen's torch be lit at glowing eyes and fanned to flame with the soft sighs of desiring souls; so—"On with the dance."

Having formally taken the ministers of America under

my apostolic protection, I feel that I am, in some degree, responsible for their errors—that it is my duty to give Brother Lowber a little gratuitous advice. If all other ministers who are denouncing dancing and kindred social customs—whose significance they cannot comprehend—should hear and heed, so much the better. I have thought seriously of calling them together for a course of lectures on the mortal sin of trying to nullify the teachings of the great Nazarene; but the time is not yet opportune.

Do not take it for granted that whatever pleases the people originated in perdition. As the whole is greater than a part, so is it wiser. The cumulative wisdom of sixty centuries—the customs of both savagery and civilization—approves the dance as a healthy method of diversion. True piety does not consist in preventing other people enjoying themselves. If you realize that you cannot indulge in progressive euchre without becoming a shoe-string gambler or bunco-steerer, or visit a ball-room without contracting an uncontrollable desire to see what Parkhurst saw and feel what Parkhurst felt, just spread your pin-feathers and fly from temptation instead of imitating the Son of Man by valiantly facing and overcoming it; but bear ever in mind that in the making of man the Almighty employs more than one kind of clay. Instead of wasting your strength trying to abolish the ball-room—an institution whose good equals its evil—turn your batteries upon those which are wholly bad. Battle against Frauds and Fakes, Hypocrites and Humbugs. Assail Poverty, Ignorance and Crime, hell's great triumvirate. When these arch-angels of evil are driven from the earth it will be time enough to abolish the social dance, burn the euchre-deck, destroy the stage and protect the Christian Sabbath from "desecration" by peddlers of hokey-pokey and popcorn balls. Doubtless the devil sometimes lurks in the ball-room; but before seeking him there, oh my brethren, let us be sure he is not snugly ensconced in the church, unctuously crying amen to the utterances of some perspiring pulpiteer who is trying to lead the armies of Israel off on a wild chase after some harmless jack-o'-lantern —while the legions of evil overrun the earth. Don't make grand-stand plays from the pulpit. Notoriety may be necessary to an actor, but does not increase the sphere of usefulness of a Campbellite preacher. If you really desire to enlarge the Lord's vineyard so as to include the unprofitable soil of Galveston Island—and are quite sure the Wharf company will not seize the Ship of Zion in part payment of the dockage—squeeze the groans and moans and chronic heartaches out of your faith and fill it to overflowing with sunshine and with flowers. Millions of tender-hearted people remain away from church simply because they cannot bear to witness the chronic gloom of those who have made their peace with God—the unhappiness of those poor creatures who are doomed to inherit an orthodox heaven. Preach that God is love; that our Father in Heaven, who watches over the very sparrows, wants his children to enjoy themselves even here on earth, and gives the means if they will but wisely employ them. Teach the religion of good living, which is also right living—the religion of beauty and joy and use. Hitch your chariot to a star instead of to a mole, and fill the land with light instead of darkness, with hope instead of despair. Think you the Creator poured his splendors forth on land and sea for eyes all dimmed with tears? that he filled the bul-bul's pulsing throat with melody divine and composed old ocean's never ceasing anthem for those deafened with their own moans?

I wouldn't preach five minutes to a man who looked as tho' his religion was hurting him—who seemed sorry he was going to be saved. When I deliver the "glad tidings of great joy" to a fellow mortal I want him to act like a poor miserable pariah who's just drawn the capital prize in a lottery, instead of treating the message as tho' it were a protested draft. And when I get thro' pumping saving grace into him I want him to go out into the world and add to its gladness instead of its gloom. I want him to object to bear-baiting because it hurts bruin, and not because it pleases the boys. No matter whether I make a Campbellite of him or a sure-enough Baptist, I want him to recognize a brother Christian in every man who is trying, in spirit and in truth, to serve the Lord. And having expended my time and energy to snatch him as a brand from the burning and formally enroll him in the army of Israel, if I find that he's such a consummate ass as to keep blazing away with his little escopeta at progressive euchre, the arm-clutch, the stage, ball-room and other unimportant social beetles, while the legions of Lucifer, with visors down and spears in rest are crowding us to the wall, I'll take a club and kill him.

THE A. P. A. IDIOCY.

DEFAMATION OF AMERICAN DAILIES.

Perhaps the most ominous of the signs of the times, so far as this Republic is concerned, is the birth of that organization known as the American Protective Association. True, the order is not formidable as yet—is of but little importance in the world of politics; but history teaches that the more ridiculous a craze or foolish a fad, the more readily it finds a following. Of course the A. P. A. cannot long survive. It's a child of Darkness and must perish with the coming of the Dawn. There is no valid reason for its existence, and the law of social as well as of physical evolution makes it imperative that the useless and unfit should perish from the earth. So perished Know-nothingism, and so will pass this new avatar of religious bigotry and political folly which has found a temporary lodgment in a land boasting liberty of conscience, beneath the flag of the free. But, though the days of the A. P. A. be few and full of trouble, it may, like the cholera scourge, or an epidemic of diarrhoea, do an infinite deal of harm before it is eradicated. Its tendency is to promote a religious war and wreck the mighty political fabric bequeathed us by our fathers, to crush religious liberty and turn back the hands on the dial of time a thousand years. Its avowed object is the practical disfranchisement of Catholics, not only in this country, but throughout the world. The movement has already become "international," if we may credit the boasts of its leaders, which proves that it was not begotten of American patriotism, as at first pretended, but born of religious bigotry. The following paragraph, taken from the illiterate and intolerant address of the president of the supreme council of the order, delivered at Milwaukee last May, is suggestive:

If coming generations are to be secure in the enjoyment of their liberties, we must drive the enemy not from the United States to Canada, nor from Canada to the United States—not from the new world to the old, nor from the old to the new—we must drive them off the face of the earth; must destroy the devil's brood, root and branch, by the mighty power of A. P. A.ism.

Think of an "international," of an "universal American Protective Association"—of Americans, interested only in preserving intact the liberties bequeathed them by those sworn enemies of monarchy, the Revolutionary heroes, assisting the Czar of Russia to preserve his crown and the Akhoond of Swat his harem! The movement is not "American;" it is Protestant, pure and simple. Its *raison d'etre* is religious instead of political. Its object is not the enforcement of the fundamental law of the land, which declares that "No religious test shall ever be required as a qualification to any office of public trust under the United States;" but, by uniting all Protestant denominations in an "anti-Papist" crusade, to "destroy the devil's brood, root and branch"—to "drive them off the face of the earth." Unless all signs be misleading and the utterances of its duly accredited leaders mere doting jargon, it is the spiritual rather than the supposed temporal power of the Pope that is troubling the A. P. A. That organization is warring upon Roman Catholic theology far more vindictively than upon "Roman Catholic corruption" in politics. Its agony is fully as great when a Protestant sends his child to a convent school as when "Papal emissaries" capture a municipal government. Pat's sister in a nunnery gives it as much concern as Pat himself on the police force. It harangues with far more gusto of the immortality of some unworthy priest than of the election of a "Papist" constable in a Catholic precinct.

Patriotic Americans have much to say anent the necessity of suppressing such blatant anarchists as Herr Most and Lucy Parsons; yet the doctrines enunciated by the A. P. A. are infinitely more dangerous to the peace and perpetuity of the Republic. Their avowed object is the division of the American people into two hostile classes—and Christ assures us that "Every kingdom divided against itself is brought to desolation." If this be true, either the A. P. A. or the government born of our fathers' blood and sanctified by our mothers' tears, must be destroyed. If we accept the dicta of the Deity we must class the A. P. A. organizers with Johann Most and Benedict Arnold. Nor are these enemies of the American government willing to wait for the disfranchisement of their Catholic fellow citizens by due process of law—the change of the federal constitution by peaceful methods and passage of a disabling act by a fanatical congress. They are already preaching war—a war of extermination! Here is a paragraph—clipped at random —from the most pretentious A. P. A. journal extant, the official organ of the order at San Francisco:

In Rochester, New York, a bad A. P. A. man shot and killed a good Catholic. The chief regret is that he had not a magazine gun instead of a single shooter.

A thousand similar expressions might be culled from the

utterances of A. P. A. orators and editors, signifying that the Protestant who murders a Catholic pleases God and renders his country a service—that having killed one Catholic he should be encouraged to slaughter more. Evidently we would have a delightful Christian love-feast should the A. P. A. become strong enough to safely embark in the wholesale butchery business—in the name of a loving Christ and the federal constitution! But let an American citizen who sees the plan of salvation thro' a different telescope—and who has a sister or daughter in a convent— shy a brick at some foul-mouthed blackguard for calumniating the Roman Catholic sisterhoods, and forthwith a terrible wail goes up from this "noble order of Christian patriots" that the Pope is trying to throttle free speech by means of a pretorian guard of brutal bulldozers. The A. P. A. willfully and with malice prepense provokes the Catholic until forbearance ceases to be a virtue, then points to his violence as an evidence of Papal iniquity. A large proportion of American Catholics are of the combative Irish blood. The terrible injustice which Ireland has for centuries suffered at the hands of orthodox England has not made them particularly friendly to the Protestant faith; yet so deeply are they imbued with American ideas; such respect have they for the right of free speech, that A. P. A. orators and editors may defame them in every possible manner— may question their patriotism and revile their religion—and do so in comparative safety. The patience of the American Catholics under the jeers and sneers, the willful calumnies and cowardly insults of the A. P. A. has no parallel in religious history since the persecutions suffered by the primitive Christians. Why they do not procure a few "magazine guns" and fill the hides of their persecutors so full of holes that they couldn't be stuffed with stovewood, I am unable to understand.

In the greatest exponent of A. P. Aism—in which Protestant Christianity and American patriotism are supposed to be united for the attainment of salvation here and hereafter, we find such headlines as the following: "Pap for Papist Pugs;" "A Specimen Catholic Brute;" "Fearful Roman Catholic Immorality;" "Papists and False Oaths;" "Jerked to Jesus;" "Illegitimacy in Rome;" "Romanists Lie with Impunity," etc.,—and the articles are worthy of their captions. Such is religious toleration and Christian charity as interpreted by the A. P. A.—such its idea of the cult established by Christ for the purpose of securing "peace on earth, good will to men." The proceedings of every ecumen-

ical council, the official acts of every Pope, the utterances of
every writer of Roman Catholic theology for a thousand
years have been scanned for evidence that the Mother Church
is the enemy of both civil and religious liberty—and that by
men who would disfranchise American citizens for worshipping God according to the dictates of their own conscience,
and murder them with "magazine guns" because of a difference of opinion anent the Real Presence! I am not much
in favor of a press censorship nor the abridgement of the
right of free speech; but I do think that men who persist in
a deliberate attempt to precipitate a civil war should be
hanged for treason. My bump of veneration is not so abnormal that it wears holes in the steeple crown of my Mexican hat; still I hold that the orator or editor who flagrantly
defames and systematically vilifies any religious cult considered sacred by millions of law-abiding men, is a blasphemous brute, and that it would be entirely consistent with the
American idea of liberty to clap a cast-iron muzzle on him
and lose the key.

It has been charged by the A. P. A. that the Iconoclast
is a "Baptist periodical," hence "its utterances should be regarded with suspicion by all patriotic Americans." Of
course every journal that declines to act as cat's-paw to pull
political chestnuts out of the fire, for the "Ape," is trying to
supplant an American President with an Italian Pope. I
am not surprised that, having demonstrated their ignorance
of the history of the Church of Rome and their utter inability to comprehend the genius of the American government,
the A. P. A. bosses should accuse a journal bearing the
suggestive title of Iconoclast of being a "Papal periodical."
A Catholic Iconoclast were almost as great a curiosity as a
feathered elephant—or an English organization for the protection of American liberties! With the controversy between Protestantism and Catholicism I have no more to do
than with that between Buddhism and Brahmanism. I
care never a copper whether a man takes his theology from
the Pope or Dalai-Lama, John Calvin or Joseph Smith, so
long as he doesn't persist in mixing it with American politics. But when one religious body presumes to monopolize the honors and emoluments of this government to the
exclusion of another; when an attempt is made in the name
of any religious cult or creed to override the constitution of
our common country; when a conspiracy is entered into by
malicious busy-bodies and aspiring demagogues to disfranchise worthy American citizens because of their religious
opinions, somebody is going to get the iconoclastic gaffles

driven into them so deep that the protruding points may be utilized as a hat rack.

But the Iconoclast does not stand alone to receive the destructive thunderbolts and sizzling scorn of that "noble order of Christian patriots" which proposes to play smash with the Pope and "destroy the devil's brood, root, and branch"—by a combination of "open Bibles" and breech-loaders. The leading article in the *A. P. A. Magazine* for July—whose politico-religious mission is ladling out a very disgusting brand of "Pap for Papist Pugs"—is an "Address by Rev. J. Q. A. Henry, San Francisco." From it I clip the following paragraph:

Time forbids that I should give the extent to which the Papacy has subsidized the press. There is scarcely a daily of note throughout the entire country whose staff is not controlled by the Jesuits. At the elbow of reporter and editor sits the Jesuitical inquisitor to see that nothing is reported or published detrimental to the Papal church. It is shocking how unfair to Protestantism and diabolically sectarian the press has become. It cringes in the presence of the hierarchy, and enforces its unscrupulous bidding with the servility of a whipped spaniel.

I dislike very much to say anything disrespectful of a preacher; still, respect for "the cloth" does not overcome my suspicion that the reverend gentleman is an unmitigated liar. In fact I know from personal experience in daily journalism that such is the case. I have served on nine daily papers—ranging in importance from the St. Louis *Globe-Democrat* to the Houston *Post;* have occupied every position from police reporter to editor, and never did a Catholic priest attempt to shape one sentence of the ten thousand columns that have passed from my pencil into print. I have treated of many questions in which Catholics were deeply interested, and never did I catch a glimpse of that "Jesuitical inquisitor." Never did Catholic—priest or layman—suggest what I should say or leave unsaid; but I have had the Protestant inquisitors at my elbow often enough, God knows. They have been persistent, meddlesome, dictatorial; and whenever I declined to allow them to manage my department they tried to get me discharged. In all my journalistic experience I was never told by a Catholic priest of a scandal in a Protestant church; but just let a Catholic priest go wrong, and four-fifths of the Protestant preachers make it their business, not only to inform the press, but to insist that the affair be "shown up" in its most unfavorable aspect. These are facts with which every daily newspaper man is familiar. Call up the editors and reporters of this country and they will tell you that the Catholic priests and Jewish Rabbis meddle with their work but little; but that, with the possible exception of the pot-house politicians and crank scribblers, the Protestant clergy is the greatest nuisance with which they have to deal. That politicians and monopolists sometimes subsidize a daily paper is doubtless true; but this corruption is not carried to the extent popularly supposed. The press is often foolish, but usually honest. Of course there are corrupt men on the press, as well as in the pulpit. I have heard jackleg reporters boast of tips received from Protestant preachers to secure spread-eagle reports of their sermons; but never did I hear either editor or reporter intimate that he had received a dollar from a priest except in the way of legitimate business that would bear the light of publicity. Of course this does not prove that priests never influence the utterances of the press; but it does signify that the preachers are not in a position to point the finger of scorn.

My opinion is that the Rev. Jeremiah Querulous Ananias Henry is guilty of a deliberate calumny, and were I now editing a daily paper I would have him indicted for criminal libel and put into the penitentiary where such reckless liars and assassins of reputation properly belong. Such a gratuitous insult offered the American press simply proves that I sized the order up correctly when I labeled it the Aggregation of Pusillanimous Asses. No organization that has undertaken such a herculean task as the practical disfranchisement and reduction to political peonage of one-seventh of the American people, will, if it possess as much sense as an acephalous louse, deliberately antagonize a power that can ridicule it out of existence, that can drive it off the earth with goosequills—despite its "magazine guns." The A. P. A. has taken plenty of rope, and if it have sufficient sense to tie a knot will inevitably hang itself. And the daily press will, if it possess one glimmering spark of American manhood, assist at the obsequies. Here is an organization which has defied its power and spat in its face. What will the daily press do about it? Will it play the "whipped spaniel" and lick the feet that trample upon it? Or will it hit this politico-religious monstrosity one biff between the eyes and send it back to the foul shades of hell from which it sprung?

GROVER'S NEW GIRL.

BABIES AND BOOT-LICKS.

We gather from the press dispatches that "at precisely 4:30 p. m. by the doctor's watch," on the seventh day of the seventh month of the year of grace, 1895, a third girl baby was born to President and Mrs. Cleveland. Regardless of the Malthusian theory of population—and the existence of more girls in America than can reasonably hope to acquire dutiful husbands—we hasten to extend congratulations. It is possible that a male heir would have better pleased our "liege, lord and sovereign born;" still, the man who holds three queens in the game of life—with the privilege of calling for cards—should feel encouraged. The new addition to the President's household appears to have taken the Nation by surprise, and it is but now slowly recovering from the shock.

The Clevelands have evidently learned something by experience. They have learned that many daily newspapers have no appreciation of the sanctity of the family circle or respect for the modesty which is the glory of motherhood—that common decency demands that these literary vultures and foolish Boswells be kept resolutely at bay. Ere President Cleveland had been married six months, the daily press —that "professional educator" and self-styled "moulder of public opinion"—began to speculate on paternal possibilities. It was recalled that before becoming President he had acquired a procreative record of which he appeared not a little proud, and that he was not a man to weary in well-doing; hence, if by any chance, a Peeping Tom reporter caught a glimpse of Mrs. Cleveland clad in a maternity gown, or even a hot-weather Mother Hubbard, the great American Commonwealth was thrown into a state of painful expectancy bordering hysteria. The family physician was beset by interrogation points wherever he turned, while seamstresses and house-servants were subjected to rigid cross-examination by enterprising Washington correspondents who should have been humanely killed. If a midwife or obstetrician was seen about the premises the world was advised thereof by wire. If a haberdasher's boy delivered a package at the White House he was fairly mobbed by reporters eager to learn if it contained safety-pins or material available for diapers. The physique of the "first lady of the land" was observed as closely and com-

mented upon as freely as that of a Blue Grass brood-mare,
and the slightest tendency to embonpoint called forth column telegrams, editorial leaders and "smart" paragraphs.
Speculation anent the probable sex of the new-comer was
freely indulged in by papers of professed respectability, and
the approaching accouchement became the subject of conversation alike in the gilded drawing-room and the dingy
"doggery." I am told that bets were laid on the sex of the
babe to be, and pools sold on the date of its debut.

Time after time the wiseacres of the press were disappointed, but that only redoubled their vigilance. It is said
that a watched kettle never boils; but to even this rule
there are exceptions, and the Cleveland household was
eventually blessed with a babe—a fuzzy-wuzzy little barbarian, in no wise distinguishable from a thousand other babes
born on the same day. But if the little bundle of bawl that
lay mewling and puking in its nurse's arms had been a rein-
carnation of the Buddha, or even the Christ—re-born in a
mansion instead of a manger, of pseudo-patrician instead of
unquestioned proletarian parentage—the American press
could not have expressed more concern. Hourly bulletins
informed the awe-struck universe of the condition of the
mother, the state of mind of the father and progress made
by the young pilgrim.

"Baby Cleveland awoke at 11.30 and wept softly."
"The baby smiled intelligently and coo-cooed to her happy father."

These are specimen bits of the intellectual goose-liver pie
served up by our journalistic caterers to a public boasting
itself "heir of all the ages and foremost in the files of time."
What caused Baby Ruth to indulge in that soft wailing cry
which echoed and re-echoed round the world by wire, has
never been satisfactorily explained. Perhaps some faint
adumbration of an idea that, through no fault of hers, she
had been precipitated into a world where fools predominate
broke her heart. Her "coo-coo" remains as much a mystery as her tears, the attempt of etymologists to prove it an
infantile form of "cuckoo" having signally failed. By unre-
mitting attention to duty, the doctors manager to save both
mother and child—even pulled the old man through without much difficulty; but for a long time the general public
languished. The strain upon its nervous forces had been
abnormal; but the wonderful recuperative powers of nature
at length asserted themselves and society was safe. Had
the first Cleveland baby been a boy, excess of joy might
have proved fatal to a nation founded by those who taught

the equality of men and held kings in contempt. Had it been two boys the sun would not only have stood still upon some occidental Gibeon and the moon in a cisatlantic valley of Ajalon, but have stuck fast and refused thenceforth to shine upon the other half of the earth. That Mrs. Cleveland did not die of vexation, nor the male progenitor of the young "princess" go gunning for various press correspondents, "able editors" and other purveyors of such godless gush over an accomplishment to which most married couples are equal, argues a patience beside which the patriarch of Uz were but a querulous dyspeptic. The third candidate for colic and carpet tacks to appear in the "Stuffed Prophet's" household was not heralded by "scare" headlines. No pools were sold on the day it would appear, no sesterces laid by chivalrous American soverigns on the question of its sex.

"Silently as the daylight comes when night is done,
And the crimson streak on ocean's cheek grows into the great sun,"

the little wanderer from No Man's Land entered this vale of tears and unostentatiously took up life's trials. The sacred pre-natal secret was guarded as closely as tho' it were some hideous crime, lest the reporters once more come prying about kitchen windows, "pumping" garrulous serving-maids and listening at key-holes to catch the first faint cry of a new-born babe. A modest matron dislikes to have a tribe of hoodlums measuring her girdle and speculating on the probabilities of parturition; so it was not until a domestic, finding the secret too hard to hold, "told a neighbor's girl" of the new arrival that the press correspondents realized that another crisis in the world's history was at hand. But although the public was spared the vulgar speculation and barbaric horn-blowing that preceded the arrival of other babes "born in the purple," it could by no possible precaution on the part of the modest mother escape the deluge of post-natal ditch-water and disgusting hog-wash. Here is a specimen, clipped from that owl of American journalism and representative "public educator," the Dallas *News*:

Cosy Gray Gables was batned in warm sunlight to-day and the early existence of the new Miss Cleveland, the personage in whom the residents of Buzzard's Bay are most interested, is marked by bright, pleasant weather. Dr. Bryant reported that Mrs. Cleveland and the little one are resting quietly and that everything is progressing finely. He will add nothing except that the newcomer is a "fine little girl." In company with Joseph Jefferson, Mr. Cleveland spent nearly all day trout fishing at East Sandwich, where Mr. Jefferson has a private stream. The party left early in the day and did not return until nearly 6 o'clock. Ruth and Esther did not drive with their nurses to the village this noon, as they have done almost every day since their arrival at Gray Gables, nor were the horses sent to the postoffice; but a messenger was dispatched on foot after the mail. The children remained at their play, often chattering as they ran about the piazzas and lawn over the little sister so recently introduced to them. Both children seem delighted with the idea of having another little one in the household.

The existence of "warm sunlight" on a July day will strike the average reader as a phenomenon well worth recording—even wiring across the continent. Warm sunlight and wet water prove that nothing is impossible in Nature. We are pleased to learn that the omens were auspicious at the birth of the Cleveland babe, portending prosperity and a life all whose paths are peace. Had one J. S. Hogg been born while the warm sunlight gilded the paternal cabin with supernal glory and rested like a benediction upon the softly murmuring pines, instead of in the midst of a March storm that knocked the pillows out of broken window panes and piled the cow-path with broken boughs and general rubbish until it resembled an interior view of Riggins' head, or the English language after a criminal assault upon it by " J. K. Street, journalist"—whoever that may be,—what a world of woe and worry, trials and tribulations might have been spared the Lone Star State! That Dr. Bryant declines to give it further information than that the babe may some day wear bloomers—and "everything is progressing finely"—is the apology which the press offers the public for not furnishing full particulars. The doctor's curt refusal to divulge all the delicate secrets of the sick-room to be exploited in double-leaded type is probably a great disappointment to many people; still it entitles him to the eternal gratitude of every mother, present and potential. The same spirit of morbid curiosity which caused crowds to assemble to see *le Grande Monarque* dress and undress himself largely prevails even among the American people, where it has been so prurient that the daily press finds it profitable to violate the canons of common decency. That President Cleveland should almost immediately leave the house, not to devote a few moments to important public business, but to spend the entire day trout-fishing in a play-actor's "private stream" (where is Henry George?) while his new-born babe was battling for a hold on life and the mother far within the pale of danger, would suggest subterbrutishness to any but a press correspondent. But then we must not judge by the highest altruistic standard a man who runs largely to bowels and little to brains. The gander carefully guards his unfledged goslings, the tiger keeps watch and ward over his pur-blind progeny, but who ever saw Taurus take an active interest in the new-born bovine?

But more important than all else, perhaps, is the information afforded us by an enlightened public press to the effect that Ruth and Esther did not drive to the village with their nurses, as was their wont, but remained at play, "chattering as they ran about the piazzas and lawn over the little sister so recently introduced to them." (Lindley Murray being already dead, the architect of the foregoing sentence in our "great public educator" cannot be indicted for homicide.) We might have expected them to discuss Mother Goose's Melodies, Coin's Financial School, the latest society novel and other light literature adapted to nascent minds. The fact that they preferred to talk of something tangible—to discuss conditions rather than theories—proves that they have risen above that photoplasmic or rudimentary state of the mental faculties occupied by the Trilbyites, the patrons of the Houston *Post* and those semi-vegetable polyps who absorb a kind of intellectual circus lemonade—with a sock in it—from that great tank of orthodox wiggletails yclept the *Baptist Standard*. We are pleased to learn that Ruth and Esther approved of the newcomer. Had they decided that it was *de trop* of course it would be instantly killed—or perhaps consigned to the tender care of Baylor University to be "educated for Baptist missionary work in Brazil."

We are further informed that "the horses were not sent to the postoffice, but a messenger was dispatched on foot after the mail." How fortunate that in raking the great round earth for rubbish, the Associated Press—that busy collector of compost—caught this important item! Otherwise, should the world wobble in its orbit and "planets and suns flame lawless thro' the sky," we might never suspect the reason. Given a cause, even Dr. Burleson might figure out an effect. We know now that the nigger employed at Gray Gables to go errands actually hoofed it to the post-office and "toted" the presidential mail-pouch, instead of driving—that he did not even ride a bike or bestride a brindle mule. Thus day by day does the diurnal press add to the mighty domain of human Knowledge and drive the monster Ignorance further into the desert. Knowledge is power, if we may believe the old copy-books, and the Archimedean lever may yet move the world.

But why criticise the press for performing its legitimate

function—that of industriously catering to a depraved public appetite for toads? If the people did not crave and pay for such intellectual ditch-water it would not be collected at great expense and pumped into them—much as the Lagado doctor inflated the colicky canine!"

The birth of babies in the Cleveland household is of no more importance than the appearance on this planet of what a high official of the present plutocratic administration calls "the spawn of the wayside cabin"—of which Lincoln was an example. In fact, if we may judge the future by the past, the "spawn" is likely to fill a larger niche in this world's economy than is the offspring of My-Policy Presidents; yet the press of this country—where every man is supposed to be a sovereign—indulge in more unmitigated gush over a Cleveland babe than does that of Russia over the birth of an hereditary Tsar. In Great Britian when a woman is confined whose kid, by any possibility short of a revolution, may come to the crowd, a high state officer is required to attend the accouchement, while the people testify their loyalty to the reigning family by votes of thanks—for the unavoidable—and a liberal *largesse* to the young princeling or dukeling who, if born in a manger like the Man of Galilee, might eat grass. We have not quite reached that state of intellectual servility where we pension the babes of our political boss, but are tending rapidly in that direction. From the Penobscot to Jim Well's town on the lower Rio Grande, toadyism is rapidly taking the place of American independence, and in this respect at least the public press is "in the vanguard of human progress." It is comforting to reflect that there was no typographical fanfaronade when Shakespeare and Burns were born—that Grant and Napoleon stormed their first breastworks without attracting the attention of the press. Even the coming into the world of the Immaculate Son of God was not at the time considered nearly so important as the birth of Cleveland's last baby. But then his Father was not in politics—did not appoint postmasters nor dispose of public bonds to syndicates on private bids.

BAYLOR IN BAD BUSINESS.

The case of Steen Morris, charged with outraging the 14-year-old "ward of the Baptist church" while she was an inmate of Baylor College, has been heard in the lower court and the defendant held to await the action of the grand jury. It is not difficult to predict the final outcome of the case. The complainant is a stranger in a strange land, an ignorant child—despite her three years at Baylor—deserted by that pious crew of hypocrites who persuaded her to leave her faraway Brazilian home and commit herself to the tender care of the Baptist church of Texas. The defendant is brother to the pious son-in-law of Baylor's president, and all the power and "pull" of that institution are being exerted to save him from the penitentiary. It is a case of weakness vs. strength, of ignorance vs. knowledge, the good name of a fatherless girl vs. the reputation of a powerful denomination and a pretentious college. Antonia Teixeira cannot cast a single vote; the Baptist church holds the political destiny —and offices—of this judicial district in the hollow of its hand. Of course she may get justice—but it's a 100 to 1 shot.

It may be presumed that all the important evidence for both prosecution and defense was introduced at the preliminary trial. It simply amounted to an accusation by the one and a denial by the other. No corroborating testimony of any importance was introduced by either. It is simply the word of a child-mother against that of a modern Joseph. That the girl acquired a contract to raise a kid while she was being equipped for Brazilian missionary work in Dr. Burleson's kitchen, and that the party of the first part was not a coon, as the Rev. S. L. Morris, in the plenitude of his Baptist charity tried to make it appear, but some lecherous white man who was allowed to range at will among the female inmates of Baylor, is all that has been established beyond the peradventure of a doubt.

Steen Morris may be innocent; but the question naturally arises: If he never had carnal intercourse with the child why does she accuse him of being the father of her illegitimate babe? What has she to gain by shielding the real criminal and accusing an innocent man of the terrible crime? She is evidently not seeking to recover pecuniary damages, for Morris has no money. She cannot expect to coerce him into marrying her, for he is already a benedict. Her accusation is evidently not the result of enmity, for she entered no complaint against him until requested by the court to disclose the author of her disgrace. Why then did she accuse the defendant and stick to her story despite the efforts of the Burlesons and the Morrises to bluff and bully-rag her into a recantation? Men of wealth or distinction are sometimes wrongly accused of sexual crimes by brazen adventuresses; but Morris is neither wealthy nor distinguished, and it is inconceivable that a child in short dresses should learn to play the adventuress in a Baptist college—or even in Dr. Burleson's kitchen.

Of course the public may be wrong in denouncing Morris as the guilty man. He may be a veritable Sir Galahad or he-Dian. He may be physically incapable of such a crime; or the girl whom Dr. Burleson would have us believe was "crazy after the boys," may have caught the good young man and ravished him *vie et armis*. We really cannot be certain of anything in this world. The Iconoclast would not prejudice the case of Morris. It simply desires that justice be done. If he is proven to be innocent it will gladly record that fact; if he is proven guilty it will insist that he be hanged. If he is guilty it goes without saying that there is a conspiracy to shield a criminal regardless of the good name of the girl, and its principals should be made to feel the strong hand of the law. Whether the child was outraged or freely gave her consent to carnal intercourse matters much from a legal, but none from a moral standpoint. She was 14 years old when ruined, and at that time the law raising the age of consent to 15 was not in effect. What would be a capital crime to-day might have been simple seduction a year ago; still the fact remains that, whatever the law of the land, a lecherous brute who will ruin a child of 14, with or without her consent, should not be allowed to live. He should first be subjected to the surgeon's knife, lashed naked thro' the streets with a whip of scorpions, then hanged higher than Haman and his foul carcass fed to the buzzards.

Whether Steen Morris be guilty or innocent; whether he be convicted or acquitted, Baylor College will have to answer at the bar of public opinion for its brutal and unchristian treatment of the Brazilian girl. She was committed to its care, a child of 13, unversed in this world's wickedness. She was utterly alone, and Baylor was to be father and mother, sister and brother to her until she developed into noble womanhood and was safely returned to her kindred across far seas, consecrated to the cause of Christ. Instead of being carefully educated she was consigned to the kitchen. Instead of being tenderly guarded she was permitted to become enciente—it was at first said by a "coon." Instead of being kindly cared for after this dire mishap and an effort made to bring her back into the fold—granting that she willfully went astray—she was bundled out of Baylor like so much carrion and never an effort made to bring her destroyer to justice. When compelled to disclose him the aged president of Baylor denounced her as a thief and branded her in the public prints as a bawd. During her confinement she was shown less consideration by Baylor than is due a wolf about to become a mother—and she the duly ordained "ward of the Baptist church!" There is not water enough in all the oceans to wash the dark stain from the escutcheon of this Baptist college; there are not words enough in the English language to convince the American people that Baylor is a proper custodian for their daughters. The credit of the Morris family may be preserved; Steen may escape the penitentiary; the unfortunate girl and her Baptist bastard may disappear from the face of the earth, but Baylor college will stink forever in the nostrils of Christendom—it is "damned to everlasting fame."

* * *

Since the above was put in type the defendant has carried his case by habeas corpus before the district judge, and that official—a worthy Baptist brother—has rendered a Scotch verdict and ordered the release without bail of the alleged rapist. One judicial tribunal, after an exhaustive hearing of the case, decided that the girl was telling the truth and ordered the defendant held; another, after a cursory examination of the matter, and without calling the complainant to combat the witnesses for the defense, ordered that he be discharged. So ends the suit. No one will be punished for the ruin of Antonia Teixeira, the "ward of the Baptist Church." The grand jury will understand that it were useless to take cognizance of the case—that it will get no assistance from her self-constituted guardians in rounding up the criminal. Somebody is guilty, but he'll go scot free; for in the eyes of these good people female virtue seems of little worth and lawless venery but a venial fault. Baylor considers that it has done its duty by the innocent child committed to its care in establishing, to the satisfaction of the court, not who is, but who is not responsible for her ruin. And Waco's morning paper—one of those "great public educators"—of the Baptist school—fairly chortles in its joy because no one will suffer for Antonia's shame—evidently thinks the debauchment of a child a matter of little importance which "prejudice has stirred into a great stink!" Right royally are Tom Ochiltree's kind of men "standing together!" Well has it been said that there may be much religion and no morality, tomes of law and little justice. Poor Antonia! Miserable little waif, adrift among the Baptist wolves! She can now beg money of publicans and sinners to carry her back to her native land, and there lay her ill-begotten babe on her old mother's breast—as her diploma from Baylor! She can seek sanctuary in the Catholic church—which her fond parents left to tread a primrose path to Christ—and there find help and human sympathy; or she can take herself to the Reservation and there pursue that "missionary work" for which three years in a Baptist college have so eminently qualified her. Whatever her future, the great world will go on much the same. Dr. Burleson will doubtless continue to "weep and pray" over erring girls—then pillory them in the public press. The Baptists will continue to send missionaries to Brazil to teach the heteroscian heathen what to do with their young daughters, and the godly people to rail at prize-fighting as a public disgrace—while Antonia Teixeira clasps her fatherless babe to her childish breast, bedews its face with bitter tears and wonders if God knows there's such a place as Texas.

THE JURY SYSTEM.

ANOTHER VENERABLE NUISANCE.

There is at present almost as much talk of reforming the jury system as of reforming the tariff. Why "reform" the jury system? Why not abolish it altogether?

The jury system, like the habeas corpus act, has long been regarded as one of the "great bulwarks of our liberties." And such it undoubtedly was when the greed of princes and prelates threatened to grind us like grain between the upper and nether millstones; when an absolute monarchy on one hand and an intolerant and presumptuous prelacy on the other were trying to fix their cursed fetters upon the brawn and brain of all mankind. When judiciary and prelacy worked together like the upper and lower jaws of a wild beast, of which the harem of a besotted king was the stomach; when such creatures as Jeffreys wore the ermine and the Star Chamber and Court of High Commission hung like ominous shadows over every English home, then indeed was trial by jury, however defective, a thing to be thankful for, to be defended in the forum or the field. Then indeed was it the sheet-anchor of liberty, the bright bow of promise to the weak, the pillar of cloud by day and of fire by night upon which the eyes of the liberty-loving world were fixed with reverence and awe,—the rock between the tempestuous sea of anarchy and the desolate desert of abject slavery, upon which rested, with such poise as it could, the ark of the social covenant.

But "the old order changeth, yielding place to new," and we have outgrown the jury system as we have the ordeal by fire and many other forms and formulas established by the fathers and religious dogma and judicial process. The trouble is that the old order acquires a kind of prescriptive right, lingers long after the conditions which brought it into being have departed, after the day of its usefulness has declined. Time was when "sacred relics" were an invaluable aid to religion, forming a bridge, as it were, between ethnic materialism and the spirituality of the Christian cultus; but having crossed the bridge it were the part of wisdom to burn it, that we may not return. A progressive world must cast the jury system behind it, as it has cast the Ptolomaic system, polytheism, alchemy and augury, absolute monarchy and many other things once regarded as the very acme of natural or even preternatural prescience.

The genesis of the jury system is by no means certain. It first attained a systematic development in England, but whether its basic principle was introduced by Anglo-Saxon or Norseman, borrowed from the Gallic-Romans or developed from the native Celtic customs, antiquarians find difficulty in deciding. It really matters little whether we are indebted for it to the semi-mythical Alfred, the legendary Hengist, or that mailed marauder, William of Normandy, to whom titled English nincompoops and dead beats delight to trace their lineage. Certain it is that during the past five hundred years its development has been in the wrong direction, and it is not to-day so well adapted to secure justice between man and man as it was when Henry II permitted cowards to decline the trial by combat for that by assize. In olden times the jury was composed of the witnesses, was selected from among reputable citizens of the neighborhood who were supposed to know most of the cause they were called upon to decide, and who might refuse to take into consideration the testimony of any or all other witnesses. Now instead of selecting those who know most about the cause they are to pass upon, we select those who know least. Instead of "afforcing the assize" by getting twelve good men and true who will agree of their own accord, we gather twelve ignorami together and, after pumping law into them they cannot comprehend, and surfeiting them with testimony which they are incompetent to analyze or unable

to remember, we allow a dozen or so shyster lawyers to be-
fog them with their sophistry, to drive out what little of the
law and evidence may have found lodgment in their befuddled brains, then lock them up until the most obstinate
jackass in the crowd coerces the others into submission or
drives them to open revolt!

* * *

In simple cases where the law is plain and explicit, twelve
honest men, possessing a personal knowledge of the facts
and acquainted with the parties to the suit, may be expected
to render a righteous verdict; but what can we expect of a
know-knothing jury, gathered by chance, where the testimony is conflicting, the interests involved are intricate, the
law ambiguous, the attorneys adepts in the art of obfusca-
tion and the bribe-giver is ever active?

Even were our juries always composed of men of the
strictest integrity, still we might expect many miscarriages
of justice. The average citizen regards jury duty as an irk-
some task to be avoided if possible. He chafes under the
restraint, is in no condition of mind to analyze great masses
of evidence. Even if he can keep his thoughts off his neglected crops, his workshop or his store and confine them
strictly to the cause in question, his mind has had no judicial
training, and, with skillful attorneys to mislead him, he is
too apt to mistake the non-essential for the essential, or suffer his prejudices to be so played upon that his verdict, while
conscientious, is infamous.

It is safe to say that five-sixths of the verdicts rendered
by juries are compromises—are not the verdict of twelve
men, but of a minority who, being strong-willed or stubborn,
override the majority, who are chiefly interested in getting
through with the business that they may receive their discharge. And this is "the great bulwark of our liberties—
the handmaid of justice!" Why, the blundering of petit
juries long since passed into a proverb! It is as impossible
to predict from the law and the evidence what verdict a jury
will render, as where lightning will strike, or what fool
demagogue the Texas democracy will next deify. About
the only thing that can be predicted with any degree of cer-
tainty is that, if the suit is against a railway company, the
corporation will get the worst of it.

* * *

It would be some improvement, doubtless, to substitute
the majority for the unanimous rule in making up verdicts,

but there would be some loss to offset this gain. While it would rob the stupid and contrary blockhead or the "fixed" juror of his power for evil, it would also deprive the man capable of rendering an intelligible and righteous judgment of his power for good. While on the one hand it would prevent a stupid and perverted minority overriding an indifferent majority, on the other it would estop a wise and judicial-minded minority acting as a check upon a blundering or vicious majority.

The fact is, society is becoming too complex for the jury system and we must find a substitute therefor. When a nation is composed of but few people they can all assemble in council and make laws; but when they become numerous, and national interests complex, pure democracy must give place to representative government or monarchy. In a small State every freeman may properly be expected to be soldier as well as citizen; but when the hundreds swell to millions, division of labor and greater proficiency in each department becomes possible. It is as foolish to expect every citizen to leave his farm and workshop to enforce the law as it is to expect him to assist directly in the making of those laws, or to take his turn at garrisoning frontier forts.

If we can trust delegates to make our laws certainly we may trust delegates to enforce them. If we can trust to judges alone in our courts of last resort, cannot we trust to them also in the lower courts? If it be objected that such a system would lead to favoritism and abuses; if the jury system has such a hold upon the popular fancy that, despite its many shortcomings, its immediate overthrow would be impossible, why not elect our jurors and pay them as we do our magistrates and county boards? There is no magic in the number twelve, five or seven would answer equally as well. The majority rule in making up verdict might be adopted and each juror's vote made a matter of record. We could thus secure the services of men of more than average intelligence and moral standing, with some little qualification for the work, fix the responsibility of verdicts and save to the general public a vast deal of worry and waste of time. It would be vastly cheaper to the commonwealth, trials would be briefer, fewer useless witnesses would be summoned and lawyers would soon learn it to be but a waste of lung power to indulge in cheap sophistry and Ciceronian fanfaronade. While a bench of trained judges, holding their positions for life, and liberally paid, would be the best possible tribunal, if we must retain the jury system let us effect a division of labor and fix upon jurors some little responsi-

bility.   Let us put men in the jury box who at least know
a hawk from a handsaw, men who freely accept the service
instead of those who are driven into it by fear of fine and
imprisonment.

POLITICIANS AND PENSIONERS.

I was conversing with a hardy-looking machinist in
Houston who incidentally remarked that he had served in
the federal army during the civil war.

"How long?"

"Only about six months.   I enlisted near the close and
never got to see a Johnny with his war-paint on."

"Get a bounty when you enlisted?"

"Oh, yes; I got $300."

"Ever try to get a pension"?

"Sure! I was taken sick of the mumps and permanently
disabled."

"Disabled for what"?

"Well, you see, my general health was impaired.   I only
draw $6 a month, but I'm trying to get an increase."

The conversation drifted to other topics and he finally
informed me that he was the parent stem from which had
sprung twelve lusty olive branches.

"Raise your family since the war?"

"Sure."

"Work at your trade regularly?"

"Haven't lost a month's time in ten years."

"Now, hones' Injun, don't you think that a man who
came out of the war capable of continued hard labor and of
incidentally accumulating a dozen kids, has a good deal of
gall to ask the Government to pay him a pension"?

"Well, congress allowed it, and I'd be a d—n fool to refuse $72 a year that's thrown at my head."

A few years after the war I witnessed a six-day walking
match and subsequently learned that the winner was drawing a comfortable pension from Uncle Sam because of a disabled leg!   A careful investigation would probably disclose
the fact that fully forty per cent of the ex-federals now receiving pensions came out of the war better men physically
than they went in.   The pension legislation indulged in by
that omnium-gatherum of practical politicians and professional jobbers yclept the American Congress, is, beyond
the peradventure of a doubt, the most damnable outrage
ever perpetrated on a free people.

The Republican party sets the pace in the matter of pension legislation—in pandering to the "old soldier vote"—and its Democratic brother considers that it must follow suit if it would keep its nose within smelling distance of the public flesh-pots. The leaders of both parties take it for granted that the old soldier can be held in line only by liberal concessions of public pap—that the moment a subsidy is denied him he will, like a political mercenary, transfer his allegiance to the cause of the enemy. As in several states he holds the balance of power, his vote is important; hence we have the edifying spectacle of Democratic and Republican congresses vieing with each other in the building of new turn-pikes upon which he may travel to the treasury.

General Grant declared that twenty-five years after the close of the war the pension expenditures should not exceed $50,000,000 per annum; yet here it is 30 years since the cessation of hostilities, and the expenditures are three times the sum named as the maximum by the federal commander! Men who followed the flag of the confederacy are fully as liberal with the public funds when bidding for the votes of ex-federals as are the most radical of Republicans.

It is well enough to grant pensions to those who were permanently disabled in the discharge of their duties and who possess no means of support; but this promiscuous pensioning for political purposes is not only an infamous outrage upon the taxpayers, but an insult to patriotism. The pay of the federals, rank and file, was far in excess of that received by the soldiers of any European country. In addition to this, many received a liberal bounty. If a man will not fight for his country or defend his home for a salary, with a subsidy annex, without asking to be provided for all the rest of his life at public expense, his patriotism is considerably below par.

I do not believe that the federal soldiers who faced the legions of Jackson and Lee are asking to be listed as chronic paupers—that the men who "saved the country" insist on taking it in part payment of their services, then compelling us to work out the balance. It is the men who "enlisted near the close of the war"—when the bounties were biggest and the draft hardest to dodge; who "never saw a Johnny with his war-paint on;" who were "permanently disabled by the mumps"—then founded large families—and those who became professional pedestrians on pensioned legs, that consider patriotism and pie as synonyms and hold the tear jug into which practical politicians ostentatiously weep for the woes of the "old soldier."

The confederate soldier suffered far more severely than did his federal brother. In addition to catching the mumps and getting disabled legs he got his house burned down, his mules stolen and his niggers confiscated. He received no fat bounties and never saw a greenback except when he went through the pockets of some federal prisoner. He drew the enemy's fire with a great deal more regularity than he drew his pay, and when he got the latter it was good for little but gun-wadding and pastime poker; yet he has managed pretty well without a pension—has even contributed some hundreds of millions toward ameliorating the mental anguish of his erstwhile enemy.

The confederates were not playing the game of war for pensions. They did not consider the Confederacy a casualty insurance company. Some fought as a matter of duty, some for the fun of the thing, and a few, perhaps, because they couldn't help it; but none of them, so far as heard from, have threatened to spill their patriotism, renounce their political principles and kick the enacting clause out of their party unless it filled them to the nozzle with pie at the expense of the public. What little has been done by the respective states for disabled and impecunious veterans was unsolicited. The old confeds have never threatened to ruin a political party unless it assisted them to rob the country. Their patriotism is not built on a gold basis like the American greenback, but is purely a fiat affair.

TRUE LOVE'S TRIALS.

Miss Rebecca Merlindy Johnson, Assistant Editor Houston Post:

My Dear Rebecca: It has been some months since I took my pen in hand to spill my fond affection over the fairest of the fair, my sweet Rose of Sharon. During this hiatus in our communion thro' the mails you have evidently imagined that my heart has become frappe—even harbored the awful hallucination that in the rush and hurry of reforming the Texas ministry, squeezing the politics out of latter day religion and promoting harmony in the bifurcated democracy, I have actually forgotten you. I gather as much from the fact that you inform the few unfortunate readers of the *Post* that I'm a bold bad man, an "adventurer," an "ingrate," and other things not calculated to inspire respect. This only proves the old adage that the path of true love is ever a rocky one, beset with thorns and thistles, as well as rosebuds and bulbuls. You know you wronged me when you made those cruel flings. You suspected that I had transferred my affections to Dr. Mary Walker—and "hell hath no fury like a woman scorned." You were wretchedly unhappy and longed to be bitterly cruel. If I ever sinned against your youth and innocence it must have been in an uneasy hypnotic dream. Before gods and men I do declare that if you have been led astray—if your young life is blighted like a tender plant by a sneaping frost—'tis no fault of mine. If you have been guilty of unwomanly conduct, God wotteth well it was despite my counsels rather than because thereof. If your conscience hurts you, and in the stilly night there comes into your exuberant bosom a feeling that's akin to pain; if you bedew your hen-feather pillow with unavailing tears while Remorse fleshes his cruel fangs in your broken heart and makes it to bleed afresh, why lay the burden of the blame on one who gently held you back by the tail of your little alpaca coat when you yearned to fill your snowy cuticle with barrel-house booze and whoop it up in Happy Hollow? Jealousy is indeed a green-eyed monster, that makes us see things more strange than ever flitted hither and yon in a jag-cure joint. "Ingrate" I may be, for I should not have left a maid so fair and wayward in a town with Epictetus Paregoric Hill and Uncle Dan Gary, with none to keep watch and ward. When she poured out to me the wealth of her fond affection I should have stayed ever by it to see that it did not sour. Still I felt my duty done when I found you, a poor green gosling in the newspaper pasture, and played the part of a guide, philosopher and friend until you developed into a full-fledged goose. Perhaps I have been derelict, for the relations of man and woman are so delicate that it is indeed hard to draw the line where duty ends and generosity begins. Still, to err is human, to forgive divine, and I beg that Rebecca the beauteous will pass my imperfections by. In these lovers' quarrels, which will arise from time to time, like ominous clouds in a summer's sky, you should not expect me to do all the forgiving, for monopolies are contrary to law. The fact is, Rebecca, I have been compelled by cruel circumstances entirely beyond my control to forego the pleasure of feeding you with the usual allowance of compressed pansy blossoms and anacreontic poetry. I have already ravished the gardens of the gods of every fragrant flower to lay at your wayward feet—have even despoiled weald and wold of straggling blooms and woven them into garlands with which to crown you Queen of the Liars' Club.

There is not even a pale pink holly-hock left blooming alone
in some deserted garden, or hexapetalous jimson waving
its wild glories above a pile of compost that can be added
to your triumphal arch or entwined in a magic cestus for my
fin de siecle Venus.   I have overworked my muse in an effort to paint the lily and gild refined gold, exhausted the
lover's dictionary in showering sweets to the sweet and can
only stand, like another Troilus, on some beetling rampart
beneath the twinkling Pleiades, make mouths at the harvest
moon and sigh my soul out toward the distant camp where
fair Cressid lies, lulled to peaceful dreams by the drowsy
bleat of the goat editor and soporific hum of the busy gal-
linipper.   I must wait for new flowers of fancy to bloom in
the arid waste, for Orpheus to mend his lute and Pegasus to
rest his weary wings.   Forgot you, Rebecca?   As the
French novelists say when waiting for an idea, "Ah God!"
What impressionable son of Adam, having once feasted his
hungry eyes on your sylph-like form; what mortal man,
having once been awed and quite o'ercome by your statu-
esque, she-Napoleonic pose, and gazed into the dreamy
depths of your bovine eyes—those wonderful windows of
the soul thro' which it peers forth with all the unutterable
longing and aching tenderness of a bull-calf contemplating
a dewy clover-patch thro' a pair of bars—could efface, even
with a bath-brick and elbow grease, that matchless vision
from his memory!   But it is not of love and love's raptures I here would speak.   It is of matters less pleasant than
yum-yum beneath the umbrageous boughs of a china-tree
while the fragrance of the bayou comes stealing around the
trysting Pyramus and Thisbe like a benediction, that chiefly
concerns us here.   The "New Woman" craze which you
have precipitated on this unhappy land is to-day the burden
of my song.   What evil and unwomanly spirit induced you
to cast aside flowing skirts and health-bustles, beflowered
hats and French heels and appear in public places in split-
tail coat and pantaloons?   How came you to exchange the
modest name of Rebecca Merlindy for the bellicose pseudo-
nym of Rienzi Miltiades?   Did you not understand that
such an example was calculated to utterly demoralize your
sex?   Already a goodly portion of the great she-world has
taken to derby hats, shirt-waists and bloomers.   Encouraged
by your almost criminal recklessness, the softer sex becomes
year by year more masculine, more inclined to don the
breeches and transpose the "obey" clause in the marriage
contract.   You dabbled in politics—or tried to—and forthwith the woods were filled with Mary Ellen Leases.   You

wrote for the papers—by proxy, of course—and half your sex contracted an incurable case of *cacoethes scribendi.* You went on the stage and played Claude Melnotte to Mrs. Jane Brown Potter's Pauline, and now all the she-stars of the theatrical firmament want to "do" male parts and stride about the painted rocks and "set" trees in white tights and top boots. You insisted upon voting, although you knew less of political economy than does a prohibition orator, and forthwith the dear creatures became clamorous for political privileges, and one of them actually hoisted a presidential lightning-rod. Your example, Rebecca, has bred a train of ills, whose culmination even the wisest philosopher cannot foresee. Indirectly you are responsible for the bicycle habit which has the beauty of America in its remorseless grasp. True, you do not ride a bike yourself, your legs not being long enough to reach the treads, nor your dignity of that kind which can be safely trusted on rubber wheels; but other women, whose physical construction is more conservative, mount the erratic machine, light their cigarettes and go whizzing by, dazzling we poor he-things with the twinkle of their Trilby feet. You doubtless think it all a joke, Rebecca mine; but it is a jest that may prove a boomerang and knock you off the social Christmas tree. You have carried it too far and must suffer the consequences. Had you donned a pair of breeches measuring 14 inches in the leg and 75 in the beam and slipped out on a dark night for a quiet lark with Dud Bryan, Will Bailey and Whistle-trigger, you would have done little harm; but such costume continually worn in the garish light of day by a gentle maid who should be spinning her marriage linen and dreaming of orange blossoms and epithalamiums, is a bid for adverse remark. Already it is whispered that you are not a woman at all, but just a dapper little man to whom heaven has denied the glory of a beard and masculine strength of mind. The world is so prone to judge by appearances, and when made up you do look a very little like a man in some respects. Think of a young and beautiful woman suspected of being only a he-thing at a time when the ladies are taking the destiny of the world into their hands! Imagine one who was born to rule, being classed with those miserable worms of the dust who, in the years to be, will watch the baby and crochet tidies while their female lords are sitting with feet cocked up in front of swell hotels, saving the country and ogling the Josephs who saunter timidly by! But that is not all—it is not half. It is even darkly hinted that you are neither male nor female, but a peculiar and eminently unsatisfactory combination of both. To such ribaldry, fair Rebecca, does your clothing-store and gin sling habit subject you. And to think that I cannot come to your rescue —that it is one of those aggravating cases wherein a doting swain must listen to the most preposterous speculation anent the idol of his affection and hold his peace—lest he make a bad matter worse! I can only confide these facts to you, trusting that womanly tact will teach you the necessity of turning to the wall your portrait in the gallery of gold-cure graduates, and adopting some more feminine occupation than chewing plug tobacco and spitting at a mark —that you will once more go into your raiment head first. I do not chide you, Rebecca. I realize full well that you are a good girl at heart; but "evil communications corrupt good manners." There is yet hope. Mary Magdalen reformed and Trilby tried to—tho' it killed her. That latter fact should caution you to go at your work of reformation scientifically, but none the less determinedly. Will you do so, for the sake of the　　　　　　APOSTLE.

JINGOES AND JOHN BULL.

ANGLO-MANIACS VS. AMERICANS.

The brutal treatment accorded the Cornell crew in England is enough to make the blood of every true American boil, and that so hotly that Johnny would be compelled to get his gun, and get it p. d. q. Still the case does not materially differ from that of a dozen others that preceded it. It is notorious that whenever American athletes cross the briny to try conclusions with our British cousins they are flagrantly insulted, systematically robbed and not infrequently mobbed by a people posing as the very avatar of fair play. Ever since the Benicia Boy put it all over the British champion—then had to lick a job-lot of high-toned toughs—the more or less "noble Briton" has missed no opportunity to belittle and belie, blackguard and bully-rag the American athlete who chanced to be his guest. Time and again it has been demonstrated that he has as little conception of the courtesy due a stranger within his gates as has a hyena of hospitality. He boasts of his civilization and sneers at Uncle Sam as a semi-savage; yet our very Bowery toughs and Boiler avenue bums will treat a brave adversary with more consideration than will the lordlings and dukelings of Great Britain. I do not say this to disparage the English people; I simply record it as a melancholy fact which has been too frequently demonstrated to permit of denial. So brutally inhospitable are the people and press of England to American athletes, that Corbett—who is not particularly thin-skinned—declares that Peter Jackson is the only pugilist he will consent to meet on British soil. As the latter is a "coon," Corbett might hope to fairly defeat him and escape being mobbed by the ring-side roughs such as the conqueror of Sayers had to contend with; tho' he realizes full well that the sympathies of England would be with the Ethiopian—just as they would be with the devil were the prince of darkness pitted against an American pugilist.

Unquestionably some grand and noble men have been bred in England—men who would do honor even to America; but the tight little isle has an undue proportion of plug-uglies and prigs, blackguards and bullies.

In boxing and wrestling, in rowing and running America has repeatedly demonstrated her superiority; but this fact does not fully explain why her athletes are so inhospitably treated in England. John Bull's chronic belly-ache dates far back of Sayer's defeat by the Benicia Boy—it can be traced to the Boston Tea Party and Bunker Hill. The royal beast of Britain has never forgotten that once upon a time an infant Republic held him up by the beard and beat the immortal ichor out of him. That kept him on reasonably good behavior for a quarter of a century, when his impudence again rose paramount to his judgment and he was given a second prescription. The trouble with the arrogant brute to-day is that he has been allowed to go too long without a licking. For more than half a century John Bull has been turning his broad beam up to Uncle Sam and fairly begging for another blistering. He should be accommodated—and this time Columbia should drive her Cinderella so far under the old buccaneer's coat-tails that he could taste leather all the rest of his life.

But the capitulation of Cornwallis, the almost ludicrous defeat of Pakenham's veterans by Jackson's frontiersmen, and the regularity with which British athletes have been relegated to the rear by their American brethren, does not fully explain the biliousness of John Bull. We have outstripped him even further in the field of industry than in athletic sport—have defeated him even more signally in the struggle for national pre-eminence than in the squared circle. The little Republic of a century ago, struggling painfully along the Atlantic sea-board, has become the wealthiest and most powerful nation in the world—the Star of Empire is now blazing in the West. America is the commercial rival of England—a more grievous offense than even the Declaration of Independence. In every possible way John Bull makes his displeasure manifest. During our civil war the present premier declared that the disruption of this nation would inure to the commercial advantage of England—a fine sentiment truly for our "Mother Country"—and thereupon John Bull began to meddle in our family unpleasantness. He had to pay for this impertinence, and that did not strengthen the *entente cordiale* to any alarming extent. In all official intercourse with America England assumes an arrogant and dictatorial tone characteristic of that country when dealing with third and fourth-class powers. There was a time when such treatment would have been hotly resented; but the old Continentals have been succeeded by Anglo-maniacs who have never forgiven Almighty God for suffering them to be born American sovereigns instead of British subjects; who cultivate the Hinglish hawkcent,—which is about as cheerful as polishing a back-tooth with a rat-tail file—ape the waddle of the Prince of Wales and turn up their twousahs don't-cherknow whenever they hear that it is raining in "Lonnon." When these Anglo-maniacs accumulate a little money they employ some fakir to evolve from his imagination a "family tree" and hang thereon a bogus coat-of-arms. They decide that Uncle Sam's sons are not quite good enough to beget their grandchildren and buy scorbutic dukelings for their daughters to drag thro' the divorce courts. They are the same mangy mavericks who dubbed Jim Blaine a "jingoist" for advocating a foreign policy with a dash of the Declaration of Independence in it—one that would compel even England to respect the American eagle. They are the same empty peacocks who lift up their discordant voices in frantic protest when orator or editor gives utterance to a genuinely American sentiment—who have a conniption fit and fall in it whenever a Congressman suggests that John Bull be compelled to keep his meddlesome snout out of American politics. These are the featherless poll-parrots who prattle of "twisting the lion's tail" whenever it is proposed to resent an English insult—talking-machines who are witty at the expense of their country's honor. These are the unhung idiots who imagine that a nation, producing in abundance everything humanity needs, would go to hell in a handbasket if it adopted an independent currency system or an international policy which Yewrup did not approve. Why in the devil's name these birds do not fly across the ocean to their beloved England, instead of remaining to befoul their own nests, it were difficult to determine. They should be compelled to migrate, for no man who esteems another country above that from which he gets his daily bread, is fit to be buried in its soil, drowned in its waters or hanged on its trees.

Why should the foremost nation of all the world fawn at the fat feet of John Bull? We can get along much better without England than can that country without us. Columbia has proven both her intellectual and physical superiority to Britannia. Then why should she stand humble and shame-faced in her presence? America has done more for the human race in a hundred and twenty years than has England in all her hoary centuries. We could buy the miserable little island, pay for it and blow it at the moon, and the world would be none the worse. England has produced some really great men; but, like the hen that sat on the nest of door-knobs, it has taken her a terribly long time to bring off her brood. Call the roll of the great of England and America for the present century and say which the world could best afford to spare!

What we need is a million funerals among the Anglomaniacs and a little healthy Jim Blaine "jingoism" in the White House. We need a revival of that old spirit which taught that the title of American sovereign is superior to any ever borne by a British subject. We need an administration that can understand that America is to-day the greatest nation on the map of the world and does not have to dance attendance on transatlantic powers. It is time the American eagle came off the nest where he has so long been hatching dollars, and emitted a scream that would clear the atmosphere of political buzzards. It is time the Giant of the Occident was looking this world over and deciding what he is going to do with it. Is America to be a new and greater Rome, bequeathing freedom to all mankind; or will the Anglomaniacs annex it to England and ordain that the tail shall wag the dog?

THE SINGLE-TAXERS.

"GEORGEISM" REVIEWED.

Of the various political parties and economic schools now striving to solve the industrial problem, none is more enthusiastically aggressive than the so-called Single-Taxers—those who expect, by laying the burden of government altogether upon land, to compel the use or relinquishment of natural opportunities for the production of wealth. The Single-Taxers are quite sure they have discovered an industrial catholicon, and, in season and out of season, they continue, with unabated zeal and unfaltering faith, their "campaign of education," their crusade against professional landlordism. As might be expected, they are regarded with pronounced aversion by the large land-owners who, driven to bay by this bold assault on prescriptive right, are not particularly choice of their weapons of warfare, resorting to the bludgeon of invective quite as readily as to the rapier of ridicule. It proves nothing to denounce the Single-Taxers as "lunatics" and "crazy communists"—at least nothing further than the inability of their opponents to meet and overcome them in the arena of intellectual controversy. Abuse is neither argument nor good policy—individuals and political parties thrive upon it. It is recruiting the ranks of the Single-Taxers and making of the Populists a political power. Abuse is an evidence of logical weakness—is the wild ravings of vindictive ignorance.

Lest the landlord class should take fright and refuse to delve deeper here, I hasten to assure them that I am not a disciple of Henry George. He has failed to convince me; but I freely admit that his theories have never been successfully controverted. To answer such a man by calling him a "crank" were too much like the college of cardinals replying to Galileo by putting him in jail. Henry George is a world-compeller, and we must either prove the fallacy of his conclusions or eventually capitulate.

The thesis from which the Single-Tax is legitimately derived did not originate with George, nor with Quesnay or Rousseau; it is old as human history. It is an ancient idea cropping out in our nineteenth century civilization—a kind of economic atavism which goes far to prove the immortality of mind, the indestructibility of human habits. Henry George is chiefly responsible for the revival of the state landlord idea; hence it has been called by his name by ignorant editors who imagined it a new "craze."

That there is something radically wrong with our industrial system is generally conceded. Even the old political parties ostentatiously train beneath the "reform" banner, and promise the betterment of labor's sad condition. Despite the mighty increase in the wealth-producing power of labor resulting from improved machinery, the masses find the battle of life becoming ever more bitter. While those who neither toil nor spin are attired like unto Solomon in all his glory, those who ditch and delve are mere bundles of rags. While Idleness feasts Industry starves. So long as such conditions prevail attempts will be made to right the wrong, and failure to obtain relief will produce that restless discontent of which bloody revolutions are born.

The problem which confronts us is of paramount importance—a crisis in the history of the human race is at hand. Every industrial depression is becoming a greater danger, not alone to existing conditions, to established forms and formulas, but to civilization itself. There was never a time when the latter could be so easily and irremediably destroyed. The truth of this startling proposition must readily appear to whosoever will carefully consider it. When each community was an independent microcosm both progress and retrogression were slow; but science has transformed these isolated and independent communities into a mighty commercial entity. A century or two ago war, pestilence or famine might have swept away half the population of the world without materially affecting the remainder; to-day the cotton planter of Texas and the corn grower of Kansas depend for their prosperity upon the price of those staples in Europe, the mechanics of England and Germany upon the demand for their wares in the antipodes. A million independent corpuscles have been incorporated in one great organism, which is affected in every part by what befalls any of its members. It is this fact—this mighty union of forces —that made the progress of the Nineteenth century possible; and it is this that has made feasible a world-wide French Revolution that may never leave a sanctuary for civilization—no house of refuge in which may be hid away and preserved for happier times the wisdom accumulated by the toil of sixty centuries. Economists usually consider the printing press, public education and political equality as the conservators of civilization, the dynamics which will carry it ever onward and upward. They forget that the same winds that waft a proud ship to port may rip its canvas to ribbons and drive it upon the rocks. When the masses were ignorant and space had not yielded to the power of steam and the electric telegraph, empires might rise or fall, peoples attain to Roman citizenship or be reduced to Russian serfdom, and few beyond that particular corner of the continent either know or care; to-day the progress of German socialism is watched with intense interest in San Francisco, and the march of a Coxey on our national capital is bulletined in Bulgaria. Men separated by far seas are brought into close communion, agrarian and communistic movements assume an international character—the electric spark may become the beacon of universal war, may set the world ablaze.

Political sovereignty united to industrial slavery, public education for those steeped to the lips in hopeless poverty were indeed a dangerous compound. Well did Caesar say of the lean and hungry Cassius, "he thinks too much—such men are dangerous." Lean and hungry men who do not read and think are servile slaves who accept their fate like the patient ox or ass; but a well-filled head and an empty stomach were fire and gunpowder in the social ark of the covenant. When men begin to ask why some should want while others waste; when a dissatisfied growl by the Parisian *sans-culotte* is promptly echoed by the Chicago *canaille;* when the proletarians throughout the world begin to realize their strength and to regard the patrician as their natural enemy; when they have been hoodooed and humbugged by pseudo-economists and lying politicians until hope is dead and patience quite exhausted; when they realize that progress in the industrial arts means deeper poverty and education but a lamp by whose cold light they view their own wretchedness, think you our boasted civilization is safe?

Such are the conditions to-day, and enlightened self-interest should suggest to the wealthy class the wisdom of giving an impartial hearing to a man who imagines he has found why a progressive civilization breeds plutocrats and paupers—why, albeit his productive power has been multiplied, the workman continues at very death-grips with the wolf of Want. The ability and erudition of Mr. George, and the further fact that his disciples are not only many, but men of more than average intelligence and economic information, certainly entitles him to courteous consideration.

It were folly to call the Single-Tax movement a passing bubble on the political sea. Men still alive once discoursed in that vein of "the Abolition lunacy;" but despite their sneers—or perchance because thereof—it grew and gath-

ered force until able to exchange the forum for the field
and prove the supernal wisdom of its thesis with the naked
sword. In considering the future of the Single-Tax movement it must not be forgotten th'at this country is to-day
a political chaos,—and that from chaos new worlds are
evolved.

*   *   *

The proposition of Henry George is that poverty persists despite the increased productiveness of labor because
of land monopoly, which enables the land-owner to demand and obtain as rent all the joint product of capital and
labor above what will induce the former to seek investment
and the latter to accept employment. He would abolish
private ownership of land and compel each occupant to pay
a rental to the state proportioned to the desirability of his
holding. He assumes that land values are created by the
community and should not go to enrich the individual, but
be appropriated by government and employed to promote
the general welfare. This plan, he thinks, would permit the
abrogation of taxes on the products of industry, thereby
enhancing the incentive to production, abolish monopoly of
natural rescurces and insure to rich and poor access thereto
on equal terms. He insists that there is no "conflict between capital and labor;" that these productive forces are
really allies and the land monopolist their common enemy,
the efficient cause of that great inequality in the distribution
of wealth which to-day threatens the very existence of civilization.

The theory is a very attractive one; but let us measure it
by existing conditions. I freely concede that did one man
own the entire arable area of the earth the rest of the race
would be as truly his slaves as tho' he held a proprietary interest in their bodies. No matter how great their production of wealth, he could appropriate all in excess of what
would yield mere animal existence. It is as absurd to permit a monopolization of land as to permit a monopolization
of the atmosphere. But that is not the question—we need
not cross a bridge until we come to it. Does a world-
embracing land monopoly exist? And, if so, is it really responsible for the fact that the population of the globe is
dividing into two well-defined classes—millionaires and
mendicants, masters and slaves? And if Mr. George has
properly diagnosed the industrial disease, has he prescribed
the proper remedy?

It were impossible in the brief space of a magazine article to take up in detail the propositions of the apostle of state landlordism and subject each to a searching analysis; nor is it necessary to do more than call attention to a few indisputable facts to prove that the public policy he recommends would do little or nothing to ameliorate the hard conditions that behedge the toiling millions.

Although the human race has inhabited the earth for ages, there has never been a time when the arable land, the timber, coal, iron and other great sources of wealth were monopolized. Three continents, rich in natural resources and capable of supporting dense populations even tho' isolated from all other portions of the earth, have scarce felt the touch of the dominant race, are inhabited chiefly by predatory bands of savages. It is possible that the time will come when the entire available surface of the earth will be thick-settled as Massachusetts—when landlordism will become a serious problem; but we have no reason to believe that the total population has materially increased within historic times. There has ever been, perhaps always will be, a vent for overcrowded countries. Man is not confined to that locality in which he is born. Year by year migration is made easier, cheaper, the world's population rendered more mobile. Rapid and systematic transportation facilities are spreading our cities over vast areas and bringing the remote parts of the earth within easy reach of the world's markets. A difference of a shilling or two a day will move vast bodies of laborers across the ocean, an added cent of interest send capital to the antipodes. When ignorance among laborers was general, a journey of a few hundred miles a serious matter and international protection of capital practically unknown, those who could monopolize the natural resources of a populous country might grievously oppress the people; but to-day labor and capital look the world over for the best opportunity, are no longer dominated by the local landlords. The vast amount of European wealth and labor here in America, and the mighty streams of money and muscle setting towards newer countries still, should suggest to Mr. George the impossibility of landowners grievously oppressing these great factors of production until the entire earth is "fenced in."

If Mr. George desires to invest money in a great manufacturing enterprise, a hundred thriving cities are ready to donate a desirable site, and some of them will even exempt his plant from taxation for a term of years—labor and capital may produce to the utmost of their power and divide the product unvexed by the greed of their arch-enemy. If he would like to acquire a little farm, thousands of men who are "land poor" are eager to accommodate him on easy terms. If he will but give it out that he wants to buy a building lot, he'll find his front yard black with real estate men ready to convince him that the landlorders of the community do not constitute a close corporation. True, he can no longer go into Illinois or Indiana and "take up" a fertile farm; he will be required to pay for the value that has been conferred upon land by the expenditure of the wealth and energy of others. In attempting to seize more than this, the landowners drive away the population, and with it the superior advantages which give value to their holdings. When the owners of land in the heart of a city demand too much, the tendency of the trade center is to move in the direction of the least resistance. Thus, when landlordism becomes a disease, it supplies its own remedy. Land is fixed while labor and capital are not. I use the word capital here in the sense in which Mr. George employs it, as distinguished from land ownership—really a distinction without a difference. Despite the hair-splitting of those economists who would save the world by the science of definition, land employed for productive purposes and possessing a marketable value, is as much capital as the farm machinery and store buildings upon it. To distinguish rent from interest is a species of philosophizing that bakes no bread, and I am surprised that a man of Mr. George's breadth of mind should waste time on such profitless subtleties while grappling with the great industrial problem. If I have money which I desire to employ for the attainment of more wealth, I may buy a farm with it and receive *rent;* or I may loan it to another who will buy a farm with it and pay me *interest.* By whatever name the increment be called, it is dug out of the soil; hence it were ridiculous to say that the landowner is the economic enemy of the capitalist. The number of mortgages recorded in the United States would indicate that in the battle which Mr. George imagines is being waged between the two, the capitalist is more than holding his own. Capital represented by desirable land presses for employment just as does capital represented by coin; and when it cannot get much it must take little.

But, it may be asked, how comes it that thousands of fertile acres lie idle in the older states while people press forward into the wilderness? I do not say there is no local land monopoly—I say that there is no general monopoly. I have monopolized one woman and one section of land; but that does not prevent other men getting married, or acquiring farms. There are other women to be won and other sunny acres awaiting ownership. In fact, taking the world at large, the supply of both land and women seems to be in shameful excess of the demand.

Men must be governed by their means. If I have an abundance of money, I will buy a farm in that garden of the gods, Central Texas, where I may enjoy many pecuniary and social advantages; if I have but little, I will go where land is cheaper because of less desirable environment, and strive by industry and economy to acquire those conveniences which my present capital does not permit me to enjoy. If I have a million of money, I may buy and build on Fifth avenue; if I have in my pockets only a choice assortment of rectangular holes, I must content myself with a squalid tenement in Rag Alley until, by getting a compound cathartic hustle on myself, I am able to command the comforts of life. It might be asked with equal reason why great store buildings sometimes remain empty while hucksters stand on the curbstone to vend their wares; why fine residences are often tenantless while there's brisk demand for small cottages—why women wear cheap calico while bolts of silk remain unsold.

*   *   *

Let us briefly consider that "unearned increment" of which Mr. George would deprive the landholder as something to which he is not justly entitled. Ten years ago—let us say—John Smith purchased a lot in the new town of K., paying therefor $100. It is now salable at $1,000, an increase in value of $900. He has not driven a stake upon it, has not caused it to produce food or shelter for man or beast. The town has simply grown up around it and enhanced its desirability, therefore its market value. Surely here is a case of "unearned increment" upon which the public may pounce with a clear conscience! But wait a bit. Although he has not used the lot, has not Smith paid "rent" thereon to the state, county and municipality in the form of taxes? And from such taxes have not the streets been paved, schoolhouses built, government maintained and a fire department paid? And do not these things add to the desirability and market value of all land in the community? Has he not for ten years past been pouring into the public coffers of K. the product of his labor? True, if ten thousand non-residents had purchased lots in the prospective city and none had improved them there would have been no increase in value; and it is also true that Smith would not be paying taxes on a valuation of $1,000 for the continued betterment of the town. After deducting the purchase price, compound interest thereon and taxes for ten years, his profits are large; but suppose he had paid $1,000 for the lot, and, despite all the money expended to maintain it, now finds it marketable at but $100: how much unearned increment is the government entitled to? If only the increase in land values is to be taken for public uses, as proposed by Mr. George, from whence is that county or municipal government where lands are declining in value, to derive its revenue?

There are unquestionably instances where people have been enriched by a rise in land values which they did little to promote; but it may be safely assumed that the general rule of action of land owners is in the direction of self-interest—that the increase in values is due chiefly to their industry and enterprise. If it be true that "men will not take up arms in defense of a boarding-house," it is also true that they will not construct railways and canals, build factories and bridges for the benefit of a community in which they have no proprietary interest. To illustrate: A few years ago the citizens of a Texas town in which realty values were rapidly declining, raised a considerable bonus to secure a railroad. The road was built, the trade territory of the town increased, freights fell, business became brisk and realty rapidly advanced. Many people moved to the town and adjacent country to share the prosperity and by their industry made it greater. There was employment for more laborers at better wages than formerly and new opportunities for the profitable employment of capital. The newcomers profited by the enterprise of the old citizens; but were they entitled to appropriate the increase in realty values? Under a system permitting them to do so would that railroad have been built? Was the enhancement of values really unearned increment, or was it the legitimate reward of capital wisely employed?

When a number of people penetrate into a new country and subdue the wild beasts and savage men; when they create a social oasis in the wilderness, from a trade ganglion, establish a government and make it a more desirable place of residence for those who come after, are they not entitled to their reward? According to that moral law of which Mr. George talks so much, are the newcomers entitled to appropriate unto themselves the value created by the toil and sacrifice of the pioneers? And when they in turn have builded roads, established schools, and by their labor made the land still more desirable, were it either just or politic to deprive them of the fruits of their toil as something that belongs equally to any tramp who may drag his idle carcass into the community?

*   *   *

The Single Tax propaganda is simply an attempt at compromise between the Georgian theory and existing conditions—the insertion of the thin end of the wedge. Mr. George would, if possible, confiscate to the last penny "that fund arising from general growth and development," regardless of its efficient cause. Just what he would do with the surplus after defraying governmental expenses and making necessary public improvements he does not plainly say, but intimates that he would pro-rate it among the people regardless of the value of the individual in our social economy, as is the practice in Freudenstaedt, Klingenberg and other German Arcadias—that have made no material progress worth mentioning during several centuries. If that be the idea, and it can be successfully carried into execution, then indeed will Weary Willie and Dusty Rhodes find life well worth the living.

But the Single-Taxers would not go to the Georgian extreme—they would simply let down the bars. They would take from the landowner only enough "rent" for the support of government; there is to be no *largesses* distributed among the impecunious—not just yet. It is urged that this plan would not interfere with private ownership of land, but would abolish land monopoly, while the tax could be more equitable and collected at less cost than any hitherto devised. This is another plausible theory concocted without due regard to conditions. Experience has repeatedly proven that while the people will stand a heavy indirect tax without murmuring, a much lighter one direct in incidence will drive them to revolt. To illustrate: The man who pays an indirect tax of $40 a year on the liquor he drinks seldom thinks of it. Ask him about the liquor tax and the chances are he will tell you it ought to be increased; but let the government take the excise off liquor and on the first of each year compel this consumer to pay $20—and denounce it as an outrage. It profits nothing to urge that such action is illogical; theories are but intellectual gymnastics—conditions govern.

But if the Single-Tax could be inaugurated despite the prejudices of the people, would it abolish local monopolies of land? Would it even have a tendency in that direction? If it be true that every dollar expended by government must be coaxed out of the soil, torn from the mine or hewn from the forest, what difference does it make, so far as monopolization of these natural resources is concerned, whether the tax falls upon them directly or indirectly? If it be true that the government mulct would be lightened, would not monopoly of natural resources be encouraged rather than repressed? Let us say that I am paying taxes on $10,000 worth of realty, half of which is unimproved land yielding me no income, and that the annual mulct is $300; the Single-Tax is inaugurated and my buildings become exempt. My taxes—reduced, of course, by the improved system—amount to but $200, all upon land. Will I be more likely than before to place my idle land on the market for what it will bring and retire from a "speculation" supposed by the Single-Taxers to be the root of all economic evil? And if so, why? I am certainly better able than before to maintain my title, for the governmental drain upon my sources of wealth is lighter. The supply of land has not been increased nor the demand therefor diminished. In this era of machinery production is impracticable without the co-operation of capital. True, labor is the creator of capital, but it has become largely dependent upon its creature—without its assistance must return to the industrial system of the savage. This is what those economists mean who offend Mr. George by discoursing of the "wage fund." If the Single-Tax leads me to part with my idle land is the capital available for the employment of labor increased? If the purchase price comes from the sale of other land there has simply been a swapping of jack-knives; if from manufacturing or commerce, the result is the same—no capital has been added to the general stock, no new opportunities have been opened to human endeavor.

It is urged that the shifting of taxes from all other forms of wealth to land would encourage production because men would no longer be "fined" by government for building a house, constructing an engine or erecting a mill. What is taxation but the taking by government of a portion of labor's product? Land, by itself considered, can pay no taxes. All governmental burdens laid upon it must be borne by what labor compels it to yield. Taxation is a tithe taken from the bushel of corn, the bale of cotton, the barrel of flour and the bolt of cloth.   Such being the case, what boots it whether the tax be laid upon the land or the product—on the plow, the crop or the crib?   As first or last the producer of wealth must pay the tax, what difference does it make, so far as production is concerned, from which pocket it is taken?

*   *   *

There are some evils inseparable from private ownership of land; but the same may be said of every human institution yet devised.   To attribute all the ills of the industrial world to this one cause were too much like tracing bunions and baldness to the same source.   Land speculation may have had something to do with the commercial crash of '93; but it were difficult to show that its influence for evil was greater than speculation in grain and fibres, stocks and bonds.   There was a tremendous shrinkage in the market value of realty that year.   The "land monopoly" became demoralized and large holders made a desperate effort to unload at a loss,—to relinquish natural opportunities for the production of wealth—and this, the Single-Taxers say, produced the panic.   If this be true, what will happen when they deliberately bring about these very conditions again? Having undertaken to better the condition of labor and capital by compelling the great landlords to throw their holdings upon the market at bankrupt sale, they next assure us that like conditions transformed a million industrious workmen into penniless tramps and strewed the country with the wrecks of business concerns.   Did land monopoly produce the panic of 1857—when a vast public domain awaited the plow?

The fact that private ownership of land is a comparatively new thing is no argument against it   The steam engine and electric telegraph—even the Republic in which we live—are new.   Nor does it profit aught to point out that no landowner can trace his title back to the Original Producer, as can the owner of a pocket-knife or a pint of peanuts.   Mr. George truly says: "That which a man makes or produces is his own, as against all the world."   In reality man cannot "make" or "produce" a pocket-knife or a pint of peanuts, any more than he can make an acre of land or a bed of ore.   He can only transform matter into articles of utility, adding thereby to its value, and that added value, and that only, is his.   In the same manner he can, by his labor, add value to land by increasing its fertility or otherwise enhancing its desirability, and that added value is "his own, as against all the world." It is all that he claims, is all that he can sell. In time the pocket-knife becomes worthless and is relinquished; in time the value of land passes, and on the site of once populous cities the solitary herdsman tends his sheep. This being true, private ownership of land is as defensible as private ownership of corn or cattle—the title of land values is as valid as his title to any other kind of wealth which human endeavor has called into existence.

The assumption that the institution upon which Mr. George is warring makes against the interest of labor remains to be demonstrated. In matters of such moment it were unsafe to draw conclusions from a few isolated instances. The prosperous condition of New Zealand may be due to the Single-Tax, or obtain despite of it. So far as I can gather from Single-Tax literature—which seems as inexhaustible as Prohibition tracts—there is no more reason for attributing trade revival in that country to the new system than for attributing trade revival in Texas to the old. The Single-Tax were much like bread pills—calculated to do neither much good nor harm—granting, of course, that the change could be effected without alarming capital.

But the extreme of the George system, by which all increase in land values would be appropriated by the state— and to which the Single-Tax is to serve as stepping-stone— would profoundly affect industrial conditions for good or for ill. Let us consider its probable effects. We will suppose that I am by trade a farmer, and find myself in one of the older states entirely devoid of capital. Clearly there is nothing for me to do but seek employment with one more prosperous. I may then save up my wage until able to embark in business for myself, either as tenant in a populous community where land is dear, or as proprietor in a sparsely settled one where it is cheap. And I would be compelled to do the same thing under the George system, for if granted access to land I have not the capital wherewith to provide the teams and tools, shelter and sustenance necessary to make a crop. When I have accumulated a little capital I lease a farm and pay rent to an individual; under the George system I would pay rent to the state. In the first instance the amount is fixed by the law of supply and demand; in the latter I would yield to my landlord (the State) every ear of corn and every ounce of cotton in excess of what could be produced on the poorest land in cultivation. In time I buy a farm. It represents the investment of so much of the product of my labor. I may exchange it for an equal amount of other forms of wealth. Having invested my capital I expect it to yield interest as well as wages. I at once become a public-spirited citizen and strive to benefit my neighbors, because their interest and mine are commutual. I want good government, schools, and churches. I may need no protection, have no children to educate or soul to save; but I realize that these institutions add to the value of my property, enhance my capital. For the same reason I give liberally of my substance to secure railways and factories, establish newspapers and libraries, build bridges and drain pestilential marshes. The increase in the value of my land repays my enterprise and rewards my philanthropy. Under the system proposed by Mr. George I could not become a free-holder, but would remain ever a tenant. Increase in the value of land I occupied would not belong to me, but to the state; hence I would have no more interest in promoting it than would the veriest vagabond. I would be as happily situated on the outskirts of civilization as in the center of the most populous state, as prosperous 50 miles from a railway or a blacksmith shop as with these conveniences at my door, for all I gained by the advantages of location would be taken from me for the benefit of those less fortunately situated. With the chief incentive to enterprise gone, I would simply stagnate, and so would my fellows. We would have a new and greater Freudenstaedt—progressing a foot or two every four centuries.

*   *   *

The Single-Taxers who are industriously warring upon land monopoly are frightening themselves with a spectre of their own contriving. There is no such thing in existence—probably never will be. Some men own vast quantities of land; but a majority of them are willing to part with it, or portions thereof, on terms that make it as safe an investment as the purchase of any other class of property at the market price. As a rule the holders of large tracts of unused land are eager to sell the bulk of it in homestead parcels to those who will improve it and thereby add to the market value of the remainder. The "unearned increment," that lesser evil of which Mr. George complains, usually proves an effective antidote for the greater monopoly of land.

In most of the large cities we find men owning large quantities of land which yields them enormous revenues

in the way of rent. Thousands of poor people slave from
the cradle to the grave to enrich these arrogant aristocrats. Such a condition is unquestionably an evil; but
will the Single-Tax—or even the George system in its
entirety—cure it? Taking the tax off a tenement building and placing it on the land occupied has no more tendency to reduce rent than has exempting one floor from
taxation and doubling it on the next. The Single-Taxers
take it for granted that more tenement buildings would
be erected—that less land would be allowed to remain
idle. Under the present system, wherever land is available buildings are erected whenever, in the opinion of
capitalists, they will yield a good return on the investment. It is the efficient demand for buildings—a demand
backed by rent-paying ability—that causes the construction of buildings now, and the same rule would be oper-
ative under the economic system proposed by Mr. George.

Clearly the Single-Tax would not make for the betterment of the masses except in so far as, by the simplifica-
tion of government it reduced taxation. And even this
benefit, according to Mr. George, would be intercepted
by the landlords, for we have already seen that a reduction of the government of tending to abate monopoly of
natural resources, would really strengthen it. We have
also seen that the Georgian theory of state landlordism if
carried to the extent of confiscation of all land values, instead of promoting progress by insuring an equitable distribution of wealth, would really retard it by throttling individual enterprise. A nation where Georgeism was fully
applied would scarce consume itself in revolutionary fires—
it would simply petrify.

According to the census of 1890, the value of land occupied by the industrial establishments of this country
was only about one-third the value of the buildings and
machinery, less than one-third the annual wages paid.
It constituted much less than one-fourth the total assets
of those concerns. Yet Mr. George would have us believe that rent is despoiling both interest and wages—
that the tail is wagging the dog! Capital is not in business solely for its health. It is just as easy to invest
money in land as in buildings and machinery, and the
greater safety of such an investment leads men to accept
a lower interest than will induce them to embark in any
industrial enterprise. Even Mr. George notes this fact,
but its natural sequence has evidently not occurred to
him. How money invested in land values yields a smaller

return than money invested in manufacturing and merchandizing, while at the same time the landlord is robbing
all active industry, Mr. George does not explain.

It does not follow, however, that private ownership of
land is an unmixed blessing; that a man who secures title
to a few square rods in the wilderness is entitled to found
thereon a purse-proud aristocracy and compel generations yet to be to pay more than royal tribute to his heirs.
The labor of the Single-Taxers is not altogether in vain.
It has driven thousands to thinking on economic questions—and "in a multitude of counsel there is wisdom."
It serves to keep the people alive to the necessity of
guarding from the undue encroachment of concentrated
capital the great domain that has been bequeathed to
them. The political and economic systems of a country
must of necessity represent a compromise between conflicting forces which hold each other in check. Where we
have ultra-conservatives we need ultra-radicals to keep
the car of progress out of the rut; and where we have
the latter we require the former to prevent a reign of
wild experimentalism that would end in disaster. The
radicals furnish the dynamics of civilization while the
conservatives maintain the equilibrium. In the collision
of factions is generated light as well as heat, and to the
philosophic ear there is social harmony only in political
discord.

THE GRAMMAR SHARP.

A party signing himself A. L. Jenks writes the Iconoclast, pointing out a grammatical error in the last number of the great religious monthly. Thanks, Jenks. Even
the best of us will inadvertently get over on the haw side
of the median line in our syntax sometimes, and I am
so grateful to you for setting me right that I will not only
put your name in print and immortalize you as the prize
jackass of your day and generation, but tell you a little
story—in the humble hope that all your busy tribe of professional grammar sharps and pestiferous pismires will
profit by it.

I served my apprenticeship in the sanctum of a surly
editor who was long on ideas but short on grammar. One
day a putty-headed pedagogue blew in—one of those
mental microbes who spend minutes thinking what to say

and months learning how to say it. He had discovered a grammatical error in an editorial leader and was gasping like a duck with its bill full of dried mud.

"Mistah Editor," he exclaimed, "I find a grammatical ehwah in your papah this morning."

"The h—l you say!" quoth the editor, who could see no harm in taking the name of the devil or his dominions in vain. "What else did you find in the article—any ideas?"

The professor assented, and the autocrat of the sanctum continued in a voice that made the bristles of the paste-brush curl: "Well, sonny, language is the vehicle of thought, and if I have succeeded in constructing a vehicle that will carry ideas into the head of such a blankety-blanked idiot, such an irremediable ass as you are, I'll get it patented."

Do you understand, Jenks? Can you discover the beautiful moral of the story without a diagram? Right here, Jenks, I will present you—as a worthy representative of a considerable contingent of smart Alecs—with a slug of advice that is more precious than fine gold. Treasure it tenderly and transmit it as a priceless heritage to the Jenkses of the next generation: Whenever you encounter a grammatical error riding gayly along on a train of thought, "Kill it and go on." Remember that even the good Homer nods sometimes. If you aspire to be really useful go sit on the bleaching board and watch an amateur game of baseball, bestride a dry goods box and save the country, spit at a mark, preach prohibition, play croquet with a bevy of old maids, suck a cane—do anything but play grammar sharp.

Another thing, Jenks, and character this in your memory: Do not take your pen in hand and write letters to a busy editor just to display your cuteness. By so doing you encroach upon the preserves of Doc Daniels—Austin's meddlesome little itch specialist. Besides, the exasperated editor may expectorate on you and drown you.

But right here a question, Jenks: How do you get into your clothes? Do you go into them head first, then pose before an amorous looking-glass with your mouth full of pins; or do you insert yourself one leg at a time, then make frantic swipes under the bureau for collar buttons, while the circumambient ether assumes a cerulean hue? This question is important. In the unlamented erstwhile the last of the Apostles was bestride the editorial tripod of the San Antonio *Express*. One day he sorted out of his mail a kick almost as silly as yours. He had been up late—attending a prayer meeting with Albert Steve and Oscar Guessaz—and his liver was a trifle out of plumb. He jumped on that kicker and recalcitrated in return until the air was full of fragments of flesh. The next day he found in his sanctum a beautiful damosel with a chilled-steel glitter in her bright blue eye. He opined that perhaps she had called to praise his latest "Sunday Sermon" and present him with a pair of hand worked slippers several sizes too small; but he was banking on the wrong card. He thought maybe she had brought a bunch of blue forget-me-nots to lay on his shrine and to say that she had worshipped at a distance until her young heart hurt her so she could stand it no longer; but he was mistaken. She had dropped in to inform him that she was the party of the first part to the controversy aforesaid, and to lament the untimely demise of chivalry. Now, A. L. Jenks, if the front elevation of your name is Amanda Louise, please understand that this don't go; if it be Abraham Lincoln it goes with altitudinous eclat and wild acclaim.

Great God, is it possible that people will give precious time to such trifling—with the mighty Universe yet to be explored, the secret of man's origin still enshrouded in mystery, his destination a mere matter of speculation! Let grammar sharps say what they will, that phrase approaches nearest perfection which conveys, with most perspicuity and least jaw-labor, an idea from mind to mind. Mortal man cannot afford to sit down "in the conflux of two eternities" and split hairs. Life is too real, too earnest, too valuable to be wasted on the idle subtleties of word-mongers. I'd rather have Samian wine served in a goard than putrid vinegar in a goblet of gold. The purists of the present are to progressive thought what the scholastics of the past were to religion. They reduce the mind to a soulless machine which grinds no grist for the hungry multitude; they blast the fruitful fig tree with the curse of their foolish criticism; they substitute manner for matter—esteem the wretched vehicle above its priceless freight.

HEAVEN AND HELL.

Their Latitude and Longitude.

Ever since the idea of Heaven and Hell first dawned upon the mind of man, he has been trying to locate those interesting ultimates, to fix their position in the Cosmos, to mark out their metes and bounds; but despite infinite inquiry at Sibyl-caves and elsewhere, patient poring over half-articulate prophecies, much labored lucubration and study of the heavens by theologico-astronomic savants, they still hover indefinite in the great inane, a drifting Delos which no scientific Jupiter can finally fix and give a latitude and longitude. We are accustomed to think of Heaven as high above us; of Hell as far beneath our feet,—a freak of barbaric fancy that even our super-civilization cannot shake off. If Heaven be over our heads at midday, what direction at Night's high noon would we take to reach the happy home of the Gods?

Is it not possible that we are using in this search telescopes of too long a range,—looking quite over the objects sought and into inane limboes; that, in fact, we need no optical aids, being able to look into the highest Heaven and deepest Hell—even with our eyes closed; to hear celestial harp-music and the rush of wings amid the perfumed groves of Paradise; to feel Hell's hot blast beating into our very faces? Is it not possible that Hell and Heaven are even around us and within us, visual, tactual,—here or nowhere?

What is it that we denominate Heaven but Happiness; that we call Hell but Unhappiness? Then art thou not in Heaven or Hell? Is it necessary to pass the portals of the tomb, to make a long voyage on unknown seas to find Pleasure or Pain? What Pleasure cans't paint with Fancy's most skillful pencil that transcends pure Love requited? What agony, mental and physical, cans't picture greater than surrounds thee on every side? Is it not true, that even here, in this world, in this life, is found the divinest Pleasure and the most demoniac Pain—the highest Heaven and the deepest, darkest Hell that human mind can conceive? That even now we flit to and fro in Paradise, harping and hymning to an ever-present God; or wander, with blistered feet and bleeding hearts, hopeless and helpless, through the desolate regions of the damned?

Perhaps if we were all transported, Elijah-like, to the

orthodox heaven, many of us would find it much less toler-
able than this earth; would long to return and fight Life's
bitter battles all over again; to suffer an occasional touch
of that nether fire which sometimes scorches and withers
us. Really, if the celestial immigration agents have put
forth a true prospectus, it is small wonder that people cling
so tenaciously to the old homestead, or, when compelled to
move, go to a quite opposite direction. In old times it was
supposed that angels relinquished heaven for earth's pains
and pleasures—being tempted thereto by the daughters of
men; and after carefully reading such celestico-descriptive
literature as can be come at, one may well wonder that the
whole Heavenly Hierarchy did not follow them, and give to
Lucifer and his hosts his leave to return thither when they
liked.

How better can we describe Heaven than by calling it
Content; Hell than by naming it Discontent? One man is
contented with a crust—finds Heaven in half a loaf of black
bread; another is discontent with a crown—finds Hell in
the wardship of half a world. How, then, if men are to retain aught of their individuality—if they are not to be blotted out and quite new beings created in their places in
whom the first parties can take no more than an idle interest—can we expect one Heaven, even though the highest,
to please everybody? How can we expect one Hell to
prove a place of pain to the great multi-minded host that is
supposed to be drifting thither? Really the Devil and his
imps would prove quite pleasant companions to many—
kindred spirits who take a grim delight in defying Destruction itself.

Stranger than even the idea that we must leave this
world to find the face of Deity or Devil is our method of
determining who shall be given a harp in the great Hereafter, who dance to music of quite other making. We set
up an arbitrary standard of Goodness; those who comply
therewith are assuredly destined for Paradise, those who fall
short thereof as certainly devoted to Destruction. If a man
do thus-and-so he may, according to all accounts, read his
title clear to mansions in the skies; if he do not so, it will be
the worse for him in the world to come. "To the victor
belongs the crown." Granted; but how are we to determine
who are the victors—what ones of the mighty host seeking
celestial bays fought their way through fierce foes; what
ones found no gorgons and goblins in their path, but
marched gaily through their allotted term of life without
so much as a skirmish?

With fair fortune and fish blood how easy it were to be a saint! With fortune of quite another hue and every vein a fierce flaming torrent of Gehenna-fire, in which Demons dance and Lust runs riot, in which Madness mingles and Murder ever shrieks, it were not so easy. Is it not possible that some of the world's worst wage the most relentless warfare upon the great realm of Darkness and the Devil? That while others are making a holiday warfare upon and putting to flight certain mischievous little imps—Satan's light infantry—many of those we call criminals and assign to the gallows here and Hell hereafter, have for long weary years been at very death-grips with the whole Infernal Hierarchy? battling without hope of victory, of that Happiness of Despair and that God like within them that, however choked by the sulphur-fumes of war, however torn and trampled, cannot cry for quarter, will not surrender, but, through defeat after defeat, fight ever on and on!

In physical warfare, where man goes forth to strive with man, the world stops not to consider who was victor or vanquished; but rather with what courage they fought, what powers they contended withal. It were greater glory to have lost Thermopylae or the Alamo than to have won on fairer fields; yet in this struggle with Hell's puissant powers to be overcome is to merit eternal infamy! To those who stand—though they never looked on Lucifer's blazing banner—imperishable crowns; to those who fall, the execration of man, the curse of God! Around the unscarred "victors" we gather with paeans of praise, upholding their hands in every trivial trial; but let not those who bear the battle's brunt—upon whose unhappy heads burst the blue terrors of that mighty cimmerian cloud—expect either aid or comfort, love or sympathy. Alone in that black Chaos; mocked by man, torn by fiends, taught that even God is their enemy, they must struggle on to—what?

ISRAEL AS IT IS.

There was a time when to have sprung from Judah's consecrated loins was better than to be born a king; when the embattled hosts of Israel made the world tremble before their martial might, and men turned for knowledge to Zion's holy hill as the helianthus turns its face to the rising sun.

When our ancestors were but brutal barbarians, clad in

skins stripped with sharp stones from beasts scarcely less ferocious; dwelling in caves and subsisting on roots and raw meat; with no aspirations above the crudest creature comforts, no conception of immortality, no dream of man's high destiny, Solomon was making silver as the stones in the streets of Jerusalem; the Jews were worshipping the "Lord of Hosts," framing those laws which are to-day the basic principle of civilization, quelling semi-barbarous people with the sword, computing the procession of the planets and weaving into the woof of human history those imperishable gems of poesy and philosophy which the world's wisest say transcend the genius of mortal man and must, perforce, be the gracious gift of God.

Yet for twenty centuries we have regarded the Jew with suspicion, treated him as if he were of an inferior race; as though in his bosom beat the heart of an inhuman harpy, in his veins coursed the accursed blood of the wolf. For twenty centuries the Jew has suffered "the oppressor's wrong, the proud man's contumely"—has been the target at which the finger of scorn was ever pointed; the buffet of dissolute princes and purse-proud potentates; the undeserving victim of the blind wrath of the proletarian rabble; the mark at which sectarian hate and unreasoning bigotry have levelled their most vindictive shafts; despoiled, outraged, beaten with many stripes; expatriated, driven hither and thither, finding no rest for his weary feet in a world which his wisdom has done so much to humanize, to which he has given happiness here and hope hereafter

Is it possible that the Jew, who is of the blood and bone of the patriarchs and prophets, of Moses the Medianite, and those warlike Maccabees before whom the fierce Syrian soldiery fled terror-stricken from Judea's hills, is a creature fit only for our contumely, a dog to be spurned by "Christian" feet? that the children of men who, cooped up in one quarter of their beloved city and dying of starvation, defended their holy temple against Titus the Terrible and the intrepid sons of all-conquering Rome until the sacred pile was dripping with blood and ablaze with the legionary's brand, but merit the sneers of a people whose ancestors a few generations ago were plowing the Northern seas as pirates in quest of plunder, or participating in the bloody and brutal rites of the Druidical superstition?

To deny that there is a widespread antipathy to the Jew were as fatuous as to deny the existence of the sun. In most parts of the United States this antipathy is latent; but in Europe it not only manifests itself in legislation and social ethics, but frequently bursts forth in deeds of desperate violence and inhumanity on the part of the people. Even while I write, in "Christian" Russia the Jews are being despoiled and outraged—their homes given to the flames, their savings to the plunderer, their daughters to the ravisher, their throats to the knife! And the rest of the so-called Christian world mildly protests; intimates that, perhaps, after all, the Jew has a soul, at least flesh and bone, and may suffer somewhat.

While the Tsar's brutal soldiery—aided by the volunteer efforts of the Russian peasantry and such other people as consider the killing of a creditor the easiest way to discharge an honest debt—are hurrying the Jews across the frontiers, the civilized world is firing whereases, resolutions, remonstrances signed by aldermen and fledgling D. D.'s, silly tirades by alleged able editors and other trifling nonsense and cheap balderdash at his "Most Christian Majesty;" then, convinced that it has done its duty, it goes home to dinner—perhaps with a half defined feeling that nobody has any business to be a Jew! Were the people of any other race subjected to such barbarous brutality, the Christian world, so-called, would demand that it cease instantly, and demand it sword in hand.

The cause of this prejudice against the Jew, which appears to be bred in the very bone of "Christian" people of Indo-European blood, it were indeed difficult to determine. Scarcely a count in the formidable indictment which has hung over him for a hundred generations like a veritable sword of Damocles, will stand analysis. It is charged that the Jew will not intermarry with other races. In God's name, cannot a man choose a wife to suit himself without having a whole majestic universe snarling at his heels? If the dark-eyed daughters of Judah prefer their kinsmen to those who from time immemorial have persecuted them, cannot a professedly chivalrous world leave them free to choose? Is it at all strange that a people whose blood for two thousand years has been kept free from taint, should decline to pour it into that great red tide which has greedily absorbed every clean and unclean thing with which it has come in contact, whether Goth or Moor, British barbarian or American red Indian, and is now blending slowly but surely with the Ethiop and Australian Bushman?

But while the incongruous and ofttimes unclean mixture of races in Europe, and especially in America, where the great-grandsons of Charlemagne's paladins wed the great-granddaughters of expatriated sneak thieves and lousy Indian squaws—where the blood of the Capulets mingles with

that of the Cades—is of itself sufficient to give pause to
those who trace their lineage through God-fearing men and
chaste women back to the days of David, it is not the only
nor the chief cause why the Jews maintain that solidarity
which is at once the wonder of the world and the burthen
of its never-ceasing jeremiad. Their religion tends to make
the Jews chary of intermarriage with non-conformists; but
the great determining cause of their exclusiveness is the
social and political ostracism to which they have for so
many centuries been generally subjected by the "enlightened," "progressive," "Christian" nations of Europe, and
which occasionally shows its ugly front, like Discord at
Peleus' nuptial rites, in free America, where anything that
can dodge the gallows or the jail for one and twenty years
is called a sovereign,—where we buy with our millions the
bastard spawn of kings' courtesans as husbands for our
daughters!

The Jew was driven into trade and money-changing by
the edicts of Christian potentates forbidding him to acquire
title to land. In his own country before the diaspora his
chief occupation was agriculture, and the law of his religion
did not permit him to lend at interest for the relief of distress. Money is power, even in the hands of the Jew, and
it is small wonder that when he found it his only friend in
a world of fanatical foes—the only weapon with which he
could hope to win his way—in sheer self-defense he dili-
gently sought to acquire all of it possible. Money to the
Jew has ever meant much more than creature comforts;
it has meant sword and shield, bulwark and bastion—the
magic wand that metamorphoses the Medusa-face of sectarian hate into that of the oily and unctuous hypocrite.

It is small wonder that in money matters the Jew has
become preternaturally keen; small wonder that in dealing
with his enemies, actual or potential, he should prove an
exacting creditor—should acquire an unenviable reputation among his hereditary critics for sordidness and "sharp
practice." But the avarice, so-called, of the Jew, is the
result, not the cause of centuries of political and social ostracism. To abuse the Jew for "getting gain" were like
throwing a man into a tempestuous sea and cursing him for
grasping desperately at whatever may promise preservation. Numerically too weak to force recognition of his
right with the naked sword, the Jew forges his weapon of
fine gold and with it makes the proudest of Christian
potentates pay him homage with their lips while they curse
him in their hearts.

So far from being a stony-hearted, avaricious people,

as popularly supposed, the Jews are naturally the most
sympathetic and generous in the world. Who ever heard
of a Jew begging bread, going to the alms-house or suffering for creature comforts, while other members of his race
—even though strangers—knowing of his necessities, had
a crust to share or a dollar to divide? And yet we "Christians,"who prate of our liberality and pose before the world
as paragons of philanthropy, ofttimes allow our old mothers
to go "on the county" while we go on a champagne "jag;"
permit our brothers to eat the bitter bread of a stranger's
contemptuous charity, while we parade as public-spirited
citizens! Very remarkable is it that while our relatives are
usually the last in the world we desire to embark in business with, the Jew prefers his near kinsman to all others.
We know our brethren—know that they will rob and betray, "bullyrag" and beat at every opportunity. The
Jew knows his brethren and trusts his fortune to their
hands without a tremor!

Avaricious? Miserly? Little-souled? Mean? Thou fool!
The Jew is the most liberal money-spender in the world.
He calls for the best of everything and pays for it like a
prince! Did you ever hear that a Jew miser starved to
death in the midst of his millions? That one of the race of
Judah ever perished for lack of medical attendance which
he was too penurious to pay for? Yet such things are of
almost daily occurrence in this Christian land! But the
victim of the unholy lust for gain is never, no, never, a Jew.
He may hide his heart in his money-bags, but never follows
the example of Pedro Garcia and keeps his soul there also.

In every country where the Jew has been accorded the
political privileges of other people, he has proven himself
a public-spirited citizen, and his subscriptions to enterprises to promote the public welfare have been paid
promptly and without protest. While the Christian has
given his "moral support," the Jew has gone down into his
pockets and planked down the wherewithal that "makes
the world go round."

Another count in the indictment is that the Jew never
really identifies himself with the country in which he re-
sides—never becomes a patriot; that he is eager to enjoy
the rights of citizenship while shirking its responsibilities
—anxious for the protection of a flag he will not lift a hand
to defend. This is, perhaps, the most remarkable of all
the multifarious phases in which ingrained prejudice and
hereditary hatred has bodied itself forth. Although the
Jewish contingent in our eleemosynary institutions and
penitentiaries is practically nil, they are largely supported

by taxes paid by the Jewish people. True, the Jew is seldom the central figure at party primaries; his voice rarely
adds to the discordant din of partisan polemics; he is seldom seen on the stump at cross-roads or the beer-barrel
in bar-rooms, telling his fellow-citizens what to do to be
saved. He rarely makes of himself a moral bankrupt or
noisy nuisance trying to capture an office with small salary
and large stealage:—but he can generally be counted upon
to cast his ballot for the "conservative" candidate and pay
his taxes promptly. Furthermore, when he finds that
country in danger which treats him a few degrees better
than a dog, he can be depended upon to risk his life and
fortune in its defense. Compared with percentage of population, the Jewish contingent in the Federal and Confederate forces was very large, and precious few circumcised
soldiers were arrested for bounty-jumping, reprimanded
for cowardice or court-martialed for desertion. Many
Jews rose to military distinction during the civil war, and
the descendants of Miles Standish, Mad Anthony Wayne,
Light-Horse Harry Lee and Francis Marion were proud to
call them their commanders. Who can forget the services
to the South of Judah Benjamin, or the heroic fortitude
with which the Jews stood by the failing Confederacy "with
their fortunes, their lives and their sacred honor?" But
for the financial aid of the Northern Jews when the tide
of battle appeared to be turning against the Federal government and the mighty structure seemed tottering to its
fall; when the British lion was crouching for a spring, and
even France looked askance at the wounded eagle, the
mailed hand of the mighty North would have fallen nerve-
less as that of a frightened child, the stars and bars would
float south of the Ohio, and that scourge of God, negro
slavery, be fixed on this fair land forever.

Since the Jews became numerous in Europe and America there has been scarce a battlefield not dyed with Israel's
consecrated blood; scarcely a military maneuver not paid
for from Jewish purses; scarce a throne not gilded by Jewish industry; scarce a printed page upon which, directly or
indirectly, they did not set their seal; scarce a poet who did
not borrow their musical metaphors; scarce an orator who
did not tacitly acknowledge in every sentence that but for
the Jews he would have nothing to say.

From the loins of Judah have sprung more intellectual
giants than any other race or nation can boast. The roster
of those who have added to the world's wisdom, to human
happiness, stretches in an unbroken line from the present
hour back to the dawn of human history. Did you ever

stop to reflect that Spinoza, the prince of philosophers, Mendelssohn, the master of the world of music, and a host of others whom we revere as something almost more than mortal, not to mention the Christ, whom we worship as a God, were all of the race which you profess to despise? The cause of the prejudice against the Jews is multifarious. He is emphatically a child of the Orient—as different from the Occidentals as though native of another planet. The brawny and intensely practical Scotch Highlander and the mild-eyed melancholy lotus-eater could scarce be further apart from an ethnological standpoint than the Jews and the Indo-Germanic people. Race, political and religious differences bred antipathy long before the destruction of the Second Temple. Then as the Jews dispersed over Europe, came the ill-wind of business rivalry, the hatred of the debtor for the creditor class, followed by the fierce fires of religious bigotry that made of mediaeval Europe a hell upon which Caius Caligula might have looked with horror. In those fierce Gehenna-fires were forged the chains that still hold the Christian mind in thrall; in those dark days when intolerance was lord paramount, when superstition was the handmaiden of religion and the Christian cavalier drove into the ground his sword, stained with the blood of non-conforming maidens, and fell upon his knees before the reeking cross that formed the hilt; when with whip and faggot, the thumb-screw and the wheel, fanatics dragged men to the throne of Grace, or drove them to the Devil, the vulpine instinct of the Jew attained, perforce, an abnormal development, distrust of those not of his race and religion became hereditary. He found the world against him, and it is his misfortune, not his fault, that his hand is against the world.

That the spirit of the Jews has not been utterly crushed by twenty centuries of systematic oppression; that they have not withered beneath the terrible baptism of fire, degenerated into contemptible spiritless lazzaroni; that the united world has signally failed to trample them beneath its brutal feet and keep them there; that despite two thousand years of trial and temptation, of calumny, intimidation, of the most brutal outrages recorded in Time's too unhappy annals, the daughters of Judah are to-day the paragons of purity, as they have ever been of beauty, proclaims to every man with eyes to see and brain to understand, that the Jews are one of the greatest races, one of the grandest peoples that ever appeared upon the earth; that the Lord of Hosts was infinitely wiser than we when He made His covenant with them and swore by His own bright essence increate, that

through good and ill, through weal and woe, He would be
their God and they should be His people.

THE CURSE OF KISSING.

Every little while some smart Alec scientist mounts the
bema to inform a foolish world that kissing is a dangerous
pastime; that upon the roseate lips of beauty there ever
lurks the bacillus, flourishing skull and cross-bones—veritable flaming swords to keep poor Adam out of his Eden.
According to these learned men the fairest maid is loaded
to the muzzle with microbes, her kiss a Judas osculation,
betraying the sighing swain who dares to browse upon
her dewy lips, to well-nigh certain death. In the "lingering sweetness long drawn out" myriads of disease germs
are supposed to pass from mouth to mouth in true reci
procity fashion, and, falling upon new and fecund soil,
take root and flourish there until the ecstatic fools pass untimely to that bourne where all faces stand so wide ajar—
held so by eternal hosannahs—that an attempted kiss were
like dropping Hoosac Tunnel into the Mammoth Cave.
As the duly ordained guide, philosopher and friend of the
scientists—as of the clergy—the Iconoclast feels compelled
to file a protest. As the Moor of Venice intimated, there's
such a thing as knowing entirely too much. Wisdom that
knocks the yum-yum out of life, transforms the fond delights of courtship into an armed neutrality and makes of
the sensuous Vale of Cashmere a profitless desert of dead
formalities and scientific sanitation, simply to save the life
assurance companies paying an occasional premium, should
be sealed in some Pandora box or genie-casket and cast
into the sea. We cannot blame the bacteria for selecting
as roosting place the rose-bud mouths of the daughters of
men, any more than we can blame the bees for hovering
with drowsy drunken hum about the fragrant flowers; still
we were happier when we knew not of their presence—
when we could swoop blithely down upon a pair of ruby lips
working like a patent clothes-wringer in a steam laundry,
and extract hyblaean honey in great hunks without Death
riding his old white skate athwart our pansy-bed and freez-
ing the genial current of our soul with his Svengali leer.
We dislike to quarrel with science, but the tables educed
in the currency controversy now epidemic in this unhappy
land have made us doubt. Death may lurk in the lover's
kiss like a yellow-jacket in a Jersey apple; but that scien-

tist who will go about with his compound microscope, searching into this tutti-frutti of the soul for miniature monsters, is fit for treason, stratagems and spoils. He's not a credible witness and ought to be abolished. He's the Thersites of modern society, and we hope to see some wrathful Achilles take him out behind the smoke-house and talk to him in a tone of voice that would discourage a book agent or a poor relation. We don't believe a word about his little tale of osculatory woe. During a variegated experience of forty years we've never combed any tuberculosis fungi, mump microbes or diphtheritic walking delegates out of our white-horse moustache. Kissing injurious to health, forsooth! Why it's the fount of perennial youth which owl-eyed old Ponce de Leon sought among the savages, instead of filling his sails with sighs of "Gady's soft desiring strain." It's the true Brown-Sequard elixir, which makes the heart of hoary age beat forever like a boy's. It's the heaven-distilled *eau de vie* which causes the young man to forget a combination of tight boot and soft-boiled corn and makes the grisly octogenarian rise up William Riley and neigh like a two-year-old. Disease germs, indeed! Why it's nature's remedy for all the ills that flesh is heir to, *facile princeps* of *ennui* antidotes, infallible cure for that tired feeling. The latest pseudo-scientist to discover that the gentle ripple of the kiss is but a dirge, tries to set in the black o'erhanging firmament a bow of promise. He opines that all danger may be avoided if the kissing machines are carefully deodorized before and after using, and recommends that the lips be washed with some chemical compound that will make the most obstinate bacillus sorry he was born. It's a great scheme—but will it work? Will our society belles and beaux now appear equipped, each with a bottle of carbolic acid or a jug of lime water in which to soak their sweetness before effecting that exchange which is no robbery? or will each parlor be provided with a bowl of bacteria annihilator, which the young man will employ much as the careful cotton planter does Paris green? The plan of disinfection before permitting the spirits to rush together a la Tennyson at the touching of the lips, may work in Boston, perhaps; but out here in the glad, free Southwest, where we still have to catch our hare before we cook it, such an arrangement would clog the wheels of progress and perhaps extinguish Hymen's torch. Imagine the Apostle chasing the beauteous Rebecca Merlindy around a log cabin at some husking bee at the metropolis of Harris county, a swab in one hand and a gourdful of carbonated bayou water in the other! Here in Texas

a man must take his kiss with the peeling on or go without.
He has enough to do to manage the maid without bother-
ing about the bacteria. And, let scientists with their double-
geared microscopes say what they may, that man who gets
an opportunity to buzz a corn-fed beauty whose breath is
sweet as that of a brindle calf fed on clover blooms, need
not worry about bacilli. It is a feast fit for gods, so
let him fall to, without waiting to have the bloom sponged
off his peach on the foolish hypothesis that its component
parts are horned hippogriffs, icthyosauria and feathered
sea-serpents such as hover in the gloom of a gold-cure
joint at 2 g. m. If his heart fails him—if he be not willing
to chance the cold and silent tomb for the felicity of browsing for a few fleeting moments in Elysian Fields—let him
follow the example of the great and glorious G. Cleveland,
Esq., and hire a substitute. There are cases, however,
where it would be well to do considerable deodorizing before risking osculation; better still, to let the doubtful
sweets remain unplucked, as not worth the labor. This
great Yankee nation has fallen into the bad habit of promiscuous kissing—a social rite as stale, flat and every way
unprofitable as employing a community toothbrush or an
indiscriminate swapping of gum. Whether dangerous diseases may be transmitted thereby I know not; but it is
death to sentiment and provocative of nausea. A woman
should be almost as chary of her lips as of more gracious
favors. A sensitive gentleman would as soon accept a
bride from Boiler avenue as take to wife a vestal virgin
whom every lecherous libertine had "mouthed and mumbled." The practice of "kissing the bride," which still prevails in communities professing not only civilization, but
the acme of aestheticism, should be abolished by law under
severe pains and penalties. Why a modest woman, who
has done nothing worse than marry, should be compelled to
kiss a company of men and thereby sample everything from
the aroma of sour stomachs to masticated codfish, I cannot
imagine. The levite who performs the ceremony usually
consecrates the first fruits to the Lord, and what he may
chance to leave is gleaned by Tom, Dick and the Devil,
until lips that would have tempted angels to assume mortal
ills, become foul as the Valley of Hinnom—sweet incense
to offer a loving lord! I once attended a church fair in
Missouri and there found two local beauties of good family
retailing kisses to all comers at two-bits apiece—"for the
good of the cause!" "D—n a cause," quoth I, "that must
be forwarded by such foul means." I bought $5 worth of
the sacred sweetness—then hired an old farmer who en-

joyed a bad case of catarrh and had worn his solitary tooth
down to the pliocene period chewing plug tobacco and de-
positing the quotient on his beard, to receive the goods.
When half through with the job he struck for a raise of
salary! A kiss should be a sacred thing—the child of a
love that is deathless. It is the benediction of a mother,
the pledge of a sweetheart, the homage of a wife. Promiscuous kissing is a casting of pearls before swine, a brutal
prostitution of the noblest and holiest rite ever practiced
by the human race. It is a flagrant offense against all that
is noble in man and modest in woman; hence let us hope
that it is really conducive to disease—that the wage of sin
is death.

THE MAN IN THE MOON.

CRITICISM BY OUR LUNAR CONTEMPORARY.

Doubtless you have a distant acquaintance with the Man
in the Moon. He never becomes unduly familiar, never
borrows money of you or quarrels with you anent forms of
baptism,—never bores you with his political views or takes
a fiendish delight in telling you the unkind things which
others say about you. When two is company he does not
make a crowd. He is probably the oldest inhabitant, certainly the most prominent citizen of our little contempo-
rary. Our ancestors saw him as an old man bearing a lantern and bundle of faggots—going about in the bright sunlight that illumines his home, much as did our own foolish
Diogenes; but whether on the same errand, deponent saith
not. What he purposed doing with his bundle of faggots
—whether to build a fire to cook his breakfast, or broil a
heretic—was never definitely determined. The modern
almanac-makers see only the face of the old fellow—a
mildly-beaming countenance, somewhat resembling that of
Mr. Pickwick, when the moon is full, that of a disappointed
and discouraged office-seeker when the bright disc has
faded to a silver bow. For my part, I could always see
in the moon many people besides an old man toiling along
to a lunar nowhere with his bundle of faggots, or beaming
down on me with smile both childlike and bland. When
the moon is full—and quite regardless of my own condition
—I can see therein a gallant soldier and his bonny bride,
two charming ladies in confidential tete-a-tete, and the
head and shoulders of a gigantic gladiator lying fast asleep

unscreened by so much as a mosquito bar—the musical attendants of Morpheus evidently being undreamed of in his philosophy. And sometimes, again, when the moon chances to hang at a peculiar angle, this variegated population disappears and the great disc resembles a mighty medallion, with Goddess of Liberty clear-cut and distinct as on the silver dollar. The stars are there encircling her, but no E Pluribus Unum—not so much as mention of "the crime of '73." I've often thought that could the other side of the moon be seen a full-fledged American eagle would there be found, squinting one eye at the legend, In God We Trust—while keeping a close grip on his bundle of arrows. I am satisfied that could Mr. Cleveland see the moon as I sometimes do, and note its similitude to the silver dollar, he'd recommend its utter abolition by act of Congress or employ the bond-clippers to build a golden pyramid for it to rest upon, like a prize pumpkin poised on a knitting-needle—

But perchance the handsome lady is the lunar "New Woman,"—not yet provided with bike and bloomers—who has retired the old man to the nursery and herself assumed the sceptre of the night.

I have tried to point out to various people the interesting family of the Man in the Moon; but they have usually insisted that he was doing the Robinson Crusoe act—sailing through space on his silver isle in utter solitude. Being a Jeffersonian Democrat, I yield to the verdict of the majority and surrender my private opinion, even discredit the evidence of my own eyes,—quite the proper thing from a partisan standpoint—and shall take it for granted that the lunar Goddess of Liberty, like our own star-crowned and mud-bedraggled deity, is a mythus, the creature of a morbid imagination, and devote my entire attention to the time-honored Man in the Moon.

He has evidently been there ever since the swift-rolling little planet assumed its present topography—perhaps millions of years ago. From a period so remote that the mind of man can scarce conceive thereof, he has looked benignly down upon this teeming earth, with its laughter and its tears, its triumphal arches and its bitter ashes—looked and held his peace. He is accounted everybody's friend, because he is no tale-bearer, tattler and two-faced talking machine; is "the same yesterday, to-day and forever;" a fact which many men—and perchance an occasional woman, likewise—might profitably reflect upon.

Nations rise and fall; religions are born and die; the Tower of Babel lifts its spiral curves to kiss the clouds, then

crumbles into dust; Alexander conquers the world and
Mark Antony casts it away as a worthless bauble to bask
in the sensuous splendor of Cleopatra's eyes; Lisbon
earthquakes engulf their thousands and the French Revolutions flame with nether fire—the Man in the Moon observes it all and makes no sign. How different he from
the Man—or even the Woman—in the Earth! Do but let
a Cleveland babe be born, or the daughter of a prosperous
map-peddler take a bankrupt dude with bogus title to
raise, and there is universal cackle as of multitudinous flocks
of geese gone mad. Let a brace of pugilists pound each
other with pillows for a fat purse, or some poor preacher
bite at the Devil's hook, baited with an old sunbonnet, and
what a commotion:—people priding themselves on the
possession of a thinking faculty expecting the heavens to
fall, or the civilization of six thousand years to slip its
trolley-pole.   Let political parties—with adjustable platforms and gutta-percha principles—indulge in wrestling-
match, with the public flesh-pots as prize, what screeching and scrannel-piping by perspiring orators and partisan
editors—the confusion of Babel worse confounded!

Sitting silent there all these centuries and watching the
goings and comings of the children of men—their mega-
lopanous horn-tootings and turgid pufferies, their inane
bickerings and infamous back-bitings—listening to their
ape-chattering and eternal much ado about nothing—has it
occurred to the Man in the Moon, think you, that what the
human race most needs is a gold-cure for the gab habit?
How thankful he must have been when the morning stars
sang together that there were no featherless bipeds to
drown, with their foolish bawling, the celestial melody!

We are supposing, of course, that the Man in the Moon
is a living, sentient being; that the mild face so long
turned upon this planet is that of one who sees, and seeing,
understands. Does such a face look down upon us from
anywhere in the great Immensity? The priests and prophets
of all ages have assured us even so.   They have given to this
supernal being many names and attributes and habitations,
but have signally failed to fix his celestial latitude and longitude. Gods come and gods go, but the Man in the
Moon remains. He saw—if aught inanimate e'er sees—
the rise of Kishna and Kronus, of Odin and Osiris, of
Jupiter and Jove; and in serene and silent majesty he looks
down upon their ruined altars and deserted fanes.   Cults
and creeds have swayed the minds of untold millions—have
enforced themselves with sword and faggot, with poison-
cup and persecution cruel as Perdition's pains—only to be

swept by the broom of Time into the world's great rubbish-heap as intellectual trash, and from these mounds of muck new dogmas have sprung like weeds, and flourished their little day, and died—layer upon layer, like cities rising and falling upon the ruins of other cities where men have lived and loved—passing, each in its turn, into the tomb of the world's history, its traditions, its utter forgetfulness—forever lost in the murky shadows of the centuries! When Jehovah has resigned to other hands the sceptre of the universe, and the Christian cultus taken its place beside the Babylonian creeds; when antiquarians trace with infinite toil on ruined monuments and fallen pillars the history of this proud Republic, as they trace that of many a bygone nation which imagined itself one of the few, the immortal things that were not born to die; when Macauley's New Zealander muses on a broken arch of London Bridge and watches the solitary herdsman tend his sheep on the site of the world's metropolis, as he does to-day where Babylonian gardens once did hang and the lords and ladies of Nineveh rolled in gilded chariots over cloth of gold—where Carthagenia's voluptuous queen wept for unrequited love and Priam's intrepid sons begirt the altars of Ilium with burnished steel—the Man in the Moon will look down with the same imperturbable countenance that he turned upon the Buddha sitting solitary beneath the Bodhi tree, upon Hagar as she wandered forth from the tent of Abraham into the wilderness. Not a line has changed since he beamed on Pyramus and Thisbe stealing forth to their trysting place near old Ninus' tomb—not a wrinkle has been added since Joshua spiked the lunar coat-tail fast in the valley of Ajalon while he slaughtered the Amorites, despoiled their vineyards and enslaved their virgins.

If the Man in the Moon would only speak, how many things he might tell us! How the world's history would be revised and our pantheon of heroes and galaxy of saints transformed! During the dark of the moon does he hold converse with that lunar Goddess of Liberty, or New Woman we have observed there,—her gaze turned intently hitherward, as tho' watching the progress of female suffrage or studying our Parisian fashion plates? Does he, in post-prandial sociability over his wine and walnuts, chatter unrestrained with that great gladiator—who may be Hercules resting from his labors, or even the sun-god visiting his fair Salene and fallen fast asleep while waiting for her to do up her back hair or put a little celestial powder on her pale cheeks? And if so, what does he say? Can you imagine—he having so carefully watched the *genus homo* ever since his advent upon the earth—familiar with every detail of his origin and development? Is it possible that he observes us simply for his amusement; or, at most, studies us much as a naturalist might the frantic industry of a tribe of ants? When the lunar blinds are close-drawn and the stars given leave to flaunt their glories in the face of night, does he make merry at our expense? Can you imagine him saying:

"Those little bipeds, straddling painfully over the surface of our sister planet, amuse me very much. Do you know sun, moon and stars were made for their especial benefit— that these planetary microbes actually imagine the world, just as the fleas on a monster dog suppose the canine was created solely for their comfort—that the animal's frantic efforts to get rid of them are "special providences" having some mysterious tendency to promote their "ultimate good?" They really imagine themselves the only important things in this great universe of ours—that the rest is but leather and prunella.

"Poor ephemera, living their little day, then sinking back into the soil, their bodies fertilizing weeds and fattening worms! Do but observe them burrowing like moles in their mother's bosom; trying to count her ribs or determine if she have a heart of fire—to read her history in the freckles of her face. Miserable redbugs on the thick cuticle of the mighty planet! Note them sweeping the milky-way with petty tubes called telescopes, or pondering with magnifying glass over a drop of water—the world of other animalculae only somewhat smaller than themselves—then founding pretentious schools wherein they impart, with birch rod and other educational appliances, the secrets of the universe! Science born of supposition, philosophies founded upon fooleries, stuffed with infinite labor into the fat heads of half-fledged ephemera and miscalled education! And the wisest in the great owlerie cannot comprehend the fundamental principle of Nature's first and simplest law, that of gravitation; cannot tell whence he came or whither he goes—uncertain whether his ancestors were angels or apes! And yet I have seen them fall upon their fellows and do them to the death for declaring that certain frog-eyed and ass-eared animalculae were incompetent to read every riddle in the great apocalypse of nature —were not familiar with the very family affairs of the Creator of the Cosmos!"

And so might the Man in the Moon go on maundering and mumbling century after century, rehearsing our faults, laughing at our presumption—even advising Bo-otes that when weary of the chase and seeking *dolce far niente*, he would find us a curious if somewhat profitless study in bacteriology.

Of course it were unkind of the Man in the Moon to make such remarks about us; still, if we could but hear, it might do us good like a medicine—enable us to better understand our small importance in the economy of the universe; to get our heads out of the clouds and cling somewhat closer to the grass. Did you ever reflect that to the archangels—if such there be—we are even as the Lilliputians of Gulliver to the Brobdignagians—mere trifling curiosities to be kept in a case—what the doodle-bugs or itch bacilli are to us?

Suppose that while idly lounging on heaven's imperial battlements, Ithuriel, star-eyed sentinel of the great court of God, should discover Brother Cranfill, the abdominous apostle of prohibition, assiduously saving the country by spying about club-room keyholes, stirring up strife between neighbors,—an abnormal nuisance, a pestiferous blue-bottle buzzing about a putrid body politic: what think you? Would the entire celestial population crowd the jasper walls, like boys at a ball-game, to observe our poor crack-brained brother? Would they dispute anent his proper entomological classification, come insisting that he was a scarabaeus, or terrestrial tumble-bug, who had misplaced his little ball of compost and was running frantically hither and thither in search thereof? Would they send a committee to the Almighty to humbly ask why this amorphous curiosity was created?

A thousand years are to the Lord as but one day; and, by laborious inquiry and shrewd guesswork, we can trace the human race back almost a week! Another seven days on the great horologue of God and the genus homo may be gone utterly; but the planets will continue to circle round the sun, Orion and Arcturus to pour their mighty streams of sidereal glory into the great realm of darkness, the Pleiades to "twinkle like a swarm of fire-flies tangled in a silver braid." The existence of the human race is but an unimportant incident in the history of the universe—infusoria born of heat and moisture, perishing when the moisture is eliminated or the heat becomes greater or less. Had man not appeared, the mountains would have reared their rugged crests to meet the glory of the unrisen sun, the purple mists have hovered in the valleys, the rivers rolled onward to the sea and the tides ebbed and flowed—not a star would have fallen from the o'erhanging firmament, not a planet hesitated in its eternal course; there

would have been never a drop of water nor a grain of sand
more or less.

"Lords of Creation," forsooth! We are the idle sport
of Time and Space. Yesterday is forgotten and to-morrow
is unknown. We toil and strive here on our miserable
ant-hill, transforming some particles of matter—mere
planetary fungi—into various shapes; but can create nothing, destroy nothing. Yet we assume that Almighty God,
who hung the midnight heavens with patines of pure gold
and painted the rings of Saturn—that even he, Architect of
the Universe—left his eternal throne, star-gemmed, cano-
pied with clouds of incense upon which ever falls the bright
effulgence of solar systems, thro' which rolls the eternal
melody of the spheres, came down to earth and of the cold
dead clay made a miserable biped and called it his master-
piece; that he is now following it about with note-book,
jotting down the inconsequential doings of this miserable
microbe—observing with jealous solicitude how it is baptized, what the "articles" of its religion, whether it worship
as Buddhist or Baptist, Methodist or Mormon! Some of us
so believe, thereby flattering our vanity and finding comfort. Others declare there is no God, because they cannot
understand him—cannot conceive of a being without a beginning; attribute everything that is to the operation of
blind force, as tho' force itself did not have an unknown
and inconceivable genesis; as tho' force without matter
were comprehensible to the human mind—could precede
matter, and, operating on nothing, produce something!

What know the infusoria in a drop of water of Caesar
and Socrates? And what know Caesar and Socrates—
hanging, microscopic in body, infinitesimal in mind, to their
little globule of a world—of this great Universe of God
and the laws which govern it? The most industrious digging will not disclose the foundations of the earth; the
most persistent star-gazing reveals to us only a few phos-
phorescent bubbles on the bosom of Infinity's shoreless
sea. And yet we dogmatize about the Deity; build elaborate theories anent the abodes of the blessed; write sacred
books and establish religious rites which we ask the world
to accept as the embodiment of supernatural wisdom. We
have conferences and convocations, synods and ecumenical councils; we have turgid Talmages, slingers of sanctified slang, malevolent Haydens, and Cranfills puffed up
like the frog in the fable with mephitic air,—all pointing
the way to some impossible Celestial City where the "pore
mizzable worm of the dust" will become an imperishable
butterfly and flit from flower to flower, doing absolutely

nothing of any importance thro' all eternity—not even marrying or giving in marriage, a mocking-bird without a
mate! And not even Cranfill, puffing out his "fair round
belly with good capon lined"—while Gabriel and Michael
stand agaze—can locate that interesting ultimate to which
they would lead us; can only vaguely assure us that it is
"over there," or "up yonder"—up and down being relative
terms by which we describe flagstaffs, sub-cellars and such
like protuberances and depressions on the earth's surface.
Celestial City, "up yonder"—whether at noon or midnight;
haven of eternal dilettanteism and yaller dog dolce far
niente "over there"—and thousands of sleek sky-pilots
with Haydenic heads, with Cranfillian stomachs nicely
padded with fat poultry and surreptitious booze at the expense of the stupid ignorance and ingrained prejudice,
leading us thither by devious routes, with toll-gate and
oratorical affliction every seven days' journey—Colombos
exploring the inane for supposititious Cathays and impossible spice islands; blind leading the blind and both falling
into the foul ditch of blasphemous dogmatism and wallowing contented there, imagining meanwhile that they are
making progress!

And all this time a behoofed and behorned devil with
leathery wings, fiery nostrils and prehensile tail with javelin
point—a kind of unholy cross between a Pasiphaean minotaur and Cleveland mugwump—resembling nothing in the
heavens or earth or the waters under the earth, unless it
be the Chicago platform—is going to and fro in the land,
seeking new Jobs to afflict with festering sores and fool
friends; snatching up handfuls of human souls and flying
screeching with them down to Perdition—for what purpose
only he and heaven knows. Curious creature this orthodox
devil who affrights the fearful soul of the evangelist—
voluntarily spending most of his time in hell when he could
just as well spend it all in Texas. It seems that the upper
and nether powers are using this earth as recruiting ground
for their armies, Lucifer obtaining the bulk of the able-
bodied volunteers, the Lord having to content himself with
the organization of amazonian guards. What effect the
advent of the muscular "New Woman" will have upon the
strife between the hosts of heaven and hell it were difficult
to determine. She certainly does not aspire to be an angel
here, and if she follows in the footsteps of her brother
hereafter, Michael might as well close his recruiting offices
and strike his colors.

I do not undervalue human life and effort and aspiration.
I do not mock the blind struggles of mortal man to put on

immortality, to master the elements and extend the domain of his knowledge; but I do insist that those who assume that Almighty God made the solar system for our sweet sakes should be tapped for the simples. Surely the stupendous labors of the Creator were undertaken with grander object, a nobler aim than the breeding on this comparatively unimportant planet of a few harpers for heaven and a host of hoodlums for hell. A few million square miles, flat as a floor, with a fence around it to prevent our falling off; a sun ten miles in diameter and a moon the bigness of an Iowa barn were sufficient plant for the manufacture of men. Then why this infinitude of suns blazing in stellar space—this exhibition of power?

Did the Creator of all this come down to earth and flicker in bushes as a fire, exhibit himself for the delectation of the elders of Israel and spend forty days chiseling laws on tables of stone, when he could have traced them in letters of flame across the firmament? Having "made the stars also"—thrown them in as lagniappe to a hard day's labor —did he send his Son, co-ruler of the universe, to be aggravated by human ants? Go to, thou wretched babbler, and put thy gall in pickle. Pour thy story into the dull ears of ancient dames, and with its marvels rob confiding childhood of its pence to line thy paunch; but tempt not the righteous indignation of reasoning men.

All messiahs, prophets and wonder-workers were even as we; and they have passed, as we in turn shall pass, back into the broad bosom of their mother earth to await the pleasure of Him that once did call them forth; who can bid them live again—for an hour, for a year, for ages, during all eternity. Some were wiser, nobler than we, contained more of the element of Godhood, their lives a larger portion of that bright Essence Increate. Buddha the Pitiful, Moses the Leader, Mahomet the Reformer and Christ the Loving, were our teachers. They imparted to us, each in his way, all they knew of the Mystery of Life—all that, in the profound depths of their superior souls, they dreamed of man's origin, his duty and his destiny. Peace to their ashes. Tho' Time will sweep from the records of the world the story of their endeavor, and even their names sound no more in the ears of men, the good they wrought will still remain, the priceless heritage of the human race—furnishing forth the foundations for nobler cults, for purer ideals, for grander conceptions of the Most High God.

Whether man e'er do put on immortality, or his little life be rounded with ever dreamless sleep; whether he wander always in Elysian fields, or,

> "Greater than kings, than gods more glad,
> The aching craze to live ends, and life glides—
> Lifeless—to nameless quiet, nameless joy,
> Blessed Nirvana—sinless, stirless rest—
> That change which never changes,"

'tis well to have lived and loved. Down upon thy knees, aspiring pigmy, and give thanks to God thou wast not born a beast—that the best of terrestrial life is thine, with the joys of infancy, the pride of manhood and the halo of age. Take the good the gods provide and hold thy peace. If it be heaven's will that a happier world awaits thee beyond the tomb's pale portals, rejoice that thou art rewarded beyond thy deserts; if not, lie down like a tired child upon its mother's breast, and pass without a sigh into the eternal, the imperishable elements from which thou wert called—back into the great Life Ocean which is God.

> "The dew is on the lotus; rise Great Sun,
> And lift my leaf and mix me with the wave.
> Om Mani Padme Hum, the sunrise comes-
> The dewdrop slips into the shining sea!"

THE NEW WOMAN.

BEAUTY AND BLOOMERS.

The new woman is the target at which editors and artists are just now leveling a world of would-be wit and abortive ridicule. She is usually depicted in the periodicals as a biped of doubtful gender, who apes the customs and clothing of creation's lords and aspires to manage the political and social world to suit herself. She is supposed to be intensely "strong-minded" and devoid of sentiment as a bale of hay—quite the antithesis of the soft, clinging creature who once made glad the heart of man by hanging her second providence upon him and sitting contentedly down to the manipulation of buttons and the rearing of babes. According to the analytical editors, she cares never a copper for the command to be fruitful and multiply—is simply an educated ice-berg who prefers billiards and bikeing to the triumphs of beauty, club life to domestic cares, and would, if opportunity offered, use Hymen's torch in a political parade and leave the later Adam without that "helpmeet" which the good God gave him on observing his utter inability to take care of himself.

The New Woman of the smart paragraph builders and

box-wood butchers may be one differentiation of the genus;
but fortunately this species is about as rare as white black-
birds—or editors with an idea above partisan politics. The
New Woman is really a very charming creature, and there
is little likelihood that she will become either too few or too
numerous. She is simply a hard-sensed young lady who
politely but pointedly declines to play second fiddle in the
great diapason of humanity—to be bound by the foolish
fashions and inept customs that have cursed her sex for
sixty centuries. She does not object to matrimony, but
declines to regard the capture of some sap-headed dude
with a few dollars as the end and aim of her existence. Her
ideals of wifehood and motherhood are too exalted to permit
her sitting supinely down on the matrimonial block; like
Patience on a monument, and waiting for some bumptious
he-thing to straddle along who will consent to supply her
with board and clothes—in consideration of the surrender
of her freedom and the debauchment of her beauty. She
prefers to gird up her patent health corset and go out into
the world to hustle her own hash until, from the great
Somewhere of her waking dreams, her ideal comes to make
of her a loving companion instead of a legal concubine.
Calphurnia will be Caesar's wife, meriting his confidence
and dividing his care, rioting in his love and rich in his
respect, or she'll be naught to him.

Such is the New Woman, who stands forth in her
matchless beauty and modest pride, undaunted by the puny
arrows of a tribe of journalistic pigmies. For ages woman
was but man's plaything, her occupation the amusement of
his idle hours—valuable chiefly for breeding purposes. The
highest educational advantages were denied her, the professions closed against her as an incapable. Her talents were
supposed to be small, and little opportunity was offered for
their enlargement. But as the world grew wiser it became
more liberal. One by one the foolish barriers that cir-
cumscribed her usefulness have fallen, and she has pressed
eagerly forward into the widening field. If she has not
proven herself man's intellectual peer she has ceased to be
a pensioner on his bounty,—has demonstrated her ability
to earn her bread—and with independence have come
grander ideals, loftier aims, nobler womanhood.

The real New Woman is self-reliant without being mannish, modest without prudery and companionable while
avoiding that familiarity which breeds contempt. But
there is quite a different creature abroad, upon which the
press delights to confer a title to which she can lay no
claim—the fashionable butterfly and professional fad-chaser,

whose newness consists chiefly in novelty of dress, the business of whose life is to make as liberal a display of her personal charms as may be consistent with a kind of india-rubber respectability. The first has demonstrated that woman may possess brains; the latter has made it manifest that she must have legs! The latter fact has long been suspected even by the exoteric school of bashful bachelors. It has been darkly hinted from time to time by divers scientific gentlemen that woman is a bipedal being who achieves locomotion by advancing one foot before the other, instead of gliding through the air like a gilded moth or sliding about the surface of the earth like a drop of quicksilver; but it remained for the fad-follower to put her physique in evidence and thereby dispel all doubt.

Now that feminine underpinning is an accepted fact,—a truth revealed—we may pause to consider whether we are the happier for our new got knowledge. Candor compels the confession that we are not particularly grateful to the fad-follower for her startling exhibitions of locomotive loveliness—that there may be too much even of a good thing. The poet assures us that,

> "Spring would be but gloomy weather
> If there was nothing else but Spring."

And he might have told us, with equal truth, that an endless procession of perambulating living pictures would pall on the ocular appetite and produce that tired feeling. The female limb is unquestionably a thing of beauty and a joy forever; but we would have been far happier had the dizzy *fin de siecle* devotee of fashion not called the world's attention to it. Had she kept it hidden we might, in the fullness of time, have found it out ourselves and enjoyed the felicity of a glad surprise. Her gratuitous anatomical exhibit argues a lack of enterprise on the part of creation's lords that is quite exasperating.

I have no desire to interfere with the sartorial liberty of the ladies; I would simply call their attention to the fact that a costume which half reveals, half conceals the female form divine, is far more fetching than one which supplants theories with conditions and deprives Fancy of her occupation. The twinkle of a pretty foot peeping coyly forth beneath a dainty petticoat; the fleeting glimpse of a well-turned ankle in a billowy sea of lace were enough to make a stoic grab a goose-quill and reel off erotic poetry by the ream—to transform the veriest Reuben into a soulful Anacreon; but what minstrel, filled to overflowing with the divine afflatus, could tune his lyre or build an Ella Wheeler ode in honor of a pair of bloomers? Why, at sight of such an apparition immortal Pegasus would balk and buck like Mark Twain's Mexican plug! Had Petrarch's Laura worn pants the dago nightingale would have come off his perch; had Heloise donned the divided skirt no heart-sore pilgrim would pour his scalding tears into her storied urn; had Helen of Troy paddled about the Isles of Greece in *fin de siecle* bathing-suit the Bard of Chios had not tuned his immortal harp nor Priam's hoary head 'have sunk beneath the sword. Think of burning Sappho in tan-colored leggings taking the Lover's Leap; of Bonnie Annie Laurie in bloomers—of Juliet with a sea-green patch on the rear elevation of her scorched banana biking suit! Had such monstrosities appeared on Parnassus, the muses would have been stricken dumb—perhaps have drowned themselves in the Pierian Spring.

If the fashionable young female—who is no more the New Woman than she is the Old Adam—is dressing to please herself, we have nothing to say; but if she is decking out to gladden the hearts of the sterner sex we hereby advise her in strict confidence that, as the rival of the ballet-girls and vaudeville beer-slingers, she is a glittering failure. Whether biking or surf-bathing, clucking at a political hen convention or dress reform congress, she is an inartistic hermaphroditical hoo-doo that, while causing the unskillful to laugh, must make the judicious grieve. In matters sartorial progress and improvement are not always synonyms. The abbreviated skirt may be more healthful than the pyramidal petticoat; but it makes a woman an offensive freak, an eyesore to the artist, an uncanny nightmare to all men with a correct conception of the eternal fitness of things. The reckless display of personal charms by the woman of fashion—her double-entendre decollete —is not calculated to promote elevation of thought or purity of action—could occur only in a society already corrupt.

It may be urged in extenuation of the offense against the canons of good taste that modesty in costume is a mere matter of custom; that had the ladies for a century or so worn bloomers—or even breeches—the world would consider it quite the proper thing because accustomed to it; that had they suddenly exchanged such garb for the modern ball-room gown, all the prudes in bloomers — or breeches—would have tearfully protested, and the female pharisees—with leathery arms and busts built like a jaundiced clap-board—thanked God they were not as other people. This may be true, for

"That monster custom, of habits devil,"

can inure us to almost anything, however outre or inartistic. A man who had never seen a rose might regard a red holly-hock as the acme of floral perfection; having never seen a female figure tastefully draped, he might contemplate even bloomers with satisfaction; but I doubt if he could regard the wearer with that chivalric adoration which has placed woman but little lower than the angels. He would doubtless consider her "a jolly good fellow," and enjoy her society to a certain extent; but that courteous deference which distinguishes him could scarce develop—he would make few sacrifices for her sake. Had such been the fashion, love would have remained but lust and marriage simply a civil contract. Had Queen Elizabeth worn bloomers, Sir Walter Raleigh might have bridged a mudpuddle for her with his costly cloak; but more likely he would have told her to climb upon his back. Leander might have swam the tempestuous Hellespont to bask in the smiles of a beauty clad only in breeches; but I think he would have waited for the boat.

SLAVE OR SOVEREIGN.

Status of the American Citizen.

[Synopsis of an address delivered by Mr. Brann, August 10, 1895.]

Fellow citizens: If I had a million o' money—carefully protected from the income tax by a plutocratic supreme court—I would probably not be here to inquire whether you are Slaves or Sovereigns. And if you could draw your check for seven figures—with any probability of getting it cashed—you would not be here to answer. You'd do just as Dives did: lean back in your luxurious chair and absorb your sangaree, while Lazarus scratched his Populist fleas on your front steps and exploited your garbage barrels for bones. You'd turn up your patrician nose at the lowly proletaire, and if he did but hint that, having created this world's wealth, he was entitled to something better than hand-outs, you'd have an anti-communistic cat-fit and denounce him as an insolent hoodlum who should be comfortably hanged. That's human nature to a hair, and you are all human,—I suppose—even if the politicians do buy you with gas and sell you for gold.

I tell you frankly that I'm complaining, not because of the other fellow's colossal fortune, but because I can't strike the plutocratic combination. I'm dreadfully anxious

to accumulate a modest fortune—of about fifty millions—
that I may build a comfortable orphan asylum for that vast
contingent of Democratic politicians whom the next election will deprive of their "pap."

I'm no philanthropist who's trying to reform the world
for the fun of the thing—who's willing to starve to death
for the sake of an attractive tombstone. I want to so
amend industrial conditions that I won't have to hustle so
hard—and so long—between meals; and when they are
bettered for me they will be bettered for you, and for every
man who—with pick or pen, brain or brawn—honestly earns
his daily bread.

I want more holidays; more time to sit down and reflect
that it is good to be alive; more time to go fishing—not
fishing for men, but for sure-enough suckers. Here in America if the average mortal aspires to fill a long-felt want
with first-class fodder, he's got to chase the almighty dollar on week-days like a hungry coyote camping on the
trail of a corpulent jack-rabbit, and spend Sunday figuring how to circumvent his fellow-citizen. Life with the
American people is one continual hurry and rush from the
cradle to the grave. We're born in a hurry, live by electricity and die with scientific expedition. Half of us don't
take time to become acquainted with our own families.
We've even got to courting by telephone, and I expect to
see some enterprising firm put up lover's kisses in tablet
form, so that they can be carried in the vest pocket and
absorbed while we figure cent per cent or make out a
mortgage.

*   *   *

For a score of years I had been listening to the boast
of the American people that they were Sovereigns by right
divine, and at last it occurred to me to swear out a search-
warrant for my crown and go on a still-hunt for my sceptre; but soon found that the jewels of my throne-room, the
rod of my authority and my purple robe of office were con-
spicuous by their absence and I wasn't married at the time
either. The American citizen is a sovereign, not to the extent of his voice and vote, but to the exact amount of Uncle
Sam's illuminated mental anguish plasters at his command.
Money is lord paramount, Mammon our prophet, our god
the golden calf.

The dollar is indeed "almighty." It's the Archimedean
lever that lifts the ill-bred boor into select society and
places the ignorant sap-head in the United State Senate.
It makes presidents of "stuffed prophets," governors of

intellectual geese, philosophers of fools and gilds infamy
itself with supernal glory. It wrecks the altars of innocence and pollutes the fanes of the people, breaks the sword
of Justice and binds the Goddess of Liberty with chains of
gold. It is lord of the land, the uncrowned king of the
commonwealth, and its whole religious creed is comprised
in the one verse, "To him that hath shall be given and he
shall have abundance, while from him that hath not shall
be taken even that which he hath."

"We, the people, rule"—in the conventions; but our del-
egated lawmakers have a different lord. In 1892 we de-
manded "tariff reform" with a whoop that shook the imperial rafters of heaven, and declared for the minting of
gold and silver without discrimination against either metal.
But our so-called "public servants," instead of hastening
to obey our behests, spent months manufacturing excuses
for disregarding their duty. Placed between the devil of
the money power and the deep sea of public opinion, they
wobbled in and they wobbled out like a drunken boa-constrictor taking its jag to a gold cure joint. They were like
the little boy who put his trousers on t'other side to—we
couldn't tell whether they were going to school or coming
home. But our doubts were all dispelled last November.
They were coming home—and they were coming to stay.
We are the fellows who were going to school—to that
school of experience where fools are educated.

*   *   *

Slave or Sovereign? The last is an individual entity, a
controlling power, his will is law. The first goes and
comes, fetches and carries at the command of a master;
creating wealth he may not possess, bound by laws he
does not approve, dependent upon the pleasure of others
for the privilege of breaking bread. Is not the latter condition that of a majority of the American people to-day?
Are they not at the subsequent end of a financial hole, the
sides soaped and never a ladder in sight?

In a country so favored—a veritable garden of the gods,
where every prospect pleases and not even the politician
is wholly vile—the lowliest laborer should be a lord, and
each and all find life well worth the living. But it is not
so. People starve while sunny savannas, bursting with fat-
ness, yield no food; they wander houseless thro' summer's
heat and winter's cold, while great mountains of granite
comb the fleecy clouds and the forest monarch measures
strength with the thunderstorm; they flee naked and
ashamed from the face of their fellow-men while fabrics

moulder in the market-place and the song of the spindle is silent; they freeze while beneath their feet are countless tons of coal—incarnate kisses of the sun-god's fiery youth; they have never a spot of earth on which to plant a vine and watch their children play—where they may rear with loving hands lowly roof and rule, lords of a little world hemmed in by the sacred circle of a home; yet the common heritage in the human race lies fair before them and there is room enough.

The people of Texas do not realize how terrible is the industrial condition of the world to-day—how wide the gulf that separates Dives and Lazarus, how pitiful the poverty of millions of their fellow men. The Texas merchant complains of dull trade, the farmer of low prices, the mechanic of indifferent wages; yet Texas is the most favored spot on the great round earth to-day. I defy you to find another portion of the globe of equal area and population where the wealth is so well distributed, where so few people go hungry to bed without prospect of breakfast. But the grisly gorgon of Greed and the gaunt spectre of Need are coming West and South in the wake of the Star of Empire. Already Texas has begun to breed millionaires and mendicants, sovereigns and slaves. Already we have an aristocracy of money, in which *wealth* makes the man and want of it the fellow, and year by year it becomes easier for Dives to add to his hoard and for Lazarus to starve to death.

We appeal to New York for capital with which to develop our resources; and New York has it in abundance— countless millions she is eager to let out at usury; yet it is estimated that ten thousand children perish in that city every year of the world for lack of food—and how many are kept alive by the bitter bread of a contemptuous charity God only knows. In one year 3,000 children were debarred from the public schools of Chicago because of lack of clothing to cover their nakedness—and Chicago boasts herself "the typical American city." The despised Salvation Army trying to feed a thousand homeless and hungry men on the sandlots of San Francisco proves that already the curse has travelled across the continent.

And people who are not only permitted to run at large, but actually elected to office, prattle of "overproduction"— while people are starving in nakedness; proposes to eliminate pauperism and inaugurate the industrial millennium by placing fiddle-strings on the free-list or increasing the tariff-tax on toothpicks—to relieve the country of the commercial jim-jams by means of the gold cure. And the fool-killer still procrastinates!

*   *   *

The American citizen is called a sovereign—by those patriots who are preparing to sacrifice themselves on the altar of a nice fat office. And perhaps he is; but I'm free. We are frequently told that the condition of labor is better to-day than a century ago. That is half a truth, yet wholly a falsehood. A century ago the workman knew naught of many comforts and conveniences he now enjoys—when he happens to have a job; but that was one age, this quite another. Progress gives no man new wants, and the luxuries of one generation become the necessities of the next. To deny this—to limit the laborer to actual necessaries as measured by a former age—were to relegate him back to barbarism, to nomadism and nakedness. If we should be content with what our fathers had, then they should have been satisfied with the comforts enjoyed by *their* progenitors, and so on back until man digs roots with his finger nails, attires himself in a streak of red paint for winter overcoat and a few freckles for summer ulster. It is by comparison with his fellows and not with his fathers that man determines whether he's fortunate or unfortunate—whether he's receiving his proper proportion of the world's increase of wealth. A century ago there was no such glaring inequality as now exists. There were no fifty million dollar fortunes and no free-soup joints. If the workman's piano was a jews-harp and his Pullman car a spavined cayuse, his employer was not erecting palaces in which to stable his blooded stock, nor purchasing dissolute princes for his daughters to play at marriage and divorce with. If the farmer's wife wore linsey-woolsey and went barefoot to save her shoes, her neighbor did not import $5,000 gowns from "Paree" and put jeweled collars on her pet cur. The difference in the condition of Dives and Lazarus is more sharply defined than ever before. It is not so much the pitiful poverty of the many as the enormous wealth of the few that is fostering discontent. Pride dallying with Sin begot Death; willful waste is breeding Anarchy in the Womb of Want. The lords and ladies of the house of Have revel in luxury such as Lucullus never knew, while within sound of their feasting gaunt children fight like famished beasts for that which the breakfast garbage barrels afford. Private fortunes make the famed wealth of Lydia's ancient kings appear but a beggar's patrimony, while brawny giants must beg or steal and starving mothers give the withered breast to dying babes.

Labor now seeks employment, not as a right, but as a privilege. It has come to such a pitiful pass in this "land of liberty," this "refuge of the world's oppressed," that to afford a man an opportunity to employ his strength or skill in the creation of wealth, a portion of which he may retain for his own support, is regarded rather as a privilege than a free contract between American Sovereigns—an act of charity, for which the recipient should be duly grateful.

No man can be a freeman while dependent upon the good will of another for his bread and butter. He may be a Sovereign *dejure,* but he's a Slave *defacto.* And under present conditions the more labor-saving machinery he invents, the tighter he rivets his chains.

We had hoped and believed that human ingenuity was about to lift the curse laid on Adam by his angry Lord; the angel of Intellect to reimparadise the poor slave, place his fetters on nature's tireless forces and declare that never again should bread be eaten in the sweat of the brow; but man proposes—and is sued for breach of promise.

Were a man to declare labor-saving machinery and the general development of the country a curse to the poor, he would be branded as a "moss-back" or budding candidate for Bedlam; yet it is unquestionably true that the further the average individual gets from the so-called blessings of civilization—the less he is affected by our boasted industrial system—the smaller his danger of starving to death.

Many of us can remember when we had little labor-saving machinery in Texas; when railways were scarce as consistent Christians at a colored camp-meeting, goods were carried from the coast on the backs of burros and a full-dress suit consisted chiefly of buckskin breeches and a brace of angel makers. And we remember also that a pauper was a curiosity; that the very cowboys played poker at $10 ante with the sky for limit, the common laborer carried coin in his belt and the merchant had money to burn. Texas has developed wonderfully during the last few decades. We now have improved machinery—and extensive poor-farms; railways—and political rings; a $3,000,-000 capitol—and an army of unemployed. We have built fine schools and finer churches, made the black man our political brother and bought his vote. We have exchanged our buckskin for broadcloth, our hair-raising profanity for the hypocrite's whine, straight corn-juice for the champagne-jag and the hip-pocket court for the jackass verdict of the petit jury. But the cowboy now plays penny-ante on credit or shoots craps for small coin; the common laborer carries in his belt only a robust appetite, while the merchant who dodges bankruptcy for a dozen years considers himself the special favorite of fortune.

And what is true of Texas is true in greater or less degree of every State in the Union. Development, so dear to the heart of the patriotic and public-spirited citizen, has a tendency to transform an independent and moderately prosperous people into masters and slaves. But this is not the fault of labor-saving machinery, nor of capital, nor of development by itself considered. The more wealth labor creates, the more it should enjoy. When the reverse is the case distribution is at fault.

The substitution of expensive machinery for hand-labor eliminated the independent artisan. His productive power was multiplied; but his independence—his ability to care for himself without the co-operation of large capital—was gone. The wheelwright could not return to his shop nor the shoemaker to his last and live in comfort. Competition with the iron fingers of the great factory were impossible. Labor must now await the pleasure of capital—the creature has become lord of its creator. The fierce competition of idle armies forces wages down, and slowly but surely the workman is sinking back to the level occupied before the cunning brain of genius harnessed the lightning to his lathe and gave him nerves of steel and muscles of brass with which to fight his battle for bread.

With the improved machinery with which he is provided, the American workman can create as much wealth in a week as he need consume in a month; but he goes down on his knees and thanks God and the plutocracy for an opportunity to toil 300 days in the year for a bare subsistence.

*   *   *

Unfortunately, I have no catholicon for every industrial ill—but the political drug-stores are full of 'em. All you've got to do is to select your panacea, pull the cork and let peace and plenty overflow a grateful land—so we're told. Instead of the cure-me-quicks prescribed by the economic M. D.'s, I believe that our industrial system has been doped with entirely too many drugs. I'd throw physic to the dogs, exercise a little common-sense and give nature a chance. There's an old story of an Arkansaw doctor who invariably threw his patients into fits because he was master of that complaint; but the economic

M. D.'s can't even cure fits. When they attempt it the patient goes into convulsions.

Instead of going to so much trouble to bar out cheap goods by means of tariff walls, I'd bar out cheap men. If you're making monkey-wrenches at $2 a day and some fellow abroad is building 'em for 50 cents, your boss comes to you and says:

"Jim, we've got to have a tariff to keep out the product of pauper labor or our nether garment's ripped from narrative to neck-band. I can't pay you $2 and compete with an employer who pays but 50 cents."

That sounds reasonable and you swing back on the G. O. P. tow-line and lay a tariff-tax on monkey-wrenches that looms up like an old-time Democratic majority in Texas. And while you are burning ratification tar-barrels and trying to shake hands with yourself in the mirror at the Mechanic's Exchange, that 50 cent fellow crosses the briny and robs you of your bench. Your old employer is protected all right, but where do you come in? You don't come in; you simply stand out in the industrial norther. You count the railroad ties from town to town while your wife takes in washing, your daughter goes to work in a factory at two dollars a week and your son grows up an ignorant Arab and gets into ward politics or the penitentiary. You can't compete with the importation, because you've been bred to a higher standard of living. You must have meat three times a day, a newspaper at breakfast and a new book—or the Iconoclast—after supper. You must have your plunge bath and spring bed, your clean shave and Sunday shirt. How can you hope to hold your job when a man is bidding for it who takes up his belly-band for breakfast, dines on slumgullion and sucks his breath for supper; to whom literature is an unknown luxury. a bath a deplorable accident, and a crummy old blanket a comfortable bed? You can't do it, and if you'll take the Apostle's advice you'll quit trying.

No; I wouldn't prevent the immigration of worthy Europeans—men of intelligence, who dignify labor. We have millions such in America, and they are most estimable citizens. Our ancestors were all Europeans, and that man who is not proud of his parentage should have been born a beast. But I'd knock higher than Gilderoy's kite the theory that America should forever be the dumping-ground for foreign filth—that people will be warmly welcomed here whom no other country wants and the devil wouldn't have.

We have made American citizenship entirely too cheap.

We permit every creature that can poise on its hind legs and call itself a man, to sway the sceptre of American Sovereignty—to become an important factor in the formation of our public polity; and then, with this venal vote on the one hand, eager to be bought, and the plutocrat on the other anxious to buy, we wonder why it is that the invariable tendency of our laws is to make the rich man a prince and the poor man a Populist—why we are "great only in that strange spell, a name."

In this work of reform we've got to begin at the bottom —with the body politic itself. You can't make a silk purse of a sow's ear, nor Sovereigns of men who were born to be Slaves. We've got to grade up or we're gone. Only superior Intelligence is capable of self-government—Ignorance and Tyranny go hand in hand. You may theorize until the Bottomless Pit is transformed into a skating park; you may vote tariffs high or low and money hard or soft; you may inaugurate the Single-Tax or transform the American Republic into a commune, but the condition of the hewers of wood and the drawers of water will never be permanently bettered while Ignorance and Vice have access to the ballot-box.

We have carried the enchanting doctrine of "political equality" entirely too far and are paying the penalty. The rebound from the monstrous doctrine of the divine right of monarchs has hurried us into equal error. Disgusted with the rottenness of the established religion, the French people once crowned a courtesan as Goddess of Reason; maddened by the insolence of hereditary officialism, our fathers placed the rod of power in the hoodlum's reckless hand and bound upon the stupid brow of hopeless nescience Columbia's imperial crown. That the greater must guide the lesser intelligence is nature's immutable law. To deny this were to question our own right to rule the beast and God's authority to reign King of all mankind. Self-preservation will yet compel us to guard the sacred privileges of American sovereignty as jealously as did Rome her citizenship.

*   *   *

Do this, and all other needed reforms will follow as surely and as swiftly as the day-god follows the dawn. Knowledge is power. When those who vote fully understand that every dollar expended by government, federal, state or municipal, must be created by the common people—that first or last, labor must furnish it forth—we'll cease having billion-dollar Congresses. We'll cease paying a hundred and forty millions per annum in federal pensions; we'll cease wasting a King's ransom annually in pretending to "improve" intermittent creeks and impossible harbors solely for political navigation; we'll cease borrowing money in time of peace to bolster up that foolish financial fetich known as the "gold-reserve;" we'll cease making so many needless laws and paying aspiring patriots fat salaries to harass us with their enforcement; we'll cease exempting from taxation the half-million dollar church and laying a heavier mulct on the mechanic's cottage and the widow's cow; we'll cease paying preachers five dollars a minute to stand up in our legislative halls and insult Almight God with perfunctory prayers; we'll cease building so many palatial prisons where thieves and thugs may be cared for at the expense of honest people, but will divide criminals into two classes—those who should be peremptorily hanged, and those who should be whipped and turned loose to hustle their own hash. Nothing knocks the sawdust out of false sentiment so quickly as the realization that it's an expensive luxury and that we must pay the freight.

Billion-dollar Congresses, eh? Do you know what that means? There are less than fifteen million wealth creators in this country, and the last farthing of it comes out of their pockets—something over $66 apiece! If you had it in silver dollars—and I suppose that most of you would accept silver—you couldn't count it in a century. Lay the coins edge to edge and they'll belt the world. Pile them on top of each other and you'll have a silver shaft more than 1750 miles high. Sand your hands and climb it. Perchance from the top you'll see many things—among others what is oppressing the poor. And while up in that rarified atmosphere, where the vision is good and thinking probably easy, you will look around for those other pyramids of expense annually erected by state, county and municipal government, then come down firm in the faith that if this isn't a great government it ought to be, considering what it costs. No wonder the workman carries in his pocket only an elegant assortment of holes!

We're governed entirely too much—Officialism is becoming a veritable Old Man of the Sea on the neck of Labor's Sinbad. About every fifth man you meet is a public servant of some sort, and you cannot get married or buried, purchase a drink or own a dog except with a by-your-leave to the all-pervading law of the land. In some states suicide itself is an infraction of the criminal code, and if the police don't cut you down in time to put you in jail the

preachers will send you to hell. Every criminal law this
state and county and city needs can be printed in a book
no larger than the Iconoclast, and that so plain that he
who runs may read and reading understand. And when
so printed and so understood, without the possibility of
misconstruction, they could be enforced at one-fifth the
cost of the present judicial failure. We have so many
laws and so much legal machinery that when you throw a
man into the judicial hopper not even an astrologer can
tell whether he'll come out a horse-thief or only a homicide—or whether the people will weary of waiting on the
circumlocution office and take a change of venue to Judge
Lynch.

This can never be a land of religious liberty—the atheist
can never be considered as on a political parity with his
ultra-orthodox brother—until we compel church property
to bear its pro rata of the public burdens.

And right here let me say a word about the "Apostle."
I have been accused by people—for whom no cherry-tree
blooms or little hatchet is ground—of being a rank atheist
and a red-flag anarchist. It has been broadly intimated
that I'm trying to rip the Christian religion up by the
roots, rob trusting hearts of their hope and deprive the
preacher of his daily bread. Now I might just as well
confess to you that I'm no angel. If I were I'd fly out of
Texas till the bifurcated Democratic party has another
"harmony" deal. When you hear people denouncing me
as an atheist, just retire to your closet and pray, "Father
forgive them, for they know not what they do." And you
might add, that nobody cares. No mortal son of Adam's
misery can produce one line I ever wrote, or quote one
sentence I ever uttered, disrespectful of *any* religion—and
that's more than you can say of most of the ministers.

But it is not right, it is not just that the little holdings
of the poor should be relentlessly taxed and costly temples exempted—palatial edifices in which polite society
pretends to worship One who broke bread with beggars
and slept in the brush. Such an arrangement signifies
neither good religion nor good sense. It's the result of
sanctified selfishness. I believe in taxing luxuries, and a
costly church is not a necessity. At least Christ did not
think so, for he never built one.

Congregations that can afford to erect fine churches and
export saving grace to the pagans of foreign climes, can
afford to pay taxes and thereby help American heathen
out of the hole. A million men out of employment, pac-
ing our streets in grim despair; a million children coming

up in ignorance and crime; a million women hesitating between the wolf of want and the abundance of infamy, and the church—supposed to be God's ministering angel—crying, "Give, give! If you can't give much, give little. Remember the widow's mite"—so acceptable to a pauper deity.

Give for what? To build fine temples in whose sacred shadows will lurk the gaunt spectre of Famine and the grisly gorgon of Crime. To buy grand organs and costly bells to peal praises to One who had nowhere to lay his head. To pay stall-fed preachers five, ten, twenty thousand dollars a year to expound the doctrine of a poor carpenter who couldn't have kept a silver dollar in his jeans a single day while there was poverty and suffering in the world.

While the wealth-producer is robbed to pension million-aires who suffered mental anguish because of the draft, and to administer worse than useless laws, still the amount so unnecessarily abstracted would be but a mere bagatelle if labor was steadily employed and reaped its just reward. With the mighty energies of this nation in full play and the wealth remaining with its producers, we could give even all the candidates an office, with plenty to get and little to do, and still have pie in the pantry and corn in the crib. There is something more the matter than govern-mental waste—there's something *radically* wrong.

* * *

In tracing the causes of panics and periods of business depression, we invariably find our currency more or less at fault. Now don't get frightened. I'm not going to dose you with free silver nor give you the gold cure. This is neither Coin's Financial School nor a gold-bug incubator. The currency question is one you know all about. Every-body does—especially the corner-grocery politician. He understands it from A to Izzard—knows almost as much about it as a hello-girl does of the nature of electricity. Prof. Jevon truly says that "a kind of intellectual vertigo appears to sieze people when they talk of money." Per-haps the Goddess of Liberty on the silver dollar has 'em Trilbyized.

We hear a great deal of late about the "science of money." It's supposed to 'be something very esoteric—something that a fellow can only master by drawing heav-ily on his gray matter, by working his think-machine up to the limit and sweating blood. Now let me tell you that there is no "science of money," any more than there's a science of harvesting hoop-poles or fighting flies. When a man begins to give you an interminable song and dance about the science of money, just you send for the police and have him locked up as a dangerous lunatic.

Here's a ticket good for so many meals at a restaurant—an order for so much wealth; and here's a silver dollar—no 'tisn't; it's a check on a-er on a "resort;" in fact, on a saloon; an I. O. U. for 12 1-2 cents, the price of a cigar—or something—I suppose. "Man should not live by bread alone." Now what's the difference between this ticket and check and the currency issued by the government? Simply this: These are the I. O. U.'s of individual's money, the I. O. U.'s of the entire American people. These are orders for certain kinds of wealth at particular places; money is an order for all kinds of wealth at any place within the jurisdiction of the federal government. This ticket is the check of one American, drawn against his personal wealth and credit; this bill is the check of all Americans, drawn against the collective wealth and credit of the nation. That's all the difference between a cocktail check and a coin, 'between a meal ticket and a ten dollar bill. Neither is worth a rap unless it can be *redeemed*. Like sanctification caught at a camp-meeting, there must be a hereafter to it or it's a humbug. But don't you metallists take that as a premise and jump at conclusions or you're liable to sprain your logical sequence. What kind of redemption did I have in view when I acquired this che—I mean this ticket? I expected that it would be redeemed in something that would expand my surcingle and enable me to cast a shadow—in eggs and oleomargarine, corn-bread and buttermilk. And if so redeemed on demand, is it not a *good ticket*—is it not *worth its face?* What kind of redemption did I expect when I acquired this bill? I expected it to be redeemed in the necessaries of life—or possibly the luxuries. Who issued it? The government. Who's the government? The people. And when the people have given me bread and butter, tobacco and transportation, clothing and cocktails, and afforded me police protection to the extent of my ten dollars hasn't it been *redeemed* in the manner I anticipated—in the only way in which money can be redeemed? If I exchange this bill for a gold eagle what have I got? Another governmental drink-check or meal-ticket that awaits redemption. And there you have the whole "science of money," over which politicians have so long puzzled their brains that their think-tanks have got full of logical wiggletails. A dollar, whether it be made of gold, silver or paper, is simply an order which

the people in their official capacity give against all the
wealth, actual and potential, of the nation; and unless the
holder can get it promptly redeemed in food and clothing,
he's in a terribly bad fix.

* * *

Every few years our industrial system gets the jim-jams.
Capital flies to cover, factories close and labor goes tramping across the country seeking honest employment and receiving a warm welcome—from militia companies with
shotted guns.   Cheerful idiots begin to prattle of "overproduction," the economic M. D.'s to refurbish all the old
remedies, from conjure-bags to communism.   They all
know exactly what caused the "crisis" and what to do for
it; but despite the doctors the patient usually—survives.
And the M. D. who succeeds in cramming his pet panacea
down its throat claims all the credit for the recovery.   We
are slowly emerging from the crash of '93, and the cuckoos
are cock-sure that Cleveland hoodooed with that financial
rabbit-foot known as the gold-reserve—that a country
fairly bursting with wealth was saved from the demnition
bowwows by the blessed expedient of going into debt; that
labor found salvation by shouldering an added burden in
the shape of interest-bearing bonds.   Hereafter when a
burro tries to lie down beneath a load that's making him
bench-legged, we'll just pile a brick house or two on top of
him, and, with ears and tail erect, he'll strike a Nancy
Hanks gait and come cavorting down the home stretch.
When a statesman can see such things as that while wide
awake and perfectly sober, he ought to consult a doctor.
No wonder the Democratic party split wide open—transformed from an ascendent sun into a bifurcated Biela's
comet, wandering the Lord knows whither.

The gold reserve, we are told, is to "protect the credit of
our currency."   Protect it from whom?   You and I are
making no assault upon it—wouldn't hurt it for the world.
When we get a paper or silver dollar we don't trot around
to the treasury to have it "redeemed" in a slug of yellow
metal—we make a bee line for the grocery store and have
it redeemed in a side o' bacon.   Who is it that chisels desolation into the blessed gold reserve—the so-called "bulwarks of our currency?"   The fellows who want bonds—the
capitalistic, the creditor class; the men who own the
mortgages and have millions of dollars corded up in
bank—the men who have most to *lose* by any bobble in the
credit of our currency.   And every time the capitalist

tries to hoist himself with his own petard, the administration smothers the blaze with a block of interest-bearing bonds. If he wants to make a sky-rocket of himself, let him kerosense his coat-tails and apply the match. If the gold reserve were really necessary to the credit of our currency, capitalists would no more make war upon it than they would bestride a buzz-saw making a million revolutions a minute. Instead of systematically draining it they would, whenever it struck "the danger-line," gather all the gold they could get and send it on to Washington. The capitalists are not crazy; they've simply got a soft snap in that "bulwark" business and are working it for all it's worth.

Calico is sold by the yard, kerosene by the gallon, coffee by the pound. These measures are immutable, and those who buy and sell by them make their contract in perfect confidence. But suppose they altered from day to day or from year to year,—the yard ranging from 25 to 50 inches, the pound from 10 to 20 ounces; would our exchanges be effected without much friction, think you? Would not such a ridiculous system of weights and measures paralyze exchange and demoralize industry? Would not those who could juggle the system to suit themselves—buying by a long and selling by a short yard—accumulate colossal fortunes at the expense of the common people? Would we not have "panics" in plenty and "depressions" galore? Well, that is exactly what is happening to the dollar, our measure of value, the most important of all our trade tools. And mark you, a change in the purchasing power of the dollar is equivalent to an alteration of every weight and measure employed by commerce. Understand? When the purchasing power of the dollar expands or contracts it has the same effect on exchange as would the expansion or contraction of the yard, the gallon and the pound.

A shifting measure of value is the nigger in our industrial woodpile. We have got to have a measure of value that's as immutable as our measure of quantity; a dollar as reliable as an official pound; a dollar that's the same yesterday, and to-day and forever, before we see the last of these panics and periods of business depression. We have got to have a currency that will adapt itself automatically and infallibly to the requirements of commerce— that will constitute an ever-effective exchange medium—before we can obtain a smooth-working industrial machine and the maximum employment of labor.

We know from experience that gold will not supply us with such a currency, that silver will not do it, that bimet-

allism will not do it—that greenbackism, as we understand
the term, will not come within a mile of it. Then what
will do it? That's the problem. Solve it, and you forever
put an end to commercial panics in a land of plenty; you
deprive capital of its power to oppress labor; you assure
industry a constant friend where it has so often found an
insidious foe. Solve it and Columbia can furnish happy
homes for half the world—homes unhaunted by the wolf
of want, but crowned with sweet content and gilded with
freedom's glory.

For a century economists have been seeking the solution
of this all-important problem. Even conservative old
Adam Smith dreamed of the emancipation of the world
from the multifarious ills of metallic money; but we still
cling with slavish servility to the silver of Abraham and
the gold of Solomon.

* * *

I do not claim to have found the philosopher's stone, for
which so many wiser men have sought in vain; but the
currency plan I proposed in 1891—and which was again
outlined in the Iconoclast for May of this year—has been
carefully examined by the ablest financiers of Europe and
America, and they have been unable to point out a fundamental fault. It is known as the interconvertible bond-currency plan, by which our circulating media would be bottomed on the entire wealth of the nation instead of upon
fragments of metal of fluctuating value; by which the volume of the currency would depend, not upon the fecundity
of the mines, the fiat of Congress or the greed of Wall
street, but upon the needs of commerce itself. By this plan
the proportion between the money-work to be done and the
money available to do it is always the same; hence it
would afford an immutable measure of value. In studying
the plan it is well to bear in mind that our foreign trade
—that bogy-man of the metallists—has no more to do
with our currency than with our pint cups and bushel-
baskets—no more than with our language and religion;
that we can pay our foreign debts and collect our foreign
credits only in commodities; that the prattle indulged in
by the metallists anent "money that is good the world
over" is mere goose-speech—that there is no such money.
We buy and sell with England and France to the extent
of tens of millions annually; yet I haven't seen a British
guinea or a French franc in fifteen years. And if you
had a foreign coin and should go around to a resort, and
call for a glass of—er—of buttermilk, and plank the little

stranger down on the counter, the party in the white apron
and Alaska dazzler would say:

"Wot yer givin' us?"

You'd reply: "I'm giving you gold—money good the
world over."

" Wot is it—watch charm? Dis ain't no pawn shop."

"But that's money."

"Eh?"

"Money—gold coin that maketh the heart glad."

"Wot kind o' money?"

"It's a British guinea."

"Well, why don't you go to Great Britain to blow yourself?"

"But my dear sir, this is money of final payment. This
is value itself. This does not depend on the stamp of government, but circulates throughout the world on its intrinsic
merit."

"Well, it don't circulate in this joint. See?

Slam your *theories* up against *conditions* before you tie
to them.

* * *

You all know that in this country there should be no
such thing as able-bodied pauperism. You know that until the last arable acre is brought to the highest possible
cultivation, every mine developed, every forest made to
contribute to the creature comforts of man, there should be
remunerative work for all. You know that, with the aid
of wealth-creating machinery every laborer should be able
to acquire a competence to comfort his declining days.
You know that until Need is satisfied and Greed is gorged
there can be no such thing as overproduction—that under
normal conditions when there's a plethora of necessaries,
the surplus energy of the nation turns to the creation of
luxuries and the standard of living advances. You know
that with such wonderful resources, touched by the magic
wand of genius, the golden age of which poets have dreamed and for which philanthropists have prayed, should be even
at our doors.

I hope to contribute in some slight degree to the establishment of conditions that will enable us to utilize to the
utmost the free gifts of a gracious God; to the proper distribution of wealth; to the emancipation of labor, not by
the law of blind force, but enlightened self-interest—not
by riotous revolution, but peaceful evolution. I want to
see every American Citizen in very truth a Sovereign, to
whom life is a joy instead of a curse. I want to see every

rag transformed into a royal robe, every hovel into a cultured home. I want to hasten, if by ever so little, the day when we can boast with the proud sons of imperial Rome, that to be an American is greater than to be a king.

And when we so amend industrial conditions that each can find employment at profitable prices, we do more to eliminate crime and foster morality than have all the prophets and preachers, from Melchizedeck the mythical to Talmage the turgid.

No man can be either a patriot or a consistent Christian on an empty stomach—he's merely a savage animal, a dangerous beast. You must get a square meal inside of a man and a clean shirt outside of him before he's fit subject for saving grace. You must give him a bath before he's worth baptizing. And when you get him clean and well clothed, fed and housed as a reward of his own honest industry, he's not far from the Kingdom of God. But if you want to degrade a people beyond redemption; if you want to transform them into contemptible peons and whining hypocrites who encumber the earth like so much unclean vermin, educate them to feed on the crumbs from Dives' banquet-board and accept his cast-off clothing with obsequious thankfulness.

The concentration of wealth in the hands of the few and the impoverishment of the common people until it was the bread of charity or the blood of the revolution, has ever been the herald of moral decay and of national death. So passed the glory of Greece and the grandeur of Rome, and, if we may judge the future by the past, so will perish the greatest republic that ever gleamed like a priceless jewel on the skeleton hand of Time. Self-interest, humanity, patriotism, religion itself, admonish us to weigh well the problem of the hour—a problem born of human progress, forced upon us by the mighty revolution wrought in the industrial world by the giant Steam—and that problem is: Shall the average American Citizen be a Slave or a Sovereign?

Don't imagine for a moment that I'm an anarchist— that I'm going to wind up this seance by unfurling the red flag and throwing a hat-full of bombs. I admit that I haven't much respect for law—there's so much of it that when I come to spread my respect over the entire lot it's about as thin as one of Sam Jones' sermons. Still, I don't believe in strikes, and riots and bloodshed. I'm for peace —peace in its most virulent form. I've had a sneaking respect for Cleveland ever since he employed a substitute to put a kibosh on the Southern Confederacy while he remained at home to play pinocle with the pretty girls. He may not be much of a statesman in time of peace, but there's no picnic ants on his judgment in time of war.

It is time that capital and labor realized that their interests are really commutual, as interdependent as the brain and the body; time they ceased their fratricidal strife and, uniting their mighty forces under the flag of Progress, completed the conquest of the world and doomed Poverty, Ignorance and Vice—hell's great triumvirate—to banishment eternal. Unless labor is employed, capital cannot increase—it can 'only concentrate. Unless property rights are held inviolable and capital thereby encouraged to high enterprise, labor is left without a lever with which to lift itself to perfect life and must sink back to barbarism.

It is time that American citizens of alleged intelligence ceased trailing blindly in the wake of partisan bandwagons and began to seriously consider the public welfare —time they realized that the people were not made for parties, but parties for the people, and refuse to sacrifice their patriotism on the unclean altar of partisan slavery. Blind obedience to party fiat; the division of the people of one great political family into hostile camps; subjection of the public interest to partisan advantage; placing the badge of party servitude above the crown of American sovereignty—the ridiculous oriflamme of foolish division above Old Glory's star-gemmed promise of everlasting unity—have brought the first nation of all the world to the very brink of destruction.

* * *

It is difficult for people here in Texas to understand the industrial condition of the American nation to-day; to appreciate the dangers upon which it is drifting. We are too apt to imagine everybody as prosperous and conservative as ourselves; or if not so, it's because they do not vote the Democratic ticket—that panacea for all the ills that flesh is heir to. Here in Texas we have hung our second providence on the Democratic party—it has become a religion with us. If a man is orthodox in his political faith all things are forgiven him; but if there's any doubt about his Democracy we are inclined to regard him as an alien, if not an anarchist. Most of us enjoy the shadow of our own vine and fig tree—which it is impossible to mortgage. We feed three times a day, have a cocktail every morning, a clean shirt occasionally, and even when cotton goes so low it doesn't pay for the paris-green to poison the worms,

we blame it on the Lord instead of on our political leaders.
But it's different in other sections of the Union.

America contains more than a million as desperate men
as ever danced the Carmagnole or shrieked with brutal
joy when the blood of French aristocrats reddened the
guillotine. The dark alleys and unclean dives of our great
cities are crowded with dangerous *sans-cullotte,* and our
highways with hungry men eager for bread—though the
world blaze for it. Pauperism is rampant, the criminal
classes increasing and everywhere the serpent of Socialism
is leaving it's empoisoned slime. Suppose that these desperate elements find a determined leader—a modern
Marat, who will make the most of his opportunities for
evil: how many of that vast contingent now clinging
with feeble grasp to the rotten skirts of a doubtful respectability, would be swept into the seething vortex of unbridled villainy? Note the failure of public officials to protect corporate property; the necessity of calling for federal
bayonets and batteries to suppress labor riots; the dangerous unrest of the common people; the sympathy of the
farmer—that Atlas upon whose broad shoulders rests our
political and industrial world—with every quasi-military
organization that throws down the gage of battle to
the powers that be, then tell me, if you can, where Dives
may look for defenders should the rabble rise in its wrath,
the bullet supplant the ballot in the irrepressible conflict
between the Cormorant and the Commune! And what are
we doing to avert the danger? Distributing a little dole
and preaching patience to starving people; quarreling
about the advisability of "counting a quorum" or coining
a little silver seigniorage; wrangling over the " :ghts" of
a mid-Pacific prostitute to rule Celts and Saxons, and trying to so "reform" the tariff that it will yield more revenue
with less taxation! We are bowing down before various
pie-hunting political gods and electing men to Congress
who couldn't tell the Federal Constitution from Calvin's
Confession of Faith. We are sending street-corner economists to state and national conventions to evolve
from their innate ignorance and gild with their supernal
gall political platforms which we are pledged beforehand to
accept as the essence of all worldly wisdom. Our patriotism has been supplanted by partisanship, and now all
are for a party and none are for the state. On July 4 we
shout for the old flag and all the rest of the year we clamor
for an appropriation. The man who is kicked by a nightmare while dreaming of the draft demands a pension and
every burning patriot wants an office. And while our

ship of state is threading with unsteady course the stormy
straits between the Scylla of Greed and the Charybdis of
Need; its canvas torn by contending winds; its decks
swept by angry waves, we boast of the strength of our
"free institutions"—as tho' Republics had never fallen nor
revolutions erased from the map of the world proud Empires that imagined themselves immortal.

But before God I do believe this selfish and unpatriotic
age will pass, as passed the age of brutish ignorance, as
passed the age of tyranny. I believe the day will come—oh
blessed dawn!—when the angel of Intellect will banish
the devil of Demagogy; when Americans will be in spirit
and in truth a band of brothers, the wrongs of one the
concern of all; when labor will no longer fear the Cormorant nor capital the Commune—when all men will be equal
before the law wherever falls the shadow of our flag.

MARLBOROUGH-VANDERBILT MARRIAGE.

The approaching marriage of Miss Consuelo Vanderbilt
to the Duke of Marlborough is agitating the social world
from centre to circumference.   New York's Four Hundred and the fashionables of London are standing on their
hind legs and wildly waving their ears.   The alliance is
pronounced not only "the social event of the season," but
of all seasons, so far as Columbia is concerned.   The capture by Miss Gould of a French count was not a circumstance to it.   The Frenchman was only a count by courtesy,
while the "Jook" is still doing business at Sara Jennings'
old stand.   The press gave us only a few columns daily
anent the Gould-Castellane barter and sale, but it shoots
the Vanderbilt-Marlborough affair into us by the page.
The press can always be depended upon to rise equal to the
occasion, and this is too evidently the supreme crisis of
the universe.   Millions of columns have been written anent
the matter, and the deluge of intellectual bilge-water has
just begun.   If Heaven and Earth should again embrace
to beget a second Saturnus the pencil-pushers could not
be more profoundly impressed.

And who the devil are the Duke of Marlborough and
Miss Vanderbilt, that the world should hold its breath
while they make elaborate preparations to contribute, each
to the misery of the other—to share the same bed and
board?   The Duke is the lineal descendant of old John
Churchill and Sara Jennings, two of the most disreputable

ducks that ever disgraced the earth.   John utilized the
virtue of his sister to break into the British "nobility,"
fawned at the feet of her princely paramour so long as he
had power to promote his fortune, then turned traitor
and sold his services to William III, by whom he was ever
regarded with suspicion and treated with contempt.   Like
Sextus Tarquinius and Benedict Arnold, he was a soldier
of some ability; but he was more shameless than the one
and more corrupt than the other.   Arnold would not have
profited by a sister's prostitution, nor Sextus have soiled
his hand with the small wage of the common soldier.   John
Churchill, founder of the House of Marlborough, was
the Boss Tweed of his time, the prize pimp of his day and
generation.   As a traitor he was the peer of Judas Iscariot,
and he has been equalled in shameless dishonesty only by
his lineal descendants.   The only assurance we have that
the latter were not bastards is to be found in the fact that
they were one and all stamped from head to heel with the
Marlborough meanness.   It is another case of the evil men
do living after them, while the good is interred with
their bones.   Sara Jennings, his wife, was eminently worthy
so mean a mate.   She was a kind of unholy cross between
Xanthippe and Sycorax, the best hated old heifer in all
England.   Too cold-blooded to play the prostitute herself,
she was content to tend door and share in the profit of her
sister-in-law's shame.   The fiance of Miss Vanderbilt is
descended from this impure source thro' a long line of titled
cuckolds and shameless pimps, and now stands on the
ragged edge of poverty, bartering to parvenues for bread
an empty dukedom bought with a female relative's dishonor.   The late Lord Randolph Churchill, uncle of the
present duke, was unquestionably the best of the lot; but
he demonstrated of what material he was made when he
failed to rip the white liver out of Prince Collars and Cuffs
when he caught that royal popinjay *flagrante delicto* with
"Lady" Churchill, at Windsor Castle—when he accepted
the foul bawd warm from the embraces of that titled nin-
compoop and permitted her to continue to bear his name.
The father of the present duke, and his predecessor in the
title was universally conceded to be the most contemptible
cur in all Christendom.   He had more than the vices of the
original Churchill and none of his supposed virtues.   He
succeeded in wedding a respectable woman, but she was
compelled to leave him because of his general cussedness.
He then sold his title to a dizzy New York music teacher
who had managed to catch a sucker and bump his head
for several millions.   He ran through with Lil Hammersly's

boodle, was carried to the grave with the syphilis and left a beggarly title to his particularly stupid son, who is now bartering it to the Vanderbilts.

Such, in brief, is the origin and history of "the great House of Marlborough"—a plebeian family raised to the peerage by prostitution and enriched by rascality that embraced every crime in the calendar, from petty thievery to base ingratitude, from arrant hypocrisy to high treason, to be in turn pauperized by pimps, beggared by bawds. There is not a drop of pure blood in the entire family.

There has never been one of the name entitled to be called a gentleman. The record of the house is black with more than Armenian meanness, across its escutcheon falls the bar-sinister of a woman's shame. The present duke is said to be somewhat better than his degraded progenitors. Poverty makes even dukes humble. When a "nobleman" is unable to buy so much as a yellow pot to put in his boudoir he is apt to strike a moderate gait; but he is a Churchill, and "an evil tree cannot bring forth good fruit." In appearance he is a tough of the toughs. He has a head like a Bowery bouncer and the mug of an ape who has met with an accident. When he gets his grip on the Vanderbilt gold it is dollars to doughnuts he will use it as did his unlamented father the millions of the gay Lil Hammersly, who paid for the privilege of being kicked and cuffed by a genuine British "nobleman" in Blenheim Palace.

And the Vanderbilts? Two hundred years ago an ignorant Hollander squatted on a patch of land at Flat Bush, L. I., and engaged in the laudable enterprise of raising cabbages, while his better half added an occasional florin to the family hoard by peddling fish. At that time the name was taken on the installment plan, being written Van Der Bilt. Old Bilt begat a son named Jacob, who followed in the footsteps of his father, and was poor without being proud. He was also a grower of cabbages, and his gude wife not above peddling sprats from door to door and filing the proceeds away in her ample yarn sock. In the course of four generations the Van Der Bilts had accumulated sufficient boodle to buy a small ferryboat, and began at once to float on to fortune. The name was coupled up to save stationery in writing it, for none realized better than they that economy is the road to wealth. By working like the Old Harry and spending never a cent, and by the rise in land values in and around New York, the Vanderbilts became wealthy enough to exchange barter in shrimps and sprats for deals in rail-way stocks—to purchase a coronet to offset that "very ancient and fish-like smell" which has so long clung to the descendants of old Aris. Miss Consuelo is the daughter of Wm. K. Vanderbilt, a lively old bird who was recently divorced from his wife for reasons that have been kept a family secret. It is the general impression, how-ever, that it was a case of mutual fornication; that while "Willie" was going a rapid gait in dizzy "Paree," Alva was holding up her end of the line in London. Such is the lineage of the young lady who is about to purchase a descendant of old Judas Iscariot Churchill and Sara Jen-nings. She is a long, gaunt, skinny young female whose face would frighten any animal but a pauper duke out for the "dough." Her muscular arms, stub-nose and big feet proclaim her plebeian origin, while if the countenance be a true index to the intellect, she is the mental equal of a half-baked Chinese idol. If she had not been born with a silver spoon in her mouth it is doubtful if she could se-cure a position in the second row of the ballet on her shape, or a place in a steam laundry by her intelligence. But Miss Consuelo is an American. Were she the de-scendant of a Bowery tough, as homely as a hedgehog and as stupid as a Cleveland Democrat she would be in-finitely too good for the best man that ever bore the title of Duke of Marborough. We are sorry for the young lady, just as we are sorry for any calf that is being led to the shambles. She will doubtless wish a thousand times that instead of wedding the "Jooke" she followed the ex-ample of her female ancestors—married some sturdy young Dutch farmer and peddled fish. After the glamour and glitter have worn away she will wonder if the game was worth the candle. She will look at the scorbutic subject of an old woman and compare him with the sov-ereigns of her native land and wish to God that she could lose him.

"What fools these mortals be" — especially where a petty title and a little money are concerned! Most of the "great American dailies" have printed pictures of the young pair who are making such elaborate preparations to occupy the same sheets; but the New York *World* out-toadies all Toadydom. It informs an alleged intelligent world just how tall Miss Vanderbilt is, the length of her foot and such other information as might be valuable were she a Papuan slave being bartered for breeding pur-poses. It also devotes considerable space to a description of the lingerie in which she will encase her "lithe limbs"

during the honeymoon. The style is only hinted at, but we
may presume that the chemise will be provided with
handles and the under-garment patterned after Biela's
comet or the Democratic party. The fit will doubtless be
au fait. The sartorial artist will doubtless be able to properly attire any portion of her anatomy by employing the
World's measurements. We regret that our great con-
temporary has neglected to tell us anything about the
lingerie of the bridegroom-elect. But perhaps he doesn't
wear any at present. He is probably waiting for the
Vanderbilt "settlement" to provide his noble anatomy
with undershirts.

I wish the young turtle-doves well, but can scarce
pray that their tribe may increase. I trust that having
secured sufficient of the ducats hoarded up by certain
Dutch fish wives to enable him to live in comfort, the
duke will give us an imitation of a nobleman who is trying to be decent; that having purchased one of the two-
and-twenty dukedoms of the United Kingdom, the young
woman will not pattern after her giddy aunt and hang
on princes' favors to the dishonor of her husband.

The papers state that the capture of the Duke by the
Vanderbiltian millions will result in bringing the bride's
parents together again—that they will re-marry. It is a
consummation devoutly to be wished. They seem to have
been made for each other—to harmonize in tastes and
habits almost as well as did old John Churchill and Sara
Jennings. In view of the aphorism that "like takes to
like," I cannot imagine how they came to drift apart. If
Mrs. Vanderbilt is looking for a rake, Willie should
please her to perfection. If he admires dizzy females,
she's the girl for his gold. If Willie loves the rapid in
crinoline he should fairly worship his *ci-devant* wife. Let
them forgive and forget and enjoy to the utmost the
beatitude of having a sure-enough Duke for a son-in-law
—of referring to their daughter in the presence of those
stuck up Goulds as "the Duchess." Willie and Alva
should spend a few months of each year at Blenheim
Palace—a place so noted in the annals of prostitution.
Vive la Van Der Bilt! Vive la Marlborough! The representative family of American parvenues and that of European pimps in holy alliance were a combination at
which the majestic world may well stand agaze.

HUMBUGS AND HUMBUGGERY.

THE GREAT AMERICAN PRODUCT.

Satan is supposed to have been the original Humbug; but he's a back number now—must feel dreadfully antiquated and useless among so many modern improvements.

That the American people love to be humbugged long since passed into a proverb. Humbuggery may be called our national vice, our besetting sin. Like liberty, it appears to be in the very air we breathe, and we take to it as naturally as we go into politics. Our entire social system has become saturated with it. It is the main-spring of many acts we loudly praise, the lode-star of men we apotheosize, is oftimes the warp and woof even of the mantle of charity, which, like a well-filled purse—or a tariff compromise—covers a multitude of sins.

There are various kinds and classes of Humbugs; but reduced to the last analysis—stripped of the sugar-coating by which they impose on the public—they are one and all simply professors of falsehood.

I am sometimes inclined to the view that humbuggery is a disease, and that some doctor will yet discover a gold-cure for it—will demonstrate that the bad habit is due to microbes that get into a man's mind and make trouble trying to turn around, or to bacilli that bore holes in his moral character and let his honesty leak out; for the medical fraternity has gravely informed us that kleptomania (sneak-thievery by eminently respectable people) and dipsomania (sottishness by the social salt of the earth), are simply diseases that should be treated with pills and powders instead of with penitentiaries and whipping-posts. Now if a man will steal a saw-mill and go back after the site simply because his pericardium is out of plumb or his liver has gone into politics; will nurse a juicy old jag until it develops into a combined museum and menagerie, because his circulation has slipped an eccentric or his stomach got out of its natural orbit, I submit, in all seriousness that he might be physically incapacitated for telling the truth by an insidious attack on his veracity by the dreadful falsehood fungi, and that the best way to restore his moral equilibrium—to remove him from the category of chronic Humbugs—would be to fumigate him.

The Lord once attempted to check the Humbug habit

by striking liars dead; but soon saw that such a plan
would prove more fatal than a second flood—that there
wouldn't be even a Noah's Ark picnic party of us left—
and reluctantly relinquished it. Science has not yet succeeded in mastering the disease; but just give it time and
it will save the world yet—will find a medical name for
every human frailty; will be able to tell, by looking at a
man's tongue, whether he's coming down with the mugwump malaria or the office-holding hysteria, and do
something for him before it's everlastingly too late.

The very best of people have a touch of the complaint
—"the trail of the serpent is over us all." Even our young
ladies are said to be, to a certain extent, Humbugs. I
have been told that many of them wear patent complex-
ions, "boughten" bangs, and pad out scrawny forms until
they appear voluptuous Junos, and thereby deceive and
ensnare, bedazzle and beguile the unsuspecting sons, of
men. I have been told that many of them who are soft-
voiced angels before marriage can give a rusty buzz-saw
cards and spades and beat it blind after they have succeeded in landing the confiding sucker. But perhaps such
tales are only the bitter complainings of miserable
Benedicts who have been soundly beaten at their own
game of humbuggery. Marriage is, perhaps, the only
game of chance ever invented at which it is possible for
both players to lose. Too often, after much sugar-coated
deception, and many premeditated misdeals on both sides,
one draws a blank and the other a booby. After patient
angling in the matrimonial pool, one lands a stingaree
and the other a bull-head. One expects to capture a demi-
god who hits the earth only in high places; the other to
wed a wingless angel who will make his Edenic bower
one long-drawn sigh of ecstatic bliss. The result is that
one is tied up to a slattern who slouches around the
house with her hair on tins, in a dirty collar and with a
dime novel, a temper like aqua-fortis and a voice like a
cat-fight; the other a hoodlum who comes home from the
lodge at 2 g. m. and whoops and howls for her to come
down and help him hunt for the keyhole, and is then
snailed in by a policeman before she can frame a curtain
lecture or find the rolling pin.

* * *

False Pride is the father of humbuggery, the parent of
Fraud. We are Humbugs because we desire that our
fellows think us better, braver, brighter, perhaps richer
than we really are. We practice humbuggery to attain

social position to which we are entitled by neither birth nor brains, to acquire wealth for which we render no equivalent, to procure power we cannot wisely employ.

While proclaiming love of democracy we purchase peers for our daughters. While boasting liberty of speech we assail like demons those who presume to dissent from our opinions in either religion or politics.

History is full of Humbugs and liberty itself ofttimes but a gilded lie. No man is really free who is dependent upon the good will of others for employment. There can be no true liberty where Prejudice usurps the throne of Reason. Men are slaves instead of sovereigns when they suffer themselves to be held in iron thrall by political dogma or religious creed, blindly accepting the *ipse dixit* of others instead of exercising to the utmost the intelligence which God hath given them.

I have said that charity itself is ofttimes a Humbug. It is so when it becomes the handmaid of ostentation instead of the true almoner of the heart; or when men give to the poor only because it is "lending to the Lord," then expect compound interest.

That philanthropist is a fraud who, after piling up a colossal fortune at the expense of the common people, leaves it to found an educational or eleemosynary institute when death calls him across the dark river. Knowing that Charon's boat is purely a passenger packet—that it carries no freight, however precious—he drops his dollars with a sigh; but, determined to reap some benefit from boodle his itching hand can no longer hold, he decrees that it be used to found some charitable fake to prevent himself being forgotten—some pitiful institute where a few of the wretched victims of his rapacious greed may get a plate of starvation soup, or a prayer-book, and bless their benefactor's name. The very monument erected over bones of the sanctimonious old skin-flint is a fraud; flaunts a string of colossal falsehoods in the face of the world; piously points to heaven—perhaps to indicate that Satan refused to receive him and sent him back to St. Peter with a request that he make other arrangements.

* * *

Many of the martyrs whose memory we revere, of the saints we apotheosize, of the heroes we enshrine in history, are one-third fraud and two-thirds fake. The man who can grow in grace while his pet corn's in chancery, or lose an election without spilling his moral character; who can wait an hour for his dinner without walking all over the nerves of his wife, or crawl out of bed in the middle of his first nap and rustle till the cold, gray dawn with a brace of colicky kids, without broadly insinuating that he was a copper-riveted, nickel-plated, automatic, double-cylinder idiot to ever get married, is a greater hero than he that taketh a city.

The place to take the true measure of a man is not the market-place or the amen-corner, not the forum or the field, but at his fireside. There he lays aside his mask and you may learn whether he's imp or angel, king or cur, hero or Humbug. I care not what the world says of him —whether it crown him with bays or pelt him with bad eggs; I care never a copper what his reputation or religion may be: If his babes dread his home-coming and his better-half swallows her heart every time she has to ask him for a five dollar bill, he's a fraud of the first water, even tho' he prays night and morn till he's black in the face and howls hallelujah till he shakes the eternal hills. But if his children rush to the front gate to greet him, and love's own sunshine illumes the face of his wife when she hears his footfall, you can take it for granted that he's true gold, for his home's a heaven, and the Humbug never gets that near the great white throne of God. He may be a rank atheist and a red-flag anarchist, a Mormon and a mugwump; he may buy votes in blocks-of-five and bet on the election; he may deal 'em from the bottom of the deck and drink beer till he can't tell a silver dollar from a circular saw, and still be an infinitely better man than the cowardly little Humbug who's all suavity in society, but who makes his home a hell—who vents upon the hapless heads of wife and children the ill-nature he would like to inflict on his fellow-men, but dares not. I can forgive much in that fellow mortal who would rather make men swear than women weep; who would rather have the hate of the whole he-world than the contempt of his wife—who would rather call anger to the eyes of a king than fear to the face of a child.

The hero is not he that strives with the world for witness—who seeks the bubble fame at the cannon's brazen lip and risks his life that he may live forever.

"Think not that helm and harness are signs of valor true;
Peace hath higher tests of manhood than battles ever knew."

To bear with becoming grace the slings and arrows of outrageous fortune; to find our heaven in others' happiness, and for their sake to sacrifice and suffer wrongs that might be righted with a thread of steel; to live an honest

life in a land where Truth doth feed on crusts while
Falsehood fattens at Lucullean feasts, requires more true
manhood, more moral stamina, more unadulterated *sand*
than to follow a flag into the very jaws of hell or die for
the faith in the *auto da fe*. Heroes? Why unurn the
ashes of the half-forgotten dead and pore o'er the musty
pages of the past for names to glorify? If you would
find heroes grander, martyrs more noble and saints of
more sanctity than Rubens ever painted or immortal
Homer sang; who, without Achilles' armor, have slain
an hundred Hectors; without Samsonian locks have torn
the lion; without the sword of Michael have thrown down
the gage to all the embattled hosts of hell, seek not in the
musty tomes of history, but in the hearts and homes of
the self-sacrificing wives and mothers of this great
world.

"God could not be everywhere," says the proverb,
"therefore he made mothers,"

Let the heroes of history have their due; still I imagine
the world would have been much the same had Alexander
died of cholera-infantum or grown up a harmless dude.
I don't thing the earth unbalanced would from its orbit
fly had Caesar been drowned in the Rubicon, or Cleveland
never been born. I imagine that Greece would have humbled the Persian pride had there been no Thermopylae,
that Rome would have ruled the world had Scaevola's
good right hand not hissed in the Tuscan fire. It is even
possible that civilization would have stood the shocks had
"Lanky Bob" and "Gentleman Jim" met on Texas soil—
that the second-term boom of "our heroic young Christian governor" would have lost no gas. One catfish does
not make a creek nor one hero a nation. The waves do
not make the sea, but the sea furnishes forth the waves.
Leonidas were lost to history but for the three hundred
nameless braves who backed his bluff. Had there been
but one Cromwell Charles the First would have kept his
head. In Washington's deathless splendor gleams the
glory of forgotten millions, and the history of Bonaparte
is written with blood of the unknown brave.

* * *

Humbuggery, fraud, deception everywhere.

"All the world's a stage
And all the men and women merely players"—

Momus the major-domo, the millions *en masque*. Even
friendship is becoming a screaming farce, intended to pro-

mote the social fortune or fill the purse. We fawn that thrift may follow; are prodigal of sweet words because they cost nothing and swell the sails of many a rich argosy; but weigh every penny we put forth, and carefully calculate the chance of gain or loss. It's heads I win, tails you lose, and when we cannot play it on that principle we promptly jump the game.

"Who steals my purse steals trash."

That's Shakespeare.

"He that filches from me my good name . . . makes me poor indeed."

That's nonsense. Reputation is but the ephemeral dew on character's everlasting gold; but he that steals a human heart and tramples it beneath his brutal heel; he that feigns a friendship he does not feel; he that fawns upon his fellows and hugs them hard and after scandals them, is the foulest fraud in all this land of fakes, the most hideous Humbug in all hell's unclean hierarchy.

I am sometimes tempted to believe that the only friendship that will stand fire is that of a yellow dog for a pauper negro. Strike a friend for a small loan and his affection grows suddenly cold; lose your fortune and your sweetheart sends you word that she will be a sister to you; your brother will betray you for boodle, your father fight you for a foolish flag and your heirs-at-law will dance when they hear of your death; but the devotion of a yaller dog to a worthless nigger hath all seasons for its own.

* * *

But the Humbug for whom I have least use is the man who assiduously damns the Rum Demon; makes tearful temperance talks; ostentatiously votes the prohibition ticket; groans like a sick calf hit by a battering-ram whenever he sees a young man come out of a barroom; then sneaks up a dirty alley, crawls thro' the side door of a second-class saloon; calls for the cheapest whiskey in the shop, runs the glass over trying to get the worth of his money; pours it down at a gulp and scoots in a hurry lest somebody ask him to treat; who has a chronic toothache—in the stomach—which nothing but drugstore whiskey will relieve; who keeps a jug of dollar-a-gallon bug-juice hid under his bed and sneaks to it like a thieving hyena digging up a dead nigger—rents his property

for saloon purposes, then piously prays the Lord to protect the young from temptation.

*   *   *

But perhaps the prince of Humbugs, the incarnation of
fraud, the apotheosis of audacity, is the street-corner politician. He towers above his fellow fakes like Saul above
his brethren. I have been time and again instructed in
the most intricate problems of public polity—questions
that have perplexed the wisest statesmen of the world—
by men who had never read a single standard work on political economy, and who could not tell to save their souls
—granting that they possess such perishable property—
whether Adam Smith wrote the "Wealth of Nations" or
the Lord's Prayer; who were not familiar with the constitution of their own state, or the face of a receipted wash-
bill; who could scarce tell a sloop from a ship, a bill of
lading from a sight draft; a hydraulic ram from a he-goat
unless they were properly labeled. Yet no question can
arise in metaphysics or morals, government or general-
ship, upon which these great little men do not presume
to speak with the authoritative assurance of a Lord Chief
Justice—or a six-foot woman addressing a four-foot husband. They invariably know it all. They could teach
Solomon and the Seven Wise Men wisdom, and had they
been on earth when Almighty God wrote the Ten Commandments they would have moved an amendment or
drafted a minority report.

And these are the fellows who frame our political platforms and dominate our elections—whose boundless cupidity, colossal ignorance and supernal gall bring about
starvation in a land of plenty—divide the most industrious and progressive people that ever graced the footstool
of Almighty God, into bloated millionaires and groveling
mendicants.

Even patriotism has become a Humbug—has been
supplanted by partisanship, and now all are for party and
none are for the state. On July 4 we shout for the old flag,
and all the rest of the year we clamor for an appropriation. The man who is kicked by a nightmare while dreaming of the draft demands a pension and every burning patriot wants an office. Twice, yea, thrice within the memory of men now living, America has been on the very
verge of an industrial revolution, a Reign of Terror; yet
we continue to hang our second Providence on a job-lot
of politcal jacksnipes who carry their patriotism in their
pockets and their sense under their surcingles. While we

who feed three times a day; who have a cocktail every morning and a clean, shirt occasionally, are boasting of our allegiance to "the grand old party," or prating of the principles of Jeffersonian democracy—are blindly trailing in the wake of some partisan band-wagon like a brindle calf behind a Kansas hay-cart—this nation, born of our fathers' blood and sanctified by our mothers' tears, is dominated by political self-seekers who have taken for their motto, "After us the deluge."

* * *

Once after holding forth at some length on Humbugs, a physician said to me:

"Ah-er—you-ah—didn't mention the medical profession."

"No," I replied, "the power of language hath its limits."

The medical, mark you, is the noblest of all professions. It contains many learned and able men who devote their lives unselfishly to the amelioration of human misery; but I much doubt whether one-half the M. D.'s now sending people to the drug stores with cipher dispatches, could tell what was the matter with a suffering mortal were he transparent as glass and lit up by electricity. There are doctors doping people with powerful drugs, who couldn't tell whether a patient had a case of cholera-morbus or was afflicted with an incurable itch for office—who have acquired their medical information from the almanacs and could not distinguish between a bunion and a stone-bruise or find the joints in a string of sausage with a search-warrant.

I have noticed that when the doctors took to writing their prescriptions in Latin it quickly became a dead language—that when I take the poet's advice and throw physic to the dogs, their numbers rapidly decrease. But the doctors are jolly good fellows. Let it be recorded to their eternal credit, that, whatever may be their faults, precious few of them will practice in their own families. I have often wished that I was a doctor of medicine instead of a doctor of divinity. There are several fellows for whom I'd like to prescribe. There's a strong affinity between the two professions. The D. D.'s deal in faith and prayer, the M. D.'s in faith and pills.

I have been frequently asked why, in lecturing on Humbugs, I skip the lawyers. There are some subjects to which a lecturer must lead up gradually; so I discuss the doctors in my discourse on Humbugs and save the attorneys for my talk on Gall.

Even our boasted educational system is half a Humbug. Too many of our professers fondly imagine that when they have crammed the dry formulas of half a dozen sciences into a small head—perhaps designed by the Deity to furnish the directive wisdom for a scavenger cart; when they have taught a two-legged moon-calf to glibly read in certain dead languages things it can in nowise comprehend —patiently pumped into it a whole congeries of things that defy its mental digestive apparatus—that it is actually educated, if not enlightened. And perhaps it is—after the manner of the trick mule or the pig that plays cards. The attempt of Gulliver scientists to calcine ice into gunpowder were not more ridiculous than trying to transform a fool into a philosopher by the alchemy of education. If it be a waste of lather to shave an ass, what must it be to educate an idiot? True education consists in the acquirement of useful information; yet I have seen college graduates —even men sporting professional sheepskins—who couldn't tell whether Gladstone's an English statesman or an Irish policeman. They knew all about Greek roots but couldn't tell a carrot from a parsnip. They could decipher a cuneiform inscription, perhaps, and state whether a pebble belonged to the paleozoic or some other period; but couldn't tell a subpoena from a search-warrant, a box of vermicelli from a bundle of fishworms.

We pore over books too much and reflect too little; depend too much on others, too little upon ourselves. We make of our heads cold-storage warehouses for other people's ideas, instead of standing up in our own independent, god-like individuality. Bacon says that reading makes a full man. Perhaps so, but it makes a great deal of difference what a fellow's full of. Too many who fondly imagine themselves educated, much resemble Mark Twain's frog with its stomach full of shot—they are crushed to earth by the things they have swallowed.

Neither the public nor any other school system has ever produced one really great man. Those who occupy the dias-throne among the immortals, contended single-handed with the darkness of ignorance and the devil of dogmatism. Columbus scorned the schools and discovered a world. Napoleon revolutionized the science of war and made himself master of Europe. Bismarck mocked at precedent, and United Germany stood forth a giant. Jesus of Nazareth ignored the learning of the Levites, and around the world arose the fanes of a new faith.

Reading is the nurse of culture; reflection the mother of genius. Our great religions were born in the desert.

Our grandest philosophers budded and burgeoned in the wilderness. The noblest poesy that ever swept the human harpsichord was born in the brain of a beggar, came bubbling from the heart of the blind; and when all the magi of the Medes, and all the great philosophers of Greece had failed to furnish forth a jurisprudence just to all, semi-barbarous Rome laid down those laws by which, even from the grave of her glory, she still rules the majestic world.

I have been accused of being the enemy of education; but then I have been accused of almost everything; so one count more or less in the indictment doesn't matter. I am not opposed to education that is useful; but why should we pay people to fill the empty heads of fools with soap and sawdust?

Perhaps the most aggressive fraud that infests the earth is the professional atheist—the man whose chief mental stock-in-trade consists of doubt and denial of revealed religion, so-called.

About the time a youngster first feels an irresistible impulse to make a fool of himself wherever a female smiles upon him; when he's reached that critical stage in life's journey when he imagines that he knows much more than his father, he begins to doubt the religion of his mother; shrewdly asks his Sunday-school teacher who made God; demonstrates by the aid of natural history diagrams, that a large whale could in nowise swallow a small prophet— that if he did succeed in relegating him to its internal economy it were impossible for him to slosh around for three days and nights in the gastric juices without becoming much the worse for wear. He attempts to rip religion up by the roots and reform the world while you wait, but soon learns that he's got a government contract on his hands, —that the man who can drive the Deity out of the hearts and homes of this land can make a fortune turning artesian wells inside out and peddling them for telegraph poles. You can't do it, son. Religion is the backbone of the body social. Sometimes it's unbending as a boarding-house biscuit, and sometimes it's a bad quality of gutta-percha; but we couldn't get far without it. Most youths have to pass thro' a period of doubt and denial—catch the infidel humor just as they do the measles and mumps; but they eventually learn that the fear of God is the beginning of wisdom.

There was never an atheistical book written; there was never an infidel argument penned that touched the *core* of any religion, Christian or Pagan. Bibles, Korans, Zandevestas—all sacred books—are but the feeble efforts of finite man to interpret the infinite; to speak forth the unspeakable; to reduce to intelligible human characters the flame-written hieroglyphs of the sky. Who made God? Suppose, Mr. Atheist, that I find thee an answer? Who will furnish thee with an intellect to understand it? How will you comprehend the genesis of a God when the wisest man for whom Christ died cannot tell why water runs down hill instead of up—cannot understand the basic principle of the law of gravitation—cannot even guess why Gov. Culberson encouraged the managers of Corbett and Fitzsimmons to bring the mill to Texas, then knocked it out at a special session of the legislature at the expense of the general public.

An atheist once solemnly assured me that he couldn't possibly *believe* anything which he couldn't *prove;* but when I asked him what led him to take such a lively interest in the welfare of his wife's children, he became almost as angry as a Calvinist whose confession of faith had been called in question. Figure up how many things you can *prove* of those you *believe,* and you'll find that you have got to do a credit business or go into intellectual bankruptcy.

But the man who denies the existence of the Deity because he cannot comprehend his origin, is even less a Humbug than the one who knows all about him—the pitiful dogmatizer who devotes his life to the defense of some poor little guess-work interpretation of the mysterious plans of him who brings forth Mazaroth in his season and guides Arcturus with his sons.

Dogmatism is the fecund mother of doubt, a manacle on the human mind, a brake on the golden wheel of Christian progress; and every dogmatizer, whether in science, politics or religion, is consciously or unconsciously, a Humbug. You *know,* do you? Know what? And who told you? Why, the man in whose mighty intellect was stored the world's wisdom; whose words have come down to us from the distant past as oracles, o'ershadowing even Solomon and Shakespeare, wasn't quite sure of his own existence. Men frequently tell me that what they *see* they *know.* Well, they've got to drink mighty little Prohibition whisky if they do; otherwise they are liable to see things they'll need an introduction to. The wisest is he that knows only that he knows nothing. Omniscient God only knows. We— you and I—are only troubled with morbid little-ideas, sired by circumstance and dammed by folly. We don't even know

how the Democracy stands on the silver question or what
caused the slump in the late election.

* * *

The average human head, like an egg—or a crock of
clabber—absorbs the flavor of its surroundings. It is
chiefly a question of environment whether we grow up
Catholics or Protestants, Republicans or Democrats, Populists or political nondescripts. And yet we adhere to opinions we have inherited with all the tenacity of a dog to a
bone or an American miser to a ten dollar bill. We assume
that our faith political and our creed religious are founded
upon our reason, when they were really made for us by
social conditions over which we had little control. We
even succeed in humbugging ourselves into the belief that
we are the people and that wisdom will die with us, when
the fact is that our head is loaded with out-of-date lumber—
our every idea moulded or modified by barbarians who were
in the bone-yard before Methusaleh was born.

Society is a vast organism in which the individual is
but an atom. It is a monstrous tree—a veritable Ygdrasyl
—penetrating both the region of darkness and the realm
of light. Whatever its peculiarities—whether monarchical
or republican, Christian or Pagan—it is a goodly tree when
it brings forth good fruit—when its boughs bend with
Apples of Hesperides and in its grateful shade is reared
the shrine of God. Be it of what shape it may, it is an
evil tree when its fruit is Apples of Sodom and it casts
a upas-shadow upon the earth. If we cannot gather grapes
of thorns or figs of thistles, how can a society that is essentially false foster that which is literally true? The body
social, of which we proudly boast, is producing dodos instead of King Davids, peanut-politicians instead of
heaven-inspired poets, cranks instead of crusaders,
Humbugs rather than heroes. Instead of exercising
in the *campus martius* our sons cultivate the Henglish
hawkcent and the London lope. In the olden days the
glory of the young man was his strength; now it is his
chrysanthemum and his collar. And it is going from bad to
worse in a ratio of geometrical progression; for how can
effeminate men—a cane-sucking, primping, mincing, affected conglomeration of masculine inanity and asininity beget world-compellers? How can women who care much
what is on the outside and little what is on the inside of
their heads, and whom a box of lily-white, a French novel,
a poodle-dog and another dude will make superlatively
happy, suckle aught but fops and fools?

Yet we boast of progress! Progress whither? From the savage who knew nothing to the dude who knows less. From the barbarian who'd plundered your baggage, to the civilized Shylock who'd steal the very earth from under your feet. From that state wherein American sovereigns, however poor, considered themselves the equals of kings and the superiors of princes, to that moral degradation and national decay in which they purchase the scurvy spawn of petty dukes as husbands for our daughters. By the splendor of God, I'd rather be a naked Fiji Islander, dancing about a broiled missionary with a bull-ring in my nose, than a simpering "sawciety" simpleton, wearing my little intellectual apparatus to a frazzle with a study of neckties!

* * *

Some of my critics have kindly suggested that the Lord made a great mistake in not consulting me when he made the world; thereby ascertaining just how I would like to have it. I was not consulted anent the creation of the Cosmos, and perhaps it is just as well for them that I wasn't—they might not be here. Too many forget that while the Lord made the world, the devil has been busy ever since putting on the finishing touches. Why, he began on the first woman before she was a week old, and he has been playing schoolmaster to her sons ever since. I confess to a sneaking respect for Satan, for he is pre-eminently a success in his chosen profession. He's playing a desperate game against omnipotent power and is more than holding his own. He sat into the game with a cash capital of one snake; now he's got half the globe grabbed and an option on the other half.

I have been called a defender of the devil; but I hope that won't prejudice the ladies against me, as it was a woman that discovered him. I confess to the belief that Satan is a gentleman compared with some of his very humble servants. We are told that he is a fallen angel who found pride a stumbling-block—that he tripped over it and plunged down to infinite despair; but tho' he fell further than a pigeon could fly in a week, the world is full of frauds who could not climb up to his level in a month; who can no more claim kinship with him in their cussedness than a thieving hyena can say to the royal beast of Bengal, "Thou art my brother." They are not fallen angels; they are risen vermin. They didn't come down from thrones in heaven like falling stars; they crawled up from holes in the earth like vicious little pismires. What can proud Lucifer have in common with the craven hypocrite, who prays with his lips while plotting petty larceny in his heart? Imagine the lord of the lower world seeking the miscroscopic souls of men who badger, brow-beat and bully-rag their better halves for spending a dollar for a new calico dress, then blow in a dozen times as much with the dice-box in a bar-room, trying to beat some other long-eared burro out of a thimble-full of bug-juice or a schooner o' beer! I don't believe Satan wants 'em. I think if they dodged the quarantine officers and got in amongst those erstwhile angels now peopling the dark regions of the damned, the doctors of that black abode would decide that they were cholera microbes or itch-bacilli and order the place fumigated.

*   *   *

But speaking of the devil—were any of you ever in love? I'm talking about the sure-enough, old-fashioned complaint that makes a man miss meals and lose sleep, write spring poetry and misplace his appetite for plug tobacco; not of the new-fangled varioloid that yields to matrimonial treatment. There's a great deal of sugar-coated humbuggery about this thing we call love. It reminds me of the sulphur and molasses my careful Presbyterian parents used to pour into me in the gentle spring-time. I don't remember why they gave it to me; but it was probably because they didn't want it themselves. Perhaps they thought foreordination hadn't done much for me, and they had best get me used to sulphur gradually. I remember, however, that, like the average case of matrimony, it usually contained a good deal more sulphur than syrup.

Matches, we are told, are made in heaven; and I think it likely, for Satan himself is said to have originated there. I'll tell you how matches are usually made: By some horrible accident John Henry and Sarah Jane become acquainted. They have no more affinity than a practical politician and pure spring water; but they dance and flirt, fool around the front gate in the dark of the moon, sigh and talk nonsense. John Henry begins to take things for his breath and Sarah Jane for her complexion. The young goslings get wonted to each other, and first thing you know they're tied up until death or divorce doth them part. And, had they missed each other altogether, they would have been just as well—perhaps better—content with other mates and made as enthusiastic a failure of married life. Most people marry without really knowing whether they're in love or not—mistake the gregarious habit for the mystic fire of Hymen's torch, the pangs of a bad digestion for the barbed arrows from the love-god's bow.

But when a couple's really got what ailed Romeo and Juliet they're in no more doubt about it than was the man after he sat down on the circular saw to see if it was running and found it the sole proprietor of a South American revolution. They don't have to send their feelings to a chemist for analysis and classification, nor take an invoice of their affections to see if any have got away. Love is really a very serious thing. Like sea-sickness, everybody laughs at it but those who have got it. When Cupid lets slip a sure-enough shaft it goes thro' a fellow's heart like a Kansas cyclone thro' a colored camp-meeting, and all the powers of hades can never head it off.

Love is the most sacred word ever framed by celestial lips. It's the law of life, the harmony of heaven, the breath of which the universe was born, the divine essence increate of the ever-living God.

But love is like all other sweet things—unless you get the very best brand it sours awful easy.

* * *

Of all the pitiful Humbugs beneath high heaven commend me to those intellectual doodle-bugs who have become Dame Fashion's devotees and devote all their intellectuality to the science of dress—to the art of being miserable *a la mode*. Thousands are to-day sailing about in silk hats who are guiltless of undershirts, bedecked with diamonds while in debt to the butcher for the meat on their bones. Families that can scarce afford calico flaunt Parisian finery, keep costly carriages while there's a chronic hiatus in their cupboards, go hungry to bed six nights in the week that on the seventh they may spread a brave feast for fashionable fools. God have mercy on all such muttonheads. They are the natural breeders of good-for-naughts, for in such an atmosphere children grow up mentally dwarfed and morally debased.

Fashionable mothers commit their children to the care of serving-maids while they sail out to soirees and receptions—put their babes on a bottle while they swing round the social circle. No wonder their sons grow up sapheads, as destitute of backbone as a banana, as deficient in moral force as a firkin of fish. Think of an infant Napoleon nursing a rubber nozzle, of rearing a Brutus on patent baby food, of bringing a Hannibal up by hand! You can't do it.

Why, if I had a woman of that kind to wife—a fashionable butterfly whose heart was in her finery and her feathers; who neglected her home to train with a lot of intellectual tomtits whose glory was small-talk; who saved her sweetest smiles for society and her ill-temper for the family altar— I say were I tied fast to that kind of a female, do you know what I'd do? Eh? You don't? Well—neither do I.

There are some Humbugs, however, who merit our respect if not our reverence—men who are infinitely better than they would have the world believe. As the purest pearl is encased in an unseemly shell, so, too, is many a god-like soul enshrined in a breast of seeming adamant. Many a man swears because he's too proud to weep, hides a quivering soul behind the cynic's sneer, fronts the world like a savage beast at bay while his heart's a fathomless lake of tears. Tennyson tells us of a monstrous figure of complete steel and armed *cap-a-pie,* that guarded a castle gate, and by its awful name and warlike mien affrighted the fearful souls of men. But one day a dauntless knight unhorsed it and clove thro' the massy helm, when forth from the wreck there came not a demon armed with the scythe of death, but a beardless boy scarce old enough to break a pointless lance upon the village green. So, too, when with the sword Excalibur of human sympathy you shear down thro' the helm and harness of some rough-spoken man who seems to hate all human kind, you find the soul of a woman and the heart of a little child.

*   *   *

Even our religion is ofttimes a Humbug, else why is it that the good Christian woman—who says her prayers as regularly as she looks under the bed for burglars—says to the caller whom she cordially detests, "I am delighted to see you;" when she's wondering why the meddlesome old gadabout don't stay at home when she's not wanted elsewhere? Why is it that when a good brother puts a five-dollar bill in the contribution box he flashes it up so all may see the figures, but when he drops a nickel in the slot to get a little grace he lets not his right hand know what his left hand doeth? Why is it that when you strike a devout deacon for the loan of ten dollars he will swear by all the gods he hasn't got it. when his pockets are fairly bursting with big bills? If his religion is not hypocrisy— if he is not a Humbug—why doesn't he tell you in plain United States that he would rather have Uncle Sam's promise to pay than yours? Oh, people are becoming such incorrigible liars that I've about quit trying to borrow money.

Too many people presume that they are full of the grace of God when they're only bilious; that they are pious because they dislike to see other people enjoy themselves; that they are Christians because they conform to certain creeds, just as many men imagine themselves honest because they obey the laws of the land—for the purpose of keeping out of the penitentiary. They put up long prayers on Sunday; that's piety. They bamboozle a green gosling out of his birthright on Monday; that's business. They have one face with which to confront the Lord and another with which to beguile their brethren. They even acquire two voices—a brisk business accent and a Sunday whine that would make a cub wolf climb a tree. I am always suspicious of a man's piety when it makes him look as tho' he had cut a throat or scuttled a ship and was praying for a commutation of the death sentence. I could never understand why a man who can read his title clear to mansions in the skies—who holds a lien on a corner lot in the New Jerusalem—should allow that fact to hurt him.

I have great respect for true religion; but for the brand of holiness that's put on with the Sunday shirt—that makes a man cry ahmen with unction, but doesn't prevent him selling 5 and 10-cent cigars out of the same box, oleomargarine and creamery butter out of the same bucket, benzine and bourbon whiskey out of the same barrel; which makes long prayers on Sunday and gives short weights on Monday; which worries over the welfare of good looking young women, but gives the old grandames the go-by; which fathers the orphan only if he's rich and husbands the widow only if she's handsome—for that kind of Christianity I have no more use than for a mugwump governor who saddles his state with the expense of a legislative session to gratify a private grudge against a brother gambler.

That religion which sits up o'nights to agonize because a few naked niggers in equatorial Africa never heard Eve's snake story, how Job scratched himself with a broken pie-plate or the hog happened to be so full of the spirit of hades; that robs childhood of its pennies to send prayer-books to people whose redemption should begin with a bath, while in our own country every town from Cattaraugus to Kalamazoo—every city from the Arctic ocean to the Austral sea—is overrun with heathen who know naught of the grace of God or the mystery of a square meal; who prowl in the very shadow of our temples of justice, build their lairs in proximity to our public schools and within sound of the collect of our churches, is an arrant Humbug,

a crime against man, an offense to God, a curse to the
world.

*   *   *

People frequently say to me, "Brann, your attacks are
too harsh. You should use more persuasion and less
pizen." Perhaps so; but I have not yet mastered the
esoteric of choking a bad dog to death with good butter.
Persuasion is well enough if you're acourting—or in the
hands of the vigilantes; but turning it loose on the average
fraud were too much like a tenderfoot trying to move a
string of freight steers with moral suasion. He takes up
his whip, gently snaps it as tho' he feared it were loaded,
and talks to his cattle like a Boston philanthropist or a
poor relation. The steers look round at him, wonder, in a
vague way, if he's worth eating, and stand at ease. An
old freighter who's been over the "divide" and got his
profanity down to a fine art, grabs that goad, cracks it
like a rifled cannon reaching for a raw recruit and spills
a string of cuss words calculated to precipitate the final
conflagration. You expect to see him struck dead—but
those steers don't. They're firmly persuaded that he's going
to outlive 'em if they don't get down and paw gravel, and
they get a Nancy Hanks hustle on 'em. Never attempt to
move an ox-team with moral suasion, or to drown the
cohorts of the devil in the milk of human kindness. It won't
work.

*   *   *

Oh, it's possible that you may disagree with me on some
minor points of doctrine. That's your blessed privilege and
I wouldn't deprive you of it if I had the power. A pompous
old fellow once called at the office of my religious monthly
to inform me that I was radically wrong on every possible
public question. He seemed to think that I had committed
an unpardonable crime in daring to differ with him. I asked
him to be seated and whistled for the devil—the printer's
devil, the only kind we keep in the office of the Iconoclast.
I told him to procure for me a six-shooter, a sledge hammer
and a boat. My visitor became greatly alarmed.

"Wh-what are you g-going to d-do?"

"Do?" I replied. "I'm going to shoot the printers,
smash the press and throw the type into the river. What
in the name of the great Sanhedrim, is the use o' me printing a paper if I can't please you?"

Mr. Pomposity subsided somewhat, and I proceeded to
talk United States to him.

"You say I'm wrong.   Perhaps I am; but how in Halifax"—I think I said Halifax; anyhow we'll let it go at that
—"how in Halifax did you find it out?   Who installed you
as infallible pope in the realm of intellect and declared it
rank folly to run counter to the ideas that roost in your nice
fat head?"

He was one of those egotistical mental microbes or intellectual animalculae who imagine that a man must be in the
wrong if he disagrees with them.   And the woods are so
full of that class of fellows that the fool-killer has become
discouraged and jumped his job.

Those who chance to think alike get together and form
a political party, a society or a sect and take it for granted
that they've got all the wisdom of the world grabbed—that
beyond their little Rhode Island of intellect are only gibber-
ing idiots and plotting knaves.   When a man fears to subject his faith to the crucible of controversy; when he declines to submit his ideas to the ballistae and battering-
rams of cold logic, you can safely set it down that he's
either a hopeless cabbage-head or a hypocritical Humbug
—that he's a fool or a fraud, is full of buncombe or bile.

It is a difference of opinion that keeps the world from
going to the dogs.   Independence of thought, doubt of
accepted dogmas, the spirit of inquiry—the desire to *know*
—is the mighty lever that has lifted man so far above the
brute level that he has begun to claim kinship with the
Creator.   Yet we say to our brother, "Thou fool," because
he takes issue with us on the tariff, or the proper time in
the moon to plant post-holes—even insist on sending people to perdition who cannot see "the plan of salvation" thro'
our little sectarian telescope.

Men of a mind flock together just like so many gab-
bling geese, or other foolish fowl of a feather, each group
waddling in the wake of some flat-headed old gander,
squawking when he squawks and fluttering when he flies.
Because I decline to get in among the goslings and be
piloted about the intellectual goose-pond, I'm told that I
have no *policy*.   Well, I hope I haven't.   If I thought I had
I'd take something for it, dontcherknow!   When I cannot
live among my fellows without surrendering my independence—forswearing freedom of speech and liberty of
thought; without having to play the canting hypocrite or go
hungry—to fawn like a flea-bitten fice to win public favor—
I'll make me a suit of leather, take to the woods and chop bee
trees.   I'd rather my babes were born in a cane-brake and
reared on bark and wild berries, with the blood of independ-

ence burning in their veins, than spawned in a palace and
brought up boot-licks and policy players.

* * *

I am sometimes inclined to believe that Life itself is a
Humbug—that the man who makes the best of it is the
one who escaped being born. We know not whence we
came or what for, whither we go or what we'll do when
we get there. True it is that life is not altogether labor and
lees—there's some skittles and beer; but the most of us
get more shadow than sunshine, more cholera-morbus than
cream. Man born of woman is of few days and full of
politics. The moment he hits the globe he starts for the
grave, and his only visible reward for long days of labor
and nights of pain is an epitaph he can't read and a tombstone he don't want. In the first of the Seven Ages of man
he's licked, in the last he's neglected, and in all the others
he's a fair mark for the shafts of falsehood. If he don't
marry his first love, he's forever miserable, and if he does,
he wishes he were dead. By the time he has learned wisdom he leaves the world, is hustled into a hell of fire or an
orthodox heaven, and for forty years I've been trying to
figure out which of these appalling evils to avoid. In one
place the climate is hot and unhealthy, in the other the
inhabitants never entertained an original idea—believed
everything they were told. Think of having to live thro'
all eternity with the strictly orthodox—people who regard
freedom of thought as foul blasphemy, millions of immaculate bricks cast in the same mould! No wonder there's
neither marrying nor giving in marriage in heaven. Just
imagine a couple of love-sick loons having nothing to do
but spoon from everlasting to everlasting, to talk tutti-
frutti thro' all eternity—never a break or breathing spell
in the lingering sweetness long drawn out! Amelia Rives
Chanler or Ella Wheeler Wilcox couldn't stand it. Nor
could I. By the time I had lived ten thousand years with
a female who could fly, and had nothing in God's world
to do but watch me, I'd either raise a revolution or send
in my resignation. It is said that Satan had an *affaire
d'amour* while he was playing Seraph. If the object of his
affections wore feathers I don't much wonder that he went
over the garden wall.

I suspect that the orthodox heaven and hell, of which
we hear so much, are Humbugs. I should know something
of those interesting ultimates—be qualified to speak *ex
cathedra*—for a doctor of divinity recently denounced me
as a child of the devil. In that case you behold in me a

prince imperial, heir-apparent to the throne of Pluto, the potential master of more than a moiety of mankind. But don't tell anybody that I've got a title, that I belong to the oldest nobility, or all the Goulderbilts will be trying to buy me.

I promise you that when I come into my kingdom I'll devise a worse punishment than physical pain. A soul is an immaterial thing. You cannot flay it with aspic's fangs nor kerosene it and set it on fire. A material hell for immaterial mind were too ridiculous for a progressive devil. But it is not necessary to be a son of Satan to build a hell in which demons dance and sulphur-fumes asphyxiate the soul. You may transform your own home into a valley of Hinnom, a veritable Gehenna; or you may make of the humblest cot a heaven, illumed by love and gilded with God's own glory—a Beulah land where flowers forever bloom, where perfumed censors swing and music throbs and thrills sweeter far than Orphean lyre or song of Israfeel.

The orthodox heaven is a pageant of barbaric splendor, of gaudy tinsel and flaming gold to dazzle the eyes of infants. It is a land of lotus-eaters, where ambition's star is blotted from the firmament and the wild ecstacy of passion beats no longer in the blood; an Oriental heaven, a Paradise for tired people—eternal *dolce far niente* for niggers and yaller dogs. No Celt or Saxon with aspiring mind, with swelling muscles and heart that flames with the fierce joy of strong endeavor, that thrills with the sweetness of sacrifice for others' sake that swells with the mad glory of triumph in the forum or the field, could have conceived such a futile farce.

Give me a land whose skies are lead and soil is sand, yet everlasting life with those I love; give me a lodge in some vast wilderness hallowed by children's laughter; give me a cave in the mountain crag to house those dearest to my heart; give me a tent on the far frontier, where, by the lambent light of their mother's eyes, I may watch my children grow in grace and the truth of God, and I'll build a heaven grander, nobler, sweeter than was ever dreamed of by the gross materialists of bygone days.

* * *

Life is a Humbug only because we make it so. We are frauds because we are fools. This is a beautiful, a glorious world, fit habitation for sons of the Most High God. It is a fruitful mother at whose fair breast all her children may be filled. There should be never a Humbug nor a hypocrite, never a millionaire nor a mendicant on the great round globe. Labor should be but healthful exercise to develop the physical man—to furnish forth a fitting casket for the godlike mind, appropriate setting for the immortal soul. The curse of life arises from a misconception of its significance. We delve in the mine for paltry gems, explore old ocean's deep for pearls; we toil and strive for gold until the hands are worn and the heart is cold; we attire ourselves in Tyrean purples and silks of Ind and strut forth in our gilded frippery on the narrow bridge of time, between the two eternities; we despoil the thin purse of the poor to erect brazen altars and priceless fanes, when the whole earth's a sacred shrine, the universe a temple thro' which rings the voice of God and rolls the eternal melody of the spheres.

*   *   *

Perhaps it is unnecessary to state that I'm not posing as a saint. I may eventually become an angel—of some sort—but I'll wear no wings. We are accustomed to think of seraphs flying from heaven to earth, flitting from star to star—irrespective of the fact that feathers are useless where there's no atmosphere. An angel working his wings to propel himself thro' a vacuum were as ridiculous as a disembodied spirit riding a bike down a rainbow.

I do not expect to reform all Humbugs, to banish all Fakes, to exterminate all Folly. If the world should get too good, I might have to hunt another home. I can understand every crime in the calendar but the crime of greed, every lust of the flesh but the lust for gain, every sin that ever damned a soul but the sin of selfishness. By all the sacred bugs and beasts of ancient Egypt, I'd rather be a witch's cat—or even a politician—and howl in sympathy with my tribe; I'd rather be a tramp and divide my handouts with one more hungry; I'd rather be a mangy yellow dog without a master and keep the company of my kind, than to be a multi-millionaire, with the blood of a snake, the heart of a beast, and carry my soul, like Pedro Garcia, in my purse.

When I think of the three thousand children in the single city of Chicago without rags to shield their nakedness from the keen north wind; of the ten thousand innocents, such as Christ blessed, who died in New York every year of the world for lack of food; of the millions in every country whose cries go up night and day to God's great throne —not for salvation, but for soup; not for the robe of righteousness, but for a second-hand pair of pants—and then

contemplate those beside whose hoarded wealth the riches
of Lydia's ancient kings were but a beggar's patrimony,
praying to Him who reversed the law of nature to feed
the poor, I long for the mystic power to coin sentences
that sear like sulphur-flames come hot from hell, and weave
of words a whip of scorpions to lash the rascals naked thro·
the world.

We humbug our parents, the public, and then, as far as
possible, our wives; tho' the latter are seldom so blind as
they seem. The wife who cannot tell when her lord and
master is lying—whether he's been sitting up with a sick
friend or nursing a Robert-tail flush—well, she must be
the newest kind of a "New Woman," with a brain built for
bloomers and bike. The New Woman is—she is all right;
just the Old Woman in disguise, a paradox and a coat of
paint.

Whenever I tackle this subject I'm reminded of a broth
of a boy who in days agone drove the team afield on my
father's farm. One rare June day, when the sun was slowly
sinking in the west, as the novelists say—and I believe
that's where Old Sol usually sinks—he got mixed up with
a bevy of industrious bumble-bees who were no respecters
of persons—would sting an honest delver as quickly as
they'd put the gaffles to a scorbutic duke. In about two
minutes Mike came over the hill a-whooping like a segment
of the Southern Confederacy reaching for a nigger regiment, his head the size and shape of a red peck measure
that had been kicked by a roan mule.

"Sure, now, they didn't do a thing t' me," he said. "An
ould bumblebug came a bizzin' an' a buzzin' aluken fer all
the wurruld like an' Orangeman wid wings, so I up an'
hit him a biff. Thin all the 'rist av the haythen tuk up his
foight—an' Oi kem home."

Hit one Humbug and every Fraud and Fake in Christendom is ready for the fray. They attempt to crush their
critic with calumny, to defeat him with falsehood. When
you hear a fellow railing at the Iconoclast, just look
through its stock of caps and you'll find one that will fit the
knot on the end of his neck.

Truth and only truth is eternal. It was not born and
it cannot die. It may be obscured by the clouds of falsehood, or buried in the debris of brutish ignorance, but it
can never be destroyed. It exists in every atom, lives in
every flower and flames in every star. When the heavens
and the earth shall pass away and the universe return to
cosmic dust, divine truth will stand unscathed amid the
crash of matter and the wreck of worlds.

Falsehood is an amorphous monster, conceived in the brain of knaves and brought forth by the breath of fools. It's a moral pestilence, a miasmic vapor that passes, like a blast from hell, over the face of the world and is gone forever. It may leave death in its wake and disaster dire; it may place on the brow of purity the brand of the courtesan and cover the hero with the stigma of the coward; it may wreck hopes and ruin homes, cause blood to flow and hearts to break; it may pollute the altar and disgrace the throne, corrupt the courts and curse the land, but the lie cannot live forever, and when it's dead and damned there's none so poor as to do it reverence.

THE TEIXEIRA-MORRIS CASE.

H. Steen Morris, a young man who parts his name on the side, was tried in this city a few days ago on the charge of raping Antonia Teixeira, the "ward of the Baptist church," while she was being "educated" at Baylor University for missionary work among the "heathen" Catholics of Brazil. All the influence of Baylor was brought to bear in favor of the man accused of invading its supposed sacred precincts to feed his unholy lust by the debauchment of a babe. As the Baptists are all-powerful in this county, and can easily make or break any man engaged in a purely local business, his acquittal seemed a foregone conclusion. No wonder the president of Baylor gleefully rubbed his hands and predicted that the alleged rape-fiend "would have easy rolling," for to oppose the wishes of the Baptist bosses were to court a social, political and business boycott by those who boast that their cult holds a copyright on freedom of conscience. Yes, Steen was to have "easy rolling"; and when the jury dismissed him with a certificate of good moral character, Dr. Burleson was going to sue the Iconoclast for damages—in the sum of 'steen million dollars I s'pose. That's what he said—but he didn't expect that his rallikaboo bluff would ever come to the ears of the Icon. For nearly a year now Dr. Burleson has been assuring doting parents with young daughters to educate that he was just about to begin to commence to do something awfully dreadful to this great religious journal; but his horrid vengeance—like some other things—is "all in his head." Just how much of the Apostle's wealth Baylor University wants—how many golden guineas it will require to heal the hurt that honor feels—I do not know; but

I'm convinced that when he's jumped up by Baylor before a jury of his peers to demonstrate his right, as an American sovereign, to denounce a damnable crime against the innocence of childhood by super-sanctified hypocrites, tumble-bugs will give milk and frogs will grow feathers. "Conscience doth make cowards of us all." Baylor will carefully lock the closet in which it keeps its interesting collection of skeletons, and refrain from blowing in the Apostle to see if he is loaded. That's what I said.

To make assurance of "easy rolling" doubly sure, those especially interested in securing the acquittal of the accused, went to the friends and temporary guardians of the ruined girl and requested them to use their influence to secure a withdrawal of the charge that force was employed to accomplish her disgrace. As her ruin was wrought before the new law, raising the age of consent from twelve to fifteen years, went into effect, it was really an attempt, by bringing undue influence to bear on the plaintiff, to get her case dismissed while convicting her of perjury. But her friends declined to further the fraud and Antonia stuck to her original story —that she had been dragged from Dr. Burleson's kitchen by the defendant and forcibly debauched within the very shadow of Baylor. Rev. Zachariah C. Taylor and Dr. Rufus C. Burleson are two of the pious brethren who thus attempted to get Antonia to alter her testimony. The aged president admitted as much in court; but protested that he "didn't want her to swear to a falsehood." If he wanted her to swear only to the truth why did he go to such pains to alter her testimony? Certainly she knew better what accorded with the facts than he possibly could. I much fear that he is one of those "wily Jesuits" who, we are asked to believe, can lie in sixteen languages and still avoid the commission of a cardinal sin.

When the case was submitted to the jury it developed that the defendant did not have such "easy rolling" as the eminent divine had predicted. Seven of the jurors were not willing to turn him loose even to please the dominant political power, while the remaining five could not quite make up their minds that it was proper to put the brother of Dr. Burleson's pious son-in-law in the penitentiary. So the case goes over to the next term of court—while the Baylorians redouble their efforts to get the plaintiff out of the country. Rev. Zachariah C. Taylor, who brought Antonia to Texas as a companion to his wife, and afterwards wrote an article for a Waco daily—which the steering committee wisely withdrew—protesting that he knew at the time that she was a foul prostitute, is back in Brazil writing letters

imploring her to return to her kith and kin in that faraway
country. Why? He declared while here that her mother
was a courtesan and all her relatives a very bad lot. Why
should the poor girl return to such immoral surroundings
—after enjoying for three years the elevating influence of
Baylor University? Does he consider that her "education"
is complete—that illegitimate childbirth constitutes Baylor's
graduating exercises—and that she should enter at once
upon the work of converting the Brazilian Catholics? Or
does he want her to resume her duties as companion to his
wife? I do not quite understand this good man Taylor.
When he brought Antonia here he gave her a certificate
of good character. When her downfall casts a shadow
over the great Baptist University he declared that she had
been bad from babyhood, and, that, knowing this, he first
made her an inmate of his family, then consigned her to
the companionship of scores of pure young girls, well knowing—if he knows anything—that one wanton can work more
mischief among innocent maids than can a dozen men.
Then he visited her at her present home to discuss the
situation, but declined to be left alone with her, fearing
that his morals might become contaminated. Like Joseph,
he was ready to fly to avoid being ravished—after keeping
her in his household for years with full knowledge that she
was a courtesan! I much fear that Rev. Zachariah would
be a first-class fraud if God hadn't intended him for a fool.

It has been nearly a year since H. Steen Morris was
arrested for the ravishment of Antonia Teixeira. The Iconoclast gave it a little attention at the time; but as a dozen or
two people have subscribed since then, it may not be amiss
to briefly summarize the celebrated case, that new patrons
of the paper may become familiar with this crowning infamy
of the age and know what to expect should they choose to
commit their children to the care of the great Baptist sanctuary of the South.

About four years ago Rev. Zachariah C. Taylor returned
from Brazil, where he had been trying to convert the
"heathen," alias the Catholics. While in Brazil, he resided
in the same house with a widow whom he now declares
was a bawd. Whether her immorality induced the reverend
gentleman to make her house his habitat, I do not know.
He may have considered that her adherence to the Baptist
faith excused her sexual frailties, if it did not sanctify them,
for he persuaded her to allow her little daughter to accom-
pany him to Texas "to be educated for missionary work in
Brazil." The Baptists here made a great hullabaloo over
her as a brand snatched from the burning—representing the

cumulative result of the long and arduous labors of their
missionary in a "heathen" land—and formally adopted her
as the "ward" of that sanctified organization. She was a
frail little thing, about eleven years old, but small for her
age and possessed average intelligence. She was committed
to the care of President Burleson of Baylor with the understanding that, after five years of careful schooling, she
should return to Brazil and explain the heavenly water-
route to her benighted Catholic brethren. Instead of being
sent to the class-room, however, she was relegated to the
Burleson kitchen, where she served in the capacity of under-
servant. About three years later—or when she was fourteen
years old—it was discovered that her clothes didn't fit her.
That was not considered very remarkable, for such things
had happened before at Baylor. It would cost considerable
money to send her home, and of course it would never do
to let her be confined at the university—that were contrary
to the Baylorian customs in such cases; so the Burlesons
and Morrises began casting about for other accommodations
—a kind of private lying-in hospital where the babe could be
born without attracting the attention of the general public
and frightening away good paying patrons. By representing Antonia as "a girl deserving sympathy rather than
condemnation," "a child we are so sorry for"—a girl
"faithful and honest"—a poor Catholic woman was induced
to give the embryo missionary to the Popish heathen a
home and minister to her in her misfortune. Despite all
precautions, however, rumors of the affair got afloat and a
nervy justice of the peace, without the fear of the Baylorians
before his eyes, proceeded to investigate the matter. The
story of the child was so plain and straightforward that
it was accepted as true by the public. She stated, albeit
with great reluctance, that H. Steen Morris, a young man
who appears to have had the run of the Baylor preserves,
solicited her favors and, being refused, ravished her person; that she had made frequent complaints to the Burlesons; "but nothing was done about it;" that when her
condition could no longer be concealed, Rev. S. L. Morris,
son-in-law to Dr. Burleson and brother to her assailant,
had tried to bulldoze her into a confession that she was
enciente by a "coon." The remarkable fact developed at
the preliminary trial that altho' three years an inmate of
Baylor—being educated with a special view to the conversion of Catholics—she knew almost nothing—not even the
tenets of the Baptist faith, or that the ravishment of a maid
was an offense against the laws of this Christian land!

It was then that Rev. Zachariah C. Taylor came to the

front with his remarkable story anent the immorality of his
Brazilian landlady and the companion he had selected for
his wife with such care. It was then that the Burlesons
discovered that Antonia was a born thief instead of an
honest and faithful child who had met with a grievous misfortune. It was then that the reverend president of Baylor
rushed into print with a screed branding as little better than
a public bawd a child in short dresses, who to this day refers
to him as "gran'pa!" It was then that the Catholic woman
who had assumed the care of a girl ravished at Dr. Burleson's door, was besought to turn her adrift—to send her
to the home for fallen women at Fort Worth! It was then
that all the power of Baylor was exerted, not to ferret out
the criminal and bring him to the bar, but to forever blacken
the character of the little orphan and shield the alleged
author of her shame.

And it was then—by the eternal gods!—that the Iconoclast aligned its guns.

Antonia's babe was born—three pounds—white. It lived
just long enough to develop a striking resemblance to H.
Steen Morris; but of course this may have been a remarkable coincidence. It died, and was buried at the cost of the
poor people who had cared for its mother when deserted
by her contemptible *alma mater*. The Iconoclast stated at
the time that it was buried in a pauper's grave—and I'm
told it is upon this inaccuracy that Dr. Burleson hangs his
slender hope of catching me for a few mental anguish plasters. It would have been buried in the Potter's Field had
the poor people depended upon Baylor University to defray
its funeral expenses. Its mother might have died in the
throes of maternity had they relied upon the Burlesons
and the Morrises to provide medical aid. The men about
town—Catholics, Jews and Atheists—paid the doctor's bill,
while the sainted Baylorians closed their purses and sighed
for the wickedness of this world. The Catholic woman
who played a mother's part to the poor victim of anti-Cath-
olic missionary education, assures me that all the aid sent
by the sanctified was six bits in cash and an old chemise
—royal beneficence which was declined with scant courtesy.

Instead of seeking refuge in the "Reservation"—whither
she would certainly have drifted had she been so "crazy
after the boys" as Dr. Burleson asserts, or so abandoned
as Rev. Taylor tried to testify when the steering committee
choked him off—the childless little mother besought forgiveness for her enemies and patiently took up her cross.
She is toiling today in an humble but honest occupation
and enjoys the respect of all manly men and noble women.

Not one word has ever been breathed against her good name except by the holy bigots and legal hirelings who are trying to help Baylor University out of the hole. She is "faithful and honest," as the Burlesons bore witness when they wanted some one to take her off their hands and expected to keep the case out of court. That is the naked truth *in nunce* anent Antonia Teixeira's debauchment—though told by the "Apostle of the Devil."

BEANS AND BLOOD.

The South Again in the Soup.

Massachusetts has solemnly decided to hold Dixie up by the patent health-bustle, single-handed and alone, and shake her until her milk-white teeth rattle like a pair o' Portuguese castanets if she doesn't refrain from roasting nigger rape-fiends. When Massachusetts dons her war-paint and shrieks for slaughter she is too terribly awful to contemplate. Boston is already grinding the sword of Gideon and flourishing the jaw-bone of an ass over the shrinking head of the Southern Philistine. She has tucked her bloomers in her boots and bade the soul of Ossawattomie Brown resume its interesting itinerary. Again the beacon fires are brightly blazing, the clans are "gathering from the hill-side, gathering from the plain," while the ear-piercing fife and thrilling trumpety-trump of the snareskin fiddle proclaim to the wondering universe that Yankee-doodle is still something of a dandy.

Faneuil Hall has spoken, and that with no uncertain sound. On November 11 was gathered in that historic pile the chivalry of the city of salt cod,—the proud patricians of trade who trace their lineage in an unbroken line back to the witch-burners. The buck niggers who have drifted to Boston in their tireless search for social equality, were likewise present, in brotherly affiliation with long-haired excuses for white men, and howled themselves hoarse in an attempt to fire the Northern heart. The mayor did himself the honor to preside over this sweet-scented assemblage of Meddlesome Matties, who were ready to sacrifice all their relatives on the altar of racial equality and political reform. The temple of Janus was thrown wide open like a boot-jack; Ate came whooping, hot from hell; Bellona gazed into the assembled gold-browed spectacles, took a long breath and shrieked for *bella, horrida bella,* which were equivalent to asking her prandial neighbor to pass the canned blood. The orators of the evening demonstrated that, as a distributor of "livers and lights," Gov. Hogg is but an awkward amateur—that if Waite wants to ride in bright red gore he must go to Boston.

The meeting then whereased and resoluted in most abominable English to the effect that niggers, guilty of nothing worse than the ravishment of Southern white women, shall not henceforth be fricasseed—that these "beings born in the image of God are entitled to a fair trial by a jury of their peers." As their "peers" in these parts have been killed as fast as caught, this means that we must send the black beasts to Boston, where 3,000 of their mental and moral mates were recently collected in the same corral. If Almighty God resembles in personal appearance a nigger ravisher, it is small wonder that he's devoutly worshipped by the Faneuil Hall folks. They belong to that class of mangy mavericks who are utterly destitute of race pride—who concede that "a white man is as good as a nigger if he behave himself." Quite naturally, they imagine that the Deity is the prototype of Fred Douglas—that Christ was conceived from such a source by a white woman without her consent. The Faneuil Hall meeting declared in the name of Massachusetts that the Ethiopian is not an immoral race, nor addicted to the crime of rape; that the *raison d'etre* of Southern roasting-bees is to keep their noble black brother in political subjection.

It was the barbecues at Tyler and Paris, Texas, that occasioned Boston's remarkable outburst—that led to the renaissance of the erstwhile John Brown. Massachusetts will make just one mouthful of Texas, then devour the rest of Dixie. We may expect the knight-errantry of Boston before the roses bloom again. Sergeant Fight-the-Good-Fight and Captain Smite-'em-Hip-and-Thigh will swoop down upon us with a Bible in one hand and "The Sword of Bunker Hill" in the other. Not even a special session of the Legislature can keep the Puritan and the Cowboy apart. Dallas can transform the J. Harvey, Jr., into a man-o'-war and seek shelter beneath its guns, and Waco protect herself by putting up a few of those awful lithographs of the erstwhile Cotton Palace; but the rest of the state will be naked before its enemies. Mexico has an idea concealed about her person that she could whip the United States and not half try if Texas would keep out of the muss, and the South is nursing a sneaking suspicion that she could make the effete East whistle *peccavi* through her proboscis if the West would give bond to keep the peace. Of course both are mistaken. Mexico imagines that San Antonio is the "Gringo" metropolis, while the South forgets that the New Woman has appeared in Massachusetts since Lee made a monkey of McClellan. Furthermore, President Cleveland has taken up his summer residence at Buzzard's Bay, and his experience with substitutes would enable him to select a veritable Sir Launcelot. Boston does not run so largely to beans and wind as in the erstwhile—even China has adopted new military tactics.

Suppose that Texas and Massachusetts hold a conference between the lines before the ball opens with the musical

> "Rounder of the iron six-pounder,
> hurling death."

Massachusetts should not execute us without affording us an opportunity to ask forgiveness and bid the world farewell. In matters so serious as civil war it were well to carefully examine the *casus belli* before making a break. We call for a parley with a view to coming to an accommodation; for has not Job said that "all a man hath will he give for his life?" We humbly ask that the brigadier-generals of the Faneuil Hall Grand Army Corps be commissioned to confer with us—and may the pitying gods move them to compassion!

What in the devil's name does Massachusetts, or any other Northern state, know about the nigger? You have studied the coon at long range, and through the bottle-green glasses of such vindictive blatherskites as Tourgee and Cockerill. Occasionally a "smart nigger," educated at our expense, drifts to Boston and plays upon the misguided sentiment of its citizens with Munchhausenisms patterned after Uncle Tom's Cabin. The Ethiop is better treated in the South than in any other portion of the American Union. We freely tax ourselves to educate his offspring and build hospitals and asylums for his unfortunate. Now that Boston is turning up her nose at Texas, it may be well to remind her that during slavery times the niggers dreaded a Massachusetts driver worse than the devil— that to this good day the elder Ethiops have no use for the bean-eaters.

Despite the ukase of Faneuil Hall, the nigger has no more conception of morality than a hyena. There is not one buck in a hundred who will not steal a pair of pants from the white man who has given him a coat—who will not despoil his chicken coop after being presented with a capon. There is not one wench in a thousand who will not sell her supposed soul for the price of a circus ticket. Most nigger preachers will steal anything they can carry, and the only one who would not lie when the truth answered equally as well, died "befo' d' wah." You can no more educate honor and chastity into a coon than into a brindle cat. We, who know the nigger, do not expect much of him. We incur large expense to afford him every opportunity, but it is seldom that he rises above the intellectual level of a camp-meeting pulpiteer. Those who do so are usually bastards—borne by black women to soldiers from Boston. We give him our cast-off-clothes and broken vistuals. We find employment for him when more competent white labor stands idle, because we have become used to providing for his physical well-being. He was our ward for many generations, and his regard for "massa" and "missus" was little short of worship. A starving horse may obtain a square meal where a man would be turned away hungry. All recognize the helplessness of the animal and are moved to compassion. For the same reason the most worthless coon may keep fat and sleek in the Southland while his betters go hungry to bed.

The South long held the blacks in bondage, and this has been charged up against her as an unpardonable crime. It was a sin against herself, and cruelly has she suffered. The South should have permitted the Ethiop to remain in Africa, a snake-worshipping, cannibalistic savage. The civilization of the black man, such as it is, is due to his enslavement by a superior race. The motive of the American slaveholder was doubtless selfish. The North freed her slaves because she found free labor the shortest road to fortune; the South retained her niggers because unfamiliar with a great economic fact. Had slave labor proven profitable, Mayor Curtis might to-day be calling the roll of his bondsmen on Bunker Hill. Despite the efficient cause of slavery, the South may say to Sambo, as Prospero to the son of Sycorax:

> "I have used thee, filth as thou art, with human care.
> I pitied thee. When thou did'st not, savage,
> Know thy own meaning, but would'st gabble like
> A thing most brutish, I endowed thy purposes
> With words that made them known : But thy vile race,
> Though thou did'st learn, had that in't which good natures
> Could not abide to be with."

While held in slavery the negro recognized his inferiority, and no more aspired to mate with the dominant race than does the buzzard with the eagle. During the civil war the blacks were left on lonely plantations with the families of their masters while the latter went to the front.

They were precious little protection, despite the Yankee idea to the contrary; but no more fear was felt that they would invade the sanctity of their master's families than tho' they had been so many mules. I have heard of but one instance of such infamy. The negroes had not then so much as dreamed of crossing the chasm that separates them from their superiors; but when accorded their freedom and the elective franchise they began to long for social equality. Their preachers—who in *ante bellum* days were chiefly valuable for breeding purposes—wanted white wives, and as new generations arrived at the age of puberty, violations of white women by black fiends became frequent. More than a thousand reputable maids and matrons have been ravished—and many of them murdered—by black bucks during the last dozen years. White babes have been torn from the cradle and sacrificed upon the unclean altar of Ethiopian lust. No Southern woman is safe from assault beyond the reach of the six-shooter. No white babe is secure in its crib unless guarded night and day. The buck nigger is a black cloud hanging over every Southern home. The dread of our women is not death, for a worse fate may at any moment befall them.

We have tried "due process of law" on the lecherous devils "born in the image" of Boston's deity. We have put rapists in prison and given them to the gallows. We have bored them with bullets. We have hanged them between heaven and earth and left their brutish carcasses for the buzzards. We have flayed them alive, and all without effect. Having found the law a failure and respectable lynching futile, we have begun to kerosene 'em and set 'em on fire. If we cannot insure the sanctity of our homes, by the Lord God of Israel, we will have the satisfaction of making the black demons suffer all the tortures of the damned.

And Boston might as well refrain from ripping great orifices in her undershirt; for if we knew that the roasting of a negro rape-fiend would bring down upon us all the ardent admirers of Ida Wells in Old and New England,— all the powers of earth, the legions of hell and the eternal wrath of heaven, we would apply the torch and brave extermination. It were better to be dead, damned and delivered; it were better the South should be made a desert of desolation forever and a day; it were better that the owl and the jackal should make our ruined homes their habitat, than to live, a race of cowardly curs, breeding babes for black demons to debauch.

So much doth the South urge in her defense. Now stand forth, thou city of baked beans and buncombe, and answer to a counter accusation: The blood of every white babe butchered by the blacks, of every maid and matron who has suffered death and despoliation by these demons, is upon the heads of those mischievous meddlers who freed the slave and made him a political sovereign; upon the heads of those unhung idiots who have been prating of racial equality; upon the heads of such unclean cattle as those who, herded together in Faneuil Hall, compared a negro rape-fiend to the Deity, and threatened to take up arms in his defense. Just such infernal guff by ignorant gillies, whose chosen vocation is vicious intermeddling with matters anent which they know less than nothing, led the foul victims of the Paris fricassee to rip open a white babe and debauch the poor little innocent after it was dead!

It is easy enough to make excuses for the war waged upon the South in behalf of the slave. We long ago conceded that it was the result of an honest misconception. The most serious of its consequences to the South was not our broken altars and ruined fanes, not the improverishment of a people little inured to labor, nor yet the lonely graves that dot our land thick as autumn leaves; it was the transformation, as if by infernal magic, of millions of stupid slaves into American sovereigns. Improvident, idle and ignorant, it is small wonder that they become criminals and courtesans. Being political incapables, they are the easy prey of designing demagogues. The South shouldered this appalling burden uncomplainingly and proceeded to make the best of it, for the *ci-devant* master is really the freedman's best friend. Had the carpet-baggers, professional reformers and other pestiferous busy-bodies let the newmade citizen alone, it would have been infinitely better for all concerned; but they proceeded to fill his fat head with false ambitions, to preach to him that his poverty, born of idleness, was the result of persecution, to hint that no social distinction should be drawn between political equals in the same republic—that the only solution of the negro problem was miscegenation. Then followed, as a natural sequence, those conditions that have alarmed our self-constituted critics.

Educating the Ethiopian were like casting pearls before swine. You may discover jewels in the head of a toad, but you'll find no wisdom in the skull of a nigger. The "brainy black men," to whom the Bostonese point with pride, are simply featherless poll-parrots. Education only serves to make the Ethiopian impudent, more inclined to live without honest labor. Politically he is a commodity, ever for sale to the highest bidder, while industrially he isn't worth a tinker's dam when beyond white domination. The idea that the Southern whites rule the ballot-box with shot-guns is all moonshine. We can buy a nigger's vote for fifty cents, while it costs four dollars to bury him.

The black is here, and I see but one way to get rid of him, and that is to drive him *en masse* beyond the Ohio and give our nigger-loving neighbors an opportunity to test their fine theories by conditions. Boston can have the whole caboodle if the Faneuil Hall crowd will pay the freight. But it is our duty, as honest men, to give her an idea what to expect of her black "images of God." She will have to build more prisons and poor-houses. She will have to chain Bunker Hill monument to the center of gravity or they'll steal it. She will have to put sheet-iron lingerie on her marble Goddess of Liberty or some morning she'll find the old girl with her head mashed in and bearing marks of sexual violence. By all means, let Massachusetts take the nigger away from the wicked Texans and carry him in triumph to the land of racial equality, political reform and gods who resemble colored ravishers. That were much better than bruiting it about that we make bonfires of innocent blacks—both "men and women"—just to see them burn. All the niggers roasted by Texas freely confessed their guilt. They were identified beyond the peradventure of a doubt. There may have been rape fiends roasted in the South who "protested their innocence even in the very jaws of death." There have been criminals hanged, shot or beheaded in every country who declined to confess. So far as I know, there has been but one colored woman burned in the South since the war. If I remember aright she assisted a syphilitic negro lover to debauch two little girls, both less than ten years of age. Massachusetts has put a number of white women to death on the suspicion that they were witches; hence her criticism of the South seems a trifle too much like the devil rebuking sin.

Massachusetts' war talk is all damphoolishness. It were impossible to raise in the entire state a thousand men for the invasion of the South on behalf of the Senegambian. The great body of the Massachusetts people have sense enough to know that the South is civilized and that the negro is a semi-savage. In the Faneuil Hall aggregation of long-haired he-virgins there were not a dozen men who would fight their own shadows on compulsion. They represent the crank element of the Old Bay State, an element that will say more in a minute than it will stand to do in a month. The better element of Boston is not meddling in other people's business. It understands the South. It ap-

preciates the black burden under which every Southern state
is struggling. It holds female chastity in high esteem. It
rejoices whenever a ravisher is done to death. Boston runs
to brains as well as to beans and brown bread. But she is
cursed with an army of cranks whom nothing short of a
straight-jacket or a swamp-elm club will ever control. Boston has no cause to blush because of Southern roasting-
bees; but the wild yodel of her own irrepressible damphools
—"one of whom her mayor is which"—might well tinge
with shame the brazen cheek of Sodom. If Massachusetts
really wants war she should wage one of extermination on
her own busybodies. When Cleveland again hires a substitute he should select the Fool-Killer and assign him to
duty in the lobby of Faneuil Hall.

THE REPUBLIC IN DANGER.

WILL THE EAGLE CEASE TO SCREAM?

How long will the American Union endure? It is customary to speak and act as tho' it could only end with Time;
as if nothing short of the final crash of the Universe rushing
back into the formless realm of Chaos and Night could possibly subvert it.

And yet it is but a new thing—a great straddling political calf standing doubtfully upon its four wobbly legs,
the bones of which are still but gristle, the tendons mere
fatty strings. Thus it stands, fronting Time; foolishly imagining itself a winged-lion or hippogriff, one of the few
immortal things that were not born to die! Really, if it
meet with no mishap until its bones have time to harden—
until its principles still in a nebulous state are finally fixed—
it will doubtless become, if not an immortal winged-creature,
at least a fine horned-bull, able to paw up the dirt and bellow
with the proudest of bovines. But infant governments, like
other juveniles, have their perils to pass through; their
colics and cramps, measles and mumps, and it is a long cry
from the baptismal font to the *toga virilis*—from wobbly,
foolish calfhood to mastership of the herd. It were well,
perhaps, not to forget that other republics have filled earth
and heaven with their self-glorification and boasts of immortality, and then, quietly or otherwise, meandered out
into the great inane, leaving behind as monuments but a few
scraps of half intelligible history, of interest chiefly to the
foolish antiquary.

"The soul politic having departed, what can follow but that the body politic be decently interred, to avoid putrescence?"

We are no longer American citizens, brothers with commutual interests; we are capitalists and laborers, farmers and manufacturers—each class fighting desperately not to promote the general welfare, but its own selfish interest. We are divided into classes-social and classes-industrial, and the lines of demarcation are becoming ever more strongly drawn. Patriotism has been throttled by greed, fraternity by jealousy. We no longer send our best men to Congress. We do not ask what a candidate can do to make the Union stronger; we do not inquire what he knows of the science of government—but rather how deep a haul he can make on the treasury for the special behoof of our section; how large an appropriation he can secure for the "improvement" of intermittent creeks and impossible harbors; for the erection of useless public buildings; how much "protection" he can secure for our products at the expense of the rest of the nation; how many fat federal offices he can distribute among us. We are after spoils; we have made of our votes levers to pry open the public treasury; we will follow any demagogue if he but lead us to the fleshpots, reckless of the future. Where is hope? What is to prevent our plunging headlong into that mad vortex of ruin, temporal and spiritual, to which we are hastening with constantly accelerating speed? To what political party shall we turn for salvation? There are but two possessing power for good or ill, and, like two bad roads, if we take the one we are apt to regret the other. Principles? What principles does either party possess that it will not willingly sacrifice to secure the mystic sesame that makes the doors of the public treasury fly open?

Is it possible that co-operation in government, as in business, is foredoomed to failure—that here as elsewhere it is true that "too many cooks spoil the broth?" Or will the mad wreck and ruin that must inevitably follow this dividing of the national house against itself but prove a purgation by fire, from which representative government will rise, phoenix-like, purer and stronger? We shall see what we shall see.

*   *   *

Those who fear the downfall of the Republic through so-called centralizing tendencies are but striving desperately to frighten themselves with a spectre of their own contriving. The danger lies not in a strong central gov-

ernment, but in a weak one. It is not "imperialism" we
have to fear so much as the State sovereignty hydra, which
was scotched, not killed, by the Lernean serpent slayers of
'61-5. This double sovereignty of State and Nation is a
weak spot in the pillar of American government, one pregnant with danger. It made the war of 1812 a pitiful farce
—would have given us a shameful defeat within the memory of men now living had Mexico bred true fighting men
instead of beggars and lice. It has several times threatened
the integrity of the Union and once cost a million precious
lives. It has on divers occasions very nearly embroiled
us in war with foreign powers, and may do so at any time—
then handicap us, as it has ever done, in the hour of peril!
Truly was it said of old that the house divided against itself
cannot stand. So long as these United States of America
are a congeries of Nations instead of a Nation—with one
supreme head to whom all petty governors must bow—it
will be so divided, ready to melt into nothingness.

Pessimism? Not a bit of it. A pessimist, with an eye
to see and mental apparatus to digest such pabulum as the
visual nerve provides would not believe that the rickety
pile we name American Union—and brag about and rob
on every possible occasion—could stand upright a single
year; could sustain the faintest adverse wind from any
quarter of the compass whatsoever. Forty odd separate
and distinct buildings of different styles of architecture
huddled together helter-skelter under one rickety patch-
work roof, hovering aloft with painful effort, pulled at,
even shot at, the props all rotten and worm-eaten—the fact
scarce concealed by liberal paint and cheap gilding.

That the rebellion of 1861 did not bring that composite
covering down with a crash; that it did not tear apart those
grotesquely grouped Nations and scatter them to the four
winds of heaven or hades, was but an accident, happy or
otherwise, as you chance to view it. The people of the
North and South were at swords' points; a collision was
inevitable—cupping had become a necessity. The very
fact that the South was determined to get out of the Union
made the North equally as determined that, cost what it
might, the Union should be preserved intact. It was not
that the people of the North loved the Union more, but
that they loved the South less, that gave vigor, even viru-
lence, to their war cry of "the Union forever," with hurrah
boys attachment. They "had it in for the nigger drivers"
and were only too happy when the latter gave them an excuse to shuck their linen. Really, it was not so much a
question of whether the Union should be preserved as

whether John Brown's soul should be permitted to go
meandering musically on, that caused the Northerner to
gird sword on thigh and go marching from Atlanta to the
sea—doing his share meanwhile to solve the negro problem from an ethnological as well as a political standpoint.

*   *   *

Now that the negro can knock off work without asking
leave; can give over petit for grand larceny whenever he
can get elected to office—and John Brown's soul goes
marching unchallenged—Mason and Dixon's semi-mythical
line is slowly but surely fading from a grand canyon to a
mere scratch in the ground; but a new sectional line is
being drawn between the East and the West that bids fair
to make no end of trouble in the near future. The most
dangerous of all lines, however, is that being drawn ever
broader and deeper between the capitalist and the laborer;
or, to dodge the hair-splitting of political economists, between Dives and Lazarus—between the man who has millions in excess of his needs and the man whose chief capital
is an active appetite. It is along this line that the first
sputtering of that revolution which is destined to try to
the uttermost our present form of government will first be
heard—nay, is even now audible. This is a revolution, rebellion or what you will, that no marching to the sea, fall
of Richmond and the like will put down; one there is no
force able to cope withal. Once well under way, it will
run its course; no flag-flaunting, resolution by prominent
citizens, enactment of Congress—not even an appropriation will suffice to check it. The only safety for our established forms and formulas lies in their quiet but rapid
metamorphosis. Our wise men, if they would "save the
country," must no longer waste time trying to prop up
buildings that are even now tumbling down; but break the
force of the fall they may, clear away the rubbish
and supervise the erection of more useful edifices. They
must not seek so much to repress the gathering storm as
to give it direction, that it destroys not the useful with the
useless.

The workingman must be made to feel that he, too, has
a country and that it is in very truth "the land of the free
and the home of the brave"—of men courageous enough
to say to the employing capitalist: We, too, are men like
thee; we are your fellow-countrymen, not your serfs. Our
labor you can only secure by giving therefor a just proportion of its product; our votes—our manhood—you can in
nowise command. These are not for sale—or rent.

One great trouble with our government is that it is becoming too complex, too redundant. There is danger of its breaking down with its own weight. We must study to simplify it, to dispense with many of our present offices, instead of creating more. The number of our tax-eaters is becoming alarming. They already constitute a vast nonproductive army; their support is becoming a serious drain upon American industry. We have too many laws and law-makers; too much red tape that hinders rather than helps Justice in the manipulation of her sword and scales. Government, municipal, State or National, is a corporation in which every citizen is a stockholder, sharing in the gains or losses. The public service should, therefore, be reduced to a purely business basis. The demagogue who mounts dry-goods box or editorial tripod and prates about rotation in office should be gagged with his own stupid nescience. When we secure faithful and efficient servants we must keep them as long as possible instead of turning them adrift to make place at the public teat for partisan "workers." The idea that public treasure is legitimate spoil must be weeded out. It is a rank, infectious growth that is rapidly strangling all that is good in our boasted representative government.

MARRIAGE AND MISERY.

Some Sanctified Debauchery.

There are probably a million women in this land living lives of legalized prostitution; who conceive children in hate of husbands they abhor, bring them forth in bitterness of spirit to be reared in an atmosphere of discord—offspring stamped from their very inception with the die of the criminal or the courtesan. Yet the purists and pietists "view with alarm" the vast increase in the number of divorces; are weeping and wailing because women will not suffer in silence a bondage that is bestial—a prostitution pre-eminently the worst in the world, that of loveless marriage. Day and night the doleful jeremiad goes up from these pious pharisees that the laxity of American divorce laws is imperiling the morals of the people, sapping the home and threatening to topple our entire system into ruin irremediable.

And what remedy do they propose? Uniform divorce laws and a reduction of the number of causes for which marital bonds may be legally broken. This would be equivalent to enacting a law that people should not summon a physician except in certain dire exigencies. Those who would elevate public morals by repressing legal separations appear to consider lax divorce laws the cause rather than the result of marital misery. They are pounding away vigorously at the shadow, leaving the substance untouched.

These foolish philosophers appear to be harboring the hallucination that where divorce is not difficult, husbands and wives are taken on trial; that matches are made just for amusement or to gratify a prurient passion, and that women pretending to respectability change their lawful companions much as men of the world do their mistresses; also that where it is next to impossible to break the marriage bond it is regarded with greater veneration and entered into with much greater caution. Doubtless a few old roues and adventuresses might make a business of marrying if divorce could be had for the asking, but it is an insult to the better class of American women to suggest that any law could so demoralize them that they would deliberately wed men with whom they did not expect to pass their lives.

Wedlock is holy only where there exists mutual love and respect. Such unions do not need to be reinforced by strict marriage laws. They mean much more than a "civil contract;" they mean devotion unto death, and would stand unshaken if every law known to man should perish from the earth. Only such unions should endure. All others are unholy and unclean—civil contracts to commit a crime against posterity—and should be dissolved. Those who protest so bitterly against divorce, who would compel people to live together after love has flown, appear to think the marriage ceremony a thaumaturgic incantation which sanctifies debauchery, a modern correlative of the ancient rites of Bacchus.

That eminent statistician, Hon. Carroll D. Wright, has recently stated that during the twenty years ending with 1886, there were granted in the United States 328,716 decrees for divorce; that the number in 1867 was 9,937 as against 25,535 in 1886, being an increase of nearly 157 per cent., while the population of the country increased during the same period only about 60 per cent. Mr. Wright added, almost unnecessarily one would think, that "the divorce statistics do not fully indicate or measure the marital infelicity or social misery of the country; they only measure the misery which can no longer abide conditions, and when parties have the courage to publicly seek release from demoralizing burdens."

Those words in quotation are worthy serious study. "When they have the courage"—to go into court and recite their grievances, to lay bare their torn hearts to the world, to be badgered and baited by shyster lawyers, made the cynosure of the rabble, and have the degradation and despair which they would fain hide from their dearest friends, caught up by a prurient press and heralded to the four winds of heaven! Only people who have the courage can stand that kind of thing, can hope for legal relief from bonds that make life a burden. And what kind of people possess this courage? Those who least deserve relief—brazen women and brutish men. How can a high-bred gentleman go into court and brand the wife to whom he poured the whole wealth of his heart, as a wanton—confess himself that most pitiable of all objects, a cuckold? If they have children, how can he deliberately cloud their whole lives? How can a modest, sensitive woman go before a rabble and rehearse the brutal scenes that have made her home a hell? No, they cannot do it; they must suffer in silence or quietly depart, leaving their unworthy mate to explain the separation as their interest or maliciousness may suggest.

The number of divorces has indeed become appalling; but this is but a partial suppuration of the sore. It argues, not that divorce laws are too lax, but that society is rotten. Marital misery cannot be decreased by denying it relief. If a woman does not love and honor her husband above all other men, she might as well be in a brothel as compelled to share his bed. If a man does not love his wife, happiness cannot abide in that home. People who do not desire to live together should be allowed to legally separate without being compelled to go into court with their grievances. It is a matter which they alone are competent to wisely decide. They have entered into a "civil contract" to make each other happy. If either wishes to annul that contract it is *prima facie* evidence that it has not been fulfilled, is void, and should be so pronounced by the courts.

To guard against hasty and ill-considered action the law might provide that application for divorce be followed by a separation of six months, during which period the marital relations would be suspended in law and in fact. At the expiration of that period, an application that the divorce be made absolute should be followed by a decree to that effect, proper provision made for the children, if any, resulting from the union. Unquestionably such a regime would increase the number of divorces. More people would "have the courage" to seek separation from uncongenial mates if they did not have to go into court with a lingering tale of woe—to explain to all Christendom, through the columns of a sensation-seeking, garbage-grabbing press, why said mates were to them a source of misery. It would afford relief to many cultured gentlemen and refined ladies to whom our present barbarous system of procedure offers only a cure infinitely worse than the complaint.

The objections that libertines would marry young ladies with deliberate intent to secure divorces is not without weight; but we cannot well condemn those already in the Slough of Despond to remain there because to help them out will afford a few fools golden opportunity to fall in. With the law as suggested, young ladies really deserving our consideration would not be so ready to contract hasty marriages with men of whom they knew little. As matters now stand many incautious women are victimized by adventurers who do not hesitate to marry as often as opportunity offers.

While we may properly look to law-reform to relieve much of the marital misery now existing, we should strive to prevent, rather than to provide a panacea for this ill in the future. The church might profitably allow the heathen a holiday and devote a little more of its energies to teaching the American people that marriage is more than a "civil contract" that may be entered into much as one does into a contract for a car-load of cotton or a pound of putty. It should set its face like flint against "marriages of convenience;" should launch some of its thunderbolts it is now wasting on the heads of harmless agnostics, at those pious people who teach their daughters that the chief end and aim of their lives must be to marry money instead of men. Our public schools should not waste quite so much time ascertaining the number of bones in the caudal appendages of the ichthyosaurus, or determining just when the paleozoic gave place to the mesozoic, and that in turn was tumbled into the unlamented erstwhile by the cenozoic time; but should devote an hour occasionally to teaching the rising generation something of the sacredness of Lamartine's trinity—the trinity of the father, mother and child.

That is the only hope for the future. Laws cannot make a people virtuous or happy. They cannot prevent mistakes in marriages. They cannot guard the sanctity of the home.

WAR OR WIND?

UNCLE SAM AS DON QUIXOTE.

Britain's royal beast and Columbia's bald-headed bird are evidently preparing to give an interesting imitation of the historical monkey and parrot—to have "one hell of a time." President Cleveland slipped a cannon cracker into Queen Victoria's Christmas sock, and is now waiting to receive in return the courtesies of the season. The old girl has got to sand her hands, seize her soap-stick and call the ripsnortin', hades-erecting bluff of the Western warrior bold, else concede Uncle Sam's right or ability to put a red fence around the Western hemisphere and compel the royal guys of Europe to keep off the grass. The party in the Populist pants and the Tippecanoe tile is trailing the flowing narrative of his star-spangled cut-away in the middle of the road, carrying an adult cypress shingle on each shoulder and ostentatiously biting his thumbs at John Bull. He has gone deliberately forth, with a search-warrant in one hand and a forty candle-power arc light in the other, to look for trouble, and either Cranfill or Christ hath said, "Seek and ye shall find."

In browsing around, seeking whom he may devour, the British lion has encountered something he can't digest. While gaily despoiling the nests of ospreys he has inadvertently run his muzzle into the eyrie of the American eagle, and unless the brute removes it with neatness and despatch, he will be sent home with his tail frozen to his belly-band and both optics swinging in the breeze.

In my humble opinion, Cleveland made a large, piebald ass of himself when he penned that arbitrate-or-fight pronunciamento. Some public enemy had probably slipped a little gunpowder into the presidential demijohn, for Grover evidently mistook himself for that substitute who subdued the Southern Confederacy. He longed once again to hear the roar of battle and set his brisket against the bayonet— to drink hot blood out of a camp skillet and satisfy his martial soul with the glorious pomp and circumstance of war. It is difficult indeed to break these prancing war-steeds to the plow. The smell of holiday powder and the roll of the toy drum causes them to stand on their hind legs and neigh for a renascence of the days that are dead.

There is nothing for it now but to back the President's foolish bluff to the last extremity. That is the penalty we must pay for having placed at the head of Federal affairs a man more skilled in pinochle than diplomacy, who runs to belly rather than brains and drinks bourbon as if it were Weiss beer. According to reliable reports, the President sat him down in a fit of pique, and, while his "hair was pulling" penned in a few minutes that message which may involve the world in war and set back the hand on the human horologue a thousand years. His case of *katzenjammer* is likely to cost us dear. Had he embroiled us with almost any other transatlantic power, we might have crawfished out of it with credit by consigning him to a Keeley-cure establishment or lunatic asylum; but we cannot afford to temporize even a little bit with John Bull. Such a policy would be interpreted by this professional bluffer as a square backdown, and would render him more insolent and overbearing than ever.

Sooner or later, Uncle Sam has got to give his British cousin a lesson in international courtesy—has got to hold Britain's marauding beast up by the narrative and bump its fat head against Plymouth Rock until his fangs fall out— and this disagreeable duty cannot be long delayed. Another war between the two great English-speaking powers has been brewing for half a century and cannot be permanently side-tracked by even the most careful diplomacy or skilled hypocrisy. It is inscribed in the Book of Fate—either Rome or Carthage must feel upon her neck the heel of the conqueror. We might just as well settle the hash of the world's bully and leave to posterity the privilege of paying the bills. It will serve to remind them of their glorious ancestors— and, while in the throes of hysterical patriotism, they'll place all the war-bonds and greenbacks on a gold-basis and provide our whiskered orphans with liberal pensions.

The trade relations of the two countries are particularly close and mutually profitable. John Bull and Brother Jonathan wine and dine, toast and taffy each other—indulge in a great deal of gush anent the common ancestry, kindred institutions and the high destiny of the great English-speaking Brotherhood; but all the time they know they are lying like Cretans—are indulging the hypocritical courtesies of commerce, the artificial smiles and effusive hand-shakings of the shop. Ethnologically, the English and Americans are as little alike as are the Germans and the French. There is a mighty tide of English blood in America; but it has been modified by climatic conditions and the admixture of Danish and German, while the Gael has tinctured it with iron and the Celt with Tabasco sauce. England may have been our "mother country" a century or so ago; but to-day she is not even our anthropological step-dame. We are no more

Englishmen because we employ the language, than a parrot is a Baptist preacher because it stands on two legs and gabbles anent things of which it knows nothing.

We owe to England no "debt of gratitude." She has done nothing for us except to fatten upon the fruits of our industry, oppress and insult us in the day of our infancy and conspire against us in the day of our strength. Despite the "many expressions of good will," down deep in the heart of each nation is a fervent desire to humiliate the other—a feeling that needs little nursing to flame forth in hate so rancorous as to make peace impossible. John Bull has never forgotten nor forgiven the Boston tea-party and Bunker Hill. Yorktown has been a thorn in his side for a century, New Orleans is a fly in his ointment. But it is the growing commerce and the expanding power of the new Nation, born of his own brutality, that aggrieves him most. He aspires to be the autocrat of the earth; to place all nations and peoples under tribute to "the Tight Little Isle"—to make them the industrial peons of his grasping tradesmen; and day by day the truth of Napoleon's prophecy —that America was destined to put an everlasting crimp in Britain's vaulting ambition—is being driven home to the wolfish heart, the iron has entered his sordid soul. When not wrestling with Brother Jonathan for the best end of the bargain in beeves, cotton and corn, or striving, by the purchase of political Benedict Arnolds, to shape our financial system for his profit and our impoverishment, his tone is exasperating if not actually insulting. His globe-trotters take a peep at our institutions from the windows of a palace-car, enjoy our hospitality, then meander home to fill their pockets with dirty pence by pandering to anti-American prejudice by caricaturing us in stupid plays and lying periodicals. Even Charles Dickens, whom we enriched and worshiped as a god—beneath whose feet Columbia laid her shining hair—repaid our love with the base ingratitude characteristic of his brethren. In our joy at meeting the author of Little Nell we forgot that he was a Briton— that tho' he might be the brightest and the wisest, he must of necessity be "the meanest of mankind."

John Bull's pauper "nobility"—with bawds and panders for progenitors—consider American heiresses their legitimate game. Englishmen come hither in the steerage of tramp steamers and accumulate fortunes; but when their wives become *enciente* they send them across the sea that their brats may be born British subjects instead of American sovereigns, then bring back these cringing slaves of a rotten monarchy to be educated at the expense of a people whom

they profess to despise. They fatten beneath the American
flag, but when asked to bear arms in its defense, plead the
exemption of aliens. The Gael and the Celt, the Dane and
the Pole, the German and the Russ consider a flag worthy
to shield their roof-tree good enough to fight for, and become enthusiastic American citizens, ready to do and die for
the country of their adoption; but once an Englishman, always an Englishman. They are so inordinately proud of
being the "humble subjects" of a beery old female, and so
ready to pour into her ample ear their tale of woe at every
opportunity, that their presence here is a constant menace
to the peace of a nation that has afforded them an opportunity to rise superior to that state in which they were born
—to develop from grimy paupers into pot-bellied plutocrats,
from menials existing on "tips" contemptuously tossed
them by gentlemen, into pompous millionaires.

When John Bull attempts to be pleasant with us he only
succeeds in being patronizing. His diplomacy is deceit
that might shame a disciple of Machiavelli, while his friendship is bounded by the shilling. During our civil war the
present prime minister openly declared that the disruption
of this nation would make to the commercial advantage of
England, and those brutal words made him the political idol
of his coldly-calculating countrymen. And yet the Anglo-
maniacs are prattling of the "indissoluble ties that bind together the great English-speaking brotherhood," and snivel-
ing about John Bull's "friendship for Brother Jonathan!"
It is a friendship akin to that of Judas Iscariot—he kisses
only to betray.

True, these are but trifles, at which Americans, conscious
of their country's invincible strength, affect to laugh; but it
is the laugh of men who long to express their hilarity with
martial music and double-shotted guns. People in this
frame of mind can easily find a pretext for booming the
coffin trust. In fact, the official *casus belli* in nearly every
bloody struggle has been but a specious apology to the world
for letting slip the dogs of war. Petty grievances accumulate
and bitterness is fostered, until, without apparent cause,
there comes the conflagration.

I sincerely trust that the political buncombe of President
Cleveland will not prove a match in the great powder magazine; but if the sword is once drawn it should not be
sheathed while the shadow of Britain's flag falls upon one
acre of the western world. When Columbia strikes again
in the name of human liberty she must strike to kill—must
make her flag a terror to tyranny. We have already had
two wars with England, and we must make it "three times

and out." We gave the British lion a breakfast in 1776, a dinner in 1812, but the omnivorous beast is not yet satisfied. If he puts his paws under our mahogany again, we must serve him with a supper that will forever satiate his lust for Yankee gore.

Nothing short of dismemberment of the Britism Empire will put England permanently on her good behavior, and this Uncle Sam can accomplish in half the time it required to conquer the Southern Confederacy. For generations Erin, prostrate and bleeding beneath the feet of Britain's marauding beast has appealed to us for aid. We have given her our sympathy and opened to her our purse; now let us given her the sword, beneath whose keen edge her ancient enemy has learned to cower. In case of war, let it be emblazoned on every battle-flag that Ireland's autonomy is a pre-requisite to peace. Let us throw fifty thousand fighting men into the Emerald Isle, as a nucleus around which the Irish, scattered throughout the world, may rally, and strike one herculean blow for God and native land. Do this, and the Irish—who have constituted England's right arm for a hundred years—will fight this war, and they'll fight it to a finish. From every land and clime upon which shines the sun the fiery Celts will come trooping to the fray, and unless held in check by Columbia's strong hand, they'll make of Ireland's oppressor a desolation forever and a day. Twice has England allied herself with the American savages in war upon this country. While she assailed us in front, she incited the murderous redskins to attack the defenseless cabins and isolated villages scattered along our western frontier. It were but retributive justice to turn the Celts, maddened by generations of cruel outrage and brutal robbery—in their thirst for vengeance—loose in their marts of trade.

Those milk-and-water Anglo-maniacs, who are crying aloud in the mugwump press that, in case of war we would be at the mercy of England's ironclads, should be sent across the sea where they may feel safe. They are the lineal descendants of those tories who preached humble submission to crazy King George, and put their white livers on exhibition when John Bull was impressing American seamen. They told America then that she was not prepared for war, and that "the British navy would dictate terms of peace off New York and Boston." They gave an imitation of Jonah, who went bawling up and down the earth, "Yet forty days and Nineveh shall be overthrown." But despite the calamity cackling, Nineveh stood—and so did New York. The Yankee tars rigged up a lot of rotten

scows, armed them with old smooth-bores, and either captured England's terrible seventy-fours or drove them under
cover, while Washington's ragged Continentals or Old Hickory's coon-skin riflemen were making the British redcoats
and Hessian mercenaries hard to catch. The best defense
of a nation is not ships of iron and forts of stone, but hearts
of oak. With three million poverty-stricken people, the
American eagle got in its gaffles. Back of the bird o' freedom to-day are seventy millions of the same fighting stock,
and more wealth than is owned by any other nation in the
world. America has passed thro' the fiery furnace—has
been welded into one homogeneous nation. In case of
another war with England that country will not have vast
tribes of Indians and traitorous tories to assist her. She
will not find one great section of America inimical to the
other and indifferent to national glory, as in 1812. Lee's
veterans will keep step with Grant's boys in blue—will set
foot as far as who goes farthest in defense of the old flag;
and I here do prophesy that when Northern valor and
Southern chivalry make common cause—tho' the sea be
black with England's ships and her shores girt with fire—
the red tide of war will soon roll thro' London's streets and
Old Glory be planted in triumph on the Tower.

I have been called a "jingo." If by that is meant that
I am jealous of my country's honor; if by that is meant
that I am all aweary of seeing the most powerful nation
that ever graced the mighty tide of time truckle like a
whipped spaniel at the feet of a neighbor it could erase
from the map of the world; if by it is meant that I long
to hear the mighty bird o' freedom emit one scream that
will cause every arrogant monarchy on earth to hunt its
hole, and hunt it p. d. q., then I am a jingo for your Van-
dyke beard.

England is the modern Attilla, the Scourge of God, the
curse of the world. Her arrogance and insolence are only
equalled by her conscienceless cupidity. She is the avatar
of Discord, the abettor of Strife, the incarnation of Greed.
Her power must be broken before a permanent peace is
possible. Not until she is humbled in the very dust need
the poet dream of that Saturnian age, when

> "The war-drum throbs no longer,
> And the battle flags are furled
> In the parliament of man,
> The federation of the world."

America is the only power that can, single-handed and
alone, cut short the career of this professional filibuster,

and this duty seems to have been assigned to us by the Deity. Still, we might have awaited a tenable excuse for hostilities. The Monroe doctrine is a political back number that should cut no ice in our national affairs to-day. Even when first enunciated and properly interpreted, it was a piece of flamboyant nonsense not worth fighting for. We were induced to adopt it by England herself, who was jealous of other European powers, and employed us as a tool to accomplish her own ends—used as the monkey did the feline's paw, to pull chestnuts out of the fire. If Europe owned every foot of soil from the Rio Bravo to Magellan Strait, and from the St. Lawrence to Symme's Hole, the autonomy of this mighty Yankee nation would be in nowise endangered. On our own soil the world in arms would find us invincible. Uncle Sam is a giant who towers, like Saul, above his brethren. There are not men and money enough in the great round globe to trail Old Glory in the dust, or tear one gleaming star from Columbia's diadem. Seventy million Americans, who know exactly what they are here for, can breed fighting stock to fill the ranks faster than the combined armies of the earth can decimate them. We can build a Chinese wall around these United States and defend it, from generation to generation, against all the world, and at the same time grow in population and increase in wealth.

Such being the case, is it not arrant folly to say that European colonization of other American countries is inimical to our peace and safety? If we have managed to exist all these years with the British possessions abutting our entire northern border, Spain holding the key to the Gulf, and the American-hating Mexican dynasty on the southwest, why should we become panic-stricken if England adds a few malarial acres to the crown on another continent? We look idly on while generation after generation of Cubans sacrifice themselves in a futile struggle for freedom. We see a spirited and industrious people oppressed by a transatlantic power and shot to death at our very door, and if one of our citizens attempts to do for them what Lafayette did for us under similar conditions, we consign him to a dungeon, then contract a double-barreled bellyache anent the outraged Goddess of Liberty because a few thieving Venezuelans cannot agree with Great Britain anent the Guiana boundary!

It would be infinitely better for us if progressive European powers took forcible possession of all Central and South America and developed those fertile countries, instead of leaving them to a lot of lazy, semi-barbarous half-breeds, who are of less importance in the world's economy than so many agency Indians. The idea that the countries south of us are "Sister Republics," whom it is Uncle Sam's duty, as a modern Sir Tristram or Don Quixote, to protect from the bities, is all buncombe. This is the only government of the people, for the people and by the people existing in the Western World—and even it is not so to any alarming extent. There is as much liberty in Mexico as in any of the so-called republics further south; yet Diaz is as supreme on Mexican soil as the Czar at St. Petersburg. The average South American "citizen" couldn't distinguish between the elective franchise and an ichthyosaurian. Oligarchies, cabals and dictators rule the roost, and whenever a man becomes rich enough to own two dogs and an antiquated gun he revolts and grasps the reins of government. The people of those "republics" are divided into two classes—those on rule or ruin bent and those content to sit in the sun and roll corn-shuck cigarettes until an opportunity occurs to steal something which they are not too tired to carry.

In case of war we want no alliance with the so-called republics of the south. We would have to provide them with guns and grub, and neither their fighting ability nor their faithlessness justifies the expense. They are first-class assassins, but very poor soldiers. A British regiment would go through them like a thunderbolt through a swarm of gnats. Had the famous Light Brigade charged the mobilized armies of South America it would not have lost a dozen men; but the chances are that every horse would have been stolen from under it.

It is urged that an attempt on our part to enforce the Cleveland-Olney interpretation of the Monroe doctrine would bring the continental powers of Europe to England's aid. That is beyond the pale of the probabilities. Spain, France, Holland and some others do not like the Monroe doctrine a little bit; but none of them are anxious for a "go" with the giant of the Occident. Uncle Sam ran a bluff on both France and Spain, and made England herself sing small while the Southern Confederacy was in the very heyday of its power. Russia could not be drawn into an anti-American alliance, for she doesn't care an Austindam about the Monroe doctrine; but while America was entertaining Western Europe, the Great White Czar, by pushing his fortunes in the Far East, would cut out some lively work for his neighbors nearer home. France, Spain, et al., will give Great Britain their

moral support, then sit on the fence and wait for their
slice of Turkey, while discussing the balance of power.
Continental Europe has troubles of her own, and John
Bull will have to tell his to Brother Jonathan.

If war is the result of the present complication the
world will be none the worse for it; but Grover Cleveland,
like the fool who fired the Ephesian Dome, will be damned
to everlasting fame. The blood of every American patriot
who falls before the batteries of Great Britain will be
upon his head. After being for years John Bull's man
Friday, the subservient tool of Downing street, he blossoms forth as *facile princeps* of the genus "jingo." Hitherto his Anglomania has been offensive to the very mugwumps; now his Americanism slops over like a toy bucket
in a cloudburst. After truckling to England in all things
like a slave to his master, he hurries us into war with that
country without provocation or excuse—puts Uncle Sam
in the position of the fool jackass who kicked before he
was spurred. Because Great Britain desired to preserve
the Hawaiian monarchy, Cleveland exceeded his authority in a feverish attempt to degrade Old Glory and
strangle the new-born republic. He ignored the Monroe
doctrine when it was flagrantly violated under his very
nose in the case of Nicaragua, then placed upon it a
strained and hitherto unheard of construction as a pretext
for making a flamboyant war-talk that by appealing to
American patriotism would cause his political errors to be
forgiven and forgotten.

THE COMMON COURTESAN.

A Glimpse of Gehenna.

I published an article in the February number of the
Iconoclast entitled "Woman's Wickedness," which gave
many supersensitive people a shock from which they have
not yet recovered. I have no particular objection to killing that class of cattle, for I believe the good God would
be glad to get the rickety breed exterminated; but I
would not ambuscade even a canting hypocrite or sheep-
killing dog, so I here put up a sign warning the whole
pestiferous crew of Pharisees to dive no deeper here,
under pain of death, and heaven alone knows what hereafter. I am going to indulge in some plain talk, and those
who wear their modesty on their sleeve will please betake
themselves to a milder diet—one of Sam Jones' aesthetic

sermons or the quack doctor ads. in the daily papers, for instance.

In my former article I discussed how courtesans are made; here I propose to consider how they can be reclaimed. Next to learning how to do a thing is learning how not to do it. The world has had a vast and varied experience with the negative side of the question and seems to have settled it to its satisfaction that the only way to lift a woman out of hell is to bar the door of egress and shoot fireballs at her through the gratings; that the only way to persuade her to leave off her sinning is to inform her that, though she repent in sackcloth and ashes, she will never be forgiven; that the only method of elevating the fallen woman is to get after her with scorpion whips when she breaks away from the brothel and scourge her back again! This system of moral therapeutics is not without its advantages; if it seldom cures, it at least kills quicker than any other that could be devised, thus abbreviating the misery of the patient.

It were as idle to expect to eliminate Prostitution as to extirpate Poverty and Greed. Just so long as Lust runs riot in the veins of Adam's sons, women will be degraded and debauched. Just so long as Want and Wretchedness stalk like grisly phantoms through the earth women will be found who will brazenly barter their souls for gold or for bread. There are women who are wantons by nature; whom no wealth, education or moral surroundings can withhold from evil.

> "But virtue, as it never will be mov'd,
> Though lewdness court it in a shape of heaven,
> So lust, though to a radiant angel link'd,
> Will sate itself in a celestial bed
> And prey on garbage."

It were idle to talk of "reforming" women who never possessed the faintest conception of modesty; in whom the brutish nature dominates the divine; but these form a very inconsiderable portion of that vast array upon whose brows blazes the scarlet brand of the courtesan. A vast majority of these unfortunates feel their degradation as no male malefactor ever felt his disgrace; would, were it possible, wash the stains from their souls with their heart's blood. Every year of the world thousands of them, unable to further bear their weight of shame, to longer endure the fierce scourgings of the fire-whips of an avenging conscience, burst the gates of death, hide in the grave from a cold world's bitter scorn. Other escape there is none;

society will not receive them back; its doors are irrevocably closed to them. They may knock, but it will not be opened unto them; they may come on their knees, groping their way through penitential tears, but they will be spurned from its portals with foul reproach. Society made them what they are; it now sits in judgment upon them and declares that they shall be no other. From the lips of the stern judge are never heard those words, the sweetest that ever fell on mortal ears, divinest sentence that ever passed the lips of God or man, "Go and sin no more." Other criminals reform. The thief becomes an honest man; the forger lives down his crime; the manslayer purifies his bloody hands with a life-time of noble deeds; but once a courtesan always a courtesan. There is no place in all the wide world but the bagnio for the woman who has once erred,—no matter how youthful or inexperienced, how foul her betrayal.

> "No; gayer insects fluttering by
> Ne'er droop the wing o'er those that die,
> And lovlier things have mercy shown
> To every failing but their own,
> And every woe a tear can claim
> Except an erring sister's shame."

* * *

Those good people who drag her hence but plunge her into tortures beyond her powers of endurance; but place her on exhibition for the world to mock, set her up as a mark for the cold unmoving finger of scorn. Those who can stand the ordeal are seldom worth saving; are women scarce conscious of their degradation, mere animals to whom all life is alike—who care little whether they take their food from the hand of a boorish husband or a dashing paramour. Crazed by the world's contempt, by its brutal scorn, trampled beneath the feet of women not worthy to serve them as waiting maids or scullions, the most rush back into the old evil life and madly plunge to more fearful depths.

What salvation can be devised for the thousands of noble women who have fallen beneath the terrible ban of public opinion? There is only one way: to reform public opinion itself; to lift from these daughters of shame the dead weight that is crushing them down to the deepest hell; to throw open to them the gates of the upper as well as of the nether world.

Such a task will appear to many almost as hopeless as an attempt to change the ocean's tides or alter the law of gravitation; but such forget that Falsehood and Folly fade before Truth like night's black shadows before the faintest light ray that trembles from the great sun. The world is naturally honest, just, pitiful; its attitude toward the fallen woman is an unnatural one, the result of centuries of false education and fatuous religion. Pessimist as I am called, I still have sufficient faith in my fellowmen to believe that they will not persist in a grievous, a brutal crime, when they can once be made to see that it is such.

But who is to convince them? The press? The pulpit? Is not the present deplorable condition the result of their teaching? They have created a false, a vicious public opinion, before which they now cower and tremble. Is there a minister living with the courage to urge his parishioners to throw open their homes to and receive on a footing of social equality the repentant Magdalen? Is there a daily paper between the two oceans that would dare make such a suggestion,—that would, even for a fat bribe, state in its editorial columns that the most abandoned courtesan that ever made night hideous with her drunken brawling, may become the peer of the President's wife by discarding her evil ways and thenceforth living a life of purity and nobleness? Not one! Yet is it not true? If not, why not? If there is any truth in our religion, the portals of heaven will fly wide open at her approach; yet we close the door in her face! Almighty God thinks her good enough to associate with the Virgin Mary, yet we raise a devil of a row if we see her talking across the back fence to our daughters or wives! The Creator of the Cosmos is waiting to crown her amid the glad acclaim of the heavenly host; yet our nice American gentleman does not consider that she is good enough to wear his name and cook his hash! His honor would be irremediably smirched by such an alliance! Yet if he can but toll her back into the old life and be one of a hundred to visit her foul bed, his honor will not show even a fly-speck—will shine like a new tin pan at a Republican powwow! Curious this thing male bipeds are wont to call their honor!

* * *

The world, ever gross despite centuries of civilization, makes no distinction in illicit intercourse of the sexes. To it all women found even one step outside the prescribed path are equally vile, alike deserving unmitigated censure; yet from the highest to the lowest of those so outlawed and placed beneath society's ban, is a sweep as far from the highest heaven as to the deepest hell. Some of the noblest, grandest women ever sent into this dreary world by a beneficent God to brighten its cimmerian gloom are known to have lived on very intimate terms with the men they

loved, and that, too, without the formality of securing society's sanction.   Love is a celestial flame that has not yet
been educated to burn ever according to terrestrial law.
Sometimes it will overlap such fences as secular statutes
and religious dogmas and set the world on fire!   Many a
noble woman has become a man's mistress because she
could neither become his wife nor trample her heart beneath her feet at the dictates of society.   With some
women love is a higher law, before which canons of church
and State shrivel into nothingness.   No saintly anathema,
no fiat of society can disturb their devotion.   Though the
world reel, the heavens fall and black chaos come again,
they will cling closer to the shrine upon which they have
cast their hearts.   Of these we need not speak further here.
Society has no power over them for good or ill.   From
its fallible judgment they calmly and confidently appeal
to an infallible God.

For those at the other extreme, the law of whose lives
is Lust instead of Love, children of the slums, the spawn of
criminals, who were courtesans from the very cradle, there
is no hope.   There is no method by which those now ex-
istent can be successfully reached.   All that we can hope to
do, is, by improving society, to curtail the class which
breeds them.   This cannot be done by dogmatizating or
founding "homes for fallen women;" we must do our
most effective work in our industrial system.   When the
laborer's lot is made easier; when it becomes possible for
all men and women to earn an honest living, society will
have fewer crimes and courtesan-breeding "dregs."

It is that vast class of women, once as pure as the snow
but now foul as the hags of hell, yet who still retain a
shadow of that "divine shame" which distinguishes humanity from the brute, and who long to return to the upper
world,—to win back the respect they have forfeited—that
chiefly concerns us here.   Naturally the first step would be
to so reform society that it will not year by year pour
thousands upon thousands of fresh recruits into the ranks
of the fallen.   Here, too, the need of industrious reform
becomes apparent.   Bitter poverty is as potent to make
prostitutes of young women as thieves of young men.
Make it possible for every young woman to earn an honest
and respectable living and you will save more souls than
have been garnered by all the priests and preachers from
Melchizedek to Sam Jones.   You make it possible for
thousands of young women to choose between good and
evil whose only alternative now of degradation is death.
You prepare a field in which it is possible for moral max-

ims to take root. It is useless to hurl homilies at people
suffering for food and fuel while the devil is clinking his
gold pieces and dazzling their eyes with gems.

But the most effective method of checking an evil that
threatens to engulf the world, is the easiest; it is to repeat
to every repentant sinner the words of the Saviour: "Go
and sin no more." Let the past perish and be forgotten:
we will not judge you by what you have been but by what
you are. Come out of the depths! If the God who made
you forgives your transgressions, can we petty creatures,
resting in the hollow of his hand, annul his judgments?
If he says that your repentant tears have washed you white
as snow, shall we appeal from his great court to that of
Mrs. Grundy?

THE "COUNTESS" CASTELLANE.

And now a tale of woe comes drifting across the dark
blue sea—another American woman who wedded a titled
nonentity is, like Niobe, all tears. Miss Anna Gould is the
latest American girl to learn that the European "nobility"
is not composed of noble men—the new-made "countess"
is already pining for her own country. I expected it. I
confided to Anna that her "Count" was utterly no account, and advised her to use him for fish bait instead of
for breeding purposes. I counselled her to give the miserable tramp a cold "hand-out" and the marble heart. I
implored her to consider her latter end and have no dealings with titled dudes. I suggested that she spill her gilded affections on some honest American mechanic who
could be trusted to carry in the coal, come home reasonably sober, avoid the company of courtesans and sure-
thing gamblers and love her as long as there was any of
her left. But it's a sheer waste of advice to give it to a
woman. Anna found the "Count" on the matrimonial
bargain-counter and gathered him in—paid for him, much
as one might purchase a hairless Mexican pup. And the
undiscriminating dailies fairly chortled in their joy. They
informed the world that the union was a love match pure
and simple—as tho' the average daily editor could distinguish between a Cupid-shaft and an affection of the
kidneys! They slobbered over the young turtle doves
until the bridal wreath floated in the lather, and prattled
of the "holy union of two young hearts." Rodents! And
while sassiety and the press was slopping over, the Castellane family was recalcitrating like mule colts because

Miss Gould would not turn over her entire fortune to her fiance—even threatened to break off the alliance at the very steps of the altar. But the Goulds knew the market quotations of expired patents of nobility, kept a stiff upper lip, and "the great house of Castellane" grew hungry and came off its perch with the frigid hauteur of a lame parrot making a sneak on a rotten peanut. Anna captured the erstwhile coronet—encumbered by an early morning accident, such as will sometimes happen in respectable families. And now we are getting the second chapter of this "true love" tale. According to apparently reliable reports, the "Countess" Castellane is one of the most miserable of mortals. Ze count—without a coronet—is blowing in her boodle on bawds and boozers while neglecting and humiliating his wife in every possible way. So brutal in his treatment, so ostentatious his neglect of the woman who has paid for the very clothes he wears and the bread in his belly, that even the heartless cosmopolites of the wickedest city in the world profess to pity her. I have tried to be sorry for the "countess;" but I can't. I am indignant that a scrawny little French fice, who insults his own country by pretensions of "nobility" in the days of the Republic, and whose forefathers were kicked across the frontier like so many sheep-killing curs by the outraged peasantry should dare mistreat a countrywomen of mine; but reason tells me it is retributive justice. When the daughter of a mouse-trap-maker and map-peddler becomes too purse-proud to marry an American sovereign, and seeks among the syphilitic dudes of a fallen dynasty a companion for her bed, she deserves to suffer the tortures of the damned. It is a grim satisfaction to know that most of these title-hunting Yankee dunderheads get their just dues. If any American woman has wedded a European "nobleman" and "lived happily ever afterwards," I have yet to hear of it. Social clap-trap and sacerdotal ceremony cannot sanctify a contract to commit a crime against nature, nor purge "a marriage of convenience" of the taint of prostitution. The woman who barters her beauty for a title, her soul for social distinction is even more culpable than the courtesan of Boiler avenue, whose fee is a dollar bill. In both cases it is cold-blooded barter and sale, but to the crime of a loveless marriage is added the vice of hypocrisy. The bawd may be driven to sell her body for bread, but the title-hunter sacrifices her purity to gratify a prurient ambition. It is scarce to be expected that women who purchase their marital companions should make model wives—that is not a clause in the contract. The penurious "nobleman" marries such a woman not because he cares for her companionship, but because he needs money which he is too indolent to earn and too cowardly to steal. Having given her his name in exchange for a grub-stake, he feels that he has performed his part of the contract, has discharged his entire duty. He understands full well that the woman wedded him solely for his title—that it was social ambition instead of love's passion that brought her to his bed —and he heartily despises her, as all hypocrites do their fellow humbugs. There is no contempt so profound, no hatred so implacable as that with which the impoverished patrician regards the aspiring parvenu ; and scarce has the epithalamium ceased ere this feeling begins to make itself manifest. The man who weds a woman solely for her wealth cannot possibly possess the instincts of a gentleman. Tho' he wear a crown, he is at heart a human hyena, capable of any crime that requires no courage—just the kind of a creature to find a fiendish joy in torturing the helpless, in making a woman's life a hell. All the manhood which the "older nobility" of Europe ever possessed was bred out by selfish marriages and shameless bawdry years ago. Most royal families were originally established by the plunder and oppression of the weak by the strong. The "nobility" was composed of the obsequious servants of marauding sovereigns, the hired assassins of crowned hoodlums, its ranks regularly recruited from professional panders and the spawn of prostitutes. For centuries the European "nobility" was but a foul cesspool into which emptied the social sewer. The throne was surrounded by "ennobled" bastards and shameless bawds swayed the sovereign's sceptre. "An evil tree cannot bring forth good fruit." Idle lives, vicious habits and inherited disease have degraded the present "nobility" below even the brutish level of its progenitors—has transformed it into a disreputable omnium-gatherum of wife-beaters and sure-thing gamblers, scorbutic cowards and brazen cuckolds. Here and there may be found a family, lately ennobled, that has not yet become irremediably rotten ; but the tendency is almost invariably downward —each succeeding generation drifting further from the distinctive virtues of manhood. And it was one of these hoodlums that Miss Gould bought for a husband. Her marital experience is that of most American women who have traded cash for coronets. The "Countess" Castellane and the "Princess" Colonna should retire to the woodshed and mingle their tears. They might retrieve their mistakes by employing a half-grown "coon" to bump together the empty pates of their titled nincompoops until they pop like a pair of painted bladders, then marry good Texas Democrats and rear a crop of boys with brains in their heads and iron in their blood.

THE MORMONS OF MEXICO.

After suffering unremitting persecution at the hands of religious bigots for half a century, the Mormons are moving into Mexico, where, I am informed, there is little inclination to interfere with their polygamous practices. And they are repaying the hospitality of our sister republic by transforming her arid wastes into fruitful farms. A dispatch announces, as an item of news, that "they are industrious and law-abiding citizens who are aiding wonderfully in the development of the country." The same could be said of the Mormons in America so long as the religious fanatics could be kept off their collars. The United States never had better citizens than were the Mormons so long as they were let alone. Their industry, thrift and penchant for attending strictly to their own business has passed into a proverb. This much may be said of them without endorsing their religious doctrines. I have ever been undecided whether Joe Smith was a faker or a fool; but certain am I that the brutal treatment accorded him and his followers in this country should call a blush of shame to the cheek of every American citizen. It was a crime unparalleled since the persecution of the Quakers by the Puritans; was committed by a country posing as the refuge of the world's oppressed—the chief exponent of individual liberty. There was not the slightest danger that polygamy would become a serious menace to American morals; the attempt to engraft it permanently upon Anglo-Saxon civilization were as futile as the labors of the Del Rio idiot to convince men who have circumnavigated the globe, that it is flat as a cellar floor. Instead of warring upon the seraglios of the Latter Day Saints, we should have considered ways and means for the abolishment of our own bagnios. We should have gotten the beam out of our own eye before going for the mote in the optic of the Mormon. The Church of the Latter Day Saints would have quickly perished had we let it alone. A religious craze thrives on persecution—"the blood of martyrs is the seed of the church." Having mur-

dered the founder of the new faith, we drove his followers—men, women and children—into the snow-clad, bliz-
zard-cursed western waste. It was not a social convulsion
that expelled the Mormons from the older states, but religious intolerance pure and simple. New York, where
Joe Smith began his ministry, suffered a free-love colony
to exist in its midst in peaceful prosperity; but the Mormons were aggressive proselytizers and thereby evoked
the undying enmity of other religious sects. Polygamy,
as subsequently practiced, appears to have had no place in
the Mormon cult until after the murder of Joe Smith; but
they were hated and harried as vindictively by their
Christian neighbors before as after it became an accepted
tenet of their faith. They were expelled, not because of
their immorality, but because of difference with their
neighbors anent religious dogma. They abandoned their
magnificent city of Nauvoo, their fruitful farms and pleasant homes in Illinois and Missouri, and tramped resolutely a thousand miles into the wilderness, hoping that
they might there enjoy that religious liberty to which
they were entitled as American citizens. Tireless industry
soon retrieved their fallen fortunes, but with prosperity
came the development of polygamy. Utah was at once denounced as a moral plague-spot demanding heroic treatment, and the Federal officials became the agents of the
new persecution. I rejoice that polygamy exists no longer
on American soil; but the remedy adopted was infinitely
worse than the disease. Religious liberty and local self-
government are the very pillars of this Republic, and the
integrity of both was fiercely assailed in our dealings with
the Latter Day Saints.

It is questionable whether we have done the monogamic doctrine any real good by the persecution of a few
polygamists. Our crusade sufficed to call the world's attention to the fact that, while dominated by the polygamous Saints, Utah was a veritable Arcadia, practically
free of pimps and prostitutes, bloated millionaires and
groveling mendicants—strange contrast to those communities where our religious ideas and code of social
ethics have long been paramount. It has served to remind
untold millions that, while accepting the Hebrew prophets and patriarchs as God's anointed, we have persistently hounded as public enemies a people who moulded their
social life by those divine models. True, Abraham, Isaac
and Jacob lived in an age of general ignorance; but if they
had Graeco-Roman wrestling matches with angels, fed
those feathered songsters and washed their feet, we may

presume that they learned how many female bosses is
permitted to the average pilgrim—whether polygamy is
displeasing to the Lord. Of course the old dispensation
has passed away; still it is difficult to imagine the Almighty permitting a sawed-off dude like King Solomon to
have a thousand pretty women and compelling a fine
lusty animal like the Rev. Jehovah Boanerges Cranfill to
worry along with one.

Furthermore, the anti-Mormon crusade has set the anthropologists to prattling again; and, shocking as it may
seem to our modern civilization and its monogamic ideas,
they are inclined to agree with Solomon that it is difficult
for a man to get too much of a really good thing. Science
does not show much respect for modern creeds and cults,
environment and education; but tells us plainly that man
is naturally a polygamous animal—even intimates that a
thousand years of monogamy, strictly enforced, would
sweep the human race from the face of the earth. Progressive physicians inform us *sub rosa,* of course—that
loss of virility is the reward of male virtue—even prescribe an occasional violation of moral law as a preventa-
tive of impotency. This is indeed a serious matter, and I
submit it to my brother ministers and humbly ask: What
are we going to do about it? Does the Seventh Commandment repeal the imperative order issued to Adam
and Eve to be fruitful and multiply? That is a knotty
theological problem which should be decided without delay, and I move that it be referred to the faculty of Baylor
University.

Monogamy has become with us a sacred thing, the citadel of social purity; and I am in nowise responsible for
the demoralizing example of King David, the beloved of
the Lord, nor for the conclusions of science that it runs
counter to the law of man's life.

If the conclusions of the anthropologists be correct—
which I am not prepared to admit, and it were presumption to deny—the question naturally arises: Were it better for the race considered either morally or physically,
that man should have a plurality of wives, or only one legal mate and many mistresses? that he should legitima-
tize all his children and accord them a father's care, or
disown a part—turn them adrift to grow up as best they
may beneath a social blight? Were it better that their
mothers have a legal claim upon him for life, and feel that
they are within the pale of respectability, or remain the
mere creatures of his caprice and suffer a social ostracism
that is more demoralizing than the worst of marriage sys-

tems? The seraglio or the bagnio—which shall it be, oh brother ministers mine? Is the courtesan more desirable to our civilization than the concubine? We have answered this important question in one way, the Mormons in another. I believe that the Gentiles are in the right. I opine that a handful of women, who are true wives, are worth more than untold millions living lives of legalized concubinage. I believe that of monogamic marriage were born the bravest and brainest men that ever fronted destiny. Still, candor compels the admission that the polygamists have both science and the cumulative wisdom of sixty centuries on their side, while we are little more than experimentalists, who may be riding to a fall. In the discussion of all problems of such import, we should be rigidly honest with both our opponents and ourselves. In considering the relation of the sexes we should remember that marriage, the most sacred of our human institutions, had its origin in selfish lust. When men attempt to live together in communities that they may be mutually helpful, they must, perforce, make rules for the measurement and conservation of individual rights. The institution of marriage, like the law against theft, was originally intended to guarantee to each male member of the community peaceable possession and enjoyment of his property. From such an unseemly grub sprung the winged Psyche which we now worship. Female purity was not handed down from heaven like Promethean fire; it was born behind the war-club and developed with the criminal code. It is sometimes necessary to a proper understanding of the phenomena with which we are confronted, to examine the compost from which springs the Rose of Sharon. Careful examination into the origin and development of social and religious phenomena signs the death warrant of dogmatism and makes us tolerant of the ideas of others. The more a man knows the more he doubts. Wisdom stammers while Ignorance out-bawls Stentor. Fools approve or condemn according to the creeds and customs to which they are born; the philosopher rises superior to his environment and education and views human institutions and habits by the light of the whole world's history.

Polygamy has gone, but America has forever lost her reputation for religious tolerance. Columbia can pose no longer as the champion of liberty of conscience. The man who desires to worship God according to the dictates of his own conscience had best charter a balloon. The Mormons are drifting to Mexico, and while these home-builders and desert-subduers are going out at one gate, the anarchists and ignorami of Italy and Russia are rolling in at the other. Even the Mormons who remain, and have renounced polygamy, are subjected to gross indignities. We send our missionaires among the Mohammedans and Buddhists of Asia to destroy the time-honored faith of their fathers, and shield them from insult with double-shotted guns. If one of them chance to catch an o'er ripe egg in his ample ear, we shriek about "Moslem fanaticism" and demand that the government tie loose the dogs of war; but let a Mormon elder come into a Christian community and begin proselyting for his faith — even since shorn of polygamy—and he is given time to leave town. Should he stand upon the order of his going, instead of humping himself down the plank turnpike with his back to the burg, he is treated to a coat of tar and feathers, supplemented by a ride on a triangular rail. The fact is that despite our boasted civilization and prattle anent freedom of thought, we are about the most narrow-brained bigots and intolerant fanatics to be found on God's foot-stool. Our very atheists are dogmatists in their denial; our agnostics are pharisees in their pride of ignorance, while the American definition of a liberalist is a man who thinks as he durn pleases and protests against others exercising the same prerogative.

POTIPHAR'S WIFE.

STORY OF JOSEPH REVISED.

For more than six-and-thirty centuries the brand of the courtesan has rested on the brow of Potiphar's wife. The religious world persists in regarding her as an abandoned woman who wickedly strove to lead an immaculate he-virgin astray. The crime of which she stands accused is so unspeakably awful that even after the lapse of ages we cannot refer to the miserable creature without a moan. Compared with her infamous conduct old Lot's dalliance with his young daughters and David's ravishment of Uriah's wife appear but venial faults, or even shine as spotless virtues.

The story of Mrs. Potiphar's unrequited passion may be strictly true; but if so the world has changed most wondrously. It transcends the probable and rests upon such doubtful *ex parte* evidence that a modern court would give her a certificate of good character. It is not in accord with our criminal code to damn a woman on the unsupported deposition of a young dude whom she has had arrested for 'attempted ravishment. Had Joseph simply filed a general denial and proven previous good character we might suspect the madame of malicious prosecution; but he doth protest too much.

Mrs. Potiphar was doubtless a young and pretty woman. She was the wife of a wealthy and prominent official of Pharaoh's court, and those old fellows were a trifle exacting in their tastes. They sought out the handsomest women of the world to grace their homes, for sensuous love was then the supreme law of wedded life. Joseph was a young Hebrew slave belonging to Mrs. Potiphar's husband, who treated him with exceptional consideration because of his business ability. One day the lad found himself alone with the lady. The latter suddenly turned in a fire alarm, and Jacob's favorite son jogged along Josie in such hot haste that he left his garment behind. Mrs. Potiphar informed those who responded to her signal of distress that the slave had attempted a criminal assault. She is supposed to have repeated the story to her husband when he came home, and the chronicler adds, in a tone of pained surprise, that the old captain's "anger was kindled." Neither Mrs. Potiphar's husband nor her dearest female friends appear to have doubted her version of the affair, which argues that, for a woman who moved in the highest social circles, she enjoyed a reasonably good reputation.

But Joseph had a different tale to tell. He said that the poor lady became desperately enamored of his beauty and day by day assailed his continence, but that he was deaf to her amorous entreaties as Adonis to the dear blandishments of Venus Pandermos. Finally she became so importunate that he was compelled to seek safety in flight. He saved his virtue but lost his vestments. It was a narrow escape, and the poor fellow must have been dreadfully frightened. Suppose that the she-Tarquin had accomplished her hellish design, and that her victim had died of shame? She would have changed the whole current of the world's history! Old Jacob and his other interesting if less virtuous sons, would have starved to death, and there would have been neither Miracles nor Mosaic Law, Ten Commandments nor Vicarious Atonement. Talmage and other industrious exploiters of intellectual tommyrot, now ladling out saving grace for fat salaries, might be as unctuously mouthing for Mumbo Jumbo, fanning the flies off some sacred bull or bowing the knee to Baal. The Pot-

iphar-Joseph episode deserves the profoundest study.   It
was an awful crisis in the history of the human race!

How thankful we, who live in these latter days, should be
that the female rape fiend has passed into the unreturn-
ing erstwhile with the horned unicorn and dreadful hippogriff, the minotaur and other monsters that once affrighted the fearful souls of men—that sensuous sirens do
not so assail us and rip our coat-tails off in a foul attempt
to wreck our virtue and fill our lives with fierce regret.
True, the Rev. Parkhurst doth protest that he was hard
beset by beer and beauty unadorned; but he seems to have
been seeking the loaded "schooner" and listening for the
siren's dizzy song.   Had Joseph lived in Texas he could
never have persuaded Judge Lynch that the lady and not
he should be hanged.   The youngster dreamed himself into
slavery, and I opine that he dreamed himself into jail. With
the internal evidence of the story for guide, I herewith present, on behalf of Mrs. Potiphar, a revised and reasonable
version of the *affaire d'amour.*

Joseph was, the chronicler informs us, young, "a goodly
person and well favoured."   His Hebraic type of manly
beauty and mercurial temperament must have contrasted
strangely with Mrs. Potiphar's dark and stolid countrymen.   Mistress and slave were much together, the master's
duties requiring his presence near his prince.   Time hung
heavily on the lady's hands and, as an ennui antidote, she
embarked in a desperate flirtation with the handsome fellow, for Egypt's dark-eyed daughters dearly love to play
fast and loose with the hearts of men.   Of course it was
very wrong; but youth and beauty will not be strictly
bound, the opportunity seemed made for mischief, and Mrs.
Potiphar cared little for her lord—a grisly old warrior who
treated her as a pretty toy his wealth had purchased, to
be petted or put aside at pleasure.

A neglected wife whose charms attract the admiring eyes
of men may not depart one step from the straight and
narrow path, but her husband's honor stands ever within
the pale of danger.   Let that husband whose courtship
ceased at Hymen's shrine, who is a gallant abroad and a
boor at home, keep watch and ward, for homage is sweet
even to wedded women.

While Potiphar played the petty tyrant and exacted of
his wife a blind obedience, Joseph sang to her songs
she loved—plaintive tales of tender passion, of enchanted
monarchs and maids of matchless beauty.   He culled the
fairest flowers from the great garden and wove them into
garlands to deck her hair, dark as that lingering night which

Moses laid upon the Valley of the Nile. He gave her a thousand little attentions so grateful to womankind, and worshipped her, not presumptuously, but with the sacred awe of a simple desert child turning his face to greet the rising sun. They were of the same age,—that age when the heart beats in passionate rebellion against cold precepts, the blood riots in the veins like molten rubies and all life seems made for love, for day dreams golden as the dawn, for sighs and sweet companionship. What wonder that she sometimes left her lord to his heavy slumbers and crept into the cool gardens with the handsome Hebrew boy; that they walked, hand clasped in hand, beneath the tall palms that nodded knowingly, and whispered sweet nothings while the mellow moonlight quivered on the Nile and sad Philomela poured forth her plaintive song like a flood of lover's tears? All day long they were alone together, —those children of the world's youth, when life was strong and moral law was weak. When the summer sun rode high in heaven and sent his burnished shafts straight down into the white streets and swooning gardens; when the great house was closed to shut out the blinding glare and in the court cool fountains cast their grateful spray, what wonder that she bade him sit at her feet and sing the love songs of his native land, wild prototypes of those which Solomon poured from the depths of his sensuous soul to his sweet Rose of Sharon?

"Behold thou art fair, my love, behold thou art fair;
Thou hast dove's eyes, thy lips are like a thread of scarlet,
Thy breasts like young roes that feed among the lilies.
Set me as a seal upon thy heart, a seal upon thy arm,
For love is strong as death, jealousy is cruel as the grave."

The song dies out and the languorous stillness is broken only by the splashing of the fountains in the great marble basins and the drowsy hum of a bee among the blossoms. The lad's head has sunk down upon the lady's knee and she is watching the tears trembling on his drooping lashes and wondering, with a little thrill of pain, if he has a sweetheart in his own land, of whom he is so sadly dreaming. She thanks him for the song in a voice low and sweet as the musical ripple of the sacred river among the reeds— she dazzles him with her great Egyptian eyes, those ebon orbs in which ever lurks the sensuous splendor of a summer night's high moon. Her hand strays carelessly among his curls as she punctuates with sighs and tears his oft-told tale of unkind brethren, the gloomy cave, the coat of many colors dipped in blood of the slaughtered kid, the cruel goad of godless Midianite, driving him on and on thro' burning sands and 'neath a blazing sun, far from his tearful mother and mourning sire. How cruel the fates to con sign to slavery one born to be a king! His master is a hard man and covetous, but her pleadings shall yet purchase sweet liberty for old Jacob's son, that he may fulfill the high dreams of which he has told her—may answer the midnight messages of Israel's God and triumph over those wicked brethren. Perhaps—who knows?—in his own land he will become a mighty prince and treat with proud Pharaoh on equal terms. Will he remember her, his only friend in a land of foes? Will he think of her when Ammon is o'erthrown and proud Moab pays his tribute? Ah, no! When a crown of jewels blazes on his brow and the sack-cloth of the slave is exchanged for imperial purple, he'll think no more of the lonely little woman by Nilus bank, who prays that Isis will magnify his power, that Osiris will shield him when the Hebrew sword rings on the Hivite spear. He will take to wife some fair cousin of Esau's house, a maid more beauteous far than those who drink the sweet waters of the south. Old Abram's daughters are fair and have dove's eyes; their lips are as threads of scarlet and their breasts like young roes that feed among the lilies. Does not the song say so? But those of Egypt—oh, unhappy Egypt!

"Love is strong as death, jealousy is cruel as the grave."

She bends low and whispers the line upon his lips, while her fragrant breath, beating upon his cheek, sinks into his blood like the jasmines' perfume,—more dangerous to the soul than Aphrodite's kisses or Anacreon's drunken song. By such arts did Cleopatra win the master spirit of the world and make the mailed warrior her doting slave, indifferent alike to honor and to duty, content but to live and love. What wonder that the callow shepherd lad, unskilled in woman's wile, believed that his mistress loved him?—that his heart went out to the handsome coquette in a wild, passionate throb in which all Heaven's angels sang and Hell's demons shrieked!

A beautiful woman! Not the beauty of Greece, on which we gaze as upon some wondrous flower wafted from Elysian Fields, and too ethereal for this gross world; nor that of Rome, with Pallas' snow-cold bosom and retrospective eye; but the sensuous beauty of the far south, that casts a Circean spell upon the souls of men. Her eyes are not dove's eyes that softly shine along the path to Heaven, but wandering fires that light the way to Hell. Her lips are not a thread of scarlet, chaste as childhood and dewy as the dawn, but the deep sullen red of a city swept with flames. Her breasts are not like young roes that feed among the lilies, but ivory hemispheres threaded with purple fire and tinged with sunset's tawny gold. Reverently as though touching divinity's robe, Joseph caresses the wanton curls that stream like an inky storm-cloud over the shapely shoulders—he puts the little hands, heavy with costly gems, back from the tearful face and holds them with a grasp so fierce that the massy rings of beaten gold bruise the tender flesh. Mrs. Potiphar starts up, alarmed by his unwonted boldness—she reads his face with a swift glance that tells her he is no longer a lad, a pretty boy to be trifled with for the amusement of an idle hour. The Cupid's bow had faded forever from his lip and childhood's innocence from his eye; he has crossed life's Rubicon, has passed at one stride from the Vale of Youth with its trifles and its idle tears, its ignorance of sex and stainless love, to Manhood's rugged mountains, where blazes Ambition's baleful star and the fires of passion ever beat, fiercer than those that sweep Gehenna's sulphurous hills.

Even while her cheek crimsons with anger and her heart flutters with fear, the woman glories in Joseph's guilty love, sweet incense to her vanity, evidence of her peerless beauty's infernal power. She retreats a step as from the brink of an abyss, but farther she cannot fly, for there is a charm in her companion's voice, potent as old in dreams by maids who sleep in Dian's bosom, yet wilder, fiercer than trumpets blown for war. As a sailor drawn to his doom by siren song, or a bird spellbound by some noxious serpent, she advances fearfully and slow until she is swept into his strong arms and held quivering there like a splotch of foam in a swift eddy of the upper Nile. The room swims before her eyes and fills with mocking demons that welcome her to the realm of darkness; the fountains' ripple sounds like roaring thunder, in which she reads the angry warning of Egypt's gods, while beneath the accursed magic of the kisses that burn upon her lips, her blood becomes boiling wine and rushes hissing thro' a heart of vice. The mocking demons turn to angels with Joseph's handsome face and crown her with fragrant flowers: the thret'ning thunders to music sweet as Memnon's matin hymn or accepted lover's sighs, heard 'neath the harvest moon,—she is afloat upon a sapphire sea beneath a sunset sky, the West Wind's musky wing wafting her, whither she neither knows nor cares.

But the angels and the fragrant flowers, the music sweet as lover's sighs and the sapphire sea, the sunset sky and

Zephyrus' musky wing are dreams; the blistered lips and
poor bruised bosom, the womanly pride humbled in the
dust and wifely honor wounded unto death—these alone
are real! With an involuntary cry of rage and shame, a cry
that is half a prayer and half a curse—a cry that rings
and reverberates through the great sleepy house like a
maniac's shriek heard at midnight among the tombs—
she flings herself sobbing and moaning upon the marble
floor. The drowsy slave starts up as from a dream, quivering in every limb like a coward looking upon his death.
He tries to raise the groveling victim of his unbridled
lust, but she beats him back; he pleads for mercy, but she
calls him ungrateful slave, base Hebrew dog and prays all
Egypt's gods to curse her conqueror. There's a rush of
feet along the hall, there's a clash of weapons in the court,
and here and there and everywhere tearful maids are cail-
ing to their mistress, the Sweet One and Beautiful, dear
Daughter of the Dawn, Lily of the Nile, while brawny
eunuchs, barelimbed and black as Hell's own brood, are
vowing dire vengeance even upon the King himself if he
has dared to harm her. The culprit glances with haggard
face and wildly pleading eyes at the woman, once so imperial in her pride, now cowering a thing accursed, clothed
only with her shame and flood of ebon hair. The great
sun, that hung in mid-heaven like a disc of burnished brass
when she first forgot her duty, descends like a monstrous
wheel of blood upon the western desert and thro' the case-
ment pours a ruddy glow over the prostrate figure—a marble Venus blushing rosy red. Joseph casts his coarse garment over his companion as one might clothe the beauteous
dead, and turns away, the picture of Despair, the avatar of
guilty Fear.

*   *   *

Love is a dangerous game to play, and oft begun
in wanton mischief ends in woeful madness. In the first
flush of shame and rage Mrs. Potiphar was eager to punish
the siave's presumption, even tho' herself o'erwhelmed in
his ruin; but hate, tho' fierce, is a fickle flame in the female
heart, and seldom survives a single flood of tears. Already Joseph's handsome face is haunting her—already
she is dreaming o'er the happy hours by Nilus' bank, where
first he praised her wondrous beauty—beneath the nodding palms when the fireflies blazed and the bulbul poured
its song. The love that has lain latent within her bosom,
or burned with friendship's unconsuming flame, awakes like
smouldering embers fanned by desert winds and fed with
camphor wood, enveloping all her world. She longs to

leave the loveless life with her sullen lord; to cast from her
as things accursed the gaudy robes and glittering gems;
to fly with the shepherd lad to the deep cool forests of the
far east and dream her life away in some black tent or
vine-embowered cot—to take his hand in hers and wander
on to the world's extreme verge, listening to the music of
his voice. The great house, once her pride, has become a
gruesome prison, the jailor a grizzly gorgon who conjured
her with the baleful gleam of gold to cast her beauty on
Mammon's brutish shrine. She hardens her heart
against him and pities herself, as wives are wont to do who
have dragged the dear honor of their husbands in the dust—
she persuades herself that love has cast radiant glory about
her guilt and sanctified her shame. Oh woman, what a
paradox thou art! When the descending sun touched the
horizon's rim Mrs. Potiphar could have plunged a poisoned
dagger through the heart of her paramour and mocked his
dying moan; the great globe of fire has not bid the world
good night, yet she is weeping because of the bitter words
with which she drove him forth.

"Love is strong as death."

She repeats the line again and again. Oh my Israel, is
the grave the limit of thy love? Wert thou dead, fair boy,
Egypt would enclose thy sacred ashes in a golden urn and
wear it ever between her breasts—would make for thee
a living sepulchre and thou shouldst sleep in the vale of
Love, between the rosy mountains of Desire. Wert thou
dead—

The slaves! They will tell their master the wild words
she spoke against her love—against his life. She must
seal their lips, must command their silence. Too late!
Even as she lays her hand on the silver bell the heavy
tread of her husband's brass-shod feet is heard in the
long hall, ringing upon the bare stone floor in rapid, nervous rhythm, so different from the usual majestic tread of
Pharaoh's chief slaughterman. The slaves have already
spoken! A faintness as of death falls upon her; but she
is a true daughter of false Egypt, and a wiser than Potiphar
would find in her face no shadow of the fear that lies heavy
on her heart. The game is called and she must play not for
name and fame, but for love and life. Her husband confronts her, ferocity incarnate,—the great cord-like veins
of the broad, low brow and massive neck knotted and
black, his eyes blazing like the orbs of an angry lion
seen by the flickering light of a shepherd's fire. He essays
to speak, but his tongue is thick, his lips parched as one
stricken with the plague, and instead of words there comes

through his set teeth a horse, hissing sound as of the great rock serpent in its wrath. His glance falls upon Joseph's garment, the gleaming sword leaps from its sheath and he turns to seek the slave. She lays her hand lightly upon his arm, great Egypt's shield, a pillar of living brass; she nestles in the grizzly beard like some bright flower in a weird forest; she kisses the bronzed cheek as Judas did that of our dear Lord and soothes him with pretty truths that are wholly lies.

Joseph is a good boy, but sometimes over-bold. Poor child! Perhaps her beauty charmed away his senses and made him forget his duty. She bade him sing to beguile a tedious hour, and he sang of love and looked at her with such a world of worship in his eyes that she grew angry and upbraided him. Let it pass; for, by the mystic mark of Apis, she frightened the boy out of his foolish fever.

She laughs gleefully, and the gruff old soldier suffers her to take his sword, growling meanwhile that he likes not these alarms—that she has marshalled Egypt's powers to battle with a mirage. The game is won; but guilt will never rest content, and oft reveals itself by much concealment. It is passing strange, she tells him tearfully, that every male who looks upon her, whether gray-headed grand-sire or beardless boy, seems smitten with love's madness. She knows not why 'tis so. If there is in her conduct aught to challenge controversy she prays that he will tell her. The old captain's brow again grows black. He leads her where the fading light falls upon her face, and, looking down into her eyes as tho' searching out the secrets of her soul, bids her mark well his words. The wife who bears herself becomingly never hears the tempter's tone or knows aught of any love but that of her rightful lord. Pure womanhood is a wondrous shield, more potent far than swords. If she has been approached by lawless libertine, he bids her, for the honor of his house, to set a seal upon her lips, instead of bruiting her shame abroad as women are wont to do whose vanity outruns their judgment.

*   *   *

Potiphar determines to watch his wife. It had never occurred to him that she could possibly go astray; but he has learned from her own confession that she is a flirt, and he knows full well that a married coquette is half a courtesan. Suspecting that Joseph's offense is graver than his wife set forth, he casts him into prison. The inexperienced youth, believing the full extent of his guilt has been blazoned to the world, and frightened beyond his

wits by armed men and clank of chains, protests with
tears and sighs that he is more sinned against than sinning. It is the old story of Adam improved upon—he
not only damns the woman, but denies the apple.

Joseph's posterity, hating Egypt with their whole heart
and intent on glorifying Israel and Israel's God, became
the only historians of this original scandal in high life; and
thus was a youth, probably neither better nor worse than
his brethren, raised to the dignity of a demi-god, while a
vain young wife is condemned through all the ages to wear
a wanton's name. The story probably contains a moral—
which wives may look for if they will.

* * *

Of course this account of Mrs. Potiphar's seduction is
a fancy sketch; but it is a true pen-picture of what too often
happens in this fair land of ours, and may be perused with
profit by many a Benedict. The number of unfaithful
wives whose sin becomes the public shame is simply appalling; yet no criminal was ever so cautious, so adept
in the art of concealment as the woman who values her reputation above her honor. There is no secret a man will
guard with such vigilance as his *amours,* no copartner in
iniquity he will shield with such fidelity as a paramour.
The bandit may turn state's evidence, and the assassin
confess beneath the noose; but the *roue* will die protesting
that his mistress is pure as the driven snow.

And yet woman is by nature as true to her rightful
lord as the needle to the magnetic north,—as faithful to her
marriage vows as the stars to their appointed courses.
When a wife "goes astray" the chances are as one to infinity that the mis-step is her husband's fault. Love is the very
life of woman. She can no more exist without it than
the vine can climb Heavenward without support,—than it
can blossom and bear fruit without the warm kiss of the
summer sun. Woman's love is a flame that must find an
altar upon which to blaze, a god to glorify; but that sacred
fire will not forever burn 'mid fields of snow nor send up
incense sweet to an unresponsive idol, even tho' it bear
the name of husband. The man who courts the wife as
assiduously as he did his sweetheart, makes the same sacrifice to serve her, shows the same appreciation of her
efforts to please him, need never fear a rival. He is lord
paramount of her heart, and, forsaking all others, she will
cleave unto him thro' good and thro' evil, thro' weal and
thro' woe, thro' life unto death. But the man who imagines his duty done when he provides food, shelter and fine

raiment for the woman he has won; who treats her as if she were a slave who should feel honored in serving him; who vents upon her hapless head the ill-nature he would like to pour into the faces of his fellow-men, but dares not, were wise to heed the advice which Iago gave to the Moor.

Woman is more subtle than her ancient enemy, the serpent, and woe to the man who attempts to tread her beneath his feet! True it is that all women who find the hymenial rites but an unreading of that enchanted spell in which they worshipped devils as demi-gods; between whose eager lips the golden apples of Hesperides prove but Dead Sea fruit; for whom the promised Elysium looms but a parched Sahara, do not seek in forbidden fields to feed their famished hearts; but it is well for the peace of mind of many a husband who neither dotes nor doubts, that black dishonor oft goes hand in hand with blissful ignorance.

The philosophic world rejects the story of Joseph, having long ago learned that he-Dians live only in childish legend and Della-Cruscan poetry. As an ideal it reverses the natural relation of the sexes; as an example it is worse than worthless, for instead of inspiring emulation the young Hebrew's heroic continence only provokes contempt. Men worship at the shrine of Solomon's wisdom, of Moses' perseverance, of David's dauntless courage, but crown the altar of Joseph with asses' ears. Such foolish Munchhausenisms give to young girls a false idea of the opposite sex, relax their vigilance and imperil their virtue. From such ridiculous romances, solemnly approved by an owl-like priesthood, sprung that false code—so insulting to womankind—that a wife's honor is not committed to her own keeping, but to the tender care of every man with whom she comes in contact. When a wife goes wrong a hypocritical world rises in well-simulated wrath—which is too often envy—and hurls its anathema maranatha at the head of the "designing villain," as tho' his companion in crime were born without brains and reared without instruction! The "injured husband"—who probably drove his wife to the devil by studied neglect that starved her heart and wounded her vanity—is regarded with contempt if he does not "make a killing" for a crime against the social code which he would himself commit.

I paint man as I find him, not as I would have him. I did not create him, or did his Architect ask my advice; hence it is no fault of mine that his virtue's frail as ocean foam—not mine the blame that while half a god he's all a beast. Mentally and sexually man is a polygamist, and, whatever its moral value may be, monogamy does violence to the law of his being. It is a barrier against which he ever beats like some wild beast of prey against restraining bars. Give him Psyche to wife and Sappho for mistress and he were not content—would swim a river to make mad love to some freckled maid. It is likely that Leander had at home a wife he dearly loved when he lost his life trying to reach fair Hero's bower. That the Lord expects little even of the best of men when subjected to beauty's bland-ishments is proven by his partiality to various princes and patriarchs who, in matters of gallantry, may be regarded as pace-setters.

I am not the apologist of the godless rake, the defender of the *roue;* but I have small patience with those mawkish purists who persist in measuring men and women by the same standard of morals. We might as well apply the same code to the fierce Malay who runs amuck and to McAllister's fashionable pismires. We might as wisely bring to the same judgment bar Bengal's royal beast, crazed with lust for blood, and Jaques wounded deer, weeping in the purling brook. Each sex and genus must be considered by itself, for each possesses its peculiar virtues and inherent vices. In all nature God intended the male to seek, the female to be sought. These he drives with passion's fiery scourge, those he gently leads by maternal longings, and thus is the Law of Life fulfilled,—the living tide runs ever on from age to age, while divine Modesty preserves her name and habitation in the earth. A man's crown of glory is his courage, a woman's her chastity. While these remain the incense rises ever from Earth's altar to Heaven's eternal throne; but it matters not how pure the man if he be a cringing coward, how brave the woman if she be a brazen bawd. Lucrece as Caesar were infamous, and Caesar as Lucrece were a howling farce.

BRO. EARLY'S BAZOO.

THE FOREIGN MISSION FAKE.

I am always discovering something new and strange. While Prof. Roentgen is experimenting with the X ray and Dr. Depew is unearthing ante-diluvian almanac jokes, I am bringing to the garish light of day wonderful differen-tiations of the intellectual doodlebug. I am not wont to boast over-much of my services to science; still it is but

fair that I be accorded due credit for having discovered
Dr. Jehovah Boanerges Cranfill, where he lay buried in the
sub-stratum of the azoic period by the anti-prohibition
majority, and the Hon. Whoopee Kalamity Homan, of
Dallas, after he had been trodden into the quicksands
by the political bull elephant.   And now patient research
in the field of micrology has been rewarded by the addition
to my cabinet of curios of Rev. M. D. Early, superintendent
of missions for the State of Texas.   He is also managing
editor of a Baptist periodical whose name I disremember.
My discovery of Early was purely an accident.   He was
out on the "Katy" road, giving the Iconoclast a "roast" that
made the paint on the car-ceiling curl.   He lamented that
people persisted in purchasing such a paper, while that into
which he poured his sacred lucubrations would not sell.   As
he talked his indignation grew until he was telling his
troubles to the entire car.   The tearful lamentations of Jeremiah and the uncanny yodel of Jonah were as nothing to
the heart-ache which Supt. Early poured forth because of
the literary perversity of the American people.   He insisted
that he had never read a copy of the Iconoclast and would
not do so, yet declared it awfully immoral, which proves that
Early is a great man.   He does not have to acquire knowledge by patient industry like other people, but takes it by
absorption as the sponge does stale beer on a mahogany bar,
and when he wants to leak it he has only to squeeze his
nice soft head.   Like the patient ox and the megalophanous
ass, Early is guided by instinct.

I regret that the good man cannot secure patrons for
his paper.   If the copy I have seen be a fair sample, the
public is missing much by giving it the frozen face.   It is
almost as interesting and equally as coherent as the sermons of Sin-Killer Griffin, or the editorial page of the
Houston *Post*.   Reading it were like standing in the vortex
of chaos and trying to size up the phenomena.   It is the
province of intellectual topsy-turvy, where the living lie dor-
mant and the dead do gibber in the streets.   When the
writers are serious the reader is convulsed, and when they
uncork their wit the wooden tobacco signs weep.   It is
a journalistic *rara avis* that none with a taste for the bizarre
should let go by.   Now is the time to subscribe.   I am determined to work up such a circulation for the *Missionary
Mistake* that Supt. Early need no longer subsist on pennies
torn from the toy savings banks of babes.   It may be well
enough for small-fry preachers to fill their lank bellies with
candy money coaxed from kids in the name of Christ; but
a man calling himself a journalist should be above such

shameful business. Of the hundreds of thousands of dollars collected annually in this country for the ostensible purpose of informing the Ahkoond of Swat that Christ is dead, by far the greater part comes from the thin purse of poverty and the chubby hand of childhood. What becomes of this cash? I am told that $2,500 per annum goes to pay the salary of this one State Superintendent. That represents 250,000 pennies per year taken from children's pockets. If each state has a missionary superintendent and Early's is the average salary, here is a snug item of $112,500 per annum paid men by the very poor to ride about the country and advertise the Iconoclast. Then there is the national organization, the secretaries and other salaried officers, not to mention the money appropriated to the support of missionary journals guiltless of readers, and to pay pet publishing houses for the printing of tracts and other utterly useless tommyrot. Think of the little tin savings banks despoiled to supply the missionary fund! And not one dollar in three collected ever gets east of Castle Garden, while the small percentage that does sift abroad might just as well be squandered here at home, for the so-called labors of our foreign missionaries have had about as little effect on "paganism" as Bro. Early's paper on the public. It has been estimated by men who have spent much time abroad, that it cost $14,000 to convert a Buddhist to Protestant Christianity, and nearly double that sum to pull a Mussulman loose from his prophet. Yet while we are peddling high-priced saving grace in pagan lands, our own country is cursed with godless heathen and reeking with crime, and in the garrets of our great cities starving mothers give the withered breast to dying babes. It will be time enough to carry bibles to barbarians when our own children are provided with bread.

The Protestant missionaries have made precious little progress in their attempt to convert the "heathen," but they have done much to engender bitterness and precipitate fanatical outbreaks, such as those recently witnessed in China, and now making a hell of Armenia. As a rule the Catholic missionaries adapt themselves to the customs of the country and win the respect of the people. They have sufficient tact to appeal to the taste of barbarians by impressive ceremonies, and aid their understanding by the use of religious symbols, while others attempt to cram into the heads of intellectual infants abstruse tenets that puzzled even the scholastics. They substitute the host for heathen charms, the crucifix for the caaba-stone, and, by teaching savage people the gentle arts of peace, bring them gradually to a full realization of the love and power of God. How far "the plotting Jesuit stoops to conquer," what "unholy compromises he makes with heathendom" I do not know; but experience has amply proven that the Catholic missionary is, while his Protestant brother is not, capable of combating successfully the dark superstitions of semi-savagery. The former can go alone among the most murderous tribes and win his way; the latter must be protected from outrage by the double-shotted guns of his government. A Catholic mission makes for peace; a Protestant mission is a storm-center of physical strife. I am not a Catholic—all my education and environments make for Protestantism; but the whole truth should be told, however it may hurt. The reformer, like the surgeon, must sometimes be cruel in order to be kind. The Protestant missionaries begin wrong. They denounce as crass heathendom everything that runs counter to their creed, whether it be paganism or a differentiation of their own religious cult. They affect a superiority to the people they are sent to serve, insult their holiest traditions, and when this brutish folly and unbridled insolence results in violence to themselves, appeal to their home government for protection and preach a war of extermination. They are usually forced upon barbarous nations as was opium upon "Pagan China" by "Christian England," and protected by ships of war while they denounce people who dissent from their religious dogma.

About two years ago a Baptist missionary stationed in Mexico—and living on the fat of the land by the same means that Dr. Early receives his $2,500 salary—issued a pamphlet grossly insulting to the people of that Republic. He was mobbed by the outraged populace and sentenced by the courts to acquire the art of courtesy in the penitentiary. Of course a tremendous roar anent this "Mexican atrocity" was made to the American government, and the consul-general succeeded in securing his release. He protected him from the mob and landed him safely on the soil of Uncle Sam, when Mr. Missionary at once began a tirade of abuse of Catholics in general and Mexicans in particular. The diplomat said quietly: "Had Mexico given you your just deserts she would have shot you as a professional mischief-maker or caged you for life as a malicious damphool. I extricated you from the penitentiary and protected you when you were scared to death and afraid to run. My mother was a Catholic. Now take my advice and head for the rising sun."

That is a fair sample of Protestant missionary endeavor in both the Occident and the Orient. That's what the kids are giving up their toys and tidbits for! Our theological exportations belong to the same class with Early—men who condemn without investigation; who consider that in the little knots on the end of their necks God has *cached* all the wisdom of the world. They are the intellectual heirs of those Smart Alecks who condemned Christ unheard, poisoned Socrates on an idle supposition and refused to even consider the Copernican theory lest they get an idea into their fat heads that would fracture their theological hats.

GOLD, SILVER AND GAB.

Talking Our Industries to Death.

It was said of old that "speech is silver and silence is golden." Yet people wonder that Cleveland has to sell bonds to keep the "reserve" intact, while the supply of silver seems to be inexhaustible! Clearly the parity of the two metals is impossible until this generation applies a Westinghouse brake to its tireless jawbone.

The wordy war now raging between the gold and silver advocates—the "robbers" and the "repudiators," the "soaptails," and "tool of Wall Street"—indicate that the foolkiller is enjoying a furlough. Deafened by the universal din, wading neck deep in the turgid tide of dialectical ditchwater, I fain would exclaim with Mercutio, "A plague on both your houses!"

In the name of the great horned beast, what is this earsplitting, nerve-destroying cackle all about? The currency? —and not one in ten thousand of those who are forcing so much foul air thro' their faces could define a "dollar" to avoid being damned! It's a political war for pie, rather than a legitimate controversy anent our currency. There's just one jackass on earth with longer ears than the free-silver agitator who isn't after office, and that's the goldite who's weeping anent "repudiation" while he hasn't a dollar at interest. The two should be tethered out in the American desert, where their braying would disturb nobody, and they could comfortably kick each other to death. I sometimes think that the great American public keeps its head open so much that the sun shines into its bazoo and sours its brain.

There is no "currency problem" outside the minds of a few plotting politicians, who want "pap," and their dupes, who eagerly embrace every opportunity to air their ignorance. While featherless geese have gabbled, business men cut the knot of Gordius. The case of gold vs. silver is now of precious little more importance to this people than that of Bardell vs. Pickwick.

Commerce has practically removed our exchange media beyond the jurisdiction of congress, and is now giving us an elastic currency, which adapts itself automatically and infallibly to the requirements of the country. The occupation of governmental money is almost gone. It has been supplanted by what some economists call a "deposit currency," but which I prefer to nominate a mercantile money. If money be but "a tool that trade works with—an exchange medium"—then is our commercial or deposit currency, by means of which 93 per cent. of all exchanges are effected, entitled to be classed as money. However, we will not pause in the midst of the howling babelian mob to split hairs —there are too many damphools trying to "save the country" by the science of definition.

More than a hundred years ago Dr. Adam Smith, the greatest of all economists—barring, of course, those Solomonic twins, Hardy and Dudley, of Texas—advised governments that they need not worry much anent the currency, as commerce is competent to provide itself with ample exchange media; and there is certainly less occasion now than then for political intermeddling.

Year by year commercial paper has been doing more and more of our money work; year by year it has been rendering governmental currency of less and less importance, until to-day we find Cleveland and Carlisle, Stewart, Peffer, and all their paladins and peers tearing their blessed undershirts anent an exchange media employed only in the most trifling transactions, representing less than 7 per cent, of our volume of business! Think of making a red-hot, hell-roaring political "issue" anent the amount of copper in the penny! Yet the cent coinage bears about the same relation to the volume of governmental money that the latter does to the entire currency of commerce. Hundreds of millions of dollars are received and paid out every day without the shifting of a coin, the transfer of a paper dollar. Checks and drafts have so far supplanted the old-time "money current with the merchant" that the cashiers of great business concerns almost forget the existence of a national currency.

Buying and selling, it must be remembered, is but a convenient method of barter, and commerce naturally seeks the best possible intermediary. In olden time gold and silver, being indestructible commodities and representing large values in small bulk, constituted the exchange media. To avoid the trouble of weighing and testing with every trade the weight and fineness were stamped on each piece of metal, and it thus became money. As civilization progressed, paper representatives were substituted for the cumbrous metals, and exchange thereby expedited. The next improvement in the trade-tool was the bank check or draft, which is but the shadow of a shade—the promise of an individual, which may be exchanged at the option of the holder for a promise of the government. It does the necessary money-work as well as gold, and far more expeditiously than any other exchange medium yet devised.

The money issued by government amounts to about two billions. As it is equal to less than 7 per cent. of the money-work required by commerce, we may reasonably infer that it is supplemented by more than 28 billions of commercial currency, making an actual circulating media of some 30 billions; yet we are asked by the silverites to believe that the country will go to hades awhooping if half a billion more is not added to this enormous sum, while the goldites are equally certain that such inflation would amount practically to a repudiation of all debts!

I implore both parties to this idiotic controversy to be calm. Opening the mints to the white metal could not inflate, nor would the utter destruction of all silver coin contract the volume of our currency. Commerce will use no more than it needs, while, if we may believe Adam Smith and the evidence of our own eyes, it will have as much as its necessities may require. If the volume be sufficient you cannot force government money into the channels of trade without displacing an equal amount of commercial currency. Contract the volume of governmental money and commerce at once provides a substitute. It were strange indeed if the Yankee, with all his shrewdness, could not manage to "swap" corn for cotton and soap for sad-irons except by the grace of an omnium-gatherum of pot-house politicians yclept the American congress! It is to expeditiously effect exchanges that we need an intermediary —a "wheel of circulation." Whatever serves this purpose well is "good money," tho' made of the hickory shirt-tails of Texas Populists; that which serves it ill is "bad money," tho' it be gold of Ophir or pearls of Ind.

"But," I am told, "the almighty dollar must be back of every check and draft, just as it is behind the greenback and silver certificate." Quite true; but what is a dollar? It is something that was never seen of man—was never coined or counted. It is a pure abstraction, a thing supposed, a term by which we express the relative value of one commod-

ity to all other commodities. It is our unit of value, and
would stand, tho' all the gold and silver were sunk a thousand fathoms into the sea. A gold coin does not measure
the value of a bushel of corn one whit more than the corn
measures the value of the metal in the coin. The "dollar"
—the unit of value—measures both, expresses their commercial relation to all other commodities. But let us concede
the truth of the dogma of financial transubstantiation; let
us admit that 25.8 grains of gold constitute a sure-enough
dollar instead of a foolish trade fiction handed down to us
from ancient days: What then? Are our commercial checks
and governmental greenbacks based only upon the gold coin
extant in this country? or upon all the gold in the world,
coined and uncoined, mined and unmined? A promissory
note, payable in gold, is not based upon the amount of yellow metal in the possession of its maker, but on his aggregate wealth—his ability to command gold. The real basis
of our circulating media, governmental and commercial, is
the wealth of the makers. Our astute economists of the
Cleveland school, insist that unless 100 millions of gold be
kept horded up as a guarantee fund, Uncle Sam's promises
to pay will not do the money-work required of them, while
93 per cent. of all our exchanges are effected by means of a
currency made by the people from day to day, and guiltless
of a governmental guarantee.

The "currency question" is really the most ridiculous
craze that ever took possession of a supposedly intelligent
people. "Money," as the term is generally understood, is
becoming of less importance in the world's economy every
day. In a few years more our system of commercial exchanges will be so perfected that government currency will
become a curiosity.

One would suppose from the tearful plaints of the "soaptails," that the country was suffering because of a dearth of
white dollars; from the clamor of the "cuckoos" anent "our
commercial relations with gold-using countries," that our
entire foreign trade depends upon an abundance of the yellow metal. We have, in fact, more silver than can be kept
in circulation, and we cannot use one dollar of any kind in
our international trade. Our money will not circulate in
Europe, that of other countries does not pass current here.
When gold or silver crosses the Atlantic it does so as merchandise and not as money, as a commodity and not as currency.

The idea that free coinage of silver would cause a general revival of business is the merest moonshine. We already have more trade tools than trade. Money transfers

the ownership of wealth from hand to hand, just as a railway moves merchandise from place to place.   When a
company has sufficient cars for its carrying trade were not
the manager an ass to put on more and run them empty?
the theory that it would "bring us down with a crash to the
50-cent silver basis" and smash the immortal ichor out of
business, is unworthy any man of brains.   It might, in con-
formity with Gresham's law, drive out gold; but you cannot
arbitrarily change the commercial standard of value by an
alteration of less than one-seventh of our circulating media.
To a fool, a bob-tail may appear to wag a big dog; but the
wise man knows that the canine controls his caudal append-
age.   The war era certainly demonstrated to both North and
South that the unit of value may be one thing, and the circulating medium quite another.

It is urged that the silver agitation is depressing the value
of our bonds and securities held abroad.   If true, this is indeed distressing; still it might be well to allow our foreign
creditors to do half the worrying.   As we can pay our foreign debts only with our products, valued in the currency of
the country to which they are carried, the tears with which
the goldites are drowning our transatlantic creditors seem
to be a wicked waste of water.

Mexico is frequently cited as an awful example of the
evils of free silver.   Were I a sixteen-to-oner I'd weave
our sister Republic into song and sing her on every stump.
I could pour forth a strain of argentiferous melody that
would transform Peffer's whiskers into a halo of glory and
waft him into the White House, while Carlisle regretted that
he sold his presidential birthright for a bad mess of cabinet
pottage.   We are told that wages are nominally lower in
Mexico than with us, and are paid in currency one-half the
value of our coin; that the country is poverty-stricken, in
debt, and has to give two silver dollars for one of gold with
which to meet the interest on her bonds.   Granted.   Now
let's view the other side of the hen-coop awhile: For ten
years past wages have been rising in Mexico and declining
in Texas.   You can procure more of the necessaries and
comforts of life over there with a Mexican dollar than here
with an American gold dollar.   And that's no fairy tale—
I've tried it.   For instance: You can buy a better cigar for
5 cents, Mexican money, in the land of the Montezumas, than
with 15 cents gold-basis coin in McLennan county.   Mexico
pays her foreign indebtedness with her products, just as she
does her big sister on this side of the Rio Grande.   If she
sometimes buys gold with her silver "dollars" at the ratio
of two to one, she is only giving two pints for a quart, two

halves for a whole, so there's nobody hurt. The Eastern states of our Union, which are making the most noise anent the "50-cent dollar," ship their capital clear across this blessed gold-standard country and invest it in free-silver Mexico. The country is still poor and labor scandalously cheap; but it is a semi-barbarous Indian nation that is but now feeling the thrill of progress, while America has been peopled with the dominant race for more than two centuries. Skilled white workmen obtain better wages in Mexico— both nominally and relatively—than with us; common Mexican labor receives precious small pay on both sides of the Rio Grande, but the least it gets is usually more than it is worth. The plea that free silver coinage is responsible for low wages in Mexico is rank dishonesty. Spain is the "mother country" of Mexico and South America. She is on a gold, while they are on a silver basis. According to the United States consular reports, the average weekly wages paid the building trades in Spain is $3.80. In Mexico it is $10, in Peru and Venezuela $9. The same disproportion prevails in all occupations. Italy is on a gold basis, and the average weekly wages of her shoemakers is $2; in Mexico and South American countries it ranges from $9 to $12, and this disproportion extends to all occupations. Wages are five times as high in the United States as in many other countries, some on a gold, some on a silver basis, which clearly demonstrates that wages may be high or low regardless of the character of the currency. It is time the people ceased listening to these partisan blatherskites, with governmental axes to grind, and considered economic questions solely upon their merits.

It is not free silver that is pushing Mexico to the front despite the general worthlessness of her people. Her progress is chiefly due to the fact that commerce there knows pretty well what it can depend upon,—is not clapper-clawed every new moon to make a political picnic. Commerce can adapt itself to almost any condition and prosper if assured that said condition will be permanent; but when change is ever imminent capital plays a waiting game or emigrates, while labor goes hungry to bed. If we would either double our tariff tax or abolish it altogether; if we would either open our mints to the unlimited coinage of the white metal, or dispense with silver currency altogether, then adopt a constitutional amendment making it a capital offence for a congressman to even discuss these matters during the next dozen years, industry would quickly revive and America blossom like a rose. Our commerce is being killed by too much economic cackle. Everybody from "Cyclone" Davis down to the "Little Giant," from G. Cleveland up to "General" Coxey, is prescribing for the country, and prostrating it with their feculent lung power. All it needs is to be let alone. Men and brethren, go cork yourselves.

WOMAN IN JOURNALISM.

This subject is at present receiving a great deal of attention from writers of both sexes, the women insisting that they are doing much to elevate journalism, while not a few male critics flatly accuse them of bringing the craft into contempt. The time is not yet come to correctly estimate woman's worth or worthlessness in this new field of her endeavor. She is not thoroughly "broken in harness;" not educated to the elimination of sex in the practice of her profession. We have as yet few women who, in the terminology of the craft, are competent to "hold down" any department of a great daily; but we have a veritable swarm of female scribblers and scrawlers laying claim to the journalistic toga. The South can boast but one "lady journalist" in the strict construction of that term; and this rara avis in newspaperdom is a Texas product. I allude, of course, to Julia Truitt Bishop, now of New Orleans.

The late Mrs. Nicholson, also of the Crescent City, was, I believe, a newspaper proprietor and thrifty business manager rather than a working editor; and your thoroughbred newspaper man does not consider "the gang down stairs" even distantly related to the brotherhood of the "brainery." They are pariahs, altogether without the pale—mere hucksters for the creative power. Mrs. Bishop is competent to "stop a gap" in any department of a great newspaper, from the composing room to the sanctum of the chief. There's a force and finish to all her work that adds charm even to a sluggish market report and makes the most pitiful sassiety slop palatable. Her mind is peculiarly masculine. She has nothing in common with that crowd of petticoated scribblers who are "padding" so many of our Southern dailies with inane drivel. It is somewhat remarkable that in all that has been written of late about the "lady journalists" of the South her name has not been so much as mentioned. The Will Allen Dromgoozles and other noisy purveyors of literary hogwash are dragged in on every occasion; but the impression appears to be general—because she works so quietly and so well—that Madame Bishop is a man. Such women—women who do the work of men in the making of great newspapers and refrain from mounting to the housetop to exhibit themselves as abnormalities — are certainly a credit to the craft; but candor compels the admission that they are few and far between. As a rule women are either dilettanti in journalism or professional panders to an unhealthy literary appetite. Thus far the newspaper labor of the Southern ladies has been, for the most part, confined to chronicling the inconsequential doings of society, inflicting school-girl essays on an inoffensive public, organizing press clubs and throwing bouquets at themselves. Publishers employ them to keep tab on Mrs. Hamfat Krupper and sound the alarm when Chappie Chrysanthemum changes his cravat; not because they can do this work better than their brothers, but because they will do it cheaper—and a self-respecting male journalist is apt to jump such a job. A number of sensational sheets, like the unsavory nuisance known as the New York *World,* have employed women to fall off ferry-boats, get locked up in lunatic asylums or girdle the globe alone and without a change of lingerie, then spill their ever useless and ofttimes offensive experiences upon the public. Women have actually been detailed by such panders to the prurient as Josef Spewlitzer to interview pugilists, flirt in the parks with professional mashers, visit hovels of prostitution—to subject themselves not only to certain insult, but to the dangers of criminal assault—to add spice to "great family journals." The female pencil pushers of whom we hear the most are built on the model of Nellie Bly. Personally they may be pure as the lilies of the field for aught I know; but their neurasthenic slumgullion is no credit to their sex. It is even more meretricious than such putrescent papers as the *Police Gazette,* for it is usually cloaked with a specious morality that gives it *entree* to the home, while the *Gazette* stops at the 10-cent barber-shop and the nigger saloon. To call these sensation-mongers "journalists" were equivalent to designating a faith-cure fraud as a physician. According to Webster any regular writer for the press is a journalist; but the term is applied by the craft only to those who can transform a few sheets of blank paper into a mirror of the world. Col. McCullagh of the *Globe-Democrat* once defined journalism as "knowing where hell will break loose and having a reporter on the spot." Magazine and sketch writers are not journalists in the usual acceptance of the term. Unquestionably many bright and noble women are employed in minor capacities on legitimate newspapers. They are useful or they would not be retained. Some of them may develop into Greeleys or Bennetts, Danas or McCullaghs for aught I know; but while in this peculiar field of ephemeral literature a number of women have acquired unsavory notoriety, none have attained to eminence. Woman's experience in journalism has thus far proven even more unsatisfactory than her attempts upon other professions. All the great women lawyers and doctors, scientists and essayists, politicians and preachers may be counted on the fingers of the two hands. They are never path-finders in the great field of knowledge. In all the hoary centuries woman has originated no religious cult, made no great discovery, enunciated no fundamental law. As a poet, dramatist and novelist she has risen high; but far above and beyond the most exalted of her sex stand the thousand immortelles. Women are flocking into journalism and medicine in larger numbers than into the other professions. Why I know not, unless it be that these offer greatest opportunity for charlatanism. They are rapidly appropriating to themselves the dirty work of both professions—the unhealthy sensationalism of the one and abortion practice of the other. The ratio of female to male physicians is probably less than 1 to 100, yet competent authorities estimate that one-half the crimes against motherhood must be laid at the door of the "lady" doctors. The ratio of women to men in newspaper work is probably less than 1 to 12; yet a careful examination of the "great" dailies will demonstrate that at least half the intellectual slime that is befouling the land is fished out of the gutter by females.

ADAM AND EVE.

After God had expended five days creating this little dog-kennel of a world, and one in manufacturing the remainder of the majestic universe out of a job-lot of political boom material, he "planted a garden eastward in Eden, and there he put the man he had formed." Adam was at that time a bachelor, therefore, his own boss. He was monarch of all he surveyed and his right there was none yet to dispute. He could stay out and play poker all night in perfect confidence that when he fell over the picket fence at 5 g. m. he would find no vinegar-faced old female nursing a curtain lecture to keep it warm, setting her tear-jugs in order and working up a choice assortment of snuffles. There were no lightning-rod agents to inveigle him into putting $100 worth of pot metal corkscrews on a $15 barn. He didn't care a rap about the "law of rent," nor who paid the "tariff tax," and no political Buzfuz bankrupted his patience trying to explain the silver problem. He didn't have to anchor his smoke-house to the center of gravity with a log chain, set a double-barrelled bear trap in the donjon-keep of his hennery nor tie a brace of pessimistic bull-dogs in his melon patch, for the nigger preacher had not yet arrived with his adjustable morals and omnivorous mouth. No female committees of uncertain age invaded his place of business and buncoed him out of a double saw-buck for the benefit of a pastor who would expend it seeing what Parkhurst saw and feeling what Parkhurst felt. Collectors for dry-goods emporiums and military parlors did not haunt him like an accusing conscience, and the pestiferous candidate was still happily hidden in the womb of time with the picnic pismire and the partisan newspaper. Adam could express an honest opinion without colliding with the platform of his party or being persecuted by the professional heresy-hunters. He could shoot out the lights and yoop without getting into a controversy with the chicken-court and being fined one dollar for the benefit of the state and fleeced out of forty for the behoof of thieving officials. He had no collar-buttons to lose, no upper vest pockets to spill his pencils and his patience, and his breeches never bagged at the knees. There were no tailors to torment him with scraps of ancient history, no almond-eyed he-washer-woman to starch the tail of his Sunday shirt as stiff as a checkerboard.

Adam was more than 100 years old when he lost a rib and gained a wife. Genesis does not say so in exact words, but I can make nothing else of the argument. Our first parents received special instructions to "be fruitful and multiply." They were given distinctly to understand that was what they were here for. They were brimming with health and strength, for disease and death had not yet come into the world. Their blood was pure and thrilled with the passion that is the music of physical perfection—yet Adam was 130 years old when his third child was born. If Adam and Eve were of equal age a marriage in American "high life"—the mating of a scorbutic dude with a milliner's sign—could scarce make so poor a record. After the birth of Seth the first of men "begat sons and daughters" —seems to have become imbued with an ambition to found

a family. As the first years of a marriage are usually the
most fruitful, we may fairly conclude that our common
mother was an old man's darling. Woman does not appear to have been included in the original plan of creation.
She was altogether unnecessary, for if God could create one
man out of the dust of the earth without her assistance he
could make a million more—could keep on manufacturing
them as long as his dust lasted. But multiplication of
"masterpieces" was no part of the Creator's plan. Adam
was to rule the earth even as Jehovah rules the heavens. As
there is but one Lord of Heaven, there should be but one
lord of earth—one only Man, who should live forever, the
good genius of a globe created, not for a race of marauders
and murderers but for that infinitely happier life which we
denominate the lower animals. This beautiful world was
not built for politicians and preachers, kings and cuckolds;
but for the beasts and birds, the forests and the flowers, and
over all of life, animate and inanimate, the earthly image
of Almighty God was made the absolute but loving lord.
The lion should serve him and the wild deer come at his
call. The bald eagle, whose bold wings seem to fan the
noonday sun to fiercer flame, should bend from the empyrean at his bidding, and the roe bear him over land and
sea on its broad pinions. As his great Archetype rules the
Cherubim and Seraphim, so should Man, a god in miniature, reign over the earth-born, the inhabitants of a lesser
heaven. As no queen shares God's eternal throne, so none
should divide the majesty of earth's diadem. There is
neither marrying nor giving in marriage, we are told,
among the angels. They rise above sex, into the realm of
the purely spiritual, scorning the sensual joys that are the
heritage of bird and beast, for intellectual pleasures that
never pall; and why should Man, the especial object of
God's providence, be grosser than his ministers?

Were I a poet I would ask no grander theme than Adam's
first century upon the earth—that age of gold when Man
was sufficient unto himself. A century undisputed master
of the world! A century of familiar converse in Eden's
consecrated groves with the great First Cause—the om-
nipresent and omnipotent God. Picture one day of such
existence! Ambition and Avarice, Jealousy and Passion,
those demons that have deluged the world with blood and
tears, have no place in Adam's peaceful bosom. He is not
in the Grove of Daphne, where lust is law, but in the
Garden of God where love is life. His subjects, not dumb
as now, or speaking a language strange to our dull ears,
greet him as he comes forth at break of day from his

aromatic bower. A thousand feathered songsters drown his
soul in melody divine, while every bud and blossom, a living censer, sways in the balmy breath of morn and pours
forth its grateful perfume. The forest monarch lays his
massy head on Adam's knee, the spotted leopard purrs
about him and the fawn nestles between his feet. High
above the Caucasian peaks a condor poises motionless in
mid-heaven, the unrisen sun gilding him as with beaten
gold. Now the saw-like summits, cloud-kissing and crowned
with eternal snow, burst into the brilliant sea and gleam
like the brow of God, while the purple mists are drawn up
from the deep valleys as tho' the giants fain woud hide
from earth their splendors, reserving them alone for heaven.
Higher and higher wheels the great sun, driving the river
mist before it and sending down through the softly whis-
pering foliage a thousand shafts of burnished gold that seek
out the violet, drain the nectareous dew-drop from its
chalice and kiss the grape until its youthful sap changes to
empurpled blood beneath the passionate caress. In the
cool shadows by the great spring—a magic mirror in whose
pellucid depths are reflected heaven's imperial concave and
Eden's virgin splendors—God walks familiar with Adam
as with a younger brother, explains to him the use and
beauty of all that is, and spreads before his wondering
eyes Creation's mighty plan.

And yet God suspects that Adam is not content, for we
hear him soliloquizing: "It is not good that the man should
be alone." The clay of which the first of men is formed is
beginning to assert itself. He watches the panther fondling
his playful cubs, the eagle's solicitude for his imperial
brood perched on the beetling crag, and the paternal instinct awakes within him. He hears the mocking-bird
trilling to his mate, the dove pitying the loneliness of Creation's mystic lord, and a fierce longing for a companionship
dearer than he has yet known takes possession of him. To
the swarming life about him his high thoughts are in-
comprehensible; in God's presence his soul swoons beneath an intellectual glory to which he cannot rise, encumbered as he is by earthly clay. He sends his swift-
winged messenger forth to summon before his throne every
fowl of the air and every beast of the field. Down thro'
the gates of the garden they come, countless thousands, and
pass before their king. "But for Adam there was not found
a helpmeet for him." Sick at heart he turns away. The
sunset has lost its glory, the spheres their music, life its
sweetness. The beams of the moon chill his blood and
Arcturus leads forth his shining sons but to mock his bar-

renness.   The flowers that wreathe his couch stifle him with
their sensuous perfume and he flies from the nightingale's
passionate song as the slave flees the scourge.   Thro' the
dark paths and over the moss-grown boulders he stumbles
on, across the fields where the fire-flies glow like showers
of flame, beneath the tall cedars whose every sigh seems
drawn from the depths of an accepted lover's soul.   Exhausted, he sinks down where the waters burst from the
foundations of the earth and, dividing into four, seem to
reiterate in ceaseless monotone, "Behold my mighty sons."
A feeling of utter loneliness, of hopeless desolation falls
upon him, such as hammers at the heart when Death has
despoiled us of all that Life held dear.   He pillows his
head upon the sleeping lion and shields himself from the
sharp night air with the tawny mane.   A cub, already hunting in dreams, comes whining and nestles down over his
heart, while Love's brilliant star pours its splendors full
upon his face.   The long black lashes, burdened with un-
shed tears, drop low, a drowsiness falls upon him and
Adam sleeps.   The heavens are rolled together like a scroll
and God descends in the midst of a legion of Angels, brightest of whom is Lucifer, Son of the Morning, not yet forever
fallen.   "It is not good that the man should be alone."   The
fitful slumber deepens; the winds are hushed; the song of
the nightingale sinks lower and lower, then ceases with an
awe-struck sigh; the lynx and the jackal, the horned owl
and the scaly serpent slink away into the deepest wood,
while Love's emblem glows like a globe of molten gold.
Then comes a burst of melody divine, beneath which the
earth trembles like a young maid's heart when, half in
ecstacy, half in fear, she first feels burning upon her own
the bearded lips of her life's dear lord.   It is the Morning
Stars singing together!   There is a perfumed air on Adam's
cheek, sweeter than ever swooned in the rose garden of
Cashmere or the jasmine bowers of Araby the Blest; there
is a touch upon his forehead softer than the white dove's
fluttering bosom; there is a voice in his ear more musical
than Israfeel's marshaling the Faithful in fields of asphodel, crying, "Awake my lord!" and the first of men is
looking with enraptured soul upon the last, best work of an
all-wise God, a beautiful woman.

THE LOCAL OPTION LUNACY.

[Mr. Brann was billed to lecture at Hillsboro, Texas, on the eve of the local option election. The Antis took possession of the opera house and changed his subject. Following is a synopsis of his address:]

Ladies and Gentlemen: I came here to talk on "Gall," and I find that I must speak on "Prohibition"—a distinction without a difference. I hold in my hand a printed challenge from the Prohib committee to meet Hon. W. K. Homan in joint debate to-night—a challenge issued when they were well aware that I was to lecture here this evening. They felt certain that I would not forego a lecture fee to mix it with them without money and without price; but they didn't know their man. I'm always willing to make some sacrifice to secure the luxury of a red-hot intellectual scrapping match. We proposed to make it a Midshipman Easy duel, a three-cornered fight—Brothers Homan and Benson vs. the "Apostle," but they wiggled in and they wiggled out, they temporized and tergiversated until we saw there wasn't an ounce of fight in the whole Prohibition crew—that, after their flamboyant defi, we couldn't pull' em into a joint debate with a span of mules and a log-chain. I last saw Bro. Bill Homan at Hubbard City. He was getting out of town on the train I got in on—after promising that he would remain over and meet me. In his harangue the night before he told his auditors that I'd simply "abuse the church and make ugly faces." Well, I didn't abuse the church on that occasion, nor upon any other, albeit I sometimes make it a trifle uncomfortable for some of its unworthy representatives. I cannot help "making ugly faces." It's my misfortune, not my fault. I was born good and Bro. Bill was born beautiful. He's the Adonis of the rostrum, the Apollo Belvidere of the bema. He's so dodgasted "purty" that the children cry for him. Had he come to earth two thousand years ago some Grecian goddess would have stolen him. Bro. Bill couldn't make an ugly face if he tried. If he ever catches sight of his own personal pulchritude as reflected in some translucent lake, I much fear that he'll meet with the fate of Narcissus. Some of you Prohibs don't know who Narcissus was. Well, he was one of those fellows whom cold water killed.

I'm no professional anti-Prohibition spouter, and have been jumped up here without preparation; but it occurs to me that it requires no careful rehearsal of set orations before an amorous looking glass, no studied intermingling of pathos, bathos and blue fire to demolish the Prohibition fallacy. Liberty is ever won by volunteers; the shackles of political and religious slavery are forged by the hands of hirelings. Prohibition cannot withstand the light of logic, the lessons of experience, nor the crucible of the commonest kind of common sense.

Milton tells us that the angel Ithuriel found the devil "squat like a toad," distilling poison in the ear of sleeping Eve; that he touched the varmint with his spear, and forthwith Satan resumed his proper shape and fled shrieking out of Paradise. Prohibition is another evil spirit that is breeding trouble in man's Eden; but when touched by the spear-point of legitimate criticism its disguise falls away, and we see, instead of a harmless toad, a malicious Meddlesome Mattie stirring up strife and bitterness among brethren.

Whenever a man opposes the plans of the Prohibs he is forthwith denounced as an enemy of morality, a slave of the saloons, a hireling of the Anheuser-Busch Brewing Association. Well, I had rather be the emissary of the saloons than the assassin of liberty, the slave of a brewer than the blind peon of ignorant prejudice, while if morality consists in attending to my neighbor's business to the neglect of my own, then I'm ferninst it, first, last and all the time. As a good German friend of mine once remarked, "Dot beoples who lives py stones shouldn't trow some glass houses, haind id?" Who is making money out of this agitation? The professional Prohibs. Did you ever know of one of these gentry making a Prohibition speech except for filthy lucre—unless he was electioneering for office or taking subscribers for a cold-water journal? They are the cattle who are *out for the stuff;* they are the mercenaries—the men who pump foul air thro' their faces for a fee. Did you ever hear of a man getting paid for defending the doctrine of personal liberty? Did you ever see a collection taken up at an anti-prohibition meeting to pay some important spouter for pointing out to the people their political duty? (A voice: "Nix.") And you never will. These prohibition orators have the impudence to denounce me as "the peon of the rum power" while I am fighting the battles of personal liberty at my own cost, yet not a dad-burned one of 'em will open his head unless paid for his wind-power! They are "reformers" for revenue only.

I have noticed that, as a rule, men who speak against Prohibition have never been in the gutter, while those who pick up a precarious livelihood by chasing the "Rum Demon" around a stump have usually been his very humble slaves. I have noticed that the men who oppose Prohibi-

tion are usually the solid, well-to-do men of the community,
the heavy tax-payers the men upon whom the schools, the
churches and the state chiefly depend for support, while
those who champion it on the rostrum are usually living in
some way upon the industry of others. The man who has
brains enough to make money and keep it usually has too
much sense to be a Prohibitionist. It is the fellows who
have made a failure of life; who live on donations; who
weep over the world's wickedness, then take up a collection
to enable them to get to the next town; who haven't sufficient moral stamina to stay sober, that are prating of
Prohibition. If we required a property franchise you
couldn't muster five thousand Prohibition votes between
the Sabine and the Rio Grande.

And yet we are told that licensing the saloons is a bad
business investment; that it costs more than it comes to;
that the way to abolish poverty is to abrogate the liquor
license law. Strange that the Prohibs should possess such
transcendent business heads and such empty stomachs!
Doubtless the drinking of liquor adds to the cost of our judiciary; doubtless it is responsible for some crime; but the
question at issue is not one of liquor-drinking vs. teetotalism
—it is a question of drinking licensed liquor or Prohibition
aquafortis. It is not a question of reducing the cost of our
courts, but of making liquor bear its due proportion of
the burdens it foists upon the people.

I am neither the friend nor enemy of liquor, any more
than I am the enemy or friend of buttermilk. I have drank
both a third of a century and have been unable to see that
they did me any especial good or harm. I was never befuddled on the one nor foundered on the other, and have
managed to get along very well with both. Whether in
eating or drinking, a man should keep his brains above
his belt, and if he cannot do that he's a precious poor excuse for an uncrowned King, an American Sovereign.

The statistics furnished by the Prohibition orators are
fearfully and wonderfully made. It has been asserted in
this campaign that a million Americans die every year
of the world from the effects of strong drink—and all this
great army goes direct to hell. The man who made that
statement is a preacher, and presumably familiar with the
Bible; but he has evidently overlooked the story of Ananias and Saphira. I learn from the United States census
report, which I hold in my hand, that in the very year in
which this Prohibition apostle claims a million Americans
were slain by strong drink, the statistical experts could find
but 1,592 victims of John Barleycorn. The doctors have

ever claimed that more people die of over-eating than of over-drinking, and the census report bears out the assertion, for in the year in which 1592 people were filed away by "alcoholism," 30.094 deaths are accredited to "diseases of the digestive organs." What causes indigestion? Over-eating, or eating food difficult of digestion. Now I submit that if Brothers Benson, Homan, *et al,* are trying to save the people of this land from premature graves and bear the stock of the coffin trust, they should direct their crusade against indigestible food,—reduce the people of this Nation by means of statutory law to a diet of cornbread and buttermilk. Let them bring all their ballistae and battering-arms to bear upon the toothsome mince pie, the railway sandwich, the hard-boiled egg and pickled pigs' feet—that pestilence that walks in darkness. Indigestion is indeed a fruitful source of crime. It casts the black shadow of chronic pessimism athwart the sunniest soul and transforms happy homes into dens of despair. It makes men irritable, morose, and prompts them to homicide. Who can tell how much misery and crime the wretched cookery of female Prohibitionists is responsible for? How the cost of our criminal courts might be reduced if these she-reformers would but attend to their kitchens and dish up for their lords and masters grub that would more easily assimilate with the gastric juices! If a man be fit for treasons, stratagems and spoils when loaded with a half a pint of red licker, what must be the condition of his mind and morals when he's full of sodden pie, half baked beans and soda-biscuits that if fired from a cannon would kill a bull?

The theory that strong drink is an unmixed evil that must be abolished, is not in accord with the genius of this government, which would give to the individual untrammeled liberty in matters concerning only himself. Experience has proven Prohibition a rank failure and the customs of mankind from the very dawn of history brand it a rotten fraud. The people of every age and clime have used stimulants, and we may safely conclude that, despite the Prohibs, they will be employed so long as man exists upon the earth. Banish liquor and man will find a substitute—even tho' it be opium, morphine or cocaine. It is said that Thor, the great northern god of war, once tried to lift what he supposed was an old woman, but found to his sorrow that it was a mighty serpent which, in Norse mythology, encircles the world. The Prohibs are warring upon what they foolishly imagine to be frivolous habit of man, but will yet learn that they are running counter to an immutable decree of God—are trying to alter the physical constitution of the human race by means of local option elections.

So far as I am personally concerned, I would care but little if every ounce of liquor was banished from the earth and its method of manufacture forever be forgotten; but I object to having a lot of he-virgins and female wall-flowers sit at my muzzle and dictate how I shall load myself. If I'm an American sovereign I propose to be supreme autocrat of my own stomach. When I want advice regarding what I shall eat and what I shall drink I'll consult a doctor of medicine instead of a doctor of divinity.

I do not oppose Prohibition because I am the friend of liquor, but because I am the friend of liberty. I would rather see a few boozers than a race of bondmen. I am not interested in preserving the liquor traffic, but I am interested in the perpetuation of those principles that ennoble a people and make manly men—men who rely upon themselves for their social salvation rather than upon a public policy which may change with the phases of the moon or the arrival of some new demagogue from distant parts. I have but little use for men who must swing to the apron-strings of a public grand-dame or go to the dogs. Let us reserve the nursery for children. Men whom we cannot trust with the guardianship of their own appetites should not be allowed to run at large. How would you young ladies like to marry "American Sovereigns" who must be tied up, like a lot of mangy cayuses when white clover is in blossom to keep 'em from catching the "slobbers?"

But, the Prohibs inform us, the brightest men of the world are ruined by strong drink. They assure us that "it is not a question of intellect, but of appetite." What was judgment given us for if not to control our appetites? If appetite be paramount to judgment why do we hang rape-fiends? Let me tell you the idea that the brainiest men of the world die drunkards is the merest moonshine. If only men of genius drank liquor a one-horse still would supply the demand and be idle six months in the year. Take the thousand greatest men the world has produced —the Thousand Immortelles—and not 2 per cent. of them died drunkards, yet 98 per cent. of them drank liquor. If the Prohibs have ever produced an intellect of the first class they must have hidden it under a bushel. Its possessor is probably one of those village Hampdens or mute inglorious Miltons of whom the poet sings. The Prohibs don't run to great men—they run to gab.

Stripped of all its superfluous trappings, the thesis of Prohibition is simply this: "Some men drink to excess; therefore no one should be permitted to drink at all. The human race must reserve its inherent tastes and time-honored habits lest some wild-eyed jay get on a jag." The question at issue, the riddle for us to unravel, is simply this: Can we afford to sacrifice human liberty to save the sots? Is the game worth the candle, and if we burn the candle will we win the game?

The Pros assure you that Prohibition prohibits. It does. It prohibits the sale of liquor and supplies its place with coffin paint. It prohibits the sale of good, ice-cold beer and gives us forty-rod bugjuice. Theories are not worth a continental when slammed up against conditions. What I hear I take with a grain of salt; but what I see that I do know. I tell you candidly that next to a pretty woman I love a cocktail. If the liquor is good and the barkeeper understands his business, I consider it a thing to thank God for—occasionally. Like religion, a little of it is an excellent thing, but an overdose will put wheels in your head. I have never yet been in a Prohibition precinct where I needed to go thirsty if I had the price of a pint flask concealed about my person—and my stomach could stand the poison.

When high license prevailed in Hillsboro you had a dozen saloons, each contributing to the revenues of the state, the country, the municipality and the school fund. You voted local option in, and now you've thirty-two unlicensed and unregulated doggeries selling rot-gut to schoolboys and contributing not one cent to the public revenues. The cost of your courts has increased, drunkenness was never so common, brawls never so frequent. It is said that even fools can learn in the bitter school of experience; but there be idiots upon whom even such lessons are lost. But you say, "Vote local option in again and we'll elect officers who will enforce the laws." Have you yet to learn that a law cannot be enforced that is not steadily upheld by public opinion? And do you not know that there's not a considerable town in Texas where public opinion demands at all times a strict enforcement of such a law? If you really desire to have a sober city, raise a purse and hire the operators of your blind tigers to place their booze on the sidewalk in buckets, accompanied by tin dippers and signs, "Help yourself—funerals furnished free." Men would then run away from the very smell of the stuff who now sneak up dirty alleys and pay 15 cents

for the privilege of poisoning themselves. On the same
principle some men—and they are not all anti-Prohibs
either—will leave a beautiful and charming wife to mope
at home while they are flirting with some female whose
face would frighten a freight-train. Man is just like a dog
—only more so. Perhaps a marauding old muley cow
would be a better comparison. A muley cow will eat anything on this majestic earth that she can steal, from a
hickory shirt to a Prohibition newspaper, and if she can't
get it thro' her neck she will chew it and suck the juice.
That's human nature to a hair. Man values most what is
hardest to get. And until you reverse the law of nature
the legitimate effect of Prohibition will be blind tigers and
back-door sneaks, the breeding of spies and the sale and
consumption of an infinitely meaner brand of booze.

That liquor has done a vast amount of damage I freely
concede; but shall we banish everything that has added to
the mighty tide of human ills? Then what have we left?
A hole in the atmosphere. God has not bequeathed to man
an unmixed blessing since he expelled him from Paradise.
Even woman, his last, best gift, hath grievous faults. The
very first one brought into this world, according to Pagan
legend and Holy Writ, was the author of all our ills. But
for her we would be to-day in a blessed state of innocence,
where mothers-in-law and millinery bills, political issues
and itinerant preachers, mental freaks and professional
reformers, jim-jams and jag cure joints disturb us not. Instead of all this toil and trouble we would lie like gods reclining on banks of asphodel, pull the heavenly bell-cord
when hungry and live on from age to age, ever young
Apollos. Perhaps the Almighty made a mistake when he
gave to man a wife, and another when he gave him the
vine; but when he corrects 'em I'll crawl off the earth.

Woman has filled the world with war's alarms, and the
bacchic revel has ended in the brawl. Troy flamed because
Menelaus' wife was false, and Philip's all-conquering son
surrendered to the brimming bowl. Ever is our dearest
joy wedded to our direst woe. The same air that comes
stealing round our pillow, laden with the sensuous perfume of a thousand flowers, rips our towns to pieces and
turns our artesian wells inside out. The same rains that
fructify the earth pour the destructive flood. The same intellectual power that bends nature's mighty forces to
man's imperial will, enables him to trample upon his
brethren. The same reckless courage that breaks the tyrant's chain ofttimes stains the hand with a brother's
blood. The same longing for woman's sweet companion-

ship that leads these to rear happy homes—sacred shrines from which incense mounts night and day to the throne of Omnipotent God—goads those to lawless love. The empurpled juice that warms the cold heart and stirs the sluggish blood that gives to the orator lips of gold, to the poet promethean fire abused doth breed the hasty quarrel and make the god a beast.

It was said of old that a middle course is safest and best, and the axiom still holds good. All the Utopias thus far inaugurated were greased at the wrong end. The fact that since the dawn of history—aye, so far back that legend itself is lost in the shadows of the centuries—the winecup has circulated about the social board, proves that it supplies a definite, an inherent human want—that it fills a niche in the world's economy. One of the first acts of a people after passing the pale of savagery is to supply itself with stimulants. Why this is so, I do not pretend to know; but so it is, and it argues that the Prohibition apostles have tackled about as big a contract as did Dame Partington—that they had best "pluck a few feathers from the wing of their fancy wherewith to supply the tail of the judgment."

The Prohibs declare that 999 out of every 1,000 crimes are caused by liquor. Suppose this to be true: Does it take the cussedness out of liquor to drive it from the front room into the back alley? Is it not a fact that the worst brand of "fighting booze" is dispensed at the illicit doggery? But the Prohibs are as badly at sea anent their criminal statistics as in the mortuary report. Comparatively few of the great criminals of this country ever drank liquor to excess. But a small per cent. of those in our penitentiaries were confirmed drunkards when accorded the hospitality of the state. When a man is convicted of crime he naturally seeks a scapegoat. Adam threw all the blame of that apple episode on Eve, simply because liquor had not then been invented and he could not plead an Edenic jag in extenuation. I was once interviewing a man who had just been sentenced to the penitentiary for horse-theft. I thought that perhaps a cocktail would cause him to talk freer, and had one smuggled to his cell. He declined it, saying that he had never taken but one drink of liquor in his life, and that made him sick.

"But," said I, "you told the court that you were crazy drunk when you committed the crime."

"Yes," he replied, "I'd rather be thought a drunkard than a natural born d——d thief."

That led me to investigate. I interviewed the recorder

of Galveston, the chief of police, the sheriff of the county, the district attorney and several other officials. We went over the records, and the habits of each offender were carefully inquired into. As a matter of course the "drunks and disorderlies" made an imposing list; but we were unable to trace the influence of liquor in more than 3 per cent of the serious crimes committed in Galveston city and county during five years.

The great cry of the Prohibs is, "Save, the boys; remove temptation from their path." Well, that's all right, if you've got a putty boy; but if I had a boy who wanted to go on a whizz and wasn't smart enough to find the means despite all the Prohibs in Christendom, I'd send him to the insane asylum. I was reading the other day of some college youths who were watched so closely that they couldn't obtain liquor, and proceeded to fill up on illuminating gas. If the supply of gas holds out those youngsters are likely to develop into great Prohibition orators. If you want to keep your boy from filling a drunkard's grave, begin by getting a sure-enough boy— one whose brain-pan lies above instead of below his ears. Then raise him right. Don't tell him that every man who sells liquor is an emissary of hell, and that every man who drinks it is a worthless sot. If you do, he'll soon find out that you are a liar without sufficient intelligence to build a dangerous falsehood, and he'll take off the muzzle. Tell him the truth and thereby retain his confidence. Tell him that liquor is a pretty good thing to let alone, but that millions of better men than his daddy have drank it and lived and died sober and useful citizens.

Prohibtion was first tried in the Garden of Eden. It proved a failure there, and it has proven a failure ever since. It is not in accord with the Christian Bible, the fundamental law of the land or the lessons of history. Wine has been used in almost every religious rite except Mohammedanism and devil worship. St. Paul recommends it, Christ made and used it and God saved Noah while letting all the good Prohibitionists drown. The Saviour came eating and drinking. Abraham Lincoln declared Prohibition "a species of intemperance within itself" and "a blow at the very principles on which our government was founded." General Grant, Thomas Jefferson, Horatio Seymour and John Quincy Adams denounced it in unmeasured terms. Who's taking issue with these giants of the intellect? Redlicker Benson of Ingeanny, who has come all the way to Texas to tell us barbarians what to do to be saved—and incidentally pick up

enough money to pay for another "jag;" Whoopee Kalamity Homan, the pretty man of Dallas, whose chief argument is that I abuse the churches—which is an infernal falsehood; and Jehovah Boanerges Cranfill, an ex-
bum who aspires to the presidency of the United States,
but couldn't be elected pound-master in his own precinct.

I have been asked why, if as much liquor is sold under
Prohibition as under high license, the saloonists insist upon contributing to the public revenues. The answer's
dead easy. The men who engineer blind tigers vote the
Prohibition ticket. They contribute to the campaign fund.
They help pay the fees of the cold water spouters and
sputers. More liquor is sold under local option than under
high license, because of man's natural hankering for forbidden fruits; but it is sold by a different class of men
and is a different kind of booze. It is sold by chronic law-
breakers, by men who have little to lose, by toughs for
whom the bat-cage hath no terrors. The man who is capable of straddling an unlicensed keg of bug-juice in a back
room and ladling out liquid hell to little boys, is quite naturally in favor of Prohibition. A man of respectability,
and who is financially responsible for offenses, desires to
keep within the limits of the law. That's the reason that
respectable saloon men are the enemies of Prohibition.

Legalize the sale of liquor and you will have some
crime, no doubt. You will have paupers and criminals to
provide for, but you'll have a revenue to help bear the
burdens. Prohibit it and you'll have the burdens without
the revenue. Permit its sale and you will have law-abiding citizens engaged in the traffic, men who will try to
make it decent, who will take a pride in the purity of their
wares and the orderliness of their places; prohibit it, and
you will have a lot of law-breakers on the one hand selling
slumgullion made of cheap chemicals and general cussedness, and a gang of spies and informers on the other stirring up strife and entailing costly litigation.

When driven to the wall; when it is clearly demonstrated that their doctrine does not accord with the genius
of this government; when it is amply proven that where-
ever tried it has proven an expensive failure, an arrant
fraud, the Prohibs fall back upon the Bible. You may
prove five hundred different religious dogmas by the
Bible, but Prohibition is not one of them. Bro. Homan
declares that the Old Testament prohibits the drinking of
wine. It does not; but it does not make circumcision ob-
ligatory, and a sin of omission is as bad as a sin of commission. If Bro. Homan proposes to be guided by the Old

Testament I beg to suggest that he is overlooking a very important bit. The Old Testament commands no class of people to abstain from wine, except the Jewish priesthood, and they *only while performing their sacred offices*. An angel of the Lord did command the barren Manoah to stay sober awhile and she should conceive and bear a son; and I imagine that something equally as miraculous might happen to Luther Benson under similar circumstances. David recounts as one of God's mercies that he giveth water to the wild ass and wine to make glad the heart of man. Solomon sings to the wine cup with all the ardor of Anacreon, while the prophets kept the morals of Israel toned up by threats that a lapse from virtue would prove disastrous to the vineyards. St. Paul advised bishops and old women to take but little wine. He also suggested to the first that they should not fly into a passion, and to the latter that spreading false reports about their neighbors was not considered good form. The Prohibs, as a last resort, insist that the wine of Biblical days was very different from our own—a kind of circus lemonade; but it seems to have gotten in its graft on old Noah in most elegant shape. If the wine of Biblical times was so harmless why did the sacred writers consider it necessary to caution people against drunkenness, bid them be temperate in all things—while avoiding teetotalism? The only beverage I can find mentioned in the Bible that affected a man like a Prohibition drink, was that given Col. Lot in the cave by his two daughters. It accomplished what medical men assure me was a miracle—and the Prohibs run largely to the miraculous.

OLD GLORY.

(San Antonio, July 4, 1893.)

Fellow Americans—I have done pretty much everything that a man may do and dodge the penitentiary, except run for office and make Fourth of July speeches. Eulogizing the Goddess of Liberty were much like adding splendor to the sunrise or fragrance to the breath of morn. She needs no encomiast, star-crowned she stands, the glory of America, the admiration of the world.

I shall make a bid for your gratitude by being brief. In July weather the song of an electric fan and the small voice of the soda-fount were more grateful to the soul than the

grandest eloquence that ever burned on a Grady's lips of
gold. It is customary I believe on July 4 to "make the
eagle scream,"—to fight o'er again all the gory battles of
the Republic, from Lexington's defeat to the glorious victory of the last election; but I am no Gov. Waite, and
blood to horses' bridles delights me not. I would rather
at any time talk of love's encounters than of war's alarums
—rather bask in the smiles of beauty than mount barbed
steeds to fright the souls of fearful adversaries. I have ever
had a sneaking respect for Grover Cleveland for sending a
substitute to remonstrate with the Southern Confederacy
while he played progressive euchre with the pretty girls.
His patriotism may not have soared above par, but there
were no picnic ants on his judgment. Much as I love my
country, I would rather be a living president than a dead
hero.

I address you as "fellow Americans," for in this land no
man of Celtic or of Saxon blood can be an alien. Whether
he were born on the banks of the blue Danube or by Kil-
larney's lovely lakes, 'mid Scotia's rugged hills or on the
sunny vales of France, he is bound to us with ties of blood;
he hath a claim upon our country, countersigned by those
brave souls who, in the western wilds, gave to Liberty a
habitation and a name—who declared that Columbia should
ever be the refuge of the world's oppressed,—that all men,
in whatever country born, should be equal before the law
wherever falls the shadow of our flag. There has of late
arisen a strange new doctrine that we should close our ports
against the peoples of other lands, however worthy they
may be; but I say unto you that such a policy were to
betray a sacred trust confided to us by our fathers,—that
every honest man beneath high heaven, every worshipper
at Liberty's dear shrine hath an inheritance here, and when,
with uplifted hand he pledges his life, his fortune and his
sacred honor to the defense of freedom's flag he becomes
as much an American as tho' to the manner born.

On occasions such as this we of America are apt to glorify ourselves too much,—to overlook the origin of those
elements that made us great. When exulting over our
victories in war and our still more glorious triumphs in
peace, our progress and our prosperity, we should not forget that had there been no Europe there would be no great
American nation; that all the courage that beats in the
blood of Columbia's imperial sons, and all the wondrous
beauty with which her daughters are dowered; that all
the tireless energy of which she proudly boasts, and all the

genius that gilds her name with glory were nurtured for a thousand years at white bosoms beyond the ocean's brine.

The American nation is the fair flower of European civilization, the petted child of the world's old age. Princes may be jealous of her progress and tyrants read in her rise their own downfall; but the great heart of the people of every land and clime is hers; to her they turn their faces as the helianthus to the rising sun,—she is their beacon light, their star of hope, guiding them to the glories of a grander day.

It is natural, it is right that on the nation's natal day we should felicitate ourselves on the sacred privileges we enjoy—should pay the tribute of our respect to those whose courage crowned us with sovereignty and made us masters of our fate; but we should not, as too often happens, make it the occasion for senseless bravado and foolish bluster. We should rather employ it to promote good will among the nations of the earth, to link together in a kindlier brotherhood the various families of the great Caucasian race, to beat the barbarous sword into peaceful plowshares and forever banish strife.

I sometimes dream that God has, in his mercy, raised this nation up unto the world's salvation,—the immediate instrument of His grace to usher in that age of gold,

"When the war-drum throbs no longer and the battle-flags are furled,
In the parliament of man, the federation of the world."

I delight to trace in the rise and fall of nations the finger of God, and strive to read the Almighty's plan in the historic page. In the farthest east appeared the first faint light of civilization's dawn, and westward ever since the star of empire hath ta'en its way, while each succeeding nation that rose in its luminous paths like flowers in the footsteps of our dear Lord, has reached a higher plane and wrought out a grander destiny. The cycle is complete—the star now blazes in the world's extreme west, and by the law of progress which has preserved for forty centuries, here if anywhere, must we look for that millennial dawn of which poets have fondly dreamed and for which philanthropists have prayed.

The awful responsibility of leadership rests upon us. We have shattered the scepter of the tyrant and broken the shackles of the slave; we have torn the diadem from the prince's brow and placed the fasces of authority in the hands of the people; we have undertaken to lead the human race from the Slough of Despond to the Delectable Moun-

tains, where Justice reigns supreme and every son of Adam
may find life worth living. Can we make good our glorious
promises? Are we equal to the task to which we have given
our hand? Ten thousand times the world has asked this
question, but there is neither Dodona Oak nor Delphic
Oracle to make reply—the future alone can answer. All
eyes are upon us, in hope or fear, in prayer or protest. The
fierce light that beats upon a throne were as the firefly's dull
flame to the lightning's flash compared with that which
illumes the every act of this champion of human progress,
this knight par excellence, this Moses of the nations.

It is an important role which God hath assigned to us
in the great drama of life, yet into a part so pregnant with
fate we too often inject the levity of the farce. While
preaching equal rights to all and special privileges to none,
we pass laws that divide the people of this land into princes
and paupers, into masters and slaves. On July 4 we shout
for the old flag, and all the rest of the year we clamor for
an appropriation. While boasting that we are sovereigns
by right divine and equal unto kings, we hasten to lay our
hair beneath the feet of every scorbutic dude who hither
drifts,

"Stuck o'er with titles and hung around with strings."

The soldier who serves the state demands a pension,
and every burning patriot wants an office. We boast that
the people rule, and office-holders are but public servants;
yet more than a moiety of us would hang our crowns on
a hickory limb and swim a river to break into official bondage. Here in Texas seven distinguished citizens are already
chasing the governorship like a pack of hungry wolves
after a wounded fawn, while the woods are full of brunette
equines who have taken for their motto,

"They also serve who only stand and wait."

Yes, our office-holders are indeed our public servants—
and my experience with servants has been that they usually
run the whole shebang.

Theoretically we have the best government on the globe,
but it is so brutally mismanaged by our blessed public servants that it produces the same evil conditions that have
damned the worst. Even Americans whose forefathers
dined on faith at Valley Forge, or fought at Lundy's Lane,
have become so discouraged by political bossism, so heart-

sick with hope deferred that they quote approvingly those
lines of Pope,

> "For forms of government let fools contest,
> Whate'er is best administered is best."

While boasting of popular government, we suffer ourselves to be led about by self-seeking politicians like a
blind man by a scurvy poodle; we have made partisanship
paramount to patriotism—have reserved the poet's line, and
now

> "All are for a party and none are for the state."

It were well for us to make July 4 less an occasion
for self-glorification than for prayerful consideration of the
dangers upon which we are drifting in these piping times
of peace—dangers that arise, not in foreign courts and
camps, but are conceived in sin by the American plutocracy and brought forth in iniquity by our own political
bosses. We have no longer aught to fear from the outside world. Uncle Sam can, if need be, marshal forth to
battle eight million as intrepid sons as those who crowned
old Bunker Hill with flame or bathed the crests of Gettysburg with blood. Upon such a wall of oak and iron
the powers of the majestic world would beat in vain. Our
altars and our fanes are far beyond the reach of a foreign
foe; but the rock that recks not the thunderbolt nor bows
to the fierce simoon, is swept from its base by the uncon-
sidered brook.

No man can be a patriot on an empty stomach; no
country can be secure, I care not if Moses make its constitution and Solon frame its laws, when half its people
are homeless and brawny giants must beg their bread. As
far back as history's dawn the rise of the plutocracy and the
impoverishment of the common people have heralded the
downfall of the state. Thus fell imperial Rome, that once
did rule the world, and Need and Greed are the ballistae
and battering-rams that are pounding to-day with tremendous power upon every throne of Europe and rocking the
very civilization of the world from turret to foundation
stone.

We have achieved liberty, but have yet to learn in this
strange new land the true significance of life. We have
made the dollar the god of our idolatry, the Alpha and
Omega of our existence, and bow the knee to it with a
servility as abject as that of courtiers kissing the hand of
Kings. As the old pagans sometimes incorporated their
lesser in their greater deities that they might worship all

at once, so have we put the Goddess of Liberty and Saving Grace on the silver dollar that we may not forget them.

But before God, I do believe that this selfish, this Mammon-serving and unpatriotic age will pass, as passed the age of brutish ignorance, as passed the age of tyranny. I believe the day will come—oh blessed dawn!—when we'll no longer place the badge of party servitude above the crown of American sovereignty, the ridiculous oriflamme of foolish division above Old Glory's star-gemmed promise of everlasting unity; when Americans will be in spirit and in truth a band of brothers, the wrongs of one the concern of all; when brains and patriotism will take precedence of ' boodle and partisanship in our national politics; when labor will no longer fear the cormorant nor capital the commune; when every worthy and industrious citizen may spend his declining days, not in some charity ward, but in the grateful shadow of his own vine and fig-tree, the loving lord of a little world hemmed in by the sacred circle of a home. There was a time, we're told, when to be a Roman was greater than to be a King; yet there came a time when to be a Roman was to be the vassal of a slave. Change is the order of the universe and nothing stands. We must go forward or we must go backward—we must press on to grander heights, to greater glories, or see the laurels already won turn to ashes on our brow. We may sometimes slip; shadows may obscure our path; the boulders may bruise our feet; there may be months of mourning and days of agony; but however dark the night, Hope, a poising eagle, will ever burn above the unrisen morrow. Trials we may have and tribulations sore; but I say unto you, oh brothers mine, that while God reigns and the human race endures, this nation, born of our father's blood and sanctified by our mother's tears, shall never pass away.

OUR AMERICAN CZARS.

Industrial Slavery vs. Political Degradation.

It cost forty million dollars to indulge in the ridiculous mummery of crowning a man, who, for nearly two years had been universally recognized as Czar of all the Russias. That enormous amount of wealth was wasted in two weeks to gratify the pitiful vanity of a miserable mortal whom accident of birth had made sovereign of a poverty-stricken and semi-savage people. An attempt to feed the famished wretches who had gathered to witness the barbaric pageant, paid for with money wrung from their own thin purses by an iron hand, causing a stampede in which thousands were killed and other thousands crippled. Imagine a slaughtered ox cast among half a million hungry wolves, and you get an idea of what occurred beneath the glistening windows of Petrovsky Palace. It was a bread-riot, a fight for food participated in by hundreds of thousands of starving people of every age and sex, while wealth was being poured out like water by one who, ablaze with thousands of costly baubles, was solemnly proclaimed their divinely ordained guide, philosopher and friend—the father of a nation and defender of the faith! All the so-called Christian countries participated in this foolish farce, this essence of criminal idiocy, this crime against man and offense to God; yet if a man who gives half his honest earnings to feed the hungry and clothe the naked, lets slip an honest oath or dares to doubt that plunging a moral leper into a frog-pond with thaumaturgic incantations will purify his soul—will cause legions of white-robed angels to go chortling up and down the sapphire hills of heaven to the music of golden harps, while the Creator of the Cosmos makes holiday—these same Christian nations rear up on their hind legs, wildly wave their ears and bray forth their hysterical horror! When news of the terrible catastrophe was carried to the Czar "he wept." Whether he used his million dollar crown as a tear-jug I do not know; but the dispatches state that as soon as he could stop the lachrymose leaks "he danced!" Happy transition from boisterous grief to ribald joy! A woman seven times wedded could scarce have done so well! The *fete* went gaily on within the gorgeous palace, while the gaunt spectre of famine and the grisly gorgon of Death kept watch and ward without. Thus do extremes meet in merry Russia, and variety adds spice to life in the court circles of the Czar. Fortune's favorites tripped o'er cloth of gold and gorged themselves with honey of Hymettus and apples of Hesperides, while the gaunt peasants, who had fought like beasts of prey for a morsel to allay Hunger's mad'ning pangs, were piled high upon the plain. Within, all light and life and joy; without, all woe and wail. In the palace the red wine gushed, precious beyond price; on the plain a warmer tide was as freely poured as libations to the demons of Darkness and Death. And above the maudlin laughter of the bacchants and the pulsing sensuous music that makes the blood to leap like flame, drowning the groans of the wounded and the wailings for the dead,

rises the eternal cackle of the optimists that all is well—
that those who dare to doubt are either anarchists or pessimists with atribilarious livers.

* * *

The gorgeous palace and the blood soaked plain—ah,
that is Russia, where some will waste while others want;
where one is born to wield a sceptre and an hundred millions to be his beasts of burthen. How different in America where every man's a sovereign, and Liberty, Equality
and Fraternity—triune transcendent!—sits enthroned.   Is
it even so? Have we here no Palaces of Petrovsky and
plains of Khodijnskoje? No costly Kremlins and cheerless
cots?   Have we no Czars to waste in foolish *fetes* and
bacchic orgies the wealth wrung from field and forest and
mine by toiling millions? none who drain into their groaning coffers the people's earnings, then display their providence and gratify their pride by flinging an occasional
bone to those whose substance they have consumed. Have
there been no bread riots here?—no grasping by strong men
for charity doled out by idlers who earn not, yet whose
white hands are bedecked with diamonds? And do not
our Czars weep for very pity of the people's woes,—then
dance—prating meanwhile of the true faith, as tho' they
were crowned and sceptred? And do they not hold over
the toiling millions the power of life and death—sending
them to the Ice Hell of Siberia at their good pleasure, there
to endure all the tortures of the damned? Five thousand
torn and trampled before Petrovsky Palace! Why, 'tis not
the first time a crown has been baptized in blood—not the
first hecatomb slain by the demon Hunger that Pride
might vaunt herself. Why should we stand aghast when
the tragedy of a day is concentrated beneath the windows
of a palace instead of spread throughout an empire? Barbarous indeed must Russia be to give her all to feed an
empty-headed emperor and his parasites, then fight for
food doled out by him as a keeper might feed a wolfish
pack of dogs! Why do not her people assert their manhood and say to the Romanoffs: "Thus far hast thou gone
in our despoilment, but here your hand is stayed; else will
we make a hen's nest of thy crown and cage thee up, even
as great Ivan did the conquered princes." Thus do we
vaunt our "American sovereignty" and talk turgid—forgetful of the fact that 10,000 children die every year in the
single city of New York for want of food and medicine—
that we have Czars of our own, against whom we have

not yet revolted! The nearest we have come to it was the march of Coxey's army—and it kept off the grass. Herod slew perhaps a hundred babes, and his crime became one of the horrors of history. How easily people were shocked in those old days of ignorance! Were he alive to-day he might add a few thousand innocents a year to his private graveyard without attracting the attention of either the police, the pulpit or the daily press. Old Dives leaned back in his comfortable arm-chair, full of wine and walnuts, neglected to offer Lazarus a hand-out, and was sent to Hell; but that was before Talmage so revised the plan of salvation that plutocrats go to heaven in Pullman cars. Fortunes of five, ten, fifty, an hundred millions,— wealth beyond the dreams of Roman Consuls or Lydian Kings, and a mighty multitude ever on starvation's brink— or over—in this blessed land of Equality—and Christ! What think you? Are we not as much the slaves of our Money Kings as the Russians to the Romanoffs? Can you, my brother artisan, exist without the gracious permission of those who hold the purse-strings? Cannot Sir Plutus say to thee, "Go starve in the highways and hedges," and enforce obedience by the simple expedient of stopping your weekly stipend—depriving you of the privilege of producing? Are not our cities crowded with people as helpless and hopeless as those who fought for food before the Palace of Petrovsky? Is not capital steadily concentrating, becoming more powerful and pitiless? True, we do not here in the South feel the blight of this plutocratic Czarship much as yet; but it is creeping on like a social leprosy— our eleemosynary population becoming proportionately larger as the number of our millionaires increases. Are we not becoming Europeanized—Russianized—the work already far advanced in the older states, where millions cry, "You take my life when you take the means whereby I live!"

* * *

Anarchist? Nay, hold thy peace. The enemy of order is he that approves a system all whose tendencies are toward a Reign of Terror. I am not inciting the groaning multitude to "take up arms against a sea of troubles"—at most, not fire-arms. Blind indeed must be he who sees not that the American masses are being slowly enslaved. Industrial serfs they are already; political peons they are fast becoming. Money is power,—even in the realm of politics—and those possessing power will assuredly employ it. Have

we not even now our political as well as our industrial
"bosses"—to whom we are expected to yield a blind obedience? Is it not notorious that Dives may secure the passage of any law—by city council or United States senate—
that his impudence demands? Has a single political platform been framed these five-and-twenty years, by any party
having a fighting chance to win, that was not moulded
and modified by his master hand to suit a selfish purpose?
Is it not a fact that this government is to-day an Oligarchy
rather than a Republic—dominated by a coterie of plutocrats as surely as tho' they appointed both congress and
the cabinet? What then? Have we cause to vilipend the
miserable Russian people? Shall the pot animadvert upon
the complexion of the kettle? Is it worse to be subjects
de jure than *serfs de facto?* Would our boasted American
sovereignty smell the worse by any other name? A remedy? Why bless you! I am no Simon Magus, called to
renovate the world. If I do say that the Duke of Argyle
hath the itch, must I perforce, erect for him a scratching-
post? that a city was swept by a destructive storm, am I
in duty bound to tame the tornado and make it turn a
mill? Every man to his trade—and I am a doctor of divinity, not a doctor of laws.

* * *

It appears to me, however, that most of our economic
M. D.'s now trying to tone up our industrial system, have
no conception of the gravity of the disease. They are at
fault in their diagnosis—have mistaken a case of buck-
ague for a bad cold. The tariff and the currency prescriptions were too much like giving a paralytic bread pills.
Commerce can adapt itself to almost any tariff conditions
and prosper if assured of their permanency. Commerce
makes 95 per cent of its exchange media, and could easily
and safely make it all if the politicians would but cease
their meretricious intermeddling. What then? Shall we
adopt the doctrine of *laissez faire* and let the world drift
—fall back upon the physical law of the survival of the
fittest, and class as unfit and deserving extermination all
those who lack the necessary astucity to secure their own
just earnings and appropriate a portion of what rightfully
belongs to their equally industrious but less vulpine neighbors? Shall we accept the *ipse dixit* of Talmage that over-
grown fortunes are a blessing, because, forsooth, their
owners sometimes build hospitals where we may go when
poisoned by the mephitic air of Trinity Church tenements;
or endow theological colleges where grown men are edu-

cated to sing psalms, take up collections and beg the
widow's mite that they may live in luxury? Shall we agree
with Pope that "whatever" is is right," no matter how
it hurts; or listen to the Lydian notes of Andrew Carnegie
as he warbles a riant roundelay in praise of poverty, or
laments in pathetic spondees the woes of the man with
spondulix? Shall we take refuge in religion, admit that the
multiplication of millionaires and mendicants is a dispensation of that Providence which "ordereth all things well,"
and cease recalcitrating? That were indeed a satisfactory
solution of the problem—so far as the plutocrats and political Czars are concerned; but will the Samsons of Labor,
dimly conscious of his terrible strength, consent to accept
it and continue to grind the Philistinic corn of patience?
There's the rub? It was only the hope of obtaining relief
by this or the other catholicon that has kept him quiet so
long. A man will suffer much when Hope whispers that
'tis not for long—that on the morrow he will find surcease;
but when his Star of Bethlehem is proven a wandering
comet, or even an ingnis fatuus born of putrid brains, and
leading him deeper into the bog—what then? For years
the politico-economic doctors have been bamboozling him
with the faith-cure folly. When the tariff was low and times
hard they told him that by raising it they would make
things right. It was raised, and Jordan's road became even
more rocky. They told him that the high tariff iniquity
was playing Old Man of the Sea to his industrial Sinbad—
that when lowered the very mesquite bushes would grow
baked apples and the song of contentment be heard in the
land. It was lowered, and forthwith the country was filled
with idle men, while banks and business houses popped like
painted bladders. Now the tariff is to be shoved up once
more. Labor is again preparing to enter an industrial
Eden—McKinley is a new Moses who is to lead it into a
land flowing with milk and honey, where the cry of "hard
times" will be forever hushed. The same pitiful farce has
been played with the currency—gold, silver and greenbacks have been in turn the star of all our hopes and the
author of all our ills. How long will Labor submit to this
miserable hocus-pocus on the part of politicians whose
shibboleth is "pie?" And when aweary of saltatating from
tweedledum to tweedledee and back again; when tired
of turning one wretched set of rascals out to turn one even
more rapacious in; when hope deferred maketh the heart
sick, what will happen? Will the people, impoverished
and broken in spirit, sink into abject slavery, or rise in

bloody rebellion against their bosses? Until one of these
two things happens; until we either become completely
Russianized, or rally to the standard of some immortal ass
like Coxey, and, by sheer brute force wreck the very
foundations of society, we will continue to speculate upon
the cause of our industrial ills and seek a remedy.

*   *   *

We have the most fruitful land upon which the sunlight
falls, the richest in natural resources. It could support
six times its present population in comfort—aye, in luxury; yet thousands of those already here cannot wring
from the soil life's bare necessities. So much is universally conceded, and we need go no further for demonstration that there's something radically wrong. What is it?
Let the cumulative wisdom of the country answer. Talleyrand has told us that "Everybody is wiser than anybody,"—a fact confirmed by the woeful failure of single-
handed industrial "reformers!" When ill it is a step toward recovery to learn what ails us. When the industrial
machine is out of gear we should ascertain beyond the
peradventure of a doubt what put it so. Regarding the
"issues" now occupying the busy politicians, there are a
multitude of opinions. An ounce of observation is worth
a smoke-house full of theory. We meet few idle men who
can trace their loss of employment to high or low tariff,
or changes in the currency; but everywhere we meet
those who were "let out" by the introduction of labor-
saving devices. The invention of typesetting machines
flooded the land with idle printers, who were accustomed
to earn from $20 to $30 a week at the case. Few of them
were fit for anything else. They invaded the job and
country offices and the fierce competition for employment
reduced wages. During the past decade a majority of
trades have had a similar experience. Vast armies of
high-priced workmen have been pauperized, have suffered
a tremendous reduction in their purchasing power. The
butcher, the baker and the candlestick maker, dependent
upon the trade of these men, reduced the number of their
employes, thus affecting in turn other tradesmen. This
meant decreased consumption, and a decline in the prices
of products of farm and mine and factory. Under such
conditions manufacturers conspired to keep up prices by
limiting production, and, while protecting themselves, precipitate the ruin of others; banks curtail their credits, and
we have an era of hard times, entailing that lack of confidence which so easily becomes a panic. So complex is

the industrial machine, so interdependent are all its parts, that the farmer in Kansas and the planter in Texas are affected more or less by a decrease in the purchasing power of the spinners of Lowell or the hodcarriers of New York. We are continually assured by the spokesmen for the plutocracy that all is well; that wages have risen somewhat in the past twenty years and the standard of living advanced. What boots it what the average wage-rate may be to the man who cannot obtain an opportunity to earn his board? Wages have not risen, the standard of living has not advanced in equal ratio with the work-man's ability to create wealth. That will explain the glaring inequalities which exist in a country of so-called equality. Nor is this the worst phase of the matter: Be-fore the introduction of costly labor-saving machines every mechanic was practically his own master; now he is another's man, dependent upon his good will for em-ployment at any price. His independence, his sovereignty is gone, and he must stand, hat in hand, before the indus-trial czar and humbly beg permission to produce. Capital is the child of labor, but the creature hath become lord of its creator. It were idle to decry labor-saving appli-ances. The sole object of toil is the production of wealth, and whatever enhances man's productive power is, by itself considered, a blessing. The trouble is that the felicity falls with unequal incidence; that, for the slight addition to the workman's wage, he must yield his free-dom—is transformed from a social entity into a mere factor in the great industrial machine, utterly useless when out of place. A mighty force has been evolved by the genius of man, which he is not yet competent to properly control. When the car of progress was pro-pelled by mule power 'twere easy to keep pace with the procession; but when steam and electricity were applied, the industrial masses became demoralized. In other words, the work-a-day world could not promptly adapt itself to the new conditions. Skilled mechanics awoke to find their trades obsolete, their chosen occupation gone, themselves as helpless as a watchmaker among savages or a plainsman in a great city. As man's power to produce life's necessaries is enhanced, his surplus energy expends itself in the creation of luxuries—the standard of living advances; but this power has multi-plied beneath the magic wand of genius faster than re-adjustment of forces were possible. Men cling desper-ately to their old occupations, and become pauperized. If we could pause awhile matters might adjust themselves; but the Car of Progress rolls ever faster and faster—a veritable Juggernaut to millions. The division and sub-division of labor goes ever on—industrial conditions change with the rapidity of the kaleidoscope. If, in Queen Elizabeth's time, it took nine tailors to make a man, it now requires a score of workmen to make a complete mechanic. A man must be a specialist, else a vagabond —and to-morrow his specialty may have become a thing of the past. It is not lack of available land, not the "tariff atrocities" or "the crime of '73" that is reducing our erst-while independent working people to the level of serfs and entailing starvation in a land of plenty; it is the evil inherent in change, the price we are paying for our vaunted Progress; it is the subjection of the many to the grasping few by the inability of the former to produce independently. The aggregate of wealth increases, but is monopolized by those astute enough to anticipate these industrial climaxes and financially able to take advan-tage thereof. Yet we talk of equalizing advantages by a change in the tariff or currency, by the elevation of this or the other blatant ass to office? What are we going to do about it? Why, we are going to keep right on con-cocting idiotic political "issues"—plastering corns to cure cramp colic—until something breaks. That's what we *will* do; what we *should* do is a very different matter. Go ask the small-bore attorney who's running for Congress because he cannot obtain a paying practice; he can tell you exactly what to do to be saved—nay, will do the business for you if you but give him an opportunity to draw $5,000 per annum and clerk hire for distributing pumpkin seeds and postoffices. Just touch the ballot box button and he will do the rest.

We know full well that no man ever honestly earned a million dollars. The individual is unable to create such an enormous amount of wealth. If he possesses that sum it is plain that in some way he has managed to put his fingers in his neighbor's pockets. What then must we say of those who accumulate fortunes of fifty millions in one brief lifetime? What of those who inherit a talent from ancestors and, without producing so much as a shoe peg, transform it into ten? We realize that the wealth of this world should belong to those who produce it, not to impudent idlers. We know that in a country whose wonderful resources have been scarce touched there should be an opportunity for every man able and willing to work. All freely concede that, with his present wealth-producing capacity, the laborer should be to a large degree absolved from "the primal eldest curse"—be able to win a competence and at the same time have abundant leisure for the improvement of his mind and cultivation of the social graces. Thus far we are all agreed; but further will not consent to go together. Here the broad pathway divides into a multitude of tortuous paths—all leading into the same inane limboes. When we ask a remedy for our ills industrial a thousand Cagliostros deafen us with their clamor; we pull in different directions—fetching up finally at the free soup-house. If we cannot as yet determine who is in the right, we may, by a little ratiocination, decide who is in the wrong, and that were no inconsiderable gain. Next in value to knowing how to do a thing is knowing how not to do it. Reason should advise us that a worse enemy to labor and society at large than even the most grasping plutocrat is the damphool empiric who would reconstruct our entire industrial system in a day. Experience has taught us that revolutions do not go backward—that the old-world days of communism and public ownership of land are forever dead; that attempts to revive customs once generally discarded can meet with no permanent success. Common-sense proclaims that government cannot enrich us; that it is our dependent, not our patron—that it can only advance the fortune of one at the expense of all. We know from observation that it matters little what political party is in power—that each has its complement of patriots and place-warmers, philosophers and fools. The problem before us is the combination of the productive power of the new industrial system with the individual independence and just distribution of the old—to secure to each the full usufruct of his labor under conditions consistent with the most advantageous application of physical energy. It is not an easy problem—not one that can be solved off-hand by a congeries of noisy demagogues and ward-heelers calling itself a national convention and prating idly of economic principles; yet in its solution lies our salvation. It is the riddle propounded to us by the sphinx of Time, which not to read is to be destroyed; yet no Œdipus makes answer. Until there is some adjustment on common-sense lines conditions will go from bad to worse, for the simple reason that it is cheaper to produce on a large than on a small scale. Our large manufactories are absorbing or destroying the lesser; the great mercantile

establishments are crushing out the small tradesmen—
agriculture is tending to the colossal. This is inevitable,
is the very breath in the nostrils of Progress; but it renders Dives more powerful and Lazarus the more dependent. Like Doedalus, we have soared so near the sun that
the wax has melted on our wings. How to continue our
flight and avoid a catastrophe is the problem of problems. Perchance next month I will offer, not a heaven-
inspired panacea, but simply a few suggestions—if I can
persuade myself that mediocrity may make itself heard
amid the megalophanous bawling of so many who know
it all. We must remember, however, that the united efforts of Solon, Lycurgus and Sam Jones were incapable
of dragging the millennium in by the ears. McKinley
may give us an "age of gold," but scarce a Saturnian
epocha. The wisest economic coryphei are powerless to
banish poverty and want from the world. Just so long
as men are born unequal in body, mind and ambition;
just so long as commerce and industry exist upon the
earth, the palace will proudly rear its fluted columns
while Hunger shivers in the lowly cot. The capable and
provident will succeed, while the incapable and wasteful
go to the wall—and this despite all panaceas of the politicians. We must remember that any system which with-
holds from genius and industry their just reward and
bestows it upon folly and sloth, or makes the people the
wards of the State—transfers them from an industrial to
a political czar—were infinitely worse than the one under
which we live; that when we have given to all equal opportunities and assured the full usufruct of their endeavor
we have discharged our full duty to society and ourselves. Put all American citizens on an industrial parity,
then let them work out their own salvation. That's the
idea.

AN OLD MAIDS' AUCTION.

No more will precocious infants convulse their auditors
at school exhibitions by lisping that almost painfully hu-
morous "piece" entitled, The Bachelor's Auction. No more
will they stand before us in all their uncomfortable cleanli-
ness and astound fond parents and admiring friends by dron-
ing forth,

"Here's an old bachelor, who wants to buy?
   A hundred old maids make answer, 'I,' 'I!'
And all the old maids, some younger, some older,
   Each lugged an old bachelor home on her shoulder."

The times change, and we change with them. I have
before me a scorched banana hand-bill advertising an "Auction of Old Maids," under the highly respectable auspices
of the Ladies' Aid Society of the Christian Church, Lampasas, Texas. From this remarkable flyer I copy the following:

"No bids entertained for less than 25 cents nor more
than 50 cents. Each purchaser of an old maid is entitled
to two saucers of ice cream. Now is your chance!" I
should suggest! A nice, kittenish old maid at two to four
bits, according to the bidding, and a brace of iron-stone
china saucers of the best home-brewed ice cream thrown
in as lagniappe! Why didn't the Ladies' Aid Society advise me before it was everlastingly too late?—I would have
taken the entire lot. Lapped in the oleiferous luxury of
country cream, and surrounded by devoted damosels whose
charm, like wine, has improved with age, I would find
life well worth the living—would plead with the fleeting
moment in the words of Faust, "Stay, thou art so fair!"
Or I could have colonized my fair Florimels in female suffrage Kansas and re-sold 'em to Mark Hanna at a profit of
300 per cent. Ah me! there be "tides in the affairs of
men, which, taken at the flood, lead on to fortune;" but
ever does the Argos sail for the Golden Fleece ere I can get
afloat. One does not have an opportunity every day to
serve the Lord by wallowing in the fragrance of faded
flowers, contemplating ancient paintings and absorbing
sweetened frost. If the Ladies' Aid Society has any more
old maids left, whom they can recommend as suitable companions for a middle-aged but uxorious Baptist minister,
they may ship, C. O. D., a dozen or so, assorted. 'S'matter
with Lampasas as an old maids' market, that they are sold
for a song and mock-birds supplied to sing it? Has the
boom collapsed, or is the town overrun by enterprising
widows who crowd their inexperienced sisters to the wall?
Think of a woman, whose charms have grown mellow
'neath two score summer suns, standing on the auction
block "in maiden meditation fancy free" and peering from
behind her fan into the upturned faces of creation's alleged lords, while a stentor-lunged salesman offers her for
the price of an aitch-bone or boarding house hen! Imagine the unfeeling huckster of a virgin heart dilating upon
an ice cream dower—and all for a quarter-of-a-dollar. O
manhood, where is thy blush! O chivalry, where thy shame!
A toothless picaninny—of the Waco Baptist breed—would
have brought more in ante-bellum times. What disposi-

tion the reckless purchasers made of their property I am not
advised. Had the sale occurred in Constantinople the answer were easy; but the purchases may have been made
in Lampasas solely on account of the cream. Selling ladies
at auction in the name of the Lord is not a custom peculiar
to Lampasas. Last April, the Epworth Leaguers, at Suffern, N. Y., disposed of a number of females at public out-
cry to the highest bidder, and, to fire the callow heart of
youth into religious fervor, hit upon the happy expedient
of concealing their faces and allowing prospective purchasers to examine their legs. Whether the Ladies' Aid
Society of Lampasas profited by this plan, I have not learned.
If they did not, they are by no means up to date—it being
so much easier to round out with sawdust the "hose a
world too large for the shrunk shank," than to recall the
lilies and roses of auld lang syne. The fact, however,
that small bids were cheerfully received and large ones not
expected—that the sacred game was played with a two-bit
ante and 50 cent limit—argues that they entered a *caveat
emptor* by recklessly exposing the faces of those brought to
the block. That is some consolation; still, the Iconoclast,
as court of last resort in matters religious—the Phillipe
de Mornay of Protestantism—cannot sanction the sale of
maids of whatsoever age at auction—no matter what portion
of their anatomy be submitted for public inspection. It has
granted indulgences to a few churches, in sore financial distress, to sell kisses to the public at a fixed price, but it must
place sacred leg-shows under the ban, even where the petticoat reaches as low as the knee, the high-water mark of
the Epworth Leaguers. It must anathematize the sale of
old maids, as too suggestive of the devil's auctions held in
days agone in Chicago's variety dives. It feels constrained
to admonish the Epworth Leaguers and Ladies' Aid Societies that infraction of this interdict will result in excom-
munication. Ministers finding their parishioners actuated
by abnormal zeal untempered with judgment, will read this
rescript from their pulpits for three consecutive Sundays.
The Iconoclast humbly hopes that no irreparable injury has
yet been wrought to morality by those whose religious ardor
has caused them to ignore social ordinances and indulge in
aesthetic heresies—who have embraced the dangerous doctrine that the end—or even both ends—justifies the means;
but it must consider the future and estimate the evils that
are likely to flow from this growing tendency on the part
of the church to compete with the devil in this particular
province. Having once resorted to money-raising expedients

which render religion ridiculous, if not disreputable; having begun with grab-bags, raffles, cake-rings and other cutthroat gambling devices, and already gotten so far as the sacred kissing bee and sanctified leg show, where would misguided zeal lead these gnat-straining, camel-swallowers did not the Iconoclast blast with its anathema this evil in the bud? As man became sated with one appeal to his animalism they would have to resort to others even more *risque* to tempt his jaded appetite, until even the obscene orgies of ancient phallic worship were revived, and Sam Jones' open-sewer sermons and Sid Williams' guano metaphors considered affectedly euphemistic. Because the devil fishes for saints with an old sun-bonnet, we are not privileged to bait our hook with fancy hosiery in a frantic attempt to land a few sinners. Aside from questions of propriety, appeals to pruriency by the goldly seldom pay. Selling kisses—in the name of Christ—no longer appeals to this aesthetic people. It has learned by experience that a kiss snatched in public from lips defiled with the saliva of beery bums and "terbacker chawin" deacons, does not create the ecstatic deliration of the "lingering sweetness long drawn out" when you have a monopoly of the business beneath a harvest moon—does not make the blood to dance and the soul to swoon like a yum-yum snap behind the parlor door. Even the reflection that you are doing your Christian duty does not sweeten the disagreeable dose. Besides, the doctors of medicine have decided that a young woman's bussing machine should be carefully deodorized every time she changes fellows, to discourage mumps, measles and choleramorbus bacteria. When I absorb my two-bits' worth of sanctified honey-dew I examine the front elevation of the sacrificial virgin for a spot where the drug-store bloom retains its pristine brightness. If it has been all swiped off by enthusiastic elders, I draw her head tenderly but firmly down until her sunny bangs nestle on my heaving brisket, plant my apostolic imprint on the back of her snowy neck and make a break for the open air, thanking the Lord at every leap that I have both saved my soul and preserved my life. The sacred leg-show is likewise becoming stale, flat and pecuniarily unprofitable since the advent of bikes and bloomers. When one can get a surfeit of all kinds, classes and conditions of legs by simply lingering on the corner, he will not—unless he be a holiness camp-meeting neophyte—cough up much cash for the privilege of gazing at a lot of splay feet that would frighten the Salvation Army, a congeries of misshapen bandy-shanks that would give a stage-

manager the nightmare and drive a poet to drink.   An old
maids' auction—even with two plates of cream added to
every chromo—is not calculated to make the average man
empty his pockets into the coffers of Israel.   Of course the
godly might resort to bust exhibitions and bare-back auctions; but they would encounter disastrous competition in
the popular bathing resorts and fashionable ball-rooms.
What else have they to offer in their attempt to beat the
devil at his own game—to make the church as attractive
to worldlings as a Five Points' variety dive?

"THE WEDDING OF THE SEASON."

It occurred in St. Louis, August 12, at exactly 5 o'clock,
p. m.; at least it was advertised—several thousand dollars'
worth—to take place at that time, and we may presume
that it was successfully pulled off, as there was no apparent
reason for police interference.   The Republic gave it a full-
page "spread"—evidently via the business office—as advance notice, and said absolutely nothing about it on the
day following the nuptial date.   Having put up so handsomely for advance advertising, "the high contracting parties" doubtless supposed they would be given at least a column puff after the agony was over, but were doomed to
disappointment.   But if the Republic failed to throw in any
post-nuptial lagniappe, it at least did its contract work well
—made its write-up of this conspiracy against single bless-
edness as interesting as any laundry soap epic or soasyou-
dont romaunt I have yet seen.   It led off with a half-tone
pine-board portrait of the loving pair holding up a rustic
fence and spooning with the unconstrained enthusiasm of
'Arry and 'is 'Arriet.   The bride-elect is gazing out into the
gloom with a whither-am-I-drifting expression, while her
fiance peers into her face with the hungry look of a Weary
Waggles regarding a hot wienerwurst.   Next on the page
we have a full-length portrait of the woman in the case
as she appears when about to have her photograph taken,
while to her right is a jackknife sketch of her fellow suf-
ferer, apparently wondering whether he had best do the
deed or take to the woods.   Sandwiched in among fac-
similes of wedding cards, gorgeous gowns and music "composed for the memorable event," are several columns of
information concerning the people whose agreement to
occupy the same sheets is supposed to be of international

importance.   They are a Miss Marie Garesche, daughter of
William A. Garesche, a St. Louis attorney of whom I had
not hitherto heard, and a certain young man who enhances
his personal pulchritude by putting his moustache up on
curl papers, preserves his mental equipoise by parting his
hair at the equator, and is growing somewhat bowlegged
beneath the ponderous title of Count Vincent des Rioux
de Messimy.   He clerks in the St. Louis branch of a New
York jobbing concern and is known to his intimes as
"Messy."   The Republic describes him as "a handsome
gentleman with the most engaging manners;" but an "ad
man" with a fat contract to fill, always sidetracks his conscience.   The portrait of this prize beaut suggests a French
barber struggling with the glad surprise of a ten-cent tip.
His affianced is described as "a dainty creature, petite in
stature, a blonde of the purest type, with large blue-gray
eyes and delicately chiseled features;" but the artist makes
a vigorous minority report.   The portrait—which I sincerely hope does Miss Garesche rank injustice—makes her
dish-faced as a new moon, with nose like a seed-wart, weak
mouth, soup-ladle chin and a smirk calculated to frighten
anything but a French count sorely in need of cash.   Mistakes will happen, and it is possible that in the rush and
hurry incident to the occasion Papa Garesche gave the
Republic's "ad man" photos of Marie's Norwegian maid
and some becurled bargain-counter "mash;" or, in making
up the forms, the foreman may have transposed the portraits of the happy pair and those intended for the freak
page.

The pedigree of the young lady is given from prehistoric
times, and from it we gather that she, too, is of blooded
stock—that "from a long and noble ancestry, and success-
ive infusions of the bluest blood," has sprung this fairest
of the flowers.   "The Garesche family traces its origin to
the early epochs of the primitive Celts of druidical memory!"   Just how it manages all this, doesn't particularly
matter; but it is evident that its genealogical tree is a veritable Ygdrasyl, and probably antedates Adam by several
centuries.   Carlyle has given us a pen-picture of "the early
epochs of the primitive Celts," in his Sartor Resartus—
refers to Col. Garesche's distinguished ancestors as a "savage, glaring fiercely from under his fleece of hair, which
with the beard reached down to his loins, and hung round
him like a matted cloak; the rest of his body sheeted in its
natural fell—a flint-hurling, aboriginal anthropophagus!"
But the Garesches progressed gradually from the primitive

to the polite. In the course of some ages they acquired the gentle art of weaving and wearing breechclouts, and eventually became "members of the Huguenot nobility of France."

It is important to note that "Jean Garesche, great-grand-uncle of the bride's grandfather, died at Nieul in 1754." Poor old man! He didn't have a title, but he may have had a tape worm or a wen. Anyhow, he's dead—died before witnessing the crowning glory of the Garesche family, the purchase of a whole page of slop in the St. Louis Republic. Ah me! In the midst of life we are in death, and no man knoweth what kind of chronic jackassi his great grand-nephew will beget. A grand something-or-other of Col. Garesche is listed as "taking an active part against the oppressive decrees of the revolutionary powers." They appear to have been very active indeed. He fled from San Domingo to France to save his life, and when the revolutionists there began to shoot recklessly he skipped over to the United States. The French royalists were at that time great skippers, and close in their foaming wake was usually to be found the patriot tri-color of France and a Tillmanic pitchfork. Vital Marie Garesche, grand-father of William A., was given a petty job in the government land office and assigned to St. Louis. He appears to have laid the foundation of the family fortune by filing a homestead claim on what is now a portion of the city. In the course of time he was elected to the city council—and the rest was dead easy. He found time, however, despite his onerous aldermanic duties in the then insignificant city, to beget sons and daughters. One of these sons, of whom we hear little in the biographical sketch, begat "William A. Garesche, the lovely girl's father, who will give her in marriage to a nobleman of equally proud lineage!" (Will somebody please 'phone to the Southern Hotel bar to send over a Joe Rickey cocktail, with seltzer on the side? Thanks!) How nice—the marriage, I mean. Col. Garesche is a forty-second cousin to various titled Frenchmen who cannot at present realize on their patents of nobility, Gallic coats-of-arms being quoted on the Bourse as on a par with Confederate bonds. Just what the downtrodden French noblemen are doing to earn a living while the republic laughs at their pretended rights of robbery, the biographer of the Garesche family does not inform us. But we need not borrow trouble—genuine French noblemen can always find employment. They make the best of barbers, the most obsequious of waiters, while as cooks they defy competition. They possess a native delicacy of touch, a refinement of feeling, and an appreciation of the eternal verities of art that render them incomparable in the depilation of a tender face or the manipulation of a souffle. Take away our French counts and Italian princes and the American sybarite would suffer.

A few commonplace Morrisons and plebeian Browns have managed to intermingle their proletarian blood with the divine ichor which pulses in the veins of Miss Garesche; but as "pa" has boodle to throw at the birds, this misfortune may be forgiven, if not forgotten. Not much is said about the bridegroom's pedigree; but we are led to infer that, tucked away in some cosy corner of la Belle France, his "ancestral castle," rears its proud battlements. He couldn't be expected to bring both his title and his castle to this country—it might disturb the world's equilibrium. The "ad man" of the Republic—who is something of an artist at "slinging the soup"—manages to weave a very pretty romance around this blue-blooded Venus and Adonis, whose union constitutes "the wedding of the season"—makes even the hymenic torch that welded the Marlborough title to the Vanderbilt millions, and the costly pyrotechnics of Count Castellane, pale their ineffectual fires. It appears that about a decade ago, when Miss Garesche was—by her own arithmetic—of almost marriageable age, her father occupied a government position in keeping with the dignity of a man who traces this "proud lineage" back to an unbroken line through Huguenot nobles to the "primitive Celts." He was United States consul to Martinique, a West India island—fully equal in area and importance to that of which the city council of Galveston once appointed "Sandy" Musgrove governor. It is well nigh as large as a South Texas melon patch, and an equal number of niggers may be found in it on any moonlight night. His duties consisted in displaying the American flag on July Fourth and Washington's birthday, drawing his salary and taking his siestas. Count Vincent des Rioux de, etc., had some relatives perched on that insignificant knob, which, for some reason, protrudes itself out of the waters of the neo-tropics, and while swinging around in search of a situation, he placed them under tribute for a few days' fodder. He couldn't very well turn around to spit in the narrow confines of Martinique without meeting the American consul. They were kindred spirits—one the calyx, the other the corolla of the fragrant genealogical flower. They compared their "proud lineages" and found them to be on a parity. The bogus count called on the opera-bouffe consul. There "he saw a fairy child with large blue eyes and a bewitchingly tender mouth. The chit of a girl (about 14) said, 'How do you do?' and "Good afternoon,' with inimitable grace." After a careful study of what the Republic calls her portrait, I am surprised that she didn't add that Polly wanted a cracker; but perhaps we should not expect abnormal precocity of children handicapped with noble pedigrees. Her "How do you do," seems, however, to have knocked the impressionable count clear off the Christmas tree, for we are assured that "whenever the young man put aside the stern realities of life he closed his eyes and dreamed of the little girl in the faraway West Indies." In other words, when the shop was closed for the day, the blinds drawn down, the cuspidore cleaned, the sawdust swept up and his lingering eternity of a title carefully polished joint by joint and stood up in the corner, his wits would go a wool-gathering and wonder how much "dust" old man Garesche had got. A new president was elected, "the rascals were turned out"—as usual—and William A. Garesche, with the public udder remorselessly pulled out of him, returned to St. Louis and resumed the burdens of life. Six years later Count Vincent des, etc., also drifted to the Cyclone City. He once more heard the magic name of Garesche, and—probably thinking he might be invited to stay to dinner—put in an appearance. The girl had forgotten him in the effort to add a few more phrases to her vocabulary. Finding the old man to be financially well fixed, Messimy laid siege to the heart of Miss Marie, and after three long years of importunity the belle of many seasons surrendered. How glad we should all be that the St. Louis breed is to be improved, that the "blue blood" of the Gareschers, traced to the primitive anthropophagi, will not be further corrupted by admixture with that of plebeian Browns, but brought back by easy stages to that pristine purity when every daughter of the distinguished house was sired by a "primitive Celt" and dammed by dame of high degree! Happy Gareschers! Ecstatic Messimy of the vestibule train title! How pretty it is to see William A.—whose grandfather's great-uncle departed this life in 1754—throwing bouquets at the nobility of both families, bouquets that cost several hundred dollars a bunch. And what a concession to *hoi polloi* to be taken into Miss Garesche's confidence and told with what kind of lingerie she will adorn her sacred person while filling the count's cup of felicity to overflowing!

I'm not finding fault—heaven forfend! The ex-consul to the mighty empire of Martinique has a perfect right to "blow hisself" for page newspaper puffs—to exhibit his genealogical tree in Shaw's Garden if he likes; while it is the prerogative of the Republic to trade nux vomica drule and Della Cruscan drivel for good American dollars. Still, I cannot imagine the great American public filing a protest had Count Vincent des, etc., and his cerulean blooded Baby Mine slipped out to Carondolet, or over to East St. Louis while no one was looking, got hitched by a justice of the peace, regaled a few friends with keg beer and pretzels, then started blithely in to take the conceit out of the census enumerators of Chicago and perpetuate the noble name of de Messimy, instead of halting the political torch-light parade to vaunt their "purty" and proclaim that they were about to accept St. Paul's sage advice to couples similarly situated. I have no word of criticism for Miss Garesche; she is a young thing, somewhat under thirty; but William A. and the gentleman with the serial story title are old enough to know better.

It is a trifle strange that no attempt was made to trace "the proud lineage" of either bride or groom back to an aristocracy of intellect, a nobility of brains—that their pride should center in a supposed descent from various mental vacuums who were "stuck o'er with titles and hung round with strings."

They exalt their horn, not because their families have produced men who won and wore the amaranthine wreath; but because their ancestors were unimportant factors of that ignoble French "nobility" whose transcendent impudence, disgusting debaucheries and wolfish exactions drove a patient and long-suffering people to a revolt whose attendant horrors constitute the darkest page in human history. France, like the United States, has abolished patents of nobility, and for the self-same-reason—because they are badges of servility, and in a republic every citizen should be a sovereign. Imagine Americans, who have learned senators for servants, and who make and unmake the chief magistrates of the greatest nation that ever sunned itself in the smile of omnipotent God, boasting that their ancestors had to take orders from some petty princeling ruled by a prostitute! There was never but one real nobility on this earth and its acknowledged head was born in a hovel. No pompous monarch that ever wielded a sceptre was worthy to sit in the presence of Shakespeare. The proudest nobleman who followed the fortunes of Charlemagne, or danced and grimaced in the corrupt court of *le Grande Monarque* would have been honored by a careless nod from Miguel Cervantes or a kick from Bobby Burns. All the Orleanists of France could not have furnished forth the brains of the boorish Corsican. No "prince of the blood," since Trajan's pillar first marked the center of the world, was the peer of Abraham Lincoln.

Messrs. Garesche and Messimy should get "the pomp of heraldry" out of their foolish heads. Few Americans can trace their lineage back more than a century or so without finding some petty lordling or ticky-tailed princeling figuring as a member of the family; but we are striving desperately to live down the disgrace. We are trying to breed out the syphilitic "blue blood" and fill the veins of this nation of sovereigns with a healthy crimson tide, thereby insuring beautiful and noble women, and men too manly to make themselves ridiculous by boasting that their ancestors were a set of impudent thieves living upon the honest earnings of others. We aspire to membership in an aristocracy founded, not upon the bones of a French king's upper-servants, but on the honest worth of noble men and women. If the Garesches and Messimys think there is, was, or can ever be a prouder title than American sovereignty, a nobler lineage than descent from brave and brainy men and chaste and beautiful women, why did they drag their empty bellies hither? Let them be sent back across the sea, as unworthy to live one hour where falls the sacred shadow of Freedom's flag.

LOVE AS AN INTOXICANT.

Seymour, Texas, Nov. 4, 1897.
Mr. Brann: Will you please answer the following question and thereby settle a dispute in Seymour: Is love intoxicating?
CHAS. E. RUPE.

My correspondent neglects to state whether Seymour is a Prohibition town. Of course if it is and love is listed as an intoxicant, the blind god will be expatriated for the benefit of the makers of Peruna, Hostetter's Bitters and other palate ticklers, popular only at blind tigers. Why the deuce didn't the Seymourites set to work and settle this vexatious problem for themselves? Must I undertake a system of scientific experiments in order to obtain this information for the citizens of Seymour? Suppose that I do so, find that love makes drunk come, and am run in by the patrol wagon while supercharged with the tender passion: don't you see that this would militate against my usefulness as a Baptist minister? How the hell could I explain to my congregation that I was full of love instead of licker? Clearly I cannot afford to offer myself as a sacrifice upon the altar of science. Should I proceed to fall in love just to see if it would go to my head, and should it do so, my Dulcina del Toboso might marry me before I recovered my mental equipoise, and I would awaken to find my liberty a has-been and my night-key *non est*. Of course I shouldn't mind it ever so little, but it would be awfully hard on the lady. I have been baptized just to see if it would soak out any original sin; I've gone up in a balloon and down in a coal mine in the interest of science; I've ridden on the pilot of a locomotive for the sake of the sensation; I've permitted myself to be inoculated with the virus of Christian charity just to see if it would "take;" I've tampered with almost every known intoxicant, from the insidious mescal of the ertswhile Montezumas to the mountain nectar of Eastern Tennessee, but I draw the line at love. Will it intoxicate? Prithee, good sirs, I positively decline to experiment. However, if hearsay evidence be admissible I'm willing to take the stand. To the best of my knowledge and belief love will pick a man up quicker and throw him down harder than even the double-distilled brand of prohibition busthead. Like champagne at 2 g. m., it is good to look upon and pleasant to the palate; but at last it biteth like a serpent and stingeth like an able-bodied bumble-bee in a pair of blue-jean pants. Like alcoholism, love lies in wait for the young and unwary—approaches the victim so insidiously that ere he is aware of danger he's a gone sucker. The young man goeth forth in the early evening and his patent leathers. His coat-tail pockets bulge with caramels and his one silk handkerchief, perfumed with attar of roses, reposeth with studied negligence in his bosom. He saith unto himself, "I will sip the nectar of the blind deity but I will not become drunken, for verily I know when to ring myself down." He calleth upon the innocent damosel with soft eyes and lips like unto a cleft cherry when purple with its own sweetness, and she singeth unto him with a voice that hath the low sweet melody of an aeolian harp, and squozeth his hand in the gloaming, sigheth just a wee wee sigh that endeth in a blush. And behold it cometh to pass that when the gay young man doth stagger down the doorsteps of her dear father's domicile he knoweth not whether he is hoofing it to Klondyke or riding an erratic mustang into Mex-

ico. He is drunken with the sweetness of it all and glad
of it. And she? Oh she lets him down easy—sends him
an engraved invitation to her marriage with some guy with
oodles of the long green whom her parent on her mother's
side has corraled at the matrimonial bargain counter. Then
the young man has a case of what we Chermans call Katzenjammer, and swears an almighty swore never to do so
any more. But he does. When a man once contracts the
habit of being in love there's no help for him. It is a
strange stimulant which acts upon the blood like the oen-
anthic of old wine, upon the soul like the perfume of jasmine buds. He has felt its mighty spell, more potent than
the poppy's juice or the distillation of yellow corn that has
waved its golden bannerets on Kentucky's sun-kissed hills
—more strangely sweet than music heard at midnight across
a moonlit lake or the soul-sensuous dream of the lotus
eaters' land. For the spell of the poppy's dreamy drug and
the charm of the yellow corn whose spirit breeds dangerous
lightnings in the blood, the skill of man has provided a
panacea; but "love is strong as death," says David's wisest
son. Will love intoxicate? Rather! I should say that
Solomon was drunk with love when he wrote the Canticles:

"Let him kiss me with the kisses of his mouth, for thy love is
better than wine."

When a man is drunken he sees strange varieties of ser-
pents. That's what ailed Adam and Eve. They kept intoxi-
cated with their own primordial sweetness until they got the
jimmies and saw a talking snake prancing around the ever-
green aisles of Eden with legs like unto a prima donna. At
least I suppose the Edenic serpent was built that way, for
the Lord cursed it and compelled it to go on its belly all
the days of its life. Hence the Lord must have pulled its
leg. So to speak, or words to that effect. As an intoxicant
love affects one differently from liquor. A man drunk on
bourbon wants to trail his coat-tails down the middle of the
plank turnpike and advise the natives that he is in town.
The man drunk on love yearns to hide away from the busy
haunts of men and write poetry for the magazines. The
one is sentenced to ten days in the bat-cave and the other
to pay some woman's board. Verily the way of the trans-
gressor is hard. Some people manage to worry thro' life
without ever becoming drunken on either liquor or love.
They marry for money, or to secure housekeepers, and drink
pink lemonade and iced buttermilk until there's clabber in
their blood. They "like" their mates, but do not love them,

and their watery babes grow up and become Baptists. Their
affections are to the real article what dengue is to yellow
fever. Temperance is a good thing in its way; but the
man who is temperate in love is not to be trusted. The true
man or woman can no more love moderately than a powder
magazine can explode on the installment plan. When the
cup once touches their lips it is drained to the very dregs.
The chalice is not passed by human hands—the gods give
and the gods withhold. Hence it is that we ever find Love's
bacchanals beating against the social bars. We laugh at
the man who flushed with wine disregards the peace and
dignity of the state; but we frown upon the woman who
drunk with love sins against our social laws. Man's brewed
enchantments may be set aside by acts of human will; but
the wine of love creeps like a subtle perfume thro' all the
senses whether we will or no, filling the brain with madness,
the heart with fire.

A NATIONAL POEM.

The Author's Publishing Company is the name of a
New York concern that is preparing to play Maecenas to
merit and endow men of genius with what John J. Ingalls
would call "wealth beyond the dreams of avarice." It is
sending broadcast over the country what purports to be a
nameless "national poem," and chained to this acephalous
literary morceau is a proposition to pay $100 in currency
of the realm to the party suggesting the most appropriate
title. This "poem" purports to be the work of one
Ardenas Foster, who promises to supply the public with
130 pages of his poetic yearnings before the robins nest
again. We do not know who Ardenas may be; but suspect he is none other than our old friend Orie Bower, the
erstwhile "Poet of the Rockies," who has disguised himself with a clean shave, a paper dickey and a new pseu-
donym. He writes like Orie. His muse has the same
happy-go-lucky gait—a confusing compromise between
the long swinging trot of a hungry coyote and the "London lope," now so fashionable with the New York's
Anglo-Maniacal Four Hundred. His lines have the same
sensuous lilt, his song the identical dreamy cadence that
caused the Greasers to swim the Rio Grande, the jackass
rabbits to waltz on their hind legs and Major Fuel to
climb Mount Franklin's rugged steeps and reflect on his

latter end when Orie tuned his lyre and poured out his aesthetic soul in song as poet-laureate of El Paso's Mc-Ginty club. Ardenas must be Orie in disguise—or Amelie Rives Chanler seeking an antidote for her early aphrodisiacs. We have room for but one verse; but it's a crackerjack, the gem of the collection and illustrates how Ardenas can soar when he spreads his pinions and takes a header into the poetic empyrean. Those who desire to follow Ardenas in his flight can secure telescopes at this office without extra charge.

> Columbia! recurrent pregnant maid,
>   And bosom throbbing with ripe harvest-heat,
> Till multitudes from thy fresh garners feed,
>   And on thy shores Creation's races meet.

We fear that the Author's Publishing Company is not doing the proper thing. We submit that any one who can put an appropriate head on such a priceless literary torse deserves more than a hundred dollars. Ardenas is nothing if not original. A "recurring pregnant maid" is an idea with which even the immortal Bard of Avon was unacquainted. Dante never dreamed of such a thing. Milton knew naught of "recurring pregnant maids." And we confess, with a feeling akin to shame, that we had not thought of the fair sex in that light ourselves—and we have associated with Rebecca Merlindy Johnson a good deal. Ardenas is the avatar of originality. He is metaphor personified. He is poetic license with the bridle off. He explores new paths of poesy with the reckless abandon of a troubadour. He opens new vistas in literature with a simple, presto, change! But he hurries us along too fast. He doesn't allow us time to become well acquainted with the ofttimes pregnant maid before asking us to contemplate creation's races meeting on her "shores." But we suppose it is all right. Certainly nothing can be impossible to a pregnant maid. She may have not only shores, but seas and a north and south pole, for aught we know. If Ardenas says so we'll believe it. We should trust our men of genius and follow unquestioningly whithersoever they lead. We shall wait for the remainder of Ardenas Foster's book with impatience. We are anxious to see what may be the peculiarities of the rest of his maids. But we trust that he will not permit creation's races to feed on them or trample their "shores" with hob-nailed shoes. At least not while the maids are pregnant. We trust that in sending out autograph copies to the press Ardenas will not overlook the Iconoclast. If

the book contains his portrait as a frontispiece we will
be only the better pleased. There's a goat in this town
we've got it in for.

BRANN ON HUMBUGS.

[The following excerpts are from Mr. Brann's lecture at Dallas
Opera House, October 17, 1895.]

A discourse on political humbugs were incomplete
without some reference to the young man whom Texas,
in a moment of mental aberration, raised to the chief
magistracy. I learn from a sermon recently inflicted on
the long-suffering inhabitants of this city, that Son
Charles is "our heroic young Christian governor." How
he must have changed during the last few months!
Shakespeare was probably viewing the Texas politician
with prophetic eye when he declared that in the great
Drama of Life a man plays many parts. Culberson is the
only one, however, who has yet succeeded in playing
them all at one and the same time. A man who can run
with the hare politically while holding with the hounds
personally, is almost too versatile to be virtuous. "Our
heroic young Christian governor!" That preacher evidently doesn't know Charles. Or if he does his idea of
Christianity is not so altitudinous that he can stand on
its apex and keep the flies off the man in the moon.
Culberson is a politician who enjoyed excellent health
before he entered the public service. He is all things to
all men and—"nothing to nobody." He's so slippery that
he couldn't stand on the partisan platform to which he
owes his political elevation. In the last gubernatorial
election pretty much every man who voted for Culberson
felt that he hand a lead-pipe cinch on a fat office, and
the remainder were certain he would work four-and-
twenty hours a day to put in effect their pet reforms.
They are wiser now. In 1890 Charlie sailed into the at-
torney-generalship on the ample coat-tails of one J. S
Hogg, and in less than thirty days he was conspiring to
retire his chief after one term and slip into his official
shoes. The trouble appears to be that the youngster was
pulled before he was ripe—before his political integrity
had time to harden, or his crop of wild oats was well in
the ground.

Now I want it distinctly understood that I am not the

apologist of pugilism; I am the apostle of the white-winged Goddess of Peace. I always carry a cruse of oil in my hip-pocket to cast upon the troubled waters. I have a pacific effect on all with whom I come in contact. Children quit crying when they see me coming, women speak well of their neighbors, men respect each other's political opinions, preachers engage in silent prayer and the lion and the lamb lie down together. And that's no lie. But as between pugilism and hypocrisy I prefer the former. I would rather see men pound each other for a fat purse than play the canting Pharisee to promote their political fortunes.

* * *

Let us look to the record of "our heroic young Christian governor." During the four years he officiated as attorney-general he made no determined effort to enforce the law then in effect prohibiting pugilism. Prizefights were pulled off at Galveston, San Antonio, El Paso and other Texas points after having been duly advertised in the daily press. He was elevated to the chief magistracy of the State, and the slugging matches continued—mills between brawny but unskilled boxers, who relied upon brute strength, and pounded each other to a pumice to make a hoodlum holiday. Some of these meetings were especially brutal—as matches between amateur athletes are likely to be; but "our heroic young Christian governor" saw no occasion to get his Ebenezer up. He simply sawed wood—didn't care a continental whether there was a law prohibiting bruising bouts or not.

And the ministerial associations were too busy taking up collections to send Bibles and blankets, salvation and missionary soup to the pagans of the antipodes to pay much attention to these small-fry pugs. They let our blessed "Texas civilization" take care of itself, while they agonized over a job lot of lazy negroes whose souls ain't worth a sou-markee in blocks of five; who wouldn't walk into heaven if the gates were wide open, but once inside would steal the eternal throne if it wasn't spiked down. No Epworth Leaguers or Christian Endeavorers where-ased, resoluted or perorated until their tongues were worn to a frazzle, trying to "preserve the honor of our ger-ate and gal-orious State by suppressing feather-pillow pugilism." Why? I don't know; do you? Of course some carping critics declare it was because the world was not watching these brutal slugging matches between youths to pugilistic fortune and fame unknown; that it was because the professionally pious had no opportunity to make a grandstand play and get their names in print—no chance to *pose* in the eye of the universe as the conservators of our *fin de siecle* civilization. But then these Doubting Thomases are ever ready to make a mock of the righteous and put cockleburrs in the back hair of the godly. I dislike to criticise "the cloth." I am prone to believe that the preachers always do the best they know how; still, I must confess that I am unable to muster up much admiration for the brass band variety of "religion" or the tutti-frutti trademark of "respectability."

Had the belief not been bred in my bones that there is a God in Israel, these little 2x4 preachers, with their great moral hippodrome—their purblind blinking at mountains and much-ado about molehills—would drive me to infidelity. By their egregious folly, their fiery denunciation of all men who dare disagree with them, their attempt to make the State subservient to the church, to establish an *imperium in imperio*—by their mischievous meddling in matters that in nowise concern them, they are bringing the beautiful religion of Christ into contempt—are doing more to foster doubt than did all the Humes and Voltaires and Paines that ever wielded pen.

Now don't get the idea that I am antagonistic to the preachers. Far from it. I am something of a minister myself; and we who have been called to labor in the Lord's vineyard—at so much per annum—must stand together. I admire the ministers in a general way—and "whom the Lord loveth he chasteneth." I feel that it is my duty to pull them tenderly but firmly back by the little alpaca coat-tails whenever they have made mistakes —to reprove them in all gentleness when I find them fanning themselves with their ears for the amusement of the mob.

But to return to "our heroic young Christian governor." When it was first proposed to bring the great fistic carnival and a million dollars to Dallas, Gov. Culberson had nothing to say. It was popularly supposed that he understood the law and would respect it. The impression got abroad that he felt rather friendly to the enterprise because it would put 500 scudi in the depleted coffers of the public and turn a great deal of ready money loose within the confines of Texas. He may not have been directly responsible for this popular idea, but he certainly did nothing to discourage it. Arrangements were perfected, important contracts entered into, a vast amount of money invested that would prove a complete loss if the enterprise collapsed. Then Culberson began to complain. He suddenly discovered that pugilism was a brutal sport, which should be suppressed. His conversion was as instantaneous as that of Saul of Tarsus. It were an insult to the intelligence of a hopeless idiot to say he did not know the Corbett-Fitzsimmons affair would prove far less brutal than a hundred fistic encounters which he, as attorney-general and governor, had tacitly encouraged—but his jewel of consistency had evidently gone to join his diamond stud. Col. Dan Stuart didn't appear inclined to do anything to ease the young man's agony, and it rapidly went from bad to worse. The Hurt decision was rendered, and the moral volcano of "our heroic young Christian governor" began to erupt in earnest. He declared that he would override the court of criminal appeals "if men enough can be found in Texas to do it"—gave an excellent imitation of an anarchist who is hungering for canned gore. After this blood-to-horses'-bridles bluff he grew quiescent—waited, Micawber-like, for something to turn up. And still Dan Stuart didn't say a word. Then "our heroic young Christian governor" broke out in a new place. The legislature was convened in extraordinary session to prevent a brace of pugilists smashing the immortal ichor out of modern civilization. It was a great moral aggregation—almost equal to Artemus Ward's WaxWurx! I am convinced of this, for it employed two doctors of divinity—at public cost, of course—to pray over it a minute each morning, for $5 per diem each. Everybody expected the president of the Florida Athletic Club to go to Austin and make an earnest free silver speech. Even the lawmakers were looking for him; but he didn't go—and the result was what might have been expected. The law-builders with the worst private records had the most to say about public morality. Men whose I. O. U.'s are not good in a game of penny ante; whose faces are familiar to the inmates of every disreputable dive between the Sabine and the Rio Bravo; who go to their legislative duties from the gambling-room and with six-shooters in the busts of their breeches, grew tearful over the prospective "disgrace of Texas" by a manly boxing bout. Hell hath no fury like a legislative humbug scorned —while he's holding his hand behind him.

* * *

But the wrath of "our heroic young Christian governor" did not abate with the enactment of a law forbidding prizefights—such a law as he had flagrantly failed to enforce. The promoters of what the court of criminal appeals declared a lawful enterprise were arrested and dragged before the grand jury of Travis county, which appears to have taken the entire earth under its protectorate. Failing an opportunity to prosecute them for an offense against the laws of the land, the powers at Austin proceeded to prosecute them on the hypothesis that they were conspiring to wreck the universe.

And what was their offense? They had "conspired" to pay $500 into the public treasury and bring a million more to Dallas. They had "conspired" to bring several thousand respectable business men to Texas from all parts of the Union and furnished employment at good wages for hundreds of hungry men.

While I do not much admire pugilism as a profession, I must say that the promoters of the enterprise conducted themselves much better than did "our heroic young Christian governor," and those alleged saints who proposed to shoulder their little shotguns and help him override the courts—to butcher their brethren in cold blood to prevent an encounter between brawny athletes armed with pillows; to sustain "modern civilization" by transforming the metropolis of Texas into a charnel-house—to prevent, by brutal homicide in the name of Christ, their neighbors exercising those liberties accorded them by the laws of the land.

* * *

Curious, this modern civilization of which we hear so much. During the palmy days of Roman grandeur and Grecian glory, their athletes fought with the terrible cestus to win a crown of oak or laurel; but then Rome never produced a Rev. Seasholes, nor Greece a Senator Bowser. The Imperial City did manage to breed a Brutus and a Cato, but never proved equal to a Culberson Think of a Texas legislature, composed chiefly of illiterate jabberwhacks who string out the sessions interminably for the sake of the $2 a day—imagine these fellows, each with a large pendulous ear to the earth, listening for the approach of some Pegasus to carry him to Congress—teaching the aesthetics of civilization to the divine philosophers of Greece and the god-like senators of Rome! Think of Perry J. Lewis pulling the Conscript Fathers over the coals—of Senator Bowser pointing out civic duties to Socrates; of Attorney-General Crane giving Julius Caesar a piece of his mind; of Charley Culberson turning up his little two-for-a-nickel nose at the Olympian games! But perhaps that is not the game "our heroic young Christian governor" is most addicted to.

*   *   *

Prizefighting—even with pillows, for points—is bad enough, no doubt; but there are worse things. Making the Texas people pay for an abortive little second-term gubernatorial boom is one of them, and canting hypocrisy by sensation-seeking preachers is another. Can the church and state find no grander work than camping on the trail of a couple of pugilists? Are Gentleman Jim and Kangaroo Bob the upper and nether millstones between which humanity is being ground? Are these the only obstacles to the inauguration of the Golden Age—that era of Peace on Earth and Good Will to Men? The world is honeycombed with crime. Brother Seasholes says there are 800 fallen women in this city alone—and I presume he knows. But if these be half so many, what a terrible story of human degradation—more appalling even than soft-glove pugilism! Our streets swarm with able-bodied beggars—young men, most of them, whom want may drive into wickedness. Human life is cheap. Men are slain in this alleged Christian land for less silver than led Judas to betray Christ. Young girls are sold to shame, and from squalid attics comes the cry of starving babes. The Goths and Visigoths are once more gathering, imperiling civilization itself, and belief in God is fading slowly but surely from the earth. Want and wretchedness skulk in the shadows of our temples, ignorance and crime stalk abroad at high noon—the legions of Lucifer are overrunning the land, transforming God's beautiful world into a veritable Gehenna. The Field of Blood is filling, the prisons and poorhouses are overflowing—crowded with wretched creatures who dared dream of fame and fortune. The great Sea of Life is thick-strewn with wrecks—millions more drifting helpless and hopeless upon the rocks. From out the darkness there come cries for aid; men pleading for employment, women shrieking in agony of soul, little children wailing with hunger and cold. And the winds wax ever stronger, the waves run higher and higher, the wreck and wraith grow ever more pitiful, more appalling. And church and state pause in this mad vortex of chaos to prate of the ills of pugilism; to legislate and perorate anent bloodless boxing bouts; to prosecute a brace of harmless pugs. The people ask bread of the church and it gives them a stone; they ask of the state protection of

their lives and liberties, and it gives them a special session
of the legislature—shoots doodle-bugs with a Gatling gun—
and sends them the bill!

*   *   *

But to recur for a moment to the fistic carnival: Have
any of you been able to determine how the Dallas News
stood in regard to that great enterprise? Sometimes, when
I want to go on an intellectual debauch, I read the News—
or Ayer's Almanac. It appears to entertain but two opinions, namely, that Uncle Sam should black the boots of
John Bull, and that Grover Cleveland carries the brains
of the world in his beebum. This brace of abortive ideas
constitute its confession of faith—the only things of which
it feels absolutely certain. When it tackles anything else it
wobbles in and it wobbles out like an unhappy married man
trying to find his way home at five o'clock in the morning.
A great diplomat once declared that language was made
to conceal thought; but the Dallas News employs it to disguise an intellectual vacuum. It can use more language
to say less than any other publication on earth. In this
particular it is like Napoleon—it stands wrapt in the solitude of its own originality.

The eating of thirty quail in thirty days was once a popular test of human endurance; but I can propose a more cru-
cial one—one that will attract more people to Dallas than
would even the Corbett-Fitzsimmons fight. Let the people
of this city offer a fat purse for the man who can read the
editorial page of the Dallas News thirty days in succession
without degenerating into a driveling idiot. It is a mental
impossibility, of course; but perhaps my good friend
"Dorry" can be persuaded to attempt it—to hoist himself
with his own petard. No man born of woman will ever
accomplish it. Massillon would become a mental bankrupt
within the month and Socrates have to be tapped for the
simples before reaching the half-way house.

The *News* is troubled with a chronic case of Anglomania. Whenever Columbia has a controversy of any
kind with Brittania, the *News* hastens to ally itself with
the Britisher; but in matters concerning the welfare of
the city of Dallas it has little to say. It did manifest a
slight inclination to take up for the fistic enterprise—
fearfully slid one foot to terra-firma; but when the success
of the carnival became doubtful the *News* hastened to
resume its time-honored position astride the fence, and it
has hung there ever since—like a foul dish-rag across a
wire clothes line. It's the greatest journalistic 'Fraid on

the face of the earth. It doesn't dare to risk the opinion
that water is wet. But probably it isn't sure of it. It is
just as well, however, for if it did know, it couldn't leak
the information in less than a column. The editorial page
of the Dallas *News* reminds me of the Desert of Sahara
after a simoon—it is such an awful waste of space. If I
had a five-year-old boy who couldn't say more in fifteen
minutes than the Dallas *News* has said in the last dozen
years, I'd refuse to father him.

One of the greatest frauds of modern times is the pol-
icy-playing newspaper. The "Archimedean lever," as
applied to daily journalism is a fake of the first magni-
tude. There is not a morning newspaper in Texas possessing sufficient political influence to elect a pound-
master. In fact, their support will damn any politician
eternally, for the people wisely conclude that what the
alleged "great dailies" support is a pretty good thing for
them to oppose. Hogg would not have reached the governorship but for the blatant opposition of the morning
press. Its friendship for George Clark was the upas-
shadow in which he perished politically. There hasn't
been an important law enacted in Texas during the last
ten years that it didn't oppose. And yet men actually
imagine that they cannot succeed in politics, business or
letters without the assistance of that great "moulder of
public opinion!" Let me tell you that every success this
country has witnessed during the past three decades was
achieved despite the morning press. To paraphrase Owen
Meredith:

> "Let a man once show the press that he feels
> Afraid of its bark, and 'twill fly at his heels;
> Let him fearlessly face, 'twill leave him alone;
> But 'twill fawn at his feet if he flings it a bone."

A NEW YORK SAWCIETY SHEET.

Some few of my readers may have incidentally heard
of a little sawciety paper published in New York City
called *Town Topics*. Its editor, having fired a couple of
front-page malodors at me, sends me a marked copy,
thinking perhaps I may be induced to call general attention to the fact that he is on the earth. It is impossible
for me to accord a free notice to every impudent pamph-
leteer and .22-caliber editor who attacks me for advertising purposes only. Believing with Tennyson that 'tis

"weakness to be wroth with weakness," I seldom waste
any shot on sawciety sheets. Nor am I in the habit of
taking up the gage thrown down by papers that exist by
pandering to pruriency, knowing that if given time they
will stink themselves into a state of "innocuous desue-
tude." *Town Topics,* however, seems to be regarded with
some degree of toleration by New York's "h'upper suk-
kles," and may, therefore, be worth a moment's attention
as indicating the moral and mental drift of our soi-disant
"best sawciety." Social as well as medical doctors sometimes find the handling of very dirty subjects an imperative duty. *Town Topics* is what is known in the terse vernacular of Hungry Hill and Tincan Alley as a journalistic
"nancy"—a trifle too dirty for decency and too epicene for
aggressive immorality. It is one of those papers which
an imbecile may understand much better than a man of
strong mentality, because the latter seeks a *raison d' etre*
for everything. Its distinguished feature is a dreary
waste of inane tittle-tattle anent the doings and mis-
doings of uppertendom. It can tell you to a minute when
the charming, beautiful and accomplished Miss Isolde
DePeyster Hamfat-Crupper became engaged to the re-
doubtable Count Orlando Bombastico Furioso Marraroni
de Cagliostro, how many buttons she will wear on the
bifurcated garment of her wedding lingerie, and whether
the broken windows in the count's ancestral castle are
stuffed with old hats or baled hay. It knows how often
J. J. Van Alen changes his sox and with what material
the exuberant basement of T. Suffern Tailor's riding
britches are half-soled—information in nowise to be despised in this era boasting itself heir of all the ages. It
knows, and relates with many winks and nods and
sayshes and sayshes, with ostentatious concealment of
names but not of persons, how Mr. and Mrs. Stubantwist
quarreled during their honeymoon, what occasioned the
Vanderbiltian divorce, and the Drayton-Astor estrangement with the subsequent duel in which "never any died."
All of which is strengthening to the mind as drinking
sweetened wind out of a toy balloon is to the body.
Town Topics has other features in a lighter vein which
make it popular with morbid young persons just verging
on pubescence, and who need a mild purgative and plenty
of exercise in the open air. To precocious kids in the
Werterian state, *Town Topics* is a valuable *pons asinorium,*
being a very charming cross between a vermiculous
diaper and the toga virilis. Its stories are intended for

neurotics only. They have all the shudder and groan of
a nigger with the buck ague, the inexpressible longing of
a hound pup fondly eyeing a rump-bone through an im-
passable picket fence. They are dank with a helpless,
hopeless dismalness which suggests death by dope to
escape the pangs of pruriency, and have all the unctu-
osity of a hot corn-dodger slathered with sop. Its heroes
seldom do anything awfully dreadful, but this fact is
never the fault of its heroines. It is a kinetoscope exhibition of Madame Potiphar and Joseph that makes you
want to encourage the young Hebrew with a club,
Town Topics is the chief exponent of that soulful decadence
of which Oscar Wilde was the high priest. But perhaps
I do the great English pervert an injustice. He had some
inturbidated idea of attaining the beautiful through the
brutal, of going to heaven by way of hell. He saw that
the rose springs from rottenness, that sweet perfumes
are extracted from impurities, that the foul emanations
of earth make the lightnings flash and roll the thunder
drums of heaven, and was really striving in a blind way
toward better things when mired in the serbonian bogs
of his own bestiality; but the editor of the paper in question bedaubs himself with the slime of sewers, not because it nurtures beauty and fragrance, but because it
breeds malodors and maggots. A man may be pardoned
for handling muck if it be to build therewith a Jacob's
Ladder, or even a Tower of Babel to reach high heaven;
but the *Town Topics* man has no other object than that of
the barefoot schoolboy who makes a squirt up between
his toes—he simply enjoys the sensation. Not being
skilled in teratology, I am unable to assign "The Saun-
terer" to a proper place among the mental misfits and
moral abnormalities; but his articles suggest some toothless old sybarite in whom age has caused perversion instead of repentance, and whose soul is ever rioting in the
nameless infamies of the Orient. There is a faint suggestion in all his stuff, not of Margery, Moll and Meg,
but of a married sawciety beaut rolling home in a closed
hack in the early dawn, with a chappie holding her head
while the champagne and *pate de foie gras* leaves its intra-
parietal recess and drules over the front elevation of her
decollette. I can cheerfully recommend *Town Topics* to any
one in need of an aspositic, and suggest it to the "mind-
cure" mountebanks as a valuable succedaneum for *nux
vomica*. It should be the official organ of every suicide club
in the country, being well calculated to disgust every sane

man with the whole human race and make him desire a
speedy death. Such is the journalistic favorite of New
York's Four Hundred. No wonder that Gotham sawciety
has become simply a nest of epicene Anglo-maniacs and
whining Mugwumps. Should a man attempt the publication of such a paper in Texas we'd hang him, for the same
reason that we kill glandered horses, send imbeciles to
the asylum and eliminate lice.

. GODEY'S MAGAZINE FOR MOKES.

My attention has just been called to the fact that *Godey's
Lady Book—Godey's Magazine,* as it is now called—is still
upon the earth. I have before me the first copy thereof I
have seen for a quarter of a century, the second one I ever
examined. I remember well that when a kid I asked my
sister for paper of which to build a kite, and she gave me
a copy of *Godey's Lady Book,* advising me at the same
time to "tie a grindstone to it for a tail," it being, she said,
"the lightest thing in literature." I examined it and found
in it a thin, sloppy periodical, containing some hay-fever
fiction, a number of impossible fashion-plates and cholera-
morbid sauce recipes. I supposed, if I thought about it at
all, that *Godey's* had gone to the rubbish heap long ago;
but it seems that "the lightest thing in literature" has managed to keep afloat, heaven knows how or why, while
scores of better magazines have been buried. Perchance
an inscrutable providence has preserved it that it might
eventually become the fashionable magazine of the negro
aristocracy of the feminine gender, a beatitude to which it
has attained after weary pilgrimage of more than half a
century. I hasten to extend to its present publishers the
glad hand and congratulate them on their enterprise, for
I imagine that it fills what the country editor calls "a long-
felt want" and fills it brimming full. Now that it has at
last reached its intellectual and social level and is content
with its lot, it should be accorded every encouragement.
The colored women of America are certainly entitled to a
magazine; and it seems that at last there has arisen a
counterpart of Eddie Bok to sling into their yearning souls
the same class of intellectual soup which makes the *Ladies'
Home Journal* a perennial joy. And Philadelphia is just
the place for a journal devoted to fashionable colored females. Simultaneously with the arrival of *Godey's Colored*

Lady Book for July the dailies announce the wedding in
that city of a so-called respectable white woman of alleged
good family with a coon, the interesting ceremony being
performed by the rector of the Protestant Episcopal Church
of the Crucified. The name of this progressive female who
has started in to solve the race problem was Constance
Mackenzie. As she loves niggers so well, let us devoutly
pray that she will give birth to a brace of brats as often
as possible, and that all her pickaninnies will be black as
the hinges of hell. As for Rev. Villers, who performed the
ceremony, I trust that his cup of joy will be filled to overflowing by his becoming grandfather to a bevy of woolly
half-breeds, for I think it would improve the Villers' stock
to graft it on the cornfield coon. Evidently the cullud people are getting up in the pictures, and are entitled to the
very best Bokism the Godey Company can give them. I
suppose that all the articles in the July number of that
periodical will be written by negroes, as it has the subtle
flavor of an old pair of sox. "The Colored Woman of To-
day," is a subject handled by Fannie Barrie Williams, a
chipper octoroon well calculated to catch a Republican's
eye. The article is illumined with the portraits of ten "up-
to-date colored ladies," evidently ranging in complexion
from a brunette banana to a blonde canary bird. Just why
these notable black women are seven-eighths white, Fannie
does not see fit to inform us. She frankly assures us, however, that "there are thousands of cultured women of the
colored race who are worth knowing, and are prepared to
co-operate with white women in all good efforts," etc.; all
of which is quite comforting, as I was beginning to fear
that these paragons of their sex were too proud to "co-
operate" with the humble Caucasian. Fannie is quite certain that, contrary to the opinion of white people with
ample opportunity to study the Senegambian, many colored females are virtuous as Dian, lovely as Ophelia and
among "the most interesting women in the land." It may
be so; but certain it is that these superior creatures do not
trot around much in Texas. I do not find fault with Fannie for bepraising her own people to the extent of accredit-
ing them with both virtue and intelligence; but if she would
produce a few "colored ladies" with a trifle more fuligin-
osity in their faces it would reflect greater credit on the
race with which bright quadroons and chipper octoroons
are peremptorily classed. The fact that her ten samples
of estimable woomanhood are chiefly of Caucasian blood
does not say much for the progress of the blacks. An ani-

mal one part baboon and seven parts Bostonese could probably acquire a taste for beans and learn to relish Browning; but his Simian blood would be considered a curse rather than a credit. All the women with whose portraits Fannie favors us may be virtuous as the wife of Caesar; but no one of them would be a full-blood negress if she could, while the fact that she is not shows that her lineage is marked by the bar-sinister. As marriages between Caucasians and coons are not much encouraged outside the Episcopalian circles of Philadelphia, the existence of an octoroon—the *creme de la creme* of "ladies of color," presupposes at least three flagrant cases of bastardy—and Fannie can scarce complain if the white people as a rule do not expect an evil tree to bring forth good fruit. The next article in this interesting number is a novelette by one Frederick W. Pangborn, evidently a coon, for he not only makes a yaller gal his heroine, but proclaims her superior in beauty, education and general accomplishments to the average white woman. But Freddie, with all his admiration for dark-eyed Dulcinas, was not born and bred in Dixie, for he imagines that an octoroon is not necessarily part negro. He succeeds, however, in producing one by the aid of a white man and a mulatto wench, which in this part of God's creation would be regarded as very much of a miracle. Godey's contains other articles by various authors; but as the thermometer registers 90 in proximity to the ice box, I must leave further examination of Ethiopian essays until cooler weather, my nose already being, like that of Trinculo, "in great indignation." I cannot say that Godey's has improved since a sharp-tongued schoolgirl contemptuously referred to it as "the lightest thing in literature," valuable for kite-making—if a grindstone be tied to the tail; but it is a great comfort to reflect that its present burden of banalities cannot be charged up to white people. That its corps of contributors are coons. Viewed as a production of the blacks or quarter-breeds— Godey's is not half bad. Whether the publishing company be composed of coons I am not informed; nor have I been advised regarding the color of the new editor. It would have been more manly had the publishers notified their white patrons of the proposed change in the color of their "Lady;" but as they take it solely for the sauce recipes aforesaid and to keep pace with the improvements in complexion powders they will probably care little what is done with the rest of the paper. While by no means a social equality shrieker, nor much in favor of solving the race problem by fading the nigger out by fornication, I like the Ethiopian—in his place, and that place is the cotton patch. I have yet to see the nigger, male or female, full-blood or quarter-breed, who wasn't irrevocably ruined by being relieved of the necessity of manual labor. Take a buck out of the cotton and dress him in broadcloth and he isn't half worth killing. Relieve a wench of hard work and she quickly acquires the brazen swing that says, "I'se bahd." A magazine like Godey's may not help them much, but it is too epicene to do anything serious harm. If it will do the best it can and henceforth keep pictures of white women out of its pages, I'll subscribe for a copy and compel the negroes on my ranch to read it, even tho' it gives them chronic malaise and unfits them for active duty in the cotton field.

DEAN HART OF DENVER.

The dispatches state that Dean H. Martyn Hart, of St. John's Cathedral, has been caught smuggling valuable furs into this country from Canada. I am not surprised that he should attempt to defraud the United States, for he has ever been a blatant and insolent enemy of the country from whose resources an inscrutable providence permits him to fill his sacerdotal paunch. Whether he were an assisted immigrant I know not; but according to popular opinion when he arrived here from his beloved England his umbilicus was hobnobbing with his backbone. I am told that he had to leave his native land to find something to eat, and quite naturally he turned his face to "the refuge of the world's oppressed," which has transformed so many English paupers into intolerable prigs. A few rectangular American meals sufficed to develop his latest insolence, and now he is fully as offensive as the average British Leggar placed on horseback. When I last heard of this erstwhile hungry Uitlander, now grown so great on American grub, he was trying to pull the leg of the Colorado people for a "Victoria Wing" to St. Luke's Hospital—was urging them to contribute liberally to prove how glad they were that the Queen is a respectable old party instead of a foul-mouthed prostitute like certain of her predecessors. In his appeal, published in the Denver *Republican,* he said:

"The world owes the Queen an immense debt of gratitude. She has set an example of purity of life which has been an incalculable power for good to the whole society of the world. What might have been the condition of that

society to-day if the first lady of the world had not set such
an example as has thrust immorality, bribery and corruption into the shade of disrepute, who can tell? * * Every
miner in Colorado should not only perpetuate the memory
of the good Queen he has a right to be proud of, but for
precaution's sake, on his own account, he should send a
subscription," etc., etc.

England, as well as other European countries, has had
dissolute Queens without materially affecting the world's
morality.   So far back as history sheds its light the better
class of people have not been prone to form their morals on
royal models; which is just as well, perhaps, as a majority of
monarchs have been sexual sinners.   As Semiramis and
Messalina, Catherine and Elizabeth could not by their dissolute lives banish from the world the blush of modesty; as it
withstood the assaults of the founders and defenders of the
Church of England faith, it would probably have survived
had Victoria been beautiful as Anne Boleyn and passionate
as Cleopatra, instead of homely as a hedge fence in her youth
and phlegmatic as a dead catfish in her age.   I have too
much confidence in womankind to believe that one Queen,
even tho' she be a Helen of Troy instead of a gin-guzzling
gain-grabber, can wreck society irrevocably.   Nor can I see
why one whose kids and their progeny are so handsomely
provided for at public expense, and who receives some $2,-
000,000 per annum for doing nothing, unless it be for writing foolish books which nobody reads, should be especially
commended for not entering, like some of her poorly paid
predecessors, into schemes of "bribery and corruption."   It
is dead easy to be honest on $2,000,000 per annum.   As
there is a limit to the universe, there must be an *ultima
thule* even to a "good Queen's" greed.   Of course the Colorado miners have a perfect "right to be proud" of a sovereign who rolls in riches while millions of her subjects
are starving; who donated one-third of her income for *one.
day* to relieve the famine sufferers of India, who, during
her entire reign, have been ruthlessly robbed for England's
enrichment; who connived at the scheme which fastened
the single gold standard on America, filling the land with
idle men and reducing thousands of silver miners to the
verge of starvation; but it is a "right" that few of them will
exercise so long as they can keep out of the lunatic asylum.
Having in mind the proverbial thriftiness of John Bull, his
vulpine resourcefulness when there is a shilling in sight, I
became curious to know something of the hospital scheme
engineered by Dean Hart, and whether miners who gave

up their scant earnings to build the Victoria annex would be treated without cost in case of accident. The following excerpt from a letter received from a prominent citizen of Colorado throws some light on the subject, and incidentally brings out the fine points of this fat-headed fraud who now fares sumptuously every day, instead of lunching as in auld lang syne on the fog banks of London:

"It is a favorite boast of Dean Hart that he never reads an American newspaper. Although he has been pastor (or 'dean') of St. John's Cathedral for a great many years he is still an English subject, never having been naturalized, and boasts of it. He is opposed to the public school system of this country, and writes articles to the different papers of the country, condemning the system. He has all his clothing imported from England or Canada. He invariably sends his wife to England that his children may 'escape the obloquy of being born American citizens.' These facts are not mere hearsay, but are notorious. But to you they must be superfluous. I have been told that you have lectured on the subject of 'Gall,' and in order to do the subject justice you must at one time have known Dean H. Martyn Hart. St. Luke's Hospital is not by any means the only good hospital in Denver. 'There are others.' It is an adjunct (for revenue only) of St. John's Cathedral. H. Martyn Hart is grand mogul of both institutions. Their charges range from $12 per week upwards in advance and there is no deviation from this rule."

So the miner who, "for precaution's sake on his own account," contributes to the Victorian Wing of St. Luke's in honor of "the first lady of the world," can, in case of accident, secure medical attention in the same concern for "$12 per week and upwards." If he isn't prepared to pay two prices for treatment that this Good Samaritan may slip abundant shekels into its sock, he can lie out in the street and rot so far as Saint (?) Luke's is concerned. The extensive circulation of the Iconoclast in Colorado leads me to hope that I can cave in the skull of that little scheme—can prevent the miners beings buncoed out of their money. It seems to me that a man with sufficient audacity to spring such a piece of disreputable dead-beatism would renounce the ministry and go into the confidence business right—with Senator Palmer for side-partner. Had the reverend gentleman who parts his name on the side like a 10-cent dude and dodges customs duties like a professional fraud, made a practice of reading the American newspapers instead of burdening his seldom brains with the dry rot of English diurnals, he might have learned (if capable of learning anything, which seems unlikely) that Colorado is not an appendage of the British crown; also that when a gabby Uitlander attacks the educational or other institutions of this country he runs considerable risk of getting his lungs kicked out by some self-respecting American citizen.   My correspondent is unnecessarily exercised because Hart takes the precaution to have his brats born dutiful British subjects instead of independent American sovereigns.   For that he cannot be too highly commended, for the sons might resemble their soupy sire.   The Republican party conferred American sovereignty upon the coon; but a pitying providence has prevented the proudest title known to human history being further degraded by Dean Hart.   I don't know but we should encourage this humble instrument of heaven's mercy to America by contributing to the Victorian Wing of St. Luke's Hospital.   By all means let Hart and all worshipful cattle of his kind ever remain the subjects of rheumy European royalty, humbly bending their rickety marrow-bones before the foolish bogey of the "divine right of banal descendants of certain bumbards and bawds to misrule and rob; for American citizenship is already weighted with all the "obloquy" it can comfortably carry.   We have got to draw the line somewhere if we would not have the title of American sovereign become as disreputable as that of British duke.   As to Victoria being "the first lady of the world" I have nothing to say, further than that the Kanakas having conferred the same high-sounding title on their own beloved Lillikizooki, the first ladies aforesaid are welcome to settle the controversy as best they can.   Were I selected to umpire the game I would certainly award the stakes to Hart's sovereign, believing as I do that even an Anglo-Saxon descended from a brutal and crazy king must be a shade better than a saddle-colored barbarian.   Nor can I blame the Englishman for making a mighty to do because, after so many centuries, one of their monarchs has honestly earned the right to be called respectable.   Such unexpected beatitude is certainly just cause for rejoicing.   Here in America we never think of congratulating ourselves that the first lady of the land is a model of womanly virtue; for we have not, never can have experience of any other kind.   In England the reverse was so long the case that we can readily appreciate John Bull's joy at finding himself under the rule of a monarch for whose private life he need not apologize.   May Victoria live long to reign if not to rule over the so-called Anglo-Saxons, and thereby enable John

Bull to hold up his head. As P. Henry would observe, "we can only judge the future by the past," which argues that she is an oasis of respectability in a boundless desert of royal debauchery.

"UNCLE WILLIAM" CAMERON.

The Apostle takes a day off to call the world's attention to Col. William Cameron of Waco, the commercial Collossus, the Napoleon of finance, the hub around which all great enterprises revolve. In the lexicon of public opinion we find the following entry: "Col. William Cameron, an up-to-date daisy, but no dude." Having lifted himself, by his own bootstraps, out of the Serbonian bogs of poverty to the milliononic plane, it follows that Col. William Cameron knows a thing or two—is "dead onto" all the world's ways that are dark and tricks that are vain. At least we were wont to think so—to imagine our Bill sharper than a serpent's tooth, the very *creme de la creme* of the "hot stuff." We were sure of it when he put back the gubernatorial crown proffered by the Texas Republicans, nailed up his smokehouse, set a bear trap in the donjon-keep of his hennery and padlocked both the bung and the spigot of his "bar'l." But alack and alas! Our idol is broken, our Carian marble hath proven but common clay. We have worshipped what Old John Knox would call a "pented bredd" those Arabian images ridiculed by Mahomet, as "gods—a gilded stick—and bowed us to the earth before one of with flies on them."

Col. William Cameron—our Bill—recently strayed from home and was spotted by a brace of gold-brick mountebanks as "a dead easy mark." They actually passed by Col. J. S. Hogg of the Link Line, with whom the Wall Street financiers have been having fun, and selected the representative citizen of Texas' educational center as their huckleberry-do, sized him up as the sucker most likely to fly at a piece o' red flannel! It was the old, old story; older than three-card monte and the shell game, older than the flim-flam of the circus ticket seller or the bank draft for 'steen thousand dollars worked off on the railway passenger from Posey county. A guileless youth with the flavor of the untamed West on his tongue, and the secret of the "Lost Mine" of Cortez and his Conquistadores concealed about his person, discovers that

Col. Cameron is his long-lost "Uncle William" with the strawberry mark on his left arm and a forgotten goatwalk amid Arizona's wilds. Upon the latter was located the rediscovered El Dorado. Sudden joy sometimes kills; but, by exercising great self-control, Col. Cameron was able to safely pass the crisis, even to wonder in a vague way how much his new-found relative wanted. This appeared, like the "chill penury" of the poet, to freeze the genial current of the young man's soul, and he hastened to assure the man of millions that his nevvy was no homeless hobo in search of a handout. He even went so far as to doubt their consanguinity, while incidentally displaying slugs of yellow metal which he had clipped from Uncle William's Arizona mine. His Mexican body servant inspected Col. Cameron and declared him an interloper and an alien, possessing no right or title to the golden treasure protruding itself thro' Arizona's sacred soil. It looked for a moment as tho' Col. Cameron would be arrested for an attempt to swindle himself. The young man was much discouraged. He wept because he could not find his real Uncle William and pour into his lap all the gold of Ophir and all the treasures of Ind. He was only a poor illiterate boy, brought up amid the cruel cactus and uncertain mescal of the uncouth West. Perhaps his companion would consent to manage the mine, to act as treasurer for this new and greater gold reserve; or, if not, he might be able to recommend some good honest man who would do so. It was truly touching, this innocent young man from Arizona, wandering among wolves like a blind orphan girl adown the midnight Bowery. Blood is thicker than water, and Col. Cameron relented and found a snug corner for his nephew within his ample heart. He didn't care for any more money himself —a man with a million or two never does. Still, a few tons of gold would be a handy thing to have in the house in case Dick Bland forced the country to a silver basis. The spider had towed the fly into Houston and was doing the elegant. Among the young man's assets were two gold bricks, about the size of Iowa barns and assaying more than $20 to the ounce. These were but unconsidered trifles which he had brought with him, thinking he might need some small change. There was oodles of it down in Arizona—on Uncle William's ranch. Col. Cameron retired to the toilet room of the Hotel Lawlor and figured out that he was worth, at the lowest calculation, $927,000,000,000,000. The cold perspiration stood out on his forehead in half-pint drops. It would never do to throw all this gold on the market at once—Cleveland and Wall Street would encompass its demonetization on the plea that silver was the only honest money. England could take a billion, Continental Europe two billions and America almost as much by calling in and canceling the silver certificates and greenbacks; but this would scarce exhaust the top-crop. What would he do with the surplus? To turn it all loose at once would run gold down to less than a dollar a pound—would kill the goose that laid the auriferous egg—would make mining even less profitable than dealing in long-leaf pine.. Happy thought! He would make the streets of Waco the exact counterpart of those in the New Jerusalem—would pave 'em with gold bricks! That done, he could get out some extra large slugs with which to dam the Brazos and rebuild the Cotton Palace. He had always wanted to do something handsome for Waco, and here was his opportunity. He would demonstrate the truth of the adage that fact is stranger than fiction by double-discounting the long-range lies of Marco Polo anent the golden roofs of far Cathay. He remembered having read in the Iconoclast that "the surface of the earth had been merely scratched—we know not what may yet be hidden in its dark depths. Our children may shoe their mules with yellow metal from King Solomon's mines." He remembered how he had slaved and saved for half a life-time to pile up a paltry million or two, and felt sorry for himself. At this juncture his nephew called to say that a string had suddenly been discovered tied to the mine, the thither end of which was securely held by his Mexican servant. It would take a cold $25,000 to turn their El Dorado loose, and he had but $5,000. He would have to sell his gold bricks at a sacrifice to raise the remainder, unless—Here he looked wistfully at Uncle William. Yes, he would fix it; what was a miserable $20,000, when you could knock it out of the mine in a minute! But suddenly his Aladdin's lamp began to smoke and sputter. He remembered having heard somewhere that all is not gold that glitters. Uncle William actually smelt a rat—smelt it all by himself, and it was not labeled either. He was taking dinner with his nephew in the hotel dining-room when it suddenly occurred to him that not every ass wears four legs. He fixed a cold, search-warrant gaze on the young man who pretended to be bone of his bone and flesh of his flesh, and the latter wilted like a white rabbit beneath the glance of a basilisk, or a sweet-potato vine frescoed with a hoar frost. Uncle William rose, pointed his soup-spoon at the cowering wretch and hissed through his teeth, as he once saw the hero do in a play: "You're a villain." The iciness of his tone frapped the coffee in the kitchen, while the mercury dropped thro' the bottom of the tube. The young man fled and Uncle William joined in the chase, his napkin streaming on the breeze like the white plume of King Henry of Navarre. Those who saw the race will not soon forget it—the wicked wretch hoofing it up Washington Avenue, his face distorted with fear; Uncle William pursuing him with uplifted soup-spoon like an avenging Nemesis! Surely the path of the transgressor is hard.

Uncle William should come home. It is not safe for him to wander about in this wicked world. Somebody might steal him. First thing we know he'll purchase the philosopher's stone or the state right to saw sunbeams up into cypress shingles. Come home, Uncle William, before the bities get you! Alas! alas! that the leading citizen of Waco should be humbugged and hoodooed by an antediluvian fake that would not impose upon a country bumpkin from the Free State of Van Zandt! Oh, Uncle William, Uncle William, when the grass grows green and the cowslip blooms in the meadow beware of the omnivrous calf.

THE SEVENTH COMMANDMENT.

A correspondent wants to know what I think of "the Single Standard of Morals, which assumes that tampering with the Seventh Commandment is as demoralizing to men as to women."

The single standard of morals, like the single standard of money, would be a magnificent thing were there at least double the present amount of raw material for it to measure. I hope to see the day when the libertine will be relegated to the social level of the prostitute where he logically belongs; but we are not dealing now with theories, but with actual conditions. I trust that I may speak plainly on this delicate subject without offending the unco guid or giving the priorient pulpiteers a pain. I believe the sexes should be equally pure—when I make a world all my women shall be paragons of virtue, and all my men he-virgins. I'll construct no Messalinas nor Cleopatras, no Lovelaces or Sir Launcelots. I'll people the world with St. Anthonys and Penelopes, Josephs and Rebecca Merlindy Johnsings. I'll ply the soft pedal to the fierce scream of passion and pull the barbs from the arrows that whiz from the Love

God's bow. Life will not then be quite so exhilarating, but it will be much better worth the living. Meantime a little spraining of the Seventh Commandment is by no means so demoralizing to man as to woman, despite the frantic protests of those who would drag the millennium in by the ears by forcing upon society, willy nilly, the single standard of morals. Man is the grosser animal, has not so far to fall; the shock to his sensibilities is not so serious—he is not so amenable to shame. A coat of black paint ruins a marble Dian, but has little appreciable effect on an iron Hercules. Illicit intercourse is not so demoralizing to man as to woman, for the further reason that it is not considered so great a crime. An act is demoralizing or degrading in proportion as the perpetrator thereof considers it criminal, as it lowers his self-respect; and men regard their crinolinic peccancy as a venial fault, while women consider such lapses on the part of their sex as grievous sin; hence the lightning of lust scarce blackens the pillar while it shatters the vase. The moral effect of an act is determined by the prevailing standard of ethics. Were polyandry the general practice, a woman could have a multiplicity of husbands and be considered pure; where polygamy is the rule, a man may have a multitude of wives and be regarded as moral. Ethical codes ever adapt themselves to conditions. Solomon was one of the most honorable men of his age, but were he alive to-day he would be branded as a shameless lecher, a contumacious criminal. There have been religions, existing thro' long ages and extending over vast empires, in which the organs of generation were considered as sacred symbols and prostitution in the purlieus of the temple regarded as pleasing to the gods. It is easy enough for bigoted ignorance to brand those people as barbarians; but in many provinces of art and science they have ever remained our masters. "The tents of the maidens" were simply places where fair religious enthusiasts sold themselves to the first stranger who offered them a piece of silver, and laid their gains upon the altar of the gods. The robber barons of old-time Germany, the diplomatic liars of mediaeval Italy, the thieves of ancient Lacadaemon and the polygamists of Biblical Palestine considered themselves as respectable people, and as they were so regarded by their compatriots, they were not morally degraded by their deeds. But the robber and the liar, the thief and the polygamist of this age are cattle of quite another color—there has been a radical change in the moral code, the peccadillos of the past have become the crimes of the present. The cross,

once an obscene pagan symbol, has been transformed from
an emblem of reproduction into one of destruction; the
"tents of the maidens" are struck; Corinth no longer im-
plores the gods to increase the number and enhance the
beauty of its courtesans; Venus Pandemos has given place
to Our Lady of Pain, and the obscene Dionysius fled before
a crucified Christ. No more does the fair religious postu-
lant play the bacchante in flower-strewn palaces while naked
Cupids crown the brimming cup and sandalled feet beat
time on polished cedar floors to music that is the cry of
brute passion in the blood—kneeling in the cold grey dawn
upon the stones she clasps a marble cross. The wanton
worship of the flesh has passed with the world's youth; but
tho' much of man's crassness has been purged away in
Time's great crucible, he is still of the earth earthly and
clings tenaciously to his ancient prerogative of polygamy.
When he marries, society does not really expect him to
respect his oath to "forsake all others"—regards it as a for-
mal bow to the convenances, a promise with a mental
reservation annex; but it considers a woman's vow as sacred
and the breaking thereof as rankest blasphemy. He is
allowed but one wife, but he may have a score of mistresses
and society will placidly wink the other eye—until some
tearful maiden requires him to share the shame she can no
longer conceal or an "injured husband" goes a gunning.
This should not be so, but so it is. There be fools, both
male and female, who will rise up to exclaim that this is
false; but that it is Gospel truth is proven every day in the
year in every community on the American continent. Men
with reputations for licentiousness that would shame old
Silenus are cordially received in the most exclusive society.
They are found at every high-falutin' "function," bending
over the white hands of the most accomplished ladies in
the land; on every ballroom floor, encircling the waists of
debutantes; in the parlors of our best people, paying court
to their young daughters. The noblest women in this world
become their wives—fondly undertake their "reformation"
while indignantly drawing their skirts aside lest they come
in contact with the tawdry finery of females whom these
lawless satyrs have debauched. Of course when a woman
learns that her reformatory work has proven a failure, drear
and dismal, she complains bitterly, may even demand a
divorce; yet she could count upon the fingers of one hand
the hubbies whom she would trust behind a sheet of paper
with a wayward daughter. She doesn't believe a little bit
in the virtue of the genus male, yet insists that her own hus-

band be a saint—assumes that her own charms should cause
him to regard all other women with indifference, and when
she learns of his polygamous practices suffers all the pangs
of wounded pride.

If a woman be homely as a *bois d'arc* hedge she may suppose the world supercharged with St. Anthonys, for she has
not been much sought; but if she be beautiful and has
mingled much with men she realizes all too well that the
story of Joseph is a foolish romance or that Mrs. Potiphar
was quite *passe*. And tho' she be pure as a vestal virgin
of Rome's best days she secretly despises the man with
whom she does not have to stand just a little bit on the defensive. Of course she demands that her male acquaintances shall be gentlemen and treat her with due courtesy
and respect; but it nettles her not a little to learn that her
charms are altogether ignored. She likes to feel her power,
to know that she is good in the eyes of men, something
desired—that her virtue is a priceless jewel over which she
must ever keep close guard; hence she likes best the male
she is compelled to watch, while a man has absolutely no
use for wife or mistress upon whose fealty he would not lay
his life. The result is that when a woman commits one
sexual sin she puts hope behind her, her feet take hold on
hell, she sinks lower and lower until she becomes the shameless associate of bummers and bawds. She is made to feel
that she has murdered her womanhood, that the red cross
of Cain blazes upon her brow. Realizing that she is a social
outcast, a moral pariah, she becomes reckless, defiant, and
finally glories in betraying the fool who trusts her. No
matter how fair the mountain upon which she has leave to
feed, she will batten on the moor. Love was her excuse
when first she went astray, and she hugs the delusion to her
heart that Cupid can sanctify a crime; but where honor
spreads not its wings of snow love perishes in the fierce
simoon of lust. The man with whom she enters the primrose path feels that he is good as his fellows. He may watch
with a sigh her descent to the noisome regions of the
damned; but comforts himself with the reflection that she
would have found her way to hades without his help—that

> "Virtue as it never will be moved,
>   Though lewdness court it in a shape of heaven,
>   So lust, though to a radiant angel linked,
>   Will sate itself in a celestial bed,
>   And prey on garbage"—

that had he played the prude she would have found another
and perhaps a baser paramour. He knows that the stain

of lechery is on his soul but draws comfort from the fact
that such is the common heritage of his sex, forgets his
victim and struggles toward the stars.   He is financially
honest, generous, and guards the honor of wife and daughters as God's best gift.   His amorous dalliance with others
instead of weaning him from his wife, causes him to regard
her with greater veneration, to contrast her purity with his
own pollution, her virtue with another's vice.   Paradoxical
as it may appear, there are no men in this world who so reverence good women as those who are notorious for their
illicit amours.   I am not, of course, speaking of the consorts
of common courtesans, of human hogs; but of the men who
people the red-light district with their cast-off mistresses.

Pitiful as it may appear, it hurts a man more to trifle
with the Eighth Commandment once than to break the
Seventh a thousand times—he is worse demoralized by stealing a mangy mule than by ruining a maid.   The male lecher
may be in all things else a lord; the thief is considered altogether and irremediably corrupt.   Society will tolerate the
one if his offense be not too flagrant, but to the other it
refuses even the shadow of forgiveness.   For three centuries the world has been trying to explain away Shakespeare's poaching, but has not thought it worth while to even
apologize for his sexual perversity.   Washington caught his
death while keeping an assignation with a neighbor's wife;
but there's little said about it—he's still the "father of his
country," including 70 million people of all classes and
colors.   Had the "slight exposure which brought on a fatal
sickness," been the result of prowling in his neighbor's barn
instead of his boudoir his name would be anathema forevermore.   The world forgives him for debauching another
man's wife, but would never have forgiven him had he raided
the same man's henroost.   It does not mean by this that
a scrawny pullet is of more importance than family honor;
it simply means that the man who steals a pullet is a cowardly thief, while the one who ignores the advances of a
pretty woman is an incorrigible idiot.   Ben Franklin could
have mistresses scattered all over the City of Brotherly Love,
and Dan Webster consort with all the light women of Washington, and still be men of genius beneath whose imperial
feet Columbia was proud to lay her shining hair; but had
either been caught sneaking from a neighbor's woodpile with
a two-cent bundle of faggots, the world would have rung
with his infamy.   The complaint against Demosthenes is not
that he was a libertine—a man before whose honeyed eloquence maiden modesty and wifely virtue were as wax; but
that he threw away sword and shield and fled like a mule-

eared rabbit before the spears of Macedon. I digress long enough to say that I have patiently investigated the story of the great orator's flight, and am fully convinced that it was a foul political falsehood, just as the current story of Col. Ingersoll's cowardice and capture is a religious lie.

Of course society has to make an occasional example, and its moral malefience, like death, loves a shining mark. It damned Breckenridge for getting tangled up with a desiring maid in a closed carriage, and relegated him to the political wilderness, yet twice elevated to the presidency the most disreputable old Falstaff that ever vibrated between cheap beer joints and ham-fatted old washerwomen who smelled of stale soap-suds and undeodorized diapers. Cleveland "told the truth"—when he had to—and was made a little tin Jesus of by the moral jabberwocks; Breckenridge, an infinitely better and brainier man, 'fessed up—and couldn't go to Congress from the studhorse district of Kentucky. When society goes hunting for scapegoats it usually manages to get a gnat lodged in its esophagus while relegating a mangy dromedary to its internal economy.

Such are the conditions which prevail to-day; but I am far from agreeing with the dictum of Pope that "whatever is, is right." Had the world ever proceeded on that principle we would still be honoring robbers and liars, thieves and polygamists. The wider license accorded man harmonizes neither with divine law, decency, nor the canons of common sense. We place womanly virtue on a pedestal and worship it while tacitly encouraging men to destroy it. We overlook the fact that a man cannot fracture the Seventh Commandment without considerable assistance. We should adopt a loftier standard of morality, nobler ideals for men. Because he is more earthy than woman it does not follow that he should be made altogether of muck. He has made some little progress since the days of Judah and Tamar, David and Bathsheba. He no longer consorts with courtesans on the public highway, nor pens up half a hundred wives in a harem, then goes broke buying concubines. He has learned that there is such a thing as shame, assumes a virtue tho' he has it not, seeks to conceal his concupiscence. What in one age society drives to a semblance of concealment in the next it brands as criminal, hence we may hope that at no distant day the single standard of morals will become more than an irridescent dream—that Josephs will not be confined altogether to gum-chewing members of the Y. M. C. A. We may eventually reach that moral plane where the male debauchee will be considered a moral outcast; but the time is not yet, and until its advent illicit commerce will continue to be more demoralizing to women than to men.

Of course there are exceptions to the rule—there are women who rise superior to the social law. George Eliot, Queen Elizabeth, Sara Bernhardt and others have trampled the social edict beneath their feet and refused to consider themselves sinners—have laughed an outraged world to scorn and stood defiant, sufficient unto themselves. Those women were intellectual amazons whom naught but the writhen bolts of God could humble, whose genius flamed with a white light even through the dun clouds of lechery; but we cannot measure the workaday woman by the few "whose minds might, like the elements, furnish forth creation." A Bernhardt is great, not because of her social sin, but despite thereof. With her art in the all-in-all, sex but an incident. She is strong enough to mount the empyrean despite the lernean serpent-coil which drags others to perdition—to compel the world to tolerate if not forgive the black stain in her heart because of the divine radiance which encircles her head. Occasionally there is a woman who can sacrifice her purity without sinking to the slums through loss of self-respect—can still maintain the fierce battle for fame, can be grand after she has ceased to be good. Mrs. Grundy can rave, and every orthodox goose stretch forth its rubber-neck to express its disapproval; but instead of bending beneath the weight of scorn, instead of sinking into the mire of the slough upon which she has set her feet she seems like old Antaeus, to gather fresh strength from the earth with which to write her name among the immortals. Queen Elizabeth is to this good day the pride of orthodox England —she had more brains than all its other monarchs combined; yet by solemn act of parliament it was decreed that the first bastard born to the "Virgin Queen" should ascend the throne of Britain. Titus was the highest possible premium placed upon female lechery, and it was placed there after due deliberation by a "God-fearing," Catholic-hating Episcopalian parliament! Fortunately for Mrs. Wettin, the present governmental figure-head, jolly old Liz either availed herself of some of the "preventatives" so extensively advertised in "great family newspapers," or neglected to own her illegitimate offspring. I cannot help but think that a love-child by Elizabeth and the courtly Raleigh would have been a great improvement on any of the soggy-headed things spawned by the House of Hanover. I do not apologize for nor condone the sexual frailties of distinguished females; the noblest career to which any woman can aspire is that of honest wifehood, and if she attains to that she is, tho' of mediocre mind, infinitely superior to the most famous wanton.

It is worthy of remark that most distinguished women since the days of Sappho and Semiramis have been impure, while not a few great men have been remarkable for their continency. Woman has been called "the weaker vessel," and certain it is that men stand the glamor of greatness, the temptations that come with riches, the white light that beats upon a throne, much better than do Eve's fair daughters. As a man becomes great, he respects more and more the cumulative wisdom of the world, becomes obedient; as a woman becomes great she grows disdainful and rebellious. Thus it is that while in the common walks of life woman is infinitely purer than man, as we ascend into the higher realms, whether in art, letters or statecraft, we discover a tendency to reverse this law until we often find great men anchorites and great women trampling on the moral code.

There be some who explain man's larger sexual liberty on physiological grounds, excuse it on the hypothesis of necessity. Physicians of the ultra-progressive school have even gone so far as to assert that continence in man is the chief cause of impotency—have pointed out that it is usually the wives of good men who go wrong, and insisted that to the former hypothesis must be attributed the latter fact. I am unable to find any reason in physiology why such a rule should not work both ways. I have said somewhere that man is naturally polygamous, and I might have added with equal truth that woman is naturally polyandrous. The difference is that woman's sexual education began earlier and she has progressed somewhat further from "a state of nature" wherein free love is the law. Man early began to defend his prerogatives, to strengthen the moral concept of his mate with a club, to frame laws for the protection of his female property. The infraction of established custom soon came to be considered a social crime, an offense of which even the gods took cognizance. Woman's polyandrous instinct yielded somewhat to education—she was compelled to make this sacrifice upon the altar of society. Thus was female continence not a thing decreed by heaven or "natural law," but was begotten of brute force. We see a survival of the old animalistic instinct in prostitution and the all too frequent illicit intercourse prevailing in the higher walks of life. Unquestionably the Seventh Commandment is violative of natural law as applied to either sex; but most natural laws must be amended somewhat ere we can have even a semblance of civilization; hence we cannot excuse man's peccadillos on that broad plea that it's "the nature of the brute." Joseph and St. Anthony, Gautama and Sir Galahad are ideals toward which man must ever strive with all his strength if he would purge the sub-soil out of his system—would mount above the gutter where wallows the dumb beasts and take his place among the gods. The custom of thousands of years to the contrary notwithstanding, it is damnable that a wife should be compelled to share a husband's caresses with lewd women. Tennyson assures us that "as the husband is the wife is." Fortunately for society this is false; still there are thorns in the bed and rebellion in the heart of the woman who must play wife to a Lovelace or a Lancelot. It is not true that it is the wives of good men who go astray; it is the wives who are naturally corrupt or morally weak. A talented lady contributor to the Iconoclast once asserted that 'tis not for good women that men have done great deeds. Perchance this is true, for men who do great deeds are goaded thereto, not by the swish of crinoline, but by the immortal gods. Such acts are bred in the bone, are born in the blood and brain. It certainly is not for bad women that men soar at the sun, for every man worth the killing despises corruption in womankind. He worships on bended knee and with uncovered head at the shrines of Minerva and Dian, and but amuses himself by stealth at that of the Pandemian Venus. When Anthony deserted his Roman wife for Egypt's sensuous Queen, he quickly became an inervated ass and his name thenceforth was Ichabod. Great Caesar dallied with the same dusky wanton, but ever in his intrepid heart ruled that "woman above reproach." Alexander of Macedon refrained from making the wife of Persia's conquered King his mistress. Napoleon found time even among the thunders of war to write daily to his wife, and when he finally turned from her it was not to seek a fairer flame but to place a son upon the throne of France. Grant stood forth in an era of unbridled license unsullied as a god. Great men have been unfaithful to their marital vows, but it has been those of mediocre minds and india rubber morals who have cowered at the feet of mistresses—who have thrown their world away for reechy kisses shared by others. While it is true that the world's intellectual titans have seldom been he-virgins or feathered saints, they did not draw god-like inspiration from their own dishonor.

"QUO VADIS."

Yes, I've read it—and when I had finished the miserable thing my head felt as tho' full of wind and dishwater. A critic is compelled to read every book of which a foolish public makes a fad, and in this era of decadent literature and depraved taste, the task is usually equivalent to wading thro' a miasmic sewer or hoofing it over an unprofitable Sahara. If a book is only bad enough it is sure of popular success. And "Quo Vadis" is the worst of all the irremediable tommyrot over which an undiscriminating public has raved. It does not even possess the doubtful charm of artistic immorality—it sinks even below the usual level of insufferable imbecility. Where it is not morally corrupt and bestially bad, it is either puerile or blasphemous. "Quo Vadis" is the mental moon-calf, a chaotic ollapodridâ composed of the intellectual fag-ends of the universe. To the normal mind it is neither entertaining nor instructive. It is a conglomeration of meaningless words, a concatenation of absurdities, a cataclysm of nescience and nonsense. It should have been subjected to the blue-pencil of the snake-editor—then burned. The story, which occupies more than 500 dreary pages, could have been better told in a dozen newspaper columns. It is a lingering agony long drawn out. It is just such a book as I would expect a Texas editor to write while enjoying an attack of delirium-tremens. Reading it were like seining the Atlantic ocean to find a bull-frog, or fishing in one of Talmage's idiotic sermons for a nascent idea. The author is a Polander with the constructive ability of a candle-maker and the lawless imagination of a pack-peddler. He calls himself Henryk Sienkiewicz. That's the way he spells it—when he wants to pronounce it he fills his mouth with hot mush, then turns a series of somersaults. The translation is by Jeremiah Curtin, who hid from the police in the Guatemalan wilds while perpetrating his crime against the English-reading world. Mr. Henryk Sienkiewicz is an innocent looking party, altho' "Quo Vadis" is not his first offense. His head resembles a long green Georgia watermelon that had been several times "plugged," but being unripe had not been pulled. His characters are all automatons—you see the strings and hear the creaking of the pulleys as they proceed to cut fantastic capers before high heaven. You no more expect to meet one of them on the street than to see a wooden Indian in front of a tobacco store hit somebody in the head with his tomahawk. When you read the last chapter you expect to see the author take off their legs, unscrew their heads and put them away in a box with grease paints.

"Quo Vadis" is the alleged "narrative of the time of Nero," but the author evidently expended little time or labor acquainting himself with the people among whom his scenes are laid. He reminds me of that Dutch philosopher who, having never seen a lion, attempted to evolve a correct idea of one from his inner consciousness, and produced a mongrel cross between a hippogriff and a nightmare. His Nero resembles the erstwhile emperor about as much as Cataline does Chollie Boy Culberson, while his early Christians remind me of a Populist convention in Kansas. About all that the author has learned of ancient Rome is the names of the streets and the rooms in bathhouse and residence and these he repeats with the tiresome industry of a pedant, or the exasperating persistence of a poll parrot. I had to hire a nigger to swab me off with a wet towel while I read the work, and all I got out of it was a joblot of misinformation and a feverish desire to plug Mr. Henryk Sienkiewhatsky's Georgia watermelon in a new place. His plot consists of getting his heroine into one trouble after another, and the futile efforts of the hero to get her out by means of the double pull of prayer to God and perquisites to the pretorian guards. He does not, however, imitate that American humorist who undertook to write a society novel, and after getting his herone enciente and his hero in jail, gave them up as hopeless. There are some rather pretty things in the book, but they are spoiled by too much elaboration; some really dramatic scenes, but they are ruined by being made to last too long. When the author gets hold of a good thing he cannot let go. Mr. Sienkiewhatsky has undertaken to write a great religio-historico-romantico novel, but has only succeeded in making himself an insufferable nuisance. He makes Roman history just as Mark Twain's sea captain did that of the civil war—to suit himself. He supplies Sts. Peter and Paul with sermons and sayings, and pulls them about as unceremoniously as he does the rest of his puppets. From first to last he caters to the religious element, and succeeds in capturing that portion of it which cannot distinguish between Jesus Christ and Sam Jones. He evidently means no offense in picturing the early Christians as an unhappy cross between fanatics and fools, and making St. Peter neglect his holy calling to officiate as guardian angel of an *affaire d'amour*. Christians believe that the Apostle were inspired men, that their words were those given them by the Almighty. The author of "Quo Vadis" professes this faith, yet puts his own words into the mouths of Sts. Peter and Paul—presumes to think and speak for Omnipotence himself. He might as well have introduced into his narrative God and the Holy Ghost. My bump of reverence is not so large as to be abnormal; but I do insist that if Christ and the Apostles were what the church believes them to be it is blasphemy for any man to attribute to them one word not duly authenticated—that when a novelist makes them parrot his own nonsense he deserves the rebuke of the church instead of its patronage.

Petronius is the only character in the book who gives evidence of being half-way alive, and we look on incredulously while he bleeds to death, declining to believe that he really possesses blood. He is Nero's favorite, an elegant Epicurean, a dilettante, a poetaster, talented, lazy, audacious, willing to bend the pregnant hinges of the knee where thrift may follow fawning, yet not hopelessly corrupt. He fattens on Nero and flatters him thro' many a long year, then insults him when he falls from favor, and goes hence in the arms of a beautiful concubine, dies to the sound of sensuous music at his own banquet board. He is the only character in the book gifted with an ounce of brains, and he denies all the gods, lives and dies an Atheist, mocks both Jehovah and Jove, laughs at Christ and the Christians. Vinicius, his nephew, is a military tribune in love with Lygia. He is a big, powerful fellow. He quarrels with his effete uncle, and the latter, a slender man, enervated by wine and women, takes both the warrior's brawny hands in one of his and holds them until he cools off—Ward McAllister conquering Sandow! Lygia is a Christian maid, a frail, spirituelle little thing—simply "a rag and a bone and a hank of hair"—yet Vinicius, at whose feet are the most voluptuous women of Rome, including the female favorite of Nero, conceives for her an unholy passion and determines to make her his mistress. She flies from him, and he attempts to seize her and drag her to his house by force, and because she eludes him he wants her flogged! Not very promising material out of which to manufacture a hero! He finds her listening to a sermon by St. Peter, the great Apostle converts him to the true faith, and his unholy passion is transmitted into pure love by religion's great alembic. St. Peter promises her to him, but Nero concludes to have her ravished, even tho' he has to attend to that little formality himself, then feed her to the lions, and for about three hundred dreary pages there's hades to pay and no pitch hot.

Vinicius has access to Nero, and is aware of the terrible doom of his lady love, yet makes no attempt to avenge her by slipping an Arkansaw toothpick into the brisket of the royal brute. He even goes to the circus to see her destroyed and sits on a bench and moans; but a barbarian saves her life by taking a monster bull by the horns and pulling its head off—thereby proving that the age of miracles was not yet past. The hero, who had not the courage to go to his fiancee's defense and save her or die with her, enters the arena when the danger is past and solemnly covers her nakedness with his pocket handkerchief. And Lygia marries Vinicius instead of the barbarian who killed the bull. But she wasn't much of a heroine anyhow. Lygia is a canting little Goody Two-Shoes without a pint of rich blood in her whole body, while Vinicius is an ecstatic chump, much better qualified to engineer a holiness campmeeting than guard a woman's honor or promote his country's glory. With power to slay herself, Lygia goes to Nero's banquet, fully expecting to be debauched. She suffers the pretorians to throw her into a foul prison, expecting that before death she will be defiled. Eunice the pagan mistress of the godless Petronius, realizing that the hour has struck, that she must choose between death and becoming the creature of a man she does not love, stretches forth her arm to the Greek physician's steel, the blood spurts and she sinks dying upon the bosom of her lord—"her honor rooted in dishonor stands and faith unfaithful keeps her falsely true."

In the burning of Rome the author of "Quo Vadis" has imitated as best he could Bulwer's destruction of Pompeii; but his description is a mere daub, a multi-headed nightmare. There is nothing majestic, nothing awe-inspiring about it, albeit the artist sweats blood to make it awful. It reads like an amateur reporter's "spread" of the Chicago fire. His description of the martyrdom of the Christians resembles an anatomical lecture, in a dissecting room. It is a revolting picture upon which the artist lovingly dwells through long pages, until the heart faints and the soul sickens with the saturnalia of blood, the interminable bestiality. It reads like a newspaper account of a prize fight "by rounds." A true artist would have completed the picture with a few bold strokes of the pencil, well knowing that familiarity even with crime breeds contempt. The Christians of "Quo Vadis" are not men and women of mental equipoise devoted in a sane manner to the services of the Master, but wild-eyed fanatics who court destruction, believing that the more terrible their torture the brighter their crown. They want to be crucified because Christ suffered that death, and they are disappointed to learn that they are to be eaten by dogs or torn by lions, that method of destruction not affording them sufficient opportunity for suffering. Doubtless there were in the days of Nero crazy Christians who courted the cross, but we may safely assume that a vast majority of the converts of Peter and Paul were sane. The labored depiction of wholesale insanity, commingled with scenes of blood, lechery, profligacy and tyranny, are scarce calculated to make people better, hence "Quo Vadis" is not a good book. It is a dismal failure from a religious, historical and artistic standpoint, but it *sells* because a lot of irresponsible damphools have made it a fad. Its author should be condemned to the treadmill for having spewed forth such an unsavory conglomeration of ignorance and ineptitude to debauch the minds of the people. "Ben Hur" is the only religious novel I know of that is really worth the reading—and it could be improved by considerable pruning.

WILLY WALLY TO WED.

Wm. Waldorf Astor is a consistent Anglo-maniac. Instead of remaining in this blawsted bloomin' country, upon which he looks with the disdain of a well groomed ass contemplating the Iliad, he hied him to "perfidious Albion" and took up his abode in its foggy metropolis, surrounded by m'luds, whom he so much admires. It could scarce be expected that a country so new and crass as America would harmonize with the triple plated culchaw and super-aestheticism of a man who traces his proud patrician lineage and abundant lucre back to Johann Jakob Astor, the wooden-show purveyor of green coon-skins and odoriferous polecat pelts, Jamaica bug-juice and brummagem jewelry. With a cash capital of one jug of cheap rum and a shirt-tail full of glass beads, the thrifty Johann Jakob went among the Indians and founded a fortune which enabled him to buy a large slice of Manhattan Island when it was selling at four cents per acre. By feeding himself but once a day, and then with a piece of fat pork anchored to a cotton cord, half-soling his own pants with sea-weed and going barefoot in summer to save his shoes, he was able to hang to his land until the industry and enterprise of others made it worth almost a dollar an acre, when he passed it on to his posterity simply because it wasn't portable. The unearned increment accumulated from generation to generation in a ratio of geometrical progression, until his spawn became as rich as grease and slung on more unadulterated agony ithan a Washington nigger with a brass watch. Willy Wally was the flower and fruitage of the Astor family. American vulgarisms grated upon his sensitive soul like a rat-tail file drawn across a sore tooth, and he arose and fled from us as a Della-Cruscan poetess might chase her shrinking soul from a country hog-killing or the pervasive odor of ebullient soft-soap. Would to heaven that all the half-baked American slobs who worship at the shrine of European flunkeyism, and who say "eyther" and "neyther," would follow in his footsteps. The brainless inanities will breed, and we should encourage them to drop their worthless calves in a foreign country. Willy Wally has just had the "distinguished honor" of entertaining 'Is Royal 'Ighness, the Prince of Wales. His Nibs has become so well known as a crooked gambler that he can no longer steer the toothsome sucker against his sure-thing games, and is devoting his talents to the profitable industry of pulling the legs of wealthy plebs in search of social distinction. He is always in need of cash, and even the title-loving English people have tired of paying debts resulting from his debaucheries. It is well understood in England that when he honors a parvenu with his royal presence that a fat "loan" is expected, which is in reality his fee for the distinguished social favor. Willy Wally is worth $150,000,000, hence can well afford to tip this social huckster who trades upon his title. Think of the felicity of seeing himself proclaimed in all the Anglo-maniacal papers of his native land as the host of Imperial Highness! I can only wonder that Wales waited so long before tapping the purse of the Astorian plutocrat; but he may have been fighting shy in order to secure a better price. The prince is heir apparent to nothing but an empty title and the privilege of being supported by the toil of better people. The sovereign of Great Britain is a veritable Toom-ta-bard, a mere figurehead, of about as little real importance in the governmental plan as a sack of sawdust. When the Prince succeeds his mother he will be as powerless so far as matters of great moment are concerned, as he is at present. He can hock the throne, give the crown jewels to harlots and divide his time between baccarat and bawdry without throwing one cog in the governmental machinery out of gear. He is simply a beery old bum who has spent his life cheating at the gaming board, debauching

the fool wives of those who hang upon his favors and doping for the foulest of all diseases. If he pays a woman any
attention her reputation is forever ruined. His leery smile
would wither the good name of a vestal virgin. Mary An-
derson, "Our Mary," understood this and cut him cold—
snubbed him as she might an impudent coon in her native
Kentucky. He is the avatar of immorality, the beau-ideal of
dead beats, a social leper who should be compelled to herd by
himself and continually cry, "Unclen! unclean!" He has
the heart of a hyena and the instincts of an ape,—proving
him a true scion of the House of Hanover. He has done
absolutely nothing for his country but disgrace it. As if to
add insult unto injury, to pile Pelion upon Ossa, he has
brought forth a brood of brainless brats to fatten on the
public and perpetuate their father's foulness. No self-
respecting English gentleman would permit him to enter
his mule pasture or associate with his sows were he not
"stuck o'er with titles and hung round with strings." When
he visits even a peer of the realm he insists upon naming
the "ladies" who are to be invited to meet him, and turns
the mansion of his host into a harem. That is the feculent
cur who has honored the great grandson of the old Manhattan hide merchant with his imperial presence. They
were well met, if the rumor be true that Willy Wally is to
wed the widow of the late Lord Randolph Churchill, "after
the prescribed term of mourning"—for the husband she
drove to his death a year ago with her debaucheries! It will
be remembered that it was the eldest son of the Prince of
Wales who was caught in a compromising attitude with
Lady Churchill at Windsor Castle. And Mr. Astor is
proud to entertain in the house to which he will bring his
soiled bride the sire of the syphilitic little simian who debauched her! Yet this man was once an American! Let
us thank the dear Lord that he is such no longer,—that his
infamy is altogether English. May he ever remain abroad
to play Pandarus to this bogus Prince; to keep a cistern—
as Othello would say—for foul toads to knot and gender in.
Widow Churchill has indeed improved her time. Before
her dishonored husband hath rotted in his grave; before
"the prescribed term of mourning" has ended;

> "Ere yet the salt of most unrighteous tears
> Had left the flushing in her galled eyes,"

she was spooning and yum-yuming, actually engaged to be
married to another man, impatiently awaiting the end of
her "mourning" period—a tear in one eye and a wink in

the other! When wedded to the concubine of Clarence, Willy Wally can go with her to lay garlands on the grave of Lord Randolph, and there reflect that not even a descendant of old John Churchill and Sarah Jennings—who prostituted a sister to fill their purse—could abide the foulness of this bawd. Being something of a *dilettante* in literature, he might collaborate with Alfred Austin, the rhymster for royalty, in a eulogy of the titled dude whose enterprise made Lady Churchill a widow that the *facile princeps* of Anglo-maniacs might win a wife. He owes a debt of gratitude to the eldest son of the Prince of Wales for thus having paved his way to a nuptial Paradise. He should burn incense daily at the sarcophagus of the son, and recommend his lively kins-woman, Mrs. J. Coleman-Drayton, to the attention of the sire,